*Universal Sound Westerns,
1929–1946*

ALSO BY GENE BLOTTNER
AND FROM MCFARLAND

Wild Bill Elliott: A Complete Filmography (2007)

*Universal-International Westerns, 1947–1963:
The Complete Filmography* (2000; softcover 2007)

Universal Sound Westerns, 1929–1946

THE COMPLETE FILMOGRAPHY

GENE BLOTTNER

McFarland & Company, Inc., Publishers
Jefferson, North Carolina, and London

The present work is a reprint of the library bound edition of Universal Sound Westerns, 1929–1946: The Complete Filmography, *first published in 2003 by McFarland.*

LIBRARY OF CONGRESS CATALOGUING-IN-PUBLICATION DATA

Blottner, Gene, 1938–
    Universal sound westerns, 1929–1946 : the complete filmography / by Gene Blottner.
      p.   cm.
    Includes bibliographical references and index.

    ISBN 978-0-7864-6079-3
    softcover : 50# alkaline paper ∞

    1. Western films—Catalogs. 2. Universal Pictures Company—Catalogs. I. Title.
PN1995.9.W4B63   2011
016.79143'6278—dc21   2003010127

BRITISH LIBRARY CATALOGUING DATA ARE AVAILABLE

© 2003 Gene Blottner. All rights reserved

No part of this book may be reproduced or transmitted in any form or by any means, electronic or mechanical, including photocopying or recording, or by any information storage and retrieval system, without permission in writing from the publisher.

On the cover: Marlene Dietrich and James Stewart in a production still from the 1939 film *Destry Ride Again*

Manufactured in the United States of America

McFarland & Company, Inc., Publishers
  Box 611, Jefferson, North Carolina 28640
    www.mcfarlandpub.com

For Catherine

Acknowledgments

Many people assisted me in obtaining information for this book. I would like to thank the stars who had the patience to allow me to interview them either by phone, in person or via correspondence through the mail: Jane Adams; Kathryn Adams; Vivian Austin Coe; Polly Burson; Frank Coglan, Jr.; Louise Currie; Edith Fellows; Susanna Foster; Lois January; Dick Jones; Kay Linaker; Fay McKenzie; Danny Morton; Edward Norris; House Peters, Jr.; Mickey Rooney; Ann Rutherford; John Sheffield; Robert Stack; and Marilyn and Wesley Tuttle.

A special thanks to those who willingly shared their knowledge, memorabilia and information, or who helped me with my research: Charles Blottner; Walt Farmer; Michael Fitzgerald; Larry Floyd; Boyd Magers; Bill McDowell; Bill Ruehlmann; Bill Sasser; Kenneth Stier; Dr. Marvel Velasco; Fred Weiss; Tommy Wells; Tom Wyatt; Tinsley Yarbrough; the staffs of the Kirn Memorial Library and Old Dominion Library in Norfolk, Virginia; the Library of Congress; Allentown Library in Allentown, Pennsylvania; Jefferson Madison Regional Library in Charlottesville, Virginia; Bethlehem Library in Bethlehem, Pennsylvania, and especially Diana Helberg, who graciously proofread my manuscript.

Also, I would like to thank those who were kind enough to provide lobby cards or photographs: Marion Shilling, Kay Linaker, Larry Floyd, Bill McDowell and Charles Blottner.

Contents

Acknowledgments	vi
Preface	1
Historical Overview	5
The Western Films	9
The Western Short Films of Universal	389
Alphabetical Listing of Universal Sound Westerns	395
Chronological Listing of Universal Sound Westerns	401
Selected Bibliography	407
Index	411

Preface

What is a western? No one person seems to have a clear definition. Some films are obviously westerns: they take place in what is known as the Old West, with cowboys, outlaws, cavalries and Indians. Some writers and historians add Northwest logging, oil-well drilling, and pioneer and Civil war stories to the genre. Others include stories that start in the West but take place mainly in the East and feature a westerner coping with gangsters in the big city.

One hundred and eighty feature films and serials were the basis for this book. Most of the films are decidedly "B" in nature and scope. That said, majority of the films, however, were well made and delivered fine entertainment.

Most of the films covered in this book are obviously westerns and were listed in Les Adams and Buck Rainey's *The Shoot-Em-Ups* (Arlington House, 1978) or Rainey's *The Shoot-Em-Ups Ride Again* (Scarecrow Press, 1990), films listed in those books were automatically included. Ten additional feature films and three serials met my criteria as well:

FEATURE FILMS
Can't Help Singing: Listed in Phil Hardy's *The Western* (William Morrow, 1983) and Michael Pitts' *Western Movies* (McFarland, 1986).
Cowboy in Manhattan: Two web sites classify this film as a western.
The Mighty Treve: Universal's ad stated, "When the killer sprang, terror stalked the range."
Mutiny on the Blackhawk: Listed in Pitts' *Western Movies* (McFarland, 1986), the second of two stories was a reworking of *Sutter's Gold* (Universal, 1936).
The Overlanders: Listed in Pitts' *Western Movies* (McFarland, 1986).
Strictly in the Groove: Listed in Pitts' *Western Movies* (McFarland, 1986).
Timber: Listed in Pitts' *Western Movies* (McFarland, 1986).

2   PREFACE

West Bound Limited: Listed as a western mystery in Michael G. Fitzgerald's *Universal Pictures* (Arlington House, 1977), and in Pitts' *Western Movies* (McFarland, 1986).
The Wildcatter: Listed in Pitts' *Western Movies* (McFarland, 1986).
Yellowstone: Listed in Pitts' *Western Movies* (McFarland, 1986).

SERIALS

The Great Alaskan Mystery: Listed in Pitts' *Western Movies* (McFarland, 1986).
Lightning Express: One web site listed this serial as a western. In addition, one of the main characters is the western railroad detective Whispering Smith, and the story is set primarily in the west.
Scouts to the Rescue: This serial also takes place in the west and has numerous elements typical of westerns.

The author was able to view all but two of the above titles, *The Mighty Treve* and *Lightning Express*. The author read *The Mighty Treve*, which took place out West and featured a dog defending sheep against a mountain lion. In reading a synopsis of and viewing stills from *Lightning Express*, sufficient western elements were present to qualify it as a western. Therefore, both were included.

In my research, I discovered that *Ramrod*, an Enterprise production, was originally scheduled to be released by Universal. The film was completed in the fall of 1946 but was released by United Artists in May 1947. Since this production had Universal roots, it is included here.

Three other possible titles were discarded. The first, *Conflict*, with John Wayne, was set in and around lumber camps, but there was no focus on the daily activity of the loggers, and no conflict in getting the logs to market; the setting served only as a background for crooked prizefights. The second, *Mutiny in the Arctic*, with Richard Arlen and Andy Devine, was an out and out action adventure picture with no hint of western trappings. The third, *Flame of New Orleans*, with Marlene Dietrich, offered no action or western elements. Therefore, these films were not included.

The few big budget films can either be purchased at your local video store or can be viewed on American Movie Classics (AMC), Turner Classic Movies (TCM), or the Western Channel. The "B" westerns can be obtained from various video distributors.

To give the reader some insight into the entry style presentation of the films and the primary sources that were used, the following information may be helpful.

BLURBS

Above the title of each film (*Lightning Express* excepted) is an example of a "blurb" used in the advertising copy for the picture. Most release dates were taken from Adams & Rainey's *The Shoot-Em-Ups* (Arlington House, 1978). If the movie is in color, this is noted. Most of the films of this period were black and white.

Alternate Title: If a film used a title other than that given upon initial release, this title is listed. Working titles will be found in the "Notes and Commentary" section of the entry.

Cast: All cast members listed before the designation "//" were identified in either the beginning or end credits, or both. All cast members listed after that designation were identified by the author or people considered knowledgeable about the western and Universal personnel.

Credits: Each person listed received on-screen billing. Credits listed for films not viewed by the author and *For the Service* came from Jay Robert North and Stanley Ralph Ross' *The Motion Picture Guide* and Adams & Rainey's *The Shoot-Em-Ups*.

Song(s): All identifiable songs have been named. Composers and artists, if known, have also been named.

Location Filming: Kenneth Stier provided most of this information. Although most entries provide some location filming information, those that do not were filmed entirely on the Universal lot or location information is not known.

Running Time: Nash & Ross' *The Motion Picture Guide* served as a starting point. Running times will vary, depending on the source used. Les Adams, in his *Yesterday's Saturdays* periodical, demonstrated that some films had at least three different running times listed upon initial release. Running times from *More Cowboy Shooting Stars*, *Western Movies*, *The Western*, *Shoot-Em-Ups*, *The Universal Story*, and *Universal Pictures*, and videotapes from the author's collection were compared to *The Motion Picture Guide*. When there was a discrepancy in running times, in most cases the time that appeared the most won. Running times for serials came from timing the video in the author's collection.

Source: If a film was derived from a published work (e.g., a novel or story), this is stated, along with the name(s) of the author(s).

Story: This is an encapsulation of the film and not an attempt to describe every scene in detail. The author has watched all the films except *Wagon Master*, *Parade of the West*, *Lucky Larkin*, *Lightning Express*, *The Storm*, *Sons of the Saddle*, *Lasca of the Rio Grande*, *Clancy of the Mounted*, and *The Mighty Treve*, which are unavailable for viewing. The story lines of *Lightning Express* and *Clancy of the Mounted* were published in Ken Weiss' *To Be Continued* (Love's Labor Press, 2000). Dr. Mavel Velasco graciously translated *Lasca del Rio Grande*, a booklet distributed by Biblioteca Films to promote the film in Hispanic countries.

Notes and Commentary: For the most part, this information was obtained from the stars, who graciously consented to allow me to interview them, facts published in *The Hollywood Reporter*; and works by various film historians.

Reviews: To give the reader an idea of how critics received the film at the time of release, selected reviews are provided. Also, retrospective comments from various authors on the western or on film in general are included. The author was unable to find a review of *Riders of the Santa Fe*.

Summation: My overall appraisal of the film, with which I can only hope the reader might agree.

As acknowledged, photographs, title cards, and movie stills used as illustrations are courtesy of Jane Adams, Kay Linaker, Marion Shilling, Charles Blottner, Larry Floyd, Bill McDowell and the author.

Historical Overview

In 1929, the western film found a voice as *In Old Arizona* (Fox, 1929) was the first all-talking western feature film. Its star, Warner Baxter, as the Cisco Kid, won an Academy Award for Best Actor. President Carl Laemmle decided that Universal's western features should also have sound. Universal had two western stars, Hoot Gibson and Ken Maynard. Gibson had been a stalwart for Laemmle since he replaced Harry Carey as the studio's premier cowhand in 1922. Maynard had moved over from First National after starring in several successful western features.

Gibson was amenable and absorbed the cost of adding sound to his features. Maynard was harder to deal with and demanded additional production money, which he received. From the first release of the season, *The Long Long Trail*, Gibson's films were all-talking. It wasn't until Maynard's fourth film in his series, *Mountain Justice*, that his films were all-talking. Maynard's first two entries had sound effects, songs and dialog sequences while the third, *Lucky Larkin*, sported only sound effects.

In 1930, *All Quiet on the Western Front* won an Academy Award for Best Picture. In addition, Laemmle had turned over the daily responsibility for running the studio to his son, Carl, Jr.

Young Carl, flushed with the success of *All Quiet on the Western Front*, believed that Universal could now compete with MGM, Paramount and, possibly, Warner Bros. "Entertainments," including series westerns, heretofore the bread and butter of the studio, would be discontinued, and more expensive, prestigious films would be offered. Gibson and Maynard left to find work at independent studios and Universal was now without a western star for the first time in over a decade.

Serials remained a staple for Universal. Mascot was the only other studio providing cliffhangers for the movie audiences. Universal released two serials in 1930 that would be of interest to the western fan. The first was *Lightning Express*. Lane Chandler played the lead, supported by Al Ferguson as Whispering Smith, a role that would later be played by George O'Brien and Alan Ladd. The second, *The Indians Are Coming*, with western great Tim McCoy, was the first all-talking serial.

Quickly, Laemmle, Jr., received backlash from theater owners. The owners demanded the studio provide "entertainments" and Universal changed direction to give the theater owners the films they wanted. The studio needed a cowboy star, and looked to the reigning western star of the silent era, Tom Mix. In 1932, Mix starred in a series of popular westerns, beginning with *Destry Rides Again*.

Mix had to bow out of his contract with Universal after nine films. Two disastrous falls made it impossible for him to continue. Mix recommended Hoot Gibson, but Ken Maynard was chosen instead.

Although Maynard's westerns were popular with movie audiences, Laemmle had reservations about this choice. Maynard's budgets were higher than his contemporaries', with no increase in box office receipts. Some of Maynard's plots (as in *Smoking Guns*) were outrageous and difficult for audiences to believe. Maynard's contract would not be renewed, and Laemmle needed a new starring cowboy.

Laemmle didn't have far to look to find his new star. Buck Jones was starring in the serial *The Red Rider*. Jones was under contract with Columbia for his series westerns. At this time, Columbia hadn't entered serial production, and he had signed a contract to make one serial annually for Universal. He wanted to form his own production company, which would allow him to have control over his stories. Laemmle agreed to Jones' terms and he moved to Universal.

Jones was extremely popular and placed first in the inaugural *Motion Picture Herald* poll of top western stars for 1936. By the next year, Jones had slipped to third place behind Gene Autry and William Boyd. His stories had begun to stress plot over action, and were met with less critical favor.

Sutter's Gold (1936) was to be an epic for Universal. No expense was spared to bring the story of Johan Sutter and the gold rush days to cinematic life. The film would prove to be a box office disaster, due primarily to a non-western type in Edward Arnold and a rambling plot line. A subsequent picture, *Show Boat* (1936), would run into financial difficulties. The studio was forced to reorganize, and Carl Laemmle was forced to retire.

An austerity program was put into effect and Universal became known as New Universal. Jones demanded $25,000 per picture. He knew that his friend, William Boyd, received this amount to play Hopalong Cassidy at Paramount. Universal would not agree to this, and Jones, in turn, entered into a contract with an independent company that would have his films distributed by Columbia. This turned out to be an unwise decision for Jones, who was never able to match his earlier successes.

With the success of singing cowboys Gene Autry, Tex Ritter, Dick Foran and others, Universal decided to produce musical westerns. Bob Baker received the nod over Roy Rogers, who soon would be starring in westerns at Republic. Baker's westerns were pleasant but did not offer the continuous rugged action that audiences expected. Perhaps Universal's financial problems necessitated fewer action scenes.

Universal's new program proved to be ineffective and Universal decided to bring the rugged action back to its series westerns. Johnny Mack Brown succeeded Buck Jones in the studio's annual western serials and starred in their series westerns with Bob Baker and Fuzzy Knight in support.

With epics, westerns bombarding the movie theaters in 1939, Universal produced *Destry Rides Again*. The film, starring Marlene Dietrich and James Stewart, became a classic. Buoyed by the success of *Destry Rides Again*, Universal began producing medium-budget westerns with running times between 70 and 89 minutes. Some memorable titles: *When the Daltons Rode* (1940), *Trail of the Vigilantes* (1940), *Badlands of Dakota* (1941), *The Lady from Cheyenne* (1941), *The Spoilers* (1942), *Frontier Badman* (1943), *Frontier Gal* (1945) and *The Daltons Ride Again* (1946).

In 1940, Brown was Universal's number one cowboy star, and the studio looked to Dick Foran to star in their annual western serials. After two years, Foran became a jack-of-all-trades actor and appeared in horror, western, adventure and musical comedy films. After Lon Chaney toplined Universal's 1942 outdoor serial, *Overland Mail*, such lesser names as Milburn Stone, Dennis Moore, Bill Kennedy and Peter Cookson filled the bill.

For the 1942-43 season, Tex Ritter was signed to co-star with Brown. The duo was billed "The West's Greatest Star Team." With western duos and trios in vogue at the time, Universal was attempting to keep pace with the competition by giving the movie-going public more western stars for their money. After one season, Ritter took over as solo lead when Brown left to do his own series at Monogram. An injury to Ritter gave Russell Hayden the lead in a film *Frontier Law* (1943), slated for Ritter; Hayden co-starred with Ritter in *Marshal of Gunsmoke* (1944).

Ritter left after appearing in three series westerns and having a cameo in *Frontier Badman* (1943). Johnny Bond and His Red River Boys had been the musical group in Ritter's previous films, but the studio decided to use Ray Whitley and His 6-Bar Cowboys instead. The decision was not to Ritter's liking and, consequently, he left the studio to star in the Texas Rangers series at PRC.

Rod Cameron was Universal's new cowboy star. After one season Cameron was elevated to bigger-budgeted films. Kirby Grant became the studio's final "B" western star.

Universal finally produced a Technicolor western, *Can't Help Singing* (1944), a musical set rimarily on a wagon train heading for California, with Deanna Durbin. Later Technicolor westerns *Salome, Where She Danced* (1945), the previously mentioned *Frontier Gal* (1945), and *Canyon Passage* (1946) were more to the action lover's taste.

In 1945, the studio began negotiations to merge with International Pictures. By November 12, 1946, the merger was complete. The studio would be called Universal-International. Agreements were made with J. Arthur Rank to acquire and distribute prestigious British films. With this new policy, "B" westerns and serials were discontinued. Each film now had to have a minimum running time of 70 minutes.

At year's end, *The Overlanders*, filmed in Australia, was released. This was a curious but effective blend of war and western film, telling the true story of a monumentuous cattle drive over rugged Australian terrain to keep the cattle from Axis forces.

The Universal era had come to a close, at least for the next 16 years. In 1964, the studio reverted back to the original name, Universal, which it has kept to this day.

In these early sound years, Universal had some of the finest western names headlining its westerns and serials. In chronological order, there was Ken Maynard, Hoot Gibson, Tim McCoy, Tom Tyler, Tom Mix, Buck Jones, Johnny Mack Brown, Randolph Scott, John Wayne, Tex Ritter and Rod Cameron. With such stars, the studio presented to the movie-going public entertaining and exciting western fare.

The Western Films

FIRST ON THE DRAW!!
...THAT WAS THE LAW on the wild western trails of the badlands!

Arizona Cyclone

Universal (November 1941)

CAST: Tom, **Johnny Mack Brown**; Muleshoe, **Fuzzy Knight**; Claire, **Nell O'Day**; Elsie, **Kathryn Adams**; Randolph, **Herbert Rawlinson**; Quirt, **Dick Curtis**; Draper, **Robert Strange**; Jessup, **Glenn Strange**; Waters, **Carl Sepulveda**; Jack, **Charles Morrison**; Nick, **Buck Moulton**; Johnson, **Jack Clifford** and **The Notables**// "Brownie"; Sam Harvey, **Kermit Maynard**; Outlaw, **Frank Ellis**; Wagon Driver, **George Plues**

CREDITS: Director, **Joseph H. Lewis**; Associate Producer, **Will Cowan**; Screenwriter, **Sherman Lowe**; Editor, **Paul Landres**; Art Directors, **Jack Otterson and Ralph M. DeLacy**; Set Decorations, **R.A. Gausman**; Cinematographer, **Charles Van Enger**; Gowns, **Vera West**; Sound, **Bernard B. Brown and Jesse Moulin**; Musical Director, **H.J. Salter**

SONGS: "On the Trail of Tomorrow" (Rosen and Carter)—sung by **The Notables**; "Let's Go" (Rosen and Carter)—sung by **The Notables**; and "Wooden Leg Pete" (Grout)—sung by **The Notables**

LOCATION FILMING: Corriganville, California

RUNNING TIME: 57 min.

STORY: Two rival companies, one owned by Herbert Rawlinson and managed by Johnny Mack Brown, and the other run by Dick Curtis, are vying for freight hauling accounts. Curtis will use any underhanded method to achieve his means. Banker Robert Strange is backing Curtis and wants Rawlinson's line put out of business to ensure Curtis will be awarded a lucrative contract to haul materials for the Telegraph Company. Through Kathryn Adams, Brown's sweetheart, Rawlinson learns the contract will be put out for bid. Strange refuses to lend Rawlinson money to post for the required bond, citing Rawlinson's trouble with outlaws as making

Arizona Cyclone (1941) title card: ***Upper left***, Fuzzy Knight and Nell O'Day; ***upper right***, Johnny Mack Brown; ***lower right***, Dick Curtis and Johnny Mack Brown.

him a bad risk. Rawlinson knows he can borrow the money from a rival bank, so Strange has Rawlinson shot. With Rawlinson's death, his daughter, Nell O'Day, is now owner, with Brown handling her affairs. Strange makes an offer to purchase the freight line, but Brown turns him down. Strange, with help from Curtis and henchman Glenn Strange, dynamites and burns O'Day's buildings, figuring this should put her out of business. As the trio make their getaway, Brown captures Strange. The freighters salvage what they can. Brown and his men ride into town to bring Curtis and his men to justice. Curtis' men are either captured or killed. Curtis retreats into a saloon, followed by Brown. The two men engage in a fierce hand-to-hand struggle. Both men try to gain possession of Brown's pistol. The pistol discharges, killing Curtis. O'Day's company wins the hauling contract for the Telegraph Company, and Brown is made an equal partner in the company. Adams and Brown now have time for romance.

NOTES AND COMMENTARY: Kathryn Adams remembered, "The other thing I was really struck by was the fact that there was no really touching of Johnny Mack Brown. I came from a family that was very affectionate, and so it just seemed unnatural not to hold out my arms and cuddle. That was a no-no in those days."

Arizona Cyclone was remade as a Tex Williams featurette, *Prairie Pirates* (Universal-International, 1950). Footage from *Arizona Cyclone* was used also.

The song "Let's Go" can be heard in *West of Carson City* (Universal, 1940) and *Arizona Trail* (Universal, 1943). "On the Trail of Tomorrow" had been featured in *West of Carson City* (Universal, 1940) and would be utilized in *Trail to Vengeance* (Universal, 1945).

Charles Morrison was usually billed as Chuck.

The title, *Arizona Cyclone*, was previously used for a Wally Wales three-reel featurette, an Imperial release in 1934.

REVIEWS: "Good Johnny Mack Brown picture" (*Variety*, 3/11/42); "Yet another Johnny Mack Brown oater, but this one's not half bad. The direction in the action scenes is exceptionally well done" (*The Motion Picture Guide*, Nash and Ross).

SUMMATION: *Arizona Cyclone* is a good "B" western. Johnny Mack Brown is at the top of his form in this one, in both the action and acting departments. Dick Curtis makes a worthy and tough adversary for Brown. Nell O'Day gives a thoughtful and spirited performance as a young woman faced with running a business due to her father's death. The only false note in the proceedings is Fuzzy Knight's role as a hypochondriac; most of his routines just don't work. Joseph H. Lewis' edgy direction gives the film added grit. Lewis utilizes unique camera angles to give the story added visual interest.

HIS BLAZING GUNS SMOKE OUT THE RENEGADES

Arizona Trail

ALTERNATE TITLE: *Sundown Trail*; Universal (September 1943)

CAST: Johnny Trent, **Tex Ritter**; Kansas, **Fuzzy Knight**; Wayne Trent, **Dennis Moore**; Martha Brooks, **Janet Shaw**; Ace Vincent, **Jack Ingram**; Dan Trent, **Erville Alderson**; Doc Wallace, **Joseph Greene**; Matt Baker, **Glenn Strange**; Sheriff, **Dan White**; Curley, **Art Fowler**; Townsman, **Bill Wolfe**; Andy, **Johnny Bond**; Johnny Bond's Red River Boys (Wesley Tuttle, Paul Sells and Jimmie Dean Glosup)

CREDITS: Director, **Vernon Keays**; Associate Producer, **Oliver Drake**; Screenwriter, **William Lively**; Editor, **Alvin Todd**; Art Directors, **John B. Goodman and Abraham Grossman**; Set Decorations, **R.A. Gausman and Lee Smith**; Cinematographer, **William Sickner**; Special Photographic

Effects, **John P. Fulton**; Sound, **Bernard B. Brown and William Hedgcock**; Musical Director, **Paul Sawtell**

SONGS: "Let's Go" (Rosen and Carter)—sung by **Tex Ritter and Fuzzy Knight**; "Stars of the Midnight Range" (Bond)—sung by **Johnny Bond and his Red River Valley Boys**; "Ridin' Down to Santa Fe" (Bond)—sung by **Johnny Bond and his Red River Valley Boys**; "Stay Away from My Heart" (Marvin)—sung by **Tex Ritter with Johnny Bond and his Red River Valley Boys**; and "The Devil's Gonna Laugh" (Rosen and Carter)—sung by **Fuzzy Knight**

LOCATION FILMING: Corriganville, California

RUNNING TIME: 57 min.

STORY: Mustered out of the Army, Tex Ritter and his pal, Fuzzy Knight, are asked by Doctor Joseph Greene to return to Arizona. Greene wants Ritter to help his ailing father, who is being plagued by rustlers. Ritter has been estranged from his father, Erville Alderson, for fifteen years but finally consents to come. Ritter arrives at Alderson's ranch in time to prevent saloon owner Jack Ingram from shooting his father. Ingram wants to obtain Alderson's ranch at any cost. Ingram's men have been raiding Alderson's cattle. Alderson tells Ritter that Dennis Moore is his legally adopted son, and begrudgingly allows Ritter and Knight to stay on the ranch. Ritter accuses Moore of wanting him out of the way so he will inherit the ranch. The men fight, and Ritter realizes Moore is on the level. Greene is behind the rustling activities. Greene wants to control all the land and water rights in the area. Greene plots another rustling raid, which is thwarted by Ritter and Knight. Frustrated by this setback, Ingram attempts to shoot Alderson. Alderson is saved by quick thinking and action by his nurse, Janet Shaw. Ritter and Moore arrive at the ranch in time to wound Ingram as he rides from the ranch. Ritter and Moore arrest Ingram as he receives treatment from Greene. At the jail, Greene smuggles a gun to Ingram. In his escape attempt, Ingram exchanges shots with Moore. Moore is unhurt but Ingram is mortally wounded. Ritter discovers Ingram's gun contained blanks. Ingram confesses that Greene is the head of the gang. Ritter and Moore round up Greene and his gang. Both Ritter and Moore have a romantic interest in Shaw, but Shaw seems to be undecided about which man she prefers.

NOTES AND COMMENTARY: *Arizona Trail* was Tex Ritter's first solo starring western feature for Universal. The film was slated to co-star Ritter with Johnny Mack Brown. Brown's move to his solo starring series at Monogram gave Ritter the Brown role of Johnny Trent. Dennis Moore was signed for the Ritter part.

Wesley Tuttle only has a thumb and little finger on his left hand. When he was six years old, Tuttle went to work with his father, who was a butcher at a market. While his father was painting signs advertising the specials of the day, Tuttle saw some freshly ground hamburger and spotted some pieces of meat, which would be ground next. Tuttle climbed up on a stool and put not only the hamburger but also his three fingers into the grinder. He later learned how to chord left handed to play the guitar.

Jimmie Dean Glosup was the brother of western singing cowboy star Eddie Dean.

The song, "Let's Go" was previously heard in *West of Carson City* (Universal, 1940) and *Arizona Cyclone* (Universal, 1941). "Stay Away from My Heart" was later featured in *I'm from Arkansas* (PRC, 1944).

REVIEWS: "A better-than-average Ritter entry" (*The Western*, Hardy); "Fairly well done Tex Ritter vehicle" (*Western Movies*, Pitts)

SUMMATION: *Arizona Trail* is a good, fast-action "B" western. Tex Ritter and Dennis Moore capably handle the heroics, and Fuzzy Knight chips in with some pleasing comedy moments. Ritter, Knight and Johnny Bond and the Red River Valley Boys are given some better-than-average songs, and these help *Arizona Trail* achieve an above-average status. The film is well directed by Vernon Keays.

RIDIN' FOR REVENGE!
...Blasting renegades off the range...!

Bad Man from Red Butte

Universal (May, 1940)

CAST: Gils Brady/ Buck Halliday, **Johnny Mack Brown**; Gabriel Hornsby, **Bob Baker**; Spud Jenkins, **Fuzzy Knight**; Tibby Mason, **Anne Gwynne**; Skip Toddhunter, **Bill Cody Jr.**; Hal Benson, **Norman Willis**; Cochran, **Earle Hodgins**; Hank, **Roy Barcroft**; Dan Toddhunter, **Lafe McKee**; Turner, **Lloyd Ingraham**; Jitters, **Buck Moulton**; Miss Wood, **Myra McKinney**; and **Texas Jim Lewis and his Band**// Brady, **Eric Alden**; Shorty, **Frank Mitchell**; Cowboy, **Art Mix**

CREDITS: Director, **Ray Taylor**; Associate Producer, **Joseph Sanford**; Screenwriter, **Sam Robins**; Editor, **Paul Landres**; Art Directors, **Jack Otterson and Ralph M. DeLacey**; Set Decorations, **R.A. Gausman**; Cinematographer, **William Sickner**; Sound, **Bernard B. Brown and Jesse Moulin**; Musical Director, **H.J. Salter**

SONGS: "Gabby, the Lawyer" (Carter and Rosen), "Where the Prairie Meets the Sky" (Carter and Rosen)—sung by **Bob Baker**; "Little Joe, the Wrangler" (traditional)—piano solo and "We Want Hornsby" (Carter and Rosen)—sung by **Texas Jim Lewis and his Band**

LOCATION FILMING: Agoura, California

RUNNING TIME: 58 min.

STORY: In Cripple Creek, gunman Johnny Mack Brown shoots up Norman Willis' saloon and Justice of the Peace Earle Hodgins' office. Willis' men chase Brown, and in an exchange of shots, Brown is wounded. Brown is able to elude his pursuers and makes it to a deserted cabin to try to tend to his wound. Into this lawless community ride three happy-go-lucky saddle pals, surveyor Johnny Mack Brown, lawyer Bob Baker and hair tonic salesman Fuzzy Knight. Willis gets rough with rancher Lafe McKee and his grandson Bill Cody Jr. when McKee asks for an extension of his loan. Surveyor Brown steps in and whips Willis in a fistfight, and the two men become bitter enemies. Willis thinks he might have fought gunman Brown. Stageline owner Lloyd Ingraham wants surveyor Brown to route a better and faster road for his stage routes. Baker sets up his law office. Surveyor Brown's girlfriend, Anne Gwynne, arrives in Cripple Creek to teach school. The best route is through McKee's ranch. Brown offers McKee enough money to pay off his loan with Willis. In traveling to Bolder Pass, surveyor Brown comes upon the cabin with the severely wounded gunman Brown. The two men are twin brothers, and, as he dies, gunman Brown asks surveyor Brown to bring Willis to justice using legal means. Willis learns that McKee has the money to pay off the loan and sends men to steal it. In the holdup, McKee is mortally wounded. Surveyor Brown trails the outlaws to town where Willis accuses him of the crime. Hodgins incites a lynch mob, but Knight's quick thinking allows surveyor Brown to escape. Willis sends his henchman, Roy Barcroft, to take possession of McKee's ranch. Surveyor Brown interferes and captures Barcroft. Baker runs for Justice of the Peace and is elected. Surveyor Brown forces Hodgins to leave Cripple Creek. Baker holds court to bring McKee's murderer to justice. When surveyor Brown brings Barcroft to court to testify, Willis realizes he'll be brought to justice and tries to escape. Surveyor Brown gives chase, whips Willis in a rugged fistfight and brings him in to stand trial for his crimes. Now Brown has time for Gwynne, and the couple plan to wed.

NOTES AND COMMENTARY: When production ended on *Bad Man from Red Butte*, Bob Baker's tenure as a starring or co-starring cowboy star was over. Universal would utilize Baker in support roles in *Ride 'Em Cowboy* (1942), the serial *Overland Mail* (1942) and *Oklahoma Raiders* (1944). In *Cowboy*, Baker has a non-speaking role in the scene in which Ella Fitzgerald sings "A-Tisket, A-Tasket." Don't blink when you watch *Oklahoma Raiders*, or you might miss Baker's appearance. In *Mail*, Baker has a strong but relatively brief support role as Young Bill Cody, receiving fifth billing. It looked like Baker's career might have a resurgence when he landed the youthful lead in Ken Maynard and Hoot Gibson's Trail Blazers initial series entry, *Wild Horse Stampede* (Monogram, 1943), but Maynard took a strong dislike to Baker, which ended his association with Monogram.

This film was remade as *Cheyenne Roundup* (Universal, 1943), with Johnny Mack Brown again essaying a dual role. Tex Ritter was Brown's co-star in the remake.

Texas Jim Lewis receives billing as Tex Jim Lewis.

In the advertisements for *Bad Man from Red Butte*, Myra McKinney receives fifth billing but is way down in the cast when listed on the screen.

"Where the Prairie Meets the Sky" was used in *Escape from Hong Kong* (Universal, 1942), *Frontier Law* (Universal, 1943), *Twilight on the Prairie* (Universal, 1944) and *I'll Tell the World* (Universal, 1945).

REVIEWS: "Up to standard" (*Variety*, 6/12/40); "Average Johnny Mack Brown oater" (*Western Movies*, Pitts)

SUMMATION: *Bad Man from Red Butte* is a top-notch "B" western. Johnny Mack Brown is in great form handling the dual role of good guy and gunman. He especially shines in the death scene of his gunman twin. Bob Baker is given a little more to do and shows he can more than capably handle the fighting and shooting sequences. Fuzzy Knight adds some welcome comedy relief as he sells his hair tonic, garnering a few genuine laughs along the way. Norman Willis makes a tough and convincing adversary for Brown. Ray Taylor's first assignment for Brown at Universal is a sure winner, as action, acting, comedy and songs are nicely balanced.

HE'S T-N-TERROR!

Bad Men of the Border

Universal (September 1945)

CAST: Ted Cameron, **Kirby Grant**; Rockabye Jones, **Fuzzy Knight**; Delores Mendoza, **Armida**; Bart Breslow, **John Eldredge**; Marie Manning, **Barbara Sears**; Ace Morgan, **Edward M. Howard**; Jose Garcia, **Francis McDonald**; Estrella, **Soledad Jimenez**// Roy, **Edmund Cobb**; Joe, **Pierce Lyden**; Bill, **Gene Stutenroth**; Ed, **Roy Brent**; Sheriff Peters, **Glenn Strange**; Gus, **Ethan Laidlaw**; Juan, **Charles Stevens**; Sanchez, **Sam Appel**

CREDITS: Director/Associate Producer, **Wallace W. Fox**; Screenwriter, **Adele Buffington**; Editor, **Phillip Cahn**; Art Directors, **John B. Goodman and Abraham Grossman**; Set Decorators, **Russell A. Gausman and Ralph Sylos**; Cinematographer, **Maury Gertsman**; Sound, **Bernard B. Brown and Jack A. Bolger, Jr.**; Musical Director, **Mark Levant**

SONGS: "And Then I Got Married" (Rosen and Carter)—sung by **Fuzzy Knight**; and "I Would Love You" (Rosen and Carter)—sung by **Armida**

LOCATION FILMING: Iverson and Corriganville, California

RUNNING TIME: 56 min.

STORY: The stagecoach to Bordertown, a town situated on both the American and Mexican sides of the border, is carrying dancer Armida and merchandise exporter Barbara Sears. The stage is held up by undercover marshal Kirby Grant, who steals the mail pouch. Grant is working with his partner, Fuzzy Knight. In Bordertown, stagecoach driver Edmund Cobb, in league with the outlaw gang, hears Grant's voice and identifies him to badman Edward M. Howard. Howard makes a failed attempt to get rid of Grant. Grant makes a pitch to become a gang member. Armida is an undercover agent from the Mexican government under assignment to investigate cantina owner John Eldredge. Eldredge is a former convicted criminal from the Unites States who professes he's gone straight. Armida, while searching Eldredge's office, finds a secret stairway to an underground tunnel. In a room off the tunnel, Armida finds counterfeit money; which makes its way into the States concealed in merchandise exported by Eldredge's wife, Sears. Before Armida can leave for help, she is captured. Grant and Knight find the tunnel, also. Knight goes for help while Grant investigates. Hearing Grant approaching, Eldredge hides and strikes Grant from behind. Eldredge realizes the game is over, and he, Sears and his gang decide to leave the area. Grant recovers and rescues Armida. Grant, Knight and a posse pursue the counterfeiters, and finally catch up and bring them to justice. With the counterfeit gang smashed, Grant and Armida leave for El Paso to be married.

NOTES AND COMMENTARY: With Rod Cameron's promotion to bigger budgeted films, Universal tapped singer Kirby Grant to be the studio's next cowboy star. Grant, reportedly, did not like appearing in this western series. In the late '40s Grant would co-star with canine star Chinook in ten Mountie features for Monogram/Allied Artists before gaining everlasting fame as Sky King in the television series of the same name (NBC, 1951–52).

Barbara Sears, who appeared in *Badmen of the Border* and *Code of the Lawless* (Universal, 1945), became a household name as "Bobo" Rockefeller when she married into that famous family.

Gene Stutenroth would later in his career shorten his last name to Roth.

"And Then I Got Married" was previously heard in *Son of Roaring Dan* (Universal, 1940).

REVIEWS: "If one can overlook the implausible plot, Kirby Grant's initial series vehicle for Universal is acceptable entertainment" (*Western Movies*, Pitts); "Routine oater" (*The Motion Picture Guide*, Nash and Ross)

SUMMATION: Suprisingly, *Bad Men of the Border* is a good "B" western, despite having no shots fired and only one punch thrown. Thanks to a good script from Adele Buffington, and firm direction from Wallace W. Fox, Kirby Grant's first starring vehicle hits the mark. Grant scores solidly as a western hero and receives top support from the cast, especially Fuzzy Knight as his confederate and Armida as an undercover agent posing as a famous dancer. Both contribute entertaining musical numbers.

Deadwood City!
ROARING CAPITAL OF THE BEST AND THE WORST IN THE WEST!
Where life was cheap ... love was priceless ... and laws were made with lead!

Badlands of Dakota

Universal (September 1941)

CAST: Jim Holliday, **Robert Stack**; Anne Grayson, **Ann Rutherford**; Wild Bill Hickok, **Richard Dix**; Jane, **Frances Farmer**; Bob Holliday, **Broderick Crawford**; Rocky, **Hugh Herbert**; Spearfish, **Andy Devine**; Jack McCall, **Lon Chaney Jr.**; Hurricane Harry, **Fuzzy Knight**; General Custer, **Addison Richards**; and **The Jesters (Dwight Latham, Walter Carlson and Guy Bonham)**// Wong Lee, **Willie Fung**; Belle, **Jeanne Kelly**; Card Player in Deadwood, **Dick Alexander**; McCall Gang Members, **Glenn Strange** and **Carleton Young**; Grayson's Butler, **Clinton Rosemond**; Uncle Wilbur Grayson, **Samuel S. Hinds**; Jackson, **Harry Cording**; Card Player on River Boat, **Kermit Maynard**; Plainview Gunmen, **Charles King** and **Nolan Willis**; Man talking to King, **Robert Barron**; Plainview Marshal, **Alan Bridge**; Townsman, **Hank Bell**; Drunk, **Don Barclay**; Stage Guard, **Chuck Morrison**; Chapman, **Bradley Page**; Ransome, **Emmett Vogan**; Henchman, **Eddie Dew**

CREDITS: Director, **Alfred E. Green**; Assistant Director, **Vernon Keays**; Associate Producer, **George Waggner**; Story, **Harold Shumate**; Screenwriter, **Gerald Geraghty**; Additional Comedy Sequences, **Victor McLeod**; Editor, **Frank Gross**; Art Directors, **Jack Otterson** and **Harold B. MacArthur**; Set Decorator, **R.A. Gausman**; Cinematographer, **Stanley Cortez**; Gowns, **Vera West**; Sound, **Bernard B. Brown** and **Robert Pritchard**; Musical Director, **H.J. Salter**; Special Location Sequences—Director, **Ray Taylor**; Assistant Director, **Charles Gould**; Cinematographer, **William Sickner**

SONGS: "McNamarra's Band" (O'Connor and Stanford)—sung by the Jesters; "Going to Have a Big Time Tonight" (Robison)—sung by the Jesters; and "I'm Weeping Alone"—sung by **the Jesters**

LOCATION FILMING: Red Rock Canyon, California

RUNNING TIME: 74 min.

STORY: Saloon owner Broderick Crawford sends his younger brother, Robert Stack, to St. Louis as an escort for Ann Rutherford. On the journey, Stack and Rutherford fall in love and marry. When he learns of the marriage, Crawford goes on a binge and is beaten up by the ruthless Lon Chaney, Jr. Frances Farmer, who loves Crawford and always thought the two would marry, breaks up the fight. Craving action, Crawford joins Chaney's renegade outfit. Chaney's men dress as Indians when they perpetrate their lawlessness. Crawford has Stack appointed Marshal of Deadwood to humiliate him, and also in the hopes Stack will be killed so he can then marry Rutherford. Stack grows into the job and, with timely interference by Richard Dix, is able to arrest Chaney. Farmer makes an unsuccessful attempt to stop Crawford from riding with the renegades. Stack has gold shipped by stagecoach. When Crawford and the renegades (in their Indian garb) raid the coach, the posse, led by Stack, Dix and Farmer, attack the outlaws. Crawford makes a run for it; Stack bulldogs him off his horse. Stack is knocked unconscious when the men hit the ground. Crawford gets away but leaves behind his watch fob, which Stack finds. Stack questions Crawford about the watch fob, but Crawford claims he lost it in his fight with Chaney. Chaney breaks out of jail and murders Dix. Farmer warns the town that the Sioux will attack. Stack sends stage driver Fuzzy Knight to bring General Addison Richards and the cavalry. The Sioux attack Deadwood and begin burning down the town. Under cover of the fight, Chaney and Crawford plan to loot the bank. Stack tries to stop Crawford but is unable to pull the trigger. Crawford knocks Stack down and points his pistol at him. Farmer arrives and shoots Crawford, realizing this is the only way to stop his lawlessness. Chaney enters the room and is about to start shooting, when, in his dying moments, Crawford guns down Chaney. As all looks lost, the cavalry arrives. The town will have to be rebuilt, and Richards takes the cavalry off to the Little Big Horn.

NOTES AND COMMENTARY: Ann Rutherford remarked, "That picture did not make a deep impression on me, unlike *Wyoming* [Metro-Goldwyn-Mayer, 1941], where I was on location for a couple of months. I remember all the scenes very vividly. Other than Bob Stack and remembering Frances Farmer, I have no recollection of the plot or anything. It was not what we call a big 'A' production. I think the most important thing about it was it had Frances Farmer in it." Rutherford was on loan from Metro-Goldwyn-Mayer for this film.

Ann Rutherford commented on Richard Dix: "I worked with him earlier on a picture called *The Devil Is Driving* [Columbia, 1937]. He's the reason that I did not do the first Hardy picture. I had already been signed by M-G-M. He had a little too much to drink, I think, and he fell at home and broke his arm or something. They had to shoot around him. They wouldn't let me go to M-G-M when M-G-M needed me. I stayed on an extra month or two. They had to replace me in the first Hardy picture." Rutherford would portray Polly Benedict in twelve Andy Hardy episodes.

Badlands of Dakota (1941) movie still: Ann Rutherford and Robert Stack (*right*) begin to fall in love.

Footage from *Badlands of Dakota* would be used in Tex Ritter's *Marshal of Gunsmoke* (Universal, 1944), the serial *Raiders of Ghost City* (Universal, 1944) and Kirby Grant's *Gun Town* (Universal, 1946).

"Going to Have a Big Time Tonight" was heard in *National Barn Dance* (Paramount, 1944).

REVIEWS: "A surprise entertainment entry" (*Variety*, 9/10/41); "Slickly directed by Green and capably acted by a strong cast, this is a better than average western" (*The Western*, Hardy).

SUMMATION: *Badlands of Dakota* is a very enjoyable minor "A" western. The acting is first rate. Robert Stack and Anne Rutherford are good as the leads, but Richard Dix, Broderick Crawford and especially Frances Farmer steal the show. Dix shows quiet authority as "Wild Bill" Hickok. Crawford gets to "chew the scenery" as a man who loses the woman he loves and drifts into a life of crime. Farmer shows a great range of honest emotions, depicting tenderness and toughness, happiness and despair as the story calls. The added comedy scenes inserted to lengthen the picture actually work and add a measure of charm to the film. Alfred E. Green's direction is on target.

The Supreme Serial Thriller! 12 chapters packed with action.

Battling with Buffalo Bill

Universal (November 1931)

CAST: Buffalo Bill (William S. Cody), **Tom Tyler**; June Mills, **Lucile Browne**; John Mills, **William Desmond**; Dave Archer, **Rex Bell**; Jim Rodney, **Francis Ford**; Breed Johns, **George Regas**; Scout Jack Brady, **Yakima Canutt**; Joe Tempas, **Bud Osborne**; Joe Brady, **Joe Bonomo**; Ezra Purdy, **Bobby Nelson**; Chief Thunderbird, **Chief Thunderbird**; Swift Arrow, **Jim Thorpe**// Henchman, **Art Mix**; Andy, **Edmund Cobb**; Army Sergeant, **Rodney Hildebrand**; Clem Tempas, **Merrill McCormick**; Dolly, **Beulah Hutton**; and "Pardner"

CREDITS: Director, **Ray Taylor**; Assistant Producer, **Henry MacRae**; Screenwriters, **George H. Plympton** and **Ella O'Neill**; Editor, **Alvin Todd**; Cinematographer, **John Hickson**; Recording Supervisor, **C. Roy Hunter**; Synchronization, **Jack Foley**; Indian Authority, **Chief Thunderbird**

LOCATION FILMING: Walker Ranch, California

RUNNING TIME: 205 min.

CHAPTER TITLES: 1. Captured by Redskins, 2. Circling Death, 3. Between Hostile Tribes, 4. The Savage Horde, 5. The Fatal Plunge, 6. Trapped, 7. The Unseen Killer, 8. Sentenced to Death, 9. The Death Trap, 10. A Shot from Ambush, 11. The Flaming Death, 12. Cheyenne Vengeance

SOURCE: Story by **Henry MacRae**, suggested by the book **The Great West That Was** by **William F. Cody (Buffalo Bill)**

STORY: Francis Ford has incited the Cheyenne Indians to attack the town of Hard Rock so he can take over all the settlers' mining claims. William Desmond and Rex Bell have raised money to purchase a stamp mill. Ford plans to use the Blackfeet Indian tribe to stop the stamp mill from getting to Hard Rock. The Cheyennes attack Hard Rock and kidnap Desmond's daughter, Lucille Browne. Browne and Bell are in love. Frontier scout Tom Tyler rescues Browne from the Cheyennes. Not knowing Browne is safe, Desmond and Bell ride to rescue Browne and are captured by the Blackfeet. Tyler is able to rescue the two men. Tyler brings the three safely back to Hard Rock. Ford decides to seek the office of town marshal, and Bell runs against him. Ford initiates a fake gold strike. All the townsmen leave except Ford's gang members. Ford is elected marshal. Tyler realizes the site of the "strike" is the camp of the Blackfeet Indians. Tyler, Desmond and Bell ride to the aid of the townspeople, who have been besieged by the Blackfeet, and help drive off the Indians. Ford frames Bell for the murder of a prospector and the theft of his gold. Tyler is able to bring proof of Bell's innocence and saves Bell from being lynched. Tyler accuses

Ford of being behind the trouble with the Indian tribes. An attempt to kill Tyler is unsuccessful. Ford and his men leave Hard Rock and hide out. Ford learns that a wagon train bringing the stamp mill is nearing Hard Rock. Again, Ford convinces the Blackfeet to attack the wagon train. Tyler brings the cavalry to rout the Indians and save the wagon train. Tyler goes after Ford and his henchmen, George Regas and Bud Osborne. Tyler catches up with the men and, in a scuffle, finishes off Regas and Osborne. With murderous intent, Ford sneaks up on Tyler. Before Ford can carry through his threat, he is shot by Thunderbird, chief of the Cheyenne Indians. Thunderbird wants peace with the settlers, which is heartily endorsed by Desmond. Bell and Browne now have time for romance as Tyler rides off to new adventures.

NOTES AND COMMENTARY: Universal intended to have Tim McCoy star as "Buffalo Bill" Cody in *Battling with Buffalo Bill*. Before McCoy could appear in his third serial, however, he was given the opportunity to star in his own western series at Columbia. Tom Tyler was subsequently signed for the lead. Tyler had made a ten-chapter sound serial, *The Phantom of the West* (Mascot, 1930), and had been under contract to Syndicate to star in five westerns for the 1930-31 season.

As in their previous western serial, *The Indians Are Coming* (Universal, 1930), a narrator, this time dressed as a frontiersman, was used to bring the viewer up to date at the beginning of each chapter. The frontiersman had his horse tied to a hitching rail in front of a cabin. Since all the chapter introductions were shot in succession, the viewer can notice the horse getting restless. Finally, in Chapter 10, the horse disappears, not to reappear until the final chapter introduction. In case the viewer is too naive to distinguish the hero from the villain, Tom Tyler's character is described as "fearless," "heap reliable scout," "straight and strong as a pine tree" and "square shooter," while Francis Ford's character is a "coyote," a "snake," a "horn toad" and a "low down no count."

Footage from Hoot Gibson's *The Flaming Frontier* (Universal, 1926) was used in this serial, as well as most of the Universal serials that depicted Indian trouble as part of their story line.

REVIEWS: "Not much history here but there is plenty of action to make up for it in this cliffhanger" (*Western Movies*, Pitts); "A superior serial." (*The Western*, Hardy).

AUTHOR'S COMMENTS: This is a very entertaining, fast moving serial with decent cliffhanger chapter endings and resolutions. Director Ray Taylor wisely keeps his focus on action, and only includes dialogue scenes that are necessary to keep the story moving. Tom Tyler makes a fine serial hero, handling both action and dialog scenes with authority. Lucile Browne, Rex Bell, William Desmond, Frances Ford and George Regas add fine support.

He's Dynamite with a '45'! Battling outlaws for black gold!

Beyond the Pecos

ALTERNATE TITLE: *Beyond the Seven Seas*; Universal (April 1945)

CAST: Lew Remington, **Rod Cameron**; Bob Randall, **Eddie Dew**; Barnacle, **Fuzzy Knight**; Ellen Tanner, **Jennifer Holt**; Dan Muncie, **Ray Whitley**; John Heydrick, **Eugene Stutenroth**; Ed Remington, **Robert Homans**; Steve Grenfels, **Jack Ingram**; Ord Tanner, **Frank Jacquet**; Arizona, **Henry Wills**; Keno Hawkins, **Jack Rockwell**// Bill, **William Desmond**; Artie, **Artie Ortego**; Sheriff, **Dan White**; Deke, **Al Ferguson**; Pat Bobbitt, **Ray Henderson**; Dr. E.L. Crane, **Forrest Taylor**; Townsman, **Jim Thorpe**; and **Ray Whitley's Bar-6 Cowboys**

CREDITS: Director, **Lambert Hillyer**; Associate Producer, **Oliver Drake**; Story, **Jay Karth**; Screenwriter, **Bennett R. Cohen**; Editor, **Ray Snyder**; Art Directors, **John B. Goodman and Abraham Grossman**; Set Decorators, **Russell A. Gausman and Ray L. Jeffers**; Cinematographer, **Maury Gertsman**; Sound, **Bernard B. Brown and Jess Moulin**; Musical Director, **Paul Sawtell**

SONGS: "High, Wide and Handsome" (Ritter and Choate)—sung by **Ray Whitely and His Bar-6 Cowboys**; "Blow the Man Down" (Traditional)—sung by **Fuzzy Knight**; "Dusty Trails" (Sheely, Sheely and List)—sung by **Ray Whitely and His Bar-6 Cowboys**; "Call of the Range" (Rosen and Carter)—sung by **Ray Whitely and His Bar-6 Cowboys**; plus "Schubert's Serenade" (Schubert) and "Moonlight Sonata" (Beethoven)—played as piano solos by **Eugene Stutenroth**

LOCATION FILMING: Corriganville, California

RUNNING TIME: 58 min.

STORY: The feud between the ranches of Rod Cameron and Eddie Dew has flared up again. Cameron had left Mesa City a few years earlier to avoid bloodshed and because he thought Jennifer Holt preferred Dew to him. Receiving a letter to return home, an unsuccessful attempt is made on Cameron's life by Jack Ingram and two henchmen. Cameron is left on foot and meets tonic salesman and former seaman Fuzzy Knight, who gives him a ride into Mesa City on his ship on wheels. In Mesa City, painter Eugene Stutenroth, the man instigating the feud, sees Cameron go into the saloon. Stutenroth has henchman Jack Ingram find Dew and tell him Cameron's in town. The two men meet and fight, with Cameron emerging as the victor. Cameron and Knight go to the ranch to talk with Cameron's father, Robert Homans. Riding along is Stutenroth, who has business with Homans. At the ranch is Holt, with her father, lawyer Frank Jacquet. Jacquet tells Homans he'll have to call in the loan he made Homans. Stutenroth offers to purchase the ranch. Cameron refuses and then asks Jacquet and Holt to leave the ranch. Cameron believes a third party is stirring up the feud. Jacquet doesn't want to ruin his old friend Homans, and goes to Stutenroth to back out of their deal to grab Homans' ranch. Stutenroth tells Jacquet he can get out of their arrangement only by selling Homans' note to him. Jacquet replies and asks for water. Ingram poisons the water. Jacquet leaves Stutenroth's house and is accosted by Cameron. As he is about to explain everything, Jacquet keels over and dies. Ingram, on the spot, accuses Cameron of poisoning Jacquet. Cameron refuses to be arrested and makes a get a way with Knight. In the chase, a bullet grazes Cameron's hand. Knight is about to treat Cameron's hand with one of his tonics when Cameron notices an oily smell. Knight tells Cameron that he got the water from a spring on Homans' ranch. Cameron realizes that Stutenroth wants the ranch because of valuable oil deposits. Cameron and Knight search Stutenroth's house and find a glass and a pitcher, both emitting a funny smell. The two men go to the coroner's in-

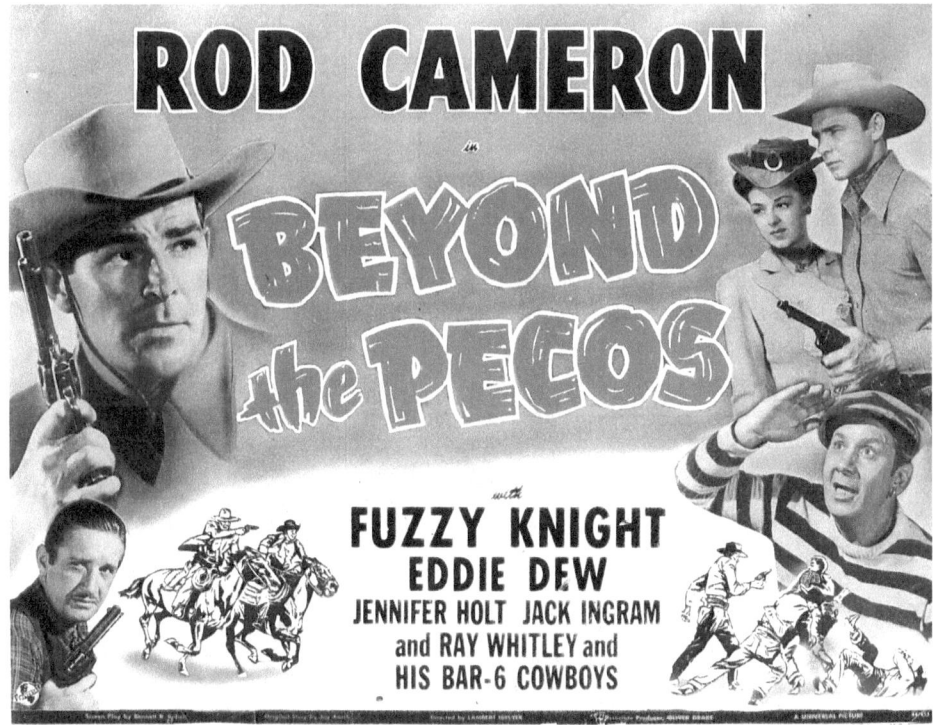

Beyond the Pecos (1945) title card: **Left *(top to bottom)*,** Rod Cameron, Jack Ingram; **right *(top to bottom)*,** Eddie Dew, Jennifer Holt, and Fuzzy Knight.

quest where Ingram is on the witness stand. Cameron asks if he could question Ingram. Ingram becomes nervous and requests a glass of water. Knight pours the water and, after Ingram has taken a long swallow, sets the mysterious pitcher down beside Ingram. Ingram, fearing he's been poisoned, confesses and implicates Stutenroth. Stutenroth, realizing the game is lost, shoots Ingram and escapes with his henchmen. Cameron, Dew and a posse give chase, with Knight bringing up the rear in his ship on wheels. Stutenroth and his men gain an almost impregnable position. Knight solves the problem by blasting the outlaws with cannon fire. Confused and stunned, Stutenroth and his men are quickly rounded up by Cameron, Dew and the posse. Peace now reigns in Mesa City, and Cameron and Holt plan to marry.

NOTES AND COMMENTARY: Lambert Hillyer was a director, primarily of western features, for over forty years. Beginning in the late teens until the late forties, Hillyer would direct many of the top western stars (e.g. William S. Hart, Buck Jones, Charles Starrett, Bill Elliott, Tex Ritter, Johnny Mack Brown and Jimmy Wakely). Hillyer ended out his career by directing most of the episodes of the *Cisco Kid* television series in the early fifties.

"Dusty Trails" can be heard in *Shady Lady* (Universal, 1945), and "*Call of the Range*" was utilized in *Man from Montana* (Universal, 1941), *Frontier Law* (Universal, 1943) and *Gunman's Code* (Universal, 1946).

The main villain in *Beyond the Pecos*, Eugene Stutenroth, would become better known in films as Gene Roth.

REVIEWS: "Stout Rod Cameron vehicle nicely helmed by veteran director Lambert Hillyer" (*Western Movies*, Pitts); "Some good action sequences overcome a stereotyped script." (*The Motion Picture Guide*, Nash and Ross).

SUMMATION: *Beyond the Pecos* is a fast-paced, action-packed "B" western with Rod Cameron in fine form. Fuzzy Knight is on target with his comedy and logical support to hero Cameron. The rest of the cast lends able support, with Eugene Stutenroth standing out as a "cultured" villain. Veteran director Lambert Hillyer knows his westerns and keeps this one at a high interest level for action fans.

He was a riding, fighting fool of a man with a girl to guard and blackmailers to get!
He was happy on a wild mustang and happier in a wild shebang!

Black Aces

Universal (September 1937); A Buck Jones Production

CAST: Ted Ames, **Buck Jones**; Sandy McKenzie, **Kay Linaker**; Homer Truesdale, **Robert Frazer**; Henry Kline, **Raymond Brown**; Len Stoddard, **Fred MacKaye**; Wolf Whalen, **Robert Kortman**; Bridge Guard, **Ben Corbett**; Boyd Lomis, **W.E. Lawrence**; Ike, **Frank Campeau**; Hank Farnum, **Bob McKenzie**; Sheriff Potter, **Chas. Le Moyne**; Outlaw, **Lee Shumway**; Joe, **Arthur Van Slyke**; Jesse Walker, **Charles King**; Jake Stoddard, **Bernard Phillips**; and "Silver"

CREDITS: Director, **Buck Jones**; Story, **Stephen Payne**; Screenwriter, **Frances Guihan**; Editor, **Bernard Loftus**; Art Directors, **Ralph Berger** and **Frank Smith**; Cinematographers, **Allen Thompson** and **William Sickner**; Sound, **L. John Myers**

LOCATION FILMING: Kernville, California

RUNNING TIME: 59 min.

SOURCE: Novel by **Stephen Payne**

STORY: Ranch owners are being sent Black Aces in the mail telling them to pay ten thousand dollars or be killed. Happy-go-lucky cowboy Buck Jones receives a Black Ace but chooses to ignore the threat. Since Jones chooses not to improve his ranch, his girlfriend, Kay Linaker, breaks off their relationship. Jones goes to town and is enticed to sit in on a card game run by Fred MacKaye. Jones loses his ranch. MacKaye's brother, Bernard Phillips, goes to Jones' ranch as he gathers his belongings. Phillips goes to the barn and is murdered. Jones is wanted for the crime. A Black Ace is sent to Linaker's ranch, threatening her father, who is out of town. Linaker and rancher Raymond Brown borrow money from banker Robert Frazier. Brown surrenders the money. Jones goes to Brown's ranch where W.E. Lawrence attempts to arrest Jones. Jones is able to escape on Lawrence's horse. In the saddlebags, Jones finds the money Brown gave to the Black Ace gang and returns it to Brown. Robert Kortman captures Jones and takes him to the hideout to be questioned by Fred MacKaye, a member of the Black Ace gang. Jones escapes and guesses that the gang's main hideout is in the Basin. Linaker, while out riding, sees men she suspects to be Black Ace members and decides to follow them. Seeing Jones' horse, Silver, Linaker sends her horse to her ranch with a note to bring help. Silver goes with Linaker's horse. Linaker goes to the hideout and is captured. Jones also makes his way to the hideout. Silver and Linaker's horse arrive at Linaker's ranch. Sheriff Charles Le Moyne and Linaker's cowhands are at the ranch. The men do not see the note, but Silver gets the men to follow him. Frazier, the Black Ace leader, shows up at the hideout to split the extortion money. Kortman and his gang plan to leave the area, taking Linaker with them. The posse arrives and corrals the gang members as Jones battles Kortman in the cabin and rescues Linaker. Frazier is detained and tries to deny having any association with the gang. Linaker tells Le Moyne that Frazier is the leader. Frazier slaps Linaker, and Jones defeats Frazier in a fistfight. During the fight, Jones tells Linaker he's now a businessman; and now they will be lifetime partners.

NOTES AND COMMENTARY: Kay Linaker's comments on *Black Aces*, "I had always wanted to do a western. To me, doing a western was synonymous with the old fear of doing a Little Eva and Uncle Tom show. I kept saying to my agent, 'I'd like to do a western.' One day he called me and he said, 'Do you still have this bug in your bonnet about doing a western?' I said, 'Yes, I do.' He said, 'You have an appointment with Buck Jones, who needs an actress. This is a good part, I understand.' I went out to see Buck Jones. He was producing at Universal as well as starring in this. Buck Jones was one of God's good gentlemen. He was a fine, prime human being. I was totally charmed and took the part. We went up to do the exteriors first. It was a fantastic experience. I was the only woman on the picture. I didn't have a stand-in. I didn't have a hairdresser. I didn't have a wardrobe girl. I was the only woman up there. I did have a double, and she was a double who had worked with me before. Her name was Aileen Goodwin. Her greatest claim to fame was she doubled in *Gone with the Wind* (Selznick/Metro-Goldwyn-Mayer) and fell down the stairs. She fell down the stairs for Scarlet. She was a charming person. My part said that I would cross a swinging bridge above the Kern River. The morning that we were going to shoot this I was out on location with the company and the director. Buck was out briefly to explain what he wanted done with the second unit. So I was sitting, waiting for him to come back so we could work. Les Selander, who was the director, came over to me and said, 'You know, we're not doing anything much. Why don't you cross the bridge now?' I said, 'Fine.' Because the director told you to do something and you did it. I crossed the bridge. The bridge was, perhaps, about two blocks long or a little better. It was about thirty five or forty feet above the Kern River. The Kern River, at this time, was a mass of foam tumbling down the hill and going up to the bridge. I had never gone across a swinging bridge in my life. I didn't realize that when you step on one of those bridges, the planking comes up to meet your foot on the next step. Also, the bridge was swinging from side to side. It was only one handhold on the bridge. That was to be grabbed going across the bridge, it was to be grabbed by your left hand. I was to cross the bridge and on the other side of the bridge I was to pick a hat from one of the heavies. Earlier, I had a gunfight with this heavy and had managed to take his hat and tie him up and disarm him. So the only thing we had to do was have me just climb up on the bridge with this hat on my head. It had no chinstrap, and it was a man's hat and it was big. I had no choice but to hold it on my head with my other hand. I had my left hand on the rail, and my right hand was holding the hat on my head. I came across the bridge. Just as I stepped off the bridge, Buck and Aileen came back from the second unit. When I stepped off the bridge, Buck looked at me and said, 'Are you all right?' I said, 'Yes, I'm fine.' He stepped over to Les and said, 'Why did you tell her to do that?' He said, 'I thought we'd save a little time and get a little bit ahead of schedule.' He said, 'You realize that she is insured by Lloyds of London, and she's not supposed to do anything like that. And this could ruin our relationship with Lloyds of London. Besides, the only reason that she did it was because she's the kind of an actress who feels the director knows what he's doing. But for your information, you don't know what you're doing and please, I want you to go back to Los Angeles right now. I never want you to come into my office again.' Les Selander didn't work for about eight years." (Author's note: Selander left Universal for Harry Sherman's Hopalong Cassidy productions for Paramount. In the forties and fifties, Selander worked at RKO, Republic, Columbia, Allied Artists and Monogram. He finally returned to Universal to direct *The Raiders* [Universal-International, 1952]. Selander directed into the late sixties, ending his career with *Arizona Bushwackers* [Paramount, 1968].)

Kay Linaker related another incident: "Buck and I stayed at the home of the owners of the hotel. I was downstairs, and he was upstairs. We had all our meals in the restaurant. It was a lovely arrangement. In the evening, there was a juke box in the bar, which was the dining room, too. We would listen to the music and chat for a short time. We never stayed very late. This one evening, about the third or fourth evening we were there, the music was playing. The guys were dancing with one another. Everybody was having a nice time. I was dancing with Buck; all of a sudden I felt him jolt. There was a man punching him. Buck had fought three or four professional bouts one time in his life. That made his fists a lethal weapon. He could only shoulder whoever came up to him. He couldn't hit anybody. He dragged me over and pushed me across the bar. The bartender was down at one end of the bar, but his wife was right there. She handed me a heavy napkin with two big salt and pepper shakers in it. It was knotted. She said, 'If anyone comes near you, swing this at them.' She vanished. I saw the bartender crawling on his hands and knees with a gun. These people [the intruders] were miners and had evidently got a load on. They were very upset because they weren't being used as extras. Only the cattlemen

Black Aces (1937) photograph: Kay Linaker and Buck Jones in a tense moment (courtesy of Kay Linaker).

were being used as extras. They came over and were going to wipe out the company. I stayed behind the bar and watched this thing happen. Somebody yelled, 'Hey, Rube.' Within seconds, all the men, who had already gone to bed, came across in their nightclothes. I had never seen a man in their nightshirt before in my life. You never saw such a lovely barroom brawl. It was just wonderful. The company beat the living thunder out of these guys. When they had them on the run, went out and picked up their car, it was a little truck, and they turned it over on its top. It was known for years as the Battle of Kernville."

Kay Linaker had another experience, this time a little more personal. She related, "I'm the only woman on the company. We are out one day, and lunch had been brought. Because I'm the only woman, they didn't have a facility for me. Sometime after lunch, along about two o'clock, I had to use the ladies room. I looked over and saw there was this nice hill and there were some rock outcroppings. I figured if I climbed up that hill and went around the corner behind the rock, if I couldn't see the company, they couldn't see me. I went up the hill. I was dressed in Levi's. I had a gun belt on. I, also, had a heavy western belt.

Under this I wore a leotard, which you always wore when you were doing any horseback riding. It was kind of a girdle thing that went from your knees to just under your ribs. I got up there. I couldn't see the company so I knew the company couldn't see me. I undid all these buckles and buttons and pulled the whole arrangement down. I was relieving myself when, all of a sudden, I heard [a noise]. I looked between my legs and there was a snake striking at the stream of water. They say you cannot run with your pants around your knees, but that is a damn lie. I ran down that hill and when I got in sight of the company, I screamed, 'Don't look.' Of course, every head swiveled and then every head swiveled right back. I got behind the prop truck and pulled myself all together. I had to walk out and sit down in a chair with all these gentlemen. I walked out, sat down, and no one said a word to me. We got to my next scene, I get up. I rehearse it. We do it. We do another set up. I'm not in that one. No one says 'Boo' to me. We did another scene. The scene was over. The fellows said, 'That was great, Katie. Fine.' At supper that night, Buck and I are sitting at this long table. People start to excuse themselves. We're still sitting there, having coffee. All of a sudden, Buck said, 'Kate, how big was the snake?' I said, 'I don't know. It was gargantuous.' He said, 'I thought it had to be. Nothing would have sent you down the hill, other than a snake.' And it was never discussed. No one ever teased me."

Kay Linaker remembered another humorous incident. In the scene, Linaker had been captured and she was to throw a canteen at a lamp, extinguishing it. Linaker professed an inability to aim and hit a target. She was told just to throw the canteen, and someone off camera would then hit the lamp. Linaker remembers, "I sat up on the bed and threw the canteen. I hit the lamp and cut it right in two. The kerosene is all over the floor. The lamp was lighted, and we got this fire all over the place. They grabbed the fire extinguishers and put out the fire." Linaker was kidded about her throwing ability after that.

REVIEWS: "Grade A Buck Jones western." (*Variety*, 8/25/37); "This is one of the best of the films directed and produced by Jones." (*The Western*, Hardy)

SUMMATION: This is a very good Buck Jones western, one of his best. Jones is quite believable as a happy-go-lucky cowhand who finally settles down. Kay Linaker brings a depth to her performance not usually seen in a "B" western, with an excellent performance. Cinematographers Allan Thompson and William Sickner's camerawork is exceptional, as the vistas of Kernville add immeasurably to the enjoyment of the picture. Jones and the uncredited Lesley Selander direct with film hands.

A Four-Fisted Action Sock!

Black Bandit

Universal (September 1938)

CAST: Bob, **Bob Baker**; Jane, **Marjorie Reynolds**; Weepy, **Hal Taliaferro**; Don, **Bob Baker**; Allen, **Jack Rockwell**; Sheriff, **Forrest Taylor**; Johnson, **Glenn Strange**; Ramsay, **Arthur Van Slyke**; Cash, **Carleton Young**; Evans, **Dick Dickinson**; Young Bob, **Schuyler Standish**; Young Don, **Rex Downing**// Deputy, **Jack Ingram**; Tom, **Tom London**; Outlaw, **Slim Whitaker**

CREDITS: Director, **George Waggner**; Assistant Director, **Glenn Cook**; Story/Screenwriter, **Joseph West**; Editor, **Carl Pierson**; Technical Director, **Albert Greenwood**; Sound, **Bernard B. Brown** and **Robert Pritchard**; Musical Director/Arranger, **Frank Sanucci**

SONGS: "Starlight on the Prairie" (Allan)—sung by **Bob Baker and male chorus**; "A Cowboy's Song for Sale" (Allan)—sung by **Bob Baker**; "My Old Paint Pony an' Me" (Allan)—sung by **Bob Baker**; and "Dusty an' Dry" (Allan)—sung by **Bob Baker**

LOCATION FILMING: Iverson, Andy Jauregui Ranch and Brandeis Ranch, California

RUNNING TIME: 60 min.

STORY: Bob Baker as the Black Bandit, with his henchman Carleton Young, leads a notorious gang of rustlers. Bandit Baker crosses the state line to continue his outlawry in a territory for which his twin brother is sheriff. Sheriff Baker is about to propose to Marjorie Reynolds when her father, Jack Rockwell, tells him there is rustling activity and Sheriff Forrest Taylor wants to see him. Taylor can't believe the resemblance between the Black Bandit and Sheriff Baker. Sheriff Baker and his old pal, Hal Taliaferro, know that means Baker's brother has finally shown up. Sheriff Baker wants to find his brother and try to straighten him out. After a rustling raid, Bandit Baker needs a horse and picks out one at Rockwell's ranch. Bell, thinking he's Sheriff Baker, allows him to take a horse. The ranchers think Sheriff Baker could be the Black Bandit, and Baker refuses to defend himself. Sheriff Baker rides off to confront his brother, which he's able to do. Goaded into a fistfight by Bandit Baker, Sheriff Baker wins and forces his brother to change clothes. Sheriff Baker goes to Young to figure a way to stop the rustling and protect his brother. Bandit Baker is mistaken for the sheriff and is captured by the ranchers. Reynolds cuts Bandit Baker loose and convinces him to help his brother. Young realizes he's facing the sheriff and gets the drop on him. Bandit Baker shows up, followed by a posse. Young goes to fight the posse while Bandit Baker states he'll take care of his brother. His brother knocks out Sheriff Baker and changes clothes with him. Young shoots Bandit Baker thinking he's the sheriff. Sheriff Baker shoots Young. Reynolds had ridden with the posse, and Bandit Baker's last words are to tell Reynolds to take care of his brother.

NOTES AND COMMENTARY: Hal Taliaferro was earlier known as western ace Wally Wales, who starred in "B" western series entries for Big 4 (1930–31) and Imperial (1934). As Taliaferro, he subsequently played sidekicks, villains and character parts in western films.

The working title for *The Black Bandit* was *Twins of the West*.

Screenwriter Joseph West was the pseudonym for director George Waggner.

Bob Baker would sing "Dry and Dusty" two films later, in *Prairie Justice* (Universal, 1938). "Starlight on the Prairie' would also be heard in *Prairie Justice*, and Johnny Bond and His Red River Boys would do the honors in *Oklahoma Raiders* (Universal, 1944).

Even though Bob Baker's voice can clearly be heard as the ranch hands sing "Starlight on the Prairie," Baker wasn't officially in the movie yet. His role was being portrayed by child actor Schuyler Standish.

REVIEWS: "A singing actioner, a little slow, but otherwise a good enough bronctrot for the trade." (*Variety*, 9/21/38); "Good production values add greatly to this Bob Baker series entry." (*Western Movies*, Pitts)

SUMMATION: *The Black Bandit* is a pretty good Bob Baker western feature. Baker gives acceptable performances as the sheriff and bandit leader. Hal Taliaferro, as Sheriff Baker's old friend, and Marjorie Reynolds, as Sheriff Baker's girl, add nice support.

FISTS FLY!
GUNS BOOM!
KNIVES FLASH!

Border Brigands

Universal (June 1935); A Buck Jones Production

CAST: Buck Barry, **Buck Jones**; Diane, **Lona Andre**; Conyda, **Fred Kohler**; Rocky O'Leary, **Frank Rice**; Sisk, **Hank Bell**; Commissioner Barry, **Edward Keane**; Commissioner Winston, **J.P. McGowan**; Big Carrie, **Gertrude Astor**; and "Silver"// Slig, **Slim Whitaker**; Gang Member, **Lew Meehan**

CREDITS: Director, **Nick Grinde**; Producer, **Irving Starr**; Screenwriter, **Stuart Anthony**; Art Director, **Ralph Berger**; Editor, **Bernard Loftus**; Cinematographers, **William Sickner** and **Allen Thompson**; Sound, **Buddy Myers**

LOCATION FILMING: Big Bear, California

RUNNING TIME: 56 min.

STORY: Fred Kohler and his gang

raid another Canadian border town and retreat to the United States. The Mounted Police have only been able to arrest one gang member, Kohler's brother, who is scheduled to be executed. Kohler sends a note to Commissioner Edward Keane promising retaliation if his brother is hanged. On patrol, Keane's brother, Buck Jones, and his pal, Frank Rice, see a galloping rider. Investigating, Jones finds the rider is a girl, Lona Andre, who crosses the border into the States illegally before Jones can stop her. Irritated because Andre taunts him about the incident, Jones kisses her. Meanwhile, as Kohler's brother is to be hanged, Kohler gains entrance to Keane's office and shoots him when his brother dies. Jones and Rice obtain a leave of absence so they can bring Kohler to justice. After taking money from three of Kohler's hirelings, Jones returns the money to Kohler at the local saloon. Jones and Rice become members of the gang. Andre works as a dancer at the saloon. Kohler tells Jones that Andre is his girl, but Jones and Andre begin to spend time together and fall in love. Jones comes up with a plan to draw Kohler into Canada and sends Rice to alert the Mounted Police. Jones hits Kohler and tells him that he's a

Border Brigands (1935) movie still: Fred Kohler (***left***) pulls a gun on Buck Jones (***right***) in a dispute over stolen money, as Hank Bell watches.

Mountie. Jones begins riding into Canada, with Kohler and his men in pursuit. As Kohler and his men enter Canada, a fierce gun battle erupts between the two factions. All the gang members are killed or captured, except Kohler, who retreats to the saloon in the States to wait for Jones. Jones is able to get to Kohler and a tough fistfight ensues. There is a struggle for a gun, which discharges, killing Kohler. Jones and Andre plan to marry.

NOTES AND COMMENTARY: With this Universal western, Jones is now billed simply as Buck; and the production company is simply Buck Jones.

There is an interesting first scene with Fred Kohler. Kohler and his men enter an apparently deserted Canadian town. Kohler sends his men to ransack various businesses while Kohler and an aide take on the bank. As the bandits leave the bank, a man walks up carrying a mail sack and is promptly hit on the head by Kohler; and the sack is taken. Another gang member walks into the scene, throws his stolen goods on the ground, turns and walks away. Kohler then shoots the man in the back. The sequence is played with no dialogue explaining the actions of the gang member who gets killed. The scene was lifted from Ken Maynard's *The Fiddlin' Buckaroo* (Universal, 1933), except in the Maynard film the action takes place in a U.S. city where the gang member questions the wisdom of stealing mail, which would put Federal authorities on their trail. The Mounted Police would be after Kohler's gang—mail or no mail.

The film has an interesting tag line, part of which states, "Knives Flash!" No knives can be seen in this picture.

REVIEWS: "Routine B." (*Motion Picture Guide*, Nash and Ross); "Well done for its sort." (*Variety*, 6/26/35)

SUMMATION: *Border Brigands* is a below average Buck Jones western. Burdened with a choppy script, it plays like pages were discarded. Competent acting can't save this one. Jones is okay with the heroics; and Lona Andre is decorative. Fred Kohler pulls off his part nicely, even displaying a decent French Canadian accent. Frank Rice chips in with good low key comedy in his sidekick role. The bottom line: the direction, cinematography and acting are up to par, but the script does this film in.

Two-Gun Range Rider Staking Down Killers with Hot-Lead Slugs! Wildcat Fighter!

Border Wolves

Universal (February 1938)

CAST: Rusty, **Bob Baker**; Mary Jo, **Constance Moore**; Clem, **Fuzzy Knight**; Jimmie, **Dickie Jones**; Ling Wong, **Willie Fung**; Judge Coleman, **Oscar O'Shea**; Dawson, **Frank Campeau**; Deputy Sheriff, **Glenn Strange**; Jailer, **Ed Cassidy**; MacKay, **Jack Montgomery**; Jack Carson, **Dick Dorrell**// John Benton, **Arthur Van Slyke**; Outlaws, **Frank Ellis** and **Jack Kirk**; Woman at O'Shea's Cabin, **Georgia O'Dell**

CREDITS: Director, **Joseph H. Lewis**; Assistant Director, **Glenn Cook**; Story/Screenwriter, **Norton S. Parker**; Editors, **Charles Craft**; Art Director, **Charles Clague**; Cinematographer, **Harry Neumann**; Sound Technicians, **Robt. Pritchard** and **Jesse Bastian**; Musical Director/Arranger, **Frank Sanucci**

SONGS: "Ridin' the Trail Again" (Taconis and Gayne)—sung by **Bob Baker**; "Blaze Away, Cowboy" (Taconis and Gayne)—sung by **Bob Baker**; "Bowlegged Bill" (Taconis and Gayne)—sung by **Fuzzy Knight**; "Wyoming Moon" (Taconis and Gayne)—sung by **Fuzzy Knight, Bob Baker and Constance Moore;** and "Ridin' the Owl Hoot Trail" (Taconis and Gayne)—sung by **male chorus.**

LOCATION FILMING: Agoura and Kernville, California

RUNNING TIME: 56 min.

STORY: Bob Baker and Fuzzy Knight come across a wagon train massacre committed by Dick Dorrell and his gang. Baker is accused of being the leader of the outlaw gang, and he and Knight are sentenced to hang. Valley Falls Sheriff Edward Cassidy releases Baker and Knight from jail and sends them to Judge Oscar O'Shea's cabin. O'Shea tells the men he knows they are innocent, and that the guilty party is his son Dorrell. He asks Baker and Knight to clear their name by bringing Dorrell to him for justice. Traveling as fugitives from justice, Baker and Knight ride the "hoot owl" trail in their quest to find Dorrell. En route, Baker meets Constance Moore, daughter of stage line owner Arthur Van Slyke; her brother Dickie Jones; and their cook, Willie Fung. Baker and Knight find Dorrell's camp and learn he has plans to steal a large gold shipment. On trying to reach Moore, Baker is arrested by Sheriff Jack Montgomery. Knight rides to bring O'Shea to save Baker's life but finds O'Shea has died. When being escorted to Valley Falls by Montgomery and his deputy, Glenn Strange, Baker meets Moore, who tells him she plans to be on the stagecoach targeted by Dorrell. Fung follows Baker and his captors, and frees him. Baker and Fung get the drop on Montgomery and Strange, and force them to ride to the place of the impending holdup. Dorrell and his men attack the stage. Baker, Montgomery, Strange, Fung and a posse swoop down on the robbers. In the skirmish, Baker shoots Dorrell. Montgomery is about to arrest Baker again when Knight shows up with Cassidy, who clears Baker's name. Baker and Moore plan to wed.

NOTES AND COMMENTARY: *Border Wolves* was remade as a Tex Williams featurette, *Coyote Canyon* (Universal-International, 1949).

REVIEWS: "Some fancy camera work from director Joseph H. Lewis, and star Bob Baker's personality and songs make this one add up to a more than passable outing." (*Western Movies*, Pitts); "Muddled singing cowboy stuff." *Motion Picture Guide*, Nash and Ross

SUMMATION: *Border Wolves* is a decidedly above average "B" western, thanks primarily to director Joseph H. Lewis' edgy direction and inventive camera angles. Bob Baker carries off the hero's role in fine style, and Fuzzy Knight chips in as a character actor rather than the standard sidekick to the film's benefit. A unique bit of scriptwriting in having Willie Fung lead the posse into the final battle with the outlaws is not enough to off set the quick demise of outlaw Dick Dorrell by Baker. A direct confrontation between antagonists Baker and Dorrell would have lifted this film higher.

SIZZLING SIX SHOOTERS BOSS THE TOWN...
BLAZING 45'S SMOKE OUT THE OUTLAWS

Boss of Boomtown

Universal (May, 1944)

CAST: Steve, **Rod Cameron**; Jim, **Tom Tyler**; Chatter, **Fuzzy Knight**; Dale, **Vivian Austin**; Clark, **Ray Whitley**; Ridgeway, **Jack Ingram**; Brett, **Robert Barron**; Minerva, **Marie Austin**; Dunne, **Max Wagner**; Cornwall, **Sam Flint**; Yuma, **Richard Alexander**; and **Ray Whitley's Bar Six Cowboys** (**Ezra Paulette**, **Lem Giles** and **Charley Quirt**)// Saloon Girl, **Beverlee Mitchell**; Captain T.S. Hiller, **Forrest Taylor**; Saloon Patrons, **Tex Cooper** and **Hank Bell**; Stage Driver, **George Plues**

CREDITS: Director, **Ray Taylor**; Associate Producer, **Oliver Drake**; Screenwriter, **William Lively**; Editor, **Ted Kent**; Art Directors, **John B. Goodman** and **Abraham Grossman**; Set Decorators, **Russell A. Gausman** and **Leigh Smith**; Cinematographer, **William Sickner**; Sound, **Bernard B. Brown** and **Jess Moulin**

SONGS: "Texas" (Marvin)—sung by **Ray Whitley and His Bar Six Cowboys**; "My Proud Beauty" (Marvin)—sung by **Marie Austin**; "Streets of Laredo" (traditional)—sung by **Ray Whitley and His Bar Six Cow-**

boys; and "Ninety-Nine Days" (Marvin)—sung by **Ray Whitley and His Bar Six Cowboys**

LOCATION FILMING: Corriganville, California

RUNNING TIME: 56 min.

STORY: Rod Cameron, Tom Tyler and Fuzzy Knight have been discharged from the Army but decide to reenlist. Tyler reenlists. Special Investigator Sam Flint recruits Cameron and Knight to help him break up the gang that has been preying on miners, stealing payrolls and gold ore. Cameron, as a masked bandit, steals a mine payroll and then flashes a lot of money at a saloon run by Vivian Austin and Jack Ingram. Tyler catches Cameron after he's robbed the bank. Cameron knocks out Tyler. Ingram and his henchman; Richard Alexander, force Cameron to enter the back of the saloon. After a fistfight between Cameron and the two outlaws over the money Cameron has stolen is stopped by Knight, the men decide to work together to steal the Army Relief Fund. Cameron insists he must meet the man behind the lawlessness before he will outline how the money can be stolen. On the way to meet the boss, Tyler arrests Cameron. Knight and Flint meet the boss, mine owner Robert Barron. Flint outlines Cameron's plan. Knight and Flint leave Barron's mine to meet the gang at the robbery site. Barron tells Ingram to kill the men. Ingram fires two shots; one wounds Flint, and the other misses Knight. Knight falls off his horse as if shot, and Ingram thinks both men are dead. Barron readies his men to rob the Army funds. Knight brings the wounded man to Army headquarters, where he is arrested. Cameron and Knight make their escape, and Tyler is instructed to bring both men back. Cameron and Knight reach the holdup site and begin firing at the outlaws. Tyler and his men arrive and help Cameron fight the holdup men. Barron and Ingram try to escape with the money. Cameron and Tyler give chase and bring both men to justice. With their names cleared, Cameron and Knight reenlist.

NOTES AND COMMENTARY: Rod Cameron took over for Tex Ritter as Universal's starring cowboy. The studio had interviewed over eighteen prospective leading men, and Bill Williams was the leading candidate. Feeling Williams did not look like a cowboy, he was assigned to a murder mystery. Cameron had made a good impression on action fans as a serial star in *G-Men Vs. the Black Dragon* (Republic, 1943) and *Secret Service in Darkest Africa* (Republic, 1943) and looked like a western star. Cameron would star in over 36 western films over the next 25 years. With a change in studio executives years later, Williams was signed to star in the *Kit Carson* TV series.

The series was placed on a temporary hiatus when Universal ran short of negative stock. Associate Producer Oliver Drake was laid off during the period. Drake went to work for the Alexander Stern Production company and wrote and directed two films in the Texas Rangers series, *Border Buckaroos* (PRC, 1943) and *Trail of Terror* (PRC, 1943).

Boss of Boomtown (1944) title card: *Upper left,* Vivian Austin; *lower left to center,* Tom Tyler, Fuzzy Knight, Rod Cameron; *upper right,* Rod Cameron.

Ray Whitley's group was known as the 6 Bar Cowboys from its inception. Advertising listed the correct group name, but the onscreen credits changed the group's name to the Bar Six Cowboys, a moniker which would stick for the remainder of the series. Whitley and his 6 Bar Cowboys replaced Johnny Bond and His Red River Boys as the music group in Universal series western features.

Tom Tyler was at the end of his starring career. Tyler would make *Sing Me a Song of Texas* (Columbia, 1945) before drifting into support roles, mostly villainous in nature, before retiring from motion pictures in 1953. Arthritis ended Tyler's life the following year. Tyler had been a prolific western star, toplining 67 features from 1929 to 1945. Having starred in six serials, Tyler was known for his vivid portrayals of Captain Marvel in *Adventures of Captain Marvel* (Republic, 1940) and *The Phantom* (Columbia, 1943).

REVIEWS: "Rod Cameron's first genre starring western is an entertaining one and will appeal to fans because Tom Tyler is costarred and the two make a good duo." (*Western Movies*, Pitts)

SUMMATION: Rod Cameron's first

starring western film is a good one. Cameron makes a good western star and is ably assisted by veterans Tom Tyler and Fuzzy Knight. Cameron and Tyler register well as Quirt and Flagg-like characters, while Knight provides decent comedy relief. Vivian Austin makes a very attractive leading lady. Robert Barron, Jack Ingram and Richard Alexander capably handle the villainy. Director Ray Taylor, cinematographer William Sickner and screenwriter William Lively are right on target.

FIGHTING FOR THE LAW...AND HIS LIFE!..
...The wildest action you've ever thrilled to!

Boss of Bullion City

Universal (January 1941)

CAST: Tom, **Johnny Mack Brown**; Burt, **Fuzzy Knight**; Martha, **Nell O'Day**; Linda, **Maria Montez**; Sheriff, **Harry Woods**; Wallace, **Melvin Lang**; Steve, **Dick Alexander**; Mike, **Earle Hodgins**; Tug, **Karl Hackett**; Mario, **George Humbert**// Card Playing Cowboy, **Kermit Maynard**; Musicians, **The Guadalajara Trio**; Miner, **Frank Ellis**

CREDITS: Director, **Ray Taylor**; Story, **Arthur St. Claire**; Screenwriters, **Arthur St. Claire** and **Victor McLeod**; Editor, **Paul Landres**; Art Directors, **Jack Otterson** and **Harold H. MacArthur**; Set Decorator, **R.A. Gausman**; Cinematographer, **William Sickner**; Sound, **Bernard B. Brown** and **Glenn Anderson**; Musical Director, **H.J. Salter**

SONGS: "Mi Morina" [My Brunette] (Castellon)—sung by **The Guadalajara Trio;** and "La Cucaracha" (traditional)—sung by **The Guadalajara Trio**

LOCATION FILMING: Iverson, California

RUNNING TIME: 61 min.

STORY: Johnny Mack Brown and Fuzzy Knight journey to Bullion City to start up a newspaper. Bullion City is a hotbed of lawlessness. Sheriff Harry Woods advises Brown to soft-peddle the outlawry in his editorials, but Brown refuses. It becomes apparent to Brown that all the holdups occur when Woods sends Deputy Melvin Lang out of town. Brown robs the stage office safe before the outlaws arrive. Brown and Lang set a trap for Woods. Woods and his men hold up a stagecoach. Brown and the posse arrive on the scene. Woods tries to accuse Brown of the robbery, but henchman Karl Hackett exposes Woods as the gang leader.

NOTES AND COMMENTARY: Maria Montez signed a term contract with Universal at $150 a week. *Boss of Bullion City* was Montez' first film. The film was held back, and the John Barrymore comedy *The Invisible Woman* (Universal, 1940) became her first movie seen by the movie going public. After supporting roles in a half dozen films, Montez won the lead in *Arabian Nights* (Universal, 1942). She quickly became the Queen of Technicolor until she balked at appearing in *Frontier Gal* (Universal, 1945) with Rod Cameron. One reason given was that Montez no longer wanted to make films with co-stars named Jon Hall or Rod Cameron. Yvonne De Carlo starred in that film and soon replaced Montez as Universal's reigning beauty. Ironically, Montez' last film with Universal was a period western, *Pirates of Monterey* (Universal, 1947), with, you guessed it, Rod Cameron.

"La Cucaracha" had been used in *When a Man Sees Red* (Universal, 1934), *Law for Tombstone* (Universal, 1937), and *Outlaw Express* (Universal, 1938), and would be performed by Paula Kelly and the Modernaires in the musical short *Frontier Frolic* (Universal, 1946).

REVIEWS: "Well produced entry in the Johnny Mack Brown series." (*Western Movies*, Pitts); "Western shows Brown at his straight shooting best." (*Motion Picture Guide*, Nash and Ross)

SUMMATION: *Boss of Bullion City* is a fairly interesting Johnny Mack Brown vehicle. The story is greatly wounded by Fuzzy Knight's "funny" business and a slightly disjointed plot. Brown himself is at top form in the acting and action sequences. The fight sequence between Brown and badman Dick Alexander is excellently choreographed and a highlight of the film. Beautiful actresses Maria Montez and Nell O'Day are pretty much wasted in their roles. One of the great badmen of the screen, Harry Woods, makes an excellent adversary for Brown; but a punch-up between the men at the finale would have been in order. The action scenes are first rate, but the script furnished by Arthur St. Clair and Victor McLeod, and the direction by the usually reliable Ray Taylor, needs propping up. This one should have been better.

GUN-SMOKE AND HANG-ROPE!
...rule the reddened plains as the Telegraph fights West!

Boss of Hangtown Mesa

Universal (August 1942)
CAST: Steve Collins, **Johnny Mack Brown**; Dr. J. Wellington Dingle, **Fuzzy Knight**; Judge Ezra Binns, **William Farnum**; Bert Lawler, **Rex Lease**; Betty Wilkins, **Helen Deverell**; Utah Kid, **Hugh Prosser**; Flash Hollister, **Robert Barron**; Clint Rayner, **Michael Vallon**; John Wilkins, **Henry Hall**; Clem, **Fred Kohler Jr.**; and **Pals of the Golden West,** with **Nora Lou Martin**// Sheriff Rogers, **Jack C. Smith**; Tom, **Mickey Simpson**; Town Tough, **Frank Hagney**

CREDITS: Director, **Joseph H. Lewis**; Associate Producer/Screenwriter, **Oliver Drake**; Editor, **Maurice Wright**; Art Directors, **Jack Otterson and Ralph M. DeLacy**; Set Decorators, **R.A. Gausman** and **Ira Webb**; Cinematographer, **Charles Van Enger**; Sound, **Bernard B. Brown and Jess Moulin**; Musical Director, **H.J. Salter**

SONGS: "Ain't Got Nothin' and Nothin' Worries Me" (Rosen and Drake)—sung by **Fuzzy Knight**; "Trail Dreamin'" (Rosen, Wakely and Drake)—sung by the **Pals of the Golden West, with Nora Lou Martin**; "Pappy Was a Gunman" (Drake)—sung by **Fuzzy Knight;** and "Song of the Prairie" (Rosen and Carter)—sung by the **Pals of the Golden West, with Nora Lou Martin**

LOCATION FILMING: Corriganville, California

RUNNING TIME: 58 min.

STORY: Hugh Prosser, one step ahead of a posse, forces Johnny Mack Brown to change clothes with him (Prosser's clothes are too distinctive and identify him on sight). Prosser also finds a letter introducing Brown as an engineer to the Telegraph Company and stating that there is $25,000 available for men and supplies. Prosser plans to impersonate Brown and take the money. Brown is left on foot but finds the camp of tonic peddler Fuzzy Knight, who will take him to Hangtown Mesa in his show wagon. The Telegraph Company has been beset with accidents and delays that threaten the completion of their construction within the contract period. Judge William Farnum, lawyer Michael Vallon and saloon owner Robert Barron are the ringleaders behind all the troubles. Prosser arrives at the construction camp and presents construction boss Henry Hall with Brown's papers and asks for the $25,000 in one lump sum. As Hall opens the safe, a telegraph message comes through. Hall asks Prosser to answer it. When Prosser is unable to comply, Hall realizes Prosser is an impostor, but Prosser shoots Hall and takes the money. As Prosser rides away, he is shot in the shoulder by Hall's niece, Helen Deverell. Prosser hides in the rocks while his wound mends. Brown and Knight arrive in Hangtown Mesa. After a mix-up, Brown has a conversation with Barron, who thinks Brown is Prosser because of his clothes, and tells him to report to Rex Lease, foreman for the Telegraph Company, and assist him in sabotaging operations. Brown is hired and convinces Deverell to make him Engineer in Charge of Construction. Brown begins to find ways to meet the contract deadline, which bothers Lease. Prosser's wound finally mends, and he rides into town to find Farnum. Farnum and his confederates realize Brown is the actual engineer sent to complete the telegraph line. Seeing Brown in town, the outlaws try to kill or capture him. Brown hides in Knight's wagon but is discovered, and both men are captured. Prosser takes Brown and Knight to a hideout while Barron, Lease and their henchmen raid and destroy all the equipment in the construction camp. Knight knocks out Prosser in a short fight and frees Brown. Brown is able to get a telegraph message to Deverell to bring all her men to the construction camp. Brown and Knight arrive, and with Deverell and the men, stage an ambush. The ambush is successful, the raiders are wiped out, and Brown captures Barron and Lease. Brown sends Knight to have the sheriff arrest Farnum and Vallon. Deverell meets the contract deadline and is awarded another. With Brown to help her, Deverell accepts.

NOTES AND COMMENTARY: *Boss of Hangtown Mesa* was the last solo starring film for Johnny Mack Brown at Universal. With his next release, *Deep in the Heart of Texas* (Universal, 1942), Brown would be co-starred with Tex Ritter for seven features.

"Trail Dreaming" is sung in **The Lone Star Trail** (Universal, 1943) and **Trigger Trail** (Universal, 1944). "Song of the Prairie" had been vocalized in **Riders of Pasco Basin** (Universal, 1940), and "Ain't Got Nothing and Nothin' Worries Me" would be heard in **Cheyenne Roundup** (Universal, 1943).

The plot of *Boss of Hangtown Mesa* was fused with the plot of *Tenting Tonight on the Old Camp Ground* (Universal, 1943) to make up the screenplay for *The Old Texas Trail* (Universal, 1944).

REVIEWS: "Above average western in the Johnny Mack Brown series." (*Variety*, 9/16/42); "Typically plotted entry in the Johnny Mack Brown series, but this one has a plethora of music." (*Western Movies*, Pitts)

SUMMATION: *Boss of Hangtown Mesa* is a slightly complicated but above average Johnny Mack Brown western. Brown, as usual, is the stalwart hero, relying more on brains and guns than his fists in this one. Fuzzy Knight contributes one of his better efforts in the series, even besting bad man Hugh Prosser in a short fight. Joseph H. Lewis' direction is okay, but not as edgy and inventive as in earlier features.

He made TOUGH *Forgers gunshot* SHY!

Boss of Lonely Valley

Universal (November 1937); A Buck Jones Production

CAST: Steve Hanson, **Buck Jones**; Sonny Lowrey, **Dick Holland**; Retta Lowrey, **Muriel Evans**; Jim Lynch, **Harvey Clark**; Jake Wagner, **Walter Miller**; Peter Starr, **Lee Phelps**; Sam Leavitt, **Matty Fain**; Aunt Martha Wiggins, **Grace Goodall**; Suds, **Ezra Paulette**; Lottie, **Virginia Dabney**; Slim, **Ted Adams**; Joe Bishop; and "Silver"// Hank, **Hank Worden**; Singing Ranch Hand, **Red Hightower**

CREDITS: Director, **Ray Taylor**; Story, **Forrest Brown**; Screenwriter,

Frances Guihan; Editor, **Bernard Loftus**; Art Director, **Ralph Berger**; Cinematographers, **Allen Thompson** and **John Hickson**; Sound, **L. John Myers**

Songs: "Singing Swinging Cowboy"—sung by **Red Hightower** and "Abide with Me" (Lyte and Monk)—played by **Virginia Dabney**

Location Filming: Kernville and Newhall, California, and the Prudential studio town set.

Running Time: 60 min.

Source: Novel by **Forrest Brown**

Story: A warning note is delivered to Muriel Evans too late to prevent the murder of the new preacher. Evans finds his body in the church. Saloonkeeper Walter Miller tells Evans that he holds a bill of sale for her property and that she'll have to move. Evans tells Buck Jones, who is in love with her, that she doesn't trust Miller. Miller wanted the preacher out of town and didn't like it when Evans came to the preacher's defense. Jones, working with undercover government agent Harvey Clark, decides to investigate. Knowing that Jones is likely to interfere with his plans, Miller intends to murder Jones. Jones and Clark investigate the church and find a tunnel that leads from the church to Miller's office. Realizing Miller must be the outlaw leader, and fearing for Evans' safety, Jones has Evans and her younger brother, Dick Holland, move to Jones' ranch. Miller sets a trap for Jones. Jones is able to capture Ted Adams, the man sent to kill Jones, and make Miller think both he and Adams perished in a fall into a river. Miller has a forger, Matty Fain, draw up papers on Jones' ranch (Fain had forged the bill of sale on Evans' ranch). Fain decides to leave town but is captured by Jones and Clark. Miller tries to take possession of the ranch but instead finds Jones very much alive and retreats to his saloon in town. Adams tells Jones that he had a change of heart and wants to help him bring Miller to justice. Jones, Clark and Adams ride to town with Jones' cowhands. Using the tunnel from the church, Jones finds the saloon girls sequestered in Miller's office. Jones has Adams take one of the girls to the church to play hymns on the church organ. Another henchman is captured and made to ring the church bells. The music and bells unnerve all the outlaws, who make a break for freedom. Miller, alone and undaunted, goes to his office to clean out his safe. Jones overpowers Miller in a short fight. Now Jones and Evans plan to wed.

Notes and Commentary: Child actor Dick Holland became a soap opera mainstay, portraying the second Joey Roberts in *The Guiding Light* (CBS, 1953) and then the second Donald Hughes in *As the World Turns* (CBS, 1956–62). Holland was the second lead in the live sci-fi children's program *Operation Neptune* (NBC, 1953). In 1970, Holland was the head writer for the TV series *A World Apart* (ABC). This program was well written and acted, and dealt with important issues that had surfaced by the seventies (e.g. racial prejudice, teenage pregnancy and cults).

The author was unable to ascertain a character name for Joe Bishop.

Boss of Lonley Valley (1937) movie still: Buck Jones (*right*) holds the wounded Dick Holland in his arms as Harry Clark and Muriel Evans look on anxiously.

Bishop receives onscreen billing in this film and *Sudden Bill Dorn* (Universal, 1937). Most film historians choose not to mention Bishop's name in the discussion of these films.

REVIEWS: "Lacking in cohesion, poorly directed and acted, this latest of Buck Jones' horse oprys is substandard." (*Variety*, 12/29/37); "Badly directed and incoherently scripted." (*The Motion Picture Guide*, Nash and Ross)

SUMMATION: As barely acceptable entertainment, this Buck Jones vehicle is saddled with ludicrous plot devices. The story asks us to believe that because a preacher has been murdered, the gang responsible would flee in fear from the playing of a hymn on the church organ. The script again fails to play fair when in two instances bullets fired point blank at Jones somehow fail to hit the mark; but that's okay, the script fails to hit the mark also. Acting by the principals is adequate while the usually competent director, Ray Taylor, just goes through the motions on this one. Truly, this is far from Jones' best.

A Four-Fisted Entertainment Sock!

The Boss Rider of Gun Creek

Universal (November 1936); A Buck Jones Production

CAST: Larry Day/Gary Elliott, **Buck Jones**; Starr Landerson, **Muriel Evans**; Pop Greer, **Harvey Clark**; Doc Northrup, **Alphonse Ethier**; Sheriff Blaine, **Tom Chatterton**; Lafe Turner, **Josef Swickard**; Ed Randall, **Ernest Hilliard**; Lawyer, **Edw. Keene**; Red Vale, **Mahlon Hamilton**; Sheriff Len Morrison, **Lee Phelps**; Slim, **Allan Sears**; Blackie, **Wm. Lawrence**; MacGregor, **Edward Hearn,** and "Silver"// Judge, **Allan Cavan**; Danny, **Iron Eyes Cody**

CREDITS: Director, **Lesley Selander**; Story, **E.B. Mann**; Screenwriter, **Frances Guihan**; Editor, **Bernard Loftus**; Art Directors, **Ralph Berger** and **Frank Smith**; Cinematographers, **Allen Thompson** and **Herbert Kirkpatrick**; Sound, **Buddy Myers**

LOCATION FILMING: Kernville, California

RUNNING TIME: 60 min.

STORY: Rodeo performer Buck Jones is arrested and convicted for murder. Actually, a ranch owner who looks exactly like Jones committed the crime. Jones is sentenced to life in prison, but Jones' pal, Harvey Clark, frees Jones as he's being transported to prison. Clark had been investigating the murder and had sent a letter to Jones' double telling him Clark has information concerning the murder. Jones' double is to meet Clark at Iron Eyes Cody's cabin. At the cabin, it is evident that both men are identical in appearance. Clark has the men switch clothes. Sheriff Tom Chatterton shows up at the cabin and gets the drop on Clark and Jones' double. Jones' double lunges at Chatterton. Chatterton fires and kills him. Jones decides to impersonate his double and rides to the double's ranch. En route, Jones sees that Muriel Evans' horses have run away, and Jones lifts Evans from the wagon. When Jones tries to stop the wagon, Silver slips and Jones is rendered unconscious as he slides down a steep embankment. Pretending amnesia, Jones learns that his double holds a mortgage on Evans' ranch and that her cattle are being stolen. Through his doctor, Alphonse Ethier, Jones begins proceedings to purchase Evans' ranch, at a top price. Jones, also, finds that businessman Ernest Hilliard and local sheriff Lee Phelps are in on the scheme to obtain Evans' ranch, which contains a valuable gold deposit. Cowhands on Jones' double's ranch have been stealing Evans cattle to prevent her from using them to obtain money to pay off the mortgage. When Clark comes to the area, both Ethier and Evans realize Jones is impersonating his double. The cowhands come to the same conclusion when Jones rides a horse that his double could never ride. This information is given to Hilliard and Phelps, who send for Chatterton to arrest Jones. Instead, Chatterton tells Jones he knows Jones is innocent and that Jones' double was the guilty party. Jones gets word that the cattle are being moved. Jones, Chatterton and Clark ride to stop them. In the ensuing a gunfight all the rustlers are shot. Before one of the rustlers dies, he implicates Hilliard and Phelps as the leaders. Both men are arrested. Now Jones and Evans have time for romance.

NOTES AND COMMENTARY: Harvey Clark, a minor sidekick in "B" westerns, began his movie career with *The Darkening Trail* (Mutual, 1915), which starred William S. Hart. Buck Jones used Clark in four of his Universal features. When George Hayes had a contract dispute with Harry Sherman over the Hopalong Cassidy series and was out for two entries, Clark was one of two men who replaced him. Clark died of a heart attack on July 19, 1938, at age 52.

REVIEWS: "Fair to middling western yarn with a mystery-on-the-range angle creeping in." (*Variety*, 12/16/36); "Confusing, below average B-western." (*The Motion Picture Guide*, Nash and Ross)

SUMMATION: Buck Jones tackles a dual role and pulls it off in fine style in this complicated and often confusing "B" western. In *The Boss Rider of Gun Creek*, Jones plays both a stalwart hero and a cowardly killer. Thanks to Jones, the film comes in as slightly above average. More action, especially in the finale, would be needed to lift this picture to the preferred western class. The supporting cast acquits itself capably, with special mention going to Muriel Evans, who handles the lead feminine role with distinction. Director Lesley Selander directs capably under the restrictions given him by screenwriter Frances Guihan's script.

---

*Lightning-Loaded Action!
It's a thrill-packed medley of bullets and ballads!*

Bury Me Not on the Lone Prairie

Universal (March, 1941)
CAST: Joe, **Johnny Mack Brown**; Lem, **Fuzzy Knight**; Edna, **Nell O'Day**; Dorothy, **Kathryn Adams**; Red, **Harry Cording**; Tiger, **Jack Rockwell**; Mustang, **Ernie Adams**; Sheriff, **Ed Cassidy**; Bob, **Don House**; Braffet, **Pat O'Brien**; Walker, **Lee Shumway**; Barney, **Jim Corey**; Wendel, **Frank O'Connor**; Lambert, **William Desmond**; Calvert, **Bud Osborne**; Jimmy Wakely and his Rough Riders (**Johnny Bond** and **Dick Reinhart**); Moose, **Slim**

Whitaker; Deputy Sheriff, **Kermit Maynard**; Poker Player, **Bob Kortman**; Outlaws, **Charles King** and **Ethan Laidlaw**

CREDITS: Director, **Ray Taylor**; Story, **Sherman Lowe**; Screenwriters, **Sherman Lowe and Victor McLeod**; Editor, **Charles Maynard**; Art Directors, **Jack Otterson and Harold MacArthur**; Set Decorator, **R.A. Gausman**; Cinematographer, **Jerome Ash**; Sound, **Bernard B. Brown and Jess Moulin**; Musical Director, **H.J. Salter**

SONGS: "I'm a Happy Cowboy" (Wakely)—sung by **Jimmy Wakely and his Rough Riders**; "Bury Me Not on the Lone Prairie" (traditional)—sung by **Jimmy Wakely and his Rough Riders;** and "The Bears Give Me the Bird" (Rosen and Carter)—sung by **Fuzzy Knight**

LOCATION FILMING: Iverson, California

RUNNING TIME: 57 min.

STORY: Three miners, Don House, Pat O'Brien and Lee Shumway, discover gold. Their discovery is noticed by three disgruntled men, Harry Cording, Jack Rockwell and Ernie Adams, who murder the miners and jump their claim. Johnny Mack Brown, brother of House, is determine to find the killers. Cording is afraid Brown will be successful and makes an unsuccessful attempt to dry gulch him. Cording and his partners are unable to find the mother lode and plan to leave the area. By accident, Brown's friend, Fuzzy Knight, finds the strike. Knight fills a saddlebag with nuggets and recklessly rides to register the claim. Knight falls from the saddle and is rendered unconscious. Cording and his pals investigate and find the gold. Knight is taken to the outlaw's cabin. Upon regaining consciousness, Knight has no memory of the gold strike and thinks he's a Confederate officer. Unable to help Knight regain his memory, Cording and Rockwell lure O'Day to the cabin, thinking she might have knowledge of the claim. Brown believes Cording is behind the murders. Kathryn Adams, Brown's sweetheart, tells Brown that O'Day rode off with Cording. Brown rides to help O'Day. When O'Day discovers Cording's true purpose, she makes a break for it, and Cording and Rockwell are unable to catch her. Cording and Rockwell decide to clear out and return to the cabin. Brown has found the cabin and is waiting for Cording and Rockwell. There is a fight, chase and fight before Brown brings Cording, Rockwell and Adams to justice. In the scuffle, Knight regains his memory. Knight and O'Day are rich. Brown will manage their claim and settle down with Adams.

NOTES AND COMMENTARY: The song "The Bears Gives Me the Bird" has its roots in medieval times. It began with the Battle of Agincourt between the French and English. The French, believing they would be victorious, decided to cut off the middle finger of all English archers, preventing them from participating in future encounters. The longbow of the English was made from the wood of the English Yew tree, and the archer's drawing of the long bow was known as plucking the yew or pluck yew. The English won the battle, and the bowmen mocked the French by waving their middle finger and telling them they could still pluck yew. The difficult consonant cluster at the beginning of the taunt changed to an easier 'f' sound, and the term over time has taken on the meaning of an intimate encounter. This gesture is also known as " giving the bird" because of the pheasant feathers used with the longbow. Songwriters Rosen and Carter used the correct connotation for this phrase, as the bears taunt Knight for his ineptitude at bear hunting.

Fuzzy Knight would sing "The Bears Give Me the Bird" again, in *Frontier Law* (Universal, 1943).

Kathryn Adams talked of her role in westerns: "I was the kind of gentle heroine. I didn't ride so I don't know if that was the reason. I think I projected the gentle, nice girl. The idea of being a vigorous, outdoor girl was not the way I was cast. "

On handling a buckboard: "That was really, really interesting. I thought, this was really a part of history. On climbing up to it, I didn't have any problem doing that but hanging on. The buckboard tore down the road with the camera alongside of it, as they did then, and looking as if you were not going to bounce off totally. That was much more scary than actually getting on the horses. I didn't scare easily, a good outdoor Minnesota girl. I wasn't really frightened, but it wasn't the easiest thing in the world to do."

On horseback riding: "I got a lot of reassurance from not only the crew but the other cast. No one, in any way, poked fun at me for not being able to ride a horse. They kept telling me the horses know what to do. So, all I had to do was hang on."

On Johnny Mack Brown: "He was really a gentleman, very kind. I remember him very well. There was a group of stills that we made with his horse. I wish I still had some of those because they were really quite nice."

On Fuzzy Knight: "He, too, was good. The one regret that I have, I didn't have much ambition for what I was doing and certainly not very much, if any, aggression. But I had wished if that I had asked if I could not sing with him. Because I did have a good voice."

On Nell O'Day: "There was a young horsewoman; but I didn't think her name was Nell O'Day, who was small and was an excellent rider. She had a seventeen hand Irish jumper that she owned. I went to a number of horse shows and watched her ride. She was so small. Interesting that I remember this, the reason that she didn't win the Blue Ribbon was because they [the judges] said the horse pulled her. She was so small that it looked like the horse was pulling her. I don't know that it was, I didn't know that much about it."

The actor Pat O'Brien isn't the noted actor of many fine films. The actor in this film was usually billed as Pat J. O'Brien.

REVIEWS: "A routine western." (*The Motion Picture Guide*, Nash and Ross); "Good Johnny Mack Brown series entry with both action and music." (*Western Movies*, Pitts)

SUMMATION: *Bury Me Not on the Lone Prairie* is a sub-par western that not even Johnny Mack Brown can save. Brown and Nell O'Day give good performances, but Fuzzy Knight receives too much footage. Knight's amnesia sequences are inane and not worthy of his talents. The story line for a good film just isn't there.

DEANNA...in TECHNICOLOR for the First Time! With the Miracle Melodies of JEROME KERN! It's the thrill....your eyes will prize forever....the most wonderful musical of all!

Can't Help Singing

Universal (December 1944)

CAST: Caroline, **Deanna Durbin**; Lawlor, **Robert Paige**; Gregory, **Akim Tamiroff**; Latham, **David Bruce**; Koppa, **Leonid Kinskey**; Miss McLean, **June Vincent**; Senator Frost, **Ray Collins**; Sad Sam, **Andrew Tombes**; Carstairs, **Thomas Gomez**; Aunt Cissy, **Clara Blandick**; Bigelow, **Olin Howlin**; Marshal, **George Cleveland**// Captain, **George Eldredge**; Gunman, **Harry Woods**; Army Officers, **Dennis Moore** and **George J. Lewis**; Lemuel, **Roscoe Ates**; Lemuel's wife, **Almira Sessons**; Bath House Attendant, **Jody Gilbert**; Barber, **Irving Bacon**; Woman at Bath House, **Renee Riano**; Saloon Owner, **George Lloyd**; Pioneers, **William Desmond** and **Richard Alexander**; Mrs. Carstairs, **Nana Bryant**; Indian, **Frank Lackteen**; Mexican Who Buys a Bell, **Jay Norvello**

CREDITS: Director, **Frank Ryan**; Assistant Director, **William Holland**; Producer, **Felix Jackson**; Associate Producer, **Frank Shaw**; Screenwriters, **Lewis R. Foster** and **Frank Ryan**; Editor, **Ted J. Kent**; Art Directors, **John B. Goodman** and **Robert Clatworthy**; Set Decorators, **Russell A. Gausman** and **Edward R. Robinson**; Cinematographers, **Woody Bredell** and **W. Howard Greene**; Costumes, **Walter Plunkett**; Make Up, **Jack P. Pierce**; Sound, **Bernard B. Brown** and **Joe Lapis**; Musical Director/Musical Score, **H.J. Salter**; Orchestrations, **Frank Skinner**; Musical Director for Miss Durbin, **Edgar Fairchild**; Vocal Coach, **Andre de Segurola**; Technicolor Color Consultant, **Natalie Kalmus**; Associate Technicolor Color Consultant, **William Fritzsche**

SONGS: "Can't Help Singing" (Kern and Harburg)—sung by **Deanna Durbin**; "Elbow Room" (Kern and Harburg) sung by **chorus**; "Can't Help Singing" (Kern and Harburg)—sung by **Deanna Durbin**, **Robert Paige** and **Irving Bacon** and chorus; "Any Moment Now" (Kern and Harburg)—sung by **Deanna**

Durbin; "Swing Your Sweetheart" (Kern and Harburg)—sung by chorus; "More and More" (Kern and Harburg)—sung by **Deanna Durbin**; "Californ-i-ay" (Kern and Harburg)—sung by **Robert Paige**, **Deanna Durbin** and **chorus**; "Medley (Californ-i-ay, More and More and Can't Help Singing)"—sung by **Deanna Durbin**, **Robert Paige** and **chorus**; plus instrumentals "March" (Kern) and "Honky-Tonk" (Kern)

LOCATION FILMING: Navajo Lake, Utah

COLOR PROCESS: Technicolor
RUNNING TIME: 89 min.
SOURCE: "Girl of the Oregon Trail" by Samuel J. and Curtis B. Warshawsky, and the story "Carolina" by John Klover and Leo Townsend.

STORY: Deanna Durbin and Lt. David Bruce are in love. Durbin's father, Ray Collins, disapproves of Bruce and has him transferred to guard Thomas Gomez' mine in Sonora. Durbin travels west and meets gambler Robert Paige. Together they join a wagon train traveling to California. Paige thinks Durbin is planning to marry Gomez. As they go farther west, Durbin and Paige begin to fall in love. Learning Bruce has been stationed in Fort

Can't Help Singing (1944) movie still: Deanna Durbin and Rogert Paige (*center*) arrive in California.

Bridger, Durbin leaves the wagon train. Paige decides to fight for Durbin's love and rides to her side. In Fort Bridger, Durbin is told Bruce is now in California, and Durbin plans to return east. On Paige's arrival, Durbin knows she loves him and they plan to start a new life in California. In California, Paige first believes Durbin was to marry Gomez. Then Bruce rides up and tries to claim Durbin as his bride. To top it all, Collins shows up and decides he likes Paige. Through all the confusion, Paige and Durbin know they love each other and will marry.

NOTES AND COMMENTARY: *Can't Help Singing* was Universal's first western filmed in color. This was also Deanna Durbin's first film in color, and her first film as a blonde.

"More and More" received an Academy Award nomination for Best Song, which lost out to "It Might as Well Be Spring" from *State Fair* (20th Century Fox, 1945). The film *Can't Help Singing* received a nomination for Scoring of a Musical Picture. *Anchors Aweigh* (Metro-Goldwyn-Mayer, 1945) won the Academy Award.

Jerome Kern and Harburg wrote three additional songs, *"I'll Follow Your Smile," "There'll Come a Day"* and *"Once in a Million Moons,"* that were not used in the film.

REVIEWS: "Bright, colorful filmusical." (*Variety*, 12/20/44); "Spritely musical-comedy-Western which will delight Deanna Durbin fans." (*Western Movies*, Pitts)

SUMMATION: *Can't Help Singing* is a bright, sparkling comedy musical set in the old west. Deanna Durbin is wonderful; her singing of Kern and Harburg's marvelous score is superb. Robert Paige makes a good leading man, and his voice rises to the occasion. Akim Tamiroff and Leonid Kinskey add a nice comedic touch to the proceedings. Director Frank Ryan does a fine job bringing the story to the screen while focusing primarily on Durbin. A special nod should be given to cinematographers Woody Bredell and W. Howard Greene, as they beautifully capture the scenic vistas to enhance the story.

Saturday Evening Post Sensation! Best-Selling Novel!
Now— GREAT MOTION PICTURE ENTERTAINMENT!
MAN AGAINST MAN ... in the fight to rule!
MAN AGAINST WOMAN ... in the fight to love!
MAN AGAINST WILDERNESS ... in the fight to live!

Canyon Passage

Universal (July 1946)

CAST: Logan Stuart, **Dana Andrews**; George Camrose, **Brian Donlevy**; Lucy Overmire, **Susan Hayward**; Caroline Marsh, **Patricia Roc**; Honey Bragg, **Ward Bond**; Hi Linnet; **Hoagy Carmichael**; Mrs. Overmire, **Fay Holden**; Jonas Overmire, **Stanley Ridges**; Johnny Steele, **Lloyd Bridges**; Ben Dance, **Andy Devine**; Vane Blazier, **Victor Cutler**; Marta Lestrade, **Rose Hobart**; Clenchfield, **Halliwell Hobbes**; Gray Bartlett, **James Cardwell**; Jack Lestrade, **Onslow Stevens**; Asa Dance, **Tad Devine**; Bushrod Dance, **Denny Devine**// Cornelius, **Peter Whitney**; Portland Storekeeper, **Chester Clute**; McLane, **Harry Shannon**; Mrs. Dance, **Dorothy Peterson**; Townsman, **Tex Cooper**; Neal Howison, **Ray Teal**; Harry Stutchell, **Ralph Peters**; Lisa, **Virginia Patton**; Preacher, **Frank Ferguson**; Indian Spokesman, **Chief Yowlachie**; Miners, **Richard Alexander**, **Karl Hackett** and **Eugene Stutenroth**; Mack McIver, **Wallace Scott**; Judge, **Erville Alderson**; Cobb, **Francis McDonald**

CREDITS: Director, **Jacques Tourneur**; Assistant Director, **Fred Frank**; Producer, **Walter Wanger**; Associate Producer, **Alexander Golitzen**; Screenwriter, Ernest Pascal; Dialogue Director, **Anthony Jowett**; Editor, **Milton Carruth**; Art Directors, **John B. Goodman** and **Richard H. Riedel**; Set Decorators, **Russell A. Gausman** and **Leigh Smith**; Cinematographer, **Edward Cronjager**; Special Photography, **D.S. Horsley**; Costumes, **Travis Banton**; Makeup, **Jack P. Pierce**; Hair Stylist, **Carmen Dirigo**; Sound, **Bernard B. Brown** and **William Hedgcock**; Musical Director, **Frank Skinner**; Technicolor Color Director, **Natalie Kalmus**; Associate Technicolor Color Director, **William Fritzsche**

SONGS: "Rogue River Valley" (Carmichael)—sung by **Hoagy Carmichael**; "Silver Saddle" (Carmichael)—sung by **Hoagy Carmichael**; "I'm Getting Married in the Morning" (Carmichael)—sung by **Hoagy Carmichael** and **Andy Devine**; and "Ole Buttermilk Sky" (Brooks and Carmichael)—sung by **Hoagy Carmichael**

LOCATION FILMING: Bend, Oregon

COLOR PROCESS: **Technicolor**

RUNNING TIME: 92 min.

SOURCE: Novel *Canyon Passage* by **Ernest Haycox**, which was first published in the *Saturday Evening Post*.

52 CANYON PASSAGE

STORY: From Portland, Oregon, freighter and trader Dana Andrews brings Susan Hayward, gold coins and other supplies to Jacksonville. Andrews had made a powerful enemy of the brutish Ward Bond when Andrews saw him near the scene of two murders. Hayward is returning to Jacksonville to eventually marry ex-press agent Brian Donlevy, while Andrews plans to wed Patricia Roc, an Englishwoman living with Andy Devine's family. Bond goads Andrews into a brutal fistfight. Andrews, using a bottle, chairs and his fists, is finally able to overcome Bond. Donlevy, addicted to gambling, has been using miners' funds stored in his company's safe. Donlevy's losses have mounted up, but Andrews gives his friend money to pay them off on the condition he'll stop gambling. Donlevy's gambling craze overcomes him. Donlevy takes gold dust belonging to miner Wallace Scott, which he loses in a card game. Scott appears and tells Donlevy he'll come for his dust the following morning. Frightened, afraid to be exposed as a thief, in desperation Donlevy resorts to murder

Canyon Passage (1946) screen card: Ward Bond (*left*) and Dana Andrews square off in a tough fistfight. Among the spectators are Lloyd Bridges (*second left*) and Richard Alexander (*center, bareheaded*). *Left border:* Brian Donlevy (*top left*), and Dana Andrews and Susan Hayward (*bottom left*).

to remain free. Andrews, about to leave on a trip to San Francisco, and knowing Donlevy has been playing in a crooked card game, tells gambler Onslow Stevens to return the money before Andrews returns. Wanting to settle elsewhere, Donlevy pressures Hayward to set a wedding date. Hayward promises to marry Donlevy on her return from San Francisco with a wedding gown. On the trail, Bond ambushes Andrews and Hayward. Stevens, who wants to keep the gold dust taken from Donlevy, had informed Bond of Andrews' trip. In the aftermath of the ambush, Andrews and Hayward discover they love each other—but in vain, since both are promised to others. Bond, frustrated in his unsuccessful attempt to kill Andrews, ravages and murders a young Indian maiden. Returning to Jacksonville, Andrews finds Donlevy has been accused of Scott's murder, and the miners are trying him. Donlevy is found guilty and will be hanged. Andrews tries to prevent mob rule and wants Donlevy tried in a real court of law. Word comes of an Indian uprising. Settlers are being murdered and their cabins burned. Amid the confusion, Andrews helps Donlevy escape. Andrews leads the townspeople and miners in a counterattack against the Indians. At Devine's cabin, the men find that Devine and his oldest son have been killed, and Roc has wandered into the woods. Bond, running for his life, seeks refuge at the cabin. Well-placed bullets from Andrews' pistol turns Bond back into the woods. Andrews and the men find Roc. The Indians catch up to Bond and kill, then scalp him. Roc realizes she wants to marry a man of the soil, not Andrews. Returning to Jacksonville, Andrews sees his trading post burned to the ground and learns that Donlevy was killed by miners in his escape attempt. Andrews starts a journey to San Francisco to raise funds to start over, with Hayward at his side.

NOTES AND COMMENTARY: Jacques Tourneur found *Canyon Passage* easier to direct than films composed of mainly indoor scenes. Tourneur felt outdoor scenes were less challenging to him than scenes with three or four people in a room.

Canyon Passage marked the screen debut of actress Patricia Roc.

"Ole Buttermilk Sky" received an Academy Award nomination for Best Song, but lost out to "On the Atchison, Topeka and the Santa Fe" from *The Harvey Girls* (Metro-Goldwyn-Mayer, 1946).

In her distinguished career, Susan Hayward received five Academy Award nominations, for: *Smash-Up: The Story of a Woman* (Universal-International, 1947), *My Foolish Heart* (RKO, 1950), *With a Song in My Heart* (20th Century Fox, 1952), *I'll Cry Tomorrow* (Metro-Goldwyn-Mayer, 1956) and *I Want to Live* (United Artists, 1958). For the last named production, Hayward took home the Oscar for Best Actress.

REVIEWS: "Beautifully Technicolored high-budget western." (*Variety*, 7/24/46); "Beautifully produced feature showing both the glory and harshness of frontier life;

a very good motion picture." (*Western Movies*, Pitts)

SUMMATION: *Canyon Passage* is a good, solid western that fails to reach classic status. Dana Andrews hands in a nifty performance as a man who has visions of a civilized west. Susan Hayward gives a fiery performance as a frontier woman promised to one man but in love with another. Brian Donlevy demonstrates his acting skill as a basically honest but greedy individual driven to desperation by his addiction to gambling. Ward Bond, Lloyd Bridges and Andy Devine head an impressive supporting cast. Hoagie Carmichael chips in with four nice songs, including the classic "Ole Buttermilk Sky." The story, however, is too episodic in nature to become a truly great film, and the screenplay is too compressed to allow full character development. There is a nicely choreographed fight between Andrews and Bond, and some good action develops in the climactic Indian uprising, but too much happens off camera (e.g. the deaths of Wallace Scott, Devine and Bond; the ravaging of an Indian maiden; and the burning of Andrews' store). Director Jacques Tourneur does a good job with the flawed script, and cinematographers Edward Cronjager and D.S. Horsley capture the magnificent splendor of the Bend, Oregon, area.

Wild ... Wide Open ... Wyoming!
The WEST'S GREATEST STAR TEAM!

Cheyenne Roundup

Universal (April 1943)

CAST: Gil Brandon and Buck Brandon, **Johnny Mack Brown**; Steve Rawlins, **Tex Ritter**; Cal Cawkins, **Fuzzy Knight**; Ellen Randall, **Jennifer Holt**; Blackie Dawson, **Harry Woods**; Slim Layton, **Roy Barcroft**; Judge Hickenbottom, **Robert Barron**; Bonanza, **Budd Buster**; Perkins, **Gil Patric;** and The **Jimmy Wakely Trio** (**Jimmy Wakely, Johnny Bond** and **Scotty Harrel**)// Pony Express Rider, **Kenne Duncan**; Townsman, **William Desmond**; Henchman, **Kermit Maynard**

CREDITS: Director, **Ray Taylor**; Associate Producer, **Oliver Drake**; Screenwriters, **Elmer Clifton** and **Bernard McConville**; Editor, **Otto Ludwig**; Art Director, **Jack Otterson** and **Ralph M. DeLacy**; Set Decorators, **R.A. Gausman** and **E.R. Robinson**; Cinematography, **William Sickner**; Sound, **Bernard B. Brown** and **Jess Moulin**; Musical Director, **H.J. Salter**

SONGS: "Ain't Got Nothin' and Nothin' Worries Me" (O. Drake, Rosen and Wakely)—sung by **Fuzzy Knight**; "Rootin' Tootin' Cowboy"

(Wakely)—sung by **The Jimmy Wakely Trio**; "Rose of the Hills" (O. Drake and Rosen)—sung by **Tex Ritter** and **The Jimmy Wakely Trio**; and "We Want Rawlins" (Rosen and Carter)—sung by **The Jimmy Wakely Trio**

LOCATION FILMING: Iverson and Agoura, California

RUNNING TIME: 59 min.

STORY: Tex Ritter, Marshal of Mesquite, runs badman Johnny Mack Brown and his confederates, Harry Woods, Roy Barcroft and Robert Barron, out of town. The men ride to the ghost town of El Dorado, owned by Fuzzy Knight. Thinking to revive the town by spreading false rumors about a gold strike, Brown buys 51 percent interest in the town. But gold is really discovered and the ghost town springs to life. Badman Brown and his cronies are behind all the lawlessness. Badman Brown's fiancée, Jennifer Holt, comes to El Dorado to marry Brown. The good citizens make Knight send a letter asking Ritter to resign his post in Mesquite and come to El Dorado. Badman Brown learns about the letter and rides to Mesquite to have it out with Ritter. Ritter puts badman Brown on the run with a serious wound. Badman Brown makes it to a cabin where he tries to take care of his wound. Good guy Brown has been searching for Brown and stumbles upon the cabin where his brother lies wounded. Bad guy Brown dies. With his last words, badman Brown repents and asks his brother to make El Dorado a decent place to live. Ritter has spotted the cabin, and he meets good guy Brown and asks him to impersonate his brother. Good guy Brown agrees, and he and Ritter return to El Dorado. Good guy Brown has cooked up a scheme for Ritter to run for sheriff, while professing to have turned crooked for the money. Woods doesn't want women around their business and tells good guy Brown to call off the wedding. As the election is running in Ritter's favor, good guy Brown tells Holt that he's her fiancé's twin brother. Barron had followed good guy Brown and rides to tell Woods. Woods decides to break up the election. Good guy Brown comes to town in time, and with Ritter and the honest citizens, brings Woods and his gang to justice. Good guy Brown and Holt marry and go on their honeymoon.

NOTES AND COMMENTARY: *Cheyenne Roundup* is a remake of *Bad Man from Red Butte* (Universal, 1940), which also starred Johnny Mack Brown. Footage from *Bad Man* is used in the confrontation between the two brothers and the bad Brown's subsequent death. The scene where Brown chases down the Pony Express rider, and the saloon brawl at the film's climax, was lifted from *West of Carson City* (Universal, 1940).

There were a couple of production lapses in the film. Johnny Mack Brown leaves to confront Tex Ritter in Mesquite. He leaves clean shaven, but upon arriving he sports a dark scruffy beard. In the scene where the vigilantes ride into town after Budd Buster has been shot, Jennifer Holt can be clearly seen in the group.

"Ain't Got Nothin' and Nothin'

Cheyenne Roundup (1943) movie still: Tex Ritter (*left center*) rounds up Robert Barron (*fourth left*) while Johnny Mack Brown (*fifth right*) does the same to Harry Woods (*right center*). Roy Barcroft (*center*), Jennifer Holt (*third right*) and Johnny Bond (*fourth right*) watch.

Worries Me" had been sung by Fuzzy Knight previously in *Boss of Hangtown Mesa* (Universal, 1942).

In the credits, Robert Barron's character name is listed as Hickenbottom, while in the film his name is simply Hicken.

REVIEWS: "Fair fodder for the action fans." (*Variety*, 4/14/43); "Satisfactory Johnny Mack Brown–Tex Ritter remake of *Bad Man from Red Butte*." (*Western Movies*, Pitts)

SUMMATION: *Cheyenne Roundup* is not a bad little film, even allowing for production lapses and excessive use of stock footage. Johnny Mack Brown plays a dual role this time out and does a fine job. Tex Ritter's part is downsized to secondary status (like the Bob Baker roles in Brown's first Universal series). Jennifer Holt shines as the prospective bride of the badman Brown. Fuzzy Knight has more of a character role in this one, and is effective. The villainy rests in the capable hands of Harry Woods, Roy Barcroft and Robert Barron. Ray Taylor directs with confidence, and the result is an entertaining, but minor, film.

BORN TO FIGHT!
and living by fist and gun!

Chip of the Flying U

Universal (November 1939)

CAST: "Chip" Bennett, **Johnny Mack Brown**; "Dusty," **Bob Baker**; "Weary," **Fuzzy Knight**; Margaret Whitmore, **Doris Weston**; J.G. Whitmore, **Forrest Taylor**; Duncan, **Anthony Warde**; Hennessy, **Karl Hackett**; Wilson, **Henry Hall**; Miss Robinson, **Claire Whitney**; Sheriff, **Ferris Taylor**; "Red," **Cecil Kellogg**; and **The Texas Rangers** (**Robert "Captain Bob" Crawford**, **Edward "Tookie" Cronenbold**, **Francis "Irish" Mahaney** and **Roderic "Dave" May**)// Slim, **Kermit Maynard**; Cowhand, **Hank Worden**; Station Agent, **Victor Potel**; Outlaw, **Chuck Morrison**; Townsman, **Hank Bell**

CREDITS: Director, **Ralph Staub**; Screenwriters, **Larry Rhine** and **Andrew Bennison**; Editor, **Louis Sackin**; Art Directors, **Jack Otterson** and **Harold MacArthur**; Set Decorator, **R.A. Gausman**; Cinematographer, **William Sickner**; Sound, **Bernard B. Brown** and **Jess Moulin**; Musical Director, **Charles Previn**

SONGS: "I Had a Gal and Her Name Was Sue"—sung by **The Texas Rangers**; "Ride On" (Carter and Rosen)—sung by **Bob Baker** and **The Texas Rangers**; "Git Along" (Carter and Rosen)—sung by **Bob Baker**; "I'm a Texas Cowboy"—sung by **The Texas Rangers**; "Aches and Pains"—sung by **Fuzzy Knight**; "Oh, Susanna" (Foster)—played by **Bob Baker** and **Fuzzy Knight**; "Mr. Moon"—sung by **Bob Baker** (Carter and Rosen)

LOCATION FILMING: Iverson, Andy Jauregui Ranch, California

RUNNING TIME: 55 min.

SOURCE: Novel *Chip of the Flying U* by **B.M. Bower** (Bertha "Muzzy" Sinclair)

STORY: Anthony Warde, a neighboring rancher, offers to purchase Forrest Taylor's ranch. Johnny Mack Brown, Taylor's foreman, had advised Taylor not to sell. Warde wants the ranch because it's adjacent to a cove, which will make it easier for Warde to supply stolen munitions to a foreign agent. Warde has a cache of munitions stored in a deserted shack on Taylor's ranch. Taylor's sister, Doris Weston, now a physician, comes to live at the ranch. Brown and Weston get off to a rocky start in their relationship. Brown rides to the bank to collect his pay and leave. As banker Henry Hall opens the safe, Warde's henchman, Karl Hackett, breaks in, steals the payroll money and shoots Hall. Warde knows the loss of the money might change Taylor's mind about selling his ranch. Brown chases Hackett, who throws the moneybag in the deserted shack before he eludes Brown. Because of the robbery, Brown decides to remain on the ranch. During roundup, Brown finds the stolen money and brings it to Weston. Weston, still not completely trusting Brown, puts her medical bag in the safe and the moneybag in Taylor's desk. Brown and Knight capture Hackett and another henchman, Chuck Morrison. Warde shows his true colors; at gunpoint he forces Brown to release his men, and forces Weston to open the safe. Warde and his men escape with Weston's medical bag. Brown and a posse begin a systematic search of the area to find Warde and his henchmen. Left behind at the ranch, Weston and ranch hand Fuzzy Knight decide to investigate the deserted shack. The outlaws capture Weston. Knight is left at the shack and sees the foreign agents reach the shack to take the munitions to a ship waiting in the cove. Knight goes for help and finds Brown and the posse. The posse rides to the shack. In the ensuing gunfight, Knight fires a bullet that ignites the munitions, destroying the shack and its occupants. Brown rescues Weston after defeating Warde in a fistfight. Brown and Weston have fallen in love and plan to marry.

NOTES AND COMMENTARY: *Chip of the Flying U* was written by Bertha Muzzy Sinclair under the pseudonym B.M. Bower. The novel had three previous screen treatments, the first with Tom Mix (Selig, 1914); the second, retitled *The Galloping Dude* (1920), with Bud Osborne; and the third with Hoot Gibson (Universal, 1926). Gibson also starred in the sequel, *King of the Rodeo* (Universal, 1928).

Johnny Mack Brown swapped his white horse for Rebel, a palomino, in this film. Brown would ride a palomino for the rest of his long western starring career.

In the third episode of this western series, Bob Baker was relegated to the role of back-up cowboy. In one scene Brown decides to trail two suspected lawbreakers. He chooses Fuzzy Knight to go along instead of the more virile Baker. Baker must have been reading the handwriting on the wall that his career at Universal, as a star, was over.

"Mr. Moon" was sung by Frances Langford in *Cowboy in Manhattan* (Universal, 1943). "Oh, Susanna" would be featured in *The Fiddlin' Buckaroo* (Universal, 1933), *Law for Tombstone* (Universal, 1937), *Courage of the West* (Universal, 1937), *Desperate Trails* (Universal, 1939) and *Rawhide Rangers* (Universal, 1941).

The destruction of the shack would be used again later, in the series entry *Riders of Pasco Basin* (Universal, 1940).

REVIEWS: "Top notch entertainment for devotees of prairie mellers." (*Variety*, 1/24/40); "Above average, considering the tired story line." (*The Motion Picture Guide*, Nash and Ross)

SUMMATION: *Chip of the Flying U* is a good, fast-paced western adventure, with Johnny Mack Brown in fine form as the primary hero. Fuzzy Knight's comedy is on target. Bob Baker's scenes are pretty much relegated to his musical numbers. Anthony Warde, Karl Hackett and Chuck Morrison are a capable bunch of villains. Doris Weston is a pert and pleasant leading lady. Director Ralph Staub keeps the action flowing, to the audience's delight.

12 chapters cram-jam full of excitement and sensational surprises.

Clancy of the Mounted

Universal / Adventure Pictures (January 1933)

CAST: Sergeant Tom Clancy, **Tom Tyler**; Ann Louise, **Jacqueline Wells**; Steve Clancy, **Earl McCarthy**; Dan Morgan, **William Desmond**; Maureen Clancy, **Rosalie Roy**; "Black" MacDougal, **William L. Thomas**; Pierre LaRue, **Leon Duval**; Inspector Cabot, **Francis Ford**; Constable MacGregor, **Tom London**; Constable McIntosh, **Edmund Cobb**; Wolf Fang, **Frank Lackteen**; Outlaw, **Steve Clemente**

CREDITS: Director, **Ray Taylor**; Producer, **Henry MacRae**; Screenwriters, **Ella O'Neill**, **Basil Dickey** and **Harry Hoyt**

CHAPTER TITLES: 1. Toll of the Rapids, 2. Brother Against Brother, 3. Ambuscade, 4. The Storm, 5. A Desperate Chance, 6. The Wolf's Fangs, 7. The Night Attack, 8. Crashing Timber, 9. Fingerprints, 10. The Breed Strikes, 11. The Crimson Jacket, 12. Journey's End

SOURCE: Poem "Clancy of the Mounted Police" by **Robert W. Service**

STORY: Leon Duval and William L. Thorne murder a miner to gain possession of a silver and radium mine, and frame Earl McCarthy for the crime. McCarthy decides to hide out until the real culprits can be arrested. McCarthy's brother, Tom Tyler, who is a sergeant in the Royal Mounted Canadian Police, is given the assignment to arrest McCarthy. Jacqueline Wells, the murdered man's daughter and heir to the mine, is coming to the Canadian Northwest to claim her inheritance. Duval makes an attempt to murder Wells but fails. Tyler locates McCarthy and finally persuades him that it would be in his best interest to turn himself in. Wells believes in McCarthy and decides to work with Tyler to prove his innocence. Working together through many obstacles and dangers, Tyler and Wells become romantically involved. From numerous clues, Tyler begins to suspect Thorne of the murder and confronts him. The men fight, and Thorne escapes dressed as a mounted policeman. Duval, thinking the mountie is Tyler, fires a shot that mortally wounds Thorne. Duval is later killed in an explosion meant for Tyler. Before dying, Thorne confesses that McCarthy was framed for the miner's murder.

NOTES AND COMMENTARY: Jacqueline Wells was billed as Diane Duval early in her career. Later she used the name by which she was probably best known, Julie Bishop.

The screenplay of *Clancy of the Mounted* was miles removed from Robert W. Service's famous poem. In Service's poem, Clancy journeys into the wilds to rescue a starving and crazy man. Clancy finds the man and begins his return to civilization through a furious blizzard. The cold

Clancy of the Mounted (1933) movie still: Tom Tyler (*center*) and Jacqueline Wells (*left center*) discuss an unidentified wounded man while an unidentified mounted policeman looks on.

kills the sled dogs. Clancy carries the man in his arms the rest of the way to the Mounted Police barracks. The blizzard takes its toll on Clancy, resulting in the loss of his toes and mind.

Tom Tyler was a formidable serial hero. In the early days of sound, Tyler was the star of one serial for Mascot and four cliffhangers for Universal. But Tyler would gain everlasting fame in serial history in the forties, playing the title roles in *Adventures of Captain Marvel* (Republic, 1941) and *The Phantom* (Columbia, 1943), two favorites of devotees of comic books and/or comic strips.

REVIEWS: "Tom Tyler fans will love this action packed cliffhanger." (*Western Movies*, Pitts)

SUMMATION: This serial was not available for viewing by the author.

He's Two-Gun Terror!
Blasting the Outlaws Out of the West!

Code of the Lawless

ALTERNATIVE TITLE: *The Mysterious Stranger*; Universal (October 1945)

CAST: Grant Carter, **Kirby Grant**; Bonanza, **Fuzzy Knight**; Julie Randall, **Poni Adams**; Lester Ward, **Hugh Prosser**; Ruth Monroe, **Barbara Sears**; Bart Rogan, **Edward M. Howard**; Chad Hilton Sr., **Stanley Andrews**; Chad Hilton Jr., **Rune H. Hultman**// Nelson, **Edmund Cobb**; Judd, **Bob McKenzie**; Crenshaw, **Rex Lease**; Reb, **Carey Harrison**; Rancher, **Fred Graham**; Perkins, **Pietro Sosso**; Sam, **Roy Brent**; Pete, **Pierce Lyden**; Rufe, **Budd Buster**

CREDITS: Director / Producer, **Wallace A. Fox**; Screenwriter, **Patricia Harper**; Editor, **Saul A. Goodkind**; Art Directors, **John B. Goodman** and **Abraham Grossman**; Set Decorators, **Russell A. Gausman** and **Ralph Warrington**; Cinematographer, **Maury Gertsman**; Sound, **Bernard B. Brown** and **Jess Moulin**; Musical Director, **Milton Rosen**

SONGS: "Jack and Jill"—sung by **Fuzzy Knight**

LOCATION FILMING: Iverson, California

RUNNING TIME: 60 min.

STORY: Stanley Andrews' corporation controls the ranches in the Pecos Territory, setting tax rates and supply prices. Unknown to Andrews, who is recuperating from an illness, his manager, Hugh Prosser, is gouging the ranchers. Prosser's set-up is jeopardized when Andrews' son, Rune H. Hultman, returns home after an absence of more than twenty years. Prosser has Hultman ambushed, but the shot only wounds him. Wandering cowboy Kirby Grant takes Hultman to Fuzzy Knight's cabin for medical attention. Grant takes Hultman's identification and decides to pose as Andrews' son. With Knight's help, Grant uncovers evidence that Prosser is behind the rancher's troubles. Prosser's henchman, Edward M. Howard, kills Andrews. Prosser and Andrews' nurse, Barbara Sears, are prepared to swear that Grant is the murderer. Grant convinces Prosser that greater profits are in store if they foreclose on the ranches and resell them. Grant instructs Knight to tell the ranchers that if they hold an election to become part of the Arizona territory, they could petition to own their ranches outright. Hultman recovers from his wounds and comes to town. Grant then reveals he is a special investigator for the Department of the Interior and arrests Prosser, Sear and Howard. Arizona becomes a territory, and the ranchers have clear title to their ranches.

NOTES AND COMMENTARY: Jane Adams (billed here as "Poni Adams") remembered Kirby Grant fondly and had this to say about him: "He rates

Code of the Lawless (1945) title card: **Left side (*top to bottom*)**, Kirby Grant, Fuzzy Knight, Poni Adams, Edward M. Howard, Hugh Prosser. In a Universal art department slip-up, the rider on horseback (***bottom left***) is Johnny Mack Brown, who doesn't even appear in the film.

very high in my opinion. I thought he was just a perfect gentleman. I was lucky to work with Johnny Mack Brown, Duncan Renaldo and Kirby because they were all great guys, full of charm and southern gentlemen, except for Duncan, and he was just great."

Jane Adams commented on Fuzzy Knight: "He was wonderful and funny. He was the funniest man, a real comic. He was funny all the time."

Code of the Lawless was very loosely based on *Son of Roaring Dan* (Universal, 1940).

REVIEWS: "Not a very distinguished effort." (*Motion Picture Guide*, Nash and Ross)

SUMMATION: *Code of the Lawless* is a pleasant western that should have been better. The montage sequence at the beginning is unnecessary, since it doesn't pertain to the story line. The movie starts well, with some adequate action sequences. Then, except for one quick scene, the action disappears. The ending is a mild round up of the principle villains. Kirby Grant looks like a good cowboy star, but the screenwriters need to place him in more action sequences. Fuzzy Knight is a decided asset as Grant's sidekick, eschewing juvenile comedy for characterization. Of the supporting cast, only Stanley Andrews gives an above average performance. The lovely Poni (later Jane) Adams is present for decoration only. It looks like the budget wasn't there to deliver a top flight western feature.

The fighting cowboy of today gets his information by radio—and rescues the girl of his dreams from the terror of the West in the wildest, most exciting, fastest, TALKING Western picture filmed to date. See the King of Cowboys in action—IT'S A TREAT!

The Concentratin' Kid

Universal-Jewel (October 1930)

CAST: The Concentratin' Kid (Bill Evans), **Hoot Gibson**; Betty Lou, **Kathryn Crawford**; Foreman Blaine, **Duke R. Lee**; Campbell, **Jim Mason**; C.C. Stile, **Robert E. Homans**// Announcer, **Fred Gilman**

CREDITS: Director, **Arthur Rosson**; Producer, **Hoot Gibson**; Story, **Harold Tarshis** and **Charles Saxton**; Screenwriter, **Harold Tarshis**; Editor, **Gilmore Walker**; Art Director, **David Garber**; Cinematographer, **Harry Neumann**; Recording Supervisor, **C. Roy Hunter**; Synchronization and Score, **David Broekman**

SONG: "I Want My Man of the Golden West"—sung by **Kathryn Crawford**

LOCATION FILMING: Conejo and the Walker Ranch, California

RUNNING TIME: 57 min.

STORY: Cowhand Hoot Gibson makes a bet with the other cowhands that he will not only meet radio singer Kathryn Crawford but will marry her. Crawford comes to town with a traveling troupe headed by Robert E. Homans. Barber Jim Mason tries to get romantic with Crawford. Gibson, unaware Crawford is the woman he wants to meet, sends Mason on his way. Mason is the leader of the gang responsible for rustling activities in the area. After mistaking another singer for the woman he wants to meet, Gibson finally realizes Crawford is the one and begins taking her out. Mason tells Crawford about Gibson's bet with the cowhands. Gibson asks Crawford to marry him. Crawford, incensed over the bet, refuses to have anything to do with Gibson. Afterwards Crawford regrets her decision, since she's really in love with Gibson. Mason plans to make one big haul and rustle all the stock when the troupe makes their final broadcast, since every cowhand will be in attendance. Using a ruse, Mason kidnaps Crawford; but Gibson learns of the kidnapping and rides after them. Gibson makes the rustlers think a posse has caught up with them, and the rustlers retreat. Then Gibson rescues Crawford from Mason. The cowhands listen to the wedding ceremony between Gibson and Crawford over the radio.

NOTES AND COMMENTARY: This was Hoot Gibson's final film for Universal.

REVIEWS: "Gibson's final film for Universal, and one of his funniest." (*The Western*, Pitts); "Fun early talkie from Hoot Gibson." (*Western Movies*, Pitts)

SUMMATION: This is a good Hoot Gibson vehicle with a decided emphasis on comedy. Gibson turns in a nifty performance, adroitly balancing the light and action filled moments. Kathryn Crawford matches up well with Gibson, shining in the scene in which she conveys her emotions over losing Gibson while singing "I Want My Man of the Golden West."

THE WORLD SINGS "HOWDY" WITH THE GREATEST WESTERN HERO OF THEM ALL!
Ride with him as he pitches a painted pony across sagebrush wilderness in a hurricane clean-up of western banditry!

Courage of the West

Universal (December 1937)

CAST: Jack Saunders, **Bob Baker**; Buck Saunders, **J. Farrell MacDonald**; Beth Andrews, **Lois January**; Hank Givens, **Fuzzy Knight**; Al Wilkins, **Harry Woods**; Rufe Lambert, **Carl Stockdale**; Jackie Wilkins, **Buddy Cox**; Washington Official, **Forrest Taylor**; Abraham Lincoln, **Albert Russell**; U.S. Marshal, **Jack Montgomery**// Secretary of State Stanton, **Charles K. French**; Secretary of State Seward, **Thomas Monk**; George Wilkins, **Oscar Gahan**; Ranger, **Glenn Strange**; Steve, **Jack Kirk**; Murphy, **Richard Cramer**; Mine Driver, **Tom London**

CREDITS: Director, **Joseph H. Lewis**; Assistant Director, **Glenn Cook**; Screenwriter, **Norton S. Parker**; Editor, **Charles Craft**; Art Director, **Charles Clague**; Sound, **Robert Pritchard** and **Jesse Bastian**; Musical Director/Arrangements, **Frank Sanucci**

SONGS: "Oh, Susanna" (Foster)—sung by **male chorus**; "Restin' Beside the Trail" (Allan)—sung by **male chorus**; "Rangers' Song" (Allan)—sung by **Bob Baker**, **Buddy Cox** and male chorus; "Rangers' Song" (reprise)—sung by **Bob Baker** and **male chorus**; "Song of the Trail" (Allan)—sung by **Bob Baker** and male chorus; "I'll Build a Ranch House on the Range" (Allan)—sung by **Bob Baker**; and "Rangers' Song" (reprise)—sung by **male chorus**

LOCATION FILMING: Lone Pine, California, and the Virginia & Truckee Railway in the Virginia City area, Nevada

RUNNING TIME: 56 min.

STORY: J. Farrell MacDonald is commissioned by President Albert Russell to operate as a "Free Ranger" and combat lawlessness in the west. MacDonald tracks down the notorious bandit Harry Woods. Woods is scheduled to hang for his crimes. MacDonald decides to adopt Woods' son and raise him as his own. Woods escapes from jail on the day he's supposed to be hung and reportedly goes to Mexico. Growing to manhood, MacDonald's son, Bob Baker, follows in his father's footsteps and becomes a Free Ranger. Baker meets rancher Lois January, who is driving a herd of horses to her ranch across the border in California. Baker and January begin to fall in love, so Baker decides to escort January to the state line. January meets her foreman, Harry Woods. Woods also is the outside contact for Carl Stockdale's outlaw gang. MacDonald is given the assignment to break up the gang. Baker sets a trap for Stockdale, but Stockdale eludes the trap and takes the gold shipment. Baker and his friend Knight follow Woods' trail to January's ranch. Only Baker goes to the ranch, but Knight recognizes Woods as he surveys the ranch through a telescope. Knight tells only MacDonald about Woods. Stockdale plans to rob a large gold shipment in town. Woods tells Stockdale that the Free Rangers have pulled out of the area; and he'll lure Baker into a trap, where he'll be killed. Woods believes Baker is MacDonald's son. As MacDonald arrives at January's ranch, Stockdale and his men steal the gold in town. MacDonald walks onto January's ranch and is shot by Woods. Woods gloats to MacDonald that Baker is riding into a trap. MacDonald tells Woods that Baker is his son. Woods asks MacDonald never to reveal to Baker that he is his real father and rides to save Baker. Outlaws have Baker in their sights, but Woods arrives, and he and Baker dispatch the outlaws. Knight sees Stockdale and his men riding from town. Actually, the Free Rangers are close by and soon pursue the robbers. Stockdale comes to the place where Baker and Woods are to change horses. Woods decides to help Baker bring in Stockdale's gang. Woods stampedes the horses but is mortally wounded by Stockdale. Baker then shoots Stockdale. The Free Rangers arrive and capture the gang. Woods dies in Baker's arms, now finally at peace. MacDonald recovers from his wound and takes command of the Rangers. Baker resigns from the Rangers to stay with January and run her ranch.

NOTES AND COMMENTARY: Bob Baker became Universal's singing cowboy star, winning out over Leonard Slye (Roy Rogers), Stuart Hamblin and Willie Phelps. Initially Universal wanted to name their new star Tex Baker. Baker, whose real name was Leland "Tumble" Weed, disagreed because he wasn't from Texas, and Bob was the name they settled upon.

Lois January commented on *Courage of the West*: "I liked that one better than a lot of them." Of Bob Baker she said, "He was sweet and nice. He was a little [nervous]) but it

Courage of the West (1937) scene card: Bob Baker cradles a dying Harry Woods as Fuzzy Knight (*center*) leads the Free Rangers to the rescue. *Left border*, Bob Baker.

didn't disturb me. He was not as tuned up." She labeled Fuzzy Knight "a delight. He was fun. Technically, professionally, he was always there. He always knew his lines. In those days, sometimes we made up our own lines."

On her career, Lois January remembered, "I didn't have a manager and I didn't have an agent. In those days, if you didn't have those, at least a real good agent or a good manager, you got tossed about. I was not that interested in becoming a cinema star. I was just having fun. I enjoyed my work. I wasn't a businesswoman. Had I been more of a businessperson and hired a good manager or agent, I would have done much better. But I never took it that seriously. When you don't take something to heart and really go at it, if you pardon the expression, it becomes sort of half-assed."

Trem Carr was the producer for the Bob Baker series but did not receive onscreen credit. Carr had John Wayne under contract at the time but decided to go with singing cowboy Baker.

Fleming Allen wrote the original songs for ten of the twelve solo starring Bob Baker western films at Universal. Allen had been the music director for the WLS radio station from 1931 to 1933. For the next two years, Allan was on the production staff at the NBC Studios in Chicago. Then Allan became a Hollywood songwriter.

"Oh, Susanna" had been heard in *The Fiddlin' Buckaroo* (Universal, 1933) and *Law for Tombstone* (Universal, 1937), and would be heard again in *Desperate Trails* (Universal, 1939), *Chip of the Flying U* (Universal, 1939) and *Rawhide Rangers* (Universal, 1941). Bob Baker would sing "Song of the Trail" in *Guilty Trails* (Universal, 1938).

When Bob Baker made personal appearances, he was billed as "The Singing Western Star Champion Rodeo Bronc Rider!" His backup group was called the Free Rangers.

REVIEWS: "Virile western fare; western thriller with Bob Baker clicking as cowboy balladeer." (*Variety*, 12/8/37); "This is the best one of them [Baker's series], thanks to Lewis' inspired direction." (*The Motion Picture Guide*, Nash and Ross)

SUMMATION: *Courage of the West*, Bob Baker's first starring western, comes out strong and ends up a winner. Baker acquits himself well and shows he should have been a major cowboy star. For insurance, J. Farrell MacDonald and Harry Woods were cast as Baker's adoptive and natural father, respectively, and both give stellar performances. Fuzzy Knight is quite good in his character role as MacDonald and Baker's friend and confidant. Joseph H. Lewis shows his directorial talent; he moves the plot forward forcefully while incorporating sweeping action scenes to bolster the story.

If you crave action with your laughs, by all means see HOOT GIBSON *in*
Courtin' Wildcats.
Here's a picture that's bigger, better and funnier than any you've
seen in a blue moon.

Courtin' Wildcats

Universal-Jewel (December 1929)

CAST: Clarence Butts, **Hoot Gibson**; Calamity Jane, **Eugenia Gilbert**; McLaren, **Monte Montague**; Mr. Butts, **Joseph Girard**; Doctor, **James Farley**; McKenzie, **Harry Todd**; Quid Johnson, **John Oscar**; Professor, **Lon Poff**; Mulvey, **Pete Morrison**// Strongman, **Joe Bonomo**; Gorilla, **Joe Bonomo**; Fugitive, **Jim Corey**; Show Worker, **Frank Ellis**; Cowboy, **Ben Corbett**

CREDITS: Director, **Jerome Storm**; Producer, **Hoot Gibson**; Screenwriter, **Dudley McKenna**; Editor, **Gilmore Walker**; Art Director, **David Garber**; Recording Supervisor, **C. Roy Hunter**; Synchronization and Score, **David Broekman**;

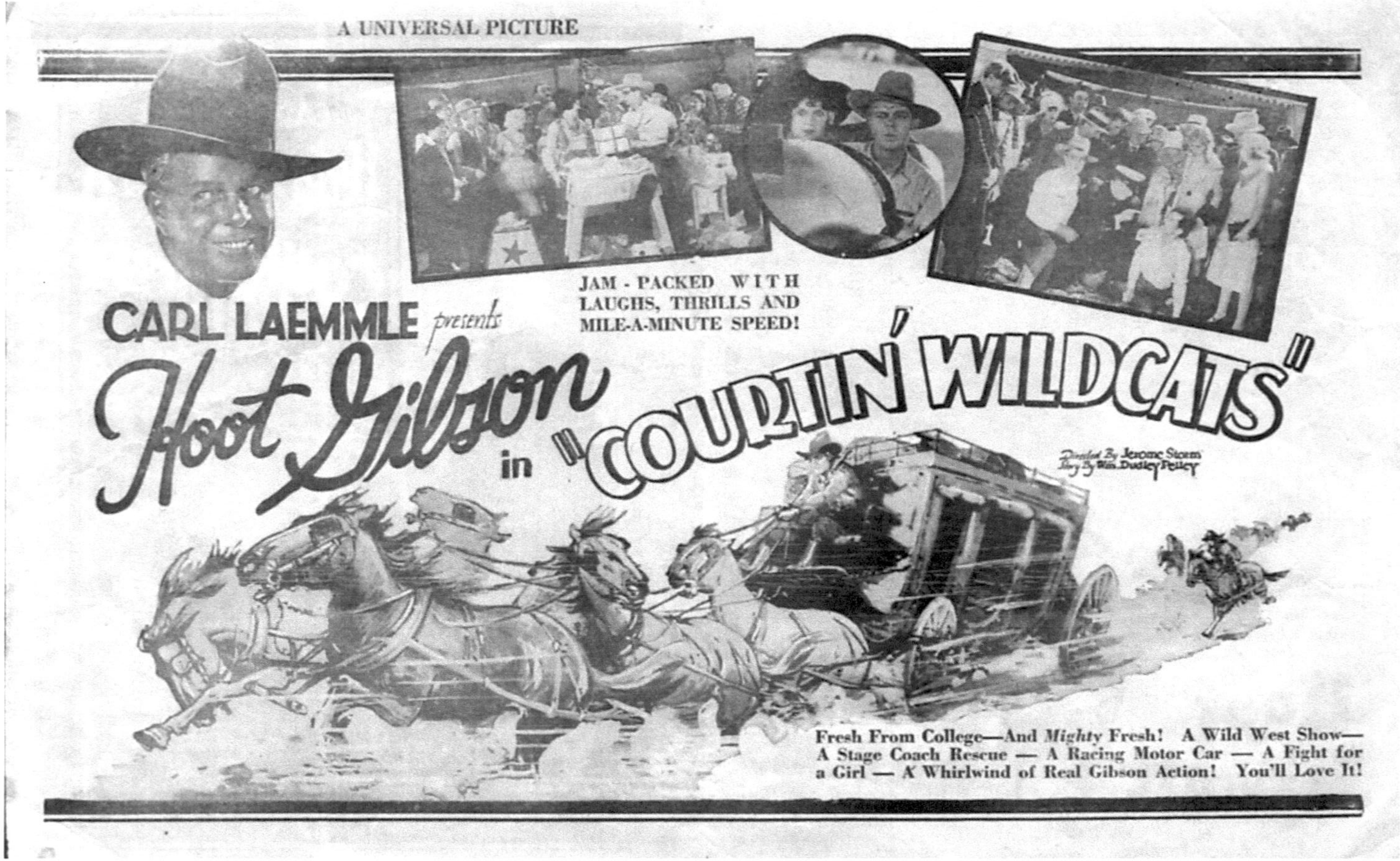

A UNIVERSAL PICTURE

CARL LAEMMLE presents

Hoot Gibson in "COURTIN WILDCATS"

JAM-PACKED WITH LAUGHS, THRILLS AND MILE-A-MINUTE SPEED!

Fresh From College—And Mighty Fresh! A Wild West Show—A Stage Coach Rescue — A Racing Motor Car — A Fight for a Girl — A Whirlwind of Real Gibson Action! You'll Love It!

Recorded, **Western Electric Equipment**

RUNNING TIME: 56 min.

LOCATION FILMING: Fillmore—Saugus area, California

SOURCE: Story "Courtin' Calamity" by **William Dudley Pelly**

STORY: College student Hoot Gibson pretends to be sickly to avoid working in a foundry owned by his father, Joseph Girard. Girard has Doctor James Farley give Gibson a thorough physical. Farley finds that Gibson has been faking, and he needs hard work to build him up. Farley arranges for Gibson to work at a Wild West Show for the summer. Gibson falls for Eugenia Gilbert, the show's sharpshooter. Gilbert is a man-hater since a man worked his way into her father's confidence and stole his money. Gibson sets out to tame the wildcat, Gilbert, and have her eat oats out of his hand. A fugitive from the law, Jim Corey, takes refuge in Gilbert's tent. This is the man who fleeced her father, so she shoots him. Thinking she had killed Corey, she makes a getaway on horseback. Corey is only wounded, and the police chase Gilbert to tell her that she's a heroine. Gibson catches up to Gilbert in his sports car. Gilbert transfers to Gibson's car. Gibson begins driving like a maniac until she eats oats from his hand. Realizing Gibson is really in love with her, Gilbert consents to marry him.

NOTES AND COMMENTARY: During the filming of *Courtin' Wildcats*, Universal set up a complete circus, with lollipops and pink lemonade, that served as a haven for children who lived in the vicinity of the studio.

Courtin' Wildcats was also released as a silent film.

REVIEWS: "Usual tenderfoot-to-toughguy tedium." (*Motion Picture Guide*, Nash and Ross); "Fitting opera for the deserted western fans." (*Variety*, 12/5/29)

SUMMATION: *Courtin' Wildcats* is a slight comedy vehicle for Hoot Gibson. Except for some scenes of Gibson performing in the Wild West show, most of Gibson's comedy falls flat. The screenplay never convinces us that Gibson and Gilbert are really in love, and the ending, with Gibson driving his sports car into the church, is absurd. No one, from actors, director, screenwriter on down, distinguishes themselves with this one.

Opposite: Courtin' Wildcats (1929) herald: *left*, Hoot Gibson portrait; *left center*, Hoot Gibson gives a present to Eugenia Gilbert; *right center*, Eugenia Gilbert and Hoot Gibson in Gibson's sports car; *right*, Hoot Gibson (*left center*) realizes Gilbert only wounded Jim Corey (*on ground*).

Pals! Buck and a Boy!
He was only a little feller, but he had what it takes to make a great man,
and Buck fought to give him every chance!

The Cowboy and the Kid

Universal (May 1936); A Buck Jones Production

CAST: Steve Davis, **Buck Jones**; Jimmy Thomas, **Billy Burrud**; June Caldwell, **Dorothy Revier**; Jess Watson, **Harry Worth**; Doctor Wilson, **Oliver Eckhardt**; Mrs. Wilson, **Mary Merch**; Judge Talbot, **Burr Caruth**; Jim Thomas, **Kernan Cripps**; Sheriff Bailey, **Lafe McKee**; "**Silver**"// Foreman, **Lew Meehan**; Townsman, **Charles King**; Mandy, **Mildred Gober**; Hotel Manager, **Henry Roquemore**; Sheriff Morton, **Dick Rush**

CREDITS: Director, **Ray Taylor**; Story, **Buck Jones**; Screenwriter, **Frances Guihan**; Editor, **Bernard Loftis**; Art Director, **Ralph Berger**; Cinematography, **Allen Thompson** and **Herbert Fitzpatrick**; Sound, **Buddy Myers**

LOCATION FILMING: Agoura and Malibu Lake, California

RUNNING TIME: 58 min.

STORY: Buck Jones is a cowboy down on his luck when he comes upon a small herd of thirsty cattle. Jones decides to shoot a hole in a nearby above-ground water line so the cattle can have water. This action wreaks havoc throughout the community. Water Company Manager Harry Worth decides to blame the trouble on rancher Kernan Cripps. Foreman Lee Meehan and his men are sent to teach Cripps a lesson. Cripps is gunned down as his young son, Bill Burrud, watches. Jones comes to the ranch and learns that Cripps was blamed for his actions. Jones tells Burrud that *he* burst the water line. Burrud responds that the men would have shot his father anyway since Worth wants the ranch. Since Burrud is now an orphan, Jones decides to take care of him. Jones believes Worth's interest indicates there may be gold or oil on the ranch. Burrud is enrolled in school, and Jones meets his teacher, Dorothy Revier. Worth has been courting Revier and has persuaded her to loan him $200 of the school's money, which he says he'll repay when she needs it. The school board decides to build an addition to the school and sets up a meeting in which the school money will be counted to see if they have sufficient funds. Revier gives a note to Jones to take to Worth to have the money returned. Worth is not in his office, so when it's time for the meeting, Revier runs away in disgrace and makes an unsuccessful suicide attempt. Jones, finally, finds Worth, who throws the note away. Jones then asks Worth for the money. There is a short fight, with Jones the victor. Jones rides away with Burrud, believing he's in trouble. When Worth tries to make people believe Jones robbed him, a sheriff from a neighboring county recognizes Worth as a bank robber. The decision is made that Jones should get the thousand dollar reward money. With this money, Jones, Revier and Burrud become a family; and they plan to look for riches on the Cripps ranch.

NOTES AND COMMENTARY: *The Cowboy and the Kid* is a remake of *Just Pals* (Fox, 1920) with Tom Mix.

Buck Jones takes a white hat from Harry Worth's office so he'll match the stock shot from a John Wayne Lone Star/Monogram western of a horse and rider jumping into a body of water.

REVIEWS: "Feeble." (*Variety*, 7/29/36); "Misguided attempt to emphasize atmosphere and character at the expense of action." (The *Western*, Hardy)

SUMMATION: Buck Jones tries to bring something different to the screen in *The Cowboy and the Kid*, but the final result is a below par mishmash of pathos and comedy. Villainy takes a back seat in this feature. No one pays the penalty for Kernan Cripps' death. Villain Worth is brought to justice for bank robbery and not murder. Jones' acting is par for the course. But the acting of young Billy Burrud and leading lady Dorothy Revier at times is reminiscent of the silent screen era. Director Ray Taylor can't do much with this one except hang on until its bumpy conclusion.

BROADWAY GOES COW-BOOGIE!
...with Herds of Honeys and Howls of Glee!

Cowboy in Manhattan

Universal (April 1943)

CAST: Bob Allen, **Robert Paige**; Babs Lee, **Frances Langford**; Hank, **Leon Errol**; Ace Robbins, **Walter Catlett**; Louie, **Joe Sawyer**; Mitzi, **Jennifer Holt**; Wild Bill, **George Cleveland**; Higgins, **Will Wright**; Tommy, **Dorothy Granger**; Potter, **Lorin Baker**; Count Kardos, **Marek Windheim**; Headwaiter, **Jack Mulhall**; Cab Driver, **Matt McHugh**; Mac, **Tommy Mack**; Bill, **Billy Nelson**// 2nd Cab Driver, **Stanley Price**

CREDITS: Director, **Frank Woodruff**; Associate Producer, **Paul Malvern**; Story, **William Thomas, Maxwell Shane** and **Warren Wilson**; Screenwriter, **Warren Wilson**; Editor, **Fred R. Feitshans Jr.**; Art Director, **John Goodman** and **Ralph De Lacey**; Set Decorators, **R.A. Gausman** and **Ira S. Webb**; Gowns, **Vera West**; Sound, **Bernard B. Brown** and **Joe Lapis**; Musical Director, **Charles Previn**; Choreographer, **Aida Broadbent**

SONGS: "Whistle Your Blues to a Bluebird" (Carter and Rosen)—sung by **Frances Langford**; "Whistle Your Blues to a Bluebird" (reprise)—sung by **Frances Langford**; "Well, Need I Say More" (Carter and Rosen)—sung by **Robert Paige** and **Frances Langford**; "Private Cowboy Jones" (Carter and Rosen)—sung by **Robert Paige** and **Frances Langford**; "Mr. Moon" (Carter and Rosen)—sung by **Frances Langford** and **chorus**; "Well, Need I Say More" (reprise)—sung by **Frances Langford**; "A Cowboy Is Happy" (Carter and Rosen)—sung by **chorus;** and "Private Cowboy Jones" (reprise)—sung by **Frances Langford** and **chorus**

RUNNING TIME: 59 min.

STORY: Walter Catlett and Leon Errol are producing a play, *Sweetheart of Texas*, to glorify the state of Texas. Wealthy Texans are backing the play. The play stars Frances Langford, who tells Catlett that if he pulls one more phony publicity stunt regarding her private life, she'll walk out. The play is to open on Broadway on December 29th, the date Texas joined the Union. Catlett runs into a problem: ticket sellers don't want to handle the play because of two other important events that same night. Songwriter Robert Paige offers a solution: hire someone to pretend to be a rich Texan who's fallen for Langford, and tell the press he's purchased all the tickets for the first week. This will not only give Paige a chance to substitute some of his songs but create an aura that will have the public clamoring for admission. As the week ends, Langford and Paige have fallen in love. Paige wants to tell Langford the truth about the stunt and that he really loves her, in the presence of Catlett. As Langford arrives, she hears Paige and Catlett talking and concludes this has been another of Catlett's publicity stunts. Langford goes into hiding. Paige thinks she's been kidnapped and, through nightclub owner Joe Sawyer, finds out where she is. Meanwhile, the Texas backers learn the rich Texan is Paige, nephew of one of the backers, George Cleveland. Cleveland knows Paige hasn't any money and flies to New York to investigate. Cleveland arrives in time to follow Paige to the house where Langford is staying. Paige barges into the house, whips the "kidnap men," and brings her to the theater. Langford realizes Paige is really in love with her. Langford gets to the show as the curtain is about to go up. The show's a big hit. Cleveland sees that Paige is a real two-fisted Texan and plans to give him two million dollars.

NOTES AND COMMENTARY: A similar story was used for *You're a Sweetheart* (Universal, 1937), with Alice Faye and George Murphy.

The song "A Cowboy is Happy" was sung by Nell O'Day in *Rawhide Rangers* (Universal, 1941), and by Claire Carleton and Fuzzy Knight in *Gun Town* (Universal, 1946). "Mr. Moon" was previously sung by Bob Baker in *Chip of the Flying U* (Universal, 1939).

REVIEWS: "Sufficient brightness in lines, situation and numbers to carry through as an above-par dual supporter." (*Variety*, 4/17/43); "Tired tale." (*The Motion Picture Guide*, Nash and Ross)

SUMMATION: *A Cowboy in Manhattan* is an entertaining show.

Frances Langford is delightful. She brings an exuberance to the film that lifts it to above average status. With her fine singing voice, Langford takes very average songs and embellishes them with something special to make them very listenable. Robert Paige is just fine as Langford's love interest. George Cleveland, as Paige's uncle, adds some welcome humor. This is just a "B" musical, but Frank Woodruff directs lovingly, and it shows.

The King of All Cowboys in His Latest Action Thriller
A Tornado of Action of Ranchers Fighting and Rustlers Plundering with This Six Shooting Son Leading the Way

The Crimson Trail

Universal (March 1935); A Charles Buck Jones Production

CAST: Billy Carter, **Charles Buck Jones**; Kitty Bellair, **Polly Ann Young**; Luke Long, **Ward Bond**; Loco, **John Bleifer**; Paul, **Paul Fix**; Jim Bellair, **Carl Stockdale**; Frank Carter, **Charles K. French**; Tom, **Charles Brinley**; Cal, **Bob Kortman**; Jack, **Bud Osborne**// "Silver"

CREDITS: Director, **Al Raboch**; Producer, **Irving Starr**; Screenwriter, **Jack Natteford**; Editor, **Bernard Loftus**; Art Director, **Ralph Berger**; Cinematography, **John Hickson** and **William Sickner**; Sound, **Dick Tyler**

LOCATION FILMING: Kernville, Iverson's Ranch and Bronson Canyon, California

RUNNING TIME: 58 min.

SOURCE: Story by **Wilton West**, published in *Thrilling Ranch Stories*

STORY: Two rival ranchers are having problems with rustling. One rancher, Carl Stockdale, is shot from ambush. Buck Jones, co-owner of the rival ranch with his uncle, Charles French, helps Stockdale's daughter, Polly Ann Young, get Stockdale back to his ranch. Stockdale tells Jones that his foreman, Ward Bond, pulled the trigger; and Jones tells Young that he'll prove he and French aren't rustlers. Jones trails the men who shot Stockdale to their hideout. As Jones is about to get the drop on them, gang member John Bleifer captures Jones. Bleifer is crazy and loves to push people off high cliffs. Bond tells Bleifer that when the fire in the fireplace goes out he can dispose of Jones. Because of Stockdale's wound, ranch hands Paul Fix and Charles Brinley lead the other Stockdale cow hands in a raid on French's ranch. Young is powerless to stop them. Meanwhile, Jones works free of his bonds and escapes from the cabin. The Stockdale men capture French and take him to the Stockdale ranch. Bond rides to the Stockdale ranch, kidnaps Young, and takes here to the hideout. When Bond leaves the cabin for a moment, Young falls into the hands of Bleifer, who immediately adores her. Bond comes for Young, but Bleifer tries to protect Young and is shot by Bond. Bond rides away with Young but is seen by Jones. Jones catches up to Bond, and a terrific fistfight ensues, with Bond knocking out Jones. As Bond prepares to finish Jones off, Bleifer shows up. In the last act of his life, Bleifer shoots Bond. With the rustling threat ended, Stockdale and French become fast friends, while Jones and Young plan to marry.

NOTES AND COMMENTARY: The fancy gunbelt worn by Ward Bond in this film had been purchased from Ken Maynard. Bond was unhappy playing bad guys against Buck Jones and Maynard. He thought he had the stuff to be a western hero.

Polly Ann Young was the older sister of Academy Award–winning actress Loretta Young.

REVIEWS: "Proof that an endless flow of action with only a touch of plot can be an effective piece of entertainment. One of the better westerns." (*Motion Picture Guide*, Nash and Ross); "This Buck Jones subject holds attention." (*Variety*, 3/20/35)

SUMMATION: This is a good Buck Jones western. The simple plot of a crooked foreman causing trouble between two ranch owners is enhanced by the performances of Jones, Polly Ann Young and John Bleifer. Jones is perfect as the hero. Young has a more in-depth part than most leading ladies in "B" westerns and pulls it off in fine style. Bleifer is good as one of the few genuinely insane villains in "B" westerns, a part usually seen at Universal in their horror films. To the plot's credit, boss badman Ward Bond whips Jones in the climactic fistfight. To the plot's detriment, Bleifer appears out of nowhere to revenge himself on Bond by shooting him and saving Jones. Also, there is a bit too much footage of Jones and Silver riding across the plains.

"THE DALTONS ARE RIDING!"
Terror Cry of the Old West...
as history's most reckless, ruthless renegades strike again!

The Daltons Ride Again

Universal (November 1945)
CAST: Emmett Dalton, **Alan Curtis**; Grat Dalton, **Lon Chaney**; Bob Dalton, **Kent Taylor**; Ben Dalton, **Noah Beery Jr.**; Mary Bohannon, **Martha O'Driscoll**; Jeff, **Jess Barker**; McKenna, **Thomas Gomez**; Mike Bohannon, **John Litel**; Graham, **Milburn Stone**; Wilkins, **Walter Sande**; Sheriff, **Douglas Dumbrille**// Tex Walters, **Stanley Andrews**; Mrs. Walters, **Virginia Brissac**; Mrs.

Bohannon, **Ruth Lee**; Haines, **Charles F. Miller**; Bartender, **Monte Montague**; Townsmen, **Dick Alexander, George Chesebro, Jack Rockwell** and **Ed Cassidy**; Posse Member, **Robert Wilke**; Rider, **Ethan Laidlaw**; Coffeyville Townsman, **Henry Hall**

CREDITS: Director, **Ray Taylor**; Assistant Director, **William Tummel**; Producer, **Howard Welsch**; Screenwriters, **Roy Chanslor** and **Paul Gangelin**; Additional Dialogue, **Henry Blankfort**; Dialogue Director, **Willard Holland**; Editor, **Paul Landres**; Art Directors, **John B. Goodman** and **Harold H. MacArthur**; Set Decorators, **Russell A. Gausman** and **Arthur D. Leddy**; Cinematographer, **Charles Van Enger**; Gowns, **Vera West**; Makeup, **Jack P. Pierce**; Sound, **Bernard B. Brown** and **Jess Moulin**; Musical Director, **Frank Skinner**

SONG: "I'll Take You Home Again, Kathleen" (traditional)—sung by **Ruth Lee**

LOCATION FILMING: Iverson and Agoura, California

RUNNING TIME: 72 min.

STORY: On their way to the Argentines, brothers Alan Curtis, Lon Chaney, Kent Taylor and Noah Beery Jr., wanted by the law, stop in Skeleton Creek to rest at Stanley Andrews' ranch. Andrews is having trouble with the Land Company, which won't allow him to extend his note. Andrews finds a buyer for some of his cattle, but Walter Sande, henchman for the Land Company, starts a prairie fire, which destroys Andrews' cattle and kills Andrews. The brothers help Andrews' wife, Virginia Brissac, retain her ranch. In Skeleton Creek, Curtis and Martha O'Driscoll, daughter of newspaper editor John Litel, have fallen in love. Sande sees horses at Litel's house and, realizing they belong to the outlaw brothers, informs Sheriff Douglas Dumbrille. Town drunk Thomas Gomez overhears the conversation and helps the brothers escape. Gomez, in reality the man behind the lawless activity, doesn't want the brothers captured. He plans to have his men raid the ranches he seeks to control and blame the carnage on the brothers. Having control of the ranches will allow the Land Company to demand top dollar for a railroad right-of-way. Unaware of the lawless activity, Curtis decides to give himself up, serve his time and then marry O'Driscoll. O'Driscoll finds Chaney, Taylor and Beery, and tells them Curtis is riding into trouble, and that they have been blamed for crimes they didn't commit. The brothers help Curtis escape a lynch mob. The brothers take incriminating evidence from the Land Office to Litel. Gomez realizes Litel must have the evidence and goes to the newspaper office, where he shoots Litel and retrieves the papers. At the coroner's inquest, the brothers are blamed for Litel's death. Litel's assistant, Jess Barker, speaks up in behalf of the brothers but has no evidence to confirm his story. The brothers dynamite the Land Office safe and bring the evidence to the inquest. Gomez, realizing all is lost, starts a gunfight but is wounded, and the Land Office henchmen are either killed or captured. Curtis gives himself up. Chaney, Taylor and Beery head for the Argentines but decide to rob the Coffeyville bank to give them traveling money. The brothers are seen riding to Coffeyville, and Dumbrille is notified. Realizing his brothers will be shot down, Curtis desperately rides to head them off. Arriving as his brothers leave the bank, the townspeople open fire. Guns blaze, and only Curtis is left alive. Curtis is sentenced to life imprisonment. O'Driscoll vows to wait for Curtis and seek a parole.

NOTES AND COMMENTARY: The prairie fire sequence was originally seen in *Frontier Badman* (Universal, 1943), and was also used in *Riders of the Santa Fe* (Universal, 1944) and *Nevada Trail* (Universal-International, 1949).

"I'll Take You Home Again, Kathleen" was used in *West Bound Limited* (Universal, 1937) and *The Spoilers* (Universal, 1942).

REVIEWS: "Action-packed outdoor melodrama." (*Variety*, 10/21/45); "Compact and very entertaining 'B' outing, with the four stars doing excellent work as the Daltons." (*Western Movies*, Pitts)

SUMMATION: *The Daltons Ride Again* is a good, fast-moving western. Bolstered by a fine ensemble cast, headed by Alan Curtis, Lon Chaney, Kent Taylor and Noah Beery Jr., and good direction by veteran Ray Taylor, the results add up to fine entertainment. Even though the story is told in flashback, Taylor manages to generate tension and suspense. Great stunt work and exciting chases add to the fun.

Double Dynamite!
Blasts the Trails of Texas!

Deep in the Heart of Texas

Universal (September 1942)

CAST: Jim Mallory, **Johnny Mack Brown**; Brent Gordon, **Tex Ritter**; "Happy" T. Snodgrass, **Fuzzy Knight**; Nan Taylor, **Jennifer Holt**; Col. Mallory, **William Farnum**; Idaho, **Harry Woods**; Sneed, **Kenneth Harlan**; Jonathan Taylor, **Pat O'Malley**; Franklin, **Roy Brent**; Mathews, **Edmund Cobb**; Judge Peabody, **Earle Hodgins,** and **the Jimmy Wakely Trio (Jimmy Wakely, Johnny Bond** and **Scotty Harrel**)// Stagecoach Driver, **George Plues**; Jail Sentries, **Budd Buster** and **Joe Phillips**

CREDITS: Director, **Elmer Clifton**; Associate Producer/ Screenwriter, **Oliver Drake**; Adaptation, **Grace Norton**; Editor, **Maurice Wright**; Art Directors, **Jack Otterson** and **Harold MacArthur**; Set Decorators, **R.A. Gausman** and **Edward R. Robinson**; Cinematographer, **Harry Newman**; Sound, **Bernard B. Brown** and **William Hedgcock**; Musical Director, **H.J. Salter**

SONGS: "Deep in the Heart of Texas" (Swander and Hershey)—sung by **Fuzzy Knight** and **George Plues**; "Song of the Sage" (Bond)—sung by **the Jimmy Wakely Trio**; "Sweet Genevieve" (traditional)—sung by **Fuzzy Knight**; "Cowboy's Lament" (traditional)—sung by **Tex Ritter** and **the Jimmy Wakely Trio**; "Deep in the Heart of Texas" (reprise)—sung by **chorus**

LOCATION FILMING: Corriganville, California

RUNNING TIME: 62 min.

STORY: After the close of the Civil War, Johnny Mack Brown and gunsmith Fuzzy Knight journey to Freedom City, the capital of the new Republic of the Rio Grande. The republic has declared itself to be a separate country from the State of Texas. With Kenneth Harlan, Harry Woods and Earle Hodgins on his council, William Farnum rules the area with an iron fist. Lawlessness runs rampant, and Brown and Knight attempt to prevent Harlan and his henchmen from lynching newspaper editor Pat O'Malley. Brown and Knight are being overwhelmed by Harlan's men when Tex Ritter lends a hand, sending out a hail of bullets that puts the renegades on the run. Brown is later arrested for his part in the incident and is taken to Farnum. Farnum and Brown are father and son. Brown can't believe the vicious things said about his father and welcomes the chance to take the position as Commissioner of Public Affairs to make certain justice is meted fairly. Brown tries to convince O'Malley and his daughter, Jennifer Holt, of his sincerity but is unsuccessful. Ritter, an agent of the State of Texas, requests they give Brown an opportunity to prove himself. At a Citizens Committee meeting, Harlan sends henchman Edmund Cobb and some renegades to raid and burn a ranch. Ritter and some men are waiting, and all of Harlan's men are captured. The men are brought to the meeting, where Brown tells Ritter the men will be tried and, if found guilty, punished. After the meeting, Farnum issues order to destroy O'Malley's newspaper equipment, and to release Cobb and his henchmen. Brown breaks with Farnum and rides to warn O'Malley. Before the equipment can be removed from the premises, Harlan, Cobb and their men arrive. A fight ensues, Brown shoots Cobb, the equipment is destroyed and Brown is arrested for murder. Farnum demands Harlan release Brown, but Harlan refuses. A power struggle begins over who will rule the republic. Farnum seeks out Ritter and asks him to save his son. Ritter agrees—on the condition that Farnum dissolves the republic. Realizing the republic is not worth Brown's death, he agrees. Ritter has Knight "fix" the renegades' guns so they cannot fire. Ritter and Knight break Brown out of jail. The ranchers ride on the town and, with the townspeople's help, capture all of the renegades. Brown, Ritter and Knight ride to Farnum's hacienda. Farnum has proposed the dissolution of the Republic of the Rio Grande. A battle begins, Harlan shoots Farnum, and Brown kills Har-

Deep in the Heart of Texas (1942) movie still: Johnny Mack Brown (***right***) tries to convince newspaperman Pat O'Malley and Jennifer Holt that justice will now be meted fairly.

lan. Then Brown and Ritter engage in fistfights with Woods and Hodgins, and the two council members are taken into custody. This area again becomes a part of Texas, and Brown and Holt fall in love.

NOTES AND COMMENTARY: The song "Deep in the Heart of Texas" was initially purchased for this picture; but Universal took the song away to use in their bigger budgeted film, *Men of Texas* (Universal, 1942). It turned out that the song interfered with the dramatic mood of that film and it was returned to their "B" western unit.

This was Tex Ritter's first western at Universal. Ritter had just completed a series at Columbia with Bill Elliott and wanted his own starring series. Universal promised Ritter his own solo starring series upon completion of seven features with Johnny Mack Brown, plus the opportunity to appear in their big budget western films. This agreement was contingent upon the studio picking up his option.

The working title and intended release title of the Gene Autry western feature *Heart of the Rio Grande* was *Deep in the Heart of Texas*. Universal beat Republic to the punch, making this was one of the few times

Republic lost out on a song to be used as a title for one of their motion pictures.

"Song of the Sage" was first heard in the John Mack Brown serial *Wild West Days* (Universal, 1937).

Cinematographer Harry Newman had previously been billed as Harry Neumann.

REVIEWS: "Good drama, action and nice music make this one fine viewing." (*Western Movies*, Pitts); "Mediocre western." (*Variety*, 9/9/42)

SUMMATION: *Deep in the Heart of Texas* is an ambitious "B" western. There is almost too much story to cram into a budget western time frame, but good acting and action see this one through. Johnny Mack Brown and Tex Ritter share the spotlight, and each one shines, especially Brown in the scene in which his father (William Farnum) dies. Fuzzy Knight delivers some mild comedy, but on the whole, the script allows him to play his part fairly straight, to good advantage to the story. Only the miscasting of veteran bad man Harry Woods as an oafish lout sounds a sour note. Elmer Clifton directs confidently and allows the story to properly develop. Although good, the film could have been better if Universal had spent a little more time and care to develop the characterization of the principals.

---

3 ACTION CHAMPS...
With blazing guns and flying fists they routed rustlers from a lawless land!

Desperate Trails

Universal (September 1939)

CAST: Steve Hayden, **Johnny Mack Brown**; Clem, **Bob Baker**; Cousin Willie, **Fuzzy Knight**; Judith Lantry, **Frances Robinson**; Big Bill Tanner, **Russell Simpson**; Malenkthy Culp, **Clarence Wilson**; Ortega, **Charles Stevens**; Lon, **Ralph Dunn**; Nebraska, **Horace Murphy**; Mrs. Plunkett, **Fern Emmett**; Marshall Cort, **Ed Cassidy**; Rosita, **Anita Camargo**; Sonny, **Bill Cody, Jr.**// Joe, **W.H. McCauley**; Lantry Cowhand, **Frank Ellis**

CREDITS: Director/Producer, **Albert Ray**; Screenwriter, **Andrew Ben**nison; Editor, **Louis Sackin**; Art Directors, **Jack Otterson** and **Ralph M. DeLacy**; Set Decorator, **R.A. Gausman**; Cinematographer, **Jerome Ash**; Sound, **Bernard B. Brown** and **William Hedgcock**; Musical Director, **Charles Previn**

SONGS: "Oh, Susanna" (Foster) — sung by **Fuzzy Knight**; "Ridin' Home" (McHugh and Adamson) — sung by **Bob Baker**; "Ridin' Home" (reprise) — sung by **Bob Baker** and chorus

LOCATION FILMING: Tuolumme County, Kernville, and Lake Sherwood, California

RUNNING TIME: 58 min.

SOURCE: Story "Christmas Eve at Pilot Butte" by **Courtney Riley Cooper**

STORY: Sheriff Russell Simpson is behind the lawless activity in the territory. Simpson plans to have his men hold up the stagecoach bringing five thousand dollars he needs to pay off a forged mortgage on Frances Robinson's ranch. Johnny Mack Brown takes the mail pouch before Simpson's hirelings can steal it. The outlaws chase Brown; but displaying uncanny accuracy with his rifle, Brown shoots all three men out of their saddles. Brown is working with Marshall Ed Cassidy to break up the lawlessness, and is directed to work out of Frances Robinson's ranch as a friend of foreman Fuzzy Knight. Robinson returns home from the East; to cover his duplicity, Simpson directs henchman Charles Stevens to arrange a fatal accident for Robinson. Brown is able to thwart the attempt, and he and Robinson take an immediate liking to each other. When Robinson's horses are stolen, Brown takes over as her foreman, and fires Ralph Dunn and the rest of the cowhands. Brown is able to hire Bob Baker and some other honest cowboys. Brown believes Simpson is the head of the outlaws and follows him to banker Clarence Wilson's house. There he overhears their conversation regarding a supposedly deserted barn. Wilson is Simpson's confederate and had forged the mortgage to Robinson's ranch. Brown and Baker break into the barn and discover Robinson's rustled horses. Arriving at the barn, Dunn and his men spot the duo and give chase. Brown quickly turns the tables and captures Dunn, forcing him to confess and name Simpson and Wilson as the leaders. Brown brings Dunn into town. Simpson and Wilson know all is lost and make an escape attempt that is foiled by Brown. When Marshall Cassidy tries to send Brown on another mission, Robinson tells him that Brown is now working for her.

NOTES AND COMMENTARY: Previews and advertisements led viewers to believe a new trio western series had burst upon the scene. Like the Hopalong Cassidy series, there would be one predominant hero, and here it would be John Mack Brown. From the first entry, Bob Baker was relegated to a back-up role. With this film, Fuzzy Knight would become Universal's resident comic sidekick. Knight would be featured in forty-five additional "B" series westerns, riding with Brown, Tex Ritter, Russell Hayden, Rod Cameron, Eddie Dew and Kirby Grant, before Universal shut down their "B" picture unit.

Various trade papers announced that Johnny Mack Brown, Bob Baker and Fuzzy Knight would star in seven entries. Baker's contract at Universal expired, so *Ragtime Cowboy Joe* (Universal, 1940) was made without him. Albert Ray, formerly a writer at 20th Century Fox, would produce the series.

The scene in which Baker and Knight sabotage wagons and buckboards to prevent the townspeople from becoming a lynch mob would be used again in *Man from Montana* (Universal, 1941).

Stuntman Eddie Parker doubled Ralph Dunn in the fight scene with Brown.

"Oh, Susanna" would be heard in five other Universal westerns: *The Fiddlin' Buckaroo* (1933), *Law for Tombstone* (1937), *Courage of the West* (1937), *Chip of the Flying U* (1939) and *Rawhide Rangers* (1941). "Ridin' Home" would be used in *Road Agent* (Universal, 1941), *Strictly in the Groove* (Universal, 1943), *Tenting Tonight on the Old Camp Ground* (Universal, 1943) and *Senorita from the West* (Universal, 1945).

Background music for *Desperate Trails* consisted of music lifted from various Universal serials.

Posters and advertisements had Brown's name as Johnny Mack, but the film's credits billed him as John Mack. Beginning with the next entry, *Oklahoma Frontier* (Universal, 1939), Brown would be called Johnny Mack for the rest of his career.

The title, *Desperate Trails*, had been used by Universal in 1921 for a Harry Carey western directed by John Ford.

REVIEWS: "A well-plotted story, a good cast and plenty of action, with nicely-maintained suspense." (*Variety*, 8/16/39); "Johnny Mack Brown's first Universal series film, and it is a good one." (*Western Movies*, Pitts)

SUMMATION: *Desperate Trails* is a good "B" western. This film introduces John Mack Brown as Universal's cowboy star. Browns reign would last until his departure to Monogram in 1943. Brown was an action star with acting ability, and he proves it in this entry. Co-stars Fuzzy Knight and Bob Baker are relegated to secondary status. Frances Robinson makes a nice leading lady. Russell Simpson shines as the ruthless gang boss, while Clarence Wilson convinces as a thief afraid of his own shadow. Director Albert Ray paces the film to good effect, with the only false note being the hokey close-up shots of Brown, Robinson and Baker during the reprise of the song "Ridin' Home."

TOM MIX TALKS for the first time on any screen, in the smashing picture made from a famous novel!
THE STORY OF A MAN, FALSELY ACCUSED, WHO RIDES AGAIN FOR A JUST REVENGE!

Destry Rides Again

ALTERNATE TITLE: *Justice Rides Again*; Universal (April 1932)

CAST: Tom Destry, **Tom Mix**; Sally Dangerfield, **Claudia Dell**; Temperance Worker, **ZaSu Pitts**; Sheriff Wendell, **Stanley Fields**; Brent, **Earle Foxe**; Warren, **Edward Piel Sr.**; Judd Ogden, **Francis Ford**; Clifton, **Frederic Howard**; Willie, **George Ernest**; The Judge, **John**

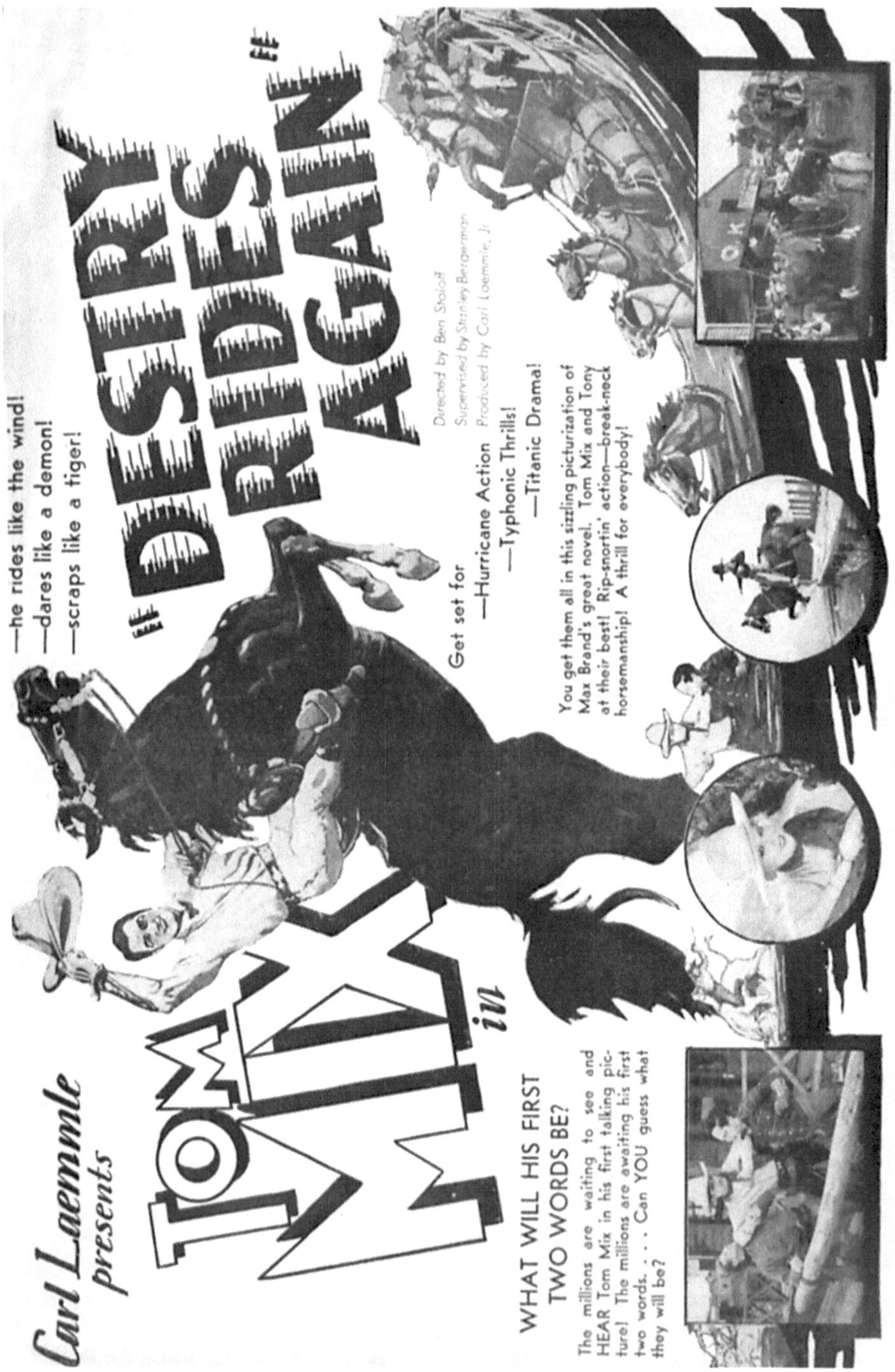

Ince; Mr. Dangerfield, **Edward Le Saint**; Foreman of Jury, **Charles K. French**; and **Tony**

CREDITS: Director, **Ben Stoloff**; Producer, **Carl Laemmle Jr.**; Associate Producer, **Stanley Bergerman**; Dialogue, **Robert Keith**; Continuity, **Isadore Bernstein**; Scenario Editor, **Richard Schayer**; Supervising Film Editor, **Maurice Pivar**; Editor, **Arthur Hilton**; Art Director, **Thomas F. O'Neill**; Cinematographer, **Daniel B. Clark**; Recording Supervisor, **C. Roy Hunter**

LOCATION FILMING: French Ranch, Newhall, Las Turas Ranch, and El Segundo, California

RUNNING TIME: 61 min.

SOURCE: Novel "Destry Rides Again" by **Max Brand**

STORY: Tom Mix, a partner in a stage line with Earle Foxe, is running for sheriff against incumbent Stanley Fields. Foxe is the secret leader of the outlaw gang terrorizing the area. Fields and his deputies are members of his gang. Foxe wants Mix out of the way and frames Mix for murder so Fields will be re-elected; and also to try to win Mix's girlfriend, Claudia Dell, for himself. Mix is sent to prison, but Dell remains faithful. Dell's father, Edward Le Saint, petitions the governor for a pardon for Mix. Knowing that Mix threatened to find out who framed him, witnesses Fields, Francis Ford, Frederic Howard, Edward Piel Sr. and others hide out. On his return to town, Mix pretends to be a sick and beaten man with no stomach for violence. Foxe is taken in by Mix's performance and tells his men it's all right to return to town. Mix soon shows that his sickness was an act, and Fields attempts to escape Mix's wrath. Mix catches up with Fields at Le Saint's ranch. As Fields is about to reveal the man behind the frame-up, he is shot by one of Foxe's men. When Mix leaves the ranch, Foxe sends Piel and two men after Mix. The men catch up with Mix, but Mix is able to turn the tables. Piel is forced to reveal his leader's name. Mix finds Foxe trying to force his attentions on Dell at Le Saint's ranch. Mix bests Foxe in a terrific fistfight. Now Mix has time to pay attention to Dell.

NOTES AND COMMENTARY: *Destry Rides Again* was Tom Mix's first sound western feature. To generate interest in this film, Universal embarked on a campaign to have children guess what Mix's first two words would be. In the film, schoolchildren are waiting at recess to see their hero. Mix rides up to the children and says, "Hello, kids."

The O.K. Livery Stable and Corral used in *Law and Order* (Universal, 1932) can be seen in the town sequences.

In some newspaper advertisements and on some lobby cards, Andy Devine was listed as appearing as a

Opposite: **Destry Rides Again** (1932) herald: *Left,* Tom Mix (*center*) breaks up a fake fight between an unidentified actor (*left*) and Frederic Howard (*right*); *left center,* Claudia Dell; *center,* Tom Mix, Frederic Howard; *right center,* Tom Mix on Tony; *right,* Tom Mix brings in three stage robbers.

stagecoach passenger in *Destry Rides Again*. Devine does not receive on-screen billing, nor can he be seen in the stagecoach sequence in this film.

Universal used the title *Destry Rides Again* as a vehicle for Marlene Dietrich and James Stewart in 1939. This was not a remake of the Tom Mix vehicle but possibly could be called a sequel. Stewart plays the son of the famous fighting sheriff Tom Destry. Both films noted that their story was based on Max Brand's novel.

Tom Mix was reunited here with his favorite cinematographer, Daniel B. Clark. Clark photographed Mix during his career at Fox studios. When Mix moved to FBO (Film Booking Office) for his final silent series, Fox would not allow Clark out of his contract and join Mix.

REVIEWS: "Tom Mix's first sound feature and it is a good one, proving why he is one of the all-time great stars of the genre." (*Western Movies*, Pitts); "Destry, in spite of good mounting, does not come up to modern standard." (*Variety*, 6/21/32)

SUMMATION: Tom Mix is in fine form in his initial sound western feature. With a swiftly moving story and Mix handling the heroics, the film is decidedly above average. Stanley Fields acquits himself well as the crooked sheriff, and Claudia Dell is in fine form as the woman Mix loves. Screenwriters Robert Keith, Isadore Bernstein and Richard Schayer do a nice job of adapting Brand's story to a "B" western format; it even, at times, resembles its source.

LEAD AND LEGS RULED THE SIN CITY OF THE WEST!

Destry Rides Again

Universal (December 1939); A Joe Pasternak Production

CAST: Frenchy, **Marlene Dietrich**; Tom Destry, Jr., **James Stewart**; Boris, **Mischa Auer**; Washington Dimsdale, **Charles Winninger**; Kent, **Brian Donlevy**; Gyp Watson, **Allen Jenkins**; Bugs Watson, **Warren Hymer**; Janice Tyndall, **Irene Hervey**; Lily Belle, **Una Merkel**; Loupgerou, **Billy Gilbert**; Judge Slade, **Samuel S. Hinds**; Jack Tyndall, **Jack Carson**; Lem Claggett, **Tom Fadden**; Sophie Clagett, **Virginia Brissac**; Rockwell, **Edmund MacDonald**; Clara, **Lillian Yarbo**; Sheriff Keogh, **Joe King**; Claggett Boy, **Dickie Jones**; Claggett Girl, **Ann Todd**// Stage Driver, **Richard Alexander**; Rowdy Cowboy, **Harry Cording**, Doctor, **Bob McKenzie**; Mrs. DeWitt, **Minerva Urecal**; Cowboy, **William Steele**; Pianist, **Billy Bletcher**; Dancer, **Carmen D'Antonio**; Jugglers, **Loren Brown** and **Harold DeGarro**; Young Boy, **Bill**

Cody, Jr.; Turner, **Lloyd Ingraham**; Bartender, **Philo McCullough**; Saloon Patron, **George Chesebro**; Cowhand, **Kermit Maynard**

CREDITS: Director, **George Marshall**; Assistant Director, **Vernon Keays**; Associate Producer, **Islin Auster**; Story, **Felix Jackson**; Screenwriters, **Felix Jackson, Gertrude Purcell** and **Henry Myers**; Editor, **Milton Carruth**; Art Directors, **Jack Otterson** and **Martin Obzina**; Set Decoration, **R.A. Gausman**; Cinematographer, **Hal Mohr**; Gowns, **Vera West**; Sound, **Bernard B. Brown** and **Robert Pritchard**; Musical Director, **Charles Previn**; Musical Score, **Frank Skinner**

SONGS: "Little Joe" (Loesser and Hollander)—sung by **Marlene Dietrich, male chorus and Charles Winninger**; "You've Got That Look" (Loesser and Hollander)—sung by **Marlene Dietrich**; "The Boys in the Back Room" (Loesser and Hollander)—sung by **Marlene Dietrich**; "Little Joe" (reprise)—sung by **children's chorus**

RUNNING TIME: 94 min.

SOURCE: Novel "Destry Rides Again" by **Max Brand**

STORY: With entertainer Marlene Dietrich's help, saloon owner Brian Donlevy wins the deed to Tom Fadden's ranch in a crooked card game. When Sheriff Joe King investigates, shots are heard; and crooked mayor Samuel S. Hinds subsequently announces King has left town suddenly. A new sheriff is needed, and Hinds appoints town drunk Charles Winninger. Winninger takes the job seriously and sends for the son of a famous sheriff, James Stewart. Winninger expects a rip-roaring, ready-for-action lawman, but instead gets a quiet, mild-mannered individual who doesn't carry a gun. Against Winninger's better judgment, he swears Stewart in as Deputy Sheriff. Donlevy lays siege to Fadden's ranch to take possession. With the ownership of Fadden's ranch, Donlevy can now levy a charge on all cattle driven to the market through this area. Stewart persuades Fadden and his family to leave the ranch, but now becomes interested in King's disappearance. Stewart visits Dietrich, and she lets it slip that King was taken care of. Dietrich is falling in love with Stewart, and he cares for her. Townsman Mischa Auer becomes a second deputy. Stewart tells Donlevy he's found a body in good condition. Donlevy sends henchman Allen Jenkins to see if King's body is still where it was left. Winninger and Auer arrest Jenkins and recover the body. Cattleman Jack Carson is arrested for not paying the levy on cattle moved through lands controlled by Donlevy. Stewart and Carson's sister, Irene Hervey, make Carson see he must pay the money to Donlevy. Auer lets it slip that a federal judge will try Jenkins instead of Hinds. Dietrich gets Stewart out of way when Donlevy's men break Jenkins out of jail. In the jailbreak, Winninger is shot in the back. Stewart buckles on his father's guns. With help from Carson, Fadden and other townspeople, Stewart attacks the saloon. With a pitched battle going on in front, Stewart is able to sneak in from an upper story. Dietrich goes to the women of the town and organizes a march on the saloon. All the women carry clubs and swarm through the saloon, immobilizing all of Donlevy's henchmen. Donlevy reaches an upper floor to get a bead on Stewart. Dietrich sees what Donlevy is doing and throws herself in front of Stewart in time to take the bullet meant for him. Stewart's return fire ends Donlevy's lawless career. With Bottle Neck now a peaceful town, Stewart has time to romance Hervey.

NOTES AND COMMENTARY: Music from the score of *Destry Rides Again* would find its way into many Universal "B" westerns and serials. The song "Little Joe" would be used in *Bad Man from Red Butte* (Universal, 1940), *Man from Montana* (Universal, 1941), *Little Joe, the Wrangler* (Universal, 1942) and *The Old Texas Trail* (Universal, 1944).

Frank Loesser is one of this country's great songwriters. With some moderate early hits in the late thirties and early forties, Loesser wrote "Praise the Lord and Pass the Ammunition" in 1942. Loesser than served in the military. Upon discharge, Loesser wrote songs for Hollywood features, winning an Academy Award for "Baby It's Cold Outside" from *Neptune's Daughter* (Metro-Goldwyn-Mayer, 1949). Loesser went to Broadway, writing the score for *Where's Charley, Guys and Dolls*. In 1961, his production *How to Succeed in Business Without Really Trying* captured a Pulitzer Prize, a Tony and Drama Critics Award for best musical.

Even though the film was advertised as being adapted from the Max Brand novel, nothing from that novel, except the title, was actually used. Felix Jackson's original story was the basis for this film *and* the Audie Murphy remake, *Destry* (Universal—International, 1955), which was also directed by George Marshall. This could possibly be called a sequel to Tom Mix's *Destry Rides Again* (Universal, 1932), with James Stewart playing Mix's son.

Marlene Dietrich and Una Merkel performed their famous fight scene themselves. The actresses were supposed to start the fight and then let the stunt doubles take over. But Dietrich and Merkel kept going until the fight was finished and Stewart poured the water on them. The scene was accomplished in one continuous take.

Plot elements of *Destry Rides Again* were the basis for the Tex Williams featurette *Nevada Trail*.

REVIEWS: "It's just plain, good entertainment, primed with action and laughs and human sentiment." (*Variety*, 12/6/39); "Dietrich steals the picture, aided by Marshall's relaxed direction and Stewart's charming support." (*The Western*, Hardy)

SUMMATION: *Destry Rides Again* is a great movie, a comedy western classic. Marlene Dietrich and James Stewart are outstanding as the leads. Both convey the emotions necessary to make their characters three-dimensional. In the outstanding supporting cast, Charles Winniger and Mischa Auer are standouts. Winninger believably transforms his character of the town drunk into a

Destry Rides Again (1939) movie still: Marlene Dietrich, James Stewart.

man who has the nerve to do his job, no matter how difficult. Auer adds the right comedy touch without turning into a caricature or buffoon. George Marshall's on-target directorial touch, balances well the comedy scenes with the drama needed to sustain audience interest. Dietrich chips in with three outstanding musical numbers, two of them, "You've Got That Look" and "The Boys in the Back Room," becoming a part of her repertoire.

KING OF THE DIAMOND SMUGGLERS!

Diamond Frontier

Universal (October, 1940)

CAST: Terrance Regan, **Victor McLaglen**; Dr. Charles Clayton, **John Loder**; Jeanne Krueger, **Anne Nagel**; Noah, **Cecil Kellaway**; Jan De Winter, **Philip Dorn**; Derek Bluje, **Francis Ford**; Travers, **Hugh Sothern**; Willem, **Ferris Taylor**; Matt Campbell, **J. Anthony Hughes**; Julia Bloem, **Evelyn Selbie**; Piet Bloem, **Lionel Belmore**; Hamilton, **John Ellis**; Judge, **Ed Stanley**; Mrs. Willem, **Dorothy Vaughan**; Kendis, **Bill Ruhl**; Morgan, **Skelton Knaggs**; Kohler, **Dewey Robinson**; Baron La Rocque, **Sigfried Arno**// "Laddie"; Prisoner, **John Harmon**; Mine Guard, **Al Bridge**

CREDITS: Director, **Harold Schuster**; Associate Producer, **Marshall Grant**; Screenwriters, **Edmund Hartman** and **Stanley Rubin**; Editor, **W. Donn Hayes**; Art Directors, **Jack Otterson** and **Harold H. MacArthur**; Set Decorator, **R.A. Gausman**; Gowns, **Vera West**; Cinematographer, **Milton Krasner**; Sound, **Bernard B. Brown** and **William Hedgcock**; Music Director, **H.J. Salter**

RUNNING TIME: 73 min.

SOURCE: Story "A Modern Monte Cristo" by **Edmund Hartmann** and **Stanley Rubin**

STORY: John Loder returns to Ammersrand, a Dutch village in South Africa, from Medical College in England. Loder is interested in practicing medicine and settling down with his sweetheart, Anne Nagel. Lawlessness has become rampart in the community due to a diamond rush. Victor McLaglan, Philip Dorn and Ferris Taylor are behind the lawlessness, as they steal diamonds, jump claims and sell the stolen diamonds. Loder calls a meeting of the diggers and community members to establish law and order. McLaglan feels threatened and has Loder framed for dealing in stolen diamonds. Loder is sentenced to ten years of hard labor in a penal colony. In his seventh year of imprisonment, Loder makes friends with fellow prisoner Sigfried Arno. McLaglan still regards Loder as a threat and makes arrangements to have him killed in an escape attempt. Loder and Arno are given the chance to escape. Arno is shot and, before dying, gives Loder a map to his wealth. Loder makes the guards think he was killed and is able to escape into the jungle. In his journey through the jungle, hermit Cecil Kellaway befriends Loder. Kellaway decides to help Loder in his quest for revenge. Arno's wealth gives Loder the means to exact his vengeance. In disguise, Loder and Kellaway return to Ammersrand where only Loder's dog, Laddie, and Gwynne immediately recognize him. Gwynne joins Loder in his revenge quest and helps pave the way for his acceptance in the community. McLaglan controls all the water in the area. Loder and Kellaway decide to dynamite the dam to make water available for everyone. Dorn tries to prevent Loder's action but instead perishes in the explosion. Loder and Kellaway bring proof of Taylor's illegal diamond activities and give him a chance to write a full confession. Taylor, instead, commits suicide. McLaglan decides to burn out all the small diggers and take over the claims. McLagan and his men engage the diggers in a terrific struggle. Loder rides to the battle to confront McLaglan. McLaglan takes aim at Loder; but before McLaglan can fire, Kellaway shoots him. A witness is found to exonerate Loder. Loder and Nagel plan to marry, while Kellaway returns to his jungle home.

NOTES AND COMMENTARY: Even though Philip Dorn is called Jan De Winter in *Diamond Frontier*, the screen credits list his role as Stafford.

REVIEWS: "An improbable yarn, with only occasional excitement, little suspense and a set of obvious characters." (*Variety*, 10/9/40); "The film is basically a hackneyed western set in a foreign locale." (*The Motion Picture Guide*, Nash and Ross)

SUMMATION: *Diamond Frontier* is a sturdy South African western bolstered by good acting from John Loder, Victor McLaglan, Cecil Kellaway and Anne Nagle. Director Harold Schuster takes Edmund Hartman and Stanley Rubin's updated story of *The Count of Monte Cristo*, and balances action and story to hold audience interest. A weakness in the story is the too convenient manner in which Loder is cleared of all criminal charges, but Schuster races through the scenes quickly to the inevitable happy conclusion.

THEY HERDED SHEEP BUT PREYED ON MEN—
BUCK PUT HIS TWO FISTS IN!
A shooting, slugging, riding demon! He shattered the wolves of the range!

Empty Saddles

Universal (December, 1936); A Buck Jones Production

CAST: Buck Devlin, **Buck Jones**; Boots Boone, **Louise Brooks**; Swap Boone, **Harvey Clark**; Cim White, **Charles Middleton**; Jim Grant, **Lloyd Ingraham**; Kit Kress, **Frank Campeau**; Red Madden, **Earl Askam**; Vegas, **Ben Corbett**; Jasper Kade, **Niles Welch**; Eloise Hayes, **Gertrude Astor**; Madge Grant, **Claire Rochelle**; Mace, **Charles Le Moyne**; Cole, **William Lawrence;** and "**Silver**"// Accordion Player, **Frank Yaconelli**; Bass Player, **Rudy Sooter**; Madden Henchman, **Allan Sears**

CREDITS: Director, **Lesley Selander**; Story, **Cherry Wilson**;

Screenwriter, **Frances Guihan**; Editor, **Bernard Loftus**; Art Director, **Ralph Berger**; Cinematographers, **Allen Thompson** and **Herbert Kirkpatrick**; Opening Music, **Felix Mills**; Sound, **L. John Myers**

SONGS: "I Love Someone on the Texas Prairie"—sung by **Frank Yaconelli**; and "Welcome to the Empty Saddle Ranch"—sung by **Rudy Sooter**

LOCATION FILMING: Jack Garner Ranch and Keen Camp, California

RUNNING TIME: 65 min.

STORY: Buck Jones happens on a deserted ranch known by the locals as the Ranch of the Empty Saddles and the Corral de Terror. After leaving the ranch, he meets trader Harvey Clark and his daughter, Louise Brooks. They tell Jones that the ranch has a curse on it. Thirty years earlier, the owner of the ranch rode against the sheepmen, so running cattle on that range would start the old feud. Jones decides to buy the property and turn it into a dude ranch. Clark and Brooks are persuaded by Jones to help put the ranch in shape. Brooks begins to fall in love with Jones. Guests arrive at the dude ranch, and Jones arranges a mock gunfight between the cowhands and the sheepmen. The sheepmen, led by William Lawrence, use real bullets. The cowhands switch from blanks to real bullets and drive the sheepherders away. New guests, financier Lloyd Ingraham and his daughter, Claire Rochelle, arrive at the ranch. Lawrence hires Earl Askam to wreck Jones' ranch. Brooks overhears the men planning to dynamite Jones' ranch, run sheep on Jones' range and kidnap Rochelle for ransom. Jones has taken the guests on a camping trip. Brooks tells Ingraham and Clark of the desperado's plans. Ingraham gets the cowhands in town to ride against Askam. Brooks rides to warn Jones of the attempted raid on the ranch, but does not mention the kidnapping plan. Brooks changes clothes with Rochelle. Jones, Ingraham and the cowhands head off the men riding to the ranch and defeat them in a gunfight. Ingraham tells Jones that his daughter will be kidnapped. Jones rides to the campsite and finds that Askam has kidnapped Brooks instead of Rochelle. Jones races after Askam and Brooks, rescues Brooks, and whips Askam in a fistfight. Brooks starts east on a train with Rochelle. Jones discovers Brooks has always been in love with him. Jones is also in love with Brooks. Riding Silver, Jones takes Brooks off the train. The two will begin life together.

NOTES AND COMMENTARY: Leading lady Louise Brooks received accolades for two German silent films, *Pandora's Box* (1929) and *Diary of a Lost Girl* (1929), directed by G.W. Pabst. *Empty Saddles* was the start of a comeback attempt in Hollywood which quickly ended after a Three Mesquiteers entry, *Overland Stage Raiders* (Republic, 1938). Becoming reclusive, Brooks began to write about films and her career, to critical acclaim.

Louise Brooks received $300 for a week's work on *Empty Saddles*. Filming for the feature took only one week. Buck Jones wanted her as a leading lady in his Columbia days, but Brooks declined. With her fortunes in films diminished, Brooks now accepted a role in a "B" western. Publicity stated how happy Brooks was to be appearing in the film: "I wouldn't trade it for all the other roles I have ever had because I'm acting now, not just being an ornament, and I feel that, at last, I am on the road toward getting some place in pictures." Most people believed otherwise.

REVIEWS: "Well mounted Buck Jones vehicle of double interest because of Louise Brooks as the leading lady." (*Western Movies*, Pitts); "Buck Jones rides again though slowed down by flighty, involved plot." (*Variety*, 2/3/37)

SUMMATION: This is an entertaining Buck Jones vehicle, but one more suited for Gene Autry. Jones fares well as the hero, and former silent screen star Louise Brooks shines as Jones' love interest. Lesley Selander directs capably, keeping the involved story, minus the usual Jones action, moving. Selander is greatly aided by the fine cinematography of Allen Thompson and Herbert Kirkpatrick. Look at the opening credits for a marvelous 3-D effect of the scenic landscapes.

Ken Maynard—In a DIfFERENT Western drama whose cowboy music will enthrall you as its blazing action excites you.
IT'S GREAT

The Fiddlin' Buckaroo

Universal (June, 1933); A Ken Maynard Production

CAST: Fiddlin', **Ken Maynard**; Ann, **Gloria Shea**; Wolf, **Fred Kohler**; Banty, **Frank Rice**; Sheriff, **Jack Rockwell**; Kerriman, **Joe Girard**; Postmaster, **Wm. Franey**; Swede, **Slim Whitaker**; Buck, **Jack Mower**; Jailer, **Bob McKenzie**; and "Tarzan"// Station Agent, **Horace B. Carpenter**; Jack, **Jack Kirk**; Outlaws, **Bud McClure, Frank Ellis, Roy Bucko, Hank Bell, Robert Walker, Buck Bucko**; Lookout, **Ben Corbett**

CREDITS: Director, **Ken Maynard**; Screenwriter, **Nate Gatzert**; Editor, **Charles Harris**; Art Director, **Ralph Berger**; Cinematographer, **Ted McCord**; Sound, **Earl Crane**

SONGS: "The Old Chisholm Trail" (traditional)—sung by **Jack Kirk and chorus**; "Oh, Susanna" (Foster)—played by **Ken Maynard**; "Turkey in the Straw" (traditional)—played by **Ken Maynard**; "My Pretty Quadroon" (Howard and Vincent)—played by **Ken Maynard**; "Wearing of the Green" (traditional)—played by **Frank Rice**; "My Pretty Quadroon" (Howard and Vincent)—sung by **Gloria Shea**; "The Old Chisholm Trail" (traditional)—sung by **Jack Kirk and chorus**; and "The Old Chisholm Trail" (traditional)—sung

THE FIDDLIN' BACKAROO

by **Jack Kirk and chorus** ("The Old Chisholm Trail" is sung over the beginning and end credits.)

LOCATION FILMING: Lone Pine, California

RUNNING TIME: 65 min.

STORY: The townspeople gather at the railroad station to welcome back Joe Girard and his daughter, Gloria Shea. Acting as advance guard for Fred Kohler's outlaw gang, Ken Maynard and Frank Rice offer entertainment at the station. Maynard and Shea fall in love at first sight. Meanwhile, Kohler and his gang loot the town. Realizing what is happening, Sheriff Jack Rockwell arrests Maynard and Rice and leads a posse in pursuit of the outlaws. With his horse Tarzan's help, Maynard and Rice break jail. Shea refuses to believe Maynard is a bandit. Maynard goes to see Shea and tells her to trust him. Rice returns to the outlaw camp and tells Kohler that Maynard has gone to Girard's ranch. Kohler thinks it would be a good idea to kidnap Shea and hold her for ransom. When he finds that Maynard will not participate in his scheme, he has Maynard tied up and placed in a cabin that is set on fire by a thrown match. Kohler kidnaps Shea and takes her to the outlaw stronghold. Tarzan helps Maynard escape the deadly flames. Maynard sets out to free Shea. Kohler orders Maynard to go to the Girard ranch and collect the ransom money. Instead Maynard tries to rescue Shea. Rice prevents Maynard from being

The Fiddlin' Buckaroo (1933) herald: *Top left*, Ken Maynard; *right center*, Ken Maynard; *right*, Gloria Shea, Ken Maynard.

shot and receives a serious wound in the process. Rice discovers Maynard is a government agent who has infiltrated the gang to stop the mail robberies. Rice decides to throw in with Maynard and rides to the Girard ranch for help. Maynard continues his rescue attempt. Rice reaches the sheriff's posse and, as he expires, tells the men Maynard is a Government man and to follow Tarzan to the outlaw camp. Maynard closes in on Kohler; and in a terrific fight on the top of a cliff, Kohler slips and falls to his death. Maynard and Shea can now continue their romance.

NOTES AND COMMENTARY: Mary Dodge wrote the song "My Pretty Quadroon" in 1863. The song told of a slave who had no thoughts of freedom because of the love he had for his kind owner. Afterwards, the slave was sold to a cruel owner who whipped him unmercifully. In 1930, Nat Vincent rewrote the song, and gained popularity with country singers. "My Pretty Quadroon" was earlier sung by Walter Huston, Harry Carey, Russell Hopton and Raymond Hatton in *Law and Order* (Universal, 1932).

"The Old Chisholm Trail" was featured in *Parade of the West* (Universal, 1930), *Stormy* (Universal, 1935), *The Phantom Rider* (Universal, 1936) and *The Old Chisholm Trail* (Universal, 1942). "Oh, Susanna" was heard in *Law for Tombstone* (Universal, 1937), *Courage of the West* (Universal, 1937), *Desperate Trails* (Universal, 1939), *Chip of the Flying U* (1939) and *Rawhide Rangers* (Universal, 1941). "Turkey in the Straw" was played in the serial *Wild West Days* (Universal, 1937).

The sequence of events in the opening hold-up scene was later borrowed for Buck Jones' *Border Brigands* (Universal, 1935).

In the credits, Joe Girard's character name is Harriman, but in the film Girard is called Kerriman.

REVIEWS: "Nice riding, good backgrounds, fair photography and good sound, but it's still guns and gallops." (*Variety*, 1/9/34); "Only interesting for his [Maynard's] use of music." (*Motion Picture Guide*, Nash and Ross)

SUMMATION: *The Fiddlin' Buckaroo* is an above average Ken Maynard series entry. Don't be put off by the number of songs; all are short and don't impede story movement. Maynard takes care of the heroics in fine fashion, thanks in part to Tarzan's assistance. The acting is par for a series western, with the exception of Frank Rice and Fred Kohler. Rice is convincing as an outlaw who moves over to Maynard's side; and Kohler makes a fine adversary for Maynard, even showing a touch of fear as he realizes that it's now just he and Maynard, with no gang members to help him. Maynard does a good job in the director's chair. Ted McCord's fine camerawork, emphasizing the magnificent backgrounds, enhances the story.

He Crusades for Law ... with a Crashing Colt!

Fighting Bill Fargo

Universal (December 1941)

CAST: Bill, **Johnny Mack Brown**; Scoop, **Fuzzy Knight**; Linda, **Jeanne Kelly**; Hackett, **Kenneth Harlan**; Julie, **Nell O'Day**; Savage, **Ted Adams**; Scanlon, **James Blaine**; Houston, **Al Bridge**; and **the Eddie Dean Trio** // "Brownie"; Townsman, **Bud Osborne**; Clem Fillmore, **Earle Hodgins**; Judge Taylor, **Joseph Eggerton**; Henchmen, **Bob Kortman** and **Buck Moulton**; Voter, **Blackie Whiteford**; Gang Member on Lookout at Polls, **Kermit Maynard**; Poll Official, **Merrill McCormick**

CREDITS: Director, **Ray Taylor**; Associate Producer, **Will Cowan**; Story, **Paul Franklin**; Screenwriters, **Paul Franklin**, **Arthur V. Jones** and **Dorcas Cochran**; Editor, **Paul Landres**; Art Directors, **Jack Otterson** and **Ralph M. DeLacy**; Set Decorator, **R.A. Gausman**; Cinematographer, **Charles Van Enger**; Gowns, **Vera West**; Sound, **Bernard B. Brown** and **Hal Bumbaugh**; Musical Director, **H.J. Salter**

SONGS: "Welcome Home" (Rosen and Carter)—sung by **the Eddie Dean Trio**; "Happiness Corral" (Rosen and Carter)—sung by **Nell O'Day** and **the Eddie Dean Trio;** and "Geraldine" (Rosen and Carter)—sung by **the Eddie Dean Trio**

LOCATION FILMING: Iverson and Agoura, California

RUNNING TIME: 57 min.

STORY: Returning after serving three years in prison for a crime he didn't commit, Johnny Mack Brown finds lawlessness running rampart. Brown plans to resume running the local newspaper with his partner, Earle Hodgins. Hodgins was responsible for framing Brown, and is in the clutches of gang leader James Blaine. Blaine's henchman, Ted Adams, was responsible for the death of Brown's father. Brown is welcomed by his sister, Nell O'Day, his sweetheart, Jeanne Kelly, Kelly's father, Judge Joseph Eggerton, and Brown's co-worker and friend, Fuzzy Knight. Blaine's stooge, Kenneth Harlan, is seeking re-election as Sheriff. The honest townspeople are backing Al Bridge for the position. Adams kills Bridge, but Blaine claims the shooting was in self-defense. With Brown's editorials getting too hot, Blaine has Adams start a fight with Brown. Brown defends himself and comes out the victor. Adams draws his gun to shoot Brown, and O'Day knocks the gun aside to save her brother's life. Adams is arrested for attempted murder. Hodgins is nominated to run against Harlan. When Hodgins pulls a shady trick against Brown, Brown throws him off the newspaper and revokes his nomination for sheriff. Hodgins' world is shattered. When Blaine rebuffs him, Hodgins goes to Brown and confesses. While Hodgins is signing the confession in the newspaper office, Brown is lured to the door and knocked out. Adams, who had temporarily been released from jail, shoots Hodgins. As Adams pulls the trigger, Hodgins ignites flash powder and, unknown to Adams, a picture of the crime has been taken. Before he dies, Hodgins writes a note to have Knight develop the picture. Accused of murdering Hodgins, Brown refuses to be arrested and gets away. With no candidate to oppose Harlan, Eggerton decides to run for the office of Sheriff. On Election Day, Blaine closes the polls early to insure victory for his candidate. Brown sneaks back to town as Knight develops the picture. This is the evidence needed to convict Blaine and his gang. Brown and the townspeople go to the polls. Blaine and his men start a gun battle. Adams and Harlan are killed, and Brown stops Blaine from getting away. Now completely exonerated, Brown and Kelly plan to marry.

NOTES AND COMMENTARY: Fuzzy Knight rides his regular horse, Brownie, while Johnny Mack Brown eschews his palomino for a different horse in this outing.

The Universal production department slipped up on this one. In an early scene, as Johnny Mack Brown is coming into town by stagecoach, six horses are pulling the coach as it reaches town but only four horses can be seen when the coach arrives at the Stage depot.

Eddie Dean was still about four years away from his own starring western series. After winning major supporting roles behind Ken Maynard in *Harmony Trail* (Mattox, 1944) and Bob Steele in *Wildfire* (Screen Guild, 1945), Dean, possessing one of the finest singing voices of all the singing cowboys, was signed by PRC in 1945. Dean's first entries in the series were in color, but the series soon reverted to black and white. Dean made twenty starring western films, although one, *Prairie Outlaws* (PRC, 1948), was mostly made up of footage from *Wild West* (PRC, 1946). Interestingly *Wild West* was produced in color while *Prairie Outlaws* was released in black and white.

"Welcome Home" would be sung by the Jimmy Wakely Trio in *The Lone Star Trail* (Universal, 1943). "Geraldine" would be performed by Fuzzy Knight, Johnny Bond and Russell Hayden in *Frontier Law* (Universal, 1943).

The end title showing a blacksmith at an anvil was lifted from *Arizona Cyclone* (Universal, 1941).

Jeanne Kelly later changed her stage name to as Jean Brooks.

REVIEWS: "A tight, fast western, well acted. Good story and plenty of action make this western above average." (*Variety*, 5/20/42); "An above average B western." (*The Motion Picture Guide*, Nash and Ross)

SUMMATION: *Fighting Bill Fargo* is another solid entry in Johnny Mack Brown's Universal series. Brown is properly authoritative in the dramatic sequences while capably handling the action. Fuzzy Knight provides good support this time out, trying to figure out how to work a new fangled camera. Knight comes up with the key to the story while providing a few laughs along the way. Among the fine supporting cast, Earle Hodgins stands out. Hodgins' character is basically that of a weakling, and he has allowed himself to be controlled by gang leader James Blaine. When his life comes crashing down around his feet, and Blaine won't offer any help, Hodgins summons the nerve to assist Brown. When later faced with death, Hodgins dies courageously. This is a gem of a performance. Ray Taylor's direction breathes life into the characters, and the results are more than satisfactory.

To avenge his Texas Ranger pal, Ken runs into the toughest bunch of bad men north of the Rio Grande. What he does to them, when they threaten the girl of his dreams, will give you chills and fever.

The Fighting Legion

Universal (April, 1930); A Ken Maynard Production

CAST: Dave Hayes, **Ken Maynard**; Molly Williams, **Dorothy Dwan**; Dad Williams, **Harry Todd**; Cloudy Jones, **Frank Rice**; Jack Bowie, **Ernest Adams**; Burl Edwards, **Stanley Blystone**; John Blake, **Jack Fowler**; Tom Dawson, **Bob Walker**; Hook Brothers, **Les Bates, Charles Whittaker and Bill Nestell;** and "**Tarzan**"// Outlaws, **Ben Corbett** and **Frank Ellis**; Bartender, **Billy Franey**; Card Player, **Lafe McKee**; Drunken Cowboy, **Jim Corey**; Ranger, **Fred Burns**

CREDITS: Director, **Harry J. Brown**; Story/Screenwriter, **Bennett Cohen**; Titles, **Leslie Mason**; Editor, **Fred Allen**; Cinematographer, **Ted McCord**; Recording Engineer, **C. Roy Hunter**

LOCATION FILMING: Lone Pine, Lake Sherwood and the Paramount Studios Street, California

RUNNING TIME: 75 min.

STORY: Texas Ranger Bob Walker is chasing Ken Maynard and Frank Rice for shooting up a camp, when Walker's horse takes a spill. Maynard comes back to help Walker. Walker decides not to arrest Maynard and Rice, and rides from Maynard's camp. An unknown assailant shoots Walker. Maynard gets to Walker before he dies, and Walker tells him that one of the gang from Bowden shot him. Maynard decides to pose as a Texas Ranger and go to Bowden to find the murderer. "Ranger" Maynard begins to tame the town. Walker's killer, Ernest Adams, arrives in Bowden and tells his outlaw friends that Maynard is not a Ranger. Maynard admits to the town that he came to Bowden to find Walker's killer. The unsavory element attempts to lynch Maynard, but quick action by Rice allows Maynard to escape. Maynard and Rice hide out at an abandoned hacienda. When the law-abiding citizens congregate at the hacienda, Maynard joins the group and draws up a plan to expose the Ranger's killer. Maynard sends a note to the Empire Saloon stating that he will walk through the doors at midnight to get Walker's killer. In the saloon, townspeople make comments about death to Adams to unnerve him. Maynard is able to get the drop on Adams and forces him to tell who hired him. Stanley Blystone, the outlaw leader, kills Adams and tries to escape, taking Dorothy Dwan as hostage. Maynard is able to capture Blystone. Maynard becomes a Texas Ranger and plans to marry Dwan.

NOTES AND COMMENTARY: Plot elements of *Fighting Legion* were later used in *The Lone Avenger* (World Wide, 1933) with Maynard. In that later film the Hook brothers are reduced by one and become the Hawkes brothers (Charles King as Nip and Edward Brady as Tuck), who act tough but rush to help Maynard bring the bad guys to justice. The script has Maynard take refuge in the good citizens' meeting place, where he joins them and makes plans to expose the murderer.

The set for the town of Bowden was built by Paramount for their production of *The Virginian* (Paramount, 1929).

Fighting Legion was also released as a silent picture.

Ernest Adams was usually billed as Ernie Adams, and Charles Whittaker as Slim, in their respective film careers.

REVIEWS: "Good western, with Maynard given histrionic chances and while not wowing, making good." (*Variety*, 4/9/30); "More dramatic tone than was usual." (*The Western*, Hardy)

SUMMATION: *Fighting Legion* is a fast, action packed western with a psychological twist that's most evident in the scenes in which Ernest Adams' nerve is broken. All the principals acquit themselves well with a special mention of Adams' fine performance. Director Harry J. Brown moves the story nicely. Les Bates, Charles Whittaker and Bill Nestell add some good comedy as the rough, tough Hooks brothers.

JOHNNY MACK BROWN
In His Most Thrilling Serial!

Flaming Frontiers

Universal (May, 1938)

CAST: Tex Houston, **John Mack Brown**; Mary Grant, **Eleanor Hansen**; Tom Grant, **Ralph Bowman**; Jim Crosby, **William Royle**; Ace Daggett, **Charles Middleton**; Bart Eaton, **James Blaine**; Breed, **Charles Stevens**; "Buffalo Bill" Cody, **Jack Rutherford**; Andy Grant, **Eddy Waller**; Joe, **Edward Cassidy**; Jake,

Carl Hackett; Hawkins, **James Farley**; Sheriff, **Horace Murphy**; Harper, **Pat O'Brien**; Thunder Cloud, **Thunder Cloud**; Chief Spotted Elk, **Bill Hazlett**; Wolf Moran, **John Roper**; Blackie, **Charles King**; Tom Forman; Ben Hollister, **Roy Barcroft**//"Scout"; Postmaster, **Michael Slade**; Reynolds, **Frank Ellis**; Bartender, **Richard Alexander**; Dave Merkle, **Al Bridge**; Townsmen, **Horace B. Carpenter** and **Tom Steele**; Drunk, **Earle Hodgins**; Hank, **Hank Bell**; Moran Henchman, **Slim Whitaker**

CREDITS: Directors, **Ray Taylor** and **Alan James**; Associate Producer, **Henry MacRae**; Screenwriters, **Wyndham Gittens, George Plympton, Basil Dickey** and **Paul Perez**; Dialogue Director, **Ella O'Neill**; Supervising Editor, **Saul Goodkind**; Editors, **Alvin Todd, Louis Sackin** and **Joseph Gluck**; Art Director, **Ralph DeLacy**; Cinematographer, **Jerome Ash**

LOCATION FILMING: Kernville, California

RUNNING TIME: 305 min.

CHAPTER TITLES: 1. The River Runs Red; 2. Death Rides the Wind; 3. Treachery at Eagle Pass; 4. A Night of Terror; 5. Blood and Gold; 6. Trapped by Fire; 7. A Human Target; 8. The Savage Horde; 9. Toll of the Torrent; 10. In the Claws of the Cougar; 11. The Half Breed's Revenge; 12. The Indians Are Coming; 13. The Fatal Plunge; 14. Dynamite; 15. A Duel to Death

SOURCE: Story "The Tie That Binds" by **Peter B. Kyne**

STORY: Store owner James Blaine threatens to have Eddy Waller jailed for embezzlement unless his daughter, Eleanor Hansen, marries him. Frontiersman John Mack Brown has a letter from Waller's son, Ralph Bowman, with money to settle the embezzlement charges. Blaine has the letter stolen, and has Waller and Brown arrested. Hansen starts west with a wagon train to find Bowman. Brown and Waller break jail and ride to catch up with the wagon train. Blaine and his henchmen have also joined the wagon train. Brown sees an Indian smoke signal and realizes the wagon train is about to be attacked. Brown guides the train through Indian perils but is unable to prevent the death of Waller at the hands of Blaine's henchmen. The wagon train finally finds safety at a stockade. A rider brings a letter to Waller from Bowman, which Blaine intercepts. Blaine, with knowledge of a gold strike by Bowman, changes his interest from Hansen to gaining possession of the mine in Gold Creek. Refusing to surrender his claim, Blaine's men kidnap Bowman. Brown decides to help Hansen find her brother. Local saloon owner Charles Middleton takes over the operation when Blaine can't make Bowman sign over his claim. Brown rescues Bowman. In town, Bowman spots one of his kidnappers, Al Bridge. As Bridge is about to talk, Middleton's hired killer, Charles Stevens, kills Bridge. Bowman wounds Stevens as he makes his escape. With one bullet fired from his gun, Bowman is framed for murder. Brown begins to search for the real murderer. Not wanting Bowman to hang, Blaine's men break

Bowman out of jail. A friendly Indian, Thunder Cloud, helps Brown rescue Bowman. Brown captures Stevens, but Stevens is able to get free when Blaine's men attack Brown. Bowman trails Stevens but is taken captive by the killer, who takes Bowman to his claim. Stevens tells Middleton that he has captured Bowman. When Stevens returns to Bowman's claim, he is followed by two of Middleton's men. Brown comes to the claim and gets the drop on Stevens. Bowman has been taken to Middleton. Middleton pretends to be Bowman's friend and convinces Bowman to give him a half interest in the claim. Blaine realizes that Middleton must have Bowman and goes to the saloon. When Brown prevents a murder attempt on Stevens' life, Stevens tells Brown that Middleton is behind the villainy. Brown reaches Middleton's office and prevents Bowman from signing over half interest in his claim. Brown is taking Middleton to the sheriff's office when Middleton and Blaine meet in the saloon. The two villains draw and fire, with the shots bringing death to both men. Brown proposes to Hansen, who accepts.

CHAPTER 3 TREACHERY AT EAGLE PASS

Flaming Frontiers (1938) scene card: John Mack Brown (*left*) confronts Charles Stevens; *right border,* John Mack Brown.

NOTES AND COMMENTARY: Peter B. Kyne's "The Tie That Binds" was also the basis for the serial *Heroes of the West* (Universal, 1932). The plot, however, was closer to *Indians are Coming* (Universal, 1930).

Some interesting billing trivia: John Mack Brown would gain everlasting western movie fame as Johnny Mack Brown; Ralph Bowman would be better known as John Archer; Hackett's first name was usually Karl instead of Carl in the billing; Thunder Cloud usually was billed as Chief Thundercloud; and John Roper's first name in the credits was usually Jack.

Like with all Universal western serials featuring Indian attacks, footage was utilized from Hoot Gibson's serial *The Flaming Frontier* (Universal, 1926).

The hat is there and then is not there. In Chapters four and 14, John Mack Brown loses his hat; then, miraculously, the hat suddenly reappears.

REVIEWS: "There is not much logic in this serial but this is made up for by endless action." (*Western Movies*, Pitts)

SUMMATION: *Flaming Frontiers* is a slightly above average, action packed western serial. John Mack Brown makes a good serial hero, realistically performing the riding, fighting and shooting scenes. Brown is given a capable supporting cast, most notably heroine Eleanor Hansen and villain Charles Middleton. The film is saddled with a weak ending, in which villains Charles Middleton and James Blaine exchange shots, killing each other instead of having hero Brown bring both to justice. In addition, a number of the chapter resolutions use "hero's luck" to extract the hero from peril, a major flaw in most Universal serials. Directors Ray Taylor and Allan James keep the story moving at high speed, maintaining a good balance between new material and stock footage in the action sequences.

TOM MIX and TONY, JR.,
In a smashing, crashing, dashing picture presenting a PETER B. KYNE *story of red courage and sizzling action in the Mount Whitney cow country!*

Flaming Guns

Universal (December, 1932)

CAST: Tom Malone, **Tom Mix**; Henry Ramsey, **William Farnum**; Mary Ramsey, **Ruth Hall**; "Uncle" Mulford, **Clarence H. Wilson**; Hugh, **George Hackathorne**; "Red" McIntyre, **Duke Lee**; "Gabe," **Pee Wee Holmes**; and "**Tony, Jr.**"// Sheriff, **Fred Burns**; Outlaw, **Bud Osborne**; Cowboy, **Slim Whitaker**

CREDITS: Director, **Arthur Rosson**; Associate Producer, **Stanley**

Bergerman; Screenwriter, **Jack Cunningham**; Editor, **Albert Akst;** Cinematographer, **Jerry Ash**

LOCATION FILMING: Alabama Hills, Lone Pine; Big Pine, Red Rock Canyon, Bridgeport, Bishop area, Gerard, California

RUNNING TIME: 57 min.

SOURCE: Novel *Flaming Guns* by **Peter B. Kyne**

STORY: Returning home from World War I, Tom Mix gets his old job back at Clarence H. Wilson's ranch. Wilson is plagued with some minor rustling and wants Mix to stop it. Mix quickly rounds up the varmints, which impresses Wilson's old friend, William Farnum. Farnum warns Wilson to let Mix run his ranch, which is having its troubles. Mix meets Farnum, and Farnum gives him a letter making him the ranch manager. Farnum and Mix are arguing over compensation when Farnum's daughter, Ruth Hall, walks into the office. Unable to come to an agreement with Farnum, Mix decides to take Hall to lunch. Infuriated, Farnum fires Mix before he can start work. Mix and Hall have a whirlwind week making the nightclub rounds, and they begin to fall in love. Running out of money, Mix remembers the letter Farnum gave him and decides to run his ranch. The current manager, Duke Lee, is causing the ranch's troubles, primarily by rustling Farnum's cattle. Mix takes over as manager, and Lee quietly leaves. Lee and his men rustle a large herd. Mix pursues and is able to bring Lee to justice and drive the herd back to the ranch. Farnum discovers Mix is running the ranch and goes to the ranch to fire him. Seeing Mix repairing a fence the rustlers tore down, Farnum has Mix arrested without allowing him to offer an explanation. Mix vows to split Farnum's ears when he gets out of his predicament. Farnum begins to have nightmares about Mix's threat, and decides to have him released from jail. But Mix has escaped from jail, and Farnum has the sheriff surround the ranch house with deputies. Mix is able to draw the sheriff and all the deputies away from the house. Farnum sees Mix approaching the house and sends Hall out with a letter reinstating him as ranch manager. Quickly, Mix and Hall decide to go to Mexico and get married. Farnum chases after them to prevent the nuptials. Mix and Hall are able to get to the church ahead of Farnum and tie the knot. Farnum accepts Mix as a member of the family.

NOTES AND COMMENTARY: *Flaming Guns* is a remake of *The Buckaroo Kid* (Universal, 1926) with Hoot Gibson.

A novelization of *Flaming Guns* was published as a Five Star Library Book by Engle-Van-Wiseman Book Corporation as a children's book and a movie tie-in. The 152-page book featured 76 photographs from the movie.

Amusing dialog exchange between two ranch hands:

FIRST COWBOY: "I was born out of wedlock."
SECOND COWBOY: "That's mighty pretty country up there."

REVIEWS: "The weakest of Tom Mix's Universal series." (*Western Movies*, Pitts); "Not one of the star's most satisfactory efforts." (*Motion Picture Guide*, Nash and Ross)

SUMMATION: This film marked a significant change of pace for Tom Mix, as he starred in a film better suited for Hoot Gibson. In fact, Gibson made the story six years earlier. Mix plays the part with a definite flair, but he's better known for more action-oriented productions. William Farnum is adequate as the blustering businessman. Ruth Hall is quite pretty and vivacious as the object of Mix's affection. In the end, the story lets Mix down—he easily dispenses with the mild villainy and then has to play a love-starved cowboy. Ultimately, the story wastes some good actors and great scenic views of Lone Pine and other picturesque locations.

MASSACRE IN "HELL'S HALF ACRE"!
BRAINS AGAINST BULLETS! BRAWN AGAINST RED DEVILS!

For the Service

Universal (May 1936); A Buck Jones Production

CAST: Buck O'Bryan, **Buck Jones**; George Murphy, **Clifford Jones**; Capt. Murphy, **Edward Keane**; Bruce Howard, **Fred Kohler**; Penny Carson, **Beth Marion**; Jim, **Frank McGlynn**; Ben, **Ben Corbett**; Sherman, **Bob McKenzie**; Chief Big Bear, **Chief Thunderbird**; and "**Silver**"// Johnson, **Lafe McKee**; Carson, **Alfred P. James**; Parson, **Niles Welch**; Freighter, **Cactus Mack**; Renegades, **Richard Cramer**, **Allan Sears** and **Blackie Whiteford**; Indian, **Chief Thundercloud**

CREDITS: Director, **Buck Jones**; Story/Screenwriter, **Isadore Bernstein**; Cinematographers, **Allan Thompson** and **Herbert Kirkpatrick**

LOCATION FILMING: Red Rock Canyon, California

RUNNING TIME: 65 min.

STORY: After fifteen years in the east, Clifford Jones returns to the west as an Army Scout under the command of his father, Edward Keane. Keane is worried that C. Jones could still be traumatized from seeing his mother and siblings massacred by Indians. Head Scout Buck Jones tells Keane that he'll take his son under his wing. Fred Kohler and his band of renegades are terrorizing the area. Kohler sells whiskey to the Indians, which makes them a threat to the settlers. B. Jones is assigned to locate the renegade camp and asks to take C. Jones along. Renegades ambush the two scouts, but Jones has them play dead. When the renegades come into the open, B. Jones fires at the renegades, who fall to the ground. C. Jones is appalled at the violence. The renegades play dead as the two scouts did earlier. After finding the renegade camp, the scouts come upon a wagon train under attack from hostile Indians. B. Jones stays to fight, but C. Jones' nerve breaks and he rides away, but then goes to the fort for help. The settlers treat C. Jones as a hero because he brought the troops to save them. B. Jones realizes the west is not the place for C. Jones. With the help of Beth Marion, who loves C. Jones (and, in returned, is loved by him), B. Jones persuades the couple to get married and travel east. B. Jones has been assigned to escort a settler to safety, when word comes of two scouts killed by the renegades. Keane assigns C. Jones to lead the scouts to the renegade camp and then massacre them. C. Jones makes the decision to bring the renegades in for trial. B. Jones arrives before the scouts go into action and tells the scouts to follow C. Jones' orders. Outside of C. Jones' hearing, B. Jones tells the men to shoot if one shot is fired. Kohler refuses to surrender, and a gunfight breaks out. C. Jones turns to run and receives a bullet in the back. The scouts wipe out the renegades. Before he dies, C. Jones asks B. Jones not to tell anyone he was shot in the back, which B. Jones agrees to do. C. Jones is buried as a hero.

NOTES AND COMMENTARY: Footage from *The Flaming Frontier* (Universal, 1926) was utilized for the attack on the wagon train.

Clifford Jones was billed also as Phillip Trent in his screen career.

REVIEWS: "Pretty actionful Buck Jones vehicle." (*Western Movies*, Pitts); "This one of the early west has enough action and suspense to satiate the hunger of the six-gun brand fans." (*Variety*, 6/3/36)

SUMMATION: *For the Service* is a strong Buck Jones western, with the emphasis on story and characterization but still packed with plenty of action. The focus of the story is on Clifford Jones, who effectively portrays a pacifist desperately attempting to follow in the footsteps of his Army Captain father, even at the cost of his own life. Buck Jones is good as a father figure or an older brother who takes Clifford Jones under his wing. Beth Marion gives a moving performance as the young woman who loves Clifford Jones and tries to get him out of the West. Buck Jones directs capably, and is not afraid to allot significant screen time to Clifford Jones, who is the key figure in this excellent story.

His Bulls-Eye Six-Shooter Spat Flaming Law for Prairie Rats!

Forbidden Valley

Universal (February 1938)

CAST: Ring Hazzard, **Noah Beery, Jr.**; Wilda Lanning, **Frances Robinson**; Ramrod Locke, **Robert Barrat**; Matt Regan, **Fred Kohler, Sr.**; Indian Joe, **Alonzo Price**; Jeff Hazzard, **Samuel S. Hinds**; Hoke Lanning, **Stanley Andrews**; Dr. Scudd, **Spencer Charters**; Blackjack, **Charles Stevens**; Meetah, **Soledad Jimenez**; Sheriff Walcott, **Ferris Taylor**; Mrs. Scudd, **Margaret McWade**; Bagley, **Henry Hunter**; Duke Lafferty, **John Ridgely**; Brandon, **James Foran**// Mrs. Ragona, **Sarah Padden**; Corlox, **Glenn Strange**

CREDITS: Director/ Screenwriter, **Wyndham Gittens**; Producers, **Henry MacRae** and **Elmer Tambert**; Editor, **Frank Gross**; Art Directors, **Jack Otterson** and **Charles H. Clark**; Cinematographer, **Woody Bredell**; Sound, **Jess A. Moulin** and **Edwin Wetzel**; Musical Director, **Charles Previn**

SONG: "Get Along, Little Pony" (Kellogg)—sung by **John Ridgely**

LOCATION FILMING: Tuolumne County and Mammoth Lakes, California

RUNNING TIME: 67 min.

SOURCE: Novel "Mountains Are My Kingdom" by **Stuart Hardy**

STORY: Riding into the mountains, Frances Robinson, her father, Stanley Andrews, her fiancé, John Ridgely, Ridgely's foreman, Fred Kohler, Sr., and Robert Barrat spot a small herd of wild mustangs. Left behind as the others ride for a closer look, Robinson chases a small pony that races close to her. In attempting to rope the pony, Robinson is unseated from her horse, which runs away, leaving her afoot. Noah Beer, Jr. has stampeded mustangs to a hidden corral, and Robinson is directly in their path. Beery Jr. carries Robinson to safety. Beery takes Robinson to a cabin inhabited by his father, Samuel S. Hinds, and himself. Before Beery and Robinson can begin their journey to Gunsight, Hinds is killed while riding one of the wild mustangs. Hinds and Beery lived in the mountains far from civilization because Hinds was accused of a murder he didn't commit. Beery is driving mustangs to sell, as well as taking Robinson to the trail to Gunsight. A rattlesnake bites Robinson. Beery shoots the venom from Robinson's arm and gets her to a doctor. Beery has to leave his mustangs, which Kohler finds and brings to Gunsight. In town, Beery and Kohler fight over the ownership of the mustangs. Beery wins the fight and makes a deadly enemy in Kohler. Beery meets his uncle, Robert Barrat, but refuses to have anything to do with him because he didn't have faith in Hinds. Beery decides to clear his father's name. The only witness to the crime, Alonzo Price, tells Beery he can't identify the murderer. Beery starts a mustang ranch high in the mountains. Price and his wife, Soledad Jimenez, come to live at the ranch and help Beery. Kohler follows Beery and plans to wait until Beery has rounded up a large herd of mustangs, then steal the horses and kill Beery. Robinson overhears Kohler's plan and rides to Gunsight for help. Kohler attacks the ranch and shoots Price as he rides away. Then Kohler attempts to steal the mustangs; but Beery and his men are able to defend themselves. Beery and Kohler begin to stalk each other, and Kohler gains the upper hand. Before Kohler can pull the trigger for the fatal shot, a shot rings out and Kohler falls. The wounded Price had fired the shot. Barrat and a posse arrive to route the rustlers. Price tells everyone that Kohler was guilty for the crime of which Hinds had been accused. Beery learns that Robinson has broken her engagement to Ridgely, so the two can marry.

NOTES AND COMMENTARY: *Forbidden Valley* was remade as *Sierra* (Universal-International, 1950) with Audie Murphy.

In one scene John Ridgely sings "Get Along Little Pony" while accompanying himself on the guitar. He is suddenly interrupted, and the sound track plays one note after Ridgely's hands have stopped moving.

"Get Along Little Pony" was written by Kay Kellogg for the Johnny Mack Brown serial *Wild West Days* (Universal, 1937). The song would later be played by the fiddle player of the Texas Rangers in *Oklahoma Frontier* (Universal, 1939).

REVIEWS: "The kids will get a special kick out of it. For the oldsters, it may not be quite so good, but it's all right." (*Variety*, 3/30/38); "Giddens directs in the cheerfully uncluttered way that juvenile audiences found so appealing." (*The Western*, Hardy)

SUMMATION: This is a delightful motion picture. *Forbidden Valley* is a fine example of an exceptional "B" western. Stars Noah Beery, Jr. and Frances Robinson deliver sterling performances within the limits of the "B" western screenplay. The supporting cast, led by Fred Kohler, Sr. and Robert Barrat, is first rate. Cinematographer Elwood Bredell captures the beauty of the mountain ranges in glorious black and white. Wyndon Gittens directs forcefully from his own screenplay. This version is superior to the color Audie Murphy feature released by Universal-International in 1951.

A Smashing, Crashing, Dashing Drama of the West.

The Fourth Horseman

Universal (September 1932)

CAST: Tom Martin, **Tom Mix**; Molly O'Rourke, **Margaret Lindsay**; "Softy" Jones, **Fred Kohler**; "Thad" Harley, **Donald Kirke**; "Gabby," **Raymond Hatton**; "Fancy," **"Buddy" Roosevelt**; Mrs. Elmer Brown, **Grace Cunard**; Elmer Brown, **Frederick Howard**; "Baby-face," **Helen Millard**; Caleb Winter, **Captain Anderson**; Charlie, **Harry Allen**; Bill Thrasher, **Herman Nolan**; Jim, **Duke Lee**; and **Tony**// Drunk Settler, **Walter Brennan**; Outlaws, **Fred Burns** and **Bud Osborne**; Mrs. Whittum, **Martha Mattox**

CREDITS: Director, **Hamilton MacFadden**; Associate Producer, **Stanley Bergerman**; Story, **Nina Wilcox Putnam**; Screenplay, **Jack Cunningham**; Editor, **Philip Cahn**; Cinematographer, **Daniel B. Clark**

LOCATION FILMING: Iverson's Ranch, California

RUNNING TIME: 63 min.

STORY: A gang of outlaws, led by Fred Kohler, holds up a mail train. In the ghost town of Stillwell, Kohler reads a letter in which the owner, Margaret Lindsay, is advised that the town will be sold for back taxes unless they are promptly paid. Kohler decides to take over the town, revitalize it and make it a haven for new settlers, whom they plan to fleece in saloons and crooked card games. As Kohler makes the town ready, Lindsay is among the settlers traveling to Stillwell. Lindsay makes friends with Tom Mix, who is driving a herd of horses to the "ghost" town. Lindsay reaches town and sternly tells Kohler she owns the town. Kohler tells Lindsay that he will manage her properties and provide her with a steady income as long as she owns the town. Mix, immediately taking a dislike to Kohler, tries to warn Lindsay not to have any dealings with him. Lindsay begins to find that Kohler's methods are detrimental to the success of Stillwell. The settlers plan to leave, fed up with a lawless community. Lindsay goes to Kohler's saloon and tells him she wants her town back. Lindsay learns that if back taxes are not paid by noon of the following day, Kohler will take over the town. Kohler tries to prevent Lindsay from leaving. Mix intercedes and takes her from the saloon. Telling Mix about the taxes, Mix and three of his cowhands start riding for the county seat. Kohler tries to stop the men. All are intercepted except the fourth horseman, Mix, who is able to reach the county seat and pay the back taxes at the last possible moment. With the taxes paid, Mix returns to Stillwell to settle things with Kohler. With help from the settlers, Kohler's men are chased out of town and Mix brings Kohler to justice. Lindsay and Mix, who have fallen in love, now become bride and groom.

NOTES AND COMMENTARY: *The*

Fourth Horseman marked Margaret Lindsay's first leading role. Lindsay would have a long career in motion pictures (lasting until 1963), mostly as leads in "B" pictures. She is probably best remembered for her role as Nikki Porter in seven Ellery Queen mysteries for Columbia (1940–42). Lindsay was coaxed out of retirement for a farewell role in *The Chadwick Family* (Universal, 1974), a made-for-television feature.

The Fourth Horseman was loosely remade as *Ghost Town Riders* (Universal, 1938) with Bob Baker, and as a Tex Williams featurette, *Gold Strike* (Universal, 1950).

REVIEWS: "Entertaining and well made Tom Mix series vehicle." (*Western Movies*, Pitts); "A well-made western." (*Variety*, 1/31/33)

SUMMATION: This is a first-rate Tom Mix western feature. Mix excels as he adroitly handles both action and dramatic scenes. Look at Mix as he firmly delivers several humorous throwaway lines. He's a delight. Margaret Lindsay, in her first lead, is handed a part with a little more involvement and depth than is usually seen in a "B" western, and she handles it nicely. Fred Kohler proves why he was one of the screen's top "B" western villains, as he becomes a worthy adversary for Mix. Hamilton MacFadden capably handles the directorial chores, especially with the standout sequence of Mix being chased as he rides to the county seat to pay Lindsay's back taxes. Mention must to be made of Daniel B. Clark's fine camera work, with great utilization of the magnificent scenic locations.

Drama at its Boldest!
The West at its Wildest!

Frisco Sal

Universal (February 1945)

CAST: Sal, **Susanna Foster**; Dude, **Turhan Bey**; Rio, **Alan Curtis**; Bunny, **Andy Devine**; Dan, **Thomas Gomez**; Mickey, **Collette Lyons**; Doc, **Samuel S. Hinds**; Hallelujah, **Fuzzy Knight**; Billy, **Billy Green**; McKinney, **Ernie Adams**; Judge, **George Lloyd**; Eddie, **Bert Fiske**// Tour Guide, **Syd Saylor**; Clancy, **Kit Guard**; Pitchman (Spider Web), **Earle Hodgins**; Rio Henchman, **Reed Howes**; Bailiff, **Ethan Laidlaw**; Male Quartette, **Carlyle Blackwell, George Bruggeman, Robert Locke Lorraine** and **Billy Wilkerson**; Hotel Clerk, **Harry Hayden**; Saloon Patron, **Jack O'Shea**

CREDITS: Director / Producer, **George Waggner**; Assistant Director, **Charles S. Gould**; Screenwriters, **Curt Siodmak** and **Gerald Geraghty**; Editor, **Edward Curtiss**; Art Directors, **John B. Goodman** and

Robert Clatworthy; Set Decorators, **Russell A. Gausman** and **Ted Von Hemert**; Costumes, **Vera West**; Cinematographer, **Charles Van Enger**; Sound, **Bernard B. Brown** and **Glenn E. Anderson**; Musical Director, **Edward Ward**; Choreographer, **Lester Horton**; Dialogue Directors, **Stacy Keach** and **Monty Collins**

SONGS: "I Just Got In" (Berens and Brooks)—sung by **Collette Lyons, female** and **male quartet**; "Good Little Bad Little Lady" (Brooks)—sung by **Susanna Foster** and **female chorus**; "Beloved" (Ward and Waggner)—sung by **Susanna Foster** and **male quartet**; "Christmas Medley" ("Silent Night," "Hark the Herald Angels Sing" and "Come All Ye Faithful")—sung by **Susanna Foster, Samuel S. Hinds** and **chorus**; "Ace in the Hole" (Dempsey and Mitchell)—sung by **Billy Green**; "Percy" (Ward and Waggner)—sung by **Collette Lyons** and **chorus**; "Beloved" (reprise)—sung by **Susanna Foster** and **male quartet**

LOCATION FILMING: French Ranch, California

RUNNING TIME: 94 min.

STORY: Susanna Foster comes from Cambridge, Massachusetts, to the Barbary Coast to find her long lost brother. The Barbary Coast is in turmoil, with saloon owner Turhan Bey and Alan Curtis, who runs a mission as a front for illegal activities, vying for the top spot. Bey wants the two to work together, but Curtis refuses. Foster manages to get a job singing at Bey's saloon and quickly becomes the star attraction. In Bey's office, Foster receives a ring that belonged to her brother. Taking the ring to police headquarters, Foster convince Police Captain Thomas Gomez to investigate. Gomez and Foster go to Curtis for help. Curtis doesn't like Foster working for Bey. Foster and Bey begin to fall in love. Curtis claims Bey murdered Foster's brother and manufactures some incriminating evidence. Foster plans to return east, but showgirl Collette Lyons persuades her to stay. Foster confronts Bey, but he refuses to comment. At the mission, Foster finds evidence that Curtis may be her brother. Bey thinks Foster is with Curtis at the mission. Arming himself, Bey starts for the mission. Foster has returned to the saloon, and Bey stops when he hears her voice as Foster performs her number in the show. Learning that Foster returned to Bey, Curtis arms himself and goes to the saloon. Bey and Curtis have a short scuffle. Curtis' shirt is torn, and a scar is revealed that proves Curtis is Foster's brother. Bey and Foster have married, and now Bey and Curtis join together to run the Barbary Coast.

NOTES AND COMMENTARY: Susanna Foster commented on *Frisco Sal*: " I thought *Frisco Sal* ended badly, with all the rowdyism and stuff, which was western. I loved Samuel Hinds. He and I talked together on the set all the time. Alan Curtis was a great gentleman. I'm often sorry I didn't go to dinner with him. He's such a fine man and very handsome. He [Thomas Gomez] was a wonderful man. He used to make me mad on the set. They would tease him because he was interested in the girl that was in the music department. It was so embarrassing. I hated them to do things like that. When I was on the set, I sat with the crew. I enjoyed their company the most. I like real people, and that's what they were."

Susanna Foster talked about Turhan Bey: "We worked well together. He was a good friend of mine. He did something recently that irritated me a lot. We did a DVD. I did this long interview. Turhan did his interview in the morning. I didn't see that, and he stayed to see mine. When he was on the television talking, he made me sick at my stomach. I had never seen him put up such a front and be so dishonest. He worried about his image. He wasn't honest like I was. I praised him and tried to make him look good in interviews. He went through all that adversity with Lana Turner. He always felt terrible about that. I always tried to make him look good whenever I talk about him. He made me look terrible. He said, 'I couldn't stand all those high notes.' He knew better. There's a lot more than high notes, for Christ's sake. I could act." Foster remarked, "They had to take him [Bey] off the set [of *The Climax* (Universal, 1944)] because he couldn't act, couldn't work because he felt I didn't want him, didn't like him. Now that he said he didn't like that screaming in his ears, the high notes, well, hell, I tell the truth about you, you son-of-a-bitch." Foster added that Bey didn't like the fact that he didn't receive billing over the women he played opposite, like Merle Oberon.

Foster commented, "She was a bigger star."

The film, originally titled *Frisco Kate*, was scheduled to be filmed in Technicolor, with Susanna Foster, Ella Raines and Robert Paige in the starring roles. Susanna Foster related this story: "I can tell you another bad story. I never try to repeat these, but Gloria Jean insists on it. She's a very honest girl. She told me, 'Susanna, Deanna [Durbin] has cut you from getting *Frisco Sal* in color. She did the same thing to me. She had scenes cut from things I did.' Whether she did or her agent, I don't know. Deanna was never nice to me. She came in the make-up department one day and Jack [Pierce] introduced me to her. She was very condescending and short, and walked away. I was hurt. My favorite star was Jeanette MacDonald and my second favorite was Deanna Durbin and my third favorite was Sonia Henie. I was kind of hurt. I didn't think anymore about it. Other people said she was very jealous. She never said hello. Never gave me a decent word."

Susanna Foster thought highly of cinematographer Charles Van Enger and remembered, "I was very fond of him. He was a sweetheart. He said to me, 'Susanne, don't let them photograph you from a down angle, full straight on, or a little bit below you.' I had a short upper lip and my nose would get in the way of something, I don't know."

Foster had only nice things to say of her co-stars, except Andy Devine: "I didn't care for him. He was always very cold to me. I don't know why, yet he was jolly with other people."

Commenting on directors, Susanna Foster said, "I was never directed by anybody. They always left me alone. That was great." She did have one incident with George Waggner, and Foster remembers, "Hal Mohr [cinematographer for Foster on a few of her films] took care of him. He told him, 'Never talk to Susanna Foster like that, not in my presence, or that'll be the end of you.' I couldn't work that afternoon. [Waggner] was a bastard. But the rest were wonderful."

Following *Frisco Sal*, George Waggner wanted Susanna Foster for *Shady Lady* (Universal, 1945). Foster commented, "I was in a very down period. I didn't like the list of the pictures they wanted me to do. I said no. I would be draped on a stage. They wanted to start the sex stuff. I don't mind showing my figure if it's part of the story if it's handled well. I objected. Then they wanted me to do *The Countess of Monte Cristo* [Universal-International, 1948] with Sonia Henie, whom I adored. That'll be a bomb. I won't do it. They wanted me to do the one Ava Gardner did, *One Touch of Venus* [Universal-International, 1948]. They wanted to change the very essence of the story; the shop girl is the Venus. She plays both parts. Instead they had Ava Gardner play Venus and I play some shop girl. No way, that's going to be a bomb. It was a bomb. Both were terrible bombs. So I said, 'Let's call it quits.'"

Some of the songs can be heard in other films. "I Just Got In" can be heard in *Gun Town* (Universal, 1946) and "Good Little, Bad Little Lady" was used in *Ride to Hangman's Tree* (Universal). When discussing "I Just Got In" with Susanna Foster remembered that Pat Ryan sang the song.

REVIEWS: "Good escapist box-office entertainment." (*Variety*, 2/14/45); "Film vehicle for singer-actress Susanna Foster. Basically for her fans." (*Western Movies*, Pitts)

SUMMATION: *Frisco Sal* is a good period melodrama set on the infamous Barbary Coast. Susanna Foster is quite good, both in the singing and acting departments. Turhan Bey and Alan Curtis make nice leading men. Andy Devine, Thomas Gomez, Samuel S. Hinds, Collette Lyons and Fuzzy Knight head an excellent supporting cast. Musical highlights include Foster's "Christmas Medley," a stunning showstopper, Billy Green's rendition of "Ace in the Hole," and Foster's stirring rendition of "Beloved" at the film's close. George Waggner directs the film with great care and coaxes fine performances from the cast, with the result being a very entertaining film.

The Lords of a Lawless Land!
...Bolder than Jesse James! More ruthless than the Daltons! More daring than Billy the Kid!

Frontier Badmen

Universal (August 1943)

CAST: Steve, **Robert Paige**; Chris, **Anne Gwynne**; Jim, **Noah Beery, Jr.**; Claire, **Diana Barrymore**; Chinito, **Leo Carrillo**; Slim, **Andy Devine**; Ballard, **Thomas Gomez**; Cherokee, **Frank Lackteen**; Courtwright, **William Farnum**; Chango, **Lon Chaney, Jr.**// Marvin, **Charles Wagenheim**; Jerry Kimball, **Tex Ritter**; Sheriff, **Robert Homans**; Lindsay, **Arthur Loft**; Thompson, **Tom Fadden**; Randall, **Norman Willis**; Auctioneer, **Eddy Waller**; Blackie, **Stanley Price**; Outlaw, **Jack Rockwell**; Townsman, **Kermit Maynard**; Cattle Buyers, **George Eldredge** and **William Desmond**; Cowboy, **Harry Cording**; Kansas, **Kansas Moehring**; Saloon Patron, **Tex Cooper**

CREDITS: Director/ Producer, **Ford Beebe**; Screenwriters, **Gerald Geraghty** and **Morgan B. Cox**; Editor, **Fred Feitshans, Jr.**; Art Directors, **John B. Goodman** and **Ralph M. DeLacy**; Set Decorators, **R.A. Gausman** and **Lee Smith**; Cinematographer, **William Sickner**; Gowns, **Vera West**; Sound, **Bernard B. Brown** and **Charles Carroll**; Musical Director, **H.J. Salter**

SONG: "Beautiful Dreamer" (Foster)—whistled by **Lon Chaney**, Jr.

LOCATION FILMING: Monogram Ranch, Walker Ranch and Newhall, California

RUNNING TIME: 77 min.

STORY: Partners Robert Paige and Noah Beery, Jr., with top hand Andy Devine bring a herd of cattle to Abilene. In Abilene, Paige and Beery learn there's an unknown person running a combine who refuses to allow the cattle buyers to bid directly with the cattlemen. Any cattle buyer objecting is found dead. Paige decides to buck the combine and buys Anne Gwynne's cattle. Paige learns that the cattle are grazing on land owned by Arthur Loft, who tells Paige to move the cattle to lands in the public domain or pay a grazing fee. The only public domain land in the area is the streets of Abilene, and that's where the cattle are moved. In the street, Paige auctions off the cattle to one of the buyers and tells the crowd he has a clue to the man behind the combine. The mystery man is saloon owner Thomas Gomez. With his hired killer, Lon Chaney, Jr., Gomez has had his way up to this point. Gomez realizes the weak link is Loft and orders him to leave town. Devine, with two of Gwynne's top hands, Leo Carrillo and Frank Lacteen, grabs Loft before he can leave. The trio breaks Loft down, and he names Gomez as the boss. Chaney kills Loft before he can talk to the sheriff. Paige and Beery decide to oppose Gomez by starting an Independent Buyer's Exchange. Also, Paige begins to romance both Diana Barrymore, a dealer in Gomez' saloon, and Gwynne. Beery is in love with Gwynne and tells Paige to court only Gwynne if he's serious about settling down. Gwynne sees Paige with Barrymore and becomes upset, and decides to go back to Texas. Beery, on the way to pick up a herd of cattle he's purchased, tells Gwynne he's always been in love with her and not to leave Abilene. Beery confronts Paige and dissolves their partnership. Gomez decides the time has come to ambush Beery and destroy the herd. Paige learns of the ambush and warns Beery in time. Prairie fires started by Gomez' henchmen destroy the cattle. Paige forces Gomez to write a check for the loss of the cattle. Gomez' henchmen force a gunfight, and Paige is arrested for starting the trouble. A lynch mob demands Paige be turned over to them. Sheriff Robert Homans refuses, and the mob lays siege to the jail. Devine, Carrillo and Lacteen help defend the jail. Barrymore alerts Gwynne, who rides for Beery's help. A second cattle herd has been brought to Abilene for Paige and Beery. Beery stampedes the cattle through the main street of Abilene,ized dispersing the mob. Gomez and Chaney begin firing at Beery. Beery rides his horse into the saloon and is quickly followed by Gwynne. The duo begins exchanging gunfire with Gomez and Chaney. Beery and Gwynne run out of bullets. As Chaney steps from cover to kill them, Barrymore gets a pistol to Beery who shoots both Chaney and Gomez. Beery and Gwynne, and Paige and Barrymore, return to Texas for a life as ranchers.

NOTES AND COMMENTARY: Tex Ritter received prominent billing in newspaper advertisements and on lobby cards and posters, but receives no onscreen credit. Ritter's part as a cattle buyer was nothing more than a cameo appearance. This was supposed to be the first of Ritter's roles in bigger budgeted pictures. As it turned out, his other appearances at Universal were in three "B" westerns, *Arizona Trail* (1943), *Marshal of Gunsmoke* (1944) and *Oklahoma Raiders* (1944).

Footage of prairie fires and the trail herd was later used in Rod Cameron's *Riders of the Santa Fe* (Universal, 1944), *The Daltons Ride Again* (Universal, 1945) and Tex Williams' *Nevada Trail* (Universal-International, 1949).

"Beautiful Dreamer' was previously sung by **Jimmy Wakely** in *The Old Chisholm Trail* (Universal, 1942).

REVIEWS: "Actionful and exciting entry." (*Variety*, 8/11/43); "Authentic looking oater from Ford Beebe with a good script, excellent cast and plenty of action; well above average." (*Western Movies*, Pitts)

SUMMATION: *Frontier Badmen* is a good minor "A" western boasting solid acting, story, direction and action. Robert Paige is fine as the cowboy with a roving eye for the ladies, and who loves to get into a scrap. Noah Beery, Jr. is bashful with females but can take care of himself in a fight. Both men end up with lovely ladies, Diana Barrymore for Paige and Anne Gwynne for Beery. The two ladies do themselves proud. The sidekicks, Andy Devine, Leo Carrillo and Frank Lackteen, add some amusing comedy as well as capably handling the action scenes. The necessary villainy is richly supplied by Thomas Gomez and especially Lon Chaney, Jr. as a cold-blooded killer who likes to whistle and play the guitar between murders. Ford Beebe shows not only why he ranks at the top when it comes to delivering rousing action scenes, but that he can effectively direct the dramatic sequences as well.

That ever-loving lady of "Salome"…
MORE GLAMOROUS! MORE AMOROUS! MORE DANGEROUS THAN EVER!

Frontier Gal

ALTERNATE TITLE: *The Bride Wasn't Willing*; Universal (December 1945); A Fessier-Pagano Production

CAST: Lorena Dumont, **Yvonne De Carlo**; Johnny Hart, **Rod Cameron**; Big Ben, **Andy Devine**; Fuzzy, **Fuzzy Knight**; Judge Prescott, **Andrew Tombes**; Blackie, **Sheldon Leonard**; Abigail, **Clara Blandick**; Sheila Winthrop, **Jan Wiley**; Buffalo, **Jack Overman**; Cherokee, **Frank Lackteen**, Mary Ann, **Beverly Simmons**//Gracie, **Claire Carleton**; Deputies, **Eddie Dunn** and **Harold Goodwin**; Henchmen, **Rex Lease, Jack Ingram, George Eldredge, Joseph Haworth** and **Edward M. Howard**; Saloon Girls, **Joan Fulton, Jean Trent, Kerry Vaughn** and **Karen Randle**; Wing Lee, **Eddie Lee**; Saloon Patron, **Jack O'Shea**, First Brawler in Candy Shop, **Cliff Lyons**

CREDITS: Director, **Charles Lamont**; Assistant Director, **William Tummel**; Executive Producer, **Howard Benedict**; Producers / Screenwriters, **Michael Fessier** and **Ernest Pagano**; Editor, **Ray Snyder**; Art Directors, **John B. Goodman** and **Richard H. Riedel**; Set Decorators, **Russell A. Gausman** and **Oliver Emert**; Cinematographers, **George Robinson** and **Charles P. Boyle**; Special Photography, **John P. Fulton**; Costumes, **Travis Banton**; Makeup, **Jack P. Pierce**; Hair Stylist, **Carmen Dirigo**; Sound, **Bernard B. Brown** and **William Hedgcock**; Musical Director / Musical Score, **Frank Skinner**; Song Director, **H.J. Salter**; Technicolor Color Director, **Natalie Kalmus**; Associate Technicolor Color Director, **William Fritzsche**

SONGS: "What is Love" (Brooks and Fairchild)—sung by **Yvonne De Carlo**; "Johnny's Coming Home Today"—sung by **Fuzzy Knight**; "Set 'Em Up Joe" (Brooks and Fairchild)—sung by **Yvonne De Carlo; Fuzzy Knight** and **chorus**; "Set 'Em Up Joe" (reprise)—sung by **Beverly Simmons**; "Set 'Em Up Joe"

114 Frontier Gal

(reprise)—sung by **Yvonne De Carlo** and **female chorus** and **Lorena**—sung by **Fuzzy Knight**

LOCATION FILMING: Lone Pine, Sequoia National Park, Kernville and Mammoth Lakes, California

COLOR PROCESS: Technicolor

RUNNING TIME: 84 min.

STORY: Wanted for manslaughter, Rod Cameron rides into town looking for the man who murdered his partner. At the Red Horse Saloon, Cameron makes time with the beautiful saloon owner, Yvonne De Carlo, incurring the wrath of De Carlo's suitor, Sheldon Leonard. Cameron and Leonard fight, and Cameron begins to lose when Leonard's henchmen join in the fray. Blacksmith Andy Devine joins in, and he and Cameron send Leonard and his men running. Cameron and DeCarlo begin a stormy romance in which De Carlo believes Cameron wants to marry her. Cameron was just flirting and plans to marry schoolteacher Jan Wiley. Not wanting to be embarrassed, De Carlo forces Cameron to marry her at the point of a gun. De Carlo and Cameron have a tempestuous wedding night. The next morning Cameron is arrested and sent to prison for six years. Upon release, Cameron returns to the Red Horse Saloon to demand a divorce and finds he's the father of a daugh-

Frontier Gal (1945) scene card: Yvonne De Carlo sings "Set 'Em Up Joe" as saloon patrons and saloon girls watch. *Left border,* Rod Cameron, Yvonne De Carlo.

ter, Beverly Simmons. In prison, Cameron had learned Leonard is the man he's seeking and tells Leonard he is going to kill him. Simmons wants a father, and she and Cameron form an attachment, which culminates in Cameron taking Simmons to his ranch when Leonard places Simmons on the bar and has her sing. DeCarlo wants her daughter back and sends Devine (who is now sheriff), Judge Andrew Tombes and her friend Fuzzy Knight to talk with Cameron. Cameron agrees that a woman is necessary to help raise Simmons, but Cameron is thinking of Wiley while the trio thinks Cameron means De Carlo. De Carlo closes her saloon to go to Cameron's ranch and tells Leonard her plans. De Carlo is upset when she sees Wiley and her aunt, Clara Bundick, at the ranch, but finally decides to discuss the best option for Simmons with Cameron. Desiring that De Carlo live with him, Leonard kidnaps Simmons. Cameron rides in pursuit. De Carlo rides to town to get Sheriff Devine and a posse. Cameron rides into a trap and is captured. Simmons makes a break and is chased by two of Leonard's henchmen onto a dead tree overhanging a raging waterfall. The posse arrives and Leonard attempts a getaway, but Cameron jumps him. The two men fight, and finally a tremendous blow by Cameron knocks Leonard over the cliff onto the rock below. Cameron sees Simmons in danger and rescues her. Finally, Cameron has a chance to tell De Carlo he really loves her. Wiley leaves to return to teaching school.

NOTES AND COMMENTARY: Jon Hall and Maria Montez were originally scheduled to star in *Frontier Gal*. Montez, in particular, was not pleased with the assignment. Both bowed out, giving Rod Cameron and Yvonne De Carlo a chance to advance to stardom. Cameron had starred in a series of "B" westerns for Universal but after *Frontier Gal* would only work in higher budgeted sagebrush sagas. De Carlo quickly became the studio's new Queen of Technicolor. Ironically, Hall would end his association with the studio by appearing in two Cinecolor western features, *Michigan Kid* (Universal, 1947) and *The Vigilantes Return* (Universal, 1947), while Montez would be co-starred with Cameron in the outdoor Technicolor picture *Pirates of Monterey* (Universal, 1947) to terminate her career with Universal.

Stuntwoman Polly Burson began a long illustrious career with this one. Universal wanted a stunt rider for Yvonne De Carlo, and Burson fit the part, as she possessed features very similar to De Carlo's. Burson had been a rodeo trick rider since age thirteen. Burson enjoyed her career, and would leave Hollywood to travel and then return to find jobs waiting for her. Burson once left on a trip around the world; she got as far as New Zealand when she ran out of money and had to return to Hollywood. She stated that this was the only thing she began that she didn't finish.

Kernville was one of the locations chosen to film *Frontier Gal*. Kernville, a small town, is located at the mouth of the Kern River, 125 miles north of Hollywood. The area is known for its picturesque cottonwood trees. In early summer, the cottonwood pods burst, producing a synthetic snowstorm, which was not needed for *Frontier Gal*. When scenes at Kernville were required, location scouts had to determine the period when the cottonwood flew and make certain scenes were completed beforehand.

REVIEWS: "Lusty western feature satire." (*Variety*, 12/5/45); "Fun comedy western; cute little oater that established De Carlo as a star." (*The Motion Picture Guide*, Nash and Ross)

SUMMATION: *Frontier Gal* is a very well done and highly entertaining comedy-drama set in the old west. Make no mistake, it still contains enough action thrills for western fans. Rod Cameron and Yvonne De Carlo make ideal leads and project the right onscreen chemistry. Andy Devine, Andrew Tombes, Fuzzy Knight and Sheldon Leonard lend excellent support. The fine and natural performance of young Beverly Simmons adds tremendously to the movie's enjoyment. Director Charles Lamont offers sturdy direction, and cinematographers George Robinson and Charles P. Boyle capture the glorious scenic backgrounds to add extra luster to the story.

SLAPPIN' LEATHER!
SLINGIN' LEAD!

Frontier Law

Universal (November 1943)

CAST: Jim Warren, **Russell Hayden**; Ramblin' Rufe Randall, **Fuzzy Knight**; Dusty, **Dennis Moore**; Lois Rogers, **Jennifer Holt**; Hawkins, **Jack Ingram**; Rogers, **Hal Taliaferro**; Slinger, **George Eldredge**; Weasel, **I. Stanford Jolley**; Vernon, **Frank LaRue**; Bates, **Jim Farley**; Jack, **Johnny Bond**; and **Johnny Bond's Red River Boys (Paul Sells, Wesley Tuttle** and **Jimmie Dean)**// Ferrell, **Michael Vallon**; Dirk, **Art Fowler**; Coroner, **Earle Hodgins**; Sheriff, **Roy Butler**

CREDITS: Director / Screenwriter, **Elmer Clifton**; Associate Producer, **Oliver Drake**; Editor, **Edgar Zane**; Art Directors, **John B. Goodman** and **Abraham Grossman**; Set Decorators, **R.A. Gausman** and **Lee R. Smith**; Cinematographer, **William Sickner**; Sound, **Bernard B. Brown** and **Jess Moulin**; Musical Director, **Paul Sawtell**

SONGS: "The Bears Give Me the Bird" (Rosen and Carter)—sung by **Fuzzy Knight**; "Call of the Range" (Rosen and Carter)—sung by **Johnny Bond and His Red River Boys**; "Geraldine" (Rosen and Carter)—sung by **Fuzzy Knight, Johnny Bond** and Russell Hayden; "Where the Prairie Meets the Sky" (Rosen and Carter)—sung by **Johnny Bond and His Red River Boys;** and "Call of the Range" (reprise)—sung by **Johnny Bond and His Red River Boys**

LOCATION FILMING: Corriganville, California

RUNNING TIME: 55 min.

STORY: Russell Hayden rides into Toll Gate to find his boyhood pal, Dennis Moore, and persuade him to be his partner in a stageline venture. Both men had been raised to be gunslingers. Hayden has stopped wearing his gun and wants Moore to do the same. Moore has been hired to protect Jack Ingram, head of the Stockman's Protective Association. Ingram is instigating a range war between the cattlemen and sheepmen, so that when an all-out range war starts he and his men can rustle both cattle and sheep. Sheepman Hal Taliaferro shoots Ingram's partner, Michael Vallon. Jennifer Holt, Taliaferro's daughter, persuades Taliaferro to hide out until a fair trail can be insured. Holt and Hayden can testify that Taliaferro killed Vallon in self-defense. Ingram holds an inquest without notifying Holt and Hayden, and a warrant is issued against Taliaferro for murder. Hayden decides to get to the bottom of the trouble and clear Taliaferro's name. Moore advises Hayden to start packing his gun. After breaking into Ingram's office, Hayden finds a clue to Ingram's rustling activities. With cattleman Jim Farley and sheepman Frank LaRue at his side, Hayden finds proof that Ingram has been the instigator of the friction between the two factions. Hayden rides to see Moore, and finds that Moore has captured Taliaferro and is taking him to jail. Moore, true to a gunslinger's code, refuses to change sides as long he's not being double-crossed. George Eldredge, one of Ingram's hirelings, incites the cattlemen in town to lynch Taliaferro. When Moore tries to stop the mob, Ingram holds Moore prisoner. When Hayden reaches town, he finds it's time to strap on his gun. At the point of outlaw guns, Moore is forced to face Hayden in a showdown. Moore tries to warn Hayden. Hayden, not comprehending, wings Moore in the arm. With the cattlemen and sheepmen behind Hayden, Ingram tries to escape and is brought to justice by Hayden. Moore decides to become Hayden's partner in the stage line, which will run to Toll Gate so Hayden and Holt can get together.

NOTES AND COMMENTARY: At the Western Film Festival in Charlotte, Wesley Tuttle recalled how he was almost killed in the production of *Frontier Law*. Tuttle, Russell Hayden and some others were riding into town with men behind bales of hay shooting at them. Hayden and Tuttle were riding side-by-side. Tuttle comments, "The fellow on my right tried to rein his horse to the left. He shouldn't have done that because that horse hit me right in the temple with his head, the bit and everything, and knocked me cold. The horse went down. The horse went over me, thank goodness. The next thing I knew I'm lying flat on the ground, my leg back under my back and my head in Russell Hayden's lap, [with Hayden] taking care of me."

Tex Ritter was originally scheduled to star in *Frontier Law*. Shortly before filming began, Ritter fell from the second story loft in his barn. Ritter was feeding his horses, and instead of pushing the hay to the chutes, he was pulling the bale when the hook slipped past the wire. Ritter fell, landing on his left hip and thigh, sustaining torn ligaments and muscles. Associate Producer Oliver Drake had the picture ready to go and wasn't able to delay the start. Russell Hayden, "Lucky" from the Hopalong Cassidy series and his own series at Columbia, was signed to take Ritter's place. His contract with Universal stated that he would be used in other films, and he received subsequently a co-starring role with Ritter in *Marshal of Gunsmoke* (Universal, 1944), and the male lead in the serial *Lost City of the Jungle* (Universal, 1945).

The working title for this film was *Gunfighters*.

"The Bears Give Me the Bird" was sung by Fuzzy Knight in an earlier film, *Bury Me Not on the Lone Prairie* (Universal, 1941). The Eddie Dean Trio sang "Geraldine" in *Fighting Bill Fargo* (Universal, 1941). "Call of the Range" was first heard in *Man from Montana* (Universal, 1941), and would sung again in *Beyond the Pecos* (Universal, 1945) and *Gunman's Code* (Universal, 1946). "Where the Prairie Meets the Sky" can, also, be heard in *Bad Man from Red Butte* (Universal, 1940), *Escape From Hong Kong* (Universal, 1942), *Twilight on the Prairie* (Universal, 1944) and *I'll Tell the World* (Universal, 1945).

The Red River Boys' Jimmie Dean was the brother of the PRC singing cowboy star Eddie Dean.

REVIEWS: "Fair Universal programmer." (*Western Movies*, Pitts)

SUMMATION: Action ace Russell Hayden is taking over where he left off in his thrilling Columbia series—fighting, riding and shooting in a fast moving "B" western saga. Fuzzy Knight's comedy is more on the juvenile side, but his bit with villain Stan Jolley at the end will give the audience an honest laugh. Dennis Moore is fine as Hayden's gunslinging pal, but one could only wish his part had been expanded to allow greater characterization between Moore and Hayden. On the whole, Director Elmer Clifton penned a nifty screenplay. A most satisfying "B" western.

With flaming shooting irons ... swinging fists ... whirlwind riding
HE SMASHED THE VARMINTS!

Ghost Town Riders

Universal (December 1938)

CAST: Bob, **Bob Baker**; Molly, Fay Shannon; Cherokee, **Hank Worden**; Judge, **George Cleveland**; Gomer, **Forrest Taylor**; Tex, **Glenn Strange**; Slim, **Jack Kirk**; Rosebud, **Martin Turner**; Fred, **Reed Howes**; Tax Collector, **Murdock MacQuarrie**// Chad, **Chuck Baldra**; Marshal, **Bob Burns**; Townsman, **Horace B. Carpenter**; Wagon Owner, **Dick Dickinson**; Cal, **Frank Ellis**; Bud, **Merrill McCormick**; Ma, **Eva McKenzie**; Jose, **George Morrell**

CREDITS: Director, **George Waggner**; Assistant Director, **Glenn Cook**; Story/Screenwriter, **Joseph West**; Editor, **Carl Pierson**; Technical Director, **Albert Greenwood**; Cinematographer, **Harry Neumann**; Sound, **Bernard B. Brown and Joe Lapis**; Musical Director and Arranger, **Frank Sanucci**; Vocal Accompaniment, **The Texas Rangers**

SONGS: "Headin' Home" (Allan) —sung by **Bob Baker and The Texas Rangers**; "It Ain't So Rosy on the Range" (Allan)—sung by **Bob Baker, Hank Worden and The Texas Rangers;** and "Down That Old Home Trail" (Allan)—sung by **Bob Baker and The Texas Rangers**

LOCATION FILMING: Iverson and Brandeis Ranch, California

RUNNING TIME: 54 min.

STORY: Outlaws led by Forrest Taylor have taken over the ghost town of Stillwell. The lone inhabitant, George Cleveland, pretends to be mentally unbalanced to avoid giving Taylor the location of a gold mine. Taylor plans to buy the town, actually owned by Fay Shannon, for back taxes and spread a rumor of a gold strike to bring the town back to life. Bob Baker, trailherding horses to be sold, and his men stop at the town to rest for a few days. Shannon, down on her luck, shows up, hoping to find the town well and prosperous. Taylor tries to send Baker on his way, and when that fails, takes Baker and his sidekick, Hank Worden, prisoner. Cleveland frees the two men, and Baker learns about Taylor's scheme to control the town. Cleveland gives Baker enough gold to pay the back taxes. The outlaws are unsuccessful in preventing Baker from saving the town for Shannon. Baker goes back to Stillwell and brings Taylor to justice. Baker plans to return to Stillwell and Shannon after he delivers the horses.

NOTES AND COMMENTARY: Fay McKenzie (billed here as Fay Shannon) talked about westerns at Universal and said, "I had done a few westerns, independents, Poverty Row." About *Ghost Town Riders,* Fay McKenzie remembered, "The director was George Waggner. I went on an interview for the part. You want so much to get the role.

120 GHOST TOWN RIDERS

Ghost Town Riders (1938) scene card: Bob Baker (*center*) is held by Glenn Strange (*right*) and an unidentified actor, as Forrest Taylor (*left*) gloats. ***Left border***, Bob Baker.

You try to think about anything you can do that would make you stand out to the director. I had a very dear girl friend, who was his niece. She and I had been in student tour at M-G-M together and had gone to school together on the M-G-M lot. We had become real chums. I thought, I'll tell him that. Maybe he'll like me. I did do it. I said, 'I believe you're Maxine's uncle.' He said, 'You say my face is awful.' We cleared it up. They shot six at this time, maybe three. The leading women for Bob Baker were Marjorie Reynolds and Marge Champion (Marjorie Bell). Margie Bell and I have been like sisters since the 3rd grade. She, now, is still dancing, and she's in *Follies* on Broadway. I've seen the show three times. She's wonderful."

McKenzie recalled, "It seems to me there was a comedy character in it that was an African-American actor [Martin Turner]. He did the comedy in this thing. My sister went with me to a theater where it was playing. It was largely an African-American audience. It was such fun. They really enjoyed the movie. I was in a fight to save my life, and the leading man [Bob Baker] said, 'Are you all right?' Someone said, 'She's all right but look at that poor guy [villain Forrest Taylor, who lost a fist fight to Baker].'"

On parenthood in the "B" western, Fay McKenzie said, "Leading ladies in westerns have fathers. I've had some wonderful character actors play my father. You never have a mother. Very rarely does the lady have a mother. You always have a nice stalwart dad. I had some wonderful dads in my western movie career."

McKenzie remarked, "Here's a funny one. Bob Baker, the first day of shooting, came over. I hadn't even met him yet. I'm on my horse. He came over and shortened my stirrup for me because it was too long. I said, 'Oh, thank you.' He said, 'That's all right, ma'am. That's how I got my start, wrangling dudes.'"

Fay McKenzie was billed as Fay Shannon in *Ghost Town Riders*. McKenzie remembered, "I used it for a very brief time. My brother-in-law was Billy Gilbert. For some reason, he thought Fay Shannon would be a good name for me. He didn't think Fay McKenzie was going to work on the marquee. That was the only time I made a film and used that. I know I sang somewhere. He, also, did the publicity: 'Fay Shannon, the cutest little tunest.' That was the corniest, the worst. It's hysterical I ever did this."

Screenwriter Joseph West is a pseudonym for director George Waggner.

Ghost Town Riders was a remake of Tom Mix's *The Fourth Horseman* (Universal, 1932), and was remade again as a Tex Williams featurette, *Gold Strike* (Universal-International, 1950).

REVIEWS: "Pretty good Bob Baker series entry." (*Western Movies*, Pitts)

SUMMATION: Another pleasant and slightly above average western feature, *Ghost Town Riders* offers an exciting chase between Bob Baker and the outlaws. Baker makes a good western hero, and this screenplay allows him to engage in two fistic encounters with villain Forrest Taylor. Fay McKenzie (billed as Shannon in this opus) delivers an engaging and sprightly performance as the "southern damsel in distress." George Cleveland, Hank Worden and Taylor head a fine supporting cast. Again, the major knock on the Baker screenwriters is the lack of tough action, which was needed to move Baker to the upper echelon of Western Stars.

The Year's Greatest Serial!
12 Super Chapters packed with WILD THRILLS!

Gordon of Ghost City

Universal (August 1933)

CAST: Buck Gordon, **Buck Jones**; Mary Gray, **Madge Bellamy**; Rance Radigan, **Walter Miller**; Amos Gray, **Tom Ricketts**; John Mulford, **William Desmond**; The Mystery Man, **Francis Ford**; Scotty, **Edmund Cobb**; Ed Roberts, **Hugh Enfield**; Hank, **Bud Osborne**; Pete, **Ethan Laidlaw**; and "Silver"// Jeff, **Jim Corey**; Tucson Charley, **Frank Ellis**; Pat Campbell, **Tom London**; Sheriff, **Dick Rush**; Bob, **William Steele**; Bill Simpson, **Lafe McKee**; Medicine Salesman, **Harry Todd**; Renegade Indian Chief, **Jim Thorpe**; Mort, **Cecil Kellogg**; Mike, **Merrill McCormick**; Mort, **Charles Royal**; Jed Wilson, **Buck Connors**

CREDITS: Director, **Ray Taylor**; Associate Producer, **Henry MacRae**; Story, **Peter B. Kyne**; Screenwriters, **Ella O'Neill, George H. Plympton, Basil Dickey, Het Manheim** and **Harry Hoyt**; Editors, **Alvin Todd** and **Frank Gross**; Art Director, **Thomas F. O'Neill**; Cinematographer, **John Hickson**

LOCATION FILMING: Bronson Canyon, California

RUNNING TIME: 235 min.

SOURCE: Story 'Oh, Promise Me!' by **Peter B. Kyne**

CHAPTER TITLES: 1. A Lone Hand, 2. The Stampede, 3. Trapped, 4. The Man of Mystery, 5. Riding for Life, 6. Blazing Prairies, 7. Entombed in the Tunnel, 8. Stampede, 9. Flames of Fury, 10. Swimming the Torrent, 11. A Wild Ride, 12. Mystery of Ghost City

STORY: Cattle rustlers have been plaguing William Desmond's ranch. Desmond's foreman, Walter Miller, is responsible for the rustling activity. A drifter, Buck Jones, brings in two of the rustlers and is hired by Desmond to bring in the rest of the gang. A clue leads Jones to the supposedly deserted town of Ghost City. At Ghost City, Jones finds Madge Bellamy. A mystery man, Francis Ford, leaves a note on Bellamy's saddle warning her to stay out of Ghost City. Bellamy brings Jones home to meet her father, Tom Ricketts. Ricketts owns a gold mine in Ghost City. Years earlier, Ricketts was crippled and his partner killed in a mine explosion. The entrance to the mine is through a store in Ghost City. Jones agrees to help the two retain their mine. Rustlers capture Jones and Bellamy. With Silver's help, Jones gets the drop on the rustlers. Jones turns the rustlers over to Miller to take back to Desmond's ranch. Miller lets the rustlers escape. Miller, wanting to obtain the gold mine, sends men to kidnap Bellamy at Ghost City. Jones rides to the ghost town and sees Bellamy being threatened. In creeping up on the outlaws in the store, the floor gives way and Jones is

Gordon of Ghost City (1933) title card: *Left*, Buck Jones, Madge Bellamy; *upper right*, Buck Jones on Silver.

plunged into a deep well. Ford shoots at the badmen, forcing them to leave town. Bellamy helps Jones escape from the well. Miller, desperate to locate the gold, sets off some dynamite, and almost kills Jones and Bellamy. Miller makes many unsuccessful attempts to rustle Desmond's cattle and to get Jones out of the way. Jones obtains proof that Miller is behind the outlawry. Realizing Desmond knows he's the outlaw leader, Miller retreats to his hideout. Jones leads a posse to the hideout. The gang is rounded up, but Miller tries to make a getaway. Miller rides to Ghost City, followed by Jones. In Ghost City, Miller and Ford exchange shots. Miller is killed and Ford wounded. Jones takes the wounded man to Ricketts' ranch. Ford's wounds help him regain his memory, and Ford turns out to be Ricketts' lost partner. With the opening of the gold mine, Ghost City will now become a boom town. Jones and Bellamy, having fallen in love, decide to get married.

NOTES AND COMMENTARY: In 1933 Buck Jones was under contract to make series westerns for Columbia Pictures. At this time, Columbia did not have a serial department and allowed Henry MacRae to sign Jones for *Gordon of Ghost City*, Universal's summer serial for 1933.

Later in his career, Hugh Enfield would be billed as Craig Reynolds.

The screenwriters gave Buck Jones an interesting and funny line of dialogue. Talking to badman Jim Corey, Jones retorts, "I'd rock you to sleep, if I had a rock."

In Chapter eight, to match stock footage, Buck Jones does not ride Silver.

REVIEWS: "Fast paced and highly entertaining cliffhanger." (*Western Movies*, Pitts)

SUMMATION: *Gordon of Ghost City* is a very good serial with some good cliffhanger endings; unfortunately, it's also marred by a few weak cliffhanger resolutions. Buck Jones is perfect as the stalwart hero, and Madge Bellamy is well cast as the attractive heroine. Walter Miller, William Desmond and Tom Ricketts are especially fine in the good supporting cast. Director Ray Taylor paces the story nicely, with good results.

CRIME-CRACKERS VS KLONDIKE KILLERS!
...*with the world's most dangerous secret the prize!*

The Great Alaskan Mystery

Universal (January 1944)

ALTERNATE TITLE: The Great Northern Mystery

CAST: Jim Hudson, **Milburn Stone**; Ruth Miller, **Marjorie Weaver**; Bosun, **Edgar Kennedy**; Herman Brock, **Samuel S. Hinds**; Doctor Hauss, **Martin Kosleck**; Doctor Miller, **Ralph Morgan**; Bill Hudson, **Joseph Crehan**; "Grit" Hartman, **Fuzzy Knight**; Captain Greeder, **Harry Cording**; Brandon, **Anthony Warde**; Dunn, **Jack Clifford**; Grey, **William Ruhl**; Haegle, **Perc Launders**; Kurtz, **Edward Gargan**; Eskimo Chief, **Jay Norvello**; Burger, **Richard Powers**// Marshal, **Edmund Cobb**; Spy at Mine, **Ray Bennett**; Kessel, **Jack Rockwell**; Deputy Marshall, **Ben Taggart**

CREDITS: Directors, **Ray Taylor** and **Lewis D. Collins**; Associate Producer, Henry MacRae; Story, Jack Foley; Screenwriters, Maurice Tombragel and George H. Plympton; Supervising Editor, **Norman A. Cerf**; Editors, **Alvin Todd, Edgar Zane, Irving Birnbaum, Jack Dolan** and **Ace Herman**; Art Director, Ralph M. DeLacy; Dialogue Director, **Jacques Jaccard**; Cinematographers, **William Sickner** and **Harry Neumann**

LOCATION FILMING: Iverson, California

RUNNING TIME: 225 min.

CHAPTER TITLES: 1. Shipwrecked Among Icebergs, 2. Thundering Doom, 3. Battle in the Clouds, 4. Masked Murder, 5. The Bridge of

Disaster, 6. Shattering Doom, 7. Crashing Timbers, 8. In a Flaming Plane, 9. Hurtling Through Space, 10. Tricked by a Booby Trap, 11. The Tunnel of Terror, 12. Electrocuted, 13. The Boomerang

STORY: Dr. Ralph Morgan has invented a revolutionary ray gun, the Peratron, which he hopes can be used to transmit matter. The device needs a powerful radioactive mineral to make it work. Recently discharged from the service due to medical reasons, Milburn Stone suggests Morgan travel to his father Joseph Crehan's mine in Alaska to see if undefined quartz will work. Morgan's assistant, Martin Kosleck, is working with a spy network that is planning to steal Dr. Morgan's invention. Traveling by ship to Alaska, Stone, Morgan and Seaman Edgar Kennedy are left to drown when the vessel strikes an iceberg. Stone and his friends make it to an iceberg. Pilot Marjorie Weaver, Morgan's daughter and Stone's girlfriend, saves the group when she spots them and brings help in time. In Alaska Stone seeks assistance from Samuel S. Hinds, the secret head of the spy ring. Repeatedly failing to eliminate Stone, Hinds' henchman, Anthony Warde, steals the Peratron, which now proves to be a weapon of mass destruction. During another failed attempt to kill him, Stone stumbles upon the henchmen's hideout. In a pitched gun battle, Stone retrieves the Peratron. Hinds makes a final attempt to obtain the ray gun. He has Kosleck blow up a mineshaft with the Peratron, again failing to kill Stone, while Warde and his men raid the mine. Warde's men are discovered. In a pitched gunfight, all the hijackers are killed. Stone then decides it would be safer to ship the Peratron back to the States. Kosleck gains possession of the ray gun and goes straight to Hinds' office. In opening the box supposedly containing the Peratron, Hinds and Kosleck find only rocks. Stone, Weaver and Kennedy bust into the office. Hinds places all the blame on Kosleck, who retaliates by shooting Hinds. Kosleck is arrested. Weaver tells Stone it's time they got married, and Stone agrees.

NOTES AND COMMENTARY: *The Great Alaskan Mystery* utilized footage of a plane landing in fog from *Sky Raiders* (Universal, 1941), and logging operations and the cliffhanger ending from *Timber* (Universal, 1942). Most of the footage for Chapters two and three came from the German film *White Hell of Pitz Palu* (Universal, 1930).

In the cliffhanger ending for Chapter nine, Anthony Warde fires multiple shots as Milburn Stone is carried along by some river rapids. The resolution shows Warde firing one shot and Stone falling in relatively calm waters.

Chapter 10 clearly shows Milburn Stone's foot touching the booby-trapped step, setting off the explosion. The resolution has Edgar Kennedy throwing a heavy sack on the step, with Kennedy and Stone being in a separate part of the cave, sheltering them from the dynamite blast.

As Chapter 12 comes to a close, Milburn Stone, Marjorie Weaver,

Joseph Crehan and Fuzzy Knight are ascending in the mine elevator when the Peratron ray blasts the mine shaft. The resolution shows the group still on a lower level when the mine shaft is blasted. Knight finds a convenient alternate route to bring them safely to the surface.

After the explosion, two hijackers return to make certain Stone was killed. A shot repeated from Chapter nine shows Stone waiting for raiders with a rifle; but when the raiders come closer, the only weapon Stone possesses is a pistol.

Milburn Stone was best know for his role of Doc Galen Adams in the long running television series *Gunsmoke* (CBS).

REVIEWS: "Actionful wartime cliffhanger." (*Western Movies*, Pitts)

SUMMATION: *The Great Alaskan Mystery* is an above average serial, due primarily to the performances of leading man Milburn Stone and comedians Edgar Kennedy and Fuzzy Knight, both of whom deliver more thoughtful characterizations than seen in most serials. Marjorie Weaver is a standout as the leading lady and Stone's love interest. Drawbacks include the two cheat endings used for the cliffhanger resolutions for Chapters nine and 10.

A SINGING COW PUNCHER ... TURNED SWINGING MAN-PUNCHER!
He sings as softly as a summer breeze ... but swings like a tornado!

Guilty Trails

Universal (October 1938)

CAST: Bob, **Bob Baker**; Jackie, **Marjorie Reynolds**; Sundown, **Hal Taliaferro**; Martha, **Georgia O'Dell**; Brad, **Jack Rockwell**; Steve, **Carleton Young**; Dan, **Forrest Taylor**; Sheriff, **Glenn Strange**; Judge, **Murdock MacQuarrie**; Stage Driver, **Jack Kirk**// Red Eagle, **Bill Hazlett**; Greasy, **Tom London**, Stage Driver, **Jimmy Phelps**; Indian Mother, **Evelyn Selbie**

CREDITS: Director, **George Waggner**; Assistant Director, **Glenn Cook**; Story/Screenwriter, **Joseph West**; Editor, **Carl Pierson**; Technical Director, **Albert Greenwood**; Cinematography, **Gus Peterson**; Sound, **Bernard B. Brown** and **Robert Pritchard**; Musical Director/Arranger, **Frank Sanucci**

SONGS: "Song of the Trail" (Allan)—sung by **Bob Baker**; "Ring Around the Moon" (Allan)—sung by **Bob Baker**; "Home on the Plains" (Allan)—sung by **Bob Baker and male chorus**; and "Song of the Trail" (Allan)—sung by **Marjorie Reynolds and chorus**

LOCATION FILMING: Walker Ranch and Andy Jauregui Ranch, California

RUNNING TIME: 57 min.

STORY: Banker Jack Rockwell stages a fake bank robbery with the help of cowhand Carleton Young. Sheriff Bob Baker and his friend, Hal Taliaferro, pursue the fleeing Young.

Rockwell has Young ride to a spot where he can cover Young's trail. On the trail, Young's boss, Forrest Taylor, recognizes him. Seeing this, Rockwell shoots Taylor. Taylor is a good friend of Baker's and has just paid off his note on his ranch at the bank. Rockwell seizes the opportunity to switch wallets with Taylor, still keeping a note on Taylor's ranch. Baker and Taliaferro arrive on the scene and exchange shots with Rockwell. Rockwell escapes, and Baker finds Taylor's body and assumes one of his bullets killed Taylor. Remorseful over Taylor's death, Baker resigns as sheriff. Taliaferro takes charge of Taylor's ranch but needs Baker's help when Taylor's son is scheduled to arrive from the East. Baker soon finds Taylor's "son" is pretty Marjorie Reynolds. Rockwell has sent Reynolds a letter stating that ten thousand is due, and that he can find a buyer for the ranch. Baker convinces Reynolds to stay and round up enough cattle to pay off the debt. A rustling attempt leads Baker to suspect Rockwell, and Young is somehow implicated. Baker works on Young, and when Young finally begins to confess, Rockwell shoots him. Accused by Baker of shooting Young, Rockwell retaliates by telling Reynolds that Baker shot her father. Reynolds decides to sell and go back east. Baker obtains evidence that Rockwell is an embezzler. Rockwell's men rustle Reynolds' cattle. Baker sends for the sheriff and trails the herd. Rockwell gets the drop on Baker and is set to shoot him when the posse arrives. Rockwell is distracted by the posse, and Baker starts a fight with Rockwell. The posse rounds up the rustlers, while Baker brings Rockwell to justice. Baker stops Reynolds from leaving the west.

NOTES AND COMMENTARY: Universal had problems with the title of this film. On screen the title is *Guilty Trails*, while the title card tells us its *Guilty Trail*.

Bill Hazlett's character name is referred to as both Red Cloud and Red Eagle in the screenplay. In his career Hazlett was also billed as Chief Many Treaties.

Guilty Trails is a remake of John Wayne's *Texas Terror* (Lone Star/Monogram, 1934).

Bob Baker originally sang "Song of the Trail" in his first starring film, *Courage of the West* (Universal, 1937).

Jack Kirk receives billing as a stage driver but is not seen in the film.

Joseph West is a pseudonym for director George Waggner.

REVIEWS: "Bob Baker followers have a good story and the whole shooteree is a little classier than some of the past tries." (*Variety*, 10/26/38); "Pretty fair Bob Baker vehicle." (*Western Movies*, Pitts)

SUMMARY: *Guilty Trails* is a pleasant, above average western with sufficient action. Bob Baker makes a good impression as an easygoing cowboy who delivers the action goods. Hal Taliaferro registers strongly as his savvy sidekick. Marjorie Reynolds adds a pretty presence as Baker's love interest, and Jack Rockwell capably handles the villainy. The story is well directed by George Waggner from his own screenplay.

Fighting Ken drifts in among the gang that's trying to chisel a ranch—
AND OH, BOY!

Gun Justice

Universal (December 1933); A Ken Maynard Production

CAST: Ken Lance, **Ken Maynard;** Ray Marsh, **Cecilia Parker;** Sam Burkett, **Hooper Atchley**; Chris Hogan, **Walter Miller**; Jones, **William Gould**; Hank Rivers, **Jack Rockwell**; Lawyer, **Sheldon Lewis**; Denver, **Ed Brady**; Imposter, **Fred MacKaye**; Red Hogan, **Bill Dyer**; Sheriff, **Jack Richardson**; Jim Lance, **Ed Coxen**; Postmaster, **Lafe McKee**; and "Tarzan"// Miner, **Horace B. Carpenter**; Heavy Man at Slot Machine, **Robert McKenzie**; Hogan Outlaw, **Ben Corbett**; Cowhands, **Hank Bell** and **Pascale Perry**

CREDITS: Director, **Alan James**; Screenwriter, **Robert Quigley**; Editor, **Charles Harris**; Art Director, **Nate Gatzert**; Cinematographer, **Ted McCord**; Sound Supervisor, **Earl Crain**

LOCATION FILMING: Kernville, California

RUNNING TIME: 59 min.

STORY: An unknown assailant murders Ed Coxen. Coxen's will leaves his ranch to Ken Maynard and Cecilia Parker. The ranch will go to Coxen's mortal enemies, Hooper Atchley and Walter Miller, if Maynard is unable to hold on to the ranch. Atchley and Miller want Coxen's ranch because of Narrow Pass, which would aid them in driving their cattle to market. Maynard left the ranch as a child, and no one knows what he looks like or how to get in touch with him. Atchley has his foreman Ed Brady's brother, Fred MacKaye, impersonate Maynard. Maynard overhears MacKaye asking directions to Coxen's ranch and follows him to miner Horace B. Carpenter's site, where he makes MacKaye a prisoner in Carpenter's cabin. Reaching town, Maynard meets Parker at the hotel and the two begin to fall in love. Atchley finds the two and makes an offer for the ranch. Maynard acts like he would be interested in selling. Not really interested in selling, Maynard just wants to see how bad Atchley wants the ranch. As Maynard leaves the hotel, Miller tells Maynard he's taking five hundred head of cattle through Narrow Pass. Maynard plans to stop Miller, by force if necessary, with the help of Coxen's ranch hands. Carpenter has released MacKaye. Atchley tells Sheriff Jack Richardson that MacKaye is the legitimate heir and Maynard is the impostor. Richardson is unable to arrest Maynard. Maynard rides to Narrow Pass to stop Miller. Atchley sends Brady to the pass to ambush both Maynard and Miller. Brady is successful in shooting Miller, but his second shot misses Maynard. Maynard chases Brady but runs into Richardson and is captured. Richardson discovers that Maynard is a Texas

Ranger assigned to track down Coxen's murderer. Meanwhile, MacKaye convinces Parker to go to the hotel in town and see William Gould, another buyer for the ranch. Gould is working for Atchley. Parker finally decides that she will not sell. Maynard catches up to Brady at the hotel and persuades Brady to name Coxen's murderer. Brady implicates Atchley. Atchley takes a bead on Maynard but is shot by Richardson. MacKaye and Gould are arrested. Maynard and Parker embrace.

NOTES AND COMMENTARY: Universal previously used the title *Gun Justice* in 1927 for a Fred Gilman two-reel western directed by William Wyler.

A Big Little Book novelization of *Gun Justice* was published by the Whitman Publishing Company as a children's book and a movie tie-in.

REVIEWS: "Ken Maynard also produced this fairly actionful drama." (*Western Movies*, Pitts); "An absorbing sagebrush item, fast, actionful and to the point." (*Variety*, 4/3/34)

SUMMATION: *Gun Justice* is another above average entry in the Ken Maynard Universal series. Maynard impresses as the valiant hero. Cecilia Parker makes a very attractive heroine and is very effective as the part owner of the ranch. The supporting cast acquit themselves adequately. Alan James' direction keeps the story moving well to its satisfactory conclusion. Special mention should be made of Ted McCord's photography, which greatly enhances the proceedings.

TERROR ON THE WARPATH!

Gun Town

Universal (January 1946)

CAST: Kip Lewis, **Kirby Grant**; Ivory, **Fuzzy Knight**; Lucky Dorgan, **Lyle Talbot**; Belle Townley, **Claire Carleton**; "Buckskin" Jane Sawyer, **Louise Currie**; Davey Sawyer, **Gene Garrick**; Sheriff, **Earle Hodgins**; Nevada, **Ray Bennett**; Joe, **Dan White**// Saloon Patron, **Tex Cooper**

CREDITS: Director / Producer, **Wallace W. Fox**; Screenwriter, **William Lively**; Editor, **Ray Snyder**; Art Direction, **John B. Goodman** and **Abraham Grossman**; Set Decorators, **Russell A. Gausman** and **Arthur D. Leddy**; Cinematography, **Maury Gertsman**; Sound, **Bernard B. Brown** and **Vernon W. Kramer**; Musical Director, **Mark Levant**

SONGS: "A Cowboy is Happy" (Carter and Rosen)—sung by **Claire Carleton** and **Fuzzy Knight**; and "I Just Got In" (Berens and Brooks)—sung by **Claire Carleton**

LOCATION FILMING: Iverson and Red Rock Canyon, California

RUNNING TIME: 53 min.

STORY: Saloon owner Lyle Talbot

leads a gang of outlaws who masquerade as Indians and steal payroll shipments intended for Louise Currie's stage line. Currie has to complete a stage road by a certain date or lose the contract. Another stage is held up, and driver Fuzzy Knight is knocked out. The horses and driverless stage are running away when Kirby Grant boards the stage and brings the horses to a stop. Ray Bennett and Dan White, Talbot's henchmen, get the drop on Grant and blame him for the robbery. In Gun Town, the outlaws incite a mob to lynch Grant. Currie, who had seen the robbery, exonerates Grant. Claire Carleton, a passenger on the coach, arrives to help Talbot by enticing the stage line workers to stay off the job. Currie's younger brother, Gene Garrick, is the Wells Fargo agent. Falling for Carlton, Garrick inadvertently tells Carleton the date of the next payroll shipment. Talbot and his men, disguised as Indians, attack the stagecoach. Grant, Currie and a posse are waiting and drive off the holdup men. Grant chases Talbot but is rendered unconscious when he hits the ground after bulldogging Talbot from his saddle. Talbot escapes but leaves behind a matchbox belonging to Garrick. Grant questions Garrick, who states he lost the matchbox. Garrick goes to Talbot's

Gun Town (1946) scene card: Kirby Grant (*left*) talks with Louise Currie and her brother, Gene Garrick.

office and learns that Talbot is behind Currie's problems. Talbot ambushes Garrick. Before Garrick dies, he tells Grant that Talbot shot him. Grant confronts Talbot. The two men fight, with Grant the victor. Carleton hits Grant from behind, and Talbot and Carleton escape. Grant finds the stolen payroll money and has it locked up in the Wells Fargo safe. Talbot incites the Indians to attack Gun Town while he and his men loot the Wells Fargo office. The Indians attack. Grant and Currie see Talbot and a henchman enter the Wells Fargo office. There's a gun battle in the Wells Fargo office. Grant shoots the henchman, and Talbot is about to fire at Grant when a bullet from Currie's pistol ends Talbot's lawless career. Gun Town is in flames, and the victorious Indians ride away. Grant tells Currie Gun Town can be rebuilt, and she'll receive an extension on the stage contract. Grant plans to stay and help Currie.

NOTES AND COMMENTARY: Louise Currie commented on *Gun Town*, "I liked it very much. It was probably my favorite because it gave me something to do. As an actress in a western, you're usually hanging on a fence waving good bye and doing nothing but smiling. It this case, I was able to be active. I had to learn to manage all those horses, driving in on a buckboard, and that was a feat because I didn't think I could ever learn that. That took a lot of nerve and a lot of courage and verve. My life had been so different. I had been educated in Washington and New York. I wasn't very western. It was a whole new twist to my career. Then I had to learn to do the bullwhip. That certainly was not in my domain. That was an enlightening and amusing thing for me to have to do. I had to be proficient enough in order to make it look real in order for me to rescue the hero. It was very educational for me, in a different sense of the word. It was a whole new something that I could learn to do and add something to my career. That's why I really enjoyed that film so much."

Louise Currie remembered Lyle Talbot from seeing him in a play when she was growing up in Oklahoma City, and said, "I was admiring his work in that. Little did I know, at that age, I would ever be in Hollywood and playing in a western movie with him as one of the leading men and I as one of the leading ladies. I had never seen him in the interim until we met in that movie."

On Kirby Grant, Louise Currie said, "He was wonderful. He was a very, very attractive man. He had everything as far as a western star should have. I'm surprised he didn't attain more stardom than he did."

Louise Currie said of Fuzzy Knight, "He was the character of all characters. He could not do anything but a fine performance. He was so into his own characterization. He was incredibly good, always."

Louise Currie remarked on her career, "I adored it. It was more amusing to me to do the way I did. I was able to do so many [parts], so quickly and have such variety. The girls that were signed into contracts at different studios would sit there as starlets, doing nothing. Of course, some went on to big stardom. My career was so completely different; I just played one [part] after another. It was a very productive and interesting career. The big film, like *Citizen Kane* [RKO, 1941], I was on that film for three months and have about three words to say the whole film. Alan Ladd and I were in the scene in the very end of *Citizen Kane*. It, originally, was rather a nice little scene but they cut it and cut it so now it's kind of nothing. I could have done ten of my movies in that length of time. That was so indicative of a big production film. It was tedious, sitting there that long because there was so little to occupy your mind. I don't think working for those films would have ever interested me."

Gun Town is a loose remake of *Badlands of Dakota* (Universal, 1941). Footage from that film is used in the opening holdup sequence, the attack on the stage by renegade whites and the counterattack by Grant and his posse (look closely to see Robert Stack, Frances Farmer and Richard Dix), and the finale when Indians raid Gun Town and the renegades attempt to rob the Wells Fargo office.

"A Cowboy Is Happy" had been heard in *Rawhide Rangers* (Universal, 1941) and *Cowboy in Manhattan* (Universal, 1943). "I Just Got In" was used in *Frisco Sal* (Universal, 1945).

REVIEWS: "Fair western." (*Variety*, 3/20/46); "Compact Kirby Grant series vehicle with fine villainous work by Lyle Talbot." (*Western Movies*, Pitts)

SUMMATION: *Gun Town* is a good "B" western. Universal uses a lot of stock footage from *Badlands of Dakota* to give the film production values it otherwise wouldn't have. Grant is on target as the Indian Agent trying to find who's behind the stagecoach, holdups and Fuzzy Knight makes a good, savvy sidekick. The acting honors go to Louise Currie as a "Calamity Jane" frontierswoman and Lyle Talbot as a gang leader with a streak of yellow. Wallace W. Fox directs confidently from a good script by William Lively and comes up with a winner. It's to the film's credit that it is eschewed the usual Fuzzy Knight concluding pratfall, which would have broken the appropriately somber mood.

Six-Gun Fury!
Guns A-blazing...

Gunman's Code

Universal (August 1946)

CAST: Jack Douglas, **Kirby Grant**; Boscoe O'Toole, **Fuzzy Knight**; Laura Burton, **Jane Adams**; Lee Payne, **Danny Morton**; Donny Burton, **Bernard Thomas**; Sam Burton, **Charles Miller**; Ben Lewis, **Karl Hackett**; Trigger, **Frank McCarroll**

CREDITS: Director / Producer, **Wallace W. Fox**; Story, **Sherman Lowe** and **Arthur St. Claire**; Screenwriter, **William Lively**; Editor, **D. Patrick Kelly**; Art Director, **Jack Otterson** and **Frank A. Richards**; Set Decorators, **Russell A. Gausman** and **Kenneth Swartz**; Cinematographer, **Maury Gertsman**; Gowns, **Rosemary Odell**; Hair Stylist, **Carmen Dirigo**; Makeup, **Jack P. Pierce**; Sound, **Bernard B. Brown** and **Jess Moulin**; Musical Director / Musical Score, **Milton Rosen**

SONGS: "Those Happy Old Days" (Carter and Rosen)—sung by **Fuzzy Knight**; "The Door of Your Heart" (Carter and Rosen)—sung by **Kirby Grant**; and "Call of the Range" (Rosen and Carter)—sung by **Kirby Grant**

LOCATION FILMING: Iverson, California

RUNNING TIME: 57 min.

STORY: Outlaws Danny Morton, Bernard Thomas and Frank McCarroll hold up the stagecoach, killing the driver and guard and taking the strongbox. In turn, Kirby Grant and Fuzzy Knight take the strongbox from Thomas and McCarroll. Grant and Knight return the money to the bank after taking a $4000 reward, which they deposit in the bank. Grant sees saloon owner Morton, an old childhood friend. Morton advises Grant to leave town. Bank president Charles Miller wants Morton to take the job of sheriff and holds a party at his ranch to announce his choice. Grant and Knight are invited to the party. Both Grant and Morton become rivals for the affections of Miller's daughter, Jane Adams. Grant meets Thomas, Adams' brother at the party. Morton tells Miller that Grant is the stagecoach bandit and makes plans to capture him. Grant gets away and returns to the ranch, where he overhears Thomas tell Adams that Morton killed the two men. Grant and Knight reveal to Adams and Thomas that they are Wells Fargo agents, and enlist Thomas' help in bringing Morton to justice. With Thomas' help, Grant and Knight foil another stagecoach robbery attempt by Morton. Morton races to town and finds Thomas in his office. When Thomas tries to leave, Morton wounds him. Morton is ultimately trapped in his saloon by the lawmen and the townspeople. Morton warns that unless he's allowed to escape, he'll let Thomas die. Grant proposes that Morton meet him in a showdown, according to the gunman's code. Grant outdraws Morton and shoots the gun from his hand. Thomas recovers from his wound. Grant rides on to new adventures, to Adams' disappointment.

NOTES AND COMMENTARY: Danny Morton remembered Kirby Grant and remarked, "Kirby and I became close friends. He was the epitome of a gentle man."

Gunman's Code is a loose remake of *Road Agent* (Universal, 1941) with Dick Foran, Leo Carrillo and Andy Devine. Footage from that earlier film appears in *Gunman's Code*.

Fuzzy Knight earlier sang "Those Happy Old Days" in *Law and Order* (Universal, 1940), with Johnny Mack Brown. "Call of the Range" was first heard in *Man from Montana* (Universal, 1941), then in *Frontier Law* (Universal, 1943) and *Beyond the Pecos* (Universal, 1945).

REVIEWS: "Pretty fair actioner in the Kirby Grant Universal series." (*Western Movies*, Pitts); "Top effort for that [Kirby Grant's] series to date; a nice piece of work contributed by heavy Danny Morton." (*Hollywood Reporter*, 10/23/46)

SUMMATION: *Gunman's Code* is an above average "B" western highlighted by good performances from hero Kirby Grant and villain Danny Morton. Fuzzy Knight again shows he can be a fine comic sidekick when he eschews juvenile situations. Leading lady Jane Adams has a nice role as the girl who loses Grant to his job. Wallace W. Fox's direction is on the mark.

All Right, Public!
YOU'VE WANTED TO BE ENTERTAINED IN A DIFFERENT WAY
And We Are Bringing to You This Week a Drama of Grim Realism That Is
DECIDEDLY DIFFERENT
A tense drama of three bad men, a new born babe, in the wastes and desolation of Death Valley.

Hell's Heroes

ALTERNATE TITLE: *Galgenvoegel*; Universal (January 1930); A Carl Laemmle Special

CAST: Bob Sangster, **Charles Bickford**; "Barbwire" Tom Gibbons, **Raymond Hatton**; "Wild Bill" Kearney, **Fred Kohler**; Mother, **Fritzi Ridgeway**; Jose, **Jose de la Cruz**; Sheriff, **Walter James**; Carmelita, **Maria Alba**; Parson Jones, "Buck" Connors// Choir Member, **Mary Gordon**; Frank Edwards, **Edward Hearn**; Croupier, **Tom London**

CREDITS: Director, **William Wyler**; Supervising Story Chief, **C. Gardner Sullivan**; Adaption & Dialogue, **Tom Reed**; Supervising Film Editor, **Del Andrews**; Editor, **Harry Marker**; Cinematographer, **George Robinson**; Recording Supervisor, **C.**

Roy Hunter; Synronization & Score, **Davis Broekman**; Recorded, **Western Electric Equipment**

SONG: "Silent Night" (Mohr and Gruber, tr. Young)—sung by **choir and congregation**

LOCATION FILMING: Mojave Desert, Panamint Valley, Bodie and Red Rock Canyon, California

RUNNING TIME: 68 min.

SOURCE: Story "Three Godfathers" by **Peter B. Kyne**

STORY: Three outlaws, Fred Kohler, Raymond Hatton and Jo de la Cruz, ride into the town of New Jerusalem to meet their leader, Charles Bickford. The outlaws rob the bank and in the process kill the bank cashier, Edward Hearn. During the get-a-way the town preacher, "Buck" Connors, shoots two of the outlaws, killing de la Cruz and wounding Hatton. A sandstorm prevents a posse from catching the bank robbers. The storm stampedes the outlaws' horses, leaving the men afoot. They walk to the nearest water hole and find it dry. At the water hole is a covered wagon with a woman, Fritzi Ridgeway, who gives birth to a baby boy. Ridgeway asks the men to be the baby's godfathers and take her son to her husband, Hearn, not knowing these men killed him. Kohler and Hatton immediately agree. Bickford acquiesces, not intending to comply with the request. Kohler and Hatton start back to New Jerusalem with the baby. Bickford tags along, intending to leave them when they get close to town. What little water they have they save for the baby. Hatton's wound makes him unable to continue, and he stays to die in the desert. As the men walk away, a gunshot is heard. Hatton has taken his own life. With their water almost gone, Kohler elects to join his friend in the desert, leaving it up to Bickford to get the baby to town. Bickford is about to collapse when he reaches a poisoned water hole. He decides to drink the water to give him the strength to make it to New Jerusalem before he expires. Bickford makes it to town and hears the hymn, "Silent Night" coming from the church. It is Christmas Day. In his final effort, Bickford brings the child safely to the congregation.

NOTES AND COMMENTARY: Charles Bickford, under contract to MGM, was loaned to Universal to star in *Hell's Heroes*. Bickford did not want to appear in this film and reluctantly agreed to do so when Junior Laemmle consented to let Bickford rewrite the script. When Bickford showed up on location in the Mojave Desert, he found the script was basically the one he had turned down. A power struggle with director William Wyler ensued, with Bickford coming out on top when Laemmle sided with him. Bickford rewrote each scene and brought a needed realistic feel to the film. Director William Wyler was a procrastinator, causing the film to run behind schedule. Bickford was due to co-star with Greta Garbo in *Anna Christie* (Metro-Goldwyn-Mayer, 1930). Universal tried to get an extension of Bickford's contract in order to finish their film. MGM refused and Bickford reported for work on *Anna Christie*. Bickford

Hell's Heroes (1930) herald: Maria Alba.

finished *Hell's Heroes* on his own time.

When filming on location in the Mojave Desert, director William Wyler dressed in khaki shorts, a tropical helmet and cowboy boots. Charles Bickford thought the effect was ludicrous.

Fred Kohler overcame the loss of two fingers and a thumb on his right hand to become one of the top villains in "B" westerns. If this deformity was mentioned in films, it was usually explained that they had been lost in a gunfight.

This story was filmed twice previously, as *Three Godfathers* (Universal Bluebird, 1916), with Harry Carey, George Berrell and Frank Lanning, and *Marked Men* (Universal, 1920) with Harry Carey, Joe Harris and Ted Brooks. It would be remade as *Three Godfathers* (Metro-Goldwyn-Mayer, 1936), starring Chester Morris, Lewis Stone and Walter Brennan; as *3 Godfathers* (Argosy/Metro-Goldwyn-Mayer, 1948), with John Wayne, Pedro Armendariz and Harry Carey Jr.; and as a TV movie, *The Godchild* (ABC-TV/ Metro-Goldwyn-Mayer, 1974), with Jack Palance, Jack Warden and Keith Carradine. Noted director John Ford helmed the 1920 and 1948 versions.

Hell's Heroes was William Wyler's first sound feature film.

Jose de la Cruz received billing as Jo de la Cruz.

The hymn, "Silent Night" was announced as "Holy Night" in this picture.

REVIEWS: "An excellent western that deserves more critical attention." (*The Motion Picture Guide*, Nash and Ross); "Gripping and real, unusually well cast and directed." (*Variety*, 1/1/30)

SUMMATION: *Hell's Heroes* is very good but grim retelling of the oft-filmed Peter B. Kyne story, effectively directed by William Wyler, who coaxes exceptional performances from his three godfathers, Raymond Hatton, Fred Kohler and, especially, Charles Bickford, as the leader of the outlaw band. Cinematographer George Robinson does an excellent job of capturing the stark vastness of the desert, enhancing the story.

From a Story by Peter B. Kyne

Heroes of the West

Universal (June 1932)

CAST: Noah Blaine, **Noah Beery, Jr.**; Ann Blaine, **Diane Duval**; Tom Crosby, **Onslow Stevens**; John Blaine, **William Desmond**; Martha Blaine, **Martha Mattox**; Rance Judd, **Philo McCullough**; Butch Gore, **Harry Tenbrook**; Buckskin Joe, **Frank Lackteen**; Bart Eaton, **Edmund Cobb**; Missouri, **Jules Cowles**; Captain Donovan, **Francis Ford**; Thunderbird, **Chief Thunderbird**// Flo, **Grace Cunard**; Rawhide Riley, **Ben Corbett**; Jim, **Jim Corey**; Railroad Worker, **Monte Montague**; Gang Members, **Art Mix** and **Slim Whitaker**; Townsman, **Tex Cooper**

CREDITS: Director, **Ray Taylor**; Associate Producer, **Henry MacRae**; Screenwriters, **Ella O'Neil, George Plympton, Basil Dickey** and **Joe Roach**; Editors, **Edward and Alvin Todd**; Cinematographer, **John Hickson**; Sound, **C. Roy Hunter** and **Jack Foley**

LOCATION FILMING: Bronson Canyon, Agoura and Walker Ranch, California

RUNNING TIME: 215 min.

CHAPTER TITLES: 1. Blazing the Trail, 2. The Red Peril, 3. The Avalanche, 4. A Shot from the Dark, 5. The Hold-Up, 6. Captured by Indians, 7. Flaming Arrows, 8. Frontier Justice, 9. The Iron Master, 10. Thundering Death, 11. Thundering Hoofs, 12. End of the Trail

SOURCE: Novel "The Tie That Binds" by **Peter B. Kyne**

STORY: William Desmond, responsible for the building of a railroad, is behind schedule and in danger of losing his contract. His construction engineer, Philo McCullough, is behind the delays. Desmond hires Onslow Stevens as boss of operations. Helping Desmond is his son, Noah Beery, Jr., and his daughter, Diane Duval. McCullough sends Frank Lackteen to ambush Stevens, but Lackteen's attempt is foiled by Beery. Stevens discovers that Harry Tenbrook, in McCullough's employ, is causing some of the delays and fires him. McCullough continues to incite the local Indian tribe to attack the railroad. With help from Beery, railroad worker Edmund Cobb and frontiersman Jules Cowles, Stevens prevents the Indians from stopping the railroad's progress. Cobb assists Stevens, even though the two are at odds with each other. Tenbrook, now working in the open, has his men attack Stevens and some railroad men. Beery drives off Tenbrook and his men. With two weeks left to complete their portion of the railroad, McCullough tries to turn Desmond against Stevens. Stevens learns that McCullough is plotting to delay the railroad. The two men engage in a vicious fistfight, with Stevens emerging victorious. Desmond demands that Stevens and McCullough work together. Cobb and Beery find proof that McCullough is behind all the railroad's trouble. Stevens, McCullough and Cobb have a wagon race to determine who is the best teamster. Noticing that Stevens' traces have been tampered with, Cobb risks his life to repair them. Stevens is then able to win the race. Cobb then shows Stevens proof of McCullough's guilt. Stevens fires McCullough and orders him to leave camp. Stevens and Cobb become friends. McCullough believes Tenbrook provided the evidence of his guilt. He goes to Tenbrook's hideout and shoots him. The dying Tenbrook, in return, draws his gun and kills McCullough. With the railroad completed, Stevens and Duval plan to marry.

NOTES AND COMMENTARY: Diane Duval was later billed as Jacqueline Wells and Julie Bishop.

Ella O'Neil was usually billed as Ella O' Neill.

Peter B. Kyne's novel "The Tie That Binds," also served as the basis for the serial *Flaming Frontiers* (Universal, 1938), with John Mack Brown.

REVIEWS: "Fair Universal serial with a more interesting cast than plot." (*Western Movies*, Pitts)

AUTHOR'S COMMENTS: *Heroes of the West* is a good serial, even though a tighter screenplay would have resulted in a superior chapter play. Ray Taylor directs efficiently, keeping the serial moving at a fast clip and adroitly interweaving the stock footage. The heroes, Noah Beery, Jr., Onslow Stevens and Edmund Cobb, acquit themselves well, both in the dialogue and action sequences. Diane Duval makes a spunky and attractive heroine. The villainy is in the capable hands of Philo McCullough, Harry Tenbrook and Frank Lackteen. The screenplay leaves a few questions unanswered (e.g. why were there no attempts to sabotage the building of the railroad in the final weeks of construction?), and a confrontation between Stevens and McCullough would have been more satisfying than having McCullough and Tenbrook shoot each other. In any event, the serial is well worth viewing.

Flying Fists, Barking Guns, Terrific Forest Fires— and Tom in the Midst of It All!

Hidden Gold

Universal (November 1932)

CAST: Tom Marley, **Tom Mix**; Nora Lane, **Judith Barrie**; Spike, **Raymond Hatton**; Big Ben Cooper, **Eddie Gribbon**; Doc Griffen, **Donald Kirke**; Jones, **Wallis Clark**; Roy Moore; and "Tony Jr." (The Miracle Horse)// The Chief, **Edward LeSaint**; Deputy, **Bud Osborne**

CREDITS: Director, **Arthur Rosson**; Story, **Jack Natteford**; Screenwriters, **Jack Natteford** and **James Mulhauser**; Cinematographer, **Daniel B. Clark**

LOCATION FILMING: Garner Ranch, Lake Hamet and Kernville, California

RUNNING TIME: 60 min.

STORY: Using Raymond Hatton's car, Hatton and two confederates, Donald Kirke and Eddie Gribbon, hold up a bank. The bank robbers are soon captured, but the money is not recovered. Because of the robbery, the bank has to close. This move adversely affects Judith Barrie's ranch, and money is badly needed. Barrie's foreman, Tom Mix, takes up prizefighting to earn money for Barrie's ranch. Because of the bank robbers' connection with the fight game, Mix is enlisted to help recover the stolen money. Mix is placed in the bank robbers' cell and begins to win their confidence. Kirke, Gribbon and Hatton break jail, taking Mix with them. Mix leads the robbers to Barrie's ranch, where he provides horses for them. Barrie sees Mix and the gangsters, and warns him that the authorities are looking for them. Kirke decides to take Barrie with them as they travel to the stolen money. The party stops to rest when the posse begins to close in. Hastily leaving, Hatton inadvertently spreads the campfire instead of putting it out. The campfire becomes a major forest fire. Kirke recovers the money and, wanting the cash for himself, shoots Hatton and Gribbon, wounding both men. Kirke escapes into the raging fire, with Mix in pursuit. Mix catches up with Kirke and takes the money from him. Barrie gets to safety and sends Tony to help Mix. Tony finds Mix, and they reach safety, being able to save only Hatton. Both Kirke and Gribbon perish in the fire. Mix is now able to square himself with the law and the bank. Mix finally marries Barrie.

NOTES AND COMMENTARY: Tom Mix was seriously injured in the making of this motion picture. Tony Jr. stepped in a gopher hole, and both horse and rider fell to the ground. Mix suffered an injured hip and three broken ribs.

The working title for *Hidden Gold* was *Oh Promise Me*.

Hidden Gold (Paramount, 1940) was the title for a Hopalong Cassidy western with William Boyd. The Mix and Boyd pictures had different storylines.

REVIEWS: "Should make for audience acceptance with more than enough to please more exacting customers." (*Variety*, 3/28/33); "This is not one of Tom Mix's better sound films." (*Western Movies*, Pitts)

SUMMATION: *Hidden Gold* is an okay Tom Mix film, which at times resembles a gangster/prison story. Mix is fine as the stalwart hero, and the rest of the cast perform capably. Director Arthur Rosson paces the story nicely, finally generating a little suspense in the forest fire sequence.

A WHIRLWIND OF WESTERN ACTION!
Daring Thrills with Fighting Ken in a Dual Role!
See Him RIDE! SHOOT! FIGHT!

Honor of the Range

Universal (April 1934); A Ken Maynard Production

CAST: Ken/Clem, **Ken Maynard**; Mary, **Cecilia Parker**; Rawhide, **Fred Kohler**; Boots, **Frank Hagney**; Rocky, **Jack Rockwell**; Turner, **James Marcus**; Smokey, **Al Smith**; Charlie, **Eddie Barnes**; Pete, **Slim Whitaker**; Saloon Keeper, **Franklyn Farnum**//"Tarzan;" Man in Balcony, **Lew Kelly**; Lookout, **Ben Corbett**; Cowhands, **Wally Wales** and **Hank Bell**; Outlaws, **Jack Kirk** and **Alan Bridge**; Posse Member, **Art Mix**

CREDITS: Director, **Alan James**; Story/Screenwriter, **Nate Gatzert**; Editor, **Charles Harris**; Art Director, **Ralph Berger**; Cinematographer, **Ted McCord**, Sound, **Earl Crain**

SONGS: "Captain Jinks of the Horse Marines" (traditional)—sung by **Eddie Barnes**; "She's Only a Bird in a Gilded Cage" (Lamb and Von Tilzer)—sung by **Ken Maynard**; "Buffalo Gal" (traditional)—played by **Cecilia Parker**

LOCATION FILMING: Bronson Canyon, California

RUNNING TIME: 62 min.

STORY: Sheriff Ken Maynard and Cecilia Parker are in love. Maynard tells Parker that he plans to quit his job and buy a ranch. Parker's father, James Marcus, closes a cattle deal and insists on payment in cash. Since it's too late to deposit the money in the bank, Maynard suggests that Marcus place the money in his brother storekeeper Ken Maynard's safe until morning. Outlaw Fred Kohler persuades storekeeper Maynard to give him the combination of the safe. Storekeeper Maynard expects to share heavily in the ill-gotten gains, but Kohler doesn't plan to give him anything. Kohler takes the money. Sheriff Maynard thinks his brother might be involved in the robbery. Sheriff Maynard promises Marcus he'll bring back the money and the men responsible. Deputy Frank Hagney thinks Maynard won't bring in the gang. With some men, Hagney overpowers Maynard, takes his badge and locks him in the saloon storeroom. Thinking he'll receive a large share of money from his role in the robbery, Storekeeper Maynard tries to get Parker to go away with him. When she refuses, Storekeeper Maynard tells Parker that Sheriff Maynard has been seriously injured and is calling for her. Since Storekeeper Maynard has Sheriff Maynard's horse, Tarzan, Parker believes him. Storekeeper Maynard takes Parker to the outlaw hideout. Kohler decides to keep them prisoner. Storekeeper Maynard places a note on Tarzan's saddle and tells Tarzan to go to Sheriff Maynard. Sheriff Maynard escapes from the storeroom, transfers to Tarzan and finds the note directing him to the hideout. At the hideout, Kohler shows Storekeeper Maynard that dynamite has been planted around the entrance to the hideout. A time fuse can be set to destroy any unwelcome visitors. Parker is taken to Kohler's room, where Kohler is plans to force himself on her. Storekeeper Maynard

Honor of the Range (1934) movie still: Ken Maynard (*left*) and Fred Kohler engage in a terrific fistfight as Cecilia Parker plays the organ to cover the sounds of the battle.

tries to prevent Kohler from going to the room. Kohler shoots Storekeeper Maynard, wounding him. Sheriff Maynard gains entrance to the hideout and confronts Kohler as he's trying to kiss Parker. The two men fight, and Sheriff Maynard finally knocks out Kohler. Parker shows Sheriff Maynard where Kohler stashed her father's money. Sheriff Maynard and Parker take the money and make a break for freedom. Storekeeper Maynard stays behind and sets off the dynamite trap, destroying the whole outlaw gang, at the cost of his own life. Sheriff Maynard returns the money to Marcus, and he and Parker plan to marry.

NOTES AND COMMENTARY: Influenced by Mae West's Gay Nineties setting in *She Done Him Wrong* (Paramount, 1933), Ken Maynard had music hall revue numbers incorporated into *Honor of the Range*. Authentic turn of the century songs were used.

Director Alan James was also billed as Alan J. Neitz, his given name, during his long career.

Eddie Barnes' character name is Charlie in the opening and closing credits, but it's Charley on his dressing room door.

"Buffalo Gal" was used by Ken Maynard in his production *Mountain Justice* (Universal, 1930), and was later sung by Jimmy Wakely and His Cowboy Band in *Strictly in the Groove* (Universal, 1943).

REVIEWS: "Ken Maynard handles the dual roles of the hero and villain quite well." (*Western Movies*, Pitts); "This isn't to be mistaken for the average shot-off cuff western." (*Variety*, 5/1/34)

SUMMATION: *Honor of the Range* is a top-notch Ken Maynard western. Maynard, in one of his best outings, essays a dual role, as the heroic sheriff and as the sheriff's cowardly and dishonest storekeeper brother who finally finds his honor. Fred Kohler makes a worthy adversary for Maynard. Cecilia Parker is allowed do some acting in the heroine role, and she does it well. Alan James knows how to pace a story to good effect, and he proves it in this entry.

RIDING ... FIGHTING ... SHOOTING!
With roaring guns and sledge-hammer fists he struck terror in rustlers' hearts!

Honor of the West

Universal (January 1939)

CAST: Bob, **Bob Baker**; Diane, **Marjorie Bell**; Russ, **Carleton Young**; Walker, **Forrest Taylor**; Bat, **Glenn Strange**; Tom, **Reed Howes**; Butch, **Frank Ellis**; Heck, **Jack Kirk**; Rancher, **Murdock MacQuarrie**; Farmer, **Walter Wills**; Announcer, **Arthur Thalasso**// Luke, **Tex Palmer**

CREDITS: Director, **George Wag-**

gner; Assistant Director, **Glenn Cook**; Technical Director, **Albert Greenwood**; Story/Screenplay, **Joseph West**; Editor, **Carl Pierson**; Cinematographer, **Harry Neumann**; Sound Supervisor, **Bernard B. Brown**; Sound Technician, **Joseph Lapis**; Musical Director/Arranger, **Frank Sanucci**

Songs: "As the Old Chuck-Wagon Rolls Along" (Allan)—sung by **Bob Baker**; "Pride of the Prairie" (Allan)—sung by **Bob Baker;** and "Headin' for the Ole Corral" (Allan)—sung by **Bob Baker**

Location Filming: Kernville, California

Running Time: 60 min.

Story: Marjorie Bell's fiancé, Carleton Young, has fallen in with Jack Kirk's gang of rustlers. Young's best friend is Sheriff Bob Baker. Baker and Bell are really in love, but neither wants to hurt Young's feelings. Alerted to rustling activities, Baker, with rancher Forrest Taylor and deputy Reed Howes, rides after the rustlers. Outlaw Tex Palmer, serving as lookout, spots Howes and shoots him. The rustlers scatter, with Kirk and Young riding to Young's ranch. Baker has Taylor tend to Howes and chases after Kirk and Young. Having no direct proof, Baker is unable to arrest the men. Howes' brother, lawman Glenn Strange, takes over as Baker's deputy. Before Howes dies, he names Palmer as his killer. Baker, Strange and a posse corner Palmer, who decides to surrender and comes out with his hands up. Strange guns Palmer down, avenging his brother. Baker finds proof that Young is in league with the rustlers and, rather than arrest Young, resigns as sheriff. Strange becomes the new sheriff and goes to arrest Young. Learning what Strange plans to do, Baker rides to warn Young. Young tells Bell he has to leave and hide out in Mexico. Baker catches up with Young, but Strange shows up and arrests Young. Kirk and his men had spotted Baker and followed also. A gun battle starts, and Strange is wounded. Then Young is wounded, and Baker plans to walk into Kirk's gunfire to save Young. Young knocks Baker out and takes his place. Kirk shoots Young as Bell brings a posse to round up the rustlers. Baker faces Kirk and empties his six-shooter into Kirk. With his dying breath, Young tells Baker to take care of Bell. Baker and Bell ride off hand-in-hand.

Notes And Commentary: The working title for *Honor of the West* was *Singing Sheriff*. Universal would finally use this title for a Bob Crosby vehicle in 1944.

The song played over the opening credits is "Dusty and Dry" (Allen), which Bob Baker sang in *Prairie Justice* (Universal, 1938).

Bob Baker's leading lady, Marjorie Bell, would later gain greater fame as dancer Marge Champion, who performed in countless Metro-Goldwyn-Mayer musicals with her husband Gower Champion.

Pressbooks and some reference books list Dick Dickinson and Frank O'Conner as the Grimes brothers, when, in fact, the actors are Tex Palmer and Frank Ellis.

Reviews: "Good average western

melodrama." (*Variety*, 7/26/39); "Plenty of action plus some nice songs makes this one of the better Bob Baker films." (*Western Movies*, Pitts)

SUMMATION: *Honor of the West* is a good Bob Baker western film with more fast action than what's usually found in his vehicles. Again we have a film that shows Baker as a highly capable action star and a fine western hero. The supporting cast, especially Carleton Young, Glenn Strange and Jack Kirk, is impressive, except, perhaps, for Marjorie Bell, whose performance is barely adequate. George Waggner directs in a solid, straightforward manner from his more than acceptable script.

THRILLS! ACTION! ADVENTURE!
DON'T miss the opening and succeeding chapters of this great TALKING serial. Redskins and settlers in fierce battles for possession of Westward trails... Renegade whites allied with Indians... an amazing plot against a fighting hero and his beautiful sweetheart... Action staged on the perilous plains where danger lurks around every turn... Truly the serial sensation of the century!

The Indians Are Coming!

Universal (October 1930)

CAST: Jack Manning, **Tim McCoy**; Mary Woods, **Allene Ray**; Bill Williams, **Edmund Cobb**; George Woods/Tom Woods, **Francis Ford**; Rance Carter, **Wilbur McGaugh**; Bull McGee, **Bud Osborne**; Uncle Amos, **Charles Royal**; "Pal"; and "Dynamite"// Lafe, **Lafe McKee**; Sheriff, **Frank Ellis**; Jim, **Jim Corey**; Charlie, **Charles LeMoyne**; Chief Yellow Snake, **Chief Thunderbird**; Bartender, **Monte Montague**

CREDITS: Director/Producer, **Henry MacRae**; Screenwriters, **George H. Plympton** and **Ford Beebe**; Editors, **Robert Wilcox, Edward Todd** and **Alvin Todd**; Supervisor, **William Lord Wright**; Cinematographer, **Wilfred Cline**; Synchronization and Sound, **David Broekman**; Recording Supervisor, **C. Roy Hunter**

RUNNING TIME: 221 min.

CHAPTER TITLES: 1. Pals in Buckskin, 2. A Call to Arms, 3. A Furnace of Fear, 4. The Red Terror, 5. The Circle of Death, 6. Hate's Harvest, 7. Hostages of Fear, 8. The Dagger Duel, 9. The Blast of Death, 10. Redskin's Revenge, 11. Frontiers Aflame, 12. The Trail's End

SOURCE: Book "The Great West That Was" by **William F. Cody** (**Buffalo Bill**)

STORY: Miner Francis Ford discovers gold at Gold Creek and sends Tim McCoy east to Hillsdale to bring his twin brother, Francis Ford, and his niece, Allene Ray, out west. Miner Ford gives McCoy money to pay off a debt to Wilbur McGaugh. Mc-

Gaugh plans to use this indebtedness to force Ray to marry him. McGaugh is in love with Ray, but the sentiment is not reciprocated. Arriving in Hillsdale, McCoy meets Ray but accidentally drops the money, which is recovered by McGaugh. McGaugh accuses McCoy of stealing the money. Seeing that McCoy and Ray are falling in love, McGaugh has McCoy arrested. McGaugh, Ray and brother Ford start west, unaware that the train's route will take them through hostile Indian country. Ray's uncle, Charles Royal, intercedes and gains McCoy's freedom. McCoy and Royal catch up with the wagon train. McCoy guides the wagon train, but soon the Indians attack in full strength. McCoy sends his dog, Pal, to Gold Creek to bring McCoy's friend, Edmund Cobb, and the settlers to the rescue. During the attack, McGaugh shoots brother Ford, blaming the death on the Indians. Cobb and the settlers arrive in time to chase the Indians. Overhearing a conversation between McGaugh and his men, Royal tells McCoy that McGaugh has the "stolen" money. After a rugged fistfight between McCoy and McGaugh, McCoy recovers the money. In retaliation, McGaugh kidnaps Ray and takes her to an Indian village. McGaugh demands a deed to half of miner Ford's claim for Ray's return. McCoy and Cobb rescue Ray, and Miner Ford refuses McGaugh's demands. McGaugh enlists the aid of the Indians to capture McCoy and Ray. McGaugh shoots the Indian Chief's son and places the blame on McCoy. As McCoy is about to be executed by the Indians, the son revives and the execution is halted. With the Cavalry on the way to the Indian village, McGaugh takes Ray to Gold Creek. Cobb rescues McCoy, and the two race after McGaugh, followed by the Indian Chief and his tribe. McCoy rescues Ray. The Cavalry arrives in Gold Creek to rout the Indians. As the Indians retreat, they spot McGaugh and some of his men. The Indian Chief kills McGaugh. One of McGaugh's men, Bud Osborne, has been badly wounded and begins to go crazy. Osborne makes it to miner Ford's cabin and, before succumbing to his wounds, tells Miner Ford that McGaugh killed his brother. McCoy and Cobb decide to help miner Ford and Ray with their gold claim, and McCoy and Ray now have time for romance.

NOTES AND COMMENTARY: To promote the serial, theaters gave away Indian hats to children who attended the first chapter.

The Indians Are Coming cost $160,00 to make and grossed over a million dollars.

Footage of the Indians riding during the opening credits came from Ken Maynard's *The Red Raiders* (First National, 1927). The serial was filmed entirely at Universal City, with footage liberally added from Hoot Gibson's *The Flaming Frontier* (Universal, 1926). Footage from *The Indians Are Coming* was later used in *Law and Order* (Universal, 1932), *Wheels of Destiny* (Universal, 1934), *For the Service* (Universal, 1936) and *Flaming Frontiers* (Universal, 1938).

REVIEWS: "An historically important Western." (*The Western*, Hardy)

SUMMATION: Through all the hoopla of this being Universal's first all-talking serial, *The Indians Are Coming* is only an average outing. Heroes Tim McCoy and Edmund Cobb are effective in their roles, though at times, their acting becomes stilted. Villain Wilbur McGaugh and heroine Allene Ray are unable to deliver their lines convincingly. Acting honors go to Francis Ford in a dual role, and to Bud Osborne as McGaugh's right-hand man. Both men understand how to deliver their lines, and Osborne, in particular, does a fine job in the scene in which he goes insane. The action scenes are generally up to par (thanks to stock footage), but Director Henry MacRae is out of his depth in the dramatic sequences.

GUNS make the MAN!
Two ivory-handled revolvers! One in the hands of a ruthless killer—the other a defender of the law of the West!

The Ivory Handled Gun

Universal (November 1935)

CAST: Buck Ward, **Buck Jones**; Paddy Moore, **Charlotte Wynters**; Wolverine Kid, **Walter Miller**; Pike, **Frank Rice**; Bill Ward, **Carl Stockdale**; Pat Moore, **Jos. Girard**; Young Pat Moore, **Niles Welch**; Young Bill Ward, **Eddie Phillips**; Alf Steen, **Bob Kortman**; Pete, **Lee Shumway**; Squint Barlow, **Stan Blystone**; Steve, **Ben Corbett**, Sheriff Crane, **Lafe McKee**; "Silver"// Outlaw, **Charles King**; Bartender at Brodie, **Lew Meehan**; "Big Boy," **Jim Thorpe**

CREDITS: Director, **Ray Taylor**; Producer, **Buck Jones**; Story, **Charles E. Barnes**; Screenwriter, **Jack Neville**; Editor, **Bernard Loftus**; Art Director, **Ralph Berger**; Cinematographers, **Allen Thompson** and **Herbert Kirkpatrick**; Sound, **Buddy Myers**

LOCATION FILMING: Vasquez Rocks and the Andy Juaregui Ranch, California

RUNNING TIME: 59 min.

STORY: In a card game dispute, Buck Jones refuses to draw against Joseph Girard, father of Charlotte Wynters, the girl he loves. Walter Miller had staged the card game, hoping it would lead to bloodshed. Miller is being paid by Stan Blystone to bring sheep into cattle country, and at the same time bring death or ruin to Jones and his father, Carl Stockdale. Years before, hatred between Stockdale and Miller's father resulted in the paralysis of Stockdale's legs and Miller's father's death. Stockdale gives Jones an ivory handled gun and tells him Miller has the matching gun, and there will be no peace until one man owns both guns. Wynters tells Girard that Miller wanted him dead. Girard is shot, and initially Wynters thinks Jones was responsible. Jones finds a clue implicating Miller; and he and his pal, Frank Rice, are deputized to bring Miller in. Miller plans to draw the cattlemen into a trap by lighting the signal fires that warn them that sheep are being driven to the valley. Sheep will then be brought into the rangeland. Trying to warn the ranchers, Jones is captured and taken to Miller. Miller plans to have Jones hanged for Girard's murder, but Wynters wants Jones brought to her alive. Wynters, now believing that Miller was the man who killed her father, attempts to rescue Jones but is captured. With Silver's help, Jones and Wynters escape. A signal fire is lighted, Wynters rides to warn the cattlemen, and Jones finds Rice. Jones and Rice take positions behind Miller and his gang, and start a gunfight. Caught in a crossfire, Miller's men are rounded up, but Miller escapes. Miller goes to Stockdale's ranch, where Wynters had been sent after warning the cattlemen. Jones follows Miller to the ranch, and the two men fight, struggling over Miller's ivory handled gun. Miller is killed, and Jones is apparently wounded. Wynters rushes to Jones' side. Finally one man possesses both guns, and peace reigns in the valley.

NOTES AND COMMENTARY: *The Ivory Handled Gun* was remade as *Law of the Range* (Universal, 1941) with Johnny Mack Brown. Ray Taylor directed both entries.

The music used in the final reel had been heard as the agitato theme for *Mystery Mountain* (Mascot, 1934), a serial starring Ken Maynard.

REVIEWS: "Good Buck Jones vehicle with a surprise finale." (*Western Movies*, Pitts); "Unusually intelligent oater, an interesting extension of the standard oater plots." (*The Motion Picture Guide*, Nash and Ross)

SUMMATION: *The Ivory Handled Gun* is a top flight "B" western with an adult slant. Buck Jones and Walter Miller handle their parts well and make excellent protagonists in this tough western. The sidekick, Frank Rice, plays the part as a capable ally rather than a buffoon. Charlotte Wynters, as in most of Jones' vehicles at Universal, has a pivotal role and acquits herself capably. Charles E. Barnes, with his story, and Jack Neville, with his screenplay, present a sparkling script with an ending that leaves Jones' fate up to the audience's imagination. Allen Thompson and Herbert Kirkpatrick's camera work is first rate, and director Ray Taylor puts it all together to create a memorable motion picture.

If it's action you want— Here It Is!
A roaring rodeo rider goes hot on the trail of a gang of desperadoes— a trail that leads from sawdust to alkali in a picture that will leave you breathless with excitement!

King of the Arena

Universal (June 1933); A Ken Maynard Production

CAST: Ken Kenton, **Ken Maynard**; Mary Hiller, **Lucille Browne**; Governor, **John St. Polis**; Bargoff, **Bob Kortman**; Baron Petroff, **Michael Visoroff**; Colonel Hiller, **James Marcus**; Saunders, **Jack Rockwell**; Tin Star, **Frank Rice**; Jimmy Hiller, **Bobby Nelson**; Captain Rodregis, **Jack Mower;** and "**Tarzan**"// Chief, **Edward Piel, Sr.**; Sambo, **Blue Washington**; Irate Bettor, **Wally Wales**; Cook, **Slim Whitaker**; Townsman, **Lafe McKee**; Town Merchant, **Horace B. Carpenter**; Sheriff, **Edward Coxen**; Pedro, **Steve Clemente**; Indian, **Iron Eyes Cody**

CREDITS: Director/Screenwriter, **Alan James**; Story, **Hal Berger** and **Ray Bouk**; Editor, **Charles Harris**; Art Director, **Ralph Berger**; Cinematographer, **Ted McCord**; Recording Engineer, **Dean Daily**

LOCATION FILMING: Vazquez Rocks and Newhall, California

RUNNING TIME: 61 min.

STORY: An outlaw gang led by a mystery villain, the Black Death, is looting banks and killing bank employees. The robbers use a chemical bullet that in death turns the victims black. Ranger Ken Maynard is assigned to the case. Maynard thinks there might be a connection between James Marcus' circus and the crimes, since the show always seems to be in the same vicinity as the robberies. Maynard obtains a leave of absence and takes his old job back as the star of the show. In addition, Maynard thinks he might have time to resume his romance with Marcus' daughter, Lucille Browne. Bob Kortman, who leads a band of Cossacks, is upset over being deposed as the show's headliner. Another bank is held up and the cashier is murdered by the Black Death bullet. Maynard proposes that all the circus performers' trunks be searched. Black Death pellets are found in Kortman's trunk. Kortman, realizing Maynard will find evidence to tie him to the crimes, steals the circus' money, kidnaps Browne and escapes in a plane. Maynard finds a note telling him to go to a casino in Mexico for ransom instructions. At the casino, Maynard meets rancher Michael Visoroff, who offers to help. Maynard is led into a trap by Visoroff's foreman, Steve Clemente, and is captured by Kortman. Led to a cabin, Maynard meets Visoroff, the actual leader of the outlaw band. With Tarzan's help, Maynard makes his escape without his six-guns. Circus performers, led by Frank Rice and Browne's younger brother, Bobby Nelson, have been

King of the Arena (1933) movie still: Bob Kortman (*right*) takes Ken Maynard captive.

summoned by Maynard and meet him on the trail. Kortman and his men plan to ambush the riders. In the gunfight, a slingshot belonging to Nelson falls into Maynard's empty holster. Seeing that there will be a tough fight, Kortman reports to Visoroff and is told to take the plane and machine gun the circus performers. Maynard returns to the cabin, not realizing Visoroff and Browne are in a secret underground laboratory, and gains control of Visoroff's Black Death pellets. Using Nelson's slingshot, Maynard hits the plane, causing it to crash. Maynard goes back to the cabin, finds the secret entrance to the laboratory, and whips Visoroff in a brutal fistfight. With the Black Death gang destroyed, Maynard and Browne now have time for romance.

NOTES AND COMMENTARY: Universal hired Ken Maynard to take over as their western star after Tom Mix left due to numerous injuries suffered in the making of his series. Mix had suggested Hoot Gibson as his replacement but the studio decided otherwise.

The working title for *King of the Arena* was *King of the Range*.

Footage of Ken Maynard and Jackie Hanlon from *Parade of the*

West (Universal, 1930) was utilized in King of the Arena. The Coleman Bros. Circus had already been used in Parade of the West, and since the circus was in the Hollywood area at the time of the King of the Arena shoot, it served as the Miller Circus in the film.

The plane seen in the film belonged to star Ken Maynard.

REVIEWS: "The standard amounts of action, suspense and gunplay are firmly locked into place." (*The Motion Picture Guide*, Nash and Ross); "Can't be considered superior to the average type. A lot of action, however, maintains its suspense well and will register satisfactorily with its fan class." (*Variety*, 8/29/33)

SUMMATION: Wild West thrills meet Sci-Fi chills, and Ken Maynard's return to Universal is a winner. *King of the Arena* showcases Maynard at his riding and roping best. Screenwriters Hal Berger and Ray Bouk deliver an interesting screenplay, and cinematographer Ted McCord films the story to good advantage. The acting of the principals is adequate, and Alan James' direction is just fine.

She Used a Woman's Wiles … to Tame the Wildest West!

The Lady from Cheyenne

Universal (April 1941); A Frank Lloyd Production

CAST: Annie, **Loretta Young**; Steve, **Robert Preston**; Cork, **Edward Arnold**; Hank Foreman, **Frank Craven**; Elsie, **Gladys George**; Mrs. McGuinness, **Jessie Ralph**; Stover, **Stanley Fields**; George, **Willie Best**; Governor, **Samuel S. Hinds**; Mr. McGuinness, **Spencer Charters**; Mrs. Matthews, **Clare Verdera**; Mr. Matthews, **Alan Bridge**; Clerk, **Charles Williams**; Fairchild, **Erville Alderson**; Stanton, **Emmett Vogan**; Uncle Bill, **Roger Imhof**; Dunbar, **William Davidson**; Politician, **James Kirkwood**; Turk, **Wade Boteler**// Leo, **Charles T. Aldrich**; Noisy Burkett, **Joe Sawyer**; Mitch Harrigan, **Harry Woods**; Henry C. Tribble, **Joseph Eggerton**; Barney Davies, **Harry Cording**; Mr. Amos, **Murdock MacQuarrie**; Train Passenger, **Richard Alexander**; Gertie, **Marian Martin**; Chorus Girls, **Dorothy Granger**, **Sally Payne** and **Iris Adrian**; Landlady, **Isabell Jewell**; Henchman, **Ralph Dunn**; Crowley, **Emory Parnell**; Bartender, **Ethan Laidlaw**; Reporter, **Jeff Corey**; Judge, **Charles Halton**; Townsmen, **Lloyd Ingraham** and **Tex Cooper**

CREDITS: Director/Producer, **Frank Lloyd**; Assistant Director, **Fred Frank**; Associate Producer, **Jack H. Skirball**; Story, **Jonathan Finn** and **Theresa Oaks**; Screenwriters, **Warren Duff** and **Kathryn Scola**; Dialogue

The Lady from Cheyenne   151

Director, **Franklin Gray**; Editor, **Edward Curtiss**; Art Directors, **Jack Otterson** and **John B. Goodman**; Set Decorator, **R.A. Gausman**; Cinematographer, **Milton Krasner**; Gowns, **Vera West**; Sound, **William Hedgcock** and **Edward B. Brown**; Musical Director, **Charles Previn**; Musical Score, **Frank Skinner**

SONGS: "My Country 'Tis of Thee" (traditional)—sung by **children's chorus**; "Ladies from Paree" (Lerner and Previn)—sung by **Sally Payne**

LOCATION FILMING: Mojave, California

RUNNING TIME: 87 min.

STORY: Land is being auctioned to build the town of Laraville. Robert Preston, working with Edward Arnold, conducts the auction to allow Arnold to purchase sections needed for him to control the water rights. Easterner Loretta Young upsets Arnold's plans by purchasing one section of land Arnold desires. Young builds a schoolhouse on her property. Attempting to induce Young to sell, Preston romances Young and has her ready to sell at a nice profit. Newspaperman Frank Craven stops the sale by obtaining proof of Arnold's scheme. In retaliation, the schoolhouse is burned to the ground. Craven is brutally beaten and his newspaper equipment damaged. Preston, who deplores violence, steps in and prevents further damage. Young is incensed and wants Arnold arrested, but finds that no jury would convict him. Young believes an all-women jury could mete out justice to Arnold. Young travels to Cheyenne to have a bill presented to the legislative body that would allow women to vote and serve on juries. Preston, the delegate from Laraville, tries to dissuade Young. In Cheyenne, Young gets help from Willie Best, an attendant for the legislature, and Gladys George, a chorus girl. Both are well versed in the intricacies of politics; and, through trickery, Young wins a unanimous vote for the bill. Learning that Arnold's men killed a man going through Young's property to obtain water, Preston breaks with Arnold. Arnold receives word that the suffrage bill has passed and Young is returning to Laraville. Arnold sends men to take Young from the train, but Preston brings a posse. In the scuffle, Preston is shot, but Arnold's men are captured. When the train arrives in Laraville, Young has Arnold arrested and brought to trial. An all-women jury finds Arnold guilty of all charges. Preston is leaving town, but Young rushes to his side and proposes. Since Preston is really in love with Young, he accepts.

NOTES AND COMMENTARY: Loretta Young was a popular and durable star of motion pictures and television. Young hit her stride in the late forties, winning the Best Actress Academy Award for *The Farmer's Daughter* (RKO, 1947) and an Academy Award nomination as Best Actress for her performance in *Come to the Stable* (20th Century Fox, 1949). In 1953 she hosted the long-running and popular television program first called *Letters to Loretta*, then renamed *The Loretta Young Show*

(NBC), which won Young three Emmy Awards.

Robert Preston already had a long screen careen when he played the part of Professor Howard Hill in the 1957 Broadway production of *The Music Man*. Preston won a Tony Award for his performance, and reprised the role in the 1962 Warner Brothers film version. Preston later received a Best Supporting Actor Academy Award nomination for his role of Toddie in *Victor/Victoria* (Metro-Goldwyn-Mayer, 1982).

"B" western fans recognize Sally Payne as the actress who sings "Ladies from Paree." Payne is known for her supporting roles in ten Roy Rogers films made at Republic between 1940 and 1942. Payne took over for Florence Rice as Edgar Kennedy's wife in Kennedy's two-reel comedies at RKO.

When a song was needed for children to sing in a classroom, "My Country 'Tis of Thee" was selected. It was earlier featured in *Mountain Justice* (Universal, 1930) and later in *Wild Beauty* (Universal, 1946).

REVIEWS: "Production about early women's liberation activities is fun to watch." (*Western Movies*, Pitts); "The characters are symbolically made-to-order, pushing the picture barely over the top of being average." (*The Motion Picture Guide*, Nash and Ross)

SUMMATION: *Lady from Cheyenne* is a delightful satirical western comedy centering on our political system. Loretta Young gives an engaging performance as a novice in politics who finds love at the same time. Robert Preston's charm is evident as he believably changes from a scoundrel to a man of honor. In the impressive supporting cast, Willie Best, as a political savvy individual, Gladys George, who knows how to influence politicians, and Frank Craven, as a crusading, intelligent newspaperman, are standouts. Frank Lloyd directs with a knowing, humorous touch throughout.

---

*Fiery, tempestuous, thrilling romance of the Southwestern borderland
Hard riding— quick fighting— glamorous drama!
Her eyes were like fire ... her lips like wine ... it was death to love her ... and yet no man could resist!*

Lasca of the Rio Grande

Universal (November 1931)

CAST: Jose Santa Cruz, **Leo Carrillo**; Miles Kincaid, **Johnnie Mack Brown**; Lasca, **Dorothy Burgess**; Crabapple, **Slim Summerville**; Smith, **Frank Campeau**; Jim Corey; John Ince; Tom London; and **Chris-Pin Martin**

CREDITS: Director, **Edward Laemmle**; Producer, **Samuel Bischoff**; Screenwriter, **Randall Faye**; Scenario Supervisor, **Richard Schayer**; Supervising Film Editor, **Maurice Pivar**; Editor, **Ted Kent**; Art Director, **Stanley Fleischer**; Cinematographer, **Harry Neumann**; Recording Supervisor, **C. Roy Hunter**

SONG: "Down by the Silvery Rio Grande" (Weisberg, Roden and Speidel)

RUNNING TIME: 60 min.

SOURCE: Poem "Lasca" by **Frank Duprez,** and story by **Tom Reed**

STORY: Both rancher and bandit Leo Carrillo, and Border Patrolman John Mack Brown, are in love with Dorothy Burgess, the belle of the Rio Grande country. Carrillo gave Burgess a diamond ring, signifying that she is his woman, and resents Brown's interest in Burgess. Burgess gets into an altercation with a drunk and takes out a knife to scare him. In the argument, the drunk falls on the knife and dies. Knowing she will be tried for murder, Burgess tries to get away but is captured by Brown. Brown transports Burgess to Border Patrol Headquarters to stand trial, and stops for the night to make camp. During the night Burgess seduces Brown. In the morning Brown lets Burgess escape—on the condition that she not go back to the Rio Grande and Carrillo. Brown returns to headquarters, where he's arrested and sentenced to three months in jail for letting Burgess escape. While in jail, Brown learns that Burgess is staying at Carrillo's house. Brown escapes, arrives at Carrillo's ranch and takes Burgess away at gunpoint. Carrillo and his men catch up with Brown and Burgess, and take them back to Carrillo's ranch. Carrillo makes plans to kill Brown and marry Burgess. Burgess is in love with Brown and helps him escape. The lovers have no idea that Carrillo is watching their every move and only waiting for them to make their escape attempt. It's a stormy night. Lightning starts a cattle stampede, Carrillo decides to let Brown and Burgess unknowingly ride into the midst of the stampeding herd. The next morning Carrillo and his men come upon the trampled bodies. Burgess is dead and Brown is dying. Carrillo orders his men to tend to Brown's wounds and then take the battered man to Border Patrol headquarters.

NOTES AND COMMENTARY: *Lasca of the Rio Grande* was John Mack Brown's first film after leaving Metro-Goldwyn-Mayer.

There were three previous versions of *Lasca of the Rio Grande: Lasca* (1913) *The Mad Stampede*, with Jane Bernoudy (Universal, 1917); and *Lasca,* with Frank Mayo (Universal, 1919).

Here Brown was billed as Johnnie Mack Brown instead of John Mack Brown or Johnny Mack Brown, as was customary.

REVIEWS: "Early talkie is more of a curio than anything else for genre fans." (*Western Movies*, Pitts); "An unusual theme for a program western." (*The Motion Picture Guide*, Nash and Ross)

SUMMATION: The author was unable to view this film.

AGAINST BLACK-HEARTED BORDER RUSTLERS!

The Last Stand

Universal (April 1938)

CAST: Tip, **Bob Baker**; Nancy, **Constance Moore**; Pepper, **Fuzzy Knight**; Thorn, **Earle Hodgins**; Turner, **Forrest Taylor**; Joe, **Glenn Strange**; Calhoun, **Sam Flint**; Tom, **Jimmy Phillips**; Ed, **Jack Kirk**// Posse Member, **Frank Ellis**; Ringo, **Bob Card**; Guard, **Jack Montgomery**

CREDITS: Director, **Joseph H. Lewis**; Assistant Director, **Glenn Cook**; Story, **Harry O. Hoyt**; Screenwriters, **Harry O. Hoyt** and **Norton S. Parker**; Editor, **Charles Craft**; Art Director, **Charles Clague**; Cinematographer, **Harry Neumann**; Sound, **Robert Pritchard**, **Charles Carroll** and **Edwin Wetsel**; Musical Director/Arranger, **Frank Sanucci**

SONGS: "Kid from Laredo" (Taconis and Gayne)—sung by **Bob Baker**; "Ridin' the Range Again" (Taconis and Gayne)—sung by **Bob Baker**; and "Lost Doggies" (Taconis and Gayne)—sung by **Bob Baker**

LOCATION FILMING: Agoura, Lake Sherwood, Andy Jauregui Ranch and Beale's Cut, California

RUNNING TIME: 57 min.

STORY: To track down his father's murderer, Bob Baker works his way into rustlers' gangs to tip off the authorities, with only pal Fuzzy Knight to help him. Baker is given a free hand to break up the rustling activities along the Mexican border. Rustler Glenn Strange recruits Baker and brings him to gang leader Earle Hodgins' ranch, not knowing Hodgins' daughter, Constance Moore, has returned from the East. Baker and Moore feel an immediate attraction to each other. Hodgins tells Baker to keep away from Moore, and tells Moore that Baker is a wanted man. Knight pretends to be a shady cattle buyer interested in obtaining some cattle under the market price. Baker helps Strange and his men rustle rancher Forrest Taylor's cattle. Strange shows Baker the hidden entrance to the hideout and reveals to Baker that Hodgins killed a cattlemen's association detective. Hodgins is the man for whom Baker has been searching. Baker has a plan to trap all the rustlers. Knight tells Taylor that Baker is a lawman and enlists his help in bringing the rustlers to justice. Then Knight tells Hodgins that Baker is not a notorious outlaw and was probably sent to spy on the gang. Strange and the gang rustle another herd. Baker tells Strange he'll ride ahead to the hideout and leaves just before Hodgins shows up. Knight meets Baker. Hodgins and Strange ride to overtake Baker. Baker holds the gang leaders off as Knight sets a dynamite charge, blocking the entrance to the hideout. The explosion is a signal for Taylor and a posse to swoop down on the rustlers. Realizing all is lost, Strange and Hodgins try to escape. Knight shoots Strange, and Baker ropes Hodgins from his

The Last Stand (1938) movie still: Bob Baker (*right*) battles Glenn Strange on the top of a runaway stagecoach.

horse. An angry Baker unleashes his frustration with a blow to Hodgins' head. Baker turns his back. Hodgins recovers from the blow and draws his gun. Hodgins is about to shoot Baker in the back when Knight rides onto the scene. With one well-placed bullet, Knight ends Hodgins' rustling career. Knight wants Baker to settle down. Baker answers that, with his marriage to Moore, the three will get along very well.

NOTES AND COMMENTARY: Watch the scene of outlaws Glenn Strange and his men chasing a stagecoach by a lake. Strange's horse trips over a piece of driftwood, and both horse and rider go down. The other outlaws just wave for Strange to remount and catch up, which he does.

In another interesting scene, one not normally found in a "B" western, Bob Baker has roped gang leader (and murderer of his father) Earle Hodgins. Hodgins' arms are pinned to his side, and Baker avenges himself with a solid blow to Hodgins' head. This is definitely not expected from a cowboy hero.

REVIEWS: "This new mesa figure [Bob Baker] makes this distinctive western thriller. He is aided by a good all-round cast and smart direction." (*Variety*, 6/1/38); "A triumph of craftsman over economy." (*The Western*, Hardy)

156   LAW AND ORDER (1932)

SUMMATION: *The Last Stand* is a well-directed and well-scripted "B" western. Bob Baker handles the heroic chores with distinction. Fuzzy Knight is more the character actor than the typical comedy sidekick, which is to the film's benefit. The villainy resides in the more-than-capable hands of Earle Hodgins and Glenn Strange. Cinematographer Harry Neumann's excellent photography, coupled with director Joseph H. Lewis' adroit camera placement and use of angles, greatly add to the scenes and story. This visual adeptness became a hallmark of Lewis' career as he grew into a director of note.

Four Men Against a Town of Bad Men ... and Reckless Women!
WALTER HUSTON'S *Greatest Role!*
See Him in a Romantic Red-Blooded Tale of Wild Frontier Days!

Law and Order

ALTERNATE TITLE: *Guns A-Blazin'*; Universal (March 1932)
CAST: Frame Johnson, **Walter Huston**; Brandt, **Harry Carey**; Luther Johnson, **Russell Hopton**; "Deadwood," **Raymond Hatton**; Poe Northrup, **Ralph Ince**; Walt Northrup, **Harry Woods**; Kurt Northrup, **Richard Alexander**; Judge Williams, **Russell Simpson**; Johnny Kinsman, **Andy Devine**// Sheriff Fin Elder, **Alphonse Ethier**; Ed Deal, **Dewey Robinson**; Lanky Smith, **Walter Brennan**; Saloon Girl, **Lois Wilson**; Townsman, **Art Mix**; George Dixon, **Arthur Wanzer**; Burleigh, **Richard Cramer**; Holt, **Charlie Hall**; The Parker Brothers, **D'Arcy Corrigan** and **Nelson McDowell**; Saloon Patron, **Hank Bell**
CREDITS: Director, **Edward L. Cahn**; Screenwriters, **John Huston** and **Tom Reed**; Scenario Editor, **Richard Schayer**; Supervising Film Editor, **Maurice Pivar**; Editor, **Phil Cahn**; Art Director, **John J. Hughes**; Cinematographer, **Jackson Rose**; Recording Supervisor, **C. Roy Hunter**
SONG: "My Pretty Quadroon" (Howard and Vincent)—sung by **Walter Huston, Harry Carey, Russell Hopton** and **Raymond Hatton**
LOCATION FILMING: Vasquez Rocks, Aqua Dulce, California
RUNNING TIME: 72 min.
SOURCE: Novel "Saint Johnson" by William R. Burnett
STORY: Walter Huston and his partners, Harry Carey, Russell Hopton and Raymond Hatton, ride into Tombstone as Alphonse Ethier is re-elected sheriff of Tombstone. Huston plans to give up law enforcement and settle down. Tombstone is being run by Ralph Ince and his brothers, Harry Woods and Richard Alexander. Ethier takes orders from Ince. The law-abiding citizens, headed by

Judge Russell Simpson, offer the job of Deputy Marshal to Huston, which he accepts. Bad blood quickly erupts between Huston and Ince. Huston has an ordinance passed prohibiting the carrying of firearms in Tombstone. A drunken Alexander terrorizes the local saloon, and Hopton orders him to put down his gun. In an exchange of shots, Alexander is killed. Ethier wants to arrest Hopton, but Huston refuses to turn him over. Believing that Huston and his friends are trying to take over the town, Simpson asks Huston to turn in his badge. Huston refuses and declares that he will bring law and order to Tombstone without the use of guns. Ince and his men ambush Carey, mortally wounding him. After the death of his friend, Huston tells the town that he and his friends will leave Tombstone in the morning. Tipped off that Ince, Woods and their men will be waiting to ambush them, Huston, Hopton and Hatton head for the O.K. Barn. A furious gun battle rages, and Huston is the only survivor. Huston leaves Tombstone knowing his destiny is not to settle down but to continue cleaning up lawless towns.

Law and Order (1932) movie still: Harry Carey (*center, seated*) plays cards while, *left to right*, Raymond Hatton, Walter Huston, unidentified actor, and Richard Alexander watch.

NOTES AND COMMENTARY: *Law and Order* was remade as a serial, *Wild West Days* (Universal, 1937) with John Mack Brown, and two feature films, *Law and Order* (Universal, 1940) with Johnny Mack Brown, and *Law and Order* (Universal-International, 1953) with Ronald Reagan.

Screenwriter John Huston was the son of Walter Huston. John Huston became a director with *The Maltese Falcon* (Warner Bros., 1941), for which he also wrote the screenplay. Huston later received an Academy Award for *The Treasure of Sierra Madre* (Warner Bros., 1948). Other western or western related films directed by Huston were *The Red Badge of Courage* (Metro-Goldwyn-Mayer, 1951), *The Unforgiven* (United Artists, 1960), *The Misfits* (United Artists, 1961), *Man in the Wilderness* (Warner Bros., 1971) and *The Life and Times of Judge Roy Bean* (National General, 1972).

Law and Order was retitled *Guns A-Blazin'* when reissued by Realart to avoid confusion with the Johnny Mack Brown version that had also been re-released. In addition, the marquee value of some of the cast members had changed over the years. In 1932, Harry Carey and Russell Hopton received second and third billing respectively. In the '50s reissue, Walter Brennan, who had originally not even received a screen credit, and Andy Devine, who had received ninth billing, took their places.

The film's working title was *Saint Johnson*.

The song "My Pretty Quadroon" was featured prominently in *Fiddlin' Buckaroo* (Universal, 1933). Ken Maynard played the song on his fiddle, and later, in the film, it was sung by Gloria Shea.

Footage from *The Indians Are Coming* was used for the introductory montage scenes. The montage footage of the introduction to lawless Tombstone can be seen in *Diamond Frontier* (Universal, 1940).

REVIEWS: "Well made, directed and acted, this is one of the all-time great Western films—a must see." (*Western Movies*, Pitts); "Serious well-conceived western." (*The Motion Picture Guide*, Nash and Ross)

SUMMATION: This is a superior western deserving of its classic status. Walter Huston heads an excellent cast, delivering a forceful and moving performance as a lawman who believes the six-gun is the basis for trouble in the West. Harry Carey, Russell Hopton, Raymond Hatton and the rest of the cast lend admirable support. Andy Devine's exceptional performance, as the first man to be hanged in Tombstone, deserves special mention. John Huston and Tom Reed deliver a wonderful script, which is nicely directed by Edward L. Cahn, especially in the graphic and suspenseful gunfight sequence at the O.K. Barn.

Action-Crammed Adventure!

Law and Order

ALTERNATE TITLE: *Lucky Ralston;* Universal (November 1940)

CAST: Bill Ralston, **Johnny Mack Brown**; Deadwood, **Fuzzy Knight**; Sally Dixon, **Nell O'Day**; Brant, **James Craig**; Poe Daggett, **Harry Cording**; Elder, **Earle Hodgins**; Deal, **Robert Fiske**; Jimmy, **James Dodd**; Judge Williams, **William Worthington**; Walt, **Ted Adams**; Kurt Daggett, **Ethan Laidlaw**; Stage Driver, **George Plues**; Dixon, **Harry Humphrey**// Henchmen, **Frank McCarroll** and **Kermit Maynard**; Election Official, **Lew Meehan**; Pete, **Bob Kortman**; Singing Cowboys, **the Notables**; Townsman, **Frank Ellis**; Chinese Gentleman, **Wong Chung**

CREDITS: Director, **Ray Taylor**; Screenwriter, **Sherman Lowe** and **Victor McLeod**; Editor, **Edward Curtiss**; Art Directors, **Jack Otterson** and **Harold H. MacArthur**; Set Decorator, **R.A. Gausman**; Cinematographer, **Jerome Ash**; Sound, **Bernard B. Brown** and **Jess Moulin**; Musical Director, **H.J. Salter**

SONGS: "Oklahoma's Oke With Me" (Dodd)—sung by **James Dodd** and **Nell O'Day**; and "Ride 'Im Cowboy" (Rosen and Carter)—sung by **the Notables**; and "Those Happy Old Days" (Rosen and Carter)—sung by **Fuzzy Knight**

LOCATION FILMING: Iverson, California

RUNNING TIME: 57 min.

SOURCE: Novel "Saint Johnson" by **W.R. Burnett**

STORY: Johnny Mack Brown, Fuzzy Knight and James Craig arrive in Rhyolite to find Harry Cording, with his brothers Ted Adams and Ethan Laidlaw, running the town. When rancher Harry Humphrey, an outspoken proponent of law and order, is murdered, Brown and his friends decide to help his daughter, Nell O'Day, run her ranch. O'Day's brother, James Dodd, kills one of Cording's men in self-defense. Cording plans to lynch Dodd, but Brown, taking the job as Deputy Marshal, prevents the hanging. Brown, with his deputies Knight and Craig, begins to enforce a "gun-toting" law. Brown makes deadly enemies of Cording and his brothers. Laidlaw, Adams and two henchmen spot Brown and O'Day outside of town and ambush them. Brown and O'Day return gunfire, and only Laidlaw remains alive. Laidlaw tells Cording that Brown and a large number of men began a gun battle and shot Adams down without giving him a chance to defend himself. Cording decides it's time to have it out with Brown, and starts by gunning down Craig. Brown and Knight accept Cording's challenge. Brown has Cording and his men ride out of town, with he and Knight in pursuit. In an exciting chase sequence, Brown ends Cording's lawless career while Knight takes care of Laidlaw. With Cording's reign of terror ended, Brown and Knight decide to journey to new adventures.

NOTES AND COMMENTARY: Universal first brought *Law and Order* to the screen in 1932 as an austere outing with Walter Huston in the lead. The first remake was a serial, *Wild West Days* (Universal, 1937), with Johnny Mack Brown. Universal then utilized the basic plot for Brown's "B" western series in 1941. Ronald Reagan starred in the only color version of *Law and Order* (Universal-International, 1953), the final remake to date.

Stuntman Eddie Parker doubles Johnny Mack Brown in his rugged fistfight with Harry Cording.

Footage from *Law and Order* was utilized in the Tex Williams featurette *Western Courage* (Universal-International, 1950).

James Dodd would gain his biggest fame as Jimmie Dodd, a member of Disney's Mouseketeers.

The screenwriters gave Fuzzy Knight a couple of good lines regarding Lady Luck: "I sure wish Lady Luck would smile upon me sometime, instead of making faces at me. She can make some mean faces sometime, too."

Fuzzy Knight would once again sing "Those Happy Old Days" in *Gunman's Code* (Universal, 1946).

REVIEWS: "Good Johnny Mack Brown western, crammed with action." (*Variety*, 11/27/40); "An easy going actioner." (*The Western*, Hardy)

SUMMATION: *Law and Order* is a superior "B" western, adroitly mixing exciting action sequences and good acting with some mild comedy and tuneful songs. Johnny Mack Brown gets to show his acting ability as well as his prowess in the fighting, shooting and riding sequences. Fuzzy Knight gives a restrained performance as the comedy sidekick that adds to the film's enjoyment. Other fine performances are given by James Craig, Nell O'Day and Harry Cording. Director Ray Taylor makes the most of the excellent script turned out by Sherman Lowe and Victor McLeod.

SMASHING FISTS AND POUNDING HOOFS STAMPING OUT DESPERADOES!

Law for Tombstone

Universal (October 1937); A Buck Jones Production

CAST: Alamo Bowie, **Buck Jones**; Nellie Gray, **Muriel Evans**; Doc Holliday, **Harvey Clark**; Judge Hart, **Carl Stockdale**; Jack Dunn, **Earl Hodgins**; Bull Clanton, **Alexander Cross**; Smith, **Chuck Morrison**; Marie, **Mary Carny**; Sheriff Blaine, **Chas. Le Moyne**; Slim, **Ben Corbett**; Tom Scutter, **Harold Hodge**; Pop, **Arthur Van Slyke**; Bob, **Ezra Paul-**

lette; Lee, **Francis Walker**; "Silver"// Peters, **Slim Whitaker**; Pecos, **Glenn Strange**

CREDITS: Director, **Charles Jones**; Co-Director, **W.B. Eason**; Story, **Charles M. Martin**; Screenwriter, **Frances Guihan**; Editor, **Bernard Loftus**; Art Director, **Ralph Berger**; Cinematography, **Allen Thompson** and **John Hickson**; Sound, **L. John Myers**

SONGS: "We Are the Rangers"—sung by **Ezra Paulette and male chorus**; "Texas Prairie"—sung by **Ezra Paulette and male chorus**; "We Are the Rangers" (reprise)—sung by **Ezra Paulette and male chorus**; "Red River Valley" (traditional)—sung by **male chorus**; "Little Brown Jug" (traditional)—sung by **male chorus**; "Oh Susanna" (Foster)—**instrumental**; "La Cucharacha" (traditional)—**instrumental**; "Red River Valley" (reprise)—**instrumental**; "Comin' Round the Mountain" (traditional)—**instrumental;** and "We Are the Rangers" (reprise)—sung by **Ezra Paulette**

LOCATION FILMING: Agoura and Kernville, California

RUNNING TIME: 59 min.

STORY: Arizona Ranger Buck Jones, with help from undercover agent Harvey Clark, is assigned to bring law and order to Tombstone and bring to justice the mysterious outlaw leader terrorizing the territory. The area has been plagued with numerous stagecoach robberies, so Jones trails a stage to Tombstone. When the stage is held up, Jones wounds outlaw Slim Whitaker and prevents the holdup. The mysterious leader orders his chief henchman, Alexander Cross, to kidnap Judge Carl Stockdale in order to prevent the trial from being held. Jones hides Stockdale, so two witnesses to the crime are murdered, leaving Jones and hotel owner Muriel Evans as the only remaining witnesses. The mysterious leader discovers where Stockdale is being held and has the Judge kidnapped. Clark believes Stockdale has been take to Cross' ranch. Jones and Clark rescue Stockdale and get him to court in time to try Whitaker. Realizing the trial will uncover the identity of the mysterious leader, storekeeper and "honest" citizen Earl Hodgins makes a getaway attempt, but is captured by Jones. Jones and Clark can now return to Ranger Headquarters.

NOTES AND COMMENTARY: Buck Jones previously played the role of Alamo Bowie in *Left-Handed Law* (Universal, 1937). Charles M. Martin wrote both stories.

Law for Tombstone was the most tune-filled of the Buck Jones westerns. Three songs are sung in the first reel, with Jones mouthing the words. Songs are sung or played throughout the story, with "We Are the Rangers" being sung for the third time in the last reel. "Red River Valley" can be heard in *Sandflow* (Universal, 1937), *Stagecoach Buckaroo* (Universal, 1941) and *The Silver Bullet* (Universal, 1942). "Little Brown Jug" would be heard in *Twilight on the Prairie* (Universal, 1944). "Oh, Susanna" saw service in *The Fiddlin' Buckaroo* (Universal, 1933), *Courage of the West* (Universal, 1937), *Desperate Trails*

(Universal, 1939), *Chip of the Flying U* (Universal, 1939) and *Rawhide Rangers* (Universal, 1941). "La Cucaracha" was used in *When a Man Sees Red* (Universal, 1934), *Outlaw Express* (Universal, 1938), *Boss of Bullion City* (Universal, 1941) and the short, *Frontier Frolic* (Universal, 1946).

REVIEWS: "Current release contains nothing to get excited about although it provides plenty action." (*Variety*, 12/29/37); "Sturdy Buck Jones vehicle." (*Western Movies*, Pitts)

SUMMATION: *Law for Tombstone* is a better than average "B" western, but its hardly up to Buck Jones' best. Jones takes care of the heroics adequately, with competent performances from the rest of the cast. The undemanding story isn't helped by offering such an obvious mystery villain. Superior camera work by Allen Thompson and John Hickson, and a tough, well-staged fistfight between Jones and Alexander Cross, enhances the film. The script states that the mystery villain and Jones are both excellent gunfighters, but the expected shootout between the two never materializes.

DEFYING DEATH-DEALING DESPERADOS!
A bold buckaroo blasts the bad men of the badlands!

Law of the Range

Universal (June 1941)

CAST: Steve, **Johnny Mack Brown**; Chap, **Fuzzy Knight**; Mary, **Nell O'Day**; Wolverine Kid, **Roy Harris**; Virginia, **Elaine Morey**; Edward, **Pat O'Malley**; Tim, **Hal Taliaferro**; Walt, **Charles King**; Sheriff, **Jack Rockwell**; Jamison, **Alan Bridge**; Curt, **Jerome Hart**; Emery, **Terry Frost;** and **the Texas Rangers** (**Robert "Captain Bob" Crawford, Edward "Tookie" Cronenbold, Francis "Irish" Mahaney** and **Roderic "Dave" May**)// Jeff Hobart, **Ethan Laidlaw**; Henchmen, **Slim Whitaker** and **Bob Kortman**; Saloon Singer, **Lucille Walker**; Bartender, **Bud Osborne**; Jake, **Jim Corey**

CREDITS: Director, **Ray Taylor**; Associate Producer, **Will Cowan**; Story, **Charles E. Barnes**; Screenwriter, **Sherman Lowe**; Editor, **E. Curtiss**; Art Directors, **Jack Otterson** and **Harold H. MacArthur**; Cinematographer, **Charles Van Enger**; Sound, **Bernard B. Brown** and **Jess Moulin**; Music Director, **H.J. Salter**

SONGS: "Six Gun Dan" (Crawford)—sung by **the Texas Rangers**; "I Plumb Forget" (Rosen and Carter)—sung by **Fuzzy Knight**; "Forget Your Boots and Saddles" (Rosen and Carter)—sung by **Lucille Walker** and **male chorus**; "Pals of the Prairie" (Crawford)—sung by **the Texas Rangers;** and "Pals of the Prairie" (reprise)—sung by **the Texas Rangers**

LOCATION FILMING: Iverson and Brandeis Ranch, California

RUNNING TIME: 59 min.

STORY: Roy Harris wants to take revenge on Pat O'Malley and also cause a range war so sheep can be brought into cattle country. In trying to fuel a fight between O'Malley and neighboring rancher Hal Taliaferro, Harris guns down one of Taliaferro's cowboys. Taliaferro tries to force O'Malley's son, Johnny Mack Brown, to draw, but Brown won't fight him. Brown is in love with Taliaferro's daughter, Elaine Morey. Brown learns that an attempt will be made to bring sheep into the valley, and rides to Taliaferro's ranch for his help in combating this menace. As Brown rides up, Harris shoots down Taliaferro. Taliaferro's other daughter, Nell O'Day, believes Brown is the murderer. From a spent cartridge found by Brown, the finger of guilt points to Harris. Sheriff Jack Rockwell deputizes Brown and his pal, Fuzzy Knight, to track down Harris. Harris plans to drive the sheep into the valley, light the signal fires to alert the ranchers, and then set up a trap to ambush the ranchers. Both Harris and O'Day want to capture Brown alive, Harris to kill Brown himself and O'Day to turn Brown over to the sheriff. Harris' men jump Brown and take him to a cabin used by Harris and his gang. Both Harris and O'Day arrive at the cabin. O'Day hears Harris gloating over his plans to turn the valley into sheep territory, and tries to free Brown. One of Harris' men, Ethan Laidlaw, gets the drop on O'Day and ties her up. Knight happens upon the cabin, sizes up the situation, and rescues Brown and O'Day. O'Day rides to warn the ranchers while Brown and Knight ride to the ambush spot. Brown and Knight begin firing on Harris and his men. O'Day reaches the ranchers in time, and they attack the ambushers. Harris' men are wiped out or captured. Harris makes a break for it, and Brown follows. Brown catches Harris and turns him over to Rockwell. With the threat to the cattlemen over, Brown has time to romance Morey.

NOTES AND COMMENTARY: *Law of the Range* is a remake of Buck Jones' *The Ivory Handled Gun* (Universal, 1935), also directed by Ray Taylor.

Law of the Range marked the film debut of Roy Harris. Harris was later billed as Riley Hill.

REVIEWS: "Standard western, plenty of action, clear characters and an unbroken story line. Above average Johnny Mack Brown western." (*Variety*, 7/16/41); "Sturdy Johnny Mack Brown western." (*Western Movies*, Pitts)

SUMMATION: *Law of the Range* is a good, exciting "B" western. Johnny Mack Brown handles the heroics admirably, and Nell O'Day chips in with some hard-riding sequences. Fuzzy Knight's comedy isn't too intrusive and may garner a chuckle or two. Roy Harris is fine as Brown's nemesis. Roy Taylor's direction is straightforward, with good results.

Blasting the Renegade Bandits!

Lawless Breed

ALTERNATE TITLE: *Lawless Clan;* Universal (August 1946)

CAST: Ted Everett, **Kirby Grant**; Tumbleweed, **Fuzzy Knight**; Marjorie Bradley, **Jane Adams**; Bartley / Issac Mellon, **Dick Curtis**; Cherie, **Claudia Drake**; Sanford Witherspoon, **Harry Brown**; Tim Carson, **Charles King**; Sheriff Dan Bradley, **Karl Hackett**; Deputy, **Hank Worden**// Station Agent, **Ernie Adams**

CREDITS: Director / Producer, **Wallace W. Fox**; Screenwriter, **Bob Williams**; Editor, **Otto Ludwig**; Art Directors, **Jack Otterson** and **Frank A. Richards**; Set Decorators, **Russell A. Gausman** and **Leigh Smith**; Cinematographer, **Maury Gertsman**; Gowns, **Rosemary Odell**; Hair Stylist, **Carmen Dirigo**; Makeup, **Jack P. Pierce**; Sound, **Bernard B. Brown** and **John W. Rixey**; Musical Director, **Milton Rosen**

SONGS: "Do the Oo La La" (Rosen and Carter)—sung by **Claudia Drake**; and "Bananas Make Me Tough" (Carter and Rosen)—sung by **Fuzzy Knight**

LOCATION FILMING: Iverson, California

RUNNING TIME: 58 min.

STORY: After the recent rash of bank robberies, Spearville bank president Dick Curtis decides to organize the banks to smash the outlaw gang. Kirby Grant and Fuzzy Knight ride into town, and it becomes evident to rancher Charles King that Grant is avoiding the law. King gives Grant and Knight jobs on his ranch. Finding a wanted poster in Grant's boot indicating that Grant is wanted for murder; and King tells Grant to kill Curtis. Grant discovers that his pistol is loaded with blanks, and he decides to carry out King's scheme. As Grant fires at Curtis, another shot rings out. Curtis falls and is pronounced dead. Grant and Knight are arrested for the crime. Seaman Curtis, the banker's twin, shows up in Spearville to see his brother. Learning of his brother's death, he and King incite the townsmen to storm the jail in order to lynch Grant and Knight. The sheriff's niece, Jane Adams, releases Grant and Knight, enabling them to escape. On a hunch, Grant and Knight open banker Curtis' grave and find it empty. Knowing the bank is holding a large amount of money for transfer, Grant and Knight stop a bank robbery. Grant unmasks the outlaws and reveals King and Curtis. Grant then proves banker Curtis and seaman Curtis are one and the same. Curtis makes a break on horseback, and Grant catches up to him. A fight ensues, with Curtis plunging over a cliff to his death. Grant proves he's a federal agent and now has time to devote his attention to Adams.

NOTES AND COMMENTARY: *Lawless Breed* was remade as *The Vanishing Westerner* (Republic, 1950) starring Monte Hale.

The sequence in which Fuzzy Knight lassoes Kirby Grant and Jane Adams was lifted intact from *The Masked Rider* (Universal, 1941), where Knight roped Johnny Mack Brown and Nell O'Day. Grant and Adams would be seen in the close-up shots.

Charles King finds a wanted poster in one of Kirby Grant's boots. The name on the poster is Duke Masters, an alias Grant used in *Gunman's Code* (Universal, 1946). The poster was issued by Foster Felton, a character name in Grant's *Trail to Vengeance* (Universal, 1945).

Fuzzy Knight sang "Bananas Make Me Tough" in the Johnny Mack Brown western *Man from Montana* (Universal, 1941). Vyola Vonn sang "Do the Oo La La" in the Johnny Mack Brown starrer *Ragtime Cowboy Joe* (Universal, 1940). Both Claudia Drake and Kirby Grant have musical numbers for which the author was unable to ascertain the titles. A good bet for the Grant song would be "I'm Sitting on the Outside."

REVIEWS: "Fairly good finale to Kirby Grant's Universal series." (*Western Movies*, Pitts); "Typical western outing," (*The Motion Picture Guide*, Nash and Ross)

SUMMATION: Bob Williams penned a good screenplay for this Kirby Grant vehicle, and the results are very satisfactory. Grant, again, does a good job as the stalwart hero, and sidekick Fuzzy Knight's light comedy is on the mark. The villainy rests in the capable hands of Dick Curtis and Charles King. Wallace W. Fox directs firmly and efficiently.

HE RIDES! HE FIGHTS! HE GETS HIS MAN!

Left Handed Law

Universal (April 1937); A Buck Jones Production

CAST: Alamo Bowie, **Buck Jones**; Betty Golden, **Noel Francis**; One-Shot Brady, **Matty Fain**; Sam Logan, **George Regas**; Tom Willis, **Robert Frazer**; Sheriff Grant, **Lee Phelps**; Conchita, **Nena Quartero**; John Golden, **Frank LaRue**; Pecos Brown, **Lee Shumway**; Joe Hernandez, **Frank Lackteen**; Kidnapper, **Wm. Lawrence**; Brazos, **Charles Le Moyne**; Tom Scudder, **Harold Hodge**; "Silver Jr."// Stage Driver, **Budd Buster**; Accordion Player in Cantina, **Frank Yaconelli**; Jim, **Jim Corey**; Todd, **Robert Walker**

CREDITS: Director, **Lesley Selander**; Story, **Charles M. Martin**; Screenwriter, **Frances Guihan**; Editor, **Bernard Loftus**; Art Director, **Ralph Berger**; Cinematographers, **Allen Thompson** and **William Sickner**; Sound, **L. John Myers**

SONG: "Out on the Texas Plains" (traditional)—sung by **vocal group**

LOCATION FILMING: Walker Ranch, California

RUNNING TIME: 62 min.

STORY: Ranger Buck Jones is assigned to break up Matty Fain's outlaw gang operating in the Twin Forks area. Initially refusing the assignment, Jones changes his mind when he learns he'll be working out of Frank La Rue's ranch and will be near LaRue's daughter, Noel Francis. Jones recovers cattle stolen from LaRue's ranch. One of Fain's partners, Robert Frazier, has Larue kidnapped. Frazier demands ten thousand dollars from LaRue for his release. Jones beats Frazier and forces him to tell where LaRue is being held. Frazier is arrested, and LaRue is released. Fearing the weak Frazier would tell everything about the gang, Fain has henchman Frank Lackteen murder Frazier. Jones, with Sheriff Lee Phelps' assistance, captures Lackteen. Lackteen tells Jones how to find Fain's hideout. Fain leaves his hideout minutes before Jones arrives, but Jones finds evidence linking Fain to the lawless activity in the Twin Fork area. Francis goes riding and sees Fain and henchman Robert Walker riding to the stagecoach road. Francis alerts Jones who, with hard riding, prevents the robbery. Jones shoots Walker, but Fain escapes. Before Walker dies, he tells Jones where Fain is going. Jones catches up to Fain. The two men step out of cover. Both men draw, but the fast and accurate Jones ends Fain's outlaw career. Larue gives Jones half interest in his ranch, and Jones and Francis can now spend time with each other.

NOTES AND COMMENTARY: In *Law for Tombstone* (Universal, 1937) Buck Jones would again play Alamo Bowie. Given the endings of the two films, it seems the **Tombstone** episode actually came before *Left Handed Law*, even though this film was released first.

The picture's end offers this amusing dialog exchange between Jones and Noel Francis.

FRANCIS: "Dad sort of likes you, Alamo."
JONES: "He must. He gave me half interest in your ranch."
FRANCIS: "That doesn't mean that I go with it."
JONES: "Don't get too ambitious. I'll get you sooner or later."
FRANCIS: "Oh, yeah."
JONES: "Yeah. Betty, what time we'd go to that dance tonight?"
FRANCIS: "I wouldn't go to a dance with you if you were the last man on earth. When do we leave?"

REVIEWS: "Workmanlike edition of typical Buck Jones western." (*Variety*, 5/12/37); "The small kids and the kid in us all will find enjoyment in this dust covered western filled with he-man action and the western clichés that could be gathered at the time." (*The Motion Picture Guide*, Nash and Ross)

SUMMATION: *Left Handed Law* is another good Buck Jones western. This time out, Jones likes to chase women and is not above resorting to violence when questioning bad guys. In one scene, he continues to beat a cowering Robert Frazer until Frazer confesses. Noel Francis is a comely and spunky leading lady, and works well with Jones. The chemistry between the stars makes their ultimate romance quite convincing. The story moves nicely and only stumbles briefly with a totally unnecessary sequence of Jones riding a bucking bronco. Lesley Selander directs with a strong hand, while screenwriter Frances Guihan offers two strong scenes at the picture's end. First comes a well-conceived confrontation between Jones and main badman Matty Fain (with the unusual musical score underscoring the tension between hero and villain), followed by a delicious repartee between Jones and Francis to end the story. Sequences like these make *Left Handed Law* an above average in a series western.

The Lightning Express

Universal (April 1930)

CAST: Jack Venable, **Lane Chandler**; Bobbie Van Tyme, **Louise Lorraine**; Whispering Smith, **Al Ferguson**; Kate, **Greta Granstedt**; Frank Sanger, **J. Gordon Russell**; Bill Lewellyn, **John Oscar**; Hank Pardelow, **Martin Clichy**; Floyd Griswell, **Bob Reeves**; Griswell's henchmen, **Robert Kelly** and **James Pierce**

CREDITS: Director, **Henry MacRae**; Titles, **Ford Beebe**; Cinematography, **Frank Redman**

CHAPTER TITLES: 1. A Shot in the Dark, 2. A Scream of Terror, 3. Dangerous Rails, 4. The Death Trap, 5. Tower of Terror, 6. A Call for Help, 7. The Runaway Freight, 8. The Show Down, 9. The Secret Survey, 10. Cleared Tracks

SOURCE: Story "Whispering Smith Speaks" by **Frank H. Spearman**

STORY: The B&M Railroad is blocked in its goal of extending the line to the Pacific Ocean when J. Gordon Russell, Louise Lorraine's guardian, refuses to allow the railroad to cross Lorraine's ranch land. Al Ferguson persuades Lane Chandler to abandon his wild party life to assist the railroad, and to help him investigate the death of Lorraine's father. Chandler's father built the Lightning Express, the railroad's best train. Using an alias, Chandler goes to work with the railroad as a foreman. Lorraine and Chandler fall in love, and Lorraine decides to support the railroad. The construction crew starts laying tracks across Lorraine's land. Russell goes all out in his attempt to stop construction, putting both Chandler and Lorraine's lives in danger. Chandler and Lorraine are able to escape death, thanks usually to Ferguson's timely interventions. Chandler, Lorraine and Ferguson go to Chandler's apartment in the city to find a survey needed for the completion of the line. Russell convinces Greta Granstedt to throw a wild party at the apartment. Arriving at his apartment, Chandler is forced to tell Lorraine his real name and that the partygoers are old friends of his. Russell shows up and convinces Lorraine that Chandler is no good, and Lorraine leaves with Russell. Ferguson tells Chandler the missing survey is in the apartment's wall safe. In the safe, Ferguson finds Lorraine's father's will naming Ferguson of Lorraine's guardian. Using a forged will, Russell had gained the position as Lorraine's guardian. Chandler and Ferguson race to Lorraine's home to show her the will. Russell grabs the envelope and quickly burns it. Russell and his men then surround Lorraine's house and a pitched battle ensues. Ferguson turns the tables and brings Russell and his men to justice. Ferguson then shows Lorraine her father's will and reveals that Russell burned an empty envelope. Chandler and Lorraine are married on the Lightning Express as it travels across Lorraine's land on the way to the Pacific Ocean.

NOTES AND COMMENTARY: Whispering Smith made his only literary appearance in Frank N. Spearman's "Whispering Smith" (Charles Scribner's Sons, 1906). In 1916, Spearman's novel reached the movie screen as two features, *Whispering Smith* (Signal Film Corp./Mutual Film Corp.) and *Medicine Bend* (Signal Film Corp./ Mutual Film Corp.) with director J.P. McGowan as Smith. Charles Hill Mailes played Smith in a contemporary drama, *Money Madness* (Universal, 1917). The novel was remade in 1926 as *Whispering Smith* (Metropolitan Pictures Corp./ Producers Distribution Corp.). Spearman expert Fred Weiss believes that Spearman moved to Los Angeles in the '20s and possibly did some screenwriting, which would explain the titles of Whispering Smith stories credited as the basis of the first two Smith sound features: Al Ferguson portrayed Smith in *The Lightning Express* (Universal, 1930), a 12-chapter serial; and George O'Brien was Smith in *Whispering Smith Speaks* (Fox, 1935). Jack Clifford played a character named Whispering Smith in two Renfrew of the Mounted episodes, **Sky** *Bandits* (Monogram, 1940) and *Yukon Flight* (Monogram, 1940). Alan Ladd became the definitive Smith in *Whispering Smith* (Paramount, 1948), a first rate Technicolor western story. Smith went modern in *Whispering Smith vs. Scotland Yard* (RKO, 1951), with Richard Carlson. Audie Murphy brought Smith to the television screen in 1961, but *Whispering Smith* (Revue/ NBC) was doomed from the start. Series co-star Guy Mitchell broke a shoulder, which held up production. Then Murphy had to fulfill a commitment for a motion picture, again holding up production. When the series finally debuted on television, it was highly criticized because of the violence seen in the first episode. Whispering Smith was canceled after 25 episodes. This, to date, was the last time Smith appeared on any screen, large or small.

SUMMATION: This serial was not available for viewing by the author.

Twin Tornadoes with Flaming Forty-Fives!
The west's greatest star team!

Little Joe, the Wrangler

Universal (November 1942)

CAST: Neal Wallace, **Johnny Mack Brown**; Bob Brewster, **Tex Ritter**; Little Joe Smith, **Fuzzy Knight**; Janet Hammond, **Jennifer Holt**; Mary Brewster, **Florine McKinney**; Lloyd Chapin, **James Craven**; Travis, **Hal Taliaferro**; Jeff Corey, **Glenn Strange**; and the **Jimmy Wakely Trio** (**Jimmy Wakely, Johnny Bond** and **Scotty Harrel**)// Larkin, **Ethan Laidlaw**; Charlie, **Slim Whitaker**; Mr. Hammond, **Robert F. Hill**; Miner, **Frank Ellis**; Helen, **Evelyn Cook**; Norton, **Carl Sepulvada**

CREDITS: Director, **Lewis D. Collins**; Associate Producer, **Oliver Drake**; Screenwriters, **Sherman L. Lowe** and **Elizabeth Beecher**; Editor, **Russell Schoengarth**; Art Directors, **Jack Otterson** and **Ralph M. DeLacy**; Set Decorators, **R.A. Gausman** and **J. Andrew Gilmore**; Cinematographer, **William Sickner**; Sound, **Bernard B. Brown** and **Jess Moulin**; Musical Director, **H.J. Salter**

SONGS: "Little Joe, the Wrangler" (traditional)/ "Little Joe" (Loesser and Hollander)—sung by **Fuzzy Knight**; "I'd Saddle My Pony" (Wakely)—sung by **the Jimmy Wakely Trio**; "Get Along, Little Dogies" (traditional)—sung by **the Jimmy Wakely Trio**; and "Little Joe, the Wrangler" (reprise)—sung by **Tex Ritter and the Jimmy Wakely Trio**

LOCATION FILMING: Corriganville, California

RUNNING TIME: 60 min.

STORY: Holdups and raids on the mines have plagued miners in the Lamplight vicinity. Sheriff Tex Ritter hasn't been able to discover who's behind this lawlessness. Mine owner Hal Taliaferro wants Ritter replaced. Taliaferro has been leading the raids, and he and his men attack a wagon being driven by Robert F. Hill. Johnny Mack Brown sees the attack and drives the hijackers off, but not before Hill is killed. Taliaferro and his men circle back and get the drop on Brown, and take him to Lamplight for Hill's murder. In Lamplight, Ritter puts Brown in jail. Brown tries to explain his innocence. Taliaferro incites the mob to lynch Brown. Ritter deputizes Fuzzy Knight and has Knight take Brown to his ranch. Hill's granddaughter, Jennifer Holt, is at the ranch and learns of her father's death. After the mob has been dispersed, Ritter questions Brown. Brown tries to tell Ritter he's a vice-president for the Monarch Mining Company and was sent to investigate why the Lamplight smelter was suddenly losing money. Taliaferro had removed Brown's credentials from his saddlebags and substituted ore from Hill's claim. Holt believes Brown is guilty of Hill's murder. When three of Taliaferro's men ride to the ranch,

Brown makes a break. Ritter gives chase and catches up with Brown. The two men fight, but Brown gets possession of Ritter's gun and makes Ritter listen to him. When Brown returns Ritter's pistol, Ritter decides to work with Brown to bring the lawbreakers to justice. Brown visits the smelter, but manager James Craven won't cooperate since Brown doesn't have the proper credentials. Craven has Brown travel a seldom used road to the nearest telegraph office to wire for credentials, but plans to have Taliaferro's men ambush him on the way. Fearing an ambush, Brown has Knight ride the ridge and watch for trouble. Taliaferro's men surround Brown. Knight opens fire with his rifle, and Brown escapes. Brown and Ritter now believe Craven and Taliaferro are behind the trouble. Ritter has telegraphed Monarch Mining for information on Brown and has obtained a court order to search Craven's books, but the books show nothing irregular. At Ritter's ranch, Holt receives a telegram identifying Brown. Directed to the smelter, Holt arrives and asks for Craven. Craven directs Holt to a room where Taliaferro captures her. Returning to town, Brown and Ritter learn Holt had gone to the smelter and ride back to the rescue, with a posse to follow. Craven had been storing the stolen gold, and now he and Taliaferro know it's time to take the loot and leave the area. Brown and Ritter return and, after gunfire and fistfights, bring Craven, Taliaferro and their men to justice. Brown now begins romancing Holt.

NOTES AND COMMENTARY: Footage from *Law of the Range* (Universal, 1941) was used in the montage sequence at the beginning of *Little Joe, the Wrangler*.

When Fuzzy Knight sings "Little Joe, the Wrangler," he also sings some of the lyrics of "Little Joe" sung by Marlene Dietrich in *Destry Rides Again* (Universal, 1939). "Little Joe" was sung by Butch 'n' Buddy in *Man from Montana* (Universal, 1941), and by Virginia Christine in *The Old Texas Trail* (Universal, 1944). "Get Along, Little Dogies" was featured in *Stagecoach Buckaroo* (Universal, 1941) and *Marshal of Gunsmoke* (Universal, 1944).

REVIEWS: "A better-than-average western." (*Variety*, 12/23/42); "A fast-paced punchfest." (*The Motion Picture Guide*, Nash and Ross)

SUMMATION: *Little Joe, the Wrangler* is a good, fast-moving "B" western with plenty of action. Johnny Mack Brown and Tex Ritter make a good starring duo, although it's obvious Brown will get a little more screen time than Ritter. Fuzzy Knight is pretty much on target with his comedy and does help Brown and Ritter round up the bad guys. Lewis D. Collins directs briskly to keep the action at the forefront.

Hot-Lead Vs Cold-Killers!
Fists fly! Guns roar ... as Johnny and Tex blast a band of border grafters!

The Lone Star Trail

Universal (August 1943)

CAST: Blaze Barker, **Johnny Mack Brown**; Fargo Steele, **Tex Ritter**; Angus McAngus, **Fuzzy Knight**; Jean Winters, **Jennifer Holt**; Doug Ransom, **George Eldredge**; Jonathan Bentley, **Michael Vallon**; Sheriff Waddell, **Harry Strang**; Cyrus Jenkins, **Earle Hodgins**; Dan Jason, **Jack Ingram**; Ben Slocum, **Bob Mitchum**; Steve Bannister, **Ethan Laidlaw**; and the **Jimmy Wakely Trio** (**Jimmy Wakely, Johnny Bond** and **Scotty Harrel**)// Shorty, **Billy Engle**; Bartender, **William Desmond**; Lem, **Eddie Parker**; Tax Collector, **Henry Roquemore**

CREDITS: Director, **Ray Taylor**; Associate Producer / Screenwriter, **Oliver Drake**; Story, **Victor Halperin**; Editor, **Ray Snyder**; Art Directors, **John Goodman** and **Ralph M. DeLacy**; Set Decorators, **R.A. Gausman** and **A.J. Gilmore**; Cinematographer, **William Sickner**; Sound, **Bernard B. Brown** and **Jess Moulin**; Musical Director, **H.J. Salter**

SONGS: "Welcome Home" (Rosen and Carter)—sung by **the Jimmy Wakely Trio**; "Adios Vaqueros"—sung by **the Jimmy Wakely Trio**; "I've Got to See Texas Just Once More"—sung by **Tex Ritter**; and "Trail Dreamin'" (Rosen, Wakely and Drake)—sung by **the Jimmy Wakely Trio**

LOCATION FILMING: Corriganville, California

RUNNING TIME: 57 min.

STORY: After spending two years in prison for a robbery he didn't commit, Johnny Mack Brown receives a parole. Learning Brown is returning to Dead Fall, Earle Hodgins, Bob Mitchum and Michael Vallon, whose perjured testimony helped to convict Brown, decide to leave town. The men return to Dead Fall after learning that Brown is now a coward. This is a ruse, and Brown warns the three men not to try to leave town again. Attempts are made on Brown's life, but timely interference by gunman Tex Ritter saves him. Fuzzy Knight, Jennifer Holt and George Eldredge befriend Brown. Unknown to Brown, Eldredge is behind a plot to prevent a dam from being constructed until Eldredge and his cronies own all the rangeland. To pay off back taxes on their ranch, Brown and Knight round up cattle to sell to buyer Ethan Laidlaw. Laidlaw, working with Eldredge, uses some stolen money to buy the cattle. Brown pays off the debt, but the stolen money is turned over to Sheriff Harry Strang. Strang is working with Ritter, who is a United States Marshal. Knight overhears Strang's conversation with Ritter and alerts Brown. Brown goes after Laidlaw and learns that Eldredge is the ringleader. The cowardly Vallon wants out and is murdered by Eldredge, who frames Brown for the crime.

Ritter makes an unsuccessful attempt to arrest Brown. Eldredge decides to burn the stolen money, but Brown stops him. After a brief but furious struggle, Brown brings the men to justice. Brown and Holt plan to wed.

NOTES AND COMMENTARY: *The Lone Star Trail* was the last Universal western for Johnny Mack Brown. Brown moved over to Monogram to begin a long series of westerns for that studio. By the time *The Lone Star Trail* reached theaters, two of Brown's Monogram features had already been released.

Tex Ritter was elevated to solo star billing after *The Lone Star Trail*, but either Dennis Moore or Russell Hayden would be around to share the heroics. Ritter would bolt from Universal a year later to join Dave O'Brien in the Texas Rangers series at PRC.

The plot of *The Lone Star Trail* owes more than a little to Tom Mix's *Destry Rides Again* (Universal, 1932).

Ace stuntman Tom Steele doubles Bob Mitchum in the fight sequences. Mitchum was almost ready for star status. He would play a major role and steal the show in Eddie Dew's *Beyond the Last Frontier* (Republic, 1943) before being tapped to star in his own western series at RKO.

When Earle Hodgins, Bob Mitchum and Michael Vallon receive letters informing them that they can return to Dead Fall, the same pair of hands open all three letters.

A newspaper article seen at the film's opening states that a fourth man, "Ed Swain," also testified against Brown. This character is never referred to again.

"Trail Dreamin'" was originally heard in *Boss of Hangtown Mesa* (Universal, 1942) and would be used later in *Trigger Trail* (Universal, 1944). "Welcome Home" was heard in the Johnny Mack Brown starrer *Fighting Bill Fargo* (Universal, 1941).

REVIEWS: "Action filled cowboy yarn." (*Variety*, 9/8/43); "The last and undoubtedly the best of Brown and Ritter's co-starring Westerns for Universal." (*The Western*, Hardy)

SUMMATION: This is one of the best "B" westerns, thoroughly enjoyable. Johnny Mack Brown and Tex Ritter are billed as the West's Greatest Star Team, but emphasis is clearly placed on Brown's role. Brown doesn't disappoint, as he handles the action and acting chores admirably. Ritter takes care of his part in fine fashion as well. Fuzzy Knight keeps his humor within reasonable bounds this outing and is quite amusing. Director Ray Taylor keeps the story moving and the action flowing. The well-choreographed fight sequence in which Brown and Ritter take on Mitchum, Jack Ingram and Eddie Parker is a dandy.

THE FIRST 100% ALL-TALKING OUTDOOR WESTERN
*Hear and See the Hair-Raising Rodeo— The Cross-Country Race— Wild Herds
Playing Follow the Leader— The Only Western to Ever Play on Broadway*

The Long Long Trail

Universal (September 1929)

CAST: Ramblin' Kid, **Hoot Gibson**; June, **Sally Eilers**; Ophelia, **Kathryn McGuire**; Mike Wilson, **James Mason**; Gyp, **Archie Ricks**, Skinny Rawlings, **Walter Brennan**; Uncle Josh, **Howard Truesdale**

CREDITS: Director, **Arthur Rosson**; Producer, **Hoot Gibson**; Continuity, **Howard Green**; Editor, **Gilmore Walker**; Art Director, **David Garber**; Cinematographer, **Harry Neumann**; Sychonization and Sound, **Bert Fiske**; Recording Supervisor, **C. Roy Hunter**; Sound, **Western Electric System**

LOCATION FILMING: Salinas, the French Ranch and Lake Sherwood, California

RUNNING TIME: 59 min.

SOURCE: Novel "The Ramblin' Kid" (Indianapolis, 1920) by **Earl W. Bowman**

STORY: Cowboy Hoot Gibson, pretending drunkenness, habitually plays practical jokes on the townspeople. After one such episode, Gibson learns that a pair of women are coming to live at Howard Truesdale's ranch. The women are Truesdale's niece, Sally Eilers, and her friend, Kathryn McGuire. Wanting to have nothing to do with the women, Gibson decides to capture the leader of a wild horse herd. After meeting Gibson, Eilers begins to fall in love with the cowboy. Gibson, however, spends time breaking and training the horse to ride as the ranch's entry in the annual race. James Mason's horse has been the winner for the past few years and willingly makes a large bet with Truesdale, not knowing Truesdale has the faster horse. Mason hires Archie Ricks to drug Gibson so he will be unable to ride. Gibson fights off the effects of the drug and wins the race. Because of Gibson's past actions, Truesdale and Eilers think he is drunk and refuse to listen to his explanations. Gibson decides to see how it would feel to really get drunk. As he orders his drink, he overhears an argument between Mason and Ricks. Gibson realizes that he was drugged. Mason tries to escape with all the money wagered on the race. Gibson bests both men in a fistfight, retrieving the money and winning Eilers.

NOTES AND COMMENTARY: *The Long Long Trail* is a remake of Hoot Gibson's *The Ramblin' Kid* (Universal, 1923).

Ingenue Sally Eilers would become the wife of western star Hoot Gibson on June 27, 1930. Gibson and Eilers were divorced on September 20, 1933, in the aftermath of a stormy marriage that consistently made the headlines.

Carl Laemmle asked Gibson to

The Long Long Trail (1929) movie still: Hoot Gibson (*right*), pretending to be drunk, terrorizes James Mason (*far left*) as unidentified actor (*big hat*) and Walter Brennan (*right center*) watch.

absorb the cost of adding sound to his western series, which Gibson consented to do. Due to the number of theaters that hadn't converted to the new sound medium, *The Long Long Trail* was also released as a silent picture.

Some film historians consider *The Long Long Trail* to be a part-talking motion picture. In the version I watched, all scenes feature full dialog, and I would consider the film to be all-talking.

This film marked screen great Walter Brennan's debut in a talking motion picture. Brennan would appear in over forty western features, winning an Academy Award for Best Supporting Actor in *The Westerner* (United Artists, 1940). Brennan starred in the popular TV western series, *The Guns of Will Sonnet* (ABC, 1967–1969).

REVIEWS: "Fun Hoot Gibson vehicle." (*Western Movies*, Pitts); "Conventional framework with no apparent reason for the title." (*Variety*, 11/6/29)

SUMMATION: *The Long Long Trail* is a nice vehicle for Gibson but only an average western feature. The villainy is mild, and not a shot is fired in anger. Most of the climactic fistfight happens in an enclosed room, and all the audience hears is the scuffle. The show is all Gibson, with the rest of the cast giving adequate support.

A REMARKABLE PICTURE OF THRILLS—"YOU AIN'T SEEN NOTHIN'" UNTIL YOU SEE HIM RIDE IN THE CROSS COUNTRY RACE—A TREAT FOR ALL

Lucky Larkin

Universal (March 1930); A Ken Maynard Production

CAST: Lucky Larkin, **Ken Maynard**; Emmy Lou Parkinson, **Nora Lane**; Martin Brierson, **James Farley**; Bill Parkinson, **Harry Todd**; Pete Brierson, **Paul Hurst**; Colonel Lee, **Charles Clary**; Hambone, **Blue Washington;** and "Tarzan"

CREDITS: Director, **Harry J. Brown**; Story/Screenwriter, **Marion Jackson**; Titles, **Leslie Mason**; Editor, **Fred Allen**; Cinematographer, **Ted McCord**

RUNNING TIME: 66 min.

STORY: Outlaws attempt to drive Charles Clary off his property to prevent him from entering horses in the county races. James Farley, the outlaw leader, tries to buy Clary's ranch, but Clary refuses to sell. Farley's brother, Paul Hurst, sets fire to Clary's barn, injuring the horses. Maynard suspects Farley is the man behind Clary's troubles and decides to ride Clary's pet colt, Tarzan, in the big race. Farley makes an unsuccessful attempt to have Tarzan disqualified. Maynard rides Tarzan to victory. Maynard captures Hurst and forces a confession out of him. Farley and Hurst are arrested, and Maynard marries Nora Lane, a homesteader's daughter.

NOTES AND COMMENTARY: *Lucky Larkin* was a silent film with a musical score and sound effects added so the film could be advertised as a sound feature.

REVIEWS: "Okay Ken Maynard feature." (*Western Movies*, Pitts); "Old line western, fitted to the inlands and double bills." (*Variety*, 3/12/30)

SUMMATION: *Lucky Larkin* was not available for viewing by the author.

Wildcats of the West!
Two-trigger thrills ... with a Sheriff and his Deputy in a battling saga of the sage!

Man from Montana

ALTERNATE TITLE: *Montana Justice*; Universal (September 1941)

CAST: Bob Dawson, **Johnny Mack Brown**; Grubby, **Fuzzy Knight**; Butch, **Billy Lenhart**; Buddy, **Kenneth Brown**; Linda, **Jeanne Kelly**; Sally, **Nell O'Day**; Thompson, **William Gould**; Dunham, **James Blaine**; Kohler, **Dick Alexander**; Trig, **Karl Hackett**; Dakota, **Edmund Cobb**; Decker, **Frank Ellis**; Chris, **Kermit Maynard**; Tex, **Jack Shannon**; Preston, **Murdock MacQuarrie**; Dugan, **Charles McMurphy**; and **the Kings Men**

CREDITS: Director, **Ray Taylor**; Associate Producer, **Will Cowan**; Screenwriter, **Bennett Cohen**; Editor, **Paul Landres**; Art Directors, **Jack Otterson and Ralph M. DeLacy**; Set Decorator, **R.A. Gausman**; Cinematographer, **Charles Van Enger**; Gowns, **Vera West**; Sound, **Bernard B. Brown and Jess Moulin**; Music Director, **H.J. Salter**

SONGS: "The Western Trail" (Rosen and Carter)—sung by **the Kings Men**; "Call of the Range" (Rosen and Carter)—sung by **the Kings Men**; "Bananas Make Me Tough" (Rosen and Carter)—sung by **Fuzzy Knight with Butch and Buddy**; "Little Joe the Wrangler" (Loesser and Hollander)—sung by **Butch and Buddy**

LOCATION FILMING: Agoura, California

RUNNING TIME: 57 min.

STORY: The Homestead Act of Montana has opened certain areas to settlers, causing concern among the cattlemen. Sheriff Johnny Mack Brown is determined to enforce the law. Aware of the cattlemen's animosity, Brown has the homesteaders camp outside of town. Brown hopes to influence William Gould, the largest cattleman, to allow the homesteaders to stay and avoid a range war. Jeanne Kelly, Gould's daughter, tries to make Gould see Brown's point. James Blaine wants to start a range war so he can seize all the open lands and cattle. Blaine has gunman Karl Hackett shoot Murdock MacQuarrie, the homesteader's leader, and Gould. Blaine's men steal MacQuarrie's cattle. Brown is accused of shooting Gould. MacQuarrie's Daughter, Nell O'Day, and deputy Fuzzy Knight help Brown escape so he can prove his innocence. Blaine learns that Gould was only wounded and sends Hackett to finish the job. Brown intercedes and captures Hackett. Hackett is allowed to escape, and Brown, Knight and O'Day follow Hackett to Blaine's ranch. At Blaine's ranch, Brown and O'Day find the stolen cattle. Brown tells O'Day to ride for help while Brown confronts Blaine and Hackett. Blaine's men show up and trap Brown in the bunkhouse. Help arrives in time, and Blaine and his men are rounded up.

Man from Montana (1941) scene card: Johnny Mack Brown (*left*) is in a Mexican stand-off with Karl Hackett (*center*) and James Blaine. **Left border**, Johnny Mack Brown.

Gould realizes there's room for all honest people in Montana.

NOTES AND COMMENTARY: When Jeanne Kelly later moved on to more ambitious projects, she was billed as Jean Brooks.

Billy Lenhart and Kenneth Brown were billed as Butch and Buddy. They appeared together in nine films for Universal. Butch had earlier received billing as "Bull Fiddle" Bill Lenhart in the Fred Scott western *Two-Gun Troubadour* (Spectrum, 1939).

Screenwriter Bennett Cohen dusted off his two-year-old screenplay from Charles Starrett's *Western Caravans* (Columbia, 1939) for this Johnny Mack Brown entry.

Man from Montana was remade as a Tex Williams featurette, *West of Laramie* (Universal-International, 1949), which re-used some footage from *Man from Montana*.

"The Western Trail" would be heard in *Rustler's Roundup* (Universal, 1946). "Call of the Range" would later be sung in *Frontier Law* (Universal, 1943), *Beyond the Pecos* (Universal, 1945) and *Gunman's Code* (Universal, 1946). "Bananas Make Me Tough" would serve as a comedy number for Fuzzy Knight again in *Lawless Breed* (Universal, 1946). "Little Joe the Wrangler" was first sung by Marlene Dietrich in *Destry Rides Again* (Universal, 1939) and became something of a staple for Universal, who utilized it in both *Little Joe the Wrangler* (Universal, 1942) and *The Old Texas Trail* (Universal, 1944).

REVIEWS: "Okay Johnny Mack Brown series entry." (*Western Movies*, Pitts); "A little below average." (*Variety*, 12/17/41)

SUMMATION: *Man from Montana* is an action-packed, highly entertaining Johnny Mack Brown western. The film spotlights Brown at his best—riding, fighting and shooting. Fuzzy Knight's comedy comes in small doses, and some of it actually works. In addition, Knight, this time out, looks like he could be of help to Brown. Director Ray Taylor paces this one to good effect.

THE MOUNTIES GET THEIR MAN!
...It's dynamite action drama of the northwest!

Man from Montreal

Universal (March 1940)

CAST: Clark Manning, **Richard Arlen**; Constable "Bones" Blair, **Andy Devine**; Myrna Montgomery, **Kay Sutton**; Doris Blair, **Anne Gwynne**; Ross Montgomery, **Reed Hadley**; Captain Owens, **Addison Richards**; Biff Anders, **Joseph Sawyer**; Jim Morris, **Jerry Marlowe**; Brad Owens, **Tom Whitten**; Old Jacques, **Eddy C. Waller**; Marcel Bircheaux, **Eddy Conrad**; Luther St. Paul, **William Royle**; Constable Rankin, **Lane Chandler**// Tom, **Pat Flaherty**; Pete, **Don Brodie**; Mack, **Karl Hackett**

CREDITS: Director, **Christy Cabanne**; Producer/ Story, **Ben Pivar**; Screenwriter, **Owen Francis**; Editor, **Maurice Wright**; Art Directors, **Jack Otterson** and **Harold H. MacArthur**; Set Decorations, **R.A. Gausman**; Cinematographer, **Milton Krasner**; Gowns, **Vera West**; Sound, **Bernard B. Brown** and **Robert Pritchard**; Musical Director, **Hans J. Salter**

LOCATION FILMING: Cedar Lake and Big Bear, California

RUNNING TIME: 61 min.

STORY: Kay Sutton entices fur trapper Richard Arlen to fall in love with her. Then her "brother," Reed Hadley (actually her husband), convinces Arlen to sell his furs in Montreal. Hadley is the leader of a gang of fur robbers. As Arlen leaves La Crosse to take his and Hadley's furs to Montreal, Mounties search his canoe and find stolen furs. Arlen is arrested but refuses to divulge Hadley's name. His friend, Constable Andy Devine, makes an unsuccess-

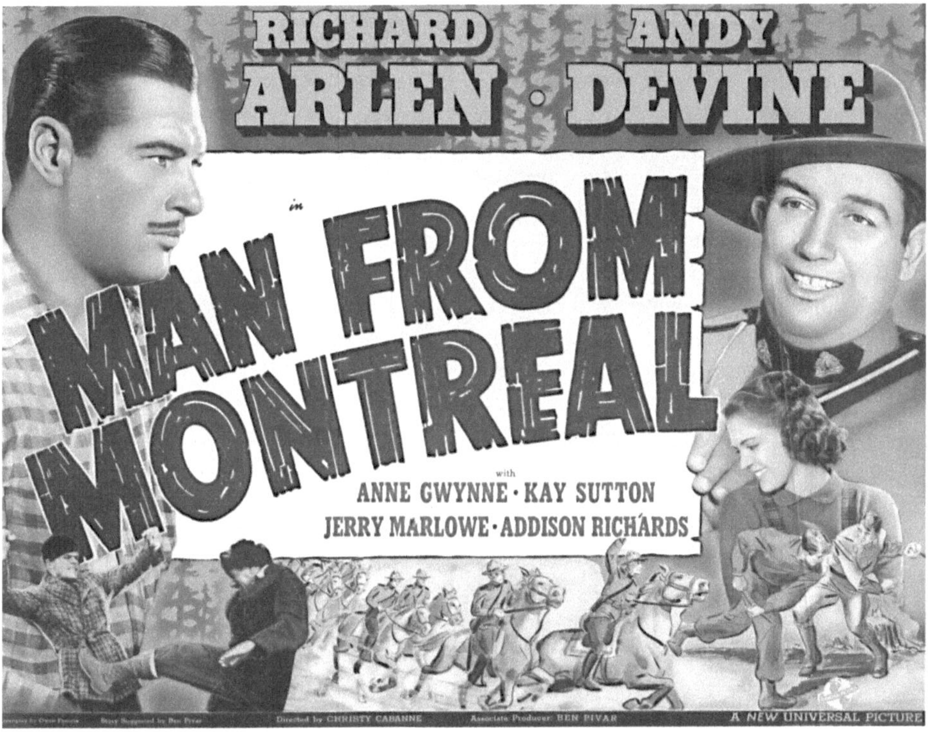

Man from Montreal (1940) scene card: *Upper left*, Richard Arlen; *lower left*, Richard Arlen (*right*) battles William Royle; *right*, Andy Devine, Anne Gwynne.

ful attempt to get Arlen to tell everything and clear his name. Devine learns that Hadley and Sutton are man and wife, and tells Arlen. Arlen breaks jail and discovers that Devine told him the truth. While Arlen is hiding out, Hadley has another fur trapper killed and places the blame on Arlen. Arlen is recaptured, but Devine and his sister, Anne Gwynne (who is in love with Arlen), help him escape. Arlen realizes that he's always loved Gwynne. Mounties spot Arlen at the scene of the murder and give chase. Arlen takes refuge in Joseph Sawyer's mine. Sawyer, a confederate of Hadley's, hides Arlen from the Mounties. Arlen tells Sawyer that Hadley is behind the fur thieves, and that he made three trips to Montreal with stolen furs. Sawyer lets it slip that Hadley and Sutton are man and wife, causing Arlen to become suspicious of Sawyer. Sawyer goes to town to see Hadley. Arlen follows Sawyer and then asks Devine to search Hadley's cabin for evidence to clear him. In the cabin Devine finds the stolen furs and overhears Hadley's plan to murder Arlen, commit a large fur robbery and place the blame on Arlen. Devine alerts the Mounties, shows them the evidence that clears Arlen, and takes them to Sawyer's claim. At the mine, Sawyer gets the drop on Hadley, planning to kill both Arlen and Hadley. Sawyer intends to take over as gang leader because Hadley had double-crossed Sawyer and his men by selling furs and not splitting the proceeds. During the argument between Hadley and Sawyer, Arlen grabs Hadley's gun and begins a gunfight with Sawyer and his men. As Arlen runs out of bullets, Devine and the Mounties arrive and capture Sawyer and his men. Hadley attempts an escape but with one solid blow by Arlen delivers Hadley to justice. With Arlen cleared of all crime, Gwynne and Arlen plan to marry.

NOTES AND COMMENTARY: One scene of interest involves Andy Devine, Tom Whitten and Pat Flaherty. Flaherty badmouths Richard Arlen, which distresses young Tom Whitten. Devine steps in and has words with Flaherty, culminating in Devine knocking Flaherty down twice. The second time Flaherty doesn't get up. Devine comments to the gathering crowd, "If I had known it would be that easy, I'd let the kid do it."

REVIEWS: "OK dualer. Strong dual entry." (*Variety*, 2/28/40); "Fast paced northwest melodrama." (*Western Movies*, Pitts)

SUMMATION: *Man from Montreal* is a good, suspenseful northwest melodrama. Richard Arlen and Andy Devine are more than capable leads and work well together. Villains Kay Sutton, Reed Hadley and Joseph Sawyer head a stellar supporting cast. Christy Cabanne directs in a straightforward, no-nonsense manner that results in an enjoyable film.

A DOUBLE DOSE OF DYNAMITE!

Marshal of Gunsmoke

ALTERNATE TITLE: *Sheriff of Gunsmoke*; Universal (January 1944)

CAST: Ward, **Tex Ritter**; Tom, **Russell Hayden**; Glow-Worm, **Fuzzy Knight**; Ellen, **Jennifer Holt**; Curtis, **Harry Woods**; Garrett, **Herbert Rawlinson**; Larkin, **Ethan Laidlaw**; Spike, **Ray Bennett**; Ezra Peters, **Michael Vallon**; Nuggett, **Ernie Adams**; Nevada, **Slim Whitaker,** and **Johnny Bond and His Red River Boys** (**Wesley Tuttle, Paul Sells** and **Jimmie Dean**)// Ed Gardner, **Dan White**; Dewey Saunders, **Bud Osborne**; Burt, **George Chesebro**; Dry Creek, **Budd Buster**; Outlaw, **Frank Ellis**

CREDITS: Director, **Vernon Keays**; Associate Producer, **Oliver Drake**; Screenwriter, **William Lively**; Editor, **Alvin Todd**; Art Directors, **John B. Goodman** and **Abraham Grossman**; Set Decorators, **R.A. Gausman** and **Leigh Smith**; Cinematographer,

Marshal of Gunsmoke (1944) title card: *Left*, Tex Ritter; *right* (*top to bottom*), Fuzzy Knight, Russell Hayden. Note: Knight's picture is from his previous effort, Frontier Law (Universal, 1943).

Harry Neumann; Sound, **Bernard B. Brown** and **Jack A. Bolger, Jr.**; Musical Director, **H.J. Salter**

SONGS: "Sundown Trail" (Marvin)—sung by **Jennifer Holt with Johnny Bond and His Red River Boys**; "My Saddle Serenade" (Bond)—sung by **Johnny Bond and His Red River Boys**; "La Golondrina" (traditional)—sung by **Jennifer Holt with Johnny Bond and His Red River Boys**; "My Saddle Serenade" (reprise)—sung by **Johnny Bond and His Red River Boys;** and "Git Along Little Dogies" (traditional)—sung by **Tex Ritter**

LOCATION FILMING: Corriganville and Monogram Ranch, California

RUNNING TIME: 58 min.

STORY: Tex Ritter arrives in Gunsmoke, and banker Herbert Rawlinson appoints him as Marshal of Gunsmoke. Rawlinson heads a law and order group who wants to incorporate the town so officials can be legally designated. Opposing Rawlinson are saloon owner Harry Woods, and Ethan Laidlaw and his gang, who want to keep a wide-open town. Ritter, with help from Fuzzy Knight, arrests Laidlaw and his gang for murder. From Jennifer Holt, a singer in Woods' saloon, Ritter learns that his brother, lawyer Russell Hayden, is returning to Gunsmoke to marry Holt. After Hayden arrives in Gunsmoke, Woods enlists Hayden's services to defend Laidlaw. Hayden gets all charges against Laidlaw and his men dropped due to testimony from witness Bud Osborne. Unknown to Hayden, the testimony is perjured. Holt breaks her engagement with Hayden. An election for incorporation is to be held the next day. Woods holds a party at his hacienda to influence people to vote against incorporation. At the party Hayden realizes that Woods is a crook and leaves to help Ritter. After Holt overhears a conversation that proves Woods duped Hayden, Woods tells her she'll be his guest at the hacienda until after the election. Woods sends Osborne to town to discredit Hayden; in the process Osborne is killed and Hayden is accused of murder. Hayden makes a break for freedom, and Ritter prevents Rawlinson from shooting Hayden. Because of this action, Rawlinson asks for Ritter's badge, which leaves Gunsmoke without any law. Hayden rides to Woods' hacienda and, with help from Ritter and Knight, frees Holt. Ritter learns that Woods has ridden to Gunsmoke and has sent men to destroy ballots coming in on the stage. Ritter sends Knight to bring the ballots in while he and Hayden go to Gunsmoke to confront Woods and his gang. Ritter, Hayden and Knight are successful. The majority of voters want the town to be incorporated. Hayden will become the town prosecutor in the case against Woods. Also, the rift between Hayden and Holt has been mended.

NOTES AND COMMENTARY: Tex Ritter's return to motion pictures after his accident found him again with a co-star. This time it was Russell Hayden, who had replaced him in *Frontier Law*. After Ritter left Monogram Pictures in 1941, he usually had to share screen time with another cowboy star. First it was Bill Elliott at Columbia, then Johnny Mack Brown at Universal. Mistakenly thinking he would be the solo star after Brown's exit to Monogram, Ritter was cast in stories written for the Brown-Ritter tandem. Even though he received top billing in *Arizona Trail* and *Oklahoma Raiders*, Dennis Moore was there to share the screen time. When Ritter left Universal for the Texas Rangers series at PRC, he had Dave O'Brien as his co-star.

Footage of Fuzzy Knight guiding the stagecoach to town by using a broken wagon tongue was previously used in *Badlands of Dakota* (Universal, 1941).

It is Jennifer Holt's singing voice that is heard in this film. Holt has stated at western film conventions that she did her own singing, and this is substantiated by Johnny Bond in his book *The Tex Ritter Story* (Chappell & Co., 1976).

"Get Along Little Dogies" was previously heard in *Stagecoach Buckaroo* (Universal, 1941) and *Little Joe, the Wrangler* (Universal, 1942). "My Saddle Serenade" was sung by Jimmy Wakely and His Rough Riders in *Pony Post*. "La Golondrina" was sung by the Guadalajara Trio in *The Masked Rider* (Universal, 1941).

REVIEWS: "Appealing Tex Ritter—Russell Hayden vehicle." (*Western Movies*, Pitts); "Action-packed." (*The Motion Picture Guide*, Nash and Ross)

SUMMATION: *Marshal of Gunsmoke* is an above average "B" western outing with plenty of action. Tex Ritter and his co-star Russell Hayden handle the heroics nicely. Fuzzy Knight's unobtrusive comedy is quite pleasing. Jennifer Holt lends a winning touch as the leading lady and shows she has a pleasant singing voice. Harry Woods again shows why he's one of "B" westerndom's top villains as he tries to best Ritter and Hayden.

A RIDIN', FIGHTIN' WHIRLWIND!
...with smoking six-guns a son of the old West rides herd on lawless border looters.

The Masked Rider

Universal (October 1941)

CAST: Larry, **Johnny Mack Brown**; Patches, **Fuzzy Knight**; Jean, **Nell O'Day**; Douglas, **Grant Withers**; Margerita, **Virginia Carroll**; Don Sebastian, **Guy D'Ennery**; Carmencita, **Carmella Cansino**; Luke, **Roy Barcroft**; Pedro, **Dick Botiller**; Pablo, **Fred Cordova**; Jose, **Al Haskell**; Manuel, **Rico de Montez**; Guard, **Bob O'Connor**; the **Guadalajara Trio**; and **Jose Cansino Dancers**

CREDITS: Director, **Ford Beebe**; Associate Producer, **Will Cowan**; Story, **Sam Robins**; Screenwriters, **Sherman Lowe** and **Victor I. McLeod**; Editor, **Jack Murray**; Art Directors, **Jack Otterson** and **Ralph M. DeLacy**; Set Decorator, **R.A. Gausman**; Cinematographer, **Charles Van Enger**; Gowns, **Vera West**; Sound, **Bernard B. Brown** and **Jess Moulin**; Musical Director, **H.J. Salter**

SONGS: "Carmencita" (Carter and Rosen)—sung by **the Guadalajara Trio**; "Cielito Lindo" (traditional)—sung by **the Guadalajara Trio**; "La Golondrina" (traditional)—sung by **the Guadalajara Trio**; "Mexican Hat Dance" (traditional)—sung by **the Guadalajara Trio**; "Cansinoble, Cansinita and Chiapanacas"—danced by the **Jose Cansino Dancers**; and "Carmenlita"—danced by **Carmela Cansino**

LOCATION FILMING: Iverson, California

RUNNING TIME: 58 min.

STORY: In Mexico, a bandit, the White Mask, and his gang have been terrorizing a silver mine owned by Guy D'Ennery and Nell O'Day. Needing money to pay off debts, D'Ennery plans to ship a load of silver. Fearing the White Mask will attack the shipment, foreman Grant Withers countermands D'Ennery's order. The White Mask and his gang attack the mine office to steal all the silver locked in the safe. The outlaw

The Masked Rider (1941) scene card: Johnny Mack Brown (*left*) ducks a punch thrown by Roy Barcroft.

gang has success in their grasp, but their plans are foiled by Johnny Mack Brown and his sidekick, Fuzzy Knight. O'Day had written her old friend, Brown, and asked him to help stop the mine holdups. O'Day introduces Brown and Knight to D'Ennery and Withers. Brown becomes acquainted with D'Ennery's daughter, Virginia Carroll, causing Withers to become very jealous. With O'Day's consent, Brown decides to deliver a shipment of silver to pay off D'Ennery's debts. In addition to needing money to pay off his men, D'Ennery owes Withers a large sum of money. Brown leads a fake pack train while Knight guides a pack train with the real ore. From his office window, Withers sees Knight leave. The White Mask stops his men from attacking Brown and leads his men to ambush Knight. Learning of Brown's plans, D'Ennery insists on joining Knight's pack train. O'Day accompanies D'Ennery. The outlaws attack. Before they can overcome Knight, D'Ennery and his men, O'Day slips away and rides to Brown for help. Knight boasts that Brown will catch up to them. The White Mask indicates that's exactly his plan, and then Brown will be killed and blamed for all the robberies. Held captive,

Knight and D'Ennery are able to get free and commandeer the freight wagon carrying the silver ore. The White Mask and his men ride in full pursuit and catch up to Knight and D'Ennery when the wagon overturns. As the bandits attack, Brown, O'Day and their men arrive and defeat the outlaws. The White Mask tries to get away but Brown quickly captures him. When the mask is removed from the bandit's face, the White Mask proves to be Withers. Brown plans to leave Mexico but is persuaded to stay by Carroll.

NOTES AND COMMENTARY: *The Masked Rider* was remade as a Tex Williams featurette, *Silver Butte* (Universal-International, 1949). Footage from *The Masked Rider* was utilized.

The sequence in which Fuzzy Knight inadvertently lassoes Johnny Mack Brown and Nell O' Day would later show up intact in Kirby Grant's western feature *Lawless Breed* (Universal, 1946). That time out, Knight ropes Grant and Jane Adams.

"Cielito Lindo" would be heard later in 1941 in *Road Agent* (Universal, 1941) and then in *Tenting Tonight on the Old Camp Ground* (Universal, 1943). Jennifer Holt, backed by Johnny Bond and His Red River Boys, sang "La Golondrina" in *Marshal of Gunsmoke* (Universal, 1944). "Mexican Hat Dance" would be featured in *Renegades of the Rio Grande* (Universal, 1945).

REVIEWS: "Plenitude of crack horsemanship and maximum of action elevate the new Johnny Mack Brown horse opera to high classification among westerns." (*Variety*, 10/8/41); "A better than average western, the standard plot is helped by dialog that is unusually witty for the genre and by Beebe's crisp direction." (*The Motion Picture Guide*, Nash and Ross)

SUMMATION: *The Masked Rider* is a solid Johnny Mack Brown vehicle with plenty of rousing action. The acting of the principals is above par for a series western, with special note going to Fuzzy Knight as Brown's sidekick. Again Knight shows that, when given the right material, he can be one of the premier western saddle pals. Knight's comedy will draw chuckles from the adult audience, while all will appreciate his ability to handle the critical action sequences. Ford Beebe directs briskly, keeping the story moving. One minor flaw: the fiesta sequence, while somewhat entertaining, should have been shortened to further heighten the tension provided by Sam Robins' story, and Sherman Lowe and Victor I. McLeod's screenplay.

The Spirit of Sam Houston
...Texas' Greatest Heritage!
Molding a Mighty State from the Reddest, Rowdiest Days of Reckless Texas' Wildest Decade!

Men of Texas

ALTERNATE TITLE: *Men of Destiny*; Universal (July 1942)

CAST: Barry Conovan, **Robert Stack**; Henry Jackson, **Broderick Crawford**; Robert Houston Scott, **Jackie Cooper**; Jane Baxter Scott, **Anne Gwynne**; Major Lamphere, **Ralph Bellamy**; Mrs. Scott, **Jane Darwell**; Sam Sawyer, **Leo Carrillo**; Colonel Scott, **John Litel**; General Sam Houston, **William Farnum**; Mrs. Sam Houston, **Janet Beecher**; Dwight Douglas, **J. Frank Hamilton**; Mrs. Olsen, **Kay Linaker**; Crittenden, **Joseph Crehan**; Silas Herbert, **Addison Richards**// Soldier, **Lane Chandler**; Rancher, **Rex Lease**; Goodrich, **Alan Bridge**; Clem, **Frank Hagney**; Raiders, **Ethan Laidlaw** and **Frank Ellis**; Townsman, **Tex Cooper**

CREDITS: Director, **Ray Enright**; Assistant Director, **Fred Frank**; Producer, **George Waggner**; Screenwriter, **Harold Shumate**; Additional Dialogue, **Richard Brooks**; Dialogue Director, **Gene Lewis**; Editor, **Clarence Kolster**; Art Directors, **Jack Otterson** and **Richard H. Riedel**; Set Decorators, **R.A. Gausman** and **R.S. Webb**; Cinematographer, **Milton Krasner**; Gowns, **Vera West**; Sound, **Bernard B. Brown** and **William Fox**; Music Director, **Edward Ware**

LOCATION FILMING: Iverson, California

RUNNING TIME: 82 min.

SOURCE: Story "Frontier" by **Harold Shumate**

STORY: Newspaper reporter Robert Stack and his photographer pal Leo Carrillo are assigned to cover the reconstruction days of Texas. Traveling to Huntsville, Stack becomes acquainted with Anne Gwynne, a die-hard Southerner who believes Texas should be a separate state from the Union. On the journey, they come upon a pregnant woman, Kay Linaker, whose husband has just been murdered, with some possessions stolen and the rest burned, leaving her stranded. Gwynne knows of a cabin a short distance away where Linaker quickly gives birth to a baby boy. Looking through the cabin, Stack finds two cases of rifles. As he mentions his findings to Gwynne, Broderick Crawford and his men ride up. Crawford is fighting for the independence of Texas and is a hero figure around the state. In Huntsville, Stack and Carrillo are offered quarters by Army Major Ralph Bellamy and Gwynne. Stack accepts Gwynne's hospitality even though he knows Gwynne only wants to watch him. Raiders rob the Huntsville bank. The banker shoots one of the raiders and in turn is shot by Crawford, lurking in the shadows.

Crawford then heads up a posse that conveniently loses the raiders' trail. Gwynne's younger brother, Jackie Cooper, is recognized as one of the raiders, but Crawford concocts an alibi that gets him released. When Stack shows a romantic interest in Gwynne, and the feelings seem to be returned, Gwynne's father orders Stack out of the house. From a raid, Carrillo noticed an unusual spur and spots that spur in the barbershop. Carrillo tells Stack. Crawford wears the spur. When Crawford understands their interest, he kidnaps the pair so he can have his own actions reported and earn favorable publicity in the newspapers. Cooper, a member of Crawford's raiders, sees that Gwynne loves Stack. Stack has made Cooper see that Crawford is serving his own interests to get rich and not the interests of Texas. Cooper helps Stack and Carrillo escape, and confronts Crawford. As Cooper starts to leave, Crawford guns Cooper down and blames the murder on Stack and Carrillo. As the mob moves to lynch the men, Bellamy shows up with a detail of cavalry and arrests Crawford. Crawford is tried and sentenced to hang. With his charisma, Crawford knows the people of Texas will not let him hang. Gwynne tells Litel the sentence is just, and only he can prevent a bloody massacre because the Army will fight to prevent Crawford from being freed. At William Farnum's grave site, the spectre of Farnum appears to tell Litel to save Texas from false patriots like Crawford. Litel, in his Confederate Officer's uniform, tells the people they're more than Texans, they're Americans, and disperses the crowd. Farnum's ghost appears to Crawford to make him understand why he has to die—because America doesn't need men who would betray their own people, but instead men who will defend freedom and democracy.

NOTES AND COMMENTARY: Kay Linaker talked about her role in *Men of Texas*: "I played a woman who had escaped from the Alamo. I was pregnant. I was having a hard time running. All of a sudden these two nice gentlemen took pity on me. They put me in their coach and started to get me to help. Unfortunately, I went into labor. They took me out of the coach, and I was lying on the side of the road. They tried to get a midwife, but nothing was working. All of a sudden I stopped this premature labor and they were able to pick me up and take me into town. Leo Carrillo was one of the gentlemen. I want you to know Leo Carrillo was a most delightful and charming person. Leo was one of the only living direct inheritors of a Land Grant through the Conquistadors. Leo was a fine, complete gentleman. He came over and started to help me up off my back on the side of the road. He said, 'Kate, it's most interesting to me. I think you're the only woman who was ever in labor for five days and gave out with nothing but cold sweat.' We had a perfectly lovely time. The young man [Robert Stack] who was playing the other part was just charming. We had a delightful time. I never saw the film." (Author's note: In the film, Linaker was the only survivor of an attack by Crawford's renegades, in the guise of keeping the Civil War alive. The coach was a public stage, which took her to a nearby shack where Linaker's character gave birth.)

On accepting her role in the film, Linaker remembered, "I was a freelance actor. Ralph Morgan was an extremely good friend of mine. I knew his daughter, Claudia, in New York. When I went to California, she called her parents and said, 'She's really a very nice kid. Take care of her.' Ralph and Daisy called me and had me to brunch the first Sunday I was in California. From that point on, they were sort of surrogate parents. We were on a picture together, I said, 'Something really puzzles me. How does it happen that you take everything that's offered to you?' He said, 'I'll tell you, Katie. Every part that is offered or every job that is offered to you in this life is a gift from the Giver of Gifts. Therefore, when it comes to you, you have an obligation to accept it and to do the very best you can with it. You are obligated to do this. If you don't, the Giver of Gifts is going to get very tired of giving you gifts; and all of a sudden, everything is going to stop.' It made great sense to me. So, from that point, whatever part was offered, I took."

The working title for this film was *Deep in the Heart of Texas*, which was ultimately used as the title for the first Johnny Mack Brown—Tex Ritter series western. The song, "Deep in the Heart of Texas" was initially purchased for the Brown-Ritter western. Universal studio brass took the song for the bigger budgeted Robert Stack western. However, the song proved to unfavorably alter the dramatic mood, so it was returned to its "B" western production unit.

Through a letter from Robert Stack's secretary, Stack professes to have no recollection of this film, nor of *Badlands of Dakota* (Universal, 1941).

REVIEWS: "Actionful. A better grade outdoor meller with historical flavor." (*Variety*, 7/8/42); "Typically slick melodrama from Universal which should please genre fans." (*Western Movies*, Pitts)

SUMMATION: *Men of Texas*, a not-too-bad little action film, tried to be an important film of epic structure but failed. The acting is merely competent, with Broderick Crawford the standout in the large cast. The film is too short to allow for the characterization needed to make this picture something special. The surreal ending (in which the ghost of Sam Houston, played by William Farnum, appears, first to guide John Litel and then to explain to Crawford why he has to hang) borders on the ludicrous. Obviously Farnum's closing speech is wartime propaganda. Nominal lead Robert Stack thanklessly stands by while Crawford, Jackie Cooper, Anne Gwynne, John Litel and Farnum propel the story to its bumbling conclusion. Ray Enright is a good action director when the material is right, but this time out, it isn't. Too bad.

Timber!
...It's a fight for life ... 'midst forest giants!

Men of the Timberland

Universal (June 1941)

CAST: Dick, **Richard Arlen**; Andy, **Andy Devine**; Kay, **Linda Hayes**; Jean, **Francis McDonald**; MacGregor, **Willard Robertson**; Lucky, **Paul E. Burns**; Tex, **Gaylord Pendleton**; Dudley, **Hardie Albright**; Withers, **Roy Harris**; Ranger, **John Ellis**// Lumberjacks in town, **Tom London** and **Ethan Laidlaw**; MacGregor's Secretary, **Jack Rice**; Café Owner, **Ralph Sanford**; Café Patron, **William Tannen**

CREDITS: Director, **John Rawlins**; Associate Producer, **Ben Pivar**; Story, **Paul Jarrico**, Screenwriters, **Maurice Tombragel** and **Griffin Jay**; Editor, **Milton Carruth**; Art Directors, **Jack Otterson** and **Ralph M. De Lacy**; Set Decorator, **R.A. Gausman**; Dialogue Director, **Maurice Wright**; Sound, **Bernard B. Brown** and **Jess Moulin**; Musical Director, **H.J. Salter**

LOCATION FILMING: Lone Pine, California

RUNNING TIME: 61 min.

STORY: Willard Robertson, with his confederate Francis McDonald, plans to strip all the timber he can to meet contracts he's signed. Linda Hayes owns one tract of land. Robertson has bribed Ranger Hardie Albright to misstate the boundaries so more timber than is allowed by law can be cut. After the timber is cut and delivered, Robertson and McDonald plan to run out on Hayes, paying her nothing. Ranger Richard Arlen is sent to the district because the timber permits look flawed. Arlen attempts to reason with Robertson to delay cutting until the permits can be checked, but Robertson refuses. Robertson hires Andy Devine and his pal Paul E. Burns to get the timber cut before the permits can be rechecked. Albright becomes frightened and is killed by McDonald. Two rangers, Gaylord Pendleton and Roy Harris, are assigned to assist Arlen. Harris dies when McDonald sends a huge log down on him, and McDonald wounds Pendleton with a rifle shot. After Arlen finishes the survey, McDonald and two of his men accost him. Seeing the unfair odds, Devine joins the fray. Devine tells McDonald and his men to clear out. Knowing the survey has been completed, McDonald sneaks into the Ranger office and burns all the papers. When Pendleton shows up, McDonald murders him. Arlen suspects McDonald and finds him in a tough saloon. When Arlen tries to get McDonald to leave with him, a fight breaks out. Devine, in the saloon with Hayes and Burns, aids Arlen in the fight. Arlen and Hayes leave by a back entrance. Devine and Burns work their way to the back, when a knife thrown by McDonald strikes Burns, killing him. Devine brings the dead man to the Ranger office where

Arlen is trying to persuade Hayes to help him bring Robertson and McDonald to justice. Devine wants to take the law into his own hands, but Arlen persuades him to work within the law. McDonald missed a crucial ledger that contains all the pertinent information. Hayes takes it to Robertson and McDonald. Arlen follows Hayes and retrieves the ledger. After Arlen leaves, Robertson sends McDonald to kill Arlen and retrieve the ledger. At the Ranger office, McDonald opens a window and is about to throw a knife into Arlen's back when the big hand of Devine prevents him. Devine and McDonald fight. McDonnell keeps things even with his knife. Devine finally rips the knife from McDonald's grasp and begins beating him until he's helpless. Arlen pulls Devine away. In the Ranger cabin, McDonald learns that Hayes was working with Arlen and can testify that Robertson sent McDonald to murder Arlen. Hayes forms her own lumber company to operate within legal boundaries, with Devine as her assistant. Arlen and Hayes begin a romance.

NOTES AND COMMENTARY: Footage of Devine and the loggers cutting trees would later be used in *Timber* (Universal, 1944), and footage without Devine would show up in the serial *The Great Alaskan Mystery* (Universal, 1944).

Roy Harris is known by most western fans as Riley Hill. Gaylord Pendleton would later billed as Steve Pendleton.

REVIEWS: "Worthwhile as a chance to see Devine in another of his humorous sidekick roles." (*The Motion Picture Guide*, Nash and Ross); "Actionful 'B' effort from Universal." (*Western Movies,* Pitts)

SUMMATION: *Men of the Timberland* is a top-notch production, possibly the best of the Richard Arlen-Andy Devine features. The acting is good in this one, with a special nod to Devine for an outstanding performance that shows his range. His reaction to the death of his pal, Paul E. Burns, is a sterling example, as pain, sorrow and anger take over. John Rawlins does himself and the picture proud with his forthright direction.

WHEN THE KILLER SPRANG, TERROR STALKED THE RANGE!

The Mighty Treve

Universal (April 1937)

CAST: "Bud" McClelland, **Noah Beery, Jr.**; Aileen Fenno, **Barbara Read**; Uncle Joel Fenno, **Samuel S. Hinds**; Mr. Davis, **Hobart Cavanaugh**; Mrs. Davis, **Alma Kruger**; Pepe, **Julian Rivero**; Slego, **Edmund Cobb**; Hibbens, **Erville Alderson**; Wilton, **Guy Usher**; Treve, "**Tuffy**"

CREDITS: Director, **Lewis D.**

Collins; Producer, **Val Paul**; Screenwriters, **Albert R. Perkins, Marcus Goodrich** and **Charles Grayson**; Editor, **Philip Cahn**; Cinematographer, **Jerome Ash**

RUNNING TIME: 68 min.

SOURCE: Novel "Treve" by **Albert Payson Terhune**

STORY: Samuel S. Hinds hires Noah Beery, Jr. and his dog Tuffy to watch over and take care of the sheep on his ranch. A vicious animal is killing sheep. Hinds believes Tuffy is to blame. Tuffy, finally, proves his innocence when he defeats a mountain lion in a terrific battle.

NOTES AND COMMENTARY: "Treve" (Grosset & Dunlap, 1924) was actually a collection of short stories that author Terhune wove into a novel. Universal took the story of Treve being mistaken for a sheep killer as the basis for this film.

The working title for *The Mighty Treve* was *Treve*.

REVIEWS: "Gripping thriller of dog's devotion." (*Variety*, 4/7/37); "Enjoyable pre–Lassie children's fare that will probably bring a tear to adult's eyes, too." (*The Motion Picture Guide*, Nash and Ross)

SUMMATION: This film was unavailable for viewing by the author.

WIDE-OPEN with Song ... and WILD with Joy!
A rhythm-rockin' round-up with These Super-Queens of Swing!

Moonlight and Cactus

Universal (September 1944)

CAST: Patty, **Patty Andrews**; Maxene, **Maxene Andrews**; Laverne, **Laverne Andrews**; Pasqualito, **Leo Carrillo**; Louise Ferguson, **Elyse Knox**; Tom Garrison, **Tom Seidel**; Punchy, **Shemp Howard**; Stubby, **Eddie Quillan**; Slugger, **Murray Alper**; Lucky, **Tom Kennedy**; Ogala, **Frank Lackteen**; Abigail, **Minerva Urecal;** and **Mitch Ayres and his Orchestra**// Amanda, **Mary O'Brien**; Elsie, **Jacqueline de Wit**

CREDITS: Director, **Edward F. Cline**; Associate Producer, **Frank Gross**; Screenwriters, **Eugene Conrad** and **Paul Gerard Smith**; Editor, **William Austin**; Art Directors, **John B. Goodman** and **Martin Obzina**; Set Decorators, **R.A. Gausman** and **Leigh Smith**; Cinematographers, **Jerome Ash**; Sound, **Bernard B. Brown** and **Charles Carroll**; Choreographer, **Charles Curran**; Orchestrator, **Vic Schoen**

SONGS: "Heave Ho My Lads, Heave Ho" (Lawrence)—played and sung by **the Mitch Ayers Orchestra**; "Send Me a Man, Amen" (Gilbert and Miller)—sung by **the Andrews Sisters**; "Wah-Hoo!" (Friend)—sung by **the Andrews Sisters, Murray Alper, Eddie Quillan, Shemp Howard** with **the Mitch Ayers Or-**

chestra; "Down in the Valley" (Luther)—sung by **the Andrews Sisters** with **the Mitch Ayers Orchestra**; "C'Mere" Baby (Gray and Jordan)—sung by **Patty Andrews**; "Home" (H. Clarkson and J. Clarkson)—sung by **the Andrews Sisters** with the **Mitch Ayers Orchestra**; "Sing" (Mooney and Prince)—sung by **the Andrews Sisters** and the **Mitch Ayers Orchestra;** and "Chiapanecas (the Mexican Hand Clapping Song)"—sung by **the Andrews Sisters** and **the Mitch Ayers Orchestra**

RUNNING TIME: 60 min.

STORY: On two weeks leave, sailor Tom Seidel takes his buddies to his ranch outside San Diego. Upon arriving, Seidel is surprised to find all the cowhands gone and the ranch being run by women. Foreman Elyse Knox asks Seidel to tour the ranch before passing judgment on the cowgirls. Seidel sees that the ranch is being run more efficiently than previously. Seidel and Knox begin to fall in love. Knox neglects to tell Seidel the ranch is plagued by rustlers, feeling she can get to the bottom of the trouble herself. The Andrews Sisters inadvertently let it slip to Seidel about the rustling. When Seidel confronts Knox, she tells him Leo Carrillo has been hired to catch the rustlers. Carrillo and his assistant, Frank Lacteen, arrive. Seidel gives them forty-eight hours to uncover the rustlers, or he will take over and find and hang each one. Carrillo becomes nervous, since it was he who took the steers. As the deadline draws near, Carrillo invites all the folks from Seidel's ranch to his hacienda for a fiesta. During the festivities Lacteen is to return the cattle. Lacteen has broken his glasses, however, and mistakenly leads the steers into the festive proceedings. Carrillo confesses that he took the cattle to make certain they were properly cared for since he didn't know how well the cowgirls could tend to them. All is forgiven, and Seidel and Knox can continue their romance.

NOTES AND COMMENTARY: The song "Wah-Hoo!" was written by Cliff Friend for a Broadway show. Friend was probably best known for "When My Dreamboat Comes Home" and "Lovesick Blues." Western singer Ray Whitley recorded "Wah-Hoo!" on February 27, 1936. In later years, "Wah-Hoo!" became a staple of the Hoosier Hot Shots.

Two years after *Moonlight and Cactus*, Elyse Knox would take the role of Ann Howe, Joe Palooka's sweetheart in Monogram's Joe Palooka series. Knox would play the role in six films from 1946 to 1949.

In 1949, Leo Carrillo would be coaxed into playing the role of Pancho for five Cisco Kid feature films released by United Artists. Carrillo, with Duncan Renaldo as Cisco, moved to television for 156 episodes. The role of Pancho is the role all western fans associate with Carrillo.

REVIEWS: "Pleasant blend of music, comedy and nonsense." (*Western Movies*, Pitts)

SUMMATION: Beginning with bright promise, *Moonlight and Cactus* quickly loses steam, becoming a below-par western musical comedy.

Elyse Knox, the Andrews Sisters and Frank Lackteen are the only bright spots in the effort. Leo Carrillo overdoes his ignorant Mexican routine, which is not helped by the labored comedy routines he's handed. The songs are pleasant, with the Andrews Sisters rendering rousing renditions of "Wa Hoo!" and the "The Mexican Hand Clapping Song." Director Edward F. Cline must have known nothing special could come from this and merely goes through the motions.

ELECTRIFYING
The wildest riding You ever saw. Ken Maynard, ace of the saddle, driving, riding behind, over and under the craziest bits of horseflesh in the entire world, in a feud story of old Kentucky.

Mountain Justice

ALTERNATE TITLE: *Kettle Creek;* Universal (May 1930); A Ken Maynard Production

CAST: Ken McTavish, **Ken Maynard**; Jud McTavish, **Otis Harlan**; Coral Harland, **Kathryn Crawford**; Lem Harland, **Paul Hurst**; Abner Harland, **Les Bates**; Judge, **Richard Carlyle**; Rusty, **Pee Wee Holmes;** and **Len Nash and His Country Boys**// Mose, **Blue Washington**; Harland Clansman, **Frank Ellis**; Man at Dance, **Frank Rice**

CREDITS: Director, **Harry J. Brown**; Assistant Director, **Mack V. Wright**; Story, **Bennett Cohen**; Screenwriters, **Lesley Mason**; Editor, **Fred Allen**; Production Manager, **Sid Rogell**; Cinematographer, **Ted McCord**; Recording Engineer, **C. Roy Hunter**; Synchronization & Sound, **David Broekman**

SONGS: "Sourwood Mountain" (Traditional)—sung by **Len Nash and His Country Boys**; "Seeing Nellie Home" (Traditional)—sung by **Kathryn Crawford, Otis Harlan** and chorus; "My Country 'Tis of Thee" (Traditional)—sung by **children's chorus**; "Buffalo Gal" (Traditional) sung by **Kathryn Crawford;** and "Dixie" (Emmett)—played by **Len Nash and His Country Boys**

LOCATION FILMING: Walker Ranch, California

RUNNING TIME: 72 min.

STORY: Cowboy Ken Maynard comes to the Kentucky backwoods community of Kettle Creek to find his father's murderer. His only clue was an unsigned letter, postmarked Kettle Creek, that his father received warning him of danger. Paul Hurst tries to force Maynard to leave town. Schoolteacher Kathryn Crawford intercedes and Maynard is allowed to stay. Hurst's brother, Les Bates, wants Maynard to stay in Kettle Creek to find out why he came. Maynard and Crawford begin to fall in love. Hurst thinks Crawford is his woman, and his hatred of Maynard grows. Crawford sends Maynard a note to meet him at the schoolhouse. Hurst intercepts the letter and then sends it on to Maynard. From the handwriting on the note, Maynard realizes that Crawford sent the warning note to his father. Hurst attempts to ambush Maynard as he arrives at the schoolhouse. Crawford grabs the rifle and the bullet misses Maynard. Maynard rushes to the schoolhouse and defeats Hurst in a furious struggle. Maynard questions Hurst about his father's death, but Hurst refuses to answer. Crawford tells Maynard she knew his father was in danger but not who wanted to murder him. Maynard allows Hurst to escape and follows him. Hurst goes to Bates. Maynard overhears Bates admit he killed his father. Maynard captures Bates, and the two men start for the railroad station. Bates' kinsmen follow and attempt to rescue him. In a wild chase, Maynard successfully eludes the men when he and Bates board a moving train leaving the station. Bates is taken to Oklahoma to stand trial for the death of Maynard's father. Later Maynard returns to Kettle Creek to marry Crawford.

NOTES AND COMMENTARY: *Mountain Justice* was also released as a silent feature.

Ken Maynard's famous horse, Tarzan, is curiously absent from this film.

Daniel Decatur Emmett has been credited with writing "Dixie." In 1993, Howard and Judith Rose Sacks proposed that a member of a musical African-American family of former slaves, the Snowdens, actually wrote this song.

"Sourwood Mountain" can be heard in *Rawhide Rangers* (Universal, 1941). "Buffalo Gal" was utilized in *Honor of the Range* (Universal, 1933) and *Strictly in the Groove* (Universal, 1943). "My Country 'Tis of Thee" was a cinematic staple for children singing in classroom settings; not only was it heard in *Mountain Justice*, but *Lady From Cheyenne* (Universal, 1941) and *Wild Beauty* (Universal, 1946) as well.

REVIEWS: "Good Ken Maynard vehicle." (*Western Movies*, Pitts); "Good for the daily grinds and kids. Plenty of action." (*Variety*, 5/21/30)

SUMMATION: Ken Maynard's first all-talking feature is a top-flight affair. Not strictly a western, but with sufficient western elements to warrant its inclusion in the genre, *Mountain Justice* provides Maynard with a good story and exciting action at the right moments. Maynard handles himself capably in the dramatic and action sequences. Maynard's fight with Paul Hurst is a gem, as is his wild ride to the railroad station with Les Bates in tow. Kathryn Crawford is on target as the love interest, and she also displays a pleasing singing voice. Director Harry J. Brown paces the story smartly, and Cinematographer Ted McCord's photography is a decided asset.

—the Action Kid himself—
You never saw a better Western picture, you never got so many thrills—and a laugh for every thrill. See this amazingly dramatic and swift story of a lone man's battle against almost impossible odds—of a stranger who rode right into the heart of a beautiful girl—and into a seething nest of outlawry!

The Mounted Stranger

Universal (February 1930); A Universal-Jewel Western

CAST: Pete Ainslee, **Hoot Gibson**; Pete (as a boy), **Buddy Hunter**; "Pop" Ainslee, **Milton Brown**; "Steve" Gary, **Fred Burns**; "White-Eye," **Jim Corey**; "Spider" Coy, **Francis Ford**; His [Spider Coy's] lookout, **Walter Patterson**; Mrs. Coy, **Francelia Billington**; "Bonita" Coy, **Louise Lorraine**

CREDITS: Director, **Arthur Rosson**; Producer, **Hoot Gibson**; Editor, **Gilmore Walker**; Art Director, **David Garber**; Cinematographer, **Harry Neumann**; Recording Supervisor, **C. Roy Hunter**; Synchronization & Score, **David Broekman**; Sound, **Western Electric Equipment**

LOCATION FILMING: Palmdale and the Mojave Desert, California

SONG: "Cielito Lindo" (Traditional)

RUNNING TIME: 65 min.

SOURCE: Story "The Ridin' Kid from Powder Ridge" by **Henry H. Knibbs**

STORY: Disliking homesteaders and feeling the open range is only for cattlemen, Fred Burns kills Milton Brown because he wouldn't leave his land. Years later, Brown's son, Hoot Gibson, catches up with Burns; Burns draws his pistol but Gibson is faster. Burns is only wounded, but Gibson thinks he's killed him. Burns vows to kill Gibson. Gibson rides to the Mexican border where he finds refuge with cantina owner Francis Ford. Ford sends Gibson to his mining claim to stay with his wife, Francelia Billington, and his daughter, Louise Lorraine. Lorraine falls in love with Gibson. Burns, now completely recovered from his wound, brings men to help him settle his score with Gibson. Gibson receives a note to come to the cantina to see Ford, but the note is designed to put him in the hands of Burns and his men. Lorraine learns of the plot and rides to warn Gibson. Burns has Gibson cornered. In helping Gibson escape, Lorraine is wounded. Gibson rides for a doctor and is spotted by Burns' men. Burns and his men chase Gibson and the doctor, who are riding double. Gibson sends the doctor to Ford's cantina. Gibson stays behind, outsmarts Burns and his men, takes one of their horses and stampedes the rest, and gets away. An argument ensues among the men left afoot in the desert, and Burns is killed by one of his own men. Lorraine recovers completely, and now Gibson and Lorraine plan to settle down together.

NOTES AND COMMENTARY: *Mounted Stranger* was a remake of *Ridin' Kid from Powder River* (Universal, 1924), with Hoot Gibson.

REVIEWS: "Good Hoot Gibson stuff, good old grind material." (*Variety*, 2/12/30); "Actionful Hoot Gibson early talkie, more serious than most of his features." (*Western Movies*, Pitts)

SUMMATION: A neat little western mixing austerity with some light comedy, *Mounted Stranger* is a fine vehicle for Hoot Gibson. Gibson, in fine form, is ably assisted by Louise Lorraine and Francis Ford. A strong storyline and quick pacing by director Arthur Rosson easily make up for the lack of action.

POUNDING ... ROARING ... BLAZING MUTINY!

Mutiny on the Blackhawk

Universal (August 1939)

CAST: Captain Robert Lawrence, **Richard Arlen**; "Slim" Collins, **Andy Devine**; Helen, **Constance Moore**; Captain, **Noah Beery**; Mate, **Guinn "Big Boy" Williams**; Wami, **Mala**; Sam Bailey, **Thurston Hall**; Tania, **Sandra Kane**; Jock, **Paul Fix**; Kit Carson, **Richard Lane**; Widow, **Mabel Anderson**; General Fremont, **Charles Trowbridge**; Sailor, **Bill Moore**; Coombs, **Byron Foulger**; General Romero, **Francisco Maran**; Parson, **Eddy Waller**; Mamo, **Mamo Clark**// Chief of Army Intelligence, **Edwin Stanley**; Bos'un, **Harry Cording**; Helmsman, **Martin Frost**; Ship's Officer, **George Lloyd**; Leader of Protesting Settlers, **Edward Le Saint**; Bill, **Murdock MacQuarrie**

CREDITS: Director, **Christy Cabanne**; Associate Producer/Story, **Ben Pivar**; Screenwriter, **Michael L. Simmons**; Editor, **Maurice Wright**; Art Directors, **Jack Otterson** and **Ralph M. DeLacy**; Set Decoration, **R.A. Gausman**; Gowns, **Vera West**; Cinematographer, **John W. Boyle**; Sound, **Bernard B. Brown** and **William Fox**; Musical Director, **Charles Previn**

RUNNING TIME: 66 min.

SOURCE: Story "In Old California" by **Ben Pivar**

STORY: Captain Richard Arlen is sent to the Sandwich Islands in the Pacific Ocean to investigate reports of slave trading to the southern states. Noah Beery, with his first mate Guinn "Big Boy" Williams, is buying island natives to sell as slaves. Arlen, suspicious of Beery, stows away on Beery's ship, the Blackhawk. Arlen is discovered aboard ship and put to work as a sailor. After making friends with Andy Devine, who believes the ship's cargo is copra, Arlen and Devine discover the hold is packed with island natives. Rations of food and water run low. Beery decides to send his cargo overboard to their deaths to insure there will be enough provisions for him and his men. Arlen plans to lead a mutiny. Williams learns of his plans and decides to kill Arlen. Devine hides Arlen until Arlen can reach the hold and free the islanders from their chains. After Williams brings all the islanders on deck, Arlen leads a mutiny to take over the ship and claps Beery, Williams and the other officers in irons. Devine becomes the new captain of the Blackhawk. The ship reaches the shores of California where Thurston Hall heads a group of settlers. Hall's mismanagement of the compound has the settlers ready to give up and return to their homes in the east. The compound's food stores are low. Arlen's intimidation, and the backing of Hall's daughter, Constance Moore, gain food for the hungry travelers. Arlen and Moore fall in love. Arlen wants enough provisions to last the journey back to the Sandwich Islands. Mexican General Francisco Maran wants Hall and the settlers to leave so the area can be claimed for Mexico. Arlen first tries to persuade Maran to assist Hall's compound and the islanders. In response, Maran issues an ultimatum that Hall has a week to vacate the compound peacefully. From scout Richard Lane, Arlen learns General Charles Trowbridge and Army troops are a short distance away. Trowbridge offers to provide the necessary provisions. Realizing Hall and the settlers plan to stay, Maran decides to attack the compound. Arlen sends Lane to seek help from Trowbridge and his Army troops while he sets traps to delay the Mexican army's assault on the compound. When all looks lost, the Army troops arrive and rout the Mexican army. Arlen tells Moore that when his assignment is completed, he will return to California. Moore decides to leave on the Blackhawk with Arlen, knowing Devine can marry them at sea.

NOTES AND COMMENTARY: The western segment of *Mutiny on the Blackhawk* is a reworking of *Sutter's Gold* (Universal, 1936); *Mutiny* even re-uses footage, primarily the battle scenes, from that earlier film. *Mutiny's* sea story segment also borrowed scenes from *Sutter's Gold*. The opening scene, for instance, was lifted from the ending of *Sutter's Gold*, showing a long-distance shot of a newspaper boy selling papers, with Edward Arnold and Lee Tracy on a park bench.

Mutiny on the Blackhawk was the first of 14 adventure yarns starring Richard Arlen and Andy Devine released between 1939 and 1941. Only *Blackhawk, Man from Montreal* (Universal, 1940) and *Men of the Timberline* (Universal, 1941) could be classified as westerns. The plots and characters had no connection from story to story. With A *Dangerous Game* (Universal, 1941), Arlen left the series. Devine was still under contract. Devine received two partners in Dick Foran and Leo Carrillo. After two entries, Foran was replaced by Don Terry, known to serial buffs as Don Winslow. Terry lasted for four films and was replaced by Metro-Goldwyn-Mayer's Dan Dailey, Jr. for the series finale, *Timber* (Universal, 1942).

REVIEWS: "Difficulty is the story never quite makes up its mind to be historic, romantic, outright western or a sea meller. Nice characterization wasted on flimsy story." (*Variety*, 8/9/39); "Weak script, the starring team manages to rise above the material because of the strong direction that keeps the action flowing." (*The Motion Picture Guide*, Nash and Ross)

SUMMATION: *Mutiny on the Blackhawk* tries hard, but the film can only be rated as average. The first half of the story, a sea story, tells a rugged tale of slave trading and mutiny to prevent mass murder of innocent islanders. Then the second half offers a flabby western whose highspot consists of recycled battle footage from *Sutter's Gold*. Richard Arlen and Andy Devine acquit themselves well. Arlen is the proper hero, while Devine adds comedy in the second half to divert the audience from the subpar storyline. The two stars receive a more than adequate support from the cast, led by slave traders Noah Beery and "Big Boy" Williams. Christy Cabannne's direction is on target when the script is good, but less so when the script lets everyone down.

YEE–OW and WA–HOO!
Here they come ... right up your old corral!
They're hitched ... in a battle of bottles and bustles...
A two-gun terror meets a gal even rarer!

My Little Chickadee

Universal (February 1940)

CAST: Flower Belle Lee, **Mae West**; Cuthbert J. Twillie, **W.C. Fields**; Jeff Badger, **Joseph Calleia**; Wayne Carter, **Dick Foran**; Aunt Lou, **Ruth Donnelly**; Mrs. Gideon, **Margaret Hamilton**; Amos Budge, **Donald Meek**; Cousin Zeb, **Fuzzy Knight**; Uncle John, **Willard Robertson**; Milton, **George Moran**; Boy, **Jack Searl**; Mrs. "Pygmy" Allen, **Fay Adler**; Gene Austin; "Candy" and "Coco"// Sheriff of Little Bend, **William B. Davidson**; Judge, **Addison Richards**; Mrs. Gideon's Co-Conspirator, **Jan Duggin**; Train Passenger, **Chester Gan**; Snoring Sheriff, **George Melford**; Hotel Clerk, **Harlan Briggs**; Squawk Mulligan, **Jimmy Conlin**; Staring Saloon Patron, **Bill Wolfe**; Gambler, **Morgan Wallace**; Pete, **Otto Hoffman**; Henchmen, **John Kelly** and **Jack Roper**; Primary Townsman, **Lloyd Ingraham**; Townsman, **Frank Ellis**; Saloon Patron, **Al Bridge**; Saloon Patron drinking Panther, **Edward Hearn**; Salvation Army Woman, **Betty Roche**; Lem, **Billy Benedict**; Miss Foster, **Anne Nagel**; School Boy, **Buster Slavan**; Deputy, **Si Jenks**

CREDITS: Director, **Edward F.

Cline; Assistant Director, **Joseph A. McDonough**; Producer, **Lester Cowan**; Screenwriters, **Mae West** and **W.C. Fields**; Editor, **Edward Curtiss**; Art Directors, **Jack Otterson** and **Martin Obzina**; Set Decorator, **R.A. Gausman**; Cinematographer, **Joseph Valentine**; Gowns, **Vera West**; Sound, **Bernard B. Brown** and **Joseph Lapis**; Musical Director, **Charles Previn**; Musical Score, **Frank Skinner**

SONG: "Willie of the Valley" (M. Drake and Oakland)—sung by **Mae West**

LOCATION FILMING: Tuolumme County and Monogram Ranch, California

RUNNING TIME: 83 min.

STORY: After being kidnapped by saloon owner Joseph Calleia as the Masked Bandit and after Calleia is seen leaving her bedroom, Mae West is run out of Little Bend as an undesirable woman. West is told she can't return until she's married and respectable. On the train to Greasewood, West meets W.C. Fields. Fields immediately falls for West; and West falls for Field's satchel, which contains a great sum of money. A "marriage" is arranged, with West persuading gambler Donald Meek to perform the ceremony. At that point, West's nemesis, Margaret Hamilton, praises her for becoming a respectable woman. In Greasewood, West sees to it that she and Fields have separate room accommodations. West also learns that Fields' money is nothing but advertising for one of his worthless products. Gambler Calleia and newspaper editor Dick Foran become rivals for West's attentions. Fields' bragging as a notorious Indian fighter gets him appointed sheriff. West's cousin, Fuzzy Knight, tells Fields that West wants her men to be bold, and that she likes men like the Masked Bandit. Fashioning a mask, Fields enters West's hotel room. West soon discovers it's Fields and not a man she loves. Leaving West's room, Fields is spotted by Hamilton who screams for help. Foran races to the jail to get Fields and sees Fields taking off his mask. Fields is arrested as the Masked Bandit and West is jailed as an accessory. West breaks jail and goes to Calleia for help. When West kisses Calleia, she knows him to be the real Masked Bandit. A lynch mob is about to hang Fields when an accurate shot from Mae West's pistol severs the rope. Then Calleia, as the Masked Bandit, rides up and throws a saddlebag full of stolen money to the crowd. Fields plans to leave Greasewood while West stays to be romanced by Calleia and Foran.

NOTES AND COMMENTARY: The current available prints of *My Little Chickadee* list Gene Austin, and Candy (Russell Hall) and Coco (Otto Heimel) in the credits, but the author was unable to spot them anywhere in the film.

In the scene in which W.C. Fields becomes acutely aware he will not be sharing the same hotel room with Mae West, Fields comments, "There's an Ethiopian in the fuel supply." Not a comment that would fly in today's politically correct world. Fields had the habit of saying, "Godfrey Daniel" when things went

200 MY LITTLE CHICKADEE

My Little Chickadee (1940) movie still: Mae West (*center*) holds the crowd at bay to allow the Masked Bandit to escape.

amiss. This was Fields' way of saying God Damn and still get past the censors.

Brad Slaven, known as "Buster" in his childhood days in films, played the student who said to Mae West, "When we was doing arithmetic on the board, when Miss Foster took sick." Slaven doesn't remember working with West, and thinks their parts were shot separately and then edited together.

Slaven, with fellow actor Billy Benedict, delivered most of the telegrams in the movies of that era. After World War II, Slaven appeared in numerous "B" westerns with Jimmy Wakely, Eddie Dean and Lash La Rue.

REVIEWS: "A hefty package of lusty humor that will click with the general audiences." (*Variety*, 2/14/40); "The classic teaming of Mae West and W.C. Fields is hardly a classic comedy but it is a pleasant affair and is well worth viewing." (*Western Movies*, Pitts)

SUMMATION: *My Little Chickadee* is a humorous and enjoyable motion picture but not the uproarious comedy one might expect with Mae West and W.C. Fields as the leads—a prime example of the sum not being equal to its parts. Both West and

Fields are fine, but neither performer is meant for sharing screen space. Joseph Calleia and Dick Foran make acceptable leading men, vying for West's affections. Margaret Hamilton is the standout in the large supporting cast. In his short bit, Donald Meek makes his moments count and registers strongly. It looks like director Edward F. Cline, wisely or unwisely, gave West and Fields their heads, as both stars completely dominate their individual scenes.

It's D-I-F-F-E-R-E-N-T!
A Wild West Show Gets Mixed Up with Bloody Politics. It's Sensational!

My Pal, the King

Universal (August 1932)

CAST: Tom Reed, **Tom Mix**; King Charles, **Mickey Rooney**; Count DeMar, **James Kirkwood**; Professor Lorenz, **Wallis Clark**; Princess Elsa, **Noel Francis**; Gretchen, **Finis Barton**; "Red," **Paul Hurst**; Baron Kluckstein, **Stuart Holmes**; Black Cloud, **James Thorpe**; Etzel, **Christian Frank**; Dowager Queen, **Clarissa Selwynne**; and "Tony"// General Wiedeman, **F. Schumann-Heink**

CREDITS: Director, **Kurt Neumann**; Story, **Richard Schayer**; Screenwriters, **Jack Natteford** and **Tom J. Crizer**

RUNNING TIME: 63 min.

STORY: Prime Minister James Kirkwood wants to raises the taxes of the people of Alvonia, most of which will go to him. Kirkwood needs the signature of the boy king, Mickey Rooney, to accomplish this. Amid the bickering of the council on the tax issue, Rooney sneaks out to see a Wild West show parade, led by Tom Mix. Rooney and Mix meet, and Mix lets Rooney ride in the parade. The two become friends. Kirkwood wants the Dowager Queen, Clarissa Selwynne, to serve as a figurehead while he becomes the power behind the throne. Rooney tells Kirkwood he will consider signing the tax bill if he is allowed to attend Mix's show. After the show, Rooney invites Mix to the palace. Mix tells Rooney he should use his position as king to help the people instead of allowing the crooked Kirkwood to run the country. Rooney decides to follow Mix's principles and tears up the tax bill. Infuriated, Kirkwood has Rooney and his teacher, Wallis Clark, kidnapped. The two are brought to Kirkwood's castle and imprisoned in the dungeon. Realizing Rooney is missing, Rooney's aunt, Noel Francis, goes to Mix for help. Mix promises to return Rooney safely, and he and his cowboys start the search. Kirkwood tries to have Clark shoot Rooney and then himself, so they

My Pal, the King (1932) herald: *Upper left*, Tom Mix on Tony; *lower left*, Tom Mix and Tony lead the Wild West show parade; *lower right* (*left to right*), Paul Hurst, unidentified actor, Tom Mix, Wallis Clark, Mickey Rooney.

could die quickly. Clark, unsuccessfully, fakes their deaths, so Kirkwood has a stone in the dungeon wall lifted to allow water to flood the cell. Mix follows the trail to Kirkwood's castle and sneak inside. Mix finds Kirkwood and, through an opening in the floor over the cell, sees Rooney and Clark trying to save themselves. Mix and Kirkwood fight, with Mix finally gaining the upper hand. Meanwhile, Mix's cowboys have gained entrance to the castle and overpowered Kirkwood's men. Mix rescues Rooney and Clark in the nick of time. Two of Mix's men "accidentally" drop Kirkwood into the water to drown. Mix and his troupe move on, but Mix promises that he will return to see Rooney some day.

NOTES AND COMMENTARY: Mickey Rooney said he was eleven years old when he made *My Pal, the King*. In this film Rooney plays a seven-year-old monarch. For the ten-day filming schedule, Rooney received $250.

The town square was actually the village set seen in *Frankenstein* (Universal, 1931).

REVIEWS: "A natural for every kid in the country. Besides that, it has plenty of adult entertainment." (*Variety*, 10/1/32); "Delightful little charmer, very natural and just a good old time at the movies." (*The Motion Picture Guide*, Nash and Ross)

SUMMATION: *My Pal, the King* is a highly enjoyable motion picture. Tom Mix switches from an old west setting to a mythical European kingdom, and the story works. Bolstered by the solid acting of Mix and Mickey Rooney, the production winds down to a most satisfying climax. The chemistry between Mix and Rooney adds immeasurably to the story's enjoyment.

JACK LONDON'S Mightiest Adventure Story!
Men Unafraid! Women Untamed!

North to the Klondike

Universal (January 1942)

CAST: John Thorn, **Broderick Crawford**; Mary Sloan, **Evelyn Ankers**; Klondike, **Andy Devine**; Nate Carson, **Lon Chaney, Jr.**; Doctor Curtis, **Lloyd Corrigan**; Waterlily, **Willie Fung**; Wellington Wong, **Keye Luke**// Tom Allen, **Stanley Andrews**; Mayme Cassidy, **Dorothy Granger**; Burt, **Monte Blue**; Lafe, **Jeff Corey**; Ben Sloan, **Roy Harris**; Settler, **George Chesebro**

CREDITS: Director, **Erle C. Kenton**; Associate Producer, **Paul Malvern**; Story, **William Castle**; Screenwriters, **Clarence Upson Young**, **Lou Sarecky** and **George Bricker**; Editor, **Ted Kent**; Art Director, **Jack Otterson** and **Ralph M. DeLacy**; Set Decorator, **R.A. Gausman**; Cinematographer, **Charles Van Enger**; Gowns, **Vera West**; Sound, **Bernard B. Brown** and **Robert Pritchard**; Musical Director, **H. J. Salter**

LOCATION FILMING: Big Bear, California

RUNNING TIME: 58 min.

SOURCE: Story "Gold Hunters of the North" by **Jack London**

STORY: Saloon owner Lon Chaney, Jr. sends for mining engineer Broderick Crawford. Chaney has discovered gold on tracts controlled by a group of settlers, and thinks conditions will prove too severe for the settlers, who will have to return home. Stanley Andrews brings supplies that will see the settlers through the harsh winter. Chaney tells Crawford there's no need for him to remain, but Crawford is nosy and decides to stay. Crawford meets Evelyn Ankers, who initially wants nothing to do with him since he came to work for Chaney. After Chaney burns the supplies. Andrews starts downstream to purchase more. Ankers' brother, Roy Harris, is settling on land close to the gold strike. Chaney offers to buy part of his property, and Harris refuses. Crawford and miner Andy Devine find Andrews' body floating in the river. Andrews had

North to the Klondike (1942) movie still: Brod Crawford (***left***), Andy Devine and Evelyn Ankers decide to keep Stanley Andrews' murder a secret from the other settlers.

been shot in the back. Crawford tells Ankers, and they hurry to find Harris. At the cabin Harris is building, he's found dead, with a bullet in his back. Keeping Andrews' death a secret from the settlers, Crawford asks friendly local doctor Lloyd Corrigan to travel the rapids by canoe to a settlement and purchase the needed supplies. By chance, Crawford discovers the cave with the gold deposits. Crawford gathers the settlers, and they march on Chaney's saloon. Crawford and Chaney engage in a brutal hand-to-hand encounter, with Crawford emerging victorious. At that moment, Corrigan returns with the supplies. The gold claim proves to be worthless. Crawford marries Ankers and settles down to a farmer's life.

NOTES AND COMMENTARY: About this time in Hollywood, Broderick Crawford and Lon Chaney, Jr. became pals and drinking buddies. Frequently, after having consumed quite a bit of alcohol, the two men enjoyed brawling with each other.

In the film, Monte Blue's character is referred to as Burt; but in one scene, Blue is called Ed.

North to the Klondike was suggested by Jack London's story, "Gold Hunters of the North," but the screenplay probably owes more of a debt to William Castle.

REVIEWS: "It's all very obvious, but with sufficient action and scenic stuff to satisfy the action audience." (*Variety*, 1/21/42); "Good adaptation of Jack London's *Gold Hunters of the North* with a dilly of a brawl between good guy Broderick Crawford and baddie Lon Chaney." (*Western Movies*, Pitts)

SUMMATION: *North to the Klondike* is a good northwoods adventure story. The film is nicely acted by the principals, with good comedy support provided by Willie Fung and Keye Luke. The picture's centerpiece comes in the form of a well-choreographed fight scene between hero Broderick Crawford and bad guy Lon Chaney, Jr. Director Erle C. Kenton keeps the story moving forward to its happy conclusion, focusing on the fistic encounter between the principals and a well-photographed and exciting canoe ride through the rapids.

---

*They Rode Like the Wind
And* SOCKED *Like a Cyclone!*

Oklahoma Frontier

Universal (October 1939)

CAST: Jeff McLeod, **Johnny Mack Brown**; Tom Rankin, **Bob Baker**; "Windy" Day, **Fuzzy Knight**; Janet Rankin, **Anne Gwynne**; George Frazier, **James Blaine**; J.W. Saunders, **Bob Kortman**; "Soapy," **Charles King**; Grimes, **Harry Tenbrook**; Sergeant, **Lane Chandler**; Judge, **Lloyd Ingraham**; "Cheyenne," **Joe De La Cruz**; Wayne, **Anthony Warde**; and **the Texas Rangers** (**Robert "Captain Bob" Crawford, Edward "Tookie" Cronenbold, Francis "Irish" Mahaney** and **Roderic "Dave" May**)// Dad Rankin, **Robert Cummings, Sr.**; Army Trooper, **Hank Bell**; Kentuck, **Al Bridge**; Drunk, **Horace Murphy**; Saloon Patrons, **George Chesebro, Frank Ellis**; Trooper, **Roy Harris**; Settler, **Richard Cramer**

CREDITS: Director/Screenwriter, **Ford Beebe**; Producer, **Albert Ray**; Editor, **Louis Sackin**; Art Directors, **Jack Otterson and Ralph M. DeLacy**; Set Decorator, **R.A. Gausman**; Cinematographer, **Jerome Ash**; Sound, **Bernard B. Brown and Jess Moulin**; Musical Director, **Hans J. Salter**

SONGS: "Get Along, Little Pony" (Kellogg) — played by **the Texas Rangers**; "Medley (Get Along Little Dogies, Buffalo Gal, Big Corral)" — sung and played by **the Texas Rangers** with **Johnny Mack Brown** on spoons; "In Old Oklahoma" — sung by **Bob Baker** and **the Texas**

Rangers; and "My Cincinnati (Ohio)"—sung by **Fuzzy Knight**

LOCATION FILMING: Agoura, California

RUNNING TIME: 58 min.

STORY: Settlers gather to participate in the Cherokee Land Rush. Among the participants are former lawmen Johnny Mack Brown and Fuzzy Knight, along with Brown's old friend Bob Baker and Baker's sister Anne Gwynne. Brown and Gwynne begin to fall in love. The section of land desired by Baker is also coveted by James Blaine, who wants that piece of land in order to control water rights in the area. Blaine makes an arrangement with Robert Kortman to obtain the tract at any cost. Learning that Brown has given Baker a map detailing a shortcut to the tract, Kortman shoots Baker, steals the map and has Brown arrested for Baker's murder. With Baker dead, Gwynne cannot participate in the land rush—unless she's the head of a household. Even though Gwynne believes Brown is a murderer, she tricks Brown into marrying her, knowing he'll be hung before the start of the land rush. Brown and Knight chastise Gwynne for her actions. Gwynne finally believes in Brown's innocence. Knight has a scheme to free Brown and enlists Gwynne's help. The plan works, and Brown and Knight are the first to reach the desired tract. Some of Kortman's men arrive, but Brown and Knight capture them, preventing them from jumping Gwynne's claim. Brown is told that Blaine is behind Baker's murder. Coming into town to confront Blaine, Brown is caught in a crossfire between Blaine and Kortman. Using a ruse, Brown wounds both Kortman and Blaine, and find evidence to prove his innocence and Blaine's guilt. Brown and Gwynne love each other and decide to settle down on the Oklahoma frontier.

NOTES AND COMMENTARY: *Oklahoma Frontier* had several working titles: *Oklahoma Kid, In Old Oklahoma* and *Outlawed Marshal*. Someone at Universal must have realized that Warner Brothers had *Oklahoma Kid* in release, with James Cagney and Humphrey Bogart.

In the credits, Fuzzy Knight's character name is noted as "Windy" Day. In the film, Johnny Mack Brown calls Knight "Frosty."

Kay Kellogg's song "Get Along Little Pony" had been heard in *Wild West Days* (Universal, 1937) and *Forbidden Valley* (Universal, 1938.

The opening scene, in which Johnny Mack Brown confronts Al Bridge was lifted almost intact from Brown's serial *Wild West Days* (Universal, 1937). In the serial, Brown intones Bridge's character name, Steve Claggett. In *Oklahoma Frontier*, Brown calls out the name Kentuck. Ironically, in the serial Brown's character name was Kentucky Wade. At the beginning of the sequence, Frank Yaconelli can be seen riding out of frame.

REVIEWS: "Competently made cowboy-and-cutthroat drama. Sturdy western." (*Variety*, 12/6/39); "Somewhat complicated oater with a good amount of action." (*Western Movies*, Pitts)

SUMMATION: *Oklahoma Frontier* is a superior "B" western that allows principals Johnny Mack Brown, Anne Gwynne and Fuzzy Knight room to act, and they respond wonderfully. Robert Kortman and James Blaine provide good villainy and prove to be formidable foes for Brown. Ford Beebe directs confidently from his own story, which provides a bizarre twist by killing off co-star Bob Baker half-way through the proceedings. The plentiful action scenes are first rate.

ROUGHEST RIDERS— TOUGHEST RAIDERS
clashing on wild-horse mesa!

Oklahoma Raiders

Universal (March 1944)

ALTERNATE TITLES: **Midnight Raiders, Riders of Oklahoma**

CAST: Steve, **Tex Ritter**; Banjo, **Fuzzy Knight**; Todd, **Dennis Moore**; Donna, **Jennifer Holt**; Arnold Drew, **Jack Ingram**; James Prescott, **George Eldredge**; Judge Masters, **John Elliott**; Sheriff Banning, **Slim Whitaker**; Higgins, **I. Stanford Jolley**; Duggan, **Dick Alexander**; Colonel, **Herbert Rawlinson**; Williams, **Ethan Laidlaw;** and **Johnny Bond and His Red River Boys** (**Paul Sells, Wesley Tuttle** and **Jimmie Dean**)// Boone Talbot, **Stephen Keyes**; Cowboy, **Bob Baker**

CREDITS: Director, **Lewis D. Collins**; Associate Producer, **Oliver Drake**; Screenwriter, **Betty Burbridge**; Editor, **Norman A. Cerf**; Art Directors, **John B. Goodman** and **Abraham Grossman**; Set Decorators, **R.A. Gausman** and **L.R. Smith**; Cinematographer, **William Sickner**; Sound, **Bernard B. Brown** and **Joe Lapis**; Musical Director, **Paul Sawtell**

SONGS: "Nelly Bly" (Foster)— sung by **Fuzzy Knight**; "Trail to Mexico"—sung by **Tex Ritter**; "Out on the Open Range"—sung by **Johnny Bond and His Red River Boys**; "A Cowboy's Dream" (Bowman and Miller)—sung by **Tex Ritter** with **Johnny Bond and His Red River Boys;** and "Starlight on the Prairie" (Allan)—sung by **Johnny Bond and His Red River Boys**

LOCATION FILMING: Corriganville, California

RUNNING TIME: 57 min.

STORY: During the Civil War, Lt. Tex Ritter and Corporal Fuzzy Knight are assigned to reestablish the supply of horses to the Cavalry from Arizona. As soon as Jack Ingram has assembled a herd of horses to be delivered, a mysterious outlaw, El Vengador, rustles them. Ritter, disguised as an out-of-work cowhand, arrives in Arizona in time to catch Ingram and two men stealing mail from the express office. In the scuffle, Ingram wounds Ritter. Ritter is being transported to receive medical care, when Ingram's henchmen, I. Stanford Jolley and Richard Alexander, try to ambush him. After the outlaws leave Ritter for dead, Jennifer Holt and Dennis Moore find him and take him to their hideout to recuperate. Ritter learns that Holt is El Vengador, and that land agent George Eldredge, with Ingram's help, took Holt's and other ranch owners' land at the point of a gun. The ranchers have been wreaking havoc on Ingram in retribution. Judge John Elliott has sent a letter to Washington to request that the courts decide who owns the land. Eldredge has this letter, which is favorable news for the ranchers. Ritter leaves the hideout and meets Knight. Ingram is hiring men for a wild horse roundup. Knight hires on, while Ritter introduces himself to Eldredge and Ingram, and states that he will go on the roundup also. Because it was dark and Ritter had a heavy beard, he is not recognized by Ingram. Moore stampedes the horses so Holt and her men can round them up. Ritter catches up with Moore and persuades him to deliver the horses to the Army. Eldredge and Ingram ride up, and Ritter has to arrest Moore. Ritter tells Holt that he will break Moore out of jail if she will surrender the horses. Jolley has incited the townspeople to lynch Moore. Knight drives his wagon through the mob to rescue Moore. Ritter, meanwhile, has obtained the needed evidence against Eldredge and Ingram. The gang is rounded up and the ranchers get their land back. Moore decides to join the Army, and Ritter promises to return to Holt at the war's end.

NOTES AND COMMENTARY: This story was first used in the Tom Keene and Julie Haydon starrer *Come on Danger* (RKO, 1932). It also served as the basis for *Renegade Ranger* (RKO, 1939) with George O'Brien and Rita Hayworth, and *Come on, Danger!* (RKO, 1942) with Tim Holt and Frances Neal. The story was later used for *Alias Billy the Kid* (Republic, 1946) with Sunset Carson and Peggy Stewart. Betty Burbridge also had a hand in the screenplay for the later production.

Oklahoma Raiders was the final film at Universal for Tex Ritter. After the completion of this picture, a decision was made to film the rest of the series the following spring. During the hiatus, Ray Whitley and his 6-Bar Cowboys had replaced Johnny Bond and His Red River Boys. When Ritter found that Bond, a close personal friend, and his group had been released, Ritter declined to appear in the final entries.

The working title for *Oklahoma Raiders* was *Wild Horse Roundup*.

"A Cowboy's Dream" can be heard in *Stormy* (Universal, 1935). "Starlight on the Prairie" was sung by Bob Baker in two films, *Black Bandit* (Universal, 1938) and *Prairie Justice* (Universal, 1938).

REVIEWS: "Very good Tex Ritter vehicle with plenty of action, a good story and supporting cast and five pleasant songs." (*Western Movies*, Pitts); "Collins' direction is forceful, and Holt proves a charming foil to Ritter's basso profundo." (*The Western*, Hardy)

SUMMATION: *Oklahoma Raiders*

is a good, fast-moving action western. Tex Ritter's singing, riding and shooting is definitely up to par, but his fight scene with badguys George Eldredge and Jack Ingram looks somewhat stilted. Fuzzy Knight had minimal comedy scenes and capably aided Ritter. Jennifer Holt is fine as the rancher's daughter turned western Robin Hood. Dennis Moore handles the secondary hero role well. Screenwriter Betty Burbridge gave Director Lewis D. Collins a nifty script, and he makes the most of it.

Range War!
Six guns roar ... as two hurricane hombres blast a trail through lawless badlands!

The Old Chisholm Trail

Universal (December 1942)

CAST: Dusty Gardner, **Johnny Mack Brown**; Montana Smith, **Tex Ritter**; Polario, **Fuzzy Knight**; Mary Lee, **Jennifer Holt**; Belle Turner, **Mady Correll**; Chief Hopping Crow, **Earle Hodgins**; Ed, **Roy Barcroft**; Joe Rankin, **Edmund Cobb**; Hank, **Budd Buster**; and **the Jimmy Wakely Trio** (**Jimmy Wakely**, **Johnny Bond** and **Scotty Harrel**)// Sheriff, **Michael Vallon**; Mike Carey, **George Sherwood**

CREDITS: Director / Screenwriter, **Elmer Clifton**; Associate Producer, **Oliver Drake**; Story, **Harry Fraser**; Editor, **Ray Snyder**; Art Directors, **Jack Otterson** and **Ralph DeLacy**; Set Decorators, **R.A. Gausman** and **A.J. Gilmore**; Cinematographer, **William Sickner**; Sound, **Bernard B. Brown** and **Jess Moulin**; Musical Director, **H.J. Salter**

SONGS: "The Old Chisholm Trail" (traditional)—sung by **Johnny Bond** and **Scotty Harrell**; "Rovin' Gambler" (traditional)—sung by **Tex Ritter**; "Beautiful Dreamer" (Foster)—sung by **Jimmy Wakely**; "Out on the Lone Star Trail"—sung by **Tex Ritter** and **the Jimmy Wakely Trio**; and "Little Sweetheart of the Rio Grande" (O.Drake, Wakely and Rosen)—sung by **the Jimmy Wakely Trio**

LOCATION FILMING: Corriganville, California

RUNNING TIME: 61 min.

STORY: Johnny Mack Brown herds cattle down the Chisholm Trail. Brown finds that the water he needs for his cattle has been fenced off. Owner Mady Correll charges an exorbitant $5 per steer to reach water, which Brown refuses to pay. Brown goes to the Lost River Trading Post, hoping to find water for his cattle. Trading post owner Jennifer Holt and her associate, gambler Tex Ritter, tell Brown that there's no water but Correll's within eighty miles. Correll has her men stampede the cattle to her water hole, and intends to charge Brown a toll for each steer that crosses her land. By accident, Brown's old friend Fuzzy Knight discovers an underground spring near the trading post. Brown makes a decision to drill for water and obtains the necessary equipment. Correll gains ownership of the equipment and won't extend usage past the original agreement. Correll sends George Sherwood to disable the equipment and force Brown to agree to her demands. Sherwood is unsuccessful; but Ritter, thinking that if the well fails Brown will leave the area, giving him an open path to Holt, sabotages the engine. Brown finds evidence that Ritter destroyed the engine, and confronts Ritter. The two men fight, with Brown the winner. Brown tells Ritter he was drilling for water so all cattlemen traveling the Chisholm Trail won't have a water shortage problem. Ritter, realizing he was wrong, concocts a scheme in which he sells some of the cattle at market price to Correll to pay the toll and obtain money to purchase a replacement engine. The well hasn't yet produced as Correll and her men ride to take away the equipment. In a pitched battle, Knight accidentally drops dynamite into the well, and water erupts. Brown, Ritter and his men gain the upper hand over Correll and her men, who are taken to jail. Ritter leaves, knowing Brown and Holt love each other.

NOTES AND COMMENTARY: The song "Rovin' Gambler" was very popular. Over the years it was recorded with great success by many artists, including the Everly Brothers, Tennessee Ernie Ford, Frankie Laine, George Hamilton IV, Jim Reeves, Hank Thompson, the New Christy Minstrels and, of course, Tex Ritter. It was sung by a male chorus in *Salome, Where She Danced* (Universal, 1945).

"The Old Chisholm Trail" has been used by Universal since the early days of sound, seeing service in *Parade of the West* (Universal, 1930), *The Fiddlin' Buckaroo* (Universal, 1933), *Stormy* (Universal, 1935) and *The Phantom Rider* (Universal, 1936). "Beautiful Dreamer" would be whistled by Lon Chaney in *Frontier Badmen*. "Little Sweetheart of the Rio Grande" was first heard in *The Silver Bullet* (Universal, 1942), and later would be sung by Ray Whitley and his Bar-6 Cowboys in *Riders of the Santa Fe* (Universal, 1944).

REVIEWS: "Standard western with the usual line of action, romance and adventure." (*Variety*, 1/20/43); "A scrappy B western." (*The Western*, Hardy)

SUMMATION: *The Old Chisholm Trail* is an above average "B" western, primarily due to Tex Ritter's unusually dark performance for a series western star. In this one, Ritter gambles, will take a drink, and allows his intense jealousy of Johnny Mack Brown's interest in Jennifer Holt to allow his dark side to emerge as he sabotages valuable drilling equipment. Brown is the ideal hero and performs well. The script allows him the bulk of the physical action, which he handles well, even besting Ritter in a fistfight. The ladies in this one are Jennifer Holt, the good girl, and Mady Correll, the bad one. Both give nice performances. Fuzzy Knight's comedy is, on the whole, acceptable. Elmer Clifton does a competent job in directing this one, with pleasing results.

A RIDING SON-OF-A-SIX-GUN!
...Keeping the Stages Rolling!

The Old Texas Trail

ALTERNATE TITLE: *Stagecoach Line;* Universal (December 1944)

CAST: Jim, **Rod Cameron**; Dave, **Eddie Dew**; Pinky, **Fuzzy Knight**; Amarillo, **Ray Whitley**; Queenie, **Virginia Christine**; Jefferson Talbot, **Joseph J. Greene**; Mary, **Marjorie Clements**; Sparks, **George Eldredge**; Gardner, **Edmund Cobb**; Sheriff, **Jack Clifford**// Howard Lane, **Harry Strang**; Rawhide Carney, **Dick Purcell**; Singer, **Merle Travis**; Pete, **George Turner**; Nevada, **Terry Frost**; and **Ray Whitley's Bar-6 Cowboys**

CREDITS: Director, **Lewis D. Collins**; Associate Director, **Oliver Drake**; Screenplay, **William Lively**; Editor, **Saul Goodkind**; Art Directors, **John B. Goodman** and **Harold H. MacArthur**; Set Decorators, **Russell A. Gausman** and **Ted Von Hemert**; Cinematographer, **William Sickner**; Sound, **Bernard B. Brown** and **Jess Moulin**; Musical Director, **Paul Sawtell**

Songs: "Riding Down That Old Texas Trail" (Allen)—sung by **Merle Travis Trio**; "Trail Dust" (Nolan, De Savis and Scrogin)—sung by **Ray Whitley, Eddie Dew and the Bar-6 Cowboys**; "Little Joe, the Wrangler" (Loesser and Hollander)—sung by **Virginia Christine**; "Polly Wolly Doodle" (Traditional)—sung by **Merle Travis Trio**

LOCATION FILMING: Iverson and Corriganville, California

RUNNING TIME: 60 min.

STORY: Texas financier Joseph J. Greene hires George Eldredge to stop the completion of Harry Strang's stagecoach road. Eldredge has henchman Dick Purcell stop a stagecoach in which Strang is a passenger. Mail employees Eddie Dew and Ray Whitley witness Purcell shoot Strang. Dew and Whitely quickly ride to the scene, and Purcell has to escape on foot. Purcell sees a lone rider, Rod Cameron, and fires a shot that creases Cameron's head. While Cameron is unconscious, Purcell switches his distinctive clothes for Cameron's more conservative garb. Cameron's clothes contain credentials identifying him as an Engineer Consultant for the stage line. Purcell gives them to Eldredge, who then has Edmund Cobb impersonate Cameron. Strang's daughter, Marjorie Clements, vows to carry on her father's work and hires Dew and Whitley to assist her. Insurance salesman Fuzzy Knight finds Cameron and brings him to Sandstone. Because of his unusual garb, Cameron is arrested and brought to trial. While Cameron was recuperating, Knight had telegraphed the stage line for duplicate credentials, which have arrived. Cameron doesn't want his true identity disclosed so that he can later ferret out the man behind the lawlessness. At the trial, saloon owner Virginia

Christine, working with Eldredge and Cobb, testifies that Cameron was not the man who shot Strang, and Cameron is released. Christine tells Cameron to work with Cobb to sabotage the road construction. Cameron is hired as Cobb's assistant and works to complete the road. Eldredge comes to Sandstone and sees Cameron, who he knows to be the real Engineer Consultant. Eldredge makes an attempt to frame Cameron for a payroll robbery. Dew had been trailing Cameron, and henchman George Turner starts shooting at both men. Dew realizes Cameron is working for the stage line. Knight's timely arrival chases away Turner. Knight had overheard Christine tell Eldredge to attack the construction camp. The three men ride to the camp, where the stagecoach with the Postal Inspector and Greene has arrived for the test run. Cameron decides to drive the coach over the uncompleted road. Cameron needs passengers, so Clements, Knight and the Postal Inspector climb aboard. Greene, who knows Eldredge will attack the coach, is forced to be the fourth passenger. Dew, Whitley and some construction men go along as outriders. Greene breaks down and tells the occupants that Eldredge will dynamite a bridge. Cameron changes his route, and Eldredge and his men attack. Dew and Whitley round up Eldredge and his henchmen. Clements receives a contract to build a stagecoach route across the State of Arizona.

NOTES AND COMMENTARY: Screenwriter William Lively took major plot elements from *Boss of Hangtown Mesa* (Universal, 1942) and *Tenting Tonight on the Old Camp Ground* (Universal, 1943) to fashion the screenplay for *The Old Texas Trail*. Footage from the climax of *Tenting Tonight* was used for the finale of *Texas Trail*. Look sharp to see Tex Ritter and Fuzzy Knight in the distance shots. Footage from *Timber* (Universal, 1942) was used in the logging montage sequence.

The song "Riding Down That Old Texas Trail" began as "Riding Down the Utah Trail" for Bob Baker in *Western Trails* (Universal, 1938) and *The Phantom Stage* (Universal, 1939). "Little Joe" was first featured in *Destry Rides Again* (Universal, 1939), with Marlene Dietrich doing the vocal honors. Virginia Christine tries to imitate La Dietrich, none too successfully.

Merle Travis, who sang two songs in *The Old Texas Trail*, would become both a noted guitarist, with his "Travis picking" style, and a famous songwriter. Travis wrote "Smoke, Smoke, Smoke" for Tex Williams, and his song "Sixteen Tons" became a big hit for Tennessee Ernie Ford. Travis was featured in the cinema classic *From Here to Eternity* (Columbia, 1953) and sang his composition "Re-enlistment Blues."

Dick Purcell's most memorable role was the comic book hero Captain America in the serial *Captain America* (Republic, 1944).

REVIEWS: "Sturdy Rod Cameron vehicle with good entertainment value." (*Western Movies*, Pitts); "A rip-snortin' 60 minutes of western clichés that raise dust in the Lone Star state." (*The Motion Picture Guide,* Nash and Ross)

SUMMATION: *The Old Texas Trail* is an above average "B" western. Rod Cameron, Eddie Dew, Fuzzy Knight and Ray Whitley make a nice quartet of heroes. Knight's mild comedy will garner a few well-deserved chuckles. Director Lewis D. Collins directs steadfastly and keeps the story interesting.

---

15 THRILL—THRONGED CHAPTERS OF EXCITING SPEED—SCORCHED ACTION!

The Oregon Trail

Universal (May 1939)

CAST: Jeff Scott, **John Mack Brown**; Margaret Mason, **Louise Stanley**, "Deadwood" Hawkins, **Fuzzy Knight**; Jimmie Clark, **Bill Cody, Jr.**; John Mason, **Ed LeSaint**; Sam Morgan, **James Blaine**; Breed, **Charles Stevens**; "Bull" Bragg, **Jack C. Smith**; Colonel Custer, **Roy Barcroft**; Dawkins, **Charles Murphy**; Slade, **Colin Kenny**; Daggett, **Forrest Taylor**; Dirk, **Charles King**; Idaho Ike, **Jim Toney**// General Sherman, **Warner Richmond**; Sergeant in Sherman's Office, **Lane Chandler**; Dan Clark, **Karl Hackett**; Colonel Terry, **Kenneth Harlan**; Pete, **Tom London**; Crowfoot, **Iron Eyes Cody**; Yellow Snake, **Richard Botiller**; Townsman, **Horace Murphy**; Trooper, **Harry Cording**; Jim Stokes, **Frank Ellis**

CREDITS: Directors, **Ford Beebe** and **Saul A. Goodkind**; Associate Producer, **Henry MacRae**; Screenwriters, **George Plympton, Basil Dickey, Edmund Kelso** and **W.W. Watson**; Dialogue, **Dorothy Cormack**; Editors, **Alvin Todd, Louis Sackin** and **Joseph Gluck**; Art Director, **Ralph DeLacy**; Cinematographers, **Jerome Ash** and **William Sickner**; Sound, **Bernard B. Brown** and **Jess Moulin**; Musical Director, **Charles Previn**

LOCATION FILMING: Kernville, California

RUNNING TIME: 280 min.

CHAPTER TITLES: 1. The Renegade's Revenge, 2. The Flaming Forest, 3. The Brink of Disaster, 4. Thundering Doom, 5. Stampede, 6. Indian Vengeance, 7. Trail of Treachery, 8. Redskin's Revenge, 9. The Avalanche of Doom, 10. The Plunge of Peril, 11. Trapped in the Flame, 12. The Baited Trap, 13. Crashing Timbers, 14. Death in the Night, 15. The End of the Trail

STORY: Scouts John Mack Brown and Fuzzy Knight are assigned by the Army to discover why large wagon trains never make it to the Oregon territory. Brown and Knight plan to join Ed LeSaint's wagon train. The wagon boss, Jack C. Smith, is in the employ of James Blaine. The un-

The Oregon Trail (1939) lobby card.

scrupulous Blaine wants no competition in his fur trading with the Indians. First, Smith leads the train in a disastrous attempt to ford a swollen river. Next, Smith places the train in the path of a prairie fire. Brown's quick actions save the wagon train, and the train pulls into Clearwater. Smith has spread the word that his wagon was the only survivor of the fire, and Brown has Smith arrested. Blaine arranges to have Smith transported by stagecoach to Fort Laramie. Brown races to the coach, not knowing Indians will attack the stage and rescue Smith. Smith is taken away by the Indians and Brown follows. Brown is unsuccessful in capturing Smith. Blaine tries to delay the wagon train's departure for a week. After this time, snows will prevent the wagon train from moving on until spring. LeSaint refuses to wait. Blaine has his men stampede the cattle, and Indians attack the train, but the settlers bravely push on. Blaine has LeSaint's daughter, Louise Stanley, kidnapped. Only LeSaint's wagon stays behind. Brown and Knight trail the kidnappers and rescue Stanley. Friendly Indians greet the train, and they decide to trade with LeSaint rather than Blaine. Blaine and some of his men ambush the friendly Indians so the word won't be spread to trade with LeSaint. Smith and another henchman, Charles Stevens, spot Brown and decide to ambush him. Instead, Brown captures Smith, and a well placed shot chases Stevens away. Smith tells Brown he'll talk when the wagon train reaches Paradise Valley. Smith is jailed, and Blaine's men attempt a jailbreak. Brown gets to the jail to fend off the attackers. A lamp crashing to the floor starts a fire, trapping both Brown and Smith. The outlaws leave Brown and Smith to die in the flames. LeSaint, Knight and the settlers rescue the men. In the confusion, Smith escapes. Blaine tells Brown that Smith is the leader of the outlaws. After a few harrowing adventures, Brown is finally able to capture Smith. Blaine sends Stevens to kill Smith, but Stevens and Smith join forces. The two men plan to take over the gang and run the territory. Through Stevens' influence, Indians capture LeSaint and Stanley. Brown and Knight rescue the prisoners, and Brown stays behind to destroy ammunition and powder stolen from Blaine. Smith tries to stop Brown, but is unsuccessful and captured. Smith tells Brown Blaine is the real leader. With help from the Cavalry, Blaine and his men are rounded up. Brown decides to give up his life as a trapper and a scout and remain with Stanley. Knight plans to keep on being a trapper.

NOTES AND COMMENTARY: The Universal screenwriters took the easy way out for the resolution to Chapter Six's cliffhanger ending. In trying to escape from an Indian village, Johnny Mack Brown and Fuzzy Knight's horses are tripped up, and Brown lays unconscious in the path of stampeding horses. The next week's episode simply showed Brown and Knight riding away from the village, with no mention of the previous week's predicament.

Notice Brown's hat during the climax of Chapter Nine. When Brown and his horse start their leap into the river, he's wearing a black hat. After landing in the river, a white hat floats away, thanks to stock footage from a John Wayne Lone Star/Monogram feature.

Footage from Hoot Gibson's *The Flaming Frontier* (Universal, 1926) is freely utilized for the *Oregon Trail*.

REVIEWS: "Actionful, but juvenile, Universal cliffhanger." (*Western Movies*, Pitts); "The serial is routine." (*The Western*, Hardy)

SUMMATION: A slipshod production, with poor continuity, overlooked plot points, and obvious cheat chapter resolutions, *The Oregon Trail* is not a cliffhanger of which Universal should be proud. The stars are first rate, however; John Mack Brown is a believable action western hero, and Fuzzy Knight registers as an intelligent sidekick. Louise Stanley is fine as the leading lady, and Bill Cody, Jr. is a decided asset to the story. The main villainy rests in the hands of James Blaine and Jack C. Smith. Unfortunately, the screenplay portrays Blaine and Smith as inept bad men, much to the detriment of the picture. The story starts out well, but at the mid-way point, usually capable screenwriters George Plympton, Basil Dickey, Edmund Kelso and W.W. Watson lose their touch, and the serial goes downhill.

He Was Galloping Justice!
Sharp-shooting for bandits rifling the Pony Express!

Outlaw Express

Universal (June 1938)

CAST: Bob, **Bob Baker**; Lorita, **Cecilia Callejo**; Andy, **Don Barclay**; Sommers, **LeRoy Mason**; Lupe, **Nina Campana**; Don Ricardo, **Martin Garralaga**; Ferguson, **Forrest Taylor**; Bill Cody, **Carlyle Moore**; Don Diego, **Julian Rivero**; Phelps, **Jack Kirk**; Ramon, **Carleton Young**; "Apache"// Army Captain, **Edward Cassidy**; Postmaster General Joseph Holt, **Arthur Van Slyke**; Chief Red Cloud, **Bill Hazlett**; Pedro, **Joe Dominguis**; Land Agent, **Horace B. Carpenter**

CREDITS: Director, **George Waggner**; Assistant Director, **Glenn Cook**; Story/ Screenwriter, **Norton S. Parker**; Editor, **Charles Craft**; Art Director, **Charles Clague**; Set Decorator, **Albert Greenwood**; Cinematographer, **Harry Neumann**; Sound, **Charles Carroll** and **Edwin Wetzel**; Music Director/Arranger, **Frank Sanucci**

SONGS: "Pony Express" (Allan)—sung by **Bob Baker**; "Out in Californi-a" (Allan)—sung by **Bob Baker** and **Don Barclay**; "Amigo Mio" (Allan)—sung by **Bob Baker**; "La Cucuracha" (traditional)—sung by **Bob Baker** and **male chorus** and danced by **Cecilia Callejo**; "Lorita" (Allan)—sung by **Bob Baker**; "Pony Express" (reprise)—sung by **Bob Baker** and **male chorus**

LOCATION FILMING: Iverson, Walker Ranch and Monogram Ranch, California

RUNNING TIME: 56 min.

STORY: Pony express riders are being killed so LeRoy Mason can obtain letters containing Spanish land grants. The grants are on their way to Washington, D.C. to be registered. Mason plans to submit forged grants so he can take over the properties. The pony express riders have been killed by Indian arrows so the blame will be thrown on the local tribe. Bob Baker and his sidekick, Don Barclay, are assigned by the U.S. Army to stop the murders. Forrest Taylor hires the duo as new riders for the Pony Express so they can work undercover. Taylor's top hand is Mason, who still feels animosity toward Baker from their Army days. Mason promises to make things difficult for Baker. Baker and Barclay are assigned to purchase horses for the Pony Express. They go to Martin Garralaga's hacienda, where Baker meets Garralaga's beautiful daughter, Cecilia Callejo. Garralaga sells Baker the horses he needs. When outlaws with forged loud grants begin taking over haciendas, Baker persuades Callejo to talk Garralaga into registering his grant. Garralaga registers his grant, which is witnessed by Mason's henchman, Carleton Young. The pony express rider carrying the grant is killed and the document stolen. Barclay overhears Mason's plan to raid the Garralaga hacienda and take possession. Baker, Barclay and the pony express riders ride to help Garralaga. Mason and his men have gained entrance to the hacienda when Baker and his men arrive. Two well placed shots by Baker end Mason's dreams of a California empire. Baker resigns from the service to run Garralaga's ranch and be with Callejo.

NOTES AND COMMENTARY: The working title for *Outlaw Express* was *Pony Express Days*.

Outlaw Express was remade as a Tex Williams featurette, *Ready to Ride* (Universal-International, 1949). Later, screenwriter Norton S. Parker used his plot of bandits stealing Spanish land grants as part of the story line for the Hopalong Cassidy feature *Three Men from Texas* (Paramount, 1940).

A particularly effective (and touching) scene comes as LeRoy Mason and his gang lay siege to Martin Garralaga's hacienda. Cecilia Callejo is tending to a wounded man, and Garralaga runs up to her. Garralaga: "I told you to stay in the house, amiga mia."

Callejo answers him with her eyes that say, "How can I leave this wounded man." Garralaga simply walks away.

"La Cucaracha" had previously been featured in *When a Man Sees Red* (Universal, 1934) and *Law for Tombstone* (Universal, 1937), and later would be utilized in *Boss of Bullion City* (Universal, 1941) and the short subject *Frontier Frolic* (Universal, 1946).

REVIEWS: "Just another hoss opry." (*Variety*, 7/20/38); "The actors are poorly cast and the story is insipid." (*The Motion Picture Guide*, Nash and Ross)

SUMMATION: This is a below average Bob Baker outing. *Outlaw Express* is pretty tame until the very end, which offers a few exciting moments before Baker dispatches villain LeRoy Mason all too quickly. Baker is okay, and Don Barclay shines as a more-than-acceptable sidekick. The acting honors go to leading lady Cecilia Callejo who says more with her eyes than her fellow actors do with words. The script by the usually reliable screenwriter Norton S. Parker is far too weak.

Filmdom's Greatest Western Star!
Riding with new speed!
Shooting with new daring!
Fighting with new fury!

Outlawed Guns

Universal (July 1935); A Buck Jones Production

CAST: Buck Rivers, **Buck Jones**; Ruth Ellsworth, **Ruth Channing**; Jingle, **Frank McGlynn, Sr.**; Jack Keeler, **Roy D'Arcy**; Babe Rivers, **Pat J. O'Brien**; Rocky Ellsworth, **Joseph W. Girard**; Marge Ellsworth, **Joan Gale**; Blacky Bates, **Lee Shumway**; Frank Davilla, **Charles King**; Harvey Daniels, **Jack Rockwell;** and "Silver"// Lynch Mob Leader, **Monte Montague**; Fireman, **Horace B. Carpenter**; Hunnicutt, **Carl Stockdale**

CREDITS: Director, **Ray Taylor**; Screenwriter, **John T. Neville**; Editor, **Bernard Loftus**; Art Director, **Ralph Berger**; Cinematographers, **William Sickner and Allen Thompson**; Sound, **Buddy Myers**

LOCATION FILMING: Kernville, California

RUNNING TIME: 62 min.

SOURCE: Story by **Cliff Farrell**, published in "Thrilling Ranch Stories"

STORY: Pat J. O'Brien falls in with Roy D'Arcy and his outlaw gang, and ends up owing D'Arcy fifteen hundred dollars in gambling debts. To repay D'Arcy, O'Brien signs a bill of sale for a thousand cows owned jointly by him and his brother, Buck Jones. Jones gets word that O'Brien has joined D'Arcy's gang and sets out with his friend, Frank McGlynn, to rescue O'Brien from an outlaw's life. After two of D'Arcy's men, Charles King and Lee Shumway, rob a stagecoach, Sheriff Joseph W. Girard receives a tip that the outlaws are hiding out in Latigo Canyon. Fearing that O'Brien is at the outlaw hideout, Jones and McGlynn try to reach the canyon before the posse but are too late. King and Shumway escape under the cover of darkness, but O'Brien is captured. Jones is able to break O'Brien out of jail, but escaping through Girard's house, O'Brien is mortally wounded by D'Arcy, who is romancing Girard's younger daughter, Joan Gale. Before O'Brien dies, he tells Jones where the stagecoach strongbox was hidden. Jones retrieves the strongbox and, upon opening it, finds only scrap iron. Jones figures that the stage line owner and D'Arcy are working together to steal the money and use the sheriff to arrest the henchmen, reducing the number of people to share in the stolen loot. Jones has McGlynn watch the stage line owner and makes him confess to his part in the robbery. Jones goes after D'Arcy, who makes a get-a-way with Gale. Jones finds this out from Gale's older sister, Ruth Channing. Jones and Channing ride to catch D'Arcy. Jones catches up with

D'Arcy. In an exchange of shots, Jones is seriously wounded and D'Arcy is killed. Channing helps Jones recover from his wound as the couple begin to fall in love.

NOTES AND COMMENTARY: Pat J. O'Brien played Buck Jones' younger brother. The "J" added to his name would differentiate him from Warner Bros. star Pat O'Brien.

REVIEWS: "Very picturesque Buck Jones story enhanced by a good story." (*Western Movies*, Pitts); "Formula heart-and-hoof pattern but well made and well cast." (*Variety*, 10/16/36)

SUMMATION: *Outlawed Guns* is a solid "B" western. Buck Jones is very good as the older brother trying to keep his younger brother, Pat J. O'Brien, from falling in with an outlaw gang. O'Brien registers strongly as the younger sibling. Frank McGlynn turns in a nice performance as a former Texas Ranger. The rest of the cast handle their roles adequately. Director Ray Taylor paces the story to good advantage, enhanced by William Sickner and Allen Thompson's fine camerawork.

15 CHAPTERS OF THUNDERING THRILLS!

Overland Mail

Universal (September 1942)

CAST: Jim Lane, **Lon Chaney**; Barbara Gilbert, **Helen Parrish**; Sierra Pete, **Noah Beery, Jr.**; "Buckskin Billy" Burke, **Don Terry**; Young Bill Cody, **Bob Baker**; Frank Chadwick, **Noah Beery, Sr.**; Tom Gilbert, **Tom Chatterton**; Puma, **Charles Stevens**; Charles Darson, **Robert Barron**; Sam Gregg, **Harry Cording**; Rose, **Marguerite De La Motte**; Lamont, **Ben Taggart**; Slade, **Jack Rockwell**; Mack, **Roy Harris**; Lem, **Carleton Young**; Jake, **Ethan Laidlaw**; Sheriff Tyler, **Jack Clifford**; Chief Black Cloud, **Chief Many Treaties**; Chief Many Moons, **Thunder Cloud**// Colonel Medford, **William Gould**; Taylor, **Forrest Taylor**; Crabtree, **Henry Hall**; Ben Bristow, **Bill Moss**; Lt. Turner, **George Sherwood**; Indian, **Iron Eyes Cody**; Renegade, **Ray Teal**; Townsman, **Jim Corey**; Miles, **Harry Tenbrook**; Pony Express Rider, **Tom Steele**; Dr. Burnside, **Charles Z. Phipps**; Captain Hinton, **Frank Pershing**; Williams, **William Desmond**

CREDITS: Directors, **Ford Beebe** and **John Rawlins**; Associate Producer, **Henry MacRae**; Story, **Johnston McCulley**; Screenwriter, **Paul Houston**; Dialogue Director, **Jacques Jaccard**; Supervising Editor, **Saul A. Goodkind**; Editors, **Alvin Todd, Louis Sackin, Joseph Gluck** and **Patrick Kelly**; Art Director, **Harold H. MacArthur**; Cinematographers, **William Sickner** and **George Robinson**

LOCATION FILMING: Kernville, California

RUNNING TIME: 273 min.

CHAPTER TITLES: 1. A Race with Disaster, 2. Flaming Havoc, 3. The Menacing Herd. 4. The Bridge of Disaster, 5. Hurled to the Depths, 6. Death at the Stake, 7. The Path of Peril, 8. Imprisoned in Flames, 9. Hidden Danger, 10. Blazing Wagons, 11. The Trail of Terror, 12. In the Claws of the Cougar, 13. The Frenzied Mob, 14. The Toll of Treachery, 15. The Mail Goes Through

STORY: Stage line and Pony Express line owner Tom Chatterton is plagued by Indian attacks on his coaches and riders, interrupting mail service going through the La Paz area. Lon Chaney, with his pals Noah Beery, Jr. and Don Terry, are assigned to find who's behind the trouble. Chatterton's old friend (and respected citizen) Noah Beery, Sr. covets the mail contract because it will be worth a million dollars to him. Working with businessman Robert Barron and cutthroats Harry Cording and Charles Stevens, Beery Sr. has directed the destruction of Chatterton's equipment, death to stage drivers and pony express riders, and the theft of the mail and other valuable cargo. Chaney and his pals accept jobs with Chatterton's company and, through their effort, conditions begin to improve. Beery Sr. directs his attention to the elimination of Chaney and his comrades but is unsuccessful. Also assisting Chaney in his efforts is Chatterton's daughter, Helen Parrish. Parrish and Chaney fall in love at first sight. Finally realizing Chatterton might prevail, Beery Sr. pretends to have been kidnapped by the renegades. A note is sent to Chatterton demanding $15,000 to save Beery Sr.'s life. Chatterton brings the money to the renegade hideout where Beery Sr. plans to have Chatterton killed. Beery Jr. had discovered a back entrance to the hideout, so Chaney, Beery Jr., Terry and a posse can get the drop on the renegades. Chaney enters the room. Guns blaze! Cording fires at Chatterton, and Chatterton falls to the floor. Chaney's bullet hits Cording. A bullet from an adjoining room is fired at Chaney, who falls to the floor. Beery Jr., Terry and the posse enter the room and wipe out the renegades. It seems that the bullets missed both Chatterton and Chaney. Both men are unharmed. Cording is badly wounded but still alive. Chaney rushes into the adjoining room to find Beery Sr. trussed up. As Cording is being taken to a doctor in La Paz, in Silver Creek, Parrish receives a letter requesting that she and her father meet Captain Frank Pershing in La Paz. All the principals reach La Paz, where Pershing takes the mail contract from Chatterton and awards it to Beery Sr. Cording has died without revealing the identity of the man behind the lawlessness. Chaney bluffs and states Cording named Barron and Berry Jr. as the gang leaders. Barron and Beery Sr. make a get-a-way in one of Chatterton's stagecoaches with Chaney, Beery Jr. and Terry in pursuit. The stagecoach overturns; Barron is killed immediately, and Beery Sr. is mortally wounded. Berry Sr., to make amends, wills all his properties to Chatterton. With the threat over, Chatterton and Parrish ask Chaney to stay on, and Chaney agrees.

NOTES AND COMMENTARY: Lon Chaney was a workhorse for Universal in the forties. In Horror films, Chaney played all the main Universal monsters—the Wolfman, the Mummy, Dracula and Frankenstein's Monster. Chaney toplined the Inner Sanctum series, and was featured in musicals, gangster films and westerns. When Dick Foran was relieved from starring in Universal's annual serial feature, Chaney received the nod. Chaney had starred in RKO's only entry in the serial market, *The Last Frontier*, in 1932. Chaney, when not in monster garb, impressed movie audiences more as a man beset with doubts and fears, or as a person with more strength than brains.

At film's end, Beery Sr. signs over all his considerable properties to Tom Chatterton as he expires, causing Lon Chaney to comment, "You know, Sierra, Chadwick wasn't such a bad sport after all." After all the problems, pain and death caused by Noah Beery, Sr. throughout 14-plus chapters it's hard to believe that statement would ever be uttered.

Lon Chaney has problems with his hat. In Chapter One, Chaney wears a black hat. Suddenly, in Chapter Two, he now sports a bright white hat. Then Chaney loses the white hat and resumes wearing the black one. In Chapter 11, Charles Stevens takes Chaney's black hat and gives it to Chief Many Treaties. Many Treaties discards the hat on the opposite shore from which Chaney emerges. Somehow, with Indians all around, Noah Beery, Jr. retrieves Chaney's hat for him.

In Chapter 14, Cording is able to gain possession of Chaney's pistol and ride off with it. As Chaney races to his horse, there is no pistol in his holster, but in the next shot Chaney's pistol is back.

Overland Mail's wagon train sequences were augmented by footage from *The Oregon Trail* (Universal, 1939) cattle stampede scenes were lifted from *Arizona* (Columbia, 1940), and the scene in which Helen Parrish's buckboard overturns had been seen earlier in *Winners of the West* (Universal, 1940).

Johnston McCulley, author of the story, is best known as the creator of the masked avenger Zorro for his novel "The Curse of Capistrano," which was first published in the Saturday August 9, 1919, edition of "All-Star Story." Douglas Fairbanks was the first screen Zorro in *Mark of Zorro* (United Artists, 1920). The first sound and color Zorro feature was *The Bold Caballero* (Republic, 1936) with Robert Livingston. Republic used the character as the basis for many serials, with the best and most faithful to the source being *Zorro's Fighting Legion* in 1939. Tyrone Power essayed the role in *Mark of Zorro* (20th Century Fox, 1940). Many Zorro features have been produced over the years, the latest being *The Mask of Zorro* (Tri-Star, 1998) with both Antonio Banderas and Anthony Hopkins as the masked avenger.

REVIEWS: "Fast paced chapterplay." (*Western Movies*, Pitts)

SUMMATION: *Overland Mail* is a slightly above average Western serial. While the action is plentiful throughout, the first six chapters have little spark. The directorial touch of Ford Beebe and John Rawlins improves over the final nine chapters, even generating some genuine suspense. There are lapses in production values, script writing, and continuity. (Chaney plays fast and loose with his hat and gun). The villains don't seem to know what they're doing, especially during the initial chapter when they plant a bomb on the coach they're having their renegades hold up. Chaney makes for an acceptable hero, but no more, while Noah Beery, Jr. and Don Terry shine with their natural and engaging performances. Fruity-voiced Noah Beery, Sr., one of filmdom's top villains, does what he can with the tired dialogue, but one grows weary hearing Beery Sr. spout the same lines about the "million dollar contract" chapter after chapter. Harry Cording makes an excellent villain, convincingly showing toughness, fear and defiance. Helen Parrish, as the spunky heroine, and Tom Chatterton, as the beleaguered stage and pony express line owner are impressive in the otherwise adequate supporting cast. *Overland Mail* is a serial that entertains but should have been much better.

ONE OF THE 3 MOST EXCITING AND IMPORTANT PICTURES OF THE YEAR!
Because it's "off the beaten track" ... because it transports you half-way 'round the world to an exciting setting never before revealed on the screen ... because it tells a story of courage and daring so humanly, so effectively that you'll be stirred as you have rarely been by any motion picture!

The Overlanders

Universal-International / J. Arthur Rank (December 1946); An Ealing Production

CAST: Dan McAlpine, **Chips Rafferty**; Bill Parsons, **John Nugent Hayward**; Mary Parsons, **Daphne Campbell**; Mrs. Parsons, **Jean Blue**; Helen Parsons, **Helen Grieve**; Corky, **John Fernside**; Sailor ("Sinbad"), **Peter Pagan**; Charlie, **Frank Ransome**; Manager, **Stan Tolhurst**; Minister, **Marshall Crosby**; Police Sergeant, **John Fegan**; Aborigine Jacky, **Clyde Combo**; Aborigine Nipper, **Henry Murdoch**

CREDITS: Director/Screenwriter, **Harry Watt**; Producer, **Michael Balcon**; Australian Associate Producer, **Ralph Smart**; Supervising Editor, **Leslie A. Norman**; Editor, **E.M. Inman Hunter**; Production Supervisor, **Jack Rix**; Technical Supervisor, **Eric Williams**; Unit Manager, **Arch Spiers**; Cinematography, **Osmond Borradaile**; Camera Operator, **Carl Kayser**; Sound, **Beresford Hallett**;

Musical Director, **Ernest Irving**; Composer, **John Ireland**; Music played by **The Philharmonic Orchestra**; Researcher, **Dora Birtles**

LOCATION FILMING: Northern Territory South and Queensland, Australia

RUNNING TIME: 91 min.

STORY: In 1942, a Japanese invasion of Northern Territory, Australia, was felt to be imminent. The decision came down to destroy the cattle herds to keep them from falling into enemy hands. One drover, Chips Rafferty, felt it would be worth the gamble to drive the cattle over the rugged terrain of Northern Territory into Queensland. Receiving permission from the Australian Meat Export Company, Rafferty began the drive with a crew consisting of an elderly drover, John Fernside, a sailor, Peter Pagan, John Nugent Hayward and his family, and two aborigines, Clyde Combo and Henry Murdoch. Hayward's oldest daughter, Daphne Campbell, and Pagan are attracted to each other, even though Campbell has a suitor who's fighting in the war. Rafferty and his group undergo many hardships: having to cross a swollen river infested with crocodiles, losing the extra horses to poisonous weeds, having to corral and break wild horses of the plains, turning the cattle that had been stampeded by dingoes, and having to cross a mountainous trail to find water. During the stampede, Pagan runs into a low hanging branch in the darkness and is knocked from his horse. Positioning himself behind a tree, Pagan is able to protect most of his body, except an arm and a leg. The injured drover is taken by Hayward's wife, Jean Blue, for medical attention. As they near the end of their destination, water is located over a bog. If the cattle rush to the water, they will be pushed into the bog and drowned. Rafferty plans to bring about a hundred cattle at a time to the water. The wind shifts, and the cattle smell the water. Rafferty and his group try to stop the cattle in their flight but see that they will be unsuccessful. Rafferty, Hayward, Fernside and Campbell race to the river and dismount, hoping to stare down the cattle. This plan works. After watering the cattle, they complete the drive. Other drovers follow with large herds. Rafferty, Campbell, Hayward and Blue return by plane to Northern Territory to begin another cattle drive. Pagan, still not fully recovered from his wounds, can only watch Campbell leave after promising to write.

NOTES AND COMMENTARY: Chips Rafferty, the Gary Cooper of Australia, reached the height of his American popularity in the late 1940s with *The Overlanders, Bush Christmas* (Ealing/Universal-International, 1947) and *Eureka Stockade* (Ealing/GFT, 1949).

The Overlanders, based on a factual incident, was Ealing Studio's first Australian production.

John Ireland, the composer of the film's musical score, is not the American actor. Although Ireland had no prior experience writing music for motion pictures, producer Michael Balcon hired him for the job.

REVIEWS: "This should come as a breath of fresh air to audiences jaded with routine pictures." (*Variety*, 9/25/46); "This is an often beautiful film that features a careful balance of both large and small moments." (*The Motion Picture Guide*, Nash and Ross)

SUMMATION: *The Overlanders* is a very good wartime western set in Australia. The impressive ensemble cast ably meets the acting demands of the story. Harry Watt's direction and screenplay is exceptional. Watt frames his scenes for maximum emotional impact, generating suspense and tension, even with the audience's knowledge that the cattle drive will be successful. Cinematographer Osmond Borradaile captures the magnificent Australian scenery, reminiscent of the vistas of the American West, and John Ireland's musical score, played to perfection by the Philharmonic Orchestra, is to be commended.

KEN MAYNARD ... *gives you the Wild West thrill of your life...
In this smashingly colorful picture of a fighting man whose prowess in the saddle lifted him from a small medicine show to stardom in the biggest Wild West attraction. See him ride the untamed "Killer!" See him crush all obstacles to help his smallboy pal! See him win the love of the champion marksman as he downs his rival.* SEE HIM IN HIS FASTEST ACTION. HE'S GREAT!

Parade of the West

Universal (January 1930); A Ken Maynard Production

CAST: Bud Rand, **Ken Maynard**; Mary Owens, **Gladys McConnell**; Professor Clayton, **Otis Harlan**; Swifty, **Frank Rice**; Shorty, **Bobbie Dunn**; Billy Rand, **Jackie Hanlon**; Copeland, **Fred Burns**; Sicily Joe, **Frank Yaconelli**; Dude, **Stanley Blystone**; Sambo, **Blue Washington**; Tarzan, "**Tarzan**"; Midnight, "**Rex**"

CREDITS: Director, **Harry Joe Brown**; Story, **Bennett Cohen**; Screenwriters, **Bennett Cohen and Lesley Mason**; Editor, **Fred Allen**; Cinematographer, **Ted McCord**; Recording Engineer; **C. Roy Hunter**

SONGS: "The Old Chisholm Trail" (traditional)—sung by **Ken Maynard**; "Down in Union County" (Spicher and Christian)—sung by **Ken Maynard** and "Sal's Got a Wooden Leg" (traditional)—sung by **Ken Maynard**

RUNNING TIME: 65 min.

STORY: Ken Maynard has the responsibility of caring for his younger brother, Jack Hanlon. Accepting an offer to join Fred Burns' Wild West Show, Maynard is to ride Rex, a wild horse. Meanwhile, Maynard and another performer, Gladys McConnell, begin to fall in love. Stanley Blystone's romantic designs on McConnell result in a fight between Maynard and Blystone, with Maynard proving victorious. Blystone decides to exact revenge and loosens the cinch on Rex when Maynard makes his ride. Maynard is thrown and trampled by Rex. Because of his injuries, Maynard must stay behind as the Wild West show moves on. Maynard writes Hanlon and McConnell. Blystone intercepts the letters, and tells everyone that Maynard is a coward. When Hanlon is taken ill, Maynard returns to the show and sets the record straight: he rides Rex and proves to Hanlon that he's not a coward, and settles affairs with Blystone.

NOTES AND COMMENTARY: *Parade of the West* was also released as a silent film.

Footage of Ken Maynard and Jackie Hanlon performing stunts in *Parade of the West* would later be used in Maynard's *King of the Arena* (Universal, 1933).

"The Old Chisholm Trail" would be heard in *The Fiddlin' Buckaroo* (Universal, 1933), *Stormy* (Universal, 1935), *The Phantom Rider* (Universal, 1936) and *The Old Chisholm Trail* (Universal, 1942).

REVIEWS: "Much padded with stock footage of bronco riding and trick roping and listlessly directed by Brown, the film doesn't fulfill the promise of Maynard's earlier part-talkies." (*The Western*, Hardy); "This is a poorly done western, padded with too much stock footage of rodeo trick-riding and roping." (*The Motion Picture Guide*, Nash and Ross)

SUMMATION: *Parade of the West* was not available for viewing by the author.

AMERICA'S CHOICE!
Here in the magnificent WESTERN ACTION SERIAL with every episode thrill-packed with dangerous adventure!
15 THRILL-PACKED CHAPTERS!

The Phantom Rider

Universal (July 1936); A Henry MacRae Production

CAST: Buck Grant, **Buck Jones**; Mary Grayson, **Marla Shelton**; Helen Moore, **Diana Gibson**; Harvey Delaney, **Harry Woods**; Judge Holmes, **Frank LaRue**; Spooky, **George Cooper**; Sheriff Mark, **Eddie Gribbon**; Shorty, **Matt McHugh**; Lizzie, **Helen Shipman**; Lew, **Wally Wales**; Steve Scott, **Joey Ray**; Jeff Grayson, **Lafe McKee**; Dirk, **James Mason**; Keeler, **Charles King**// "Silver"; Roscoe, **Charles LeMoyne**; Ezra Horner, **Charles K. French**; Gabe, **Jim Corey**; Blackie, **Lee Shumway**; Hudson, **Clem Bevins**; Tex, **Tom London**; Dance Hall Girl, **Priscilla Lawson**; Stagecoach Driver, **Hank Bell**; Saloon Singer, **Cactus Mack**; Outlaw, **Slim Whitaker**; Mr. Blake, **Orrin Burke**; Indian Chief, **Jim Thorpe**

CREDITS: Director, **Ray Taylor**; Screenwriters, **George Plympton, Basil Dickey** and **Ella O'Neill**; Editors, **Saul Goodkind, Edward Todd, Alvin Todd** and **Louis Sackin**; Art Director, **Ralph Berger**; Cinematographers, **Allen Q. Thompson** and **John Hickson**

SONGS: "Hidden Valley" (Mitchell and Stept)—sung by **Cactus Mack and His Saddle Tramps**; "Going Home" (traditional)—sung by **Cactus Mack and His Saddle Tramps**; and "The Old Chisholm Trail" (traditional)—sung by **Cactus Mack and His Saddle Tramps**

LOCATION FILMING: Walker Ranch, Lone Pine, Red Rock Canyon and Agoura, California

RUNNING TIME: 284 min.

CHAPTER TITLES: 1. Dynamite, 2. The Maddened Herd, 3. The Brink of Disaster, 4. The Phantom Rides, 5. Trapped by Outlaws, 6. Shot Down, 7. Stark Terror, 8. The Night Attack, 9. The Indian Raid, 10. Human Targets, 11. The Shaft of Doom, 12. Flaming Gold, 13. Crashing Timbers, 14. The Last Chance, 15. The Outlaw's Vengeance

STORY: The Governor has assigned State Ranger Buck Jones and Judge Frank LaRue to find the leader of the outlaw gang working in the area. Buck, disguised as the Phantom Rider, helps the homesteaders against the outlaws. Jones finds a clue that indicates the answer to the trouble may lie with the Hidden Valley Ranch, owned by Marla Shelton. The outlaws need control of all the ranches in the area because the railroad will require access for a right-of-way. Shelton's father, Lafe McKee, has disappeared. Jones finds McKee at the same time as the outlaws. In an exchange of shots, the outlaws are driven off, but McKee is mortally wounded. McKee gives Jones a wallet to give to Shelton. Jones takes the wallet to Shelton and vows to bring her father's murderer to justice. The outlaw gang tries to take the wallet from Shelton's safe. Jones, as the Phantom Rider, interferes, and claims it for himself. Jones' sidekick, George Cooper, brings La Rue to Jones' cabin, and Jones gives the wallet to La Rue for safekeeping. The outlaws try to stop the stagecoach bringing railway representative Orrin Burke to town. Jones, with help from Shelton's cowhands, stops the outlaw's scheme. The mysterious boss wants to prevent any deal between Shelton and Burke from being consummated, and to take possession of McKee's wallet. Jones asks Shelton not to sell her ranch to the railroad. Shelton agrees but then changes her mind. Shelton now has possession of the wallet. At the signing, shots ring out, and Burke is wounded. In the confusion, Jones, as the Phantom Rider, takes control of the wallet. Rancher Harry Woods, trying to help Shelton, believes Jones is the Phantom Rider. Woods sets a trap to prove that Jones and the Phantom Rider are one, but both Jones and the Phantom Rider appear—Cooper is wearing the Phantom Rider outfit. Shelton needs money to pay off the mortgage and thinks about selling the ranch. Woods tells Shelton that he will lend her ten thousand dollars.

Jones, as the Phantom Rider, advises her not to accept. In McKee's wallet are directions to a gold mine. Jones locates the mine for Shelton. Woods and his men show up, also. Through harrowing adventures, enough gold reaches town so Shelton can pay off the mortgage. The mysterious boss wants Jones and Cooper out of the way, since he now believes them to be lawmen. An attack on the two men fails, but the outlaws escape. Shelton decides to make a deal with the railroad. Before she can do this, the outlaws seize Shelton and bring her to the hideout. In trying to rescue Shelton, Jones, as the Phantom Rider, is captured, but Silver gets away. The mysterious boss turns out to be Woods. Silver leads a posse to the outlaw hideout before Shelton can sign over Hidden Valley Ranch in exchange for Jones' life. Woods and his gang are rounded up, and Jones now has time for Shelton.

NOTES AND COMMENTARY: Actress Helen Shipman was the mother of actor Brian Keith.

The James Mason in this serial is not the famous English actor.

Wally Wales, under the name Hal Taliaferro, would have a long career in films, especially in westerns and serials.

"The Old Chisholm Trail" can be heard in *Parade of the West* (Universal, 1930), *The Fiddlin' Buckaroo* (Universal, 1933), *Stormy* (Universal, 1935) and *The Old Chisholm Trail* (Universal, 1942).

REVIEWS: "Well paced serial." (*Western Movies*, Pitts)

SUMMATION: *The Phantom Rider* is a good Buck Jones serial. Jones again makes for a perfect serial hero. The serial boasts a good supporting cast, highlighted by Marla Shelton as Jones' love interest, George Cooper as his savvy sidekick, and one of the top western badmen, Harry Woods, who leads a fine group of henchmen to menace Jones. Director Ray Taylor paces the serial nicely, but the screenwriters let the story down with some weak chapter resolutions. Universal, like Columbia, could be satisfied, at times by simply having the hero dust himself off and carry on.

ROUGH RIDING BULLET BLAZING FIST FLYING ACTION!

The Phantom Stage

Universal (February 1939)

CAST: Bob, **Bob Baker**; Mary, **Marjorie Reynolds**; Grizzly, **George Cleveland**; Lawson, **Forrest Taylor**; Runt, **Ernie Adams**; Denver, **Reed Howes**; Sheriff, **Glenn Strange**; Scott, **Murdock MacQuarrie**; Stage Driver, **Jack Kirk**; Blacksmith, **Dick Rush**; Stage Guard, **Tex Palmer**

CREDITS: Director, **George Wag-**

gner; Assistant Director, **Glenn Cook**; Story/ Screenwriter, **Joseph West**; Editor, **Carl Pierson**; Technical Director, **Albert Greenwood**; Cinematographer, **Harry Neumann**; Sound, **Bernard B. Brown** and **Joseph Lapis**; Musical Director/Arranger, **Frank Sanucci**

SONGS: "Down the Road to Santa Fe" (Allan)—sung by **Bob Baker** and **George Cleveland**; "Give Me the Life of a Cow-boy" (Allan)—sung by **Bob Baker**; "We're Brandin' Today" (Allan)—sung by **Bob Baker and vocal group**; "Ridin' Down That Utah Trail" (Allan)—sung by **Bob Baker;** and "We're Rollin' Today" (Allan)—sung by **Bob Baker**

LOCATION FILMING: Kernville, California

RUNNING TIME: 57 min.

STORY: Wandering cowboys Bob Baker and George Cleveland help break up a bank robbery and save the sheriff's life, but circumstances make it look like they're part of the gang. After this narrow escape, Baker and Cleveland decide to settle town and head for Montana. The cowboys stop in Terminal City. Cleveland overhears how gold shipments leave from Medicine Hat in a strongbox, which is empty when it reaches its destination. No one wants the job as stage driver, so Cleveland volunteers Baker and himself. Forrest Taylor heads the outlaw gang that robs the coaches. He sends trunks with his confederate, Ernie Adams, inside. Blacksmith Dick Rush has rigged the strongbox to be opened from the inside. Stage owner Marjorie Reynolds tells Baker and Cleveland that failure to deliver any future shipments will result in the cancellation of her hauling contract and the end of her stage line. On the next delivery, Baker stashes the strong box in the boot instead of on top of the stage, so Adams is unable to steal this shipment. Baker and Reynolds begin to fall in love. Baker and Cleveland have the responsibility of transporting a large shipment. Taylor and his men ride on a ridge near the stagecoach road to divert Baker and Cleveland's attention. Adams is able to climb out of the trunk and into the stagecoach, Adams reach into the boot and steal the shipment. Unable to climb back into the trunk, Adams has to jump from the stage. With no weight in the trunk, it begins moving about. Baker discovers the trunk is now empty. Baker believes Taylor and Rush, who both received trunks, are responsible for the robberies but has no proof. Baker climbs into the trunk to be taken to the gang's headquarters. Taylor and Adams retrieve the trunk and are startled to find it heavy. Cleveland convinces Sheriff Glenn Strange to follow Taylor and save Baker's life. Taylor believes Baker is in the trunk; and he and Adams throw the trunk off a bridge, down a rocky embankment and into the river. Cleveland and the posse see this and ride to rescue Baker, but find only a heavy sack in the trunk. Baker is still on the wagon, hiding from Taylor and Adams. Taylor arrives at his ranch and tells his men they have to clear out quickly. Baker gets the drop on Taylor and the men, unaware that henchman Reed Howes is sneaking

The Phantom Stage (1939) movie still: Bob Baker (*top*) fires at an outlaw about to shoot the sheriff, while George Cleveland takes aim at other bank robbers.

up behind him. As Howes clubs Baker, Cleveland and the posse arrive. The posse rounds up the gang. Taylor had ducked into a barn, and now sneaks out with the intention of shooting Baker, who is staggering to his feet. Cleveland fires two quick shots, ending Taylor's lawless career. Baker and Reynolds marry and go on a honeymoon, with Cleveland in a trunk on the rear of the stage.

NOTES AND COMMENTARY: Bob Baker suffered serious facial and head injuries during the making of this film. Baker was driving a top-heavy stagecoach downhill when one of the horses decided to go its own way and pulled the other horses off the road. The brake rods buckled, the stagecoach overturned and Baker was thrown from the coach against the side of a cliff. His cowboy hat was credited for preventing damage to his skull. Ernie Adams, who was also on the coach, suffered some non-critical injuries.

The Phantom Stage was Bob Baker's final solo starring role. As Universal began their next season, Johnny Mack Brown became the top cowboy, with Baker and Fuzzy Knight in support.

Screen credits mix up Ernie Adams' and Tex Palmer's character names. Actually, Adams plays Runt and Palmer is the Stage Guard. Also, Murdock MacQuarrie's character name is listed as Scott, while everyone calls him John.

Director George Waggner and screenwriter Joseph West are one and the same person.

Universal slipped up when they picked the singing voice for George Cleveland. It was so obviously mismatched that it became unintentionally amusing.

Bob Baker originally sang "Ridin' Down That Utah Trail" in *Western Trails* (Universal, 1938).

The Phantom Stage was remade as a Tex Williams featurette, *The Fargo Phantom* (Universal-International, 1950).

REVIEWS: "A stock western in the Bob Baker series, not too well made and far less exciting than most." (*Variety*, 12/6/39); "A strange western." (*The Motion Picture Guide*, Nash and Ross)

SUMMATION: *The Phantom Stage* is another pleasant Bob Baker series western. Baker and sidekick George Cleveland handle their roles in easygoing fashion. A clever and well-paced script by director and screenwriter George Waggner keeps the interest level high, despite the lack of fast action.

Blazing GUNS BLAST A TRAIL!
Braving savages and renegades ... to make way for the Pony Express!

Pony Post

Universal (December 1940)

CAST: Cal, **Johnny Mack Brown**; Shorty, **Fuzzy Knight**; Norma, **Nell O'Day**; Alice, **Dorothy Short**; Goodwin, **Tom Chatterton**; Atkins, **Stanley Blystone**; Mack Richards, **Jack Rockwell**; Claud Richards, **Ray Teal**; Whitmore, **Kermit Maynard**; Fairweather, **Lane Chandler**; George Barber, **Eddie Cobb**; Dr. Nesbet, **Lloyd Ingraham**; Hamilton, **Charles King**; Jimmy Wakely and his Rough Riders (**Johnny Bond** and **Dick Reinhart**)// "Brownie"; Indian, **Iron Eyes Cody**

CREDITS: Director, **Ray Taylor**; Story/Screenwriter, **Sherman Lowe**; Editor, **Paul Landres**; Art Directors, **Jack Otterson** and **Harold H. MacArthur**; Set Decorator, **R.A. Gausman**; Cinematographer, **Jerome Ash**; Sound, **Bernard B. Brown** and **Glenn Anderson**; Musical Director, **H.J. Salter**

SONGS: "I Don't Like No Cows" (Rosen and Carter)—sung by **Fuzzy Knight**; "Way Back in Oklahoma" (Dean and Bond)—sung by **Jimmy Wakely and His Rough Riders**; "My Saddle Serenade" (Bond)—sung by

Jimmy Wakely and His Rough Riders; and "Ride, Ride, Ride" (Bond)—sung by **Jimmy Wakely and His Rough Riders**

LOCATION FILMING: Iverson, Corriganville and Agoura, California

RUNNING TIME: 59 min.

STORY: Stanley Blystone, the manager of the Pony Express line in Ruby Valley, has been doing a poor job. General Manager Tom Chatterton asks Johnny Mack Brown to take over. Getting wind of his impending replacement, Blystone tells brothers Jack Rockwell and Ray Teal that Chatterton is bringing a large sum of money to Ruby Valley. The holdup attempt fails when Brown spots the holdup men and chases them into a small band of unfriendly Indians. Blystone is fired but leaves only after being beaten by Brown in a fistfight. Blystone induces Rockwell and Teal to steal horses from Nell O'Day's father's way station. O'Day's father is killed in the raid and the horses are stolen. Brown and O'Day investigate and find that one of the raiders' horses has a broken horseshoe. Blystone persuades Rockwell and Teal to sell the stolen horses back to the Pony Express. Brown sees the brothers with the horses. As Brown approaches, the brothers ride off. Later in town, O'Day discovers that Teal's horse is the one with the broken horseshoe. Teal chases O'Day to where Brown is bringing in the stolen horses. Brown chases Teal back to town, where he joins Blystone and Rockwell. The renegades engage in a gunfight with Brown and O'Day. Brown shoots Teal, and O'Day guns down Rockwell. Brown brings Blystone to justice before he can escape. O'Day receives a new job with the Pony Express.

NOTES AND COMMENTARY: The song "Way Back in Oklahoma" would be sung by Eddie Dean and Roscoe Ates in *Driftin' River* (PRC, 1946). "My Saddle Serenade" would be used in *Marshal of Gunsmoke* (Universal, 1944). Listen to the piano music during the saloon scenes; Universal made use of the score from *Destry Rides Again* (Universal, 1939) by playing "(See What) The Boys in the Back Room Will Have" and "Little Joe."

In England's *Western Film Annual* (1954), western great Wild Bill Elliott listed his favorite western films, and Johnny Mack Brown's *Pony Post* made the list.

REVIEWS: "Mildly tiresome sagebrusher. Inferior western with insufficient action." (*Variety*, 12/25/40); "Tiresome, unexciting western." (*The Motion Picture Guide*, Nash and Ross)

SUMMATION: *Pony Post* is a slight western that comes in at about average, thanks to the performances of Johnny Mack Brown and Nell O'Day. The villainy is not as intricate as in other Brown westerns, but the fast pace generated by director Ray Taylor nearly compensates. The "funny" antics of Fuzzy Knight lower the film's rating. Knight's routines are unbelievable and without humor. Sherman Lowe is responsible for the story and screenplay, and should be properly ashamed of the result.

Fighting Bob Baker on a Rampage Again!
He cleaned out a nest of bandits ... and cracked every bad egg in it!

Prairie Justice

Universal (November 1938)

CAST: Bob, **Bob Baker**; Anita, **Dorothy Fay**; Alfalfa, **Hal Taliaferro**; Benson, **Jack Rockwell**; Sheriff, **Forrest Taylor**; Dry Gulch, **Carleton Young**; Haynes, **Glenn Strange**; Boots, **Jack Kirk**; Smokey, "**Wimpy**"// "**Apache**"; Jed (Stage Driver), **Jimmy Phelps**; Bert (Stage Guard), **Slim Whitaker**; Stage Line Agent, **Murdock MacQuarrie**; Chuck, **Chuck Baldra**

CREDITS: Director, **George Waggner**; Assistant Director, **Glenn Cook**; Story/ Screenwriter, **Joseph West**; Editor, **Carl Pierson**; Technical Director, **Albert Greenwood**; Cinematographer, **Gus Peterson**; Sound, **Barnard B. Brown** and **Robert Pritchard**; Musical Director/ Arranger, **Frank Sanucci**

SONGS: "Dusty an' Dry" (Allan) — sung by **Bob Baker**; "Hi' Falutin' Cowboy" (Allan) — sung by **Dorothy Fay** and **Bob Baker**; "Starlight on the Prairie" (Allan) — sung by **Bob Baker, Chuck Baldra** and **male chorus**; and "Rose of the Prairie" (Allan) — sung by **Bob Baker** and **male chorus**

LOCATION FILMING: Monogram Ranch, Andy Jauregui Ranch and Walker Ranch, California

RUNNING TIME: 58 min.

STORY: Before outlaws can rob a stagecoach, U.S. Marshal Bob Baker, posing as a bandit, takes the strongbox and hides it. Arriving in River Junction, Baker tells his father, Sheriff Forrest Taylor, and his deputy Hal Taliaferro where the strongbox is hidden. When Taylor goes for the strongbox, he is trailed by two outlaws, Carleton Young and Jack Kirk. When Taylor recovers the strongbox, Young takes deadly aim in the middle of Taylor's back and pulls the trigger of his rifle. Young is in league with rancher Jack Rockwell whose niece and half owner of the ranch, Dorothy Fay, has returned from the East. Rockwell tells Fay all the cattle have been stolen, the ranch is not doing well and she should return to the East. Baker, now posing as a wandering cowhand, has made Fay's acquaintance and persuades her to give him a job if he finds the cattle. Baker finds the herd and takes Kirk, who was guarding the cattle, into custody. Believing Baker to be harmless, Rockwell and the Citizens' Committee ask Baker to be their new sheriff, and he accepts. A large shipment of gold is scheduled to be shipped by stagecoach. Baker arranges to have a fake shipment go by stage, while Rockwell will deliver the real shipment. After the stage travels a short distance from town, Taliaferro meets it with Baker's horse. Baker and Taliaferro ride to watch Rockwell, and spy Rockwell surrendering the gold to Young and his men. But Baker had pulled a double switch, and the strongbox Young took contained only horseshoes. Baker catches up to Rockwell and tells him that he found the stolen herd and is about to round up the rustlers. Rockwell goes directly to the herd and is accosted by Baker. Rockwell tells Baker that little by little he fell under Young's control. Finding only horseshoes, Young thinks Rockwell double-crossed him and follows Rockwell to settle the score. Young sneaks up on Rockwell and sees him talking with Baker. Young decides to shoot Baker first, but Rockwell takes the bullet meant for Baker. Young attempts to escape on Rockwell's buckboard, and Baker overhauls him. The two men fight on the careening buckboard. Baker knocks Young from the vehicle, and Young is killed in the fall. Baker tells Fay that Rockwell died a hero. Baker resigns from law enforcement to marry Fay and run her ranch.

NOTES AND COMMENTARY: Earlier in his career, sidekick Hal Taliaferro had been a series western star, under the name Wally Wales. Wales made series for Big 4 in the 1930–31 season and Imperial in 1934. Taliaferro was also billed as Walt Williams in two of the Bud 'n Ben series entries for Reliable in 1934.

"Dusty an' Dry" was sung earlier by Bob Baker in *Black Bandit* (Universal, 1938). "Starlight on the Prairie" was featured in *Black Bandit* and *Oklahoma Raiders* (Universal, 1944).

George Waggner used the pseudonym Joseph West for his story and screenplay activities.

Dorothy Fay married Tex Ritter in her hometown of Prescott, Arizona, on June 14, 1941. With her marriage to Ritter, Fay wound down her show business career.

REVIEWS: "Pic, generally, is good enough to keep the Baker series moving." (*Variety*, 11/30/38); "Fair Bob Baker series vehicle." (*Western Movies*, Pitts)

SUMMATION: *Prairie Justice* is another pleasant Bob Baker outing. Baker deftly handles both the action and singing responsibilities. Dorothy Fay makes a nice leading lady and even joins Baker in one musical number. A good supporting cast of "B" western players adds to the enjoyment of the story.

A Bold Buckaroo and His Croonin' Side-Kick! In a tuneful tangle...of bullets and ballads!

Ragtime Cowboy Joe

Universal (September 1940)

CAST: Steve, **Johnny Mack Brown**; Joe, **Fuzzy Knight**; Helen, Nell O'Day; Bo, **Dick Curtis**; Mary, **Marilyn Merrick**; Virgil, **Walter Soderling**; Putt, **Roy Barcroft**; Del, **Harry Tenbrook**; Roy, **George Plues**; Sheriff, **Edward Cassidy**; Edwards, **Buck Moulton**; Duncan, **Harold Goodwin**; Osborne, **Wilfred Lucas**; Mansfield, **William Gould**; Bartender, **Bob O'Connor**; Clements, **Bud Osborne**; Foreman, **Charles Whitaker**; Hank Clayton, **Jack Clifford**; Singer, **Vyola Vonn;** and **the Texas Rangers** (Robert "Captain Bob" Crawford, Edward "Tookie" Cronenbold, Francis "Irish" Mahaney and Roderic "Dave" May)// "Ranger"; Outlaw, **Frank McCarroll**; Deputies, **Eddie Parker** and **Kermit Maynard**

CREDITS: Director, **Ray Taylor**; Screenwriter, **Sherman Lowe**; Editor, **Paul Landres**; Art Directors, **Jack Otterson** and **Harold H. MacArthur**; Set Decorator, **R.A. Gausman**; Cinematographer, **Jerome Ash**; Sound, **Bernard B. Brown** and **Glenn Anderson**

SONGS: "Ragtime Cowboy Joe" (Clarke, Muir and Abrahams)—sung by **the Texas Rangers**; "Song of the Trail Drive" (Crawford)—sung by **the Texas Rangers**; "Do the Oh La La" (Rosen and Carter)—sung by **Vyola Vonn**; "Cross-Eyed Kate" (Rosen and Carter)—sung by **Fuzzy Knight**; and "Ragtime Cowboy Joe" (reprise)—sung by **the Texas Rangers**

LOCATION FILMING: Agoura, California

RUNNING TIME: 58 min.

STORY: Dick Curtis delivers 400 head of cattle stolen from rancher Wilfred Lucas to Harold Goodwin. Lucas has trailed the stolen herd and is shot down by Curtis. Curtis finds a letter on Lucas' body stating that a Cattlemen's Association detective will arrive to investigate rustling activity. When Johnny Mack Brown rides into the area, Curtis has Brown arrested for Lucas' murder. Lawyer Walter Soderling, the leader of the rustler's gang, tells Curtis he needs Lucas' ranch to control the area; a railroad has been negotiating with Soderling for a right-of-way. Brown asks for a lawyer. Soderling and his secretary, Marilyn Merrick, plan to defend him. Merrick, who is Brown's girlfriend, slips Brown a note naming Soderling and Curtis as gang leaders. Brown breaks jail and rides to Lucas' ranch, where he offers his services to Lucas' daughter, Nell O'Day, and her foreman, Fuzzy Knight. Knight tells Brown the railroad is coming through and will save the ranch for O'Day. Soderling offers to have some of his men take O'Day's cattle to market. Brown then reveals to O'Day he's a Cattleman's Association detective and Soderling is the gang leader. Brown wants the drive to take place so the gang can be rounded up while committing a crime. Brown and Sheriff Ed Cassidy overhear Soderling tell Curtis to stampede O'Day's cattle and sell them to Goodwin. After Curtis leaves Soderling's office, Brown and Cassidy arrest Soderling. Curtis' men stampede the cattle. Brown signals Cassidy and the posse. The posse rounds up the gang members while Brown brings in Curtis. Brown and Merrick plan to get together.

NOTES AND COMMENTARY: Grant Clarke, Lewis Muir and Maurice Abrahams wrote the song "Ragtime Cowboy Joe" in 1912. Even though the song was the title of this picture, it took Alice Faye in *Hello, Frisco, Hello* (20th Century Fox, 1943), and Betty Hutton in *Incendiary Blonde* (Paramount, 1945) to make it popular again. In later years, the chorus became more noted than the verse. Grant Clarke also wrote the song "Second Hand Rose."

Ragtime Cowboy Joe was initially scheduled to be a 1939–40 release, with Johnny Mack Brown, Bob Baker and Fuzzy Knight. With the close of production of *Bad Man from Red Butte* (Universal, 1940), Baker's contract at Universal expired and he was replaced by Nell O'Day. The film was the second release of Johnny Mack Brown's 1940–41 season.

The scene in which Johnny Mack Brown stops Nell O'Day's "runaway" buckboard was used again in Kirby Grant's *Rustler's Roundup* (Universal, 1946), with Grant and Jane Adams in the close-ups.

The song "Do the Oo La La" would be sung by Claudia Drake in Kirby Grant's *The Lawless Breed* (Universal, 1946)/

Ranger was Nell O'Day's horse in the picture.

Marilyn Merrick is better known to western fans as Lynn Merrick.

REVIEWS: "Despite some apparent script uncertainty, *Ragtime Cowboy Joe* keeps moving with frequent gun battles, fistic brawls and hard riding, so it holds interest much of the way." (*Variety*, 10/2/40); "The hackneyed plot gets pretty good service from this Universal actioner." (*Western Movies*, Pitts)

SUMMATION: *Ragtime Cowboy Joe* is a slightly above average western feature that should have been much better. In the previous entries with Brown, Fuzzy Knight's role emphasized character with a touch of welcome comedy. This time out, Knight is a full-fledged comic sidekick, with the final results coming in on the dismal side. Johnny Mack Brown's ability as an action star who can act, and the spritely Nell O'Day (who can ride, rope and deliver her lines convincingly), do much to counterbalance Knight's part in the proceedings and some unbelievable coincidences in the script. It's just too much to believe that Brown's girl, Marilyn Merrick, just happens to be working for head villain Walter Soderling and can quickly tell Brown it's Soderling and Dick Curtis behind the lawlessness. To his credit, Director Ray Taylor brings the action to the foreground and paces the story quickly to cover the holes in the script.

THE GOLD FIELDS ROAR WITH WILD ADVENTURES...
...as secret agents crack down on smugglers, high-jackers and spies!

Raiders of Ghost City

Universal (July 1944)

CAST: Captain Steve Clark, **Dennis Moore**; Cathy Haines, **Wanda McKay**; Alex Morel, **Lionel Atwill**; Idaho Jones, **Joe Sawyer**; Captain Clay Randolph, **Regis Toomey**; Trina Dessard, **Virginia Christine**; Doc Blair, **Eddy C. Waller**; Carl Lawton, **Emmett Vogan**; Colonel Sewell, **Addison Richards**; Abel Rackerby, **Charles Waggenheim**; Braddock, **Jack Ingram**; Rawhide, **Edmund Cobb**; Bart, **Jack Rockwell**; Bill Jasper, **Ernie Adams**; Hank, **George Eldredge**; Lieut. Jim Clark, **Gene Garrick**// Chief Tahona, **Chief Thundercloud**; Freiderich, **George J. Lewis**; Major Graham, **William Forrest**; Major Norton, **Rex Lease**; Lane, **Pierce Lyden**; Burke, **Ray Teal**; Murdock, **Robin Short**; Saloon Patron, **John Cason**; Slim, **Budd Buster**; Dan Lake, **Joel Friedkin**; Soldier, **Dan White**; Raider at Cave, **Robert Barron**; Graton, **Gene Roth**; Garrett, **Lee Phelps**; Miner, **Tex Cooper**

CREDITS: Directors, **Ray Taylor** and **Lewis D. Collins**; Associate Producers, **Morgan B. Cox** and **Ray Taylor**; Screenwriters, **Luci Ward** and **Morgan B. Cox**; Dialogue Director, **Willard Holland**; Supervising Editor, **Norman A. Cerf**; Editors, **Alvin Todd**, **Edgar Zane**, **Irving Birnbaum**, **Jack Dolan** and **Ace Herman**; Art Director, **Harold H. MacArthur**; Cinematographers, **William Sickner** and **Harry Neumann**

LOCATION FILMING: Iverson, Brandais and Tuolumme County, Beals Cut, California

RUNNING TIME: 226 min.

CHAPTER TITLES: 1. Murder by Accident, 2. Flaming Treachery, 3. Death Rides Double, 4. Ghost City Terror, 5. The Fatal Lariat, 6. Water Rising, 7. Bullet Avalanche, 8. Death Laughs Last, 9. Cold Steel, 10. Showdown, 11. The Trail to Torture, 12. Calling All Buckboards, 13. Golden Vengeance

STORY: As the Civil War draws to a close, Captain Dennis Moore of the Secret Service has been assigned to stop gold thefts in the Oro Grande, California, area. The raiders suspected to be Southern sympathizers, are actually mercenaries under the command of Prussian spies Lionel Atwill and Virginia Christine.

Wells Fargo operative Joe Sawyer, Wells Fargo manager Wanda McKay and local doctor Eddy C. Waller aid Moore. Moore's younger brother, Gene Garrick, has infiltrated the raiders. Garrick is wounded in a raid and taken prisoner. He refuses to talk to anyone but Moore. Before Moore can receive Garrick's information, his brother is shot. Before he dies, Garrick indicates that the answer to the mystery can be found at the Golden Eagle Saloon. Moore, with his own ingenuity and Sawyer's timely interference, blunts the Prussian spies' efforts, and Atwill and Christine decide Moore must die. A clue leads Moore to San Francisco, where after cheating death, he gains a codebook that will aid in identifying Prussian spies stationed in the United States. Atwill and Christine want the gold to enable Prussia to purchase Alaska, which would again make their country a world power. When suspicion again points to the Golden Eagle Saloon, Atwill has the raiders attack the bar and take valuable papers to their hideout in Ghost City. The papers instead fall into Moore's hands, but everything is in code. Christine suggests that they in-

Raiders of Ghost City (1944) scene card: Dennis Moore (*left*) and Joe Sawyer (*right center*) are captured by Virginia Christine, Jack Rockwell (*center*) and Lionel Atwill. Left border, Edmund Cobb (*left*), unidentified actor and Jack Rockwell ride hard.

cite the Modoc Indians to go on the warpath. With this diversion, the gold can then be transported out of the area. McKay follows Christine to the hideout in Ghost City. Moore, Sawyer, Waller and the local miners come to Ghost City to search the place thoroughly. McKay tells the men the hideout is the old livery stable. As the raiders and Moore's men engage in a gunfight, the Indians attack, bent on massacring all whites. McKay rides for the cavalry, who arrive just as the Indians are about to take total control of Ghost City. During the fight, Atwill has returned to Oro Grande, where the gold has been stored all the time. Before Atwill and an accomplice, George J. Lewis, can clear out, Moore and Sawyer arrive. A fight starts, resulting in Atwill's death and Lewis' capture. Christine leaves in the gold wagon, with McKay following. During this escape attempt the wagon overturns, killing Christine. The United States begins negotiations to purchase Alaska. Moore and McKay plan to marry.

NOTES AND COMMENTARY: Dennis Moore played the hero in five other serials, *The Master Key* (Universal, 1945), *The Purple Monster Strikes* (Republic, 1945), *The Mysterious Mr. M* (Universal, 1946), *Perils of the Wilderness* (Columbia, 1956) and the final American cliffhanger, *Blazing the Overland Trail* (Columbia, 1956). Moore never made it into the top rank of western stars. He appeared as an action sidekick in the final four George Houston Lone Rider westerns and the first Bob Livingston Lone Rider sagebrusher for PRC in 1942. Next, Moore was a member of the Range Busters in four entries in 1943. He took the Tex Ritter role when Ritter's part was upgraded at Universal in 1943 due to Johnny Mack Brown's departure for his own series at Monogram. Moore's last shot at series stardom came in 1944–45, as the action cowboy in Jimmy Wakely's series at Monogram. Moore was led to believe that, should Wakely stumble, he would become the star of the series. Things came to a head when Moore, after drinking and being egged on by fellow performers, confronted Wakely at his home, brandishing a knife. A scuffle resulted; Wakely received a cut to his head before Moore could be subdued. Wakely refused to press charges. In return, Moore had to leave Los Angeles for sixty days. John James replaced Moore for the last three films in the series. Moore played support and villainous roles in Westerns until his final glory as a serial hero. Moore resumed filling supporting roles, and his final western feature film part was an appearance with Rory Calhoun in *The Domino Kid* (Columbia, 1957).

Virginia Christine is remembered fondly as Mrs. Olson in the Folgers television ads. She played the part for 21 years.

Footage from *Road Agent* (Universal, 1941) was used in the chase sequence in Chapter Eight. Chapter 12 utilized footage from *Trail of the Vigilantes* (Universal, 1941) as the buckboards raced across the plains. The Indian attack and the burning of Ghost City in Chapters 12 and 13 were initially seen in *Badlands of Dakota* (Universal, 1941).

REVIEWS: "Pretty good Universal cliffhanger enhanced by a fine cast." (*Western Movies*, Pitts)

SUMMATION: *Raiders of Ghost City* is an above average serial that falters in the final chapters. The revelation in Chapter 13 that the real gold has been stored in Oro Grande all the time is hard to swallow. The excellent cast, comprised of veterans Dennis Moore, Joe Sawyer, Lionel Atwill, Regis Toomey, Virginia Christine, Eddy C. Waller, along with some of the stellar bad guys of the "B" westerns, make the few rough spots more than bearable.

TWO RIDIN' SONS O' GUNS!

Raiders of San Joaquin

ALTERNATE TITLE: *Riders of San Joaquin;* Universal (June 1943)

CAST: Rocky Morgan, **Johnny Mack Brown**; Gil Blake, **Tex Ritter**; Eustace Clairmont, **Fuzzy Knight**; Jane Carter, **Jennifer Holt**; Bodine Carter, **Henry Hall**; Jim Blake, **Joseph Bernard**; Gus Sloan, **George Eldredge**; Rogers, **Henry Roquemore**; Morgan, **John Elliott**; Clark, **Michael Vallon**; Detective, **Jack O'Shea**; Lear, **Jack Ingram**; Johnson, **Robert Thompson**; Tanner, **Carl Sepulveda**; Tripp, **Scoop Martin**; McQuary, **Roy Brent**; Deputy, **Budd Buster** and Jimmy Wakely Trio (**Jimmy Wakely, Johnny Bond** and **Scotty Harrel**)

CREDITS: Director, **Lewis D. Collins**; Associate Producer, **Oliver Drake**; Story, **Patricia Harper**; Screenwriters, **Elmer Clifton** and **Morgan B. Cox**; Editor, **Russell Schoengarth**; Art Directors, **Jack Otterson** and **Harold H. MacArthur**; Set Decorators, **R.A. Gausman** and **A.J. Gilmore**; Cinematographer, **William Sickner**; Gowns, **Vera West**; Sound, **Bernard B. Brown** and **Jess Moulin**; Musical Director, **H.J. Salter**

SONGS: "I'd Rather Be Footloose and Free" (O. Drake) — sung by **Fuzzy Knight**; "A Carefree Cowboy" (O. Drake) — sung by **Tex Ritter**; "The Hatches and the Morgans" (O. Drake) — sung by **the Jimmy Wakely Trio** and **Fuzzy Knight**; and "Clementine" (traditional) — sung by **the Jimmy Wakely Trio**

LOCATION FILMING: Corriganville, California

RUNNING TIME: 59 min.

STORY: The Railroad is grabbing ranches by force and intimidation in the Valley Center District. Drifters Johnny Mack Brown and Fuzzy Knight arrive at Joseph Bernard's ranch to hear railroad detective Jack Ingram tell Bernard and his son, Tex Ritter, that the railroad will take the ranch. Brown learns Bernard and Henry Hall's ranches are the only ones the railroad doesn't control.

Brown meets Hall's daughter, and the two like each other immediately. A meeting is held at storekeeper Henry Roquemore's store. The ranchers select Bernard to meet with the railroad president and settle the difficulties. Henchman Carl Sepulvada guns down Bernard. Ritter kills Sepulvada in a gun duel, which makes Ritter an outlaw. Roquemore is behind the lawlessness. Fearing that his outlaw status will allow the railroad to take his ranch, Ritter deeds the property to Hall. Railroad Manager George Eldredge arrives in Valley Center. Brown reveals to Hall that he's the son of the Vice President of the railroad. Brown asks Hall to find out how much Eldredge will pay for both ranches. Eldredge forces Hall to sign over the ranches at the point of a gun. Brown retrieves all the deeds and papers from Eldredge's safe. From the papers, Brown discovers that the railroad has done significant business with Rogers, indicating he might be the man behind the lawlessness. Finally, Ritter is captured and jailed. Brown asks Hall and Holt to meet with his father, John Elliott. Eldredge and Ingram are suspicious of Brown. They follow him and discover Brown is the man who stole the deeds and papers. Brown is captured but will not tell where the papers are hidden. Knight, who's running a lunch counter in town, is keeping the papers for Brown. Knight overhears from Roquemore and Eldredge where Brown is being held. Knight breaks Ritter out of jail. Learning Hall, Holt and Elliott are on their way to Valley Center, Eldredge sends men to ambush them. Ritter and Knight arrive at the hideout to rescue Brown. A fight ensues, and Eldredge is captured. Brown forces Eldredge to change clothes with him, then forces Eldredge to ride with him to the ambush site. Eldredge's men think Eldredge is Brown and shoot him. Brown, with Ritter and Knight's help, rounds up the henchmen. Arrested, Roquemore protests his innocence, but Knight has hidden the papers in some bread he's baked, and the heat reveals Roquemore's signature on pertinent documents. With the ranches restored to their rightful owners, the railroad will make a fair offer for a right-of-way. Romance blossoms between Brown and Holt.

NOTES AND COMMENTARY: The song "Clementine" was a big hit record for Bobby Darin in 1960. The song first appeared on the album *This Is Darin*, which reached number six on the record charts. Initially, there was no thought to release the song as a single. "Clementine" was later included in the compilation album *The Bobby Darin Story*, a hit record at 18th place.

REVIEWS: "Actionful teaming of Johnny Mack Brown and Tex Ritter." (*Western Movies*, Pitts); "A winner in their [Brown and Ritter] Western series." (*Hollywood Reporter*, 4/2/43)

SUMMATION: *Raiders of San Joaquin* is another fine entry in the Johnny Mack Brown-Tex Ritter series. Again, Brown and Ritter make for stalwart heroes. Brown handles most of the fast action while Ritter receives most of the dramatic scenes.

Jennifer Holt is perfect as the rancher's daughter who finds herself falling for Brown while she believes he's double-crossed her father. Director Lewis D. Collins directs with an eye on continuous action to delight the audience.

MEN ARE SO EASY!...
A little lace
A pair of lips
A touch and they kill for you!

Ramrod

Enterprise/ United Artists (May 1947); A Harry Sherman Production

CAST: Dave Nash, **Joel McCrea**; Connie Dickason, **Veronica Lake**; Bill Schell, **Don DeFore**; Jim Crew, **Donald Crisp**; Frank Ivey, **Preston Foster**; Rose Leland, **Arleen Whelan**; Ben Dickason, **Charlie Ruggles**; Red Cates, **Lloyd Bridges**; Curley, **Nestor Paiva**; Ed Burma, **Ray Teal**; George Smedley, **Houseley Stevenson**; Link Thomas, **Robert Wood**; Walt Shipley, **Ian MacDonald**; Virg Lea, **Wally Cassell**; Mrs. Parks, **Sarah Padden**; Jess More, **Hal Taliaferro**; Bice, **Jeff Corey**; Burch Nellice, **Vic Potel**// Burt, **Holly Bane**; Bailey, **Trevor Bardette**; Annie, **Rose Higgins**; Tom Peebles, **Cliff Parkinson**; Pokey, **John Powers**; Dr. Parks, **Chick York**

CREDITS: Director, **André De Toth**; Assistant Director, **Harold Godsoe**; Producer, **Harry Sherman**; Associate Producer, **Gene Strong**; Screenwriters, **Jack Moffitt**, **Graham Baker** and **Cecile Kramer**; Editor, **Sherman A. Rose**; Production Designer, **Lionel Banks**; Set Decorator, **Allan O'Dea**; Cinematographer, **Russell Harlan**; Special Scenic Effects, **Harry Redmond, Jr.**; Costumes, **Eddie Armand**; Costumes for Miss Lake and Miss Whelan, **Edith Head**; Make Up, **Don Donaldson**; Sound, **Ben Winkler**; Musical Composer and Conductor, **Adolph Deutsch**; Musical Director, **Rudolph Polk**

LOCATION FILMING: Zion National Park area, Utah

RUNNING TIME: 94 min.

SOURCE: Novel "Ramrod" by **Luke Short**

STORY: To spite her father, Charles Ruggles, and the man her father wants her to marry, cattleman Preston Foster, Veronica Lake plans to marry small rancher Ian MacDonald and raise sheep instead of cattle. As MacDonald starts to board the stagecoach to purchase the sheep, he's stared down by Foster. MacDonald has lost face and leaves town, turning his ranch over to Lake. Lake has one cowhand, Joel McCrea, who plans to ride on. Lloyd Bridges, a Foster cowhand, goads McCrea into a fight in which Bridges is severely beaten. Foster tells McCrea to leave town whereupon McCrea takes the job as Lake's ramrod. Needing cowhands, McCrea enlists devil-may-care Don DeFore and a few of his friends. McCrea wants to fight Foster within the law. When one of Lake's cowhands receives a brutal beating, DeFore braces one of Foster's waddies and kills him. Lake wants to escalate the fight and entices DeFore to stampede her own cattle over a cliff, putting the blame on Foster. Sheriff Donald Crisp, a good friend of McCrea's, goes to Foster's ranch to arrest him. Foster, knowing he's innocent of the crime, refuses to surrender and guns Crisp down. Foster sends word that one of his men, Robert Wood, shot the sheriff and plans to ambush McCrea when he goes after Wood. McCrea shoots Wood, and, from hiding, Bridges fires at McCrea. The two men exchange shots. Bridges is killed and McCrea badly wounded. McCrea makes it to seamstress Arlene Whelan's house. Whelen and McCrea are in love, and Whelan helps McCrea. Foster searches the town to find a trace of McCrea. Whelan hides McCrea until DeFore can take him to an out of the way hideout. Lake brings supplies to the men, but a Foster cowhand follows her. Foster and his men show up, but DeFore and Lake lead them away from McCrea. Foster catches up with DeFore and fires both barrels of a shotgun into his back. At Ruggles' ranch, McCrea learns of DeFore's death and Lake's duplicity in the cattle stampede. In town, McCrea and Foster face each other. McCrea, armed with a shotgun, and is able to get close enough to avenge his friend's death. Lake tells McCrea they can run her ranch together. McCrea spurns Lake's proposition and asks Whelan to marry him.

NOTES AND COMMENTARY: Frederick Dilley Glidden, using the pseudonym Luke Short, wrote over fifty novels. His first novel to be filmed was "Ramrod." In the next twelve years, nine more novels and one short story would be produced, with such stars as Randolph Scott, Rod Cameron, Robert Taylor, Robert Mitchum and Burt Lancaster bringing his characters to life.

Ramrod was produced in the latter part of 1946 by Harry Sherman's Enterprise Productions and was intended to be a Universal-International release. With the change of command at Universal, Sherman or someone at Universal made the decision not to release the film. *Ramrod* was distributed through United Artists in May 1947. The production is now owned by Metro-Goldwyn-Mayer. This is the one western that got away from Universal.

Veronica Lake, known for her peek-a-boo hairstyle, was a leading Paramount star, noted for her roles opposite Alan Ladd in *This Gun for Hire* (Paramount, 1942), *The Glass Key* (Paramount, 1942), *The Blue Dahlia* (Paramount, 1946) and *Saigon* (Paramount, 1948). Loaned to Enterprise Productions for *Ramrod*, Lake was directed by André De Toth, who was her husband at that time. Released from Paramount Studios in 1948, De Toth arranged for Lake to have a sizable role in *Slattery's Hurricane* (20th Century Fox, 1949), which he directed. The film failed to restore Lake's superstar status, and her film career, for the most part, was over.

Ramrod was André De Toth's first endeavor in the western genre. De Toth would direct many western features in the fifties, primarily with Randolph Scott. The two would collaborate on *Man in the Saddle* (Columbia, 1951), *Carson City* (Warner Bros., 1952), *The Stranger Wore a Gun* (Columbia, 1953), *Thunder Over the Plains* (Warner Bros., 1953), *Riding Shotgun* (Warner Bros., 1954) and *The Bounty Hunter* (Warner Bros., 1954).

Joel McCrea had a three-picture contract with Harry Sherman. *Ramrod* was the second. Previously, McCrea had starred in *Buffalo Bill* (20th Century Fox, 1944), and would complete his contract by headlining *Four Faces West* (United Artists, 1948). Sherman's greatest claim to fame was as producer of the first fifty-four entries in William Boyd's Hopalong Cassidy series.

Don DeFore is beloved by television fans for his roles of Thorny in *Adventures of Ozzie and Harriett* (ABC, 1952–61) and George Baxter in *Hazel* (CBS, 1961–65).

Supporting actor Holly Bane is also known to "B" western and serial fans as Michael Ragan.

At the film's conclusion, Joel McCrea and Veronica Lake had this dialogue exchange:

McCrea: "I'm thinking about Jim Crew and Bill Schell."
Lake: "That couldn't be helped."
McCrea: "Link told me about the stampede."
Lake: "Would it make any difference if I said I was sorry, terribly sorry?"
McCrea: "Funny how people fall back on those words, 'I'm sorry.'"
Lake: "What counts now is our happiness, our freedom, the way we want to live."
McCrea: "Not we, Connie, just you. Alone."
Lake: "I don't want it alone."
McCrea: "You don't want it alone. I guess that squares everything."

Reviews: "*Ramrod* is a good western, with above par cast members." (*Variety*, 2/26/47); "A fine, little-appreciated western." (*The Motion Picture Guide*, Nash and Ross)

Summation: *Ramrod* is a good, solid western with fine acting, direction and story. Joel McCrea heads a stellar cast, providing a nice performance as a man who can't be pushed around. Veronica Lake is properly seductive as a woman who uses her feminine charms to entice men into doing her bidding. Preston Foster, as a ruthless cattleman, and Don DeFore, as a devil-may-care cowboy, turn in sparkling performances. Screenwriters Jack Moffitt, Graham Baker and Cecile Kramer deliver a script that offers believable character development, and good action and suspense. André De Toth directs with a firm hand, with satisfactory results. Cinematographer Russell Harlan, with special scenic effects by Harry Redmond, Jr., captures the scenic wonders of the Zion National Park area in Utah.

Death Rides the Trail!
...As a two-gun terror from Texas explodes into action!

Rawhide Rangers

Universal (July 1941)

CAST: Brand, **Johnny Mack Brown**; Porky, **Fuzzy Knight**; Joan, **Kathryn Adams**; Patti, **Nell O'Day**; Steve, **Roy Harris**; Blackie, **Harry Cording**; Rawlings, **Al Bridge**; Captain, **Frank Shannon**; Martin, **Ed Cassidy**; Dirk, **Bob Kortman**; Sing Lo, **Chester Gan**; Banker, **Jim Farley**; and **the Texas Rangers (Robert "Captain Bob" Crawford, Edward "Tookie" Cronenbold, Francis "Irish" Mahaney** and **Roderic "Dave" May)**// Townsmen, **Frank Ellis** and **Fred Burns**

CREDITS: Director, **Ray Taylor**; Associate Producer, **Will Cowan**; Screenwriter, **Ed Earl Repp**; Editor, **Paul Landres**; Art Directors, **Jack Otterson** and **Harold H. MacArthur**; Cinematographer, **Charles Van Enger**; Sound, **Bernard B. Brown** and **Jess Moulin**; Musical Director, **H.J. Salter**

SONGS: "Then We Go Ridin'" (Cool)—sung by **the Texas Rangers**; "Huckleberry Pie" (Rosen and Carter)—sung by **Fuzzy Knight**; "Oh, Susanna" (Foster)—sung by **Roy Harris**; "Sourwood Mountain" (Traditional)—sung by a trio; "A Cowboy is Happy" (Rosen and Carter)—sung by **Nell O'Day;** and "It's a Ranger's Life" (Cool)—sung by **the Texas Rangers**

LOCATION FILMING: Iverson, California

RUNNING TIME: 56 min.

STORY: With the Palo Verde area beset by lawlessness, Ranger Johnny Mack Brown is assigned to ferret out the outlaw leader (respected citizen Edward Cassidy). When Brown's brother, Roy Harris, dies during an attempted stagecoach holdup, Brown resigns from the Rangers. Brown starts a string of robberies, frustrating both the Rangers and Cassidy's outlaw gang. After a robbery, Cassidy's chief henchman, Harry Cording, captures Brown. Cassidy orders Cording to induce Brown to join the gang. The outlaws will pull a few more robberies, then murder Brown and blame the wave of lawlessness on him. The last job will be the robbery of the Palo Verde bank. Brown gets word to the Rangers, who lie in wait when Cording's gang reaches town. When Cording and Brown leave the bank with the money, the Rangers open fire. All the gang is killed or captured except Cording. Cording makes his way to Cassidy's office, closely followed by Brown. After a tough fistfight, Brown brings Cassidy and Cording to justice. Brown is appointed Captain of the Palo Verde post and has time to resume his romance with his sweetheart, Kathryn Adams.

NOTES AND COMMENTARY: When asked about directors, the only one Kathryn Adams could recall was this

Rawhide Rangers (1941) scene card: Johnny Mack Brown gets set to hit a terrified Harry Cording.

film's Ray Taylor, "I can see his face. I do remember him because we have this Minnesota bond thing. I don't remember really being directed [in her career in westerns]."

Frank Shannon had a long screen career but will be most remembered as Dr. Zarkov in the three Flash Gordon serials for Universal.

Fuzzy Knight would sing "Huckleberry Pie" in the Kirby Grant western *Trail to Vengeance* (Universal, 1945). "Sourwood Mountain" was featured in the Ken Maynard film *Mountain Justice* (Universal, 1930). "A Cowboy Is Happy" was sung in *Cowboy in Manhattan* (Universal, 1943) and *Gun Town* (Universal, 1946). "Oh, Susanna" saw the most service of any song in Universal westerns, showing up in five other films: *Fiddlin' Buckaroo* (Universal, 1933), *Law for Tombstone* (Universal, 1937), *Courage of the West* (Universal, 1937), *Desperate Trails* (Universal, 1939) and *Chip of the Flying U* (Universal, 1939).

In the montage sequence of Johnny Mack Brown turned "outlaw," a scene from *Law of the Range* (Universal, 1941) was used.

The credits list Kathryn Adams' character name as Joan, but she is called Joanne in the picture.

Roy Harris was also billed as Riley Hill during his tenure on the silver screen.

REVIEWS: "Standard, but slick, Johnny Mack Brown vehicle." (*Western Movies*, Pitts); "An old formula yarn is given a couple of new twists to help from being wholly mechanical." (*The Motion Picture Guide*, Nash and Ross)

SUMMATION: *Rawhide Rangers* is an above average "B" western. Johnny Mack Brown is virtually the whole show in this one, and he easily rises to the occasion. Rather than playing his usual sidekick role, Fuzzy Knight here receives only a few "comic bits" (involving his efforts to steal desserts). Knight does nothing to further the story. Some might derive a few chuckles from his antics, but Knight's scenes are only filler. Except for Nell O'Day, no one really rises above the average in the supporting cast.

The screen's outstanding man of action in a New Serial THRILLER.

The Red Rider

Universal (July 1934)

CAST: "Red" Davidson, **Buck Jones**; "Silent" Slade, **Grant Withers**; Marie Maxwell, **Marion Shilling**; Jim Breen, **Walter Miller**; Joe Portos, **Richard Cramer**; Johnny Snow, **Edmund Cobb**; Robert Maxwell, **Charles K. French**; Joan McKee, **Margaret La Marr**; Al Abel, **Monte Montague**; Bill Abel, **Jim Thorpe**; Sheriff, **William Desmond**; Mayor "Soapy" Caswell, **Lee Beggs**; Scotty McKee, **J.P. McGowan**; Prosecutor, **Frank Glendon;** and "**Silver**"// Civic Leader, **Hank Bell**; Harp, **Frank Rice**; Banty, **John Merton**; Berg, **Jim Corey**; Kelsey, **Bud Osborne**; Madden, **Al Ferguson**; Slim, **Dennis Moore**; Ranch Cook, **Chester Gan**; Indian, **Art Ardigan**; Wilson, **Art Mix**; and "**Silver, Jr.**"

CREDITS: Director, **Louis Friedlander**; Producer, **Milton Gatzert**; Associate Producer, **Henry MacRae**; Screenwriters, **George Plympton, Vin Moore, Ella O'Neill** and **Basil Dickey**; Editors, **Saul Goodkind** and **Edw. Todd**; Art Director, **Thomas O'Neill**; Cinematographer, **Richard Fryer**; Sound, **RCA Victor System**

LOCATION FILMING: Agoura and Lake Sherwood, California

RUNNING TIME: 279 min.

CHAPTER TITLES: 1. Sentenced to Die, 2. A Leap for Life, 3. The Night Attack, 4. Treacherous Ambush, 5. Trapped, 6. The Brink of Death, 7. The Fatal Plunge, 8. The Stampede, 9. The Posse Rider, 10. The Avenging Trail, 11. The Lost Diamonds, 12. Double Trouble, 13. The Night Raiders, 14. In Enemies' Hideout, 15. Brought to Justice

SOURCE: Novel "The Red Head from Sun Dog" by **W.C. Tuttle**

STORY: Grant Withers is accused of killing J.P. McGowan, the father of his girlfriend, Margaret La Mar. To settle an old grudge, Walter Miller shot McGowan. Sheriff Buck Jones is forced to arrest his friend but believes him to be innocent. Jones had found two clues, a marijuana cigarette and a piece of an envelope, which leads him to believe the murderer lives along the Mexican border. When Withers is convicted, Jones helps him break jail. Jones gives Withers his horse Silver to outdistance any posse. Jones resigns as sheriff and heads to the Mexican border to help his friend. In Secomoro, Jones spots Silver and wins him from Mexican badman Richard Cramer. Withers is working for outlaw leader Walter Miller. Cramer and Miller have involved rancher Charles K. French in a diamond scheme. French was unaware the diamonds were to be smuggled into the United States. Jones gets a job on French's ranch and meets his daughter, Marion Shilling. Jones, with cowhand Edmund Cobb and Withers, has many harrowing adventures as he looks for the diamonds and the real killer of McGowan. Jones finally finds the diamonds in the saddle he obtained when he won Silver back. In an argument between the two bandit leaders, Miller shoots Cramer. Jones chases Miller and captures him. Withers is cleared of the murder charge and plans to marry La Mar. Jones and Shilling decide to wed.

NOTES AND COMMENTARY: Marion Shilling commented about *The Red Rider*: "I thoroughly enjoyed it. It had a good plot. It kept up the interest. It had a good cast."

Remembering Buck Jones, Shilling said, "Buck Jones' charm was true and real. Nothing phony about him. He was always on time and knew his lines."

Marion Shilling did most of her own riding in the serial. Shilling remembers, "After Buck coached me, I got a lot more confident on a horse. He gave me so many good tips. He was an expert, himself. The master of horseback riding, he was a good teacher."

Buck Jones introduced Shilling to supporting actor Jim Thorpe. She was thrilled to meet the famous former athlete and Olympic Gold Medal winner. She later realized the meeting was really for Thorpe's benefit.

Marion Shilling enjoyed working with villain Walter Miller. She remembered Miller as "a very nice guy, a fine person, an excellent actor. I had been a great fan of his as a teenager, seeing him in serials. Interesting when I grew up and worked with him to think I could actually work with Walter Miller."

A few weeks after the serials completion, Shilling attended a rough-cut screening in Hollywood. "I went down. There were people standing at the entrance. 'Hi, Marian. Hi, Marian.' I didn't recognize any of them. Every one of these clean shaven, well-dressed men had been a cowboy in the movie with a beard or dirt on their face. I had to be rein-

The Red Rider (1934) photograph: Buck Jones, Marion Shilling (courtesy of Marion Shilling).

troduced all over again. They were my pals in the movie, and I didn't even recognize them."

During the filming of *The Red Rider*, Buck Jones was still negotiating a contract with Irving Briskin of Columbia Pictures. Jones had been unhappy with the stories given him at Columbia. Carl Laemmle and Carl Laemmle, Jr. had decided not to renew Ken Maynard's contract. Laemmle then offered Jones a contract to make six westerns a year, which Jones accepted.

Buck Jones had purchased the motion picture rights to the novel "The Redhead from Sun Dog" from author W.C. Tuttle, which he sold to Universal for $25,000.

In 1934, a novelization of "The Red Rider" was published as a Five Star Library Book by the Engel-Van-Wiseman Book Corporation as a children's book and a movie tie-in.

In *The Red Rider*, Monte Montague received billing as Monty Montague, and J.P. McGowan was billed as Robert McGowan. Though not billed, John Merton was known as Mert La Varre, and Dennis Moore was going by Denny Meadows at this time. Director Louis Friedlander was better known as Lew Landers in his long career. In a brief appearance in the rodeo sequence in Chapter 10, Silver Jr. is introduced.

The runaway Spanish coach sequence, plus the horse spill of Monty Montague and Jim Thorpe, were lifted from Ken Maynard's *Song of the Caballero* (Universal, 1930).

Look at Buck Jones' reaction to Marion Shilling's kiss in Chapter 10. First Jones looks stunned, then he licks his lips, cocks his hat and decides he liked it. Shilling remarked, "It was not unpleasant."

The author enjoyed henchman Bud Osborne's comment when he thinks gang leader Walter Miller has taken valuable diamonds for himself: "I hate a crook."

REVIEWS: "Top notch Buck Jones cliffhanger." (*Western Movies*, Pitts); "A routine affair." (*The Western*, Hardy)

SUMMATION: *The Red Rider* is a top flight serial. The screenplay offers subtle touches that help emphasize the characterizations of the principals. Buck Jones is totally believable as a man whose loyalty to a friend almost destroys his life. Grant Withers scores highly as Jones' best friend, falsely accused of murder. Marion Shilling handles her role with charm and the assertiveness needed to round out her part of Jones' love interest. Edmund Cobb, Walter Miller and Richard Cramer all breathe life into their roles. Louis Friedlander directs with a sure hand, eliciting good performances from the cast as he keeps the action flowing.

*A **T-N-T**WO-GUN RANGER*
...blasts the border bandits!

Renegades of the Rio Grande

ALTERNATE TITLE: *Bank Robbery;* Universal (June 1945)

CAST: Buck Emerson, **Rod Cameron**; Cal Benedict, **Eddie Dew**; Trigger Bidwell, **Fuzzy Knight**; Dolores Salezar, **Jennifer Holt**; Tex Henry, **Ray Whitley**; Bart Drummond, **Glenn Strange**; Karl Holbrook, **Edmund Cobb**; Pete Jackson, **Dick Alexander**; Maria, **Iris Clive**; Johnny Emerson, **John James**; Ray Whitley's Bar-6 Cowboys// Hank, Jack Casey; Juan, **Hal Hart**; Sheriff, **Roy Butler**; Clem, **Dick Botiller**; Outlaw, **Budd Buster**

CREDITS: Director, **Howard Bretherton**; Associate Producer, **Oliver Drake**; Screenwriter, **Ande Lamb**; Editor, **Edward Curtiss**; Art Directors, **John B. Goodman** and **Harold H. MacArthur**; Set Decorators, **Russell A. Gausman** and **Ray Jeffers**; Cinematographer, **Maury Gertsman**; Sound, **Bernard B. Brown** and **Glenn E. Anderson**; Musical Director, **Paul Sawtell**

SONGS: "Down an Old Spanish Trail"—sung by **Ray Whitley and His Bar-6 Cowboys**; "Mexican Hat Dance" (traditional)—played by **Ray Whitley and His Bar-6 Cowboys**; "Pedro, the Gay Vaquero"—sung by **Hal Hart**; "Along the Rio Grande"—sung by **Ray Whitley and His Bar-6 Cowboys**; "I'm the Son of a Son of a Son of a Gunman"—sung by **Fuzzy Knight**; and "Down an Old Spanish Trail" (reprise)—sung by **Ray Whitley and His Bar-6 Cowboys**

LOCATION FILMING: Iverson and Corriganville, California

RUNNING TIME: 56 min.

STORY: Glenn Strange and his henchman chase Rod Cameron and his brother, John James, in a running gunfight. In the exchange of shots, James is seriously wounded and Cameron is captured. Strange likes Cameron's gun belt and takes it. Strange wants the map showing the location of stolen bank money; James had participated in the robbery. When James learned that the money belonged to Jennifer Holt, he wanted to return the cash and asked Cameron to help him. Rangers Eddie Dew and Fuzzy Knight observe the wounding of James and Cameron's capture. James tells Dew and Knight that Cameron is not a gang member and was trying to return the money. The Rangers follow the outlaws' trail to their camp, where they rescue Cameron. Cameron proceeds to Holt's hacienda and tells her what he is trying to do. Dew and Knight see Strange's chief henchman, Edmund Cobb, and arrest him. The Rangers bring Cobb into Vista Grande, where he's jailed. Cameron comes to the jail and wants to handle the retrieval of the money, and needs Knight to help him. Strange and some henchmen are in the local saloon. Cameron tells

Knight he going to start a fistfight with Strange, and instructs Knight to grab his stolen gun belt when Strange takes it off. The map is hidden in the holster. In a rugged fight, Cameron defeats Strange. Knight takes the gun belt and drops it out of a window. Strange has arranged to have Cobb break jail. During his escape Cobb sees the gun belt and takes it, witnessed by Knight. Cameron and Knight ride to the outlaw camp and are captured. Strange has kidnapped Holt and brings her to the hideout. Cameron tells Holt the map is hidden at the hacienda. Strange and Cobb and a few henchmen take Cameron and Holt to get the map. Knight is left at the camp as a prisoner but is rescued by Dew and Holt's foreman, Ray Whitley. Knight tells Dew of Cameron's predicament. Dew and Knight ride to the hacienda while Whitley rides to town for a posse. Cameron has been stalling Strange. As time runs out, Dew and Knight arrive but are spotted by Strange's henchmen. A gun battle begins between the Rangers and outlaws. The diversion enables Cameron to start a fistfight with Strange and Cobb. As the fight moves to the balcony, Dew begins to mix it up with Cobb while Cameron fights Strange. Knight holds off the henchmen until the posse arrives. Cameron and Dew win their fights, and the rest of the gang is rounded up. Cameron retrieves his gun belt and gives the map to Holt. With the gang arrested, Dew and Knight ride to new adventures while Cameron romances Holt.

NOTES AND COMMENTARY: After the completion of this season's "B" western series, Rod Cameron was promoted to bigger budgeted films. Cameron would star in three more westerns at Universal before making the decision to freelance. Cameron signed with both Republic and Allied Artists to make both western and non-western action films.

With Cameron out of the series westerns, associate producer Oliver Drake was released. Drake was immediately signed by Monogram to work on Jimmy Wakely's series westerns as director, producer and sometimes screenwriter.

John James would receive his best chance at stardom when he was selected to replace Dennis Moore in Jimmy Wakely's Saddle Pals series. Unfortunately for James, after three entries Monogram dropped him from the series. Monogram executives felt Wakely now had sufficient drawing power to be a solo star.

"Mexican Hat Dance" was heard in *The Masked Rider* (Universal, 1941).

REVIEWS: "Solid Rod Cameron vehicle, which shows why he went on to bigger things." (*Western Movies*, Pitts); "Solid cast of veterans keeps this one on the trail." (*The Motion Picture Guide*, Nash and Ross)

SUMMATION: *Renegades of the Rio Grande* is hardly anything new, but so well done it rates as an above average "B" western. Rod Cameron dominates the proceedings with a good performance. Cameron receives fine support from Fuzzy Knight, Eddie Dew, Jennifer Holt and the rest of the supporting cast.

Knight, as a Texas Ranger, shows intelligence tempered with some neat humor through most of the film. With his authoritative manner, Dew shows the potential that wasn't apparent in his Republic starring series. Along the way, someone taught Dew how to throw a realistic punch, which he freely demonstrates. Holt pulls off the role of a Mexican senorita, complete with authentic accent. Glenn Strange and Edmund Cobb capably take care of the villainy. Howard Bretherton breathes life and interest into the story, with pleasant results.

IF IT HAD HOOFS— OR WHEELS— BUCK COULD RIDE IT...
And how!
You've seen him ride Horses! You've seen him ride steers! NOW— you'll freeze to your seat as Buck rides a roarin', rip snortin' racer through prairies, pavements and picket fences to win the girl he loves!

Ride 'Em Cowboy

ALTERNATE TITLE: *Cowboy Holiday;* Universal (September 1936); A Buck Jones Production

CAST: Jess Burns, **Buck Jones**; Lillian Howard, **Luana Walters**; Sam Parker, Jr., **Donald Kirke**; Chuck Morse, **George Cooper**; Jim Howard, **J.P. McGowan**; Sam Parker, **Joseph Girard**; Sheriff Stanton, **Charles Le Moyne**; Sandy Adams, **William Lawrence;** and "Silver"// Simmons (Postmaster), **Bob McKenzie**; Pete, **Hal Price**

CREDITS: Director, **Leslie Selander**; Story, **Buck Jones**; Screenwriter, **Frances Guihan**; Editor, **Bernard Loftus**; Art Director, **Ralph Berger**; Cinematographers, **Allen Q. Thompson** and **Herbert Kirkpatrick**; Sound, **Buddy Myers**

LOCATION FILMING: Rancho Maria and Sand Canyon, California

RUNNING TIME: 60 min.

STORY: The Bar X cowboys, led by happy-go-lucky Buck Jones, wreak havoc on the town of Blair on the first of every month. Jones is given the choice of staying out of town or going to jail. Jones elects to leave town, but as he leaves he drops some bullets in the stove. This is the last straw, and Sheriff Charles Le Moyne goes after Jones. Realizing he's in big trouble, Jones transfers from Silver to a moving freight train. In the freight car, Jones meets George Cooper, who is masquerading as an auto mechanic. Unknown to Jones, Cooper has the real mechanic, William Lawrence, trussed up in the car. Cooper talks Jones, who knows nothing about cars, into becoming the race car's driver. The car is being transported to rancher J.P. McGowan to compete in a race with rival rancher Joseph Girard. The fate of McGowan's ranch is at stake. At Fulton, Lawrence gets loose, but

Cooper's fast talking sees Lawrence jailed as a fugitive from the East. Jones wants out; but McGowan's daughter, Luana Walters, has complete faith that Jones will win the race. Also at stake is Walters' fate. If McGowan's car loses she will have to marry Girard's son, Donald Kirke. Kirke plans to win at any costs and sabotages McGowan's car. Cooper extorts information from Lawrence that allows Jones and Cooper to put the car back together. Kirke recognizes Jones and send for Le Moyne to arrest him, thus depriving McGowan of a driver. All Kirke would have to do would be to circle the track once and claim victory. Jones finally gets the car started and crashes through a fence and into the race. The race is close, but Jones emerges the victor. Jones pursues Kirke and finally forces Kirke to stop his car. In a short fistfight, Jones exacts vengeance. Le Moyne, Walters and McGowan arrive on the scene. Le Moyne declines to arrest Jones but tells him to stay in Fulton. McGowan hires Jones as his foreman, to Walters' obvious delight.

NOTES AND COMMENTARY: *Ride 'Em Cowboy* marked the feature directorial debut of Lesley Selander, who was billed as Leslie.

In 1936, a novelization of *Ride 'Em Cowboy* was published as a Big Little Book by the Whitman Publishing Company as a children's book and a movie tie-in.

The title of this film was later changed to *Cowboy Holiday* to avoid confusion with the Abbott and Costello film of the same name that Universal produced in 1942.

Publicity for *Ride 'Em Cowboy* made much of the fact that leading lady Luana Walters was a former "Wampus Baby Star."

REVIEWS: "This one offers such rapid action and pleasant change of background from the overworked cactus to a newer cinder path that the latitude will be forgiven." (*Variety*, 12/16/36); "This innocuous feature plays havoc with suspension of disbelief, but it is an enjoyable little romp nevertheless." (*The Motion Picture Guide*, Nash and Ross)

SUMMATION: *Ride 'Em Cowboy* is an excellent "B" western. In this outing, Buck Jones decided to do something different, and it works. Jones easily handles the dramatic and comedy scenes. George Cooper gives wonderful support as an opportunist pretending to be a mechanic. This was Lesley Selander's directorial debut, and it lands in the winner's circle.

They're Makin' a Mess of the West!
with Music! Mirth! And Madness!
They slam the frontier on its ear with herds of howls,
sock songs ... blues-busting laughter!

Ride 'Em Cowboy

Universal (February 1942)

CAST: Duke, **Bud Abbott**; Willoughby, **Lou Costello**; Bob Mitchell, **Dick Foran**; Anne Shaw, **Anne Gwynne**; Alabam, **Johnny Mack Brown**; The Merry Macs (Tom, **Judd McMichael**; Harry, **Ted McMichael**; Dick, **Joe McMichael,** and Dotty Davis, **Mary Lou Cook**); Ruby, **Ella Fitzgerald**; Sam Shaw, **Samuel S. Hinds**; Jake Rainwater, **Douglas Dumbrille**; Ace Henderson, **Morris Ankrum**// Rodeo Announcer, **Russell Hicks**; Martin Manning, **Charles Lane**; Pete Conway, **Richard Lane**; Woman at Rodeo, **Isabelle Randolph**; Rodeo Manager, **Wade Boteler**; Doctor, **Boyd Davis**; Railroad Detectives, **James Flavin** and **Eddie Dunn**; Big Cowboy, **Harry Cording**; Bus Driver, **Bob Baker**; Townsman at Train Station, **Hank Bell**; Sunbeam, **Linda Brent**; Moonbeam, **Jody Gilbert**; Ranger Captain Jack, **James Seay**; Midget, **Harry Monty**; Indian Maidens, **Carmella Cansino** and **Lee Sunrise**; Henchman, **Ralph Peters**; Indian in Car, **Iron Eyes Cody**

CREDITS: Director, **Arthur Lubin**; Assistant Director, **Gil Valle**; Associate Producer, **Alex Gottlieb**; Story, **Edmund L. Hartmann**; Screenwriters, **True Boardman** and **John Grant**; Adapter, **Harold Shumate**; Dialogue Director, **Joan Hathaway**; Editor, **Philip Cahn**; Art Directors, **Jack Otterson** and **Ralph M. DeLacy**; Set Decoration, **R.A. Gausman**; Cinematography, **John W. Boyle**; Gowns, **Vera West**; Sound, **Bernard B. Brown** and **Hal Bumbaugh**; Musical Director, **Charles Previn**; Musical Score, **Frank Skinner**; Music Supervisor, **Ted Cain**; Choreographer, **Nick Castle**

SONGS: "Give Me My Saddle" (DePaul and Raye)—sung by **Dick Foran**; "Wake Up Jacob" (DePaul and Raye)—sung by **the Merry Macs**; "A-Tisket, A-Tasket" (Feldman and Fitzgerald)—sung by **Ella Fitzgerald, the Merry Macs and cast**; "Beside the Rio Tonto Shore" (DePaul and Raye)—sung by **the Merry Macs**; "I'll Remember April" (DePaul and Raye)—sung by **Dick Foran and chorus**; "Rockin' and Reelin'" (DePaul and Raye)—sung by **the Merry Macs and Ella Fitzgerald**; "Ride 'Em, Cowboy" (DePaul and Raye)—sung by **Dick Foran, the Merry Macs and chorus**

LOCATION FILMING: Sable Ranch, California

RUNNING TIME: 86 min.

STORY: At a New York Rodeo, cowboy author Dick Foran tries to prove to critics he's an authentic son of the west by riding a horse around the arena while singing. Backstage, he quickly proves he's a tenderfoot when a steer mistakenly released from its pen by vendors Bud Abbott and Lou Costello causes Foran to fall from his saddle into the steer's path. Cowgirl Anne Gwynne, hands-on favorite to win the trick riding contest and collect a much needed ten thousand dollars, steps in and bulldogs the steer, saving Foran from harm. Gwynne injures her ankle, making it impossible for her to enter the contest. Foran tries to give Gwynne a check for ten thousand, but Gwynne refuses to accept it. Gwynne's father, Samuel S. Hinds, could use the money for his dude ranch's upkeep. Gwynne returns home and finds Foran is a guest at the ranch. Abbott and Costello, hiding from their irate boss, end up on the train and also arrive at the ranch, needing work. Foreman Johnny Mack Brown feels sorry for them and gives the boys a job. Trying to prove Foran is not a cowboy, columnist Charles Lane has entered Foran in the rodeo, riding for Hinds' ranch. As Gwynne and Foran begin to fall in love, Foran asks Gwynne to teach him to become a real cowboy. Hinds is certain of victory and bets a thousand dollars his ranch will win. Gam-

Ride 'Em Cowboy (1942) movie still: Lou Costello (*left*) and Bud Abbott notice something.

bler Morris Ankrum tells Foran about the bet, and Foran agrees to cover it at ten to one. Ankrum doesn't realize this is Foran's way of paying back Gwynne's lost prize money and thinks Foran is planning to throw the event. Ankrum bets heavily that Hinds' ranch will lose, and kidnaps both Foran and Brown to ensure he'll win his bet. In old-fashioned western action, Foran and Brown get away. During the chase, Brown is wounded in the shoulder. At the rodeo, Gwynne's trick riding has pulled Hinds' ranch close to victory; but Foran is needed to win the final event. At the last possible moment, Foran arrives and wins. Foran and Gwynne plan to marry. Throughout the story, Costello tries to avoid marrying Jody Gilbert. Costello accidentally shot an arrow into a heart on Gilbert's teepee, and in Indian custom that's a marriage proposal. Costello, with Abbott's help, spends most of his time trying to avoid the clutches of Gilbert's father, Douglas Dumbrille, and his Indian braves. Finally, Costello is forced into marriage but, to his amusement, finds that Abbott had taken Gilbert's place, unknown to Dumbrille.

NOTES AND COMMENTARY: Universal changed the title of Buck Jones' earlier *Ride 'Em Cowboy* (Universal, 1936) to *Cowboy Holiday* to avoid confusion with the Abbott and Costello film.

Ride 'Em, Cowboy was made before *Keep 'Em Flying* (Universal, 1941) but held back until February 1942. *Flying* received the earlier release to cash in on the popularity of Abbott and Costello's two previous service comedies, *Buck Privates* (Universal, 1941) and *In the Navy* (Universal, 1941).

Arthur Lubin directed Abbott and Costello's first five starring films then and called it quits. Lubin sensed the duo seemed bored, and they became difficult to work with Lubin continued to enjoy their friendship and was grateful for having had the opportunity to work with them.

The song "I'll Remember April" was one of the most beautiful to come out of Abbott and Costello's films. For a number of years in TV prints, that was the first sequence to be cut.

The swimming pool sequence was inserted to show Universal starlets in their bathing suits.

REVIEWS: "Typical Abbott and Costello film fare which adds up to the same strong box office." (*Variety*, 2/11/42); "One of the duo's better films." (*The Western*, Hardy)

SUMMATION: *Ride 'Em Cowboy* is a funny western comedy. Bud Abbott and Lou Costello's routines are amusing while the story of Dick Foran and Anne Gwynne's romance makes interesting filler between the duo's shenanigans. To add some western authenticity, Foran and cowboy star Johnny Mack Brown chip in with a little western action. Six songs are featured in the film, with the stand outs being a beautiful rendition of "I'll Remember April" by Dick Foran, a swinging "A-Tisket, A-Tasket" by Ella Fitzgerald and a jiving "Rockin' and Reelin'" by the Merry Macs. Director Arthur Lubin has paced this with an eye on fun and enjoyment for the audience.

*The Cry for Action Is Answered!
Here Is a Real Thrill Drama of the Roaring West Where Horsemanship Feats Excel!*

The Rider of Death Valley

Universal (May 1932)

ALTERNATE TITLES: **Riders of the Desert**; **Riders of Death Valley**

CAST: Tom Rigby, **Tom Mix**; Helen Joyce, **Lois Wilson**; Lew Grant, **Fred Kohler**; Doctor Larribee, **Forrest Stanley**; Betty Joyce, **Edith Fellows**; Bill Joyce, **Willard Robertson**; Tillie, **Mae Busch**; Peck, **Otis Harlan**; Gabe Dillon, **Francis Ford**; and "Tony"// Miner, **Lafe McKee**; Claim Salesman, **Richard Cramer**; Joe (Bartender), **Robert McKenzie**; Indian in town, **Iron Eyes Cody**; Townsman, **Max Ascher**

CREDITS: Director, **Albert Rogell**; Associate Producer, **Stanley Bergerman**; Story/Screenwriter, **Jack Cunningham**; Scenario Editor, **Richard Shayer**; Supervising Film Editor, **Maurice Pivar**; Editor, **Robert Carlisle**; Art Director, **Thomas F. O'Neill**; Dialogue Supervisor, **Gene Lewis**; Cinematographer, **Daniel B. Clark**; Recording Supervisor, **C. Roy Hunter**

LOCATION FILMING: Death Valley, Calabasas, Imperial County Sand Dunes, California, and the Yuma, Arizona, area

RUNNING TIME: 78 min.

STORY: Doctor Forrest Stanley learns of Willard Robertson's gold strike. With the help of his henchman, Fred Kohler, Stanley plans to jump Robertson's claim. Impetuously, Kohler hides in Robertson's cabin and, when about to be discovered, shoots Robertson. Rancher Tom Mix hears the shot and rides to Robertson's cabin. Mix rides for Stanley and finds both Stanley and Kohler on the trail. Mix sends both men to Robertson's cabin while he rides for Stanley's medical bag. At the cabin, the mortally wounded Robertson asks Stanley to give a map of his claim to his sister, Lois Wilson. Upon Robertson's death, Stanley is about to pocket the map when Mix shows up and takes possession of it. Mix divides the map into three pieces to ensure that no one reaches the claim before Wilson can take possession. Upon Wilson's arrival, Mix, not trusting Stanley and Kohler, refuses to surrender his part of the map. Instead, Mix decides that the group will travel to the claim. Mix, knowing Stanley and Kohler are waiting for their chance to kill him to obtain his portion, memorizes his section and then burns it. When the group arrives at the spot where Mix's portion of the map is needed, Mix decides to return to town so Stanley and Kohler will not see the location of the claim. An argument between Kohler and Mix causes the horses pulling the wagon to bolt, with Wilson holding on for dear life. Mix rescues Wilson, but the wagon goes over a cliff, destroying food, water and supplies. Mix gambles that water might be present at Robertson's claim and leads the group there. Finding very little water at the claim, Mix rations all water supplies. Kohler finds gold at the claim and, in his excitement, kicks over his water supply. Mix realizes that their only chance for survival is to send his horse, Tony, to his ranch for help. Since Tony doesn't want to leave his master, Mix has to beat the horse to get him to leave for the ranch. When water supplies run low, Kohler, crazed with thirst, stumbles out into the desert to die. Mix starts out on foot to meet the cowboys from his ranch. Stanley, having consumed the rest of the water at the claim, decides to dynamite some rocks in the hopes that water will be found. The heat takes its toll on Mix, and he passes out in the desert. Tony leads Mix's cowhands to him. After being revived, Mix and his men ride to the claim. Stanley has lit the dynamite fuse, unaware that Wilson is standing near the dynamite. Stanley yells for Wilson to run to safety, but Wilson is too weak to respond. Mix arrives in time to save Wilson from the blast, and falling rocks take Stanley's life. Mix revives Wilson, and the two plan to face the future together.

The Rider of Death Valley (1932) movie still: Lois Wilson refuses to listen to Tom Mix.

NOTES AND COMMENTARY: The working title for this film was *Destry of Death Valley*. Universal changed the title after the box office success of Mix's initial sound feature, *Destry Rides Again* (Universal, 1932), feeling this tie-in was no longer necessary.

When asked about *Rider of Death Valley*, Edith Fellows remarked, " I loved Tony." When Fellows came on the set and Tony was present, she would always go over and pet the horse.

One day on location, Lois Wilson decided to sit on the desert sands as she and Tom Mix had lunch. A Gila monster started crawling up Wilson's skirts. Mix, alertly, shot the poisonous reptile with a blank cartridge. Mix knew that even a blank cartridge, at close range, could do significant damage.

When Universal released their million-dollar serial, *Riders of Death Valley*, in 1941, the studio changed the title of Mix's picture to *Riders of the Desert*. World-Wide used this title also for a Bob Steele western feature in 1932.

Some ads mistakenly called the film *Riders of Death Valley*.

In 1934, a novelization of "The Rider of Death Valley" was published as a Five Star Library Book by Engel-Van-Wiseman Book Corporation as a children's book and a movie tie-in.

REVIEWS: "One of the best Tom Mix pictures to date and in it Mix turns in a swell job. There's plenty of suspense and plenty of action, with the latter intelligently restrained." (*Variety*, 8/2/32); "By common agreement Mix's finest sound film, *Rider of Death Valley* has the benefit of an unusually thoughtful script made convincing by Mix and Kohler's outstanding performance and Clark's bleak location cinematography." (*The Western*, Hardy)

SUMMATION: *Rider of Death Valley* is a gem! This is a truly exceptional "B" western that stresses plot development and characterization over the well-staged action scenes. Tom Mix has probably his finest role, as a westerner trying to protect Lois Wilson's claim. The scene in which Mix beats Tony so the horse will leave him and go for help is outstanding. It is easy to feel the love Mix has for his horse. Fred Kohler is quite convincing as a man crazed over the lack of water who wanders off into the desert to die. Wilson turns in a neat performance as a young eastern lady who learns how to endure the hardships of the desert. Of the major players, only Forrest Stanley's performance seems out of place in a film steeped with realism. Stanley relies too much on typical villainous postures that seem more of a caricature than true to life. Director Albert Rogell's direction of Jack Cunningham's superior screenplay is right on the mark, as is the excellent camerawork of Daniel B. Clark.

The Million-Dollar Thrill-Special!
With a million-dollar cast of dare-devils ... in the super-serial of all time...!
15 Super-Thrilling Chapters!

Riders of Death Valley

Universal (July 1941)

CAST: Jim Benton, **Dick Foran**; Pancho, **Leo Carrillo**; Tombstone, **Buck Jones**; Mary Morgan, **Jeanne Kelly**; Wolf Reade, **Charles Bickford**; Borax Bill, **Guinn "Big Boy" Wiliams**; Butch, **Lon Chaney, Jr.**; Smokey, **Noah Beery, Jr.**; Rance Davis, **Monte Blue**; Joseph Kirby, **James Blaine**; Tex, **Glenn Strange**; Dirk, **Roy Barcroft**; Trigger, **Jack Rockwell**; Rusty, **Ethan Laidlaw**; Pete Gump, **Richard Alexander**; Chuckawalla Charlie, **Frank Austin**; Rimrock, **Charles Thomas**; Dan Gordon, **William Hall**; Judge Knox, **James Guilfoyle**; Cactus Pete, **Ernie Adams**// "Silver"; Smokey; Lafe Hogan, **Jack Clifford**; Kate, **Ruth Rickaby**; Hank, **Ted Adams**; Salty, **Edmund Cobb**; Buck Hansen, **Ed Payson**; Blake, **Dan Rowan**; Ira Jackson, **Charles Whitaker**; Slim, **Frank Brownlee**; Graham, **James Farley**; Richards, **Jerome Harte**; Mr. Wilson, **Alonzo Price**; Bartender, **Jimmie Lucas**; Stage Driver, **Bud Osborne**; Miners, **Edward Cassidy** and **Jack Ingram**

CREDITS: Directors, **Ford Beebe** and **Ray Taylor**; Associate Producer, **Henry MacRae**; Screenwriters, **Sherman Lowe, George Plympton, Basil Dickey** and **Jack Connell**; Dialogue Director, **Jacques Jaccard**; Supervising Editor, **Saul A. Goodkind**; Editors, **Alvin Todd, Louis Sackin** and **Joseph Gluck**; Art Director, **Ralph DeLacy**; Cinematographers, **Jerome Ash** and **William Sickner**

SONGS: "Ride Along" (Rosen and Carter)—sung by **Dick Foran** and chorus

LOCATION FILMING: Red Rock Canyon and Kernville, California

RUNNING TIME: 284 min.

CHAPTER TITLES: 1. Death Marks the Trail, 2. The Menacing Herd, 3. The Plunge of Peril, 4. Flaming Fury, 5. The Avalanche of Doom, 6. Blood & Gold, 7. Death Rides the Storm, 8. Descending Doom, 9. Death Hold the Reins, 10. Devouring Flames, 11. The Fatal Blast, 12. Thundering Doom, 13. The Bridge of Disaster. 14. A Fight to the Death, 15. The Harvest of Fate

STORY: Dick Foran and his Riders of Death Valley keep most of the lawlessness in check. The Riders are made up of Buck Jones, Leo Carrillo, Guinn "Big Boy" Williams, Noah Beery, Jr. and Glenn Strange. Saloon owner James Blaine, with his confederates Monte Blue and William Hall, want to organize a Miners Protective Association to enable them to control all gold mined in Death Valley. To achieve his desires, Blaine forges an uneasy alliance with the ruthless desperado Charles Bickford. Foran is able to stop Blaine's Protective Association. Blaine's interests change when Frank Austin reaches Panamint with news of a fabulous gold strike. The effort costs Austin his life, but he's able to give Foran a map to take him to the gold strike. Foran, who grubstaked Austin, and Austin's niece, Jeanne Kelly, will be co-owners. This arrangement is fine with Foran and Kelly because they fall for each other at first sight. Bickford and his gang try repeatedly to gain possession of the map and finally succeed. It proves to be a hollow victory because the stolen map is false. The real map is in the bank's safe, and Foran has the map memorized. Austin's claim is located, and Foran wins the ensuing race to register the claim. Foran has to borrow money to mine the claim. Bickford and his men make it tough for Foran to mine and transport the ore. Blaine has forced the bank to sell the loan to him; and he will, under no circumstance, allow an extension. Foran, with Jones' help, gets the ore to the smelter. Bickford learns that Blaine wants to dissolve their partnership. Bickford decides to loot Panamint and take over the smelter. First Bickford goes to Blaine's office while Blaine confers with Blue. Bickford guns down both Blue and Blaine, but not before Blaine tells him the stage is bringing in $100,000. Foran and Jones stop the stage outside of town and have the messenger and money taken off the stage. The Riders come into town behind the stage. A gunfight erupts between Bickford's gang and the Riders. The outlaws are wiped out, with the exception of Bickford. He races across the plains, with Foran in pursuit. When Foran corrals Bickford, the outlaw knocks him down. Bickford draws a gun to finish off Foran, when a well-directed rifle shot by Jones ends Bickford's lawless career.

NOTES AND COMMENTARY: Universal billed the serial as "The Million-Dollar Thrill- Special!" Looking at the impressive cast, it's easy to figure where most of the money was spent.

Jeanne Kelly replaced Nan Grey in the lead female role.

Footage from *Stormy* (Universal, 1935) highlights the serial's wild horse herd stampede sequence. The sandstorm used for the ending of Chapter Seven was initially seen in *Flash Gordon's Trip to Mars* (Universal, 1938).

REVIEWS: "A top notch cast is the chief asset of this otherwise mediocre serial." (*Western Movies*, Pitts)

SUMMATION: *Riders of Death Valley* is a very entertaining serial, primarily due to the outstanding cast. Dick Foran handles the action chores quite adequately but can't match the droll humor of Buck Jones. Both stars are fine action heroes. Charles Bickford, one of the screen's finest actors, doesn't simply go through the motions when assigned to this serial, but gives it his best—to the betterment of the production. Jeanne Kelly is given the opportunity to shine, and she makes the most of it. The outstanding supporting cast is headed by capable performers Leo Carrillo, Guinn "Big Boy" Williams and Lon Chaney. The script, fashioned by screenwriters Sherman Lowe, George Plympton, Basil Dickey and Jack Connell, is straightforward and uncomplicated, but therein lies its charm. Director Ford Beebe and Ray Taylor place the emphasis on the cast without neglecting the action, easily keeping the audience's attention. For once in a Universal serial, some of the cliffhanger resolutions prove more than satisfactory.

Riders of Pasco Basin
...they thunder into action to rid the range of rats and renegades!

Riders of Pasco Basin

Universal (April 1940)

CAST: Lee Jameson, **Johnny Mack Brown**; Bruce Moore, **Bob Baker**; Luther, **Fuzzy Knight**; Jean Madison, **Frances Robinson**; Matthew Kirby, **Arthur Loft**; Magee, **Ted Adams**; Joel Madison, **Frank LaRue**; Caleb Scott, **William Gould**; Evans, **James Guilfoyle**; Sheriff, **Ed Cassidy**; Uncle Dan, **Lafe McKee**; Tommy Scott, **Robert Winkler**; Johnson, **Charles Morrison;** and **Rudy Sooter and the Californians**// Gunmen, **George Chesebro, Slim Whitaker** and **Frank Ellis**; Townsman, **Davy Sharpe**; Cowhand, **Kermit Maynard**; Rancher Jones, **Ed Piel, Sr.**; "Skinflint," **Robert Cord**; Townsman, **Hank Bell**

CREDITS: Director / Screenwriter, **Ford Beebe**; Art Directors, **Jack Otterson and Harold H. MacArthur**; Editor, **Louis Sackin**; Set Decorator, **R.A. Gausman**; Cinematographer, **William Sickner**; Sound, **Bernard B. Brown and Jesse Bastian**; Musical Director, **Hans J. Salter**

SONGS: "I'm Tying Up My Bridle to the Door of Your Heart" (Carter and Rosen)—sung by **Bob Baker**; "Looney Cowboy Band"—sung by **Rudy Sooter and His Californians**; "Song of the Prairie" (Carter and Rosen)—sung by **Bob Baker, with Rudy Sooter and His Californians**

LOCATION FILMING: Agoura, California

RUNNING TIME: 56 min.

STORY: Newspaper editor William Gould summons Johnny Mack Brown to Pasco Basin. Gould is opposed to Arthur Loft and James Guilfoyle's water project, and fears his life is in danger. Brown arrives to find that his girlfriend Frances Robinson's father, Frank La Rue, and Brown's best friend, Bob Baker, think the water project will be of great benefit to the ranchers in the community. Actually, Gould is right; the project is a scam, with Loft pocketing most of the money the ranchers put up while Guilfoyle plans to take possession of all mortgaged ranches, allowing him to gain control of the basin. When Gould prints another article condemning the water project, Loft has Sheriff Edward Cassidy sent out of town so his gunmen can murder Gould. Brown organizes the ranchers opposed to the project to counter Loft having his gunmen deputized. Loft and Guilfoyle poison La Rue's mind against Brown. La Rue tells Brown to stay off his ranch. After Brown leaves, Guilfoyle has his henchman, Ted Adams, shoot La Rue, wounding him. Guilfoyle blames Brown. Then Adams begins a reign of terror, making it look like the work of Brown's vigilantes. Robinson and Baker accuse Brown of the crimes. Sheriff Cassidy arrives with proof of Brown's innocence and asks Brown for his help in bringing Loft and his gunmen to justice. Brown, Baker and the vigilantes ride to town and enter into a blazing gunfight with Loft's gunmen. Seeing the tide turning against them, Loft and Guilfoyle attempt a get a way. Brown catches up and ends their lawless career with a couple of well directed punches. Baker and the vigilantes round up the gunmen. Brown and Robinson plan to marry.

NOTES AND COMMENTARY: The working title for the film was *Vigilante War*.

Universal was guilty of a couple of production lapses in the filming of *Riders of Pasco Basin*. When Johnny Mack Brown receives a letter from William Gould, the salutation is "Dear Jim"—but Brown's character name is Lee Jameson. The scene in which Gould is mortally wounded was clumsily staged. With bullets flying all around, both Brown and Gould calmly get up from their chairs to stand in the line of fire.

The scene in which a shack is blown up was lifted from an earlier film in the series, *Chip of the Flying U* (Universal, 1939).

"Song of the Prairie" would be heard again in *Boss of Hangtown Mesa* (Universal, 1942).

REVIEWS: "Regulation western produced along tried and true lines. Has sufficient action and plot situation." (*Variety*, 5/22/40); "Well done Johnny Mack Brown vehicle." (*Western Movies*, Pitts)

SUMMATION: *Riders of Pasco Basin* is an exciting western, despite some shoddy production lapses uncharacteristic of a Universal product. Bob Baker has a little more to do in this saga than used, although it's perfectly clear that Johnny Mack Brown is the primary hero. Brown is given the chance to show genuine emotion, especially in the scene in which he consoles little Robert Winkler over his father William Gould's death. Later Brown displays his anger and frustration over Arthur Loft's villainy with a well placed punch to a beaten Loft's jaw. The lovely Frances Robinson handles the role of Brown's love interest nicely. Director Ford Beebe again shows why he is considered one of the top action directors by keeping the story continually on the move.

He's Gallopin' Vengeance!
He's Wallopin' Fury!
Smashing renegade rule on the wide-open trail!

Riders of the Santa Fe

ALTERNATE TITLE: *Mile-a-Minute*; Universal (November 1944)

CAST: Marshal Matt Conway, **Rod Cameron**; Larry Anderson, **Eddie Dew**; Bullseye Johnson, **Fuzzy Knight**; Carla Anderson, **Jennifer Holt**; Hank, **Ray Whitley**; Earl Duncan, **Lane Chandler**; Ed Miller, **Earle Hodgins**; Tom Brenner, **George Douglas**; Biff Macauley, **Dick Alexander**; Otis Wade, **Budd Buster**; Luella Tucker, **Ida Moore**; Bartender, **Al Ferguson**; and **Ray Whitley's Bar-6 Cowboys**// Townsmen, **Ray Jones and Henry Wills**

CREDITS: Director, **Wallace W. Fox**; Associate Producer, **Oliver Drake**; Screenwriter, **Ande Lamb**; Editor, **Ray Snyder**; Art Directors, **John B. Goodman** and **Abraham Grossman**; Set Decorators, **Russell A. Gausman** and **Leigh Smith**; Cinematography, **Maury Gertsman**; Sound, **Bernard B. Brown** and **William Hedgcock**; Musical Director, **Paul Sawtell**

SONGS: "The Defective Detective from Deadwood" (O. Drake)—sung by **Fuzzy Knight**; "Bed Down, Bed Down, Little Dogies" (Johns, Nale and Webb)—sung by **Ray Whitley**; "Out on the Santa Fe" (Allen)—sung by **Eddie Dew and Ray Whitley's Bar 6 Cowboys**; "Little Sweetheart of the Rio Grande" (O. Drake, Wakely and Rosen)—sung by **Ray Whitley and His Bar-6 Cowboys**

LOCATION FILMING: Agoura, California

RUNNING TIME: 60 min.

STORY: Needing a mayor he can control, saloon owner and outlaw leader George Douglas nominates saloon clown Fuzzy Knight. Knight sends for lawman Rod Cameron to take the job of sheriff. Unknown to Knight, Cameron no longer carries guns to do his job. Knight swears in Cameron as sheriff and singer Ray Whitley as deputy. Douglas bought Budd Buster's ranch and had a new map drawn in which the boundaries have been changed, giving Douglas control of water in the Red Mountain area. When Eddie Dew trail herds his cattle down the Santa Fe Trail, he finds there is a charge of a dollar per steer, which he refuses to pay. Dew attempts to obtain water by force, but Cameron stops him. Cameron tells Dew to bring the cattle into Red Mountain and use water from the troughs. Cameron and Knight take Buster to the boundaries on Douglas' ranch. Buster tells Cameron that Douglas has the correct map in his office safe. Douglas' henchman, Lane Chandler, ambushes Buster and throws the blame on Dew. Dew is arrested, and Chandler incites a mob to lynch him. Cameron sends Knight to get the map from Douglas' safe. Though successful,

Knight is captured but refuses to tell where he hid the map. Knight overhears Douglas' plan to stampede Dew's cattle onto his ranch. By trickery, Knight gets free and arrives at the jail in time to turn back the lynch mob and capture Chandler. Cameron and Dew ride to impede Douglas, while Whitley forms a posse. A gunfight erupts between the lawmen and the outlaws. Seeing that the lawmen have the upper hand, Douglas and henchman Richard Alexander try to get to their horses but are stopped by Cameron and Dew. Cattle herds will now have water as they're driven over the Santa Fe Trail.

NOTES AND COMMENTARY: "The Defective Detective from Deadwood" was known as "The Defective Detective from Brooklyn" when Smiley Burnette sang the song in *Public Cowboy No. 1* (Republic, 1937). "Little Sweetheart of the Rio Grande" was featured in *The Silver Bullet* (Universal, 1942) and *The Old Chisholm Trail* (Universal, 1942).

Plot elements from *Destry Rides Again* (Universal, 1939), *The Old Chisholm Trail* (Universal, 1942) and *Frontier Badmen* (Universal, 1943) were recycled by screenwriter Ande Lamb to fashion the screenplay for *Riders of the Santa Fe*.

Riders of the Santa Fe was remade as *Nevada Trail* (Universal-International, 1949), a featurette starring Tex Williams.

SUMMATION: *Riders of the Santa Fe* is a neat little action-filled "B" western. Heroes Rod Cameron, Eddie Dew and Fuzzy Knight are effective in their roles. Knight has a funny sequence in which, with Knight dressed as villain George Douglas' old maid aunt, henchman Earle Hodgins makes a pass at him. Jennifer Holt has little to do but look decorative in this outing. George Douglas, Lane Chandler and Richard Alexander supply the villainy. Director Wallace W. Fox keeps the story on the move.

Three GOOD Bad Men!

Road Agent

ALTERNATE TITLE: *Texas Road Agent;* Universal (December 1941)

CAST: Duke, **Dick Foran**; Pancho, **Leo Carrillo**; Andy, **Andy Devine**; Patricia, **Anne Gwynne**; Leavitt, **Samuel S. Hinds**; Martin, **Richard Davies**; Lola, **Anne Nagel**; Big John, **Morris Ankrum**; Steve, **John Gallaudet**; Shayne, **Reed Hadley**; Lewis, **Eddy Waller**; Jake, **Ernie Adams**; Luke, **Lew Kelly**// Teresa, **Luana Walters**; Bank Teller, **Emmett Lynn**; Outlaws, **George J. Lewis** and **Jack Rutherford**; Ranchers, **Jack Rockwell** and **Alan Bridge**; Townsman, **Bill Wolfe**

266 ROAD AGENT

CREDITS: Director, **Charles Lamont**; Associate Producer, **Ben Pivar**; Story, **Sherman Lowe and Arthur St. Claire**; Screenwriters, **Morgan Cox, Arthur Strawn and Maurice Tombragel**; Editor, **Frank Gross**; Art Directors, **Jack Otterson and Ralph M. DeLacey**; Set Decorator, **R.A. Gausman**; Cinematographer, **Jerome Ash**; Gowns, **Vera West**; Sound, **Bernard B. Brown and Robert Pritchard**; Musical Director, **H.J. Salter**

SONGS: "Ridin' Home" (Adamson and McHugh)—sung by **Anne Nagel and Dick Foran**; "Cielito Lindo" (Fernandez)—sung by **Dick Foran**; and "Ridin' Home" (reprise)—sung by **Dick Foran**

LOCATION FILMING: Iverson, Corriganville, California

RUNNING TIME: 60 min.

STORY: Dick Foran, Leo Carrillo and Andy Devine take a strongbox from stagecoach robbers led by John Gallaudet and bury it in the local cemetery. The driver and the sheriff were murdered in the holdup, but a

Road Agent (1941) scene card: Andy Devine (*left*), Leo Carrillo and Dick Foran check the contents of the strongbox taken from the stagecoach robbers. *Left border*, Leo Carrillo; *right border*, Dick Foran (*top*), Andy Devine. Note: With the film re-issued (and retitled) as *Texas Road Agent*, Leo Carrillo now receives top billing due to his popularity as Pancho in the *Cisco Kid* television series.

passenger witnessed the murders and can identify the bandits. Ranchers are worried that the money won't show up. Foran returns the money, less 10 percent as a reward. The witness is murdered, and Foran is pegged as the killer. Anne Nagel, an old friend who sings at the local saloon, tells Foran that Morris Ankrum is behind the lawless activity. Since the townspeople don't know Foran, he poses as a ranch owner and receives an invitation to a party at banker Samuel S. Hinds' ranch. Hinds discovers Foran's true identity and sends for a posse. Warned by Hinds' daughter Anne Gwynne, who is sweet on Foran, Foran and his two companions make their escape. Returning to Hinds' ranch, the three men are captured by Hinds and Richard Davies, who is in love with Gwynne. The trio is scheduled to hang, but Nagle brings evidence of Foran's innocence. Foran tells the crowd that he came to settle things with Ankrum. Ankrum wants the money that's in the bank. Foran, Carrillo and Devine hold up the bank before Ankrum's men can. The three men then ride to Hinds' ranch. Ankrum deduces that's where Foran will head, and he and his men ride there. Davies and the townspeople also come to the ranch. A terrific gun battle ensues. Ankrum is killed and the townsmen take care of the rest of the outlaws. With the outlawry at an end, Foran reveals to Hinds that he and his men are undercover lawmen, and they ride on to new adventures.

NOTES AND COMMENTARY: *Road Agent* was later reworked as a Kirby Grant vehicle, *Gunman's Code* (Universal, 1946).

The title *Road Agent* was reused for a Tim Holt RKO western in 1952, which told a completely different story.

"Ridin' Home" was featured in *Desperate Trails* (Universal, 1939), *Strictly in the Groove* (Universal, 1943), *Tenting Tonight on the Old Camp Ground* (Universal, 1943) and *Senorita from the West* (Universal, 1945). "Cielito Lindo" can be heard in *The Masked Rider* (Universal, 1941) and *Tenting Tonight on the Old Camp Ground* (Universal, 1943).

REVIEWS: "Good action in familiar western style." (*Variety*, 12/10/41); "*Road Agent* departs little from formula, but is worth sitting through just the same." (*The Motion Picture Guide*, Nash and Ross)

SUMMATION: *Road Agent* is a good, fast-moving "B" western. Dick Foran makes for a solid action star who also possesses a fine singing voice. Foran is ably assisted by two veteran actors, Leo Carrillo and Andy Devine, who know how to mix action and comedy in the right proportions. Lovely Anne Gwynne receives more to do than most heroines in these little westerns, and turns in a neat performance. Director Charles Lamont keeps the story moving, to good advantage.

When Hoot runs up against four-footed mustang dynamite, it's just too bad—for the pony! See him wild-ride all over the place and give you a thousand other thrills in his climb from ramshackle rancher to oil millionaire.

Roaring Ranch

Universal (April 1930)

CAST: Jim Dailey, **Hoot Gibson**; Tom Marlin, **Frank Clark**; June Marlin, **Sally Eilers**; Ramsey Kane, **Wheeler Oakman**; Mrs. Morgan, **Mrs. Steele**; Bobby Morgan, **Bobby Nelson**; Marylin Morgan, **Baby Walker**; Reginald Sobieski, **Leo White**// Sheriff, **Bob Burns**; Arsonist, **Jim Corey**

CREDITS: Director/Story/Screenwriter, **B. Reeves Eason**; Producer, **Hoot Gibson**; Editor, **Gilmore Walker**; Art Director, **David Garber**; Cinematography, **Harry Neumann**; Recording Engineer, **C. Roy Hunter**; Synchronization and Sound, **David Broekman**

LOCATION FILMING: Conejo, California

RUNNING TIME: 68 min.

SOURCE: Story, "Howdy Cowboy" by **Reeves Eason**

STORY: Easygoing Hoot Gibson owns a small ranch, not knowing it's rich in oil. Unscrupulous geological surveyor Wheeler Oakland wants to purchase the land. Oakland also wants to marry Sally Eilers, daughter of wealthy rancher Frank Clark. Eilers and Gibson are in love, but Gibson won't propose because of his lack of money. Knowing Gibson won't sell his ranch to him, Oakman has Leo White make an offer for Gibson's ranch. Gibson refuses to sell. Staying at Gibson's ranch are youngster Bobby Nelson and his baby sister, Baby Walker. Gibson is caring for the children while their mother, Mrs. Steele, recovers from an accident. Oakman hires Jim Corey and another man to set fire to Gibson's ranch. Gibson is able to get the children out of the cabin. Eilers, who was with Gibson, sees two men ride from the scene. Gibson races after the two men and forces them to accompany him to Sheriff Bob Burns. With his ranch destroyed, Gibson sells his property to White. After the sale, Eilers finds there is oil on the ranch. Burns shows Gibson two halves of two hundred dollar bills found on the arsonists. Gibson confronts Oakman and White and finds the other halves of the bills. Gibson tears up the option he signed, and Burns arrests the two men. Gibson marries Eilers and becomes an oil magnate.

NOTES AND COMMENTARY: Bobby Nelson had recently completed the *Pioneer Kid* series at Universal. These were silent featurettes released during the 1929–30 season.

REVIEWS: "Well done Hoot Gibson early talkie." (*Western Movies*, Pitts); "Universal put milk and honey into this western and made it too sweet." (*Variety*, 5/21/30)

SUMMATION: *Roaring Ranch* is a first-rate Hoot Gibson western, with

Gibson ably handling the action, dramatics and comedy. Gibson is a (ahem) hoot taking care of Baby Walker. Sally Eilers chips in a fine performance as Gibson's love interest. B. Reeves Eason paces the film nicely from a nifty screenplay he also wrote.

Buck Jones' Biggest and Best Serial!
Alive with Action!
Daring with Drama!
Thundering with Thrills!

The Roaring West

Universal (July 1935)

A Henry MacRae Production

CAST: Montana Larkin, **Buck Jones**; "Silver"; Mary Parker, **Muriel Evans**; Jinglebob Morgan, **Frank McGlynn, Sr.**; Gil Gillespie, **Walter Miller**; Ann Hardy, **Eole Galli**; Clem Morgan, **Harlan Knight**; Saloon Singer, **Frank Santley**; Jim Parker, **William Desmond**; Happy, **Tiny Skelton**; Tex, **Charles King**; Steve, **Pat O'Brien**; Marco Brett, **William L. Thorne**; Shorty, **George Ovey**; Sheriff Stark, **Dick Rush**; Pete, **Slim Whitaker**; Fred Humes; Butch, **Tom London**; **Cliff Lyons**// Forest Ranger Bob, **Buddy Roosevelt**; Old Man on Stage, **Lafe McKee**; Indian Joe, **Artie Ortego**; Slim, **Jay Wilsey**; Night Deputy, **Stanley Blystone**; Land Agent, **Horace B. Carpenter**; Stage Driver, **Hank Bell**

CREDITS: Director, **Ray Taylor**; Screenwriters, **George Plympton, Nate Gatzert, Basil Dickey, Robert C. Rothafel** and **Ella O'Neill**; Editors, **Saul Goodkind, Edward Todd, Alvin Todd** and **Irving Applebaum**; Art Director, **Ralph Berger**; Cinematographers, **William Sickner** and **Richard Fryer**

SONG: "The Old Oaken Bucket" (Woodworth and Kialmark)—sung by **Fred Santley**

LOCATION FILMING: Alabama Hills in Lone Pine, Kernville, Lasky Mesa and Bronson Canyon, California

RUNNING TIMES: 282 minutes

CHAPTER TITLES: 1. The Land Rush, 2. Torrent of Terror, 3. Flaming Peril, 4. Stampede of Death, 5. Danger in the Dark, 6. Death Rides the Plain, 7. Hurled to the Depths, 8. Ravaging Flames, 9. Death Holds Reins, 10. The Fatal Blast, 11. The Baited Trap, 12. The Mystery Shot, 13. Flaming Torrents, 14. Thundering Fury, 15. The Conquering Cowpunchers

SOURCE: A magazine story by **Edward Earl Repp**

STORY: Buck Jones and Frank McGlynn, Sr. have a map showing the location of a gold mine. Ranch owner William Desmond wants the two men to work for him. Jones and Desmond's daughter, Muriel Evans, show an interest in each other. Walter Miller, Desmond's foreman, makes a copy of the map. In the land rush, Miller and his men stake claim to the land Jones wanted. McGlynn's brother, Harlan Knight, arrives with the real map. Miller frames Jones for murder and kidnaps Knight. Jones escapes from jail. Desmond tells Jones and McGlynn to hide in a ranch at Hidden Valley, unaware the outlaws are keeping Knight prisoner there. Knight frees himself and joins Jones and McGlynn. Before the men can escape, the outlaws return. A pitched battle ensues, witnessed by Evans. Evans brings Desmond and his cowhands to the rescue. In the struggle, Knight makes a break and is recaptured by Miller. The testimony of a wounded outlaw, Pat O' Brien, clears Jones of the murder charge. O'Brien becomes an ally of Jones and helps by infiltrating Miller's gang to bring back information. Knight is repeatedly kidnapped and rescued. Knight finally decides to file a claim on the gold site. Jones, McGlynn, Desmond and Evans tag along. The outlaws follow the group. The group reaches the claim and is now ready to file at the land office. Knight, Desmond and Evans head to the land office but are intercepted by Miller and his men and captured. Knight promises to show Miller the claim site if Miller frees Evans and Desmond. Before Knight can make good on his promise, all are rescued by Jones. Knight finally registers his claim. Miller makes an unsuccessful attempt to jump the claim. Knight plans to ship some of the gold to town. Miller learns about the shipment, but Jones gets the gold to town safely. Miller and his gang raid the bank, but Jones and his friends are waiting. Miller attempts to get away, but Jones catches up and whips Miller in a short fistfight. With the troubles ended, Jones has time to propose to Evans.

NOTES AND COMMENTARY: In 1935, a novelization of *The Roaring West* was published as a Big Little Book by the Whitman Publishing Company as a children's book and a movie tie-in.

Chapter Six utilized stock footage from Ken Maynard's *The Wagon Master* (Universal, 1929). Maynard and his horse Tarzan can be seen in medium and long shots.

In Chapter Five, Tiny Skelton can be seen reading the Mother Goose rhyme "Once I Saw a Little Bird."

Jay Wilsey was known as Buffalo Bill, Jr. in his starring western career.

REVIEWS: "Actionful serial starring Buck Jones." (*Western Movies*, Pitts)

SUMMATION: *The Roaring West* is another good serial with Buck Jones. Jones, the perfect hero, is aided by a fine cast headed by Muriel Evans, Walter Miller, Frank McGlynn, Sr., William Desmond and Harlan Knight. Director Ray Taylor keeps the story on the move with some nice action sequences. The major flaw in the serial is the ease in which our heroes escape death and disaster in some of the chapter resolutions. Though its lack of characterizations means that, *Roaring West* falls short of the standards set by Jones' earlier serials, it still remains good fun. And there is a nice scene in which McGlynn cries tears of happiness over Jones' escape from a forest fire. This is followed by Desmond embarrassing Jones by asking him to give Evans her dry clothes. Ostensibly, Evans is standing behind a blanket without anything on. The chemistry between Jones and Evans greatly adds to the enjoyment of the serial.

BUCK JONES—in a full-length, full-strength, smashing WESTERN FEATURE!

Rocky Rhodes

Universal (September 1934); A Charles Buck Jones Production

CAST: Rocky Rhodes, **Charles Buck Jones**; Nan Street, **Sheila Terry**; Harp Haverty, **Stanley Fields**; Dan Murtch, **Walter Miller**; John Street, **Alf P. James**; Joe Hilton, **Paul Fix**; Mrs. Rhodes, **Lydia Knott**; Stark, **Lee Shumway**; Reed, **Jack Rockwell**; Bowles, **Carl Stockdale**; Jake, **Monte Montague**; Red, **Bud Osborne**; Boggs, **Harry Semels**; and "Silver"// Stockyard Worker, **Al Ferguson**; Deputy Mike, **Robert Walker**; Doctor, **Clarence Geldart**

CREDITS: Director, **Al Raboch**; Producer, **Irving Stark**; Screenwriter, **Edward Churchill**; Editor, **Ray Snyder**; Art Director, **Ralph Berger**; Cinematographer, **Ted McCord**; Sound, **Buddy Meyer**

LOCATION FILMING: Iverson, California

RUNNING TIME: 64 min.

SOURCE: Story by **W.C. Tuttle**

STORY: Paul Fix sends a letter to Buck Jones in Chicago telling him that Walter Miller is trying to grab all the land around Cactus City, including land owned by Jones' father. Jones' pal, Stanley Fields, decides to go west with him. Arriving in Cactus City, neighboring rancher Alf P. James and his daughter, Sheila Terry, tell Jones that Miller wants their ranch, that Jones' father has been murdered, and that money needed to pay off a debt to Miller was stolen. Fix has been arrested for the crime. Miller arranges for Fix to break jail. Miller's henchman, Lee Shumway, shoots Fix in the back as he rides from the jail. Before Fix dies, he tells Jones that he didn't shoot his father. Jones swears to find Fix's murderer. James is going to be dispossessed and Terry goes to Jones for help. Jones tells Miller he must prove ownership before taking over the ranch, and tells Miller to leave. That night Shumway steals Jones' knife. The bank is robbed and the banker killed, with Jones' knife left at the scene of the crime. Jones refuses to be arrested and tells Sheriff Jack Rockwell that he will produce the killer within twenty-four hours. Miller's lawyer, Carl Stockdale, has had enough of murder and wants out. Stockdale takes money from Miller's safe. Jones shows up and accuses Stockdale of the murders. Stockdale breaks down and tells Jones that Miller had Jones' father killed. Terry had been at Jones' ranch; on her way home, her horse stumbles; injuring Terry. Miller sends two of his men to dynamite James' ranch. Terry drags herself into her home. Jones finds Miller in the saloon and tries to force a showdown. Shumway draws his gun to shoot Jones, but Fields shoots the gun out of his hand. Miller rides to James' ranch, looking for his two henchmen to help him in his fight with Jones. Jones followed Miller, and the two men fight. Terry overhears the two henchmen talking and realizes what they're doing, and drags herself out of the window to safety. Seeing that Jones is in the house, Terry calls to Jones. Jones knocks out Miller and races to Terry's side just as the dynamite explodes, destroying the house and killing Miller. Jones and Terry plan to marry.

NOTES AND COMMENTARY: This was the first feature film Jones made at Universal. Jones had starred in two serials, *Gordon of Ghost City* (Universal, 1933) and *The Red Rider* (Universal, 1934), under a separate contract to Henry MacRae. Jones began making his Universal series in August 1934.

In 1935, a novelization of *Rocky Rhodes* was published as a Five Star Library Book by the Engel-Van-Wiseman Book Corporation as a children's book and a movie tie-in.

REVIEWS: "Nice blend of action and comedy make this a very good Buck Jones outing." *Western Movies*, Pitts; "An intriguing film." (*The Western*, Hardy)

SUMMATION: *Rocky Rhodes* is a good "B" western. Buck Jones ably meets both the acting and action demands of the script. Good supporting performances are offered by Stanley Fields as Jones' gangster sidekick from Chicago and Sheila Terry as Jones' love interest. In addition, Walter Miller makes a properly nasty villain. The script is only adequate, but good acting plus Al Raboch's steady direction puts this one over in good stead.

The MOUNTIES GET THEIR MAN!
...blasting the outlaws out of the Northwest!
13 CHAPTERS of Mountainous Thrills!

The Royal Mounted Rides Again

Universal (October 1945)
CAST: Frenchy, **George Dolenz**; Wayne Decker, **Bill Kennedy**; June Bailey, **Daun Kennedy**; Bucket, **Paul E. Burns**; Taggart, **Milburn Stone**; Price, **Robert Armstrong**; Dancer, Danny Morton; Jackson Decker, **Addison Richards**; Lode MacKenzie, Tom Fadden; Bunker, **Joseph Haworth**; Madame Mysterioso, **Helen**

Bennett; Sergeant Nelson, **Joseph Crehan**; Superintendent MacDonald, **Selmer Jackson**; Ladue, **Daral Hudson**; Kent, **George Lloyd**; Grail, **George Eldredge**; Archer, **William Haade**; Bull Andrews, **Rondo Hatton**// Blackie LaRoque, **Richard Alexander**; Tom Bailey, **Guy Beach**; Red, **Matt Willis**; Nick, **Lane Chandler**; Townsman, **Guy Wilkerson**; Miner, **Ed Cassidy**; Outlaw, **Paul Birch**

CREDITS: Directors, **Ray Taylor** and **Lewis D. Collins**; Assistant Directors, **Ralph Slosser**, **Ira S. Webb** and **V.O. Smith**; Producer, **Morgan B. Cox**; Screenwriters, **Joseph O'Donnell, Tom Gibson** and **Harold C. Wire**; Dialogue Director, **Willard Holland**; Supervising Editor, **Norman A. Cerf**; Editors, **Alvin Todd, Edgar Zane, Irving Birnbaum** and **Jack Dolan**; Art Direction, **Harold MacArthur**; Cinematographers, **Jerome Ash** and **Charles Van Enger**

LOCATION FILMING: Corriganville, California

RUNNING TIME: 221 min.

CHAPTER TITLES: 1. Canaska Gold, 2. The Avalanche Trap, 3. River on Fire, 4. Skyline Target, 5. Murder Toboggan, 6. Ore Car Accident, 7. Buckboard Runaway, 8. Thundering Water, 9. Dead Men for Decoys, 10. Derringer Death, 11. Night Trail Danger, 12. Twenty Dollar Doublecross, 13. Flaming Showdown

STORY: Guy Beach discovers a pocket of gold on his mining claim. Milburn Stone, manager of Addison Richards' mining claims, is in the mine at the time of discovery and kills Beach. Stone then dynamites the tunnel so no one else can discover the gold. Stone plans to tunnel in from Richards' copper mine and steal the gold. Richards is suspected of the murder because he has a reputation for being ruthless. Richards' son, Bill Kennedy, a corporal in the Royal Canadian Mounted Police, is assigned to the case. Beach's daughter, Daun Kennedy, also thinks Richards is behind her father's death. Richards finally proves that he is not a murderer, and the suspicion falls on Stone. Saloon owner Robert Armstrong takes control of the gold theft operation by threatening to expose Stone to the police. B. Kennedy runs a bluff on Stone and Stone falls for it, proving his guilt. Stone was going to manufacture evidence that his right hand man, Joe Haworth, was the murderer. So Haworth shoots Stone as he tries to escape. Three of Stone's confederates, George Eldredge, George Lloyd and William Haade, have removed the gold from the mine but cannot move the gold out of the area because the Mounties have set up a blockade. Haworth takes a saddlebag full of gold and tries to leave the area but is arrested by B. Kennedy. Eldredge smuggles a gun to Haworth so he can attempt to escape. In an exchange of shots, B. Kennedy mortally wounds Haworth. Haworth's gun contained blanks. Eldredge takes control, killing Lloyd and Haade. He captures a number of hostages and, knowing Armstrong's saloon is a riverboat, forces Armstrong to take it out into the river. Armstrong sets fire to the boat. Eldredge temporarily gains the

upper hand, but fortunes shift and Armstrong shoots Eldredge. Armstrong tells a confederate that he'll rescue the hostages so he can be a hero, and then he can take control of the gold. This admission of guilt is heard by B. Kennedy, who then arrests Armstrong. The hostages are rescued, and B. Kennedy and D. Kennedy plan to wed.

NOTES AND COMMENTARY: One of the more interesting actors in this serial is Rondo Hatton. Hatton developed the disease, acromegalia, (which is characterized by a marked distortion of the bones of the face, skull, hands and feet), the result of being gassed on the battlefields during World War I. The usual cause is an excess of growth hormone from the pituitary gland. Hatton received small parts until he played the menacing "Hoxton Creeper" in the Sherlock Holmes mystery *The Pearl of Death* (Universal, 1945). This led to bigger roles in "B" films at Universal. Hatton had the lead in *The Brute Man* (PRC, 1946), actually produced by Universal but sold to PRC due to Hatton's failing health. The film wasn't released until eight months after his death.

Jack Randall was signed for the part of Bunker, Milburn Stone's primary henchman. Randall had been a singing cowboy star for Monogram from 1937 to 1940. The series was canceled for the 1940–41 season. Randall had appeared in some non-western roles, but *Royal Mounted Rides Again* would be his first western role since his series at Monogram. On the first day of shooting, Randall had to film a difficult riding sequence. Randall's head hit a tree branch, killing the actor. Universal then assigned Joe Haworth to the part. Haworth's first scene was to ride the same horse Randall had ridden down the same path Randall had taken. The scene was difficult to film because the horse was almost uncontrollable.

REVIEWS: "Fairly entertaining Universal serial." (*Western Movies*, Pitts)

AUTHOR'S COMMENTS: What a surprise! *Royal Mounted Rides Again* is a fast moving, enjoyable later Universal serial. The wooden Bill Kennedy has the lead; in reality he's no better or worse than other serial heroes of the mid-to-late forties. The serial offers a fine supporting cast, headed by such "B" stalwarts as Addison Richards, Robert Armstrong, Milburn Stone, Paul E. Burns, George Eldredge, George Lloyd and William Haade, which adds to the fun. Directors Ray Taylor and Lewis D. Collins keep the pace fast and furious. The screenwriters came up with some good chapter endings; and the resolutions, for the most part, are fine.

Opposite: The Royal Mounted Rides Again (1945) one sheet: Chapter 8. *Clockwise from bottom left*, George Dolenz, Milburn Stone, Bill Kennedy, and Bill Kennedy again.

If you want
ACTION * THRILLS
ROMANCE * ADVENTURE
EXCITEMENT
Don't miss any of these 12 BIG EPISODES!

Rustlers of Red Dog

Universal (January 1935)

CAST: Jack Wood, **John Mack Brown**; Mary Lee, **Joyce Compton**; "Laramie," **Raymond Hatton**; "Deacon," **Walter Miller**; "Rocky," **H.L. Woods**; "Snakey," **Fredric MacKaye**; Ira Dale, **William Desmond**; Tom Lee, **Charles K. French**; Capt. Trent, **J.P. McGowan**; Bob Lee, **Lafe McKee**; Buck, **Edmond Cobb**; Chief Grey Wolf, **Chief Thunder Cloud**; Blackhawk, **William Hazlett**; Chief Scarface, **Jim Thorpe**; Young Indian Chief at Blackhawk's Village, **Artie Ortego**; Jake, **Bud Osborne**; Hank, **Jim Corey**; Ann Darcy; **Fritzi Brunette**; Older Woman Settler, **Grace Cunard**; **Virginia Ainsworth**; Singing Group at Campfire, **the Crockett Family**// Kruger, **Monty Montague**; Al, **Al Ferguson**; Dick, **Harry Tenbrook**; Saloon Gambler, **Jerry Frank**; Wally, **Wally Wales**; Fred, **Slim Whitaker**; Outlaw, **Art Mix**

CREDITS: Director, **Louis Friedlander**; Producer, **Milton Gatzert**; Associate Producer, **Henry MacRae**; Screenwriters, **George Plympton, Basil Dickey, Ella O'Neill, Nate Gatzert** and **Vin Moore**; Editors, **Saul Goodkind, Edward Todd, Alvin Todd** and **Irving Applebaum**; Art Director, **Ralph Berger**; Cinematographers, **William Sickner** and **Richard Fryer**

LOCATION FILMING: Vasquez Rocks and Bronson, California

RUNNING TIME: 231 min.

CHAPTER TITLES: 1. Hostile Redskins, 2. Flaming Arrows, 3. Thundering Hoofs, 4. Attack at Dawn, 5. Buried Alive, 6. Flames of Vengeance, 7. Into the Depths, 8. Paths of Peril, 9. The Snake Strikes, 10. Riding Wild, 11. The Rustlers Clash, 12. Law and Order

SOURCE: Story by **Nathaniel Eddy**

STORY: H.L. Woods and his outlaw gang, the Rustlers of Red Dog, are terrorizing the area around the town of Nugget. John Mack Brown, a former lawman, and his pals, Raymond Hatton and Walter Miller, are asked by banker Charles K. French to accept the post of marshal of Nugget. Brown refuses, stating he's had enough of killing and he wants to live a peaceful life. Learning that money to start a bank in Nugget is arriving by wagon train, Woods and his chief henchman, Frederic MacKaye, make plans to steal the cash. French's brother, Lafe McKee, and French's daughter, Joyce Compton, are bringing the money to the west. From Indian smoke signals, Brown and his men know hostile Indians will attack the wagon train. The Indians attack. The settlers look to Brown and his men for guidance. Fearing the Indians will completely wipe out the train, Woods and his rustlers join the fight with Brown and the settlers. Cavalry troops arrive, rout the Indians and guide the wagon train to the fort. The Indians attack the fort. Woods locates the wagon with the bank funds. Opening the gate, Woods and his men drive the wagon through the Indians. The Indians enter the fort and capture Brown, Compton, Hatton and Woods. More cavalry come to the fort to save the surviving settlers. Through a ruse, Brown and his friends escape the Indian camp. The group comes upon Woods' men securing the money in a cave in preparation of dynamiting open the safe. When the men leave to fetch the dynamite, the quartet sneak into the cave, Compton opens the safe, and Brown and his men remove the money. Brown is able to get the money to French. Woods has Indians attack Nugget while he and his men take the money. Brown, Compton, Hatton and Miller pursue Woods and his gang, and again retrieve the cash. The exciting adventure makes Brown and Compton realize they love one another. Finally, Brown captures Woods and MacKaye, but gang members free the outlaw leaders before they can come to trial. Brown, Hatton and Miller chase the outlaws, killing all in a running gunfight. Brown plans to go prospecting, strike it rich and marry Compton.

NOTES AND COMMENTARY: Johnny Mack Brown and Raymond Hatton would work together nine years later. When they team up at Monogram from 1943 to 1948 for 44 western adventures, starting with *The Ghost Rider* (Monogram, 1943).

Rustlers of Red Dog was Brown's first serial at Universal. Previously he had starred in *Fighting with Kit Carson* at Mascot in 1933. Brown would headline three more serials in his career, *Wild West Days* (Universal, 1937), *Flaming Frontiers* (Universal, 1938) and *The Oregon Trail* (Universal, 1939).

Brown's ride for help at the conclusion of Chapter Two would be used as a cliffhanger ending for Chapter 12 of Brown's later serial *Flaming Frontiers* (Universal, 1938).

Amazingly, as Chapter Three unfolds, the script forgets about the Indians who rode into the wagon train's inner circle in the previous episode.

REVIEWS: "Actionful and entertaining Johnny Mack Brown cliffhanger." (*Western Movies*, Pitts)

SUMMATION: *Rustlers of Red Dog* delivers exactly what it promises. It gives the audience plenty of action, excitement and thrills. Johnny Mack Brown and H.L. Woods make strong and believable adversaries. Raymond Hatton and Walter Miller register solidly as Brown's sidekicks, handling the action with subtle humor that will be appreciated by the adult audience. Joyce Compton is a fetching leading lady. Director Louis Friedlander keeps the story going at full gallop. The only negative aspect is the heavy reliance on stock footage in the Indian attack sequences.

Sizzling Western Action!
See some of the fastest rodeo scenes ever filmed—drama that will keep you on the edge of your seat.

The Rustlers' Roundup

Universal (March 1933)

CAST: Tom Lawson, **Tom Mix**; Mary Brand, **Diane Sinclair**; Danny Brand, **Noah Beery, Jr.**; Bill Brett, **Douglas Dumbrille**; Dave Winters, **Roy Stewart**; Sheriff Brass, **Nelson McDowell**; Sheriff Holden, **William Desmond**; Bayhorse, **Frank Lackteen**; Homer Jones, **William Wagner**; Husky, **Pee Wee Holmes**; Sodden, **Bud Osborne**; and "Tony"// Walt, **Walter Brennan**; Rodeo Patron, **Edmund Cobb**

CREDITS: Director, **Henry MacRae**; Story, **Ella O'Neill**; Screenwriter, **Frank Howard Clark**; Editors, **Albert Akst** and **Russell F. Schoengarth**; Cinematographer, **Daniel B. Clark**

LOCATION FILMING: Lone Pine and Tuolemme County, California

RUNNING TIME: 56 min.

STORY: Rancher Tom Mix finds ways to prevent Diane Sinclair from selling the ranch she and her brother, Noah Beery, Jr., inherited upon the death of their father. Foreman Douglas Dumbrille wants Sinclair to sell the ranch to neighboring rancher Roy Stewart. Mix knows the ranch contains an underground spring that makes the property extremely valuable. Unfortunately, only Sinclair's father knew the location. Dumbrille and Stewart are the leaders of a rustling gang plaguing Sinclair and Beery. Beery overhears Dumbrille planning another cattle raid and tries to capture the rustlers. Instead, the rustlers overpower Beery and take him to their hideout. Mix learns of Beery's disappearance and tells Sinclair that he'll bring him back. Dumbrille decides that Beery should meet with a fatal accident. Mix intervenes and both men escape the rustlers' camp. Sinclair has sold six hundred horses to Stewart and will receive payment when the horses are delivered. The horses, however, are being driven to the border instead of to Stewart's ranch. Beery goes for the sheriff and a posse. The posse stops the theft of the horses and rounds up the rustlers. Beery sees Dumbrille but is unable to capture him. Mix arrives and holds Dumbrille for the sheriff. With witnesses present, Mix tricks a confession out of Dumbrille. Mix and Sinclair have fallen in love and ride off to find the location of the underground spring.

NOTES AND COMMENTARY: During the filming of *The Rustlers' Roundup*, Mix sustained another fall, damaging his rib cage, prompting his decision to end the series. Citing that the risks weren't worth appearing on the silver screen, Mix suggested that Hoot Gibson replace him. Some theaters advertised *The Rustlers' Roundup* as Tom Mix's farewell picture.

Mix requested that a scene with William Desmond be written into the film. The scene's focus was to demonstrate Desmond's ability with a six-gun.

Footage from *The Devil Horse* (Pathe, 1926) was utilized in the horse rustling sequence.

To insure that the rodeo footage would be authentic, Hoot Gibson allowed Mix to film sequences at his Round-Up Wild West Show.

REVIEWS: "Tom Mix's final series western is not up to others in his Universal series, although it is still above average." (*Western Movies*, Pitts); "It adds up to a good Mix western with above-average production values." (*The Motion Picture Guide*, Nash and Ross)

SUMMATION: *The Rustlers' Roundup* is a very pleasant "B" western with an engaging performance by Tom Mix. Mix shows that he's very adept with a quip as well as with the action scenes. Leading lady Diane Sinclair, veteran heavy Douglas Dumbrille and youthful Noah Beery, Jr. all deliver good performances. Although the plot is somewhat light on action, the story holds the interest throughout. Henry MacRae's direction is on target.

BLASTING THE BADLAND TERRORS!

Rustler's Roundup

ALTERNATIVE TITLE: **Rustler's Hideout;** Universal (August 1946)

CAST: Bob Bryan, **Kirby Grant**; Pinky Pratt, **Fuzzy Knight**; Jo Fremont, **Jane Adams**; Sheriff Fin Elder, **Earle Hodgins**; Judge Wayne, **Charles Miller**; Vic Todd, **Edmund Cobb**; Louie Todd, **Ethan Laidlaw**; Faro King, **Mauritz Hugo**; Tom Fremont, **Eddy C. Waller**; Jules Todd, **Frank Mario**// Cal Dixon, **Steve Clark**; Rancher, **Hank Bell**; Jim Walton, **Rex Lease**; Pete Hannigan, **Bud Osborne**; Gunsmith, **Budd Buster**; Doctor, **George Morrell**; Rustler, **Kermit Maynard**

CREDITS: Director / Producer, **Wallace W. Fox**; Story, **Sherman Lowe** and **Victor McLeod**; Screenwriter, **Jack Natteford**; Editor, **Saul A. Goodkind**; Art Directors, **Jack Otterson** and **Frank A. Richards**; Set Decorators, **Russell A. Gausman** and **Leigh Smith**; Cinematographer, **Maury Gertsman**; Gowns, **Vera West**; Hair Stylist, **Carmen Dirigo**; Makeup, **Jack P. Pierce**; Sound, **Bernard B. Brown** and **John W. Rixey**; Musical Director, **Milton Rosen**

SONGS: "That's the Way I Am" (Carter, Brooks and Rosen)—sung by **Fuzzy Knight** and **Kirby Grant**; "Vote for Cal Dixon" (O. Drake, Wakely and Rosen)—sung by **Jane Adams** and "The Western Trail" (Carter and Rosen)—sung by **Kirby Grant**

LOCATION FILMING: Iverson, Corriganville and Agoura, California

RUNNING TIME: 57 min.

STORY: Kirby Grant and his pal, Fuzzy Knight, find that Edmund Cobb and his brothers run the town of Rawhide. Their man, Earle Hodgins, was reelected sheriff. Knowing about Grant's law enforcement background, Judge Charles Miller asks Grant to take the job of marshal. Grant refuses, stating that he wants to buy a ranch and settle down. Cobb and his men rustle some of rancher Eddy Waller's cattle. Waller sees the theft and rides for help, but Cobb ambushes Waller. With Waller's death, Grant decides to track down the killer and to help his daughter, Jane Adams. Grant gathers proof that Cobb murdered Waller, but Hodgins refuses to arrest Cobb. Grant takes the marshal's badge and arrests Cobb. Cobb's brothers, Ethan Laidlaw and Frank Mario, and members of the outlaw gang, trap Grant and Knight in the jail in an attempt to free Cobb. Adams brings the honest ranchers to town to help the lawmen. During the battle, Cobb escapes from jail. The ranchers help Knight round up the gang, while Grant brings Cobb back to stand trial.

NOTES AND COMMENTARY: *Rustler's Roundup* seems to be a partial remake of *Law and Order* (Universal, 1940) and *The Silver Bullet* (Universal, 1942), both starring Johnny Mack Brown.

The song "Vote for Cal Dixon" was heard as "Vote for Emily Morgan" in *The Silver Bullet* (Universal, 1942). Jane Adams states that she did not sing the song "Vote for Cal Dixon." "The Western Trail" was originally heard in *Man from Montana* (Universal, 1941).

When Charles Miller calls out the names of the jurors, he says the name Pete Hannigan twice.

The scene in which Kirby Grant stops Jane Adams' "runaway" buckboard was lifted from *Ragtime Cowboy Joe* (Universal, 1940). In that one Johnny Mack Brown stops Nell O'Day's buckboard.

Footage from *Trail of the Vigilantes* (Universal, 1940) was used for the scenes in which the ranchers ride to Grant and Fuzzy Knight's aid.

REVIEWS: "Nicely paced and actionful Kirby Grant vehicle." (*Western Movies*, Pitts)

SUMMATION: *Rustler's Roundup* is a solid Kirby Grant oater, with Grant and Fuzzy Knight making a good team. Grant handles the heroics well, and Knight gives one of his best sidekick performances as he practices the art of subtle comedy. Director Wallace W. Fox nicely balances strong action, comedy and songs.

*The Tale that Set the West on Fire!
Salome!.. Lure of the West!
Loot of the Lawless!... love prize of 1000 swaggering gunmen from
Texas to the Rockies.*

Salome, Where She Danced

Universal (April 1945)

CAST: Salome, **Yvonne De Carlo**; Jim, **Rod Cameron**; Cleve, **David Bruce**; Dimitrioff, **Walter Slezak**; Von Bohlen, **Albert Dekker**; Madame Europe, **Marjorie Rambeau**; Professor Max, **J. Edward Blomberg**; Dr. Ling, **Abner Biberman**; General Lee, **John Litel**; Count Von Bismarck, **Kurt Katch**; Bartender, **Arthur Hohl**; Henderson, **Gavin Muir**; Panatela, **Nestor Paiva**; Sheriff, **Will Wright**; Henry, **Joseph Haworth**; Lafe, **Matt McHugh**; Seven Salome Girls, **Poni Adams, Barbara Bates, Daun Kennedy, Kathleen O'Malley, Karen Randle, Jean Trent** and **Kerry Vaughn**// Lineman, **Eddie Dunn**; Telegrapher, **Charles Waggenheim**; Sophia, **Sylvia Field**; Kurt (Salome's lover), **David Bruce**; Stage Driver, **Edmund Cobb**; Shotgun Guard, **Richard Alexander**; Theater Patrons, **George Chesebro, Hank Bell** and **Budd Buster**; Bartender, **George Sherwood**; Bar Girl, **Cecilia Callejo**; Deputy, **Al Ferguson**

CREDITS: Director, **Charles Lamont**; Assistant Director, **Fred Frank**; Chase Sequence Director, **Breezy Eason**; Producer, **Walter Wanger**; Associate Producer, **Alexander Golitzen**; Story, **Michael J. Phillips**; Screenwriter, **Laurence Stallings**; Dialogue Director, **Ernest Truex**; Editor, **Russell Schoengarth**; Art Directors, **John B. Goodman** and **Alexander Golitzen**; Set Decorators, **Russell A. Gausman** and **Victor A. Gangelin**; Cinematographers, **Hal Mohr** and **W. Howard Greene**; Costumes, **Vera West**; Makeup, **Jack Pierce**; Sound, **Bernard B. Brown** and **William Hedgcock**; Musical Director / Musical Score, **Edward Ward**; Choreographer, **Lester Horton**; Technicolor Color Director, **Natalie Kalmus**; Associate Technicolor Color Director, **William Fritzsche**.

SONGS: "Blue Danube" (Strauss) —danced by **Yvonne De Carlo**; Salome; "Rovin' Gambler" (traditional)—sung by **male chorus**; "O Tannebaum" (traditional)—sung by **Yvonne De Carlo and male chorus**; and "Blue Danube" (Strauss)—sung by **Yvonne De Carlo**

LOCATION FILMING: Lone Pine, California

COLOR PROCESS: Technicolor

RUNNING TIME: 90 min.

STORY: After the close of the Civil War, news correspondent Rod Cameron journeys to Berlin to report on a possible war between Prussia and Austria. Viennese entertainer Yvonne De Carlo is sent to Berlin to dance for Prussian ruler Kurt Katch. Cameron enlists De Carlo's aid to discover when Prussia will attack Austria. The information will also be sent to De Carlo's lover. Katch's aide, Albert Dekker, falls for De Carlo. De Carlo is able to give Cameron the date of the attack. Prussia brings war to Austria, and De Carlo's lover dies in battle. Dekker brands Cameron a spy and plans to have him executed. Cameron threatens to reveal that Dekker had given top secret information to De Carlo. Dekker allows Cameron to leave Prussia. Cameron takes De Carlo with him, and they travel to Drinkman Wells, Texas. Cameron, now De Carlo's manager, arranges for De Carlo to perform the dance "Salome." Bandit leader David Bruce, once a Confederate officer, and his men raid the opera house, steal the money and kidnap De Carlo. At the bandit's hideout, De Carlo notices a strange resemblance between Bruce and her dead Austrian lover. De Carlo and Bruce fall in love. Bruce returns the money and travels with Cameron and De Carlo to San Francisco. The people of Drinkman Wells change the town's name to Salome, Where She Danced. Needing money to put on a show, Cameron arranges for wealthy Walter Slezak to meet De Carlo. Slezak falls for De Carlo and agrees to finance a performance of Salome. This news reaches Dekker, who yearns to revenge himself on De Carlo for prying military secrets from him. Knowing De Carlo loves Bruce, Slezak arranges a full pardon for Bruce and his men for their crimes as stagecoach robbers, and arranges a job for Bruce as shotgun guard for the very stage line he once robbed. Dekker arrives in San Francisco on a stage that Bruce guards. Seeing Dekker, Bruce follows him to the Opera House. Dekker tells De Carlo she will either return to Prussia to face charges as a spy or live with him. Bruce confronts Dekker. They duel with swords, Bruce's quick thrust ends Dekker's life. Bruce steals a stagecoach and begins a journey to his home state of Virginia. Slezak gives chase in a police wagon, with De Carlo and Cameron following. Nifty driving allows Slezak to capture Bruce. De Carlo's coach arrives. Slezak escorts the handcuffed Bruce to De Carlo. After throwing the handcuff keys into the coach, Slezak tells the driver to take the couple to Virginia.

NOTES AND COMMENTARY: *Salome, Where She Danced* was Yvonne De Carlo's starring feature film debut. At Universal studios, De Carlo was being tested for a possible contract when Producer Walter Wanger noticed her. Wanger thought De Carlo's looks were striking and arranged for additional screen tests. De Carlo learned she had won the lead in *Salome, Where She Danced* from a newspaper article. In press releases, Wanger called De Carlo the "Most Beautiful Girl in the World."

After weeks of intense dance rehearsals, Yvonne De Carlo's toes and ankles had taken so much punishment in preparation for her routines that she required injection of Novocain to allow her to dance properly in the film.

De Carlo's greatest disappointment came in the playback of the vocal rendition of "The Blue Danube." The voice was not De Carlo's; her voice had been dubbed without her knowledge. This was the only time in De Carlo's distinguished career that the singing voice issuing from her lips would not be hers.

Jane Adams worked for the Pasadena Playhouse for four years, appeared in 26 plays and graduated with a Theater Arts degree. Adams worked on *Lux Radio Theatre* and *The Whistler* radio programs. In New York, Adams became associated with the Harry Conover Agency. Adams worked on early television programs because she had a stage background and could remember her lines. Harry Conover gave the name Poni to Adams because he thought her regular name, Betty Jane, was too ordinary. Adams' face was featured on the covers of eight magazines, plus she received a full-page photograph, wearing a very elegant gown, in *Esquire Magazine*, along with a resume of her career to that point. Producer Walter Wanger called Adams back to Hollywood to test for the lead in *Salome, Where She Danced*. Adams lost out to Yvonne De Carlo because she had no dancing experience, which the role required. Universal signed Adams to a contract and had her play one of the handmaidens in the Salome dance sequence.

"Rovin' Gambler" was performed by Tex Ritter in *The Old Chisholm Trail* (Universal, 1942). "Blue Danube" would be played by Spade Cooley and His Orchestra in *Senorita from the West* (Universal, 1945).

REVIEWS: "Beautifully filmed drama, has strong entertainment value." (*Variety*, 4/1/45); "Amusing tongue-in-cheek melodrama with Yvonne De Carlo a knockout in the title role." (*Western Movies*, Pitts)

SUMMATION: *Salome, Where She Danced* is an entertaining cult western. The film established Yvonne De Carlo as a star, and her presence shines throughout the proceedings. Rod Cameron does in a fine job as one of De Carlo's many suitors. David Bruce seems a little wooden as the man De Carlo loves. Albert Dekker, Walter Slezak and Abner Biberman give noteworthy performances in the large supporting cast. The story is episodic and seems at times pieced together. Charles Lamont's strong directorial hand ultimately makes the film satisfying.

Man—Hunting, Mystery, Mad Bravery! Breakneck Riding, a Fight to the Finish!

Sandflow

Universal (February 1937); A Buck Jones Production

CAST: Buck Hallett, **Buck Jones**; Rose Porter, **Lita Chevret**; Quayle, **Bob Kortman**; Texan, **Arthur Aylesworth**; Lane Hallett, **Robert Terry**; Joaquin, **Enrique DeRosas**; Mr. Porter, **Josef Swickard**; the Kid, **Lee Phelps**; Rillito, **Harold Hodge**; Sheriff, **Tom Chatterton**; Santone, **Arthur Van Slyke**; Parable, **Malcolm Graham**; "Silver"// Townsman, **Horace B. Carpenter**; Cowboy who captures horse, **Jack Rockwell**

CREDITS: Director, **Lesley Selander**; Story, **Cherry Wilson**; Screenwriter, **Frances Guihan**; Editor, **Bernard Loftus**; Art Director, **Ralph Berger**; Cinematographers, **Allen Thompson** and **Herbert Kirkpatrick**; Sound, **L. John Myers**

SONGS: "Home on the Range" (traditional)—sung by **Lee Phelps**; and "Red River Valley" (traditional)

LOCATION FILMING: Alabama Hills, Lone Pine, California

RUNNING TIME: 58 min.

STORY: The father of Buck Jones and Robert Terry had built up his herd with stolen cattle from three ranches. Jones has repaid the debt to two of the ranches, but is now financially ruined since the town bank failed. Wanted for murder, a wounded Terry, chased by a posse, comes to a line shack for help. Cowhand Bob Kortman wants to turn Terry in for the reward. Jones, believing Terry is innocent, hides his brother. Jones' friend, Enrique DeRosas, promises Kortman money equal to the reward if he will leave Terry alone. Terry tells Jones that he committed the murder. Jones follows Terry's horse to Terry's girl, Lita Chevret. Jones is captured and taken to a place of refuge. Terry is being cared for by DeRosas. At the refuge, Jones finds that Chevret's father, Josef Swickard, has lost his mind his bank failed; and there was another man besides Terry at the scene of the murder. Kortman is captured and brought to the refuge. Jones and Kortman plan to escape, but Kortman knocks out Jones, leaves by himself and runs into Swickard. Kortman, frightened by his appearance, hits Swickard, killing him instantly. Stealing a horse, Kortman rides away, with Jones, mounted on Silver, in pursuit. Kortman unknowingly rides to the spot where DeRosas is caring for Terry. Kortman makes an attempt to take Terry in, but Jones arrives. The two men fight. Kortman gains the upper hand only to be shot by DeRosas. Jones and DeRosas take Terry to the refuge. Jones and DeRosas plan to journey to Mexico to pay off the debt to the last ranch; but Chevret tells Jones that because of the bank's failure, the debt is paid— Swickard owned that ranch. Jones rides off, leaving Terry with Chevret.

NOTES AND COMMENTARY: Lita Chevret here received her only leading role in feature films (following eight years of minor roles, usually unbilled, at major and minor studios). She failed to make a favorable impression. Some reference books list Chevret as an Indian Squaw in the comedy-western *My Little Chickadee* (Universal, 1940), but in the current print available she can't be found by the author.

"Red River Valley" would later be heard in *Law for Tombstone* (Universal, 1937), *Stagecoach Buckaroo* (Universal, 1941) and *The Silver Bullet* (Universal, 1942).

REVIEWS: "Title of Buck Jones' latest is colorless but the film isn't, plenty of action." (*Variety*, 3/24/37); Somewhat meandering Buck Jones vehicle." (*Western Movies*, Pitts)

SUMMATION: *Sandflow* is a confusing film, failing to adequately answer all the questions it proposes, (e.g. why the murder was committed). Acting by the principals is uneven, with Buck Jones turning in a good performance while leading lady Lita Chevret and villain Bob Kortman prove uneven. At times Kortman reverts to silent screen gestures, making his part all the more ludicrous. The story is greatly enhanced by the excellent photography of cinematographers Allen Thompson and Herbert Kirkpatrick, and a well-choreographed fistfight between Jones and Kortman. Lesley Selander's usually steady direction is not evident in this below par Jones effort.

THE WEST'S BOLDEST ADVENTURE HERO!
SEE EVERY CHAPTER OF THIS NEW SERIAL FOR 13 THRILLING WEEKS

The Scarlet Horseman

Universal (January 1946)

CAST: Kirk Norris, **Peter Cookson**; Jim Bannion, **Paul Guilfoyle**; Elise Halliday, **Janet Shaw**; Carla Marquette, **Virginia Christine**; Loma, **Victoria Horne**; Amigo Manana, **Cy Kendall**; Zero Quick, **Edward M. Howard**; Idaho Jones, **Harold Goodwin**; Ballou, **Danny Morton**; Mrs. Halliday, **Helen Bennett**; Tragg, **Jack Ingram**; Kyle, **Edmund Cobb**; Panhandle, **Guy Wilkerson**; Senator Halliday, **Al Woods**; Tioga, **Fred Coby**; Pecos, **Ralph Lewis**// Indian Chief, **Forrest Lewis**; Indian Guide, **Frank Lackteen**; Saunders, **Jack Rockwell**; Dan, **Marshall Reed**; Senator Barnes, **Mauritz Hugo**; Senator Masters, **Hank Patterson**; Halliday's Maid, **Beatrice Roberts**; Jed, **Dick Curtis**; Mrs. Barnes, **Ellen Corby**; Tom Leach, **Rex Lease**; Railroad Engineer, **Stanley Blystone**; Outlaw at Rosa Rita Mine, **Ed Cassidy**; Townsman at rear of Boarding House, **Jack Kirk**; Seth,

Budd Buster; Farrow, **Ernie Adams**; Ace, **Paul Birch**; Henchman at Barn, **Pierce Lyden**; Henchman on Trail, **Hal Taliaferro**; Henchmen, **Lee Roberts** and **Frank McCarroll**

CREDITS: Directors, **Ray Taylor** and **Lewis D. Collins**; Assistant Directors, **Phil Bowles, Charles M. Bennett** and **Carl Beringer**; Producer, **Morgan B. Cox**; Screenwriters, **Joseph O'Donnell, Tom Gibson** and **Patricia Harper**; Supervising Editor, **Norman A. Cerf**; Editors, **Alvin Todd, Edgar Zane, Irving Birnbaum, Jack Dolan** and **D. Pat Kelley**; Art Director, **Harold MacArthur**; Cinematographers, **Jerome Ash** and **George Robinson**; Dialogue Director, **Willard Holland**

LOCATION FILMING: Kernville, California

RUNNING TIME: 248 min.

CHAPTER TITLES: 1. Scarlet for a Champion, 2. Dry Grass Danger, 3. Railroad Rescue, 4. Staked Plains Stampede, 5. Death Shifts Passengers, 6. Stop That Stage, 7. Blunderbuss Broadside, 8. Scarlet Doublecross, 9. Doom Beyond the Door, 10. The Edge of Danger, 11. Comanche Avalanche, 12. Staked Plains Massacre, 13. Scarlet Showdown

STORY: The Comanches go on the warpath to prevent settlers from entering the Stakes Plains country. Paul Guilfoyle, Peter Cookson and Cy Kendell are sent to the town of Forty Four to discover who is stirring up the Indians. A conspiracy is afoot to have Texas allow the Staked Plains area to become a separate state inhabited by the Comanche nation. To further that end, wives and daughters of prominent Texas state senators have been kidnapped to force the senators to draft and enact such a proposal. To keep the Comanche Indians from attacking settlers, Guilfoyle adopts the guise of the Scarlet Horseman, champion of the Comanches through the ages. Victoria Horne, a half-caste Comanche, is the power behind the Comanches, but (because of her bloodline) cannot be the actual chief. Horne is working with Virginia Christine and saloon owner Danny Morton to achieve the separate state. Freight line owner Edward M. Howard wants to be included in this scheme, knowing there's a lot of money to be made. Unknown to Horne, Christine is working to her own purposes, intending to make herself the actual ruler of the state, with the Comanches as her slaves. The Staked Plains looks to be a total desert but contains some of the most fertile and valuable land in Texas. Guilfoyle, Cookson and Wells Fargo agent Harold Goodwin place their lives in jeopardy by trying to stop the lawlessness. Finally, Goodwin decides to arrest Howard. Cookson rides to Christine's ranch to place Christine and Horne in custody. Fearing Goodwin is walking into more trouble than he can handle, Guilfoyle, as the Scarlet Horseman, rides to help him. Goodwin is about to be caught in a crossfire when the Scarlet Horseman steps in and shoots Howard and Morton. The Scarlet Horseman goes to the Comanche village and asks them to find the kidnapped women in the Staked Plains country. Goodwin rides to Christine's ranch and finds himself under Christine's gun, along with Cookson and Horne. No longer needing them alive, Christine prepares to kill them, but a timely bullet from the Scarlet Horseman's pistol knocks the gun from her hand, and Christine is placed under arrest. Horne is restored to power in the Comanche nation. Guilfoyle, Cookson and Kendall ride on to new adventures.

NOTES AND COMMENTARY: *The Scarlet Horseman* was Universal's last western serial. Released in January 1946, the ending gave promise to another thrilling chapterplay with Paul Guilfoyle, Peter Cookson and Cy Kendall. Universal would release two more serials in 1946, *Lost City of the Jungle* and *Mysterious Mr. M*, before the "B" picture unit would shut down. *The Scarlet Horseman* received heavier and more intense promotion in newspaper advertising than most of the Universal serials.

In Chapter One, Danny Morton goes to gunsmith Paul Guilfoyle's store to retrieve a firearm left for repair. Cy Kendall wheels the supposedly crippled Guilfoyle into the front of the store. Guilfoyle picks up a gun and says to Morton, "Sorry, Ballou, I know you've been bucking your tether, but when my knees ache, I rest. Anyway, one day, more or less, getting back a shooting iron never hurt anybody. There you are, all loaded. [Guilfoyle hands the gun to Morton.] You really have quick action there now. All loaded." Morton hands the gun back to Guilfoyle and was supposed to say, "I hear you can still shoot sitting down, even without practice." Instead, Morton said, " I hear you can still shit shooting down." The cast and crew broke up when Guilfoyle replied, "Shit shooting down?"

Danny Morton enjoyed playing in serials, stating, "It was like a boyhood dream come true." Morton and his brother went to see serials in the twenties. When the films were over they expected to see the actors and actresses come out from behind the screen.

When Danny Morton first auditioned for westerns and serials, he remembered, "I didn't know one end of a horse from the other, but I eventually became a good rider." Morton added, "I always made sure that I had a good stunt double, so it would make me look good."

Guy Wilkerson's character name in *The Scarlet Horseman* was Panhandle. Wilkerson, fresh from the Texas Rangers series at PRC, played Panhandle Perkins in 22 entries from 1942 to 1945.

The character of Wells Fargo agent Idaho Jones, here played by veteran actor Harold Goodwin, was initially performed by Joe Sawyer in *Raiders of Ghost City* (Universal, 1944).

Wagon train footage in Chapter Two was lifted from *The Oregon Trail* (Universal, 1939). A sequence of John Wayne crashing a train through a mine barricade in *The Spoilers* (Universal, 1942) was used as the cliffhanger ending to Chapter Three, with Peter Cookson at the throttle this time out. The cattle stampede sequence in Chapter Four was filmed from *Arizona* (Columbia, 1940). In Chapter Six, the Indians attacking a stagecoach sequence came from *Winners of the West* (Universal, 1940). Those with sharp eyes will recognize James Craig, Charles Stevens and Edmund Cobb riding hell bent for leather. Liberal footage from *The Flaming Frontier* (Universal, 1926) was used in the Indian attacks.

Dressed in black to resemble past Universal serial heroes Johnny Mack Brown, Dick Foran and Lon Chaney, Peter Cookson, in Chapter Eight, has his gun belt buckled in back, but then a scene later it's buckled in the front.

The barn explosion seen at the end of Chapter Nine had been created by Howard and Theodore Lydecker at Republic. Republic used that explosion in many of their serials and feature films.

Whenever the Scarlet Horseman returned to the stable area for his horse, he always removed the saddle. In Chapter 13, when the Horseman prepares to spring into action, his horse is already saddled and ready to go.

REVIEWS: "Pleasantly actionful chapterplay." (*Western Movies*, Pitts)

SUMMATION: Despite the almost excessive use of stock footage from previous Universal productions, *The Scarlet Horseman* proves to be an entertaining film. Paul Guilfoyle delivers a good performance as the Horseman and his alter ego, a "crippled" gunsmith. Virginia Christine and Victoria Horne are impressive as the chief villainess and a half-caste Comanche, respectively. Peter Cookson, though a little wooden, proves serviceable as the other leading man. Veteran directors Ray Taylor and Lewis D. Collins blend action, story, and stock footage into a pleasing whole.

Dynamited by Desperadoes! Captured by Indians!
Attacked by Mountain Lions! Stampeded by Thundering Hooves!
Adventure ... thrills ... breath-taking exploits by daring Boy Scouts. 12 blood-chilling chapters of exciting hair-trigger action and suspense!

Scouts to the Rescue

Universal (February 1939)

CAST: Bruce Scott, **Jackie Cooper**; Rip Rawson, **David Durand**; Skeets Scanlon, **Bill Cody, Jr.**; Mary Scanlon, **Vondell Darr**; Hal Marvin, **William Ruhl**; Hermie, **Sidney Miller**; Turk Mortensen, **Ivan Miller**; Pat Scanlon, **Edwin Stanley**; Pug O'Toole, **Ralph Dunn**; High Priest Lukolu, **George Regas**; Scoutmaster Hale, **Jack Mulhall**; Doc, **Jason Robards**; Leeka, **Dick Botiller**; Hurst, **Victor Adams**; Jim Hussey; Ken, **Frank Coglan, Jr.**; Blaine, **Emmett Vogan**; Sam Bernard; Carson, **Lee Phelps**// "Scout"; Indian, **Iron Eyes Cody**; Joe, **Eddie Parker**

CREDITS: Directors, **Ray Taylor and Alan James**; Associate Producer, **Henry MacRae**; Story, **Irving Crump** of *Boy's Life* magazine; Screenwriters, **Wyndham Gittens, George Plympton, Basil Dickey and Joseph Poland**; Supervising Editor, **Saul A. Goodkind**; Editors, **Alvin Todd and Louis Sackin**; Art Direction, **Charles Clague**; Cinematographer, **William Sickner**; Musical Director, **Charles Previn**; Dialogue Director, **Ella O'Neill**

LOCATION FILMING: Dardanelle Mountain (High Sierras), near Sacramento, CA

RUNNING TIME: 230 min.

CHAPTER TITLES: 1. Death Rides the Air, 2. Avalanche of Doom, 3. Trapped by Indians, 4. River of Doom, 5. Descending Doom, 6. Ghost Town Menace, 7. Destroyed by Dynamite, 8. Thundering Hoofs, 9. The Fire Gods Strike, 10. Battle of Ghost Town, 11. Hurtling Through Space, 12. The Boy Scouts Triumph

STORY: Gangster Ivan Miller arrives in Martinsville to retrieve a letter and map sent by Edwin Stanley's brother to Stanley. Stanley tells Miller the letter was burned. Stanley's son, Bill Cody, Jr., retrieved the map and wants to follow the directions, expecting to find buried treasure. Scout Jackie Cooper tells Cody he thinks the treasure is located in Ghost Town. G-Man William Ruhl has been assigned to investigate Stanley. In the mountains above Ghost Town dwells a mysterious Indian tribe. The treasure turns out to be a large cache of twenty-dollar bills. Cooper shows Ruhl the treasure when Ruhl arrives in Ghost Town, and the money proves to be counterfeit. "Bad boy" David Durand learns of the counterfeit money and tells Miller. Miller kidnaps Stanley, but Ruhl believes Stanley to be part of the gang. Cody is captured to pressure Stanley into cooperating and making new counterfeit plates. Cody escapes the gangsters but is captured by the mysterious Indians. Cooper rescues Cody. The counterfeiters take Stanley to a cabin. Vondell Darr, Stanley's daughter, finds the cabin but is captured. Ruhl, with Cooper's help, finds the cabin and takes Stanley and Darr to Ghost Town. In Ghost Town, Cooper is almost killed in a dynamite trap left by the gangsters to frighten the Indians. When Ruhl rushes to Cooper's aid, Stanley and Darr escape to find evidence that will prove Stanley innocent. Ruhl and Cody find Darr and Stanley. Due to Stanley's actions, Ruhl is beginning to believe he's innocent. Durand can prove Stanley's innocence, but Stanley cannot convince Durand to talk with Ruhl. The Indians capture Stanley and take him to their mountain cave. Cooper trails Stanley and the Indians, and leaves markers for Ruhl to follow. Cooper tries to free Stanley but is captured. Durand and two gangsters also follow Stanley and discover the cave has a supply of radium. Miller, in his plane, releases grenades to bring the Indians out of the cave. This gives Cooper and Stanley an opportunity to escape, with Ruhl's help. Ruhl and Stanley return to Ghost Town to destroy the counterfeiters' printing press. Gangsters, alerted by Durand, travel to Ghost Town, where a gun battle ensues between the G-Man and Stanley and the gangsters. In the woods, Durand and Cooper meet, and Cooper finally persuades Durand to come over to his side. Durand brings the Scouts, and Cooper gets ammunition to Ruhl just as he fires his last bullet. As the gangsters retreat, they kidnap Darr and take her to the mountain cabin. By a ruse, Cooper and Durand rescue Darr. Ruhl and G-Man Phelps arrive at the cabin and are attacked by Miller and his men. Cooper takes the gangsters' car and goes to Ghost Town to bring back more G-Men. The G-Men arrive in time, and the gang members are either captured or killed. Miller tries to escape in a car bur Cooper climbs aboard. The two fight and fall from the car just before it careens over a cliff. As Miller begins to gain the upper hand, Ruhl shows up to take Miller into custody. Durand joins the Boy Scouts.

NOTES AND COMMENTARY: Frank Coglan remarked about his role in *Scouts to the Rescue*, "I was Jackie Cooper's best buddy. What disappointed me in the credits, they didn't give me a picture in the original credits. They gave Sidney Miller one and all that. I couldn't control that."

When staying at the hotel near Bishop, California, some girls at the bar tried to attract the attention of Jackie Cooper, Sidney Miller and Frank Coglan. Coglan remembers, "We went back up to our room. They wanted to come up to see us. We had a suite. Jackie thought he was too old to live with his mother any more." Coglan made the excuse that they had an early call the next morning.

Frank Coglan and Jackie Cooper became best friends. Cooper remarked, "We used to go to his home and swim each Sunday with he and his mother. Except his stepfather became a kind of pain in the fanny. He was a good guy at one of the studios. He was cheating on Jackie's mother; we saw it, with the nurse. So I didn't respect him after that."

To add authenticity to the serial, newsreel footage from an actual Boy Scout Jamboree in Washington was used, and President Franklin D. Roosevelt can be seen. Also, Dr. James P. West, Chief Executive Director for the Boys Scouts, makes a few short remarks.

Vondell Darr was the victim of tragic circumstances about a year after the completion of *Scouts to the Rescue*. Walking near her home, Darr was struck on the head with a two-by-four by an unknown assailant and then raped on the sidewalk. This event ended Darr's career, one that began as a child star in the silent days.

The cliffhanger ending to Chapter Four turned out to be a harrowing experience for Jackie Cooper, Vondell Darr and Frank Coglan Jr. Traveling downstream in a canoe, the trio was to pull into a cove, but the current proved too strong and the canoe sped towards some fast-moving rapids. Coglan thought that by having everyone stay low in the canoe, they could ride out any danger. Passing close by a large rock, Cooper pushed the canoe away with his foot and the canoe capsized, throwing Cooper, Darr and Coglan into the water. Coglan made it to a large rock and grabbed Darr as she went past. Cooper was swept further downstream, about another hundred yards, before finally making it safely to shore. Crew members threw a rope to Coglan, and he and Darr were pulled to safety.

In 1939, a novelization of *Scouts to the Rescue* was published by Rand McNally as a children's book and a movie tie-in.

Look closely at a scene in Chapter 11. William Ruhl and Bill Cody, Jr. climb into the G-Men's car. An unknown object leans up against the running board, which wasn't there when the car pulled into the scene. As the car drives off, the object falls to the ground.

The scenes of rocks and boulders being dropped down the mountainside was lifted from *Sutter's Gold* (Universal, 1936). Footage of the stampeding wild horses in Chapters Eight and Nine had previously been seen in *Stormy* (Universal, 1935).

SUMMATION: *Scouts to the Rescue* is a good Universal serial, with the usual caveat: the cliffhanger resolutions allow Jackie Cooper and the other good guys to escape death too easily. Cooper gives a nice performance as the ideal Boy Scout and is properly heroic. David Durand matches Cooper as the bad boy who finally sees the light. Universal assembles a good supporting cast, with Edwin Stanley and William Ruhl the most impressive. Ray Taylor and Alan James direct briskly, and William Sickner photographs the beautiful vistas of Dardanelle Mountain to good advantage.

THE WHOLE CAST TALKS
The King of the Saddle
What a man! He outrode, outfought and outwitted one of the boldest bands that ever operated in wild old California—AND HOW! He'll keep you excited every minute he's on the screen in this smashing drama of adventure during one of the most colorful periods in American history. For downright entertainment, see and hear!

Senor Americano

Universal (November 1929); A Ken Maynard Production

CAST: Lieut. Michael Banning, **Ken Maynard**; Camelita De Acosta, **Kathryn Crawford**; Don Manuel de Acosta, **Frank Beale**; Carlos Ramirez, **Gino Corrado**; Manana, **Frank Ya**conelli; Maddox, **J.P. McGowan**; and "Tarzan"

CREDITS: Director, **Harry Joe Brown**; Producer, **Ken Maynard**; Story, **Helmer Bergman and Henry McCarty**; Screenwriters, **Bennett Ray Cohen and Lesley Mason**; Editors, **Fred Allen and Lesley Mason**; Cinematographer, **Ted McCord**

SONGS: "Estrellita" (Ponce)—sung by **Ken Maynard**

RUNNING TIME: 71 min.

STORY: Army officer Ken Maynard and his sidekick, Frank Yaconelli, sent to Southern California to investigate the lawless activity in the area, arrive at Frank Beals' ranch in time for a fiesta. Maynard and Gino Corrado quickly become rivals for the affections of Beals' daughter, Kathryn Crawford. Maynard bests Corrado in the various riding activities, winning the Golden Bridle, and is invited to the ranch that night. Maynard and Crawford begin to fall in love. J.P. McGowan is behind the outlawry, stealing grants to gain control of all the land in the area. Maynard receives a message to report to his commanding officer. McGowan sees Maynard leave the ranch and has him followed. The United States Congress has approved annexation of California as a territory, and Maynard is to carry the news to the citizens of Southern California. Upon Maynard's return, McGowen's men capture Maynard and steal the annexation proclamation. Tarzan frees Maynard, and Maynard races to Beals' ranch. At the ranch, McGowan accuses Maynard of being in league with the outlaws and has him arrested. Crawford finally believes in Maynard's innocence and learns that her father is in danger. Maynard tells her to ride for help. McGowan persuades Beals to let him hold onto the land grant for safekeeping, and then shows his true colors. Corrado realizes that McGowan had duped him, and the two men argue. Yaconelli frees Maynard. Maynard retrieves the grant and battles McGowan's men while Corrado holds McGowan at bay. Fighting valiantly, Maynard is finally overcome by the outlaws. Crawford arrives with help, and Corrado gets the drop on McGowan. Maynard and Crawford are now free to resume their romance.

NOTES AND COMMENTARY: *Senor Americano* was also released as a silent picture.

The theme song "Estrellita" was translated from the Spanish by George Gibson Davis, and was arranged by George P. Hulten.

REVIEWS: "The best of Maynard's part-talking westerns." (*The Western*, Hardy); "As a whole this film is about the best fare Ken Maynard has cooked and sure meat for western fans." (*Variety*, 1/1/30)

SUMMATION: *Senor Americano* is an exciting, well-paced western, with Maynard emulating, at times, the dashing Douglas Fairbanks. The performances of Maynard, Kathryn Crawford, Gino Corrado, Frank Yaconelli and J.P. McGowan are satisfactory. Director Harry Joe Brown makes the most of the action sequences.

She Ropes and Brands the Broadway Boys with Her Kiss-Behavin' Ways!

Senorita from the West

Universal (October 1945)

CAST: Phil Bradley, **Allan Jones**; Jeanne Blake, **Bonita Granville**; Tim Winters, **Jess Barker**; Cap, **George Cleveland**; Rosebud, **Fuzzy Knight**; Dusty, **Oscar O'Shea**; Williams Wylliams, **Renny McEvoy**; Justice of Peace; **Olin Howlin**; Kid, **Danny Mummert**; Elmer, **Bob Merrill**; Producer, **Emmett Vogan**; Taxi Driver, **Billy Nelson**; Motor Cop, **Jack Clifford**; **Spade Cooley and His Orchestra** (includes **Tex Williams**)// Moving Men, **Al Ferguson** and **Frank Hagney**; Roundup Café Patron, **Ralph Dunn**; Masseur, **Richard Alexander**; Doorman at Party, **Lane Chandler**

CREDITS: Director, **Frank Strayer**; Associate Producer, **Philip Cahn**; Screenwriter, **Howard Dimsdale**; Dialogue Director, **Stacy Keach**; Editor, **Paul Landres**; Art Directors, **John B. Goodman** and **Abraham Grossman**; Set Decorators, **Russell A. Gausman** and **Leigh Smith**; Cinematographer, **Paul Ivano**; Gowns, **Rosemary Odell**; Sound, **Bernard B. Brown** and **Robert Pritchard**; Musical Director, **Edgar Fairchild**

SONGS: "Am I in Love"—sung by **Allan Jones**; "These Hazy, Lazy Old Hills" (Blackburn and Huntly)— sung by **Bonita Granville**; "What a Change in the Weather" (Gannon and Kent)—sung by **Allan Jones and chorus**; "Blue Danube" (Strauss)— played by **Spade Cooley and His Orchestra**; "Ridin' Home" (McHugh and Adamson)—played by **Spade Cooley and His Orchestra**; "Lou Lou Louisana" (Carter and Rosen)— sung by **Bonita Granville with Spade Cooley and His Orchestra**; "Lonely Love" (Carter and R. Sinatra)—sung by **Allan Jones and chorus** and "All the Things I Wanna Say"—sung by **Bonita Granville and chorus**

RUNNING TIME: 63 min.

STORY: Unknown to Bonita Granville, her guardians, George Cleveland, Fuzzy Knight and Oscar O'Shea, have found gold and are millionaires. Granville runs away to New York to find fame as a singer but lands a job as an elevator operator at the Radio Center building. She meets two young men, Allan Jones and Jess Barker. Barker is the singing star of a radio program aimed at bobby soxers. In reality, Barker can't sing, and Jones provides the vocalizing since Jones is afraid of the actively avid young fans. Jones and Granville begin to fall in love. Barker becomes a rival for Granville's affections after he learns her guardians are millionaires, a fact of which Jones is unaware. Barker tries every dirty trick to discredit Jones and finally convinces Granville to elope. The guardians, who had aided Barker, learn that Barker is the phony and Jones is the right man for Granville. In a mad dash to Justice of the Peace

Olin Howlin's house, Jones arrives just in time to stop the marriage ceremony and claim Granville. Granville, who had begun to harbor doubts about Barker, is overjoyed.

NOTES AND COMMENTARY: The working title for this film was *Have a Heart*.

Bonita Granville is perhaps best remembered as Nancy Drew in four Warner Bros. entries (1938–39). Basically ending her screen career in 1949, she appeared in a Lassie television episode, a series she produced. Married to Jack Wrather, who produced the Lone Ranger television and radio programs, Granville took a co-starring role in the masked man's first feature length production, *The Lone Ranger* (Warner Bros., 1956).

Allan Jones enjoyed his greatest screen triumph as Jeannette MacDonald's leading man in *The Firefly* (Metro-Goldwyn-Mayer, 1937), in which he sang "The Donkey Serenade." *Senorita From the West* was the final picture for Jones under his Universal contract. Jones married actress Irene Hervey. They had a son, Jack, who became a popular recording star.

Character actor Olin Howlin was also billed as Olin Howland in a long screen career, which spanned forty years from 1918 until 1958. Howlin played in support of Bonita Granville in *Nancy Drew, Reporter* (Warner Bros., 1939), and was a regular on the television series *Circus Boy* (Screen Gems, 1956–58).

"Blue Danube" had previously been heard to good advantage, as it was danced and sung by Yvonne De Carlo in *Salome, Where She Danced*. "Riding Home" was utilized in *Desperate Trails* (Universal, 1939), *Road Agent* (Universal, 1941), *Tenting Tonight on the Old Camp Ground* (Universal, 1943) and *Strictly in the Groove* (Universal, 1943).

REVIEWS: "Pretty feeble romance." (*Variety*, 10/17/45); "Typically amusing and glossy Universal World War II product." (*Western Movies*, Pitts)

SUMMATION: *Senorita from the West* is a mediocre musical. Allan Jones and Bonita Granville are okay as the leads, but a subpar script and songs do them in. George Cleveland, Fuzzy Knight and Oscar O'Shea as Granville's guardians provide some comedy, but more is needed in this one. The best moments come courtesy of the specialty numbers by Spade Cooley and his orchestra.

Triple-Threat Trouble ... Ridin' the Range!

The Silver Bullet

Universal (April 1942)

CAST: "Silver Jim" Donovan, **Johnny Mack Brown**; Wild Bill Jones, **Fuzzy Knight**; Doctor Thad Morgan, **William Farnum**; Nancy Lee, **Jennifer Holt**; Walt Kincaid, **LeRoy Mason**; Rance Harris, **Rex Lease**; Queenie Leonard, **Grace Lenard**; Emily Morgan, **Claire Whitney**; Buck Dawson, **Charles "Slim" Whitaker**; Nevada Norton, **Michael Vallon**; Pete Sleen, **Merrill McCormick**; and **Pals of the Golden West** with **Nora Lou Martin**// Sheriff, **James Farley**; Coroner, **Lloyd Ingraham**; Townsman, **William Desmond**; Doc Winslow, **Harry Holman**; Wagon Driver, **George Plues**

CREDITS: Director, **Joseph H. Lewis**; Associate Director/ Story, **Oliver Drake**; Screenwriter, **Elizabeth Beecher**; Editor, **Maurice Wright**; Art Directors, **Jack Otterson** and **Ralph M. DeLacy**; Set Decorators, **R.A. Gausman** and **Ira Webb**; Cinematographer, **Charles Van Enger**; Sound, **Bernard B. Brown** and **Jess Moulin**; Musical Director, **H.J. Salter**

SONGS: "My Gal She Works in a Laundry" (O. Drake, Rosen and Wakely)—sung by **Fuzzy Knight**; "Little Sweetheart of the Rio Grande" (O. Drake, Rosen and Wakely)—sung by the **Pals of the Golden West with Nora Lou Martin**; "Vote for Emily Morgan" (O. Drake, Rosen and Wakely)—sung by **the Pals of the Golden West**; "Red River Valley" (traditional)—sung by **the Pals of the Golden West with Nora Lou Martin**; "Vote for Emily Morgan" (reprise)—sung by **the Pals of the Golden West with Nora Lou Martin**; and "Red River Valley" (reprise)—sung by the **Pals of the Golden West with Nora Lou Martin**.

LOCATION FILMING: Corriganville, California

RUNNING TIME: 56 min.

STORY: For five years Johnny Mack Brown has been searching for the man who murdered his father and shot a silver bullet into Brown's back. Brown wears the bullet, intent on some day to return it to the killer. Brown's journey brings him to Winchester, where businessman LeRoy Mason and doctor William Farnum are candidates for State Senator. Mason has the support of the large ranchers, while Farnum's support comes mainly from the small ranchers who hope to protect their water supply. Jennifer Holt, daughter of a large rancher, has thrown her support behind Mason. Mason is the man Brown has been seeking. Brown visits Farnum and asks if he has treated a man with a large, jagged, lightning-like scar on his left arm, and leaves a drawing of the scar. Mason, hoping to marry Holt if he's elected, asks Farnum if he can remove the scar. After hesitating for a moment, Farnum agrees to operate immediately. After the procedure, Mason notices the drawing on Farnum's desk and murders the doctor. When the drawing fails to materialize as evidence at the inquest, Brown knows the murderer lives in Winchester. Mason thinks he has the election won, but Brown suggests that Farnum's wife, Claire Whitney, run for the office. Whitney finds she has the women's support behind her (even Holt, who thinks Whitney will do a better job of protecting the rights of the small rancher). Brown gets his pal, Fuzzy Knight, and Holt to ride to the outlying ranches to remind folks to come in and vote. Mason's arm begins to trouble him, and he has doctor Harry Holman meet him at an out-of-the-way cabin and look at his arm. Holman removes the bandage, finds the scar intact, and tells Mason the scar cannot be removed. Knight, approaching the cabin to paste up an election poster, overhears everything and starts to leave to report to Brown. Mason's hirelings capture Knight and hold him captive in the cabin. Mason leaves to return to the polls, leaving Knight under guard. Holt, seeing Knight's horse, sneaks up to the cabin. Knight sees Holt and, through trickery, is able to tell her about Mason. One of the guards, Charles "Slim" Whittaker, spots Holt and gives chase. During the confusion, Knight makes his escape. Brown sees Whittaker chasing Holt and lassoes Whittaker from his horse. Holt tells Brown about Mason. Brown tells the townspeople Mason is the man he's been hunting. A gun battle erupts, with Mason the only member of his gang left alive. Mason summons the courage to meet Brown in a gun duel, but is no match for Brown. Whitney is elected State Senator, and Brown and Holt plan to marry.

NOTES AND COMMENTARY: With this film, Oliver Drake took over the reins of associate producer. Drake would write some of the screenplays and songs. Drake, also a director in his long career, would stay at Universal as associate producer for twenty entries, culminating with *Renegades of the Rio Grande* (Universal, 1945), a Rod Cameron western.

Fuzzy Knight is a would-be playwright in this film. One of the leading characters in his proposed play is the Wolverine Kid, a name from *Law of the Range* (Universal, 1941), with Johnny Mack Brown and Knight.

"Little Sweetheart of the Rio Grande" would be used in *The Old Chisholm Trail* (Universal, 1942) and *Riders of the Santa Fe* (Universal, 1944). The western favorite, "Red River Valley," saw service in *Sandflow* (Universal, 1937), *Law for Tombstone* (Universal, 1937) and *Stagecoach Buckaroo* (Universal, 1941). "Vote for Emily Morgan" later became "Vote for Cal Dixon" in *Rustler's Roundup* (Universal, 1946).

The Silver Bullet (Commodore, 1934) had previously been used as a title for a Tom Tyler western (though the plots were different).

REVIEWS: "Neat western with logical action and incidental songs." (*Variety*, 8/5/42); "The direction is taut and sharp, and that final confrontation is unforgettable." (*The Motion Picture Guide*, Nash and Ross)

SUMMATION: *The Silver Bullet* is a well-written, above average western. Johnny Mack Brown is perfect as a man of vengeance trying to return a silver bullet to the man who shot him in the back. LeRoy Mason is excellent as the man Brown seeks.

Mason's reactions as he realizes he's the only gang member left—first showing fear, and then the resolve to face Brown in a showdown—are masterful. Knight is good as a would-be playwright who throws in with Brown. Joseph H. Lewis' on-target direction allows humor to ease the tension at times, while still keeping his edgy manner, utilizing good camera effects to enhance the story.

GUNNING FOR HIS OWN BROTHER!
...for the kid who once saved his life and later died for him!

Silver Spurs

Universal (January 1936)

CAST: Jim Fentriss, **Buck Jones**; Janet Allison, **Muriel Evans**; Drag Harlan, **George Hayes**; Webb Allison, **J.P. McGowan**; Art Holden, **Robert Frazer**; Snell, **Wm. Lawrence**; Peggy Wyman, **Beth Marion**; Durango, **Earl Askam**; Yuma Kid, **Bruce Lane**; Dude, **Denny Meadows**; Station Agent, **Bob McKenzie**// "Silver"; Sheriff, **Kernan Cripps**

CREDITS: Director, **Ray Taylor**; Producer, **Buck Jones**; Story, **Charles Alden Seltzer**; Screenwriter, **Joseph Francis Poland**; Editor, **Bernard Loftus**; Art Director, **Ralph Berger**; Cinematographer, **Allen Thompson** and **Herbert Kirkpatrick**; Sound, **Buddy Myers**

LOCATION FILMING: Vasquez Rocks, Lasky Mesa and the Iverson Ranch, California

RUNNING TIME: 61 min.

STORY: Ranch owner J.P. McGowan's daughter, Muriel Evans, returns to Loma after a long stay in the east, to find the area overrun with rustlers, outlaws and gamblers. Waiting at the train station for her father, Evans receives unwelcome attention from Robert Frazier, known as "SilverSpurs." After the station receives a bank shipment, Frazier and William Lawrence steal the money and kill the bank employees. Foreman Buck Jones is sent to bring Evans to the ranch. Irked at having to wait, Evans fails to hit it off with Jones. Fearing that Frazer might have designs on Evans, Jones takes the long way to the ranch to make certain Evans arrives safely. Jones suspects Earl Askam, one of McGowan's cowhands, is in league with the rustlers and is trying to influence Bruce Lane to follow in his footsteps. Jones tries hard to convince

Lane not to ride with the outlaws, but is unsuccessful. George Hayes has been sent by the governor to bring in Frazer and makes his base at McGowan's ranch. Hayes locates Frazer's hideout on McGowan's ranch and tells McGowan that government men will bring Frazer to justice. Jones and Evans fall in love, and, while riding, see rustlers driving cattle to the outlaw hideout. Jones tells McGowan what he saw, but McGowan won't let Jones lead men to wipe out the rustlers. Waiting out on the range to meet Jones, Evans is kidnapped by Fraser. Evans has written one word, "SilverSpurs," on a rock to let Jones know what has happened to her. Frazer knows the note will bring Jones to his hideout, where he and Lawrence will wait in ambush. Hayes is finally ready to lead McGowan's men in a raid against the outlaw camp. Lane comes to the camp and learns what Frazer has in store for Jones. Lane reveals that he is Jones' brother, and he won't allow Jones to be killed. Frazer pretends to back down. Lane believes Frazer and turns his back, only to be shot down. Jones arrives and flushes Frazer into the open to be shot by Lawrence, mistaking him

Silver Spurs (1936) scene card: Buck Jones (*right*) engages in a brutal fight with Earl Askam. *Right border*, Buck Jones.

for Jones. Jones then dispatches Lawrence. Hayes and McGowan and the cowhands capture or kill the rest of the rustlers. Evans comforts a grieving Jones.

NOTES AND COMMENTARY: Denny Meadows, under the names Dennis Moore and Smokey Moore, would become a minor western star at PRC and Monogram, and a serial hero at Republic, Universal and Columbia.

The film's title on the screen is *Silverspurs* (one word), but the ads and promotional material list it as *Silver Spurs*.

REVIEWS: "It's low on two fisted action, but not a bad effort from the actors." (*The Motion Picture Guide*, Nash and Ross); "Above average western." (*Variety*, 4/1/36)

SUMMATION: *SilverSpurs* though slower paced than the usual Buck Jones western, *Silver Spurs* is none the less effective, thanks to good performances by Jones and Muriel Evans in the principal roles, and fine support by the rest of the cast. The action, when it comes, is sudden and violent. The film is thoughtfully directed by Ray Taylor.

RAW! RAWDY! RUTHLESS!
THE TOWN THAT TOOK 'EM ALL ... IN THE RECKLESS RACE FOR BLACK GOLD!
Fortunes made at the spin of a drill ... and lost at the spit of a gun!

Sin Town

Universal (September 1942)

CAST: Kye Allen, **Constance Bennett**; Dude McNair, **Broderick Crawford**; Wade Crowell, **Patric Knowles**; Laura Kirby, **Anne Gwynne**; Angelo Colina, **Leo Carrillo**; Judge Eusace Vale, **Andy Devine**; Rock Delaney, **Ward Bond**; Sheriff Bagby, **Arthur Aylesworth**; Kentucky Jones, **Ralf Harolde**; Dry Hole, **Charles Waggenheim**; Holister, **Billy Wayne**; Anderson, **Bryant Washburn**; Hansen, **Jack Mulhall**// Conductor, **Oscar O'Shea**; Porter, **Clarence Muse**; Old Timer, **Eddy Waller**; Lynch Mob Participants, **Frank Ellis** and **George J. Lewis**; Juggler, **Murray Parker**; Dance Hall Girls, **Rebel Randall** and **Jean Trent**; Mr. Carter, **Guy Usher**

CREDITS: Director, **Ray Enright**; Assistant Director, **Gil Valle**; Producer, **George Waggner**; Screenwriter, **W. Scott Darling** and **Gerald Geraghty**; Additional Dialogue, **Richard Brooks**; Dialogue Director, **Gene Lewis**; Editor, **Edward Curtiss**; Art Directors, **Jack Otterson** and **Harold H. MacArthur**; Set Decorators, **R.A. Gausman** and **A.J. Gilmore**; Cinematography, **George Robinson**; Gowns, **Vera West**; Sound, **Bernard B. Brown** and **Paul Neal**; Musical Director, **H.J. Salter**

RUNNING TIME: 74 min.

STORY: Conman Broderick

Crawford and his confederate, Constance Bennett, arrive in the Carson Town area with four oil leases purchased from Leo Carrillo for $17,000, after making Carrillo believe he was beholden to Crawford. It turns out that Carrillo was the better conman because the leases are worthless. Crawford and Bennett arrive in Carson Town in time to prevent the lynching of Ward Bond. Bond had killed the newspaper owner father of Anne Gwynne. Bond is placed in jail, awaiting trial. Because of Bond's influence over the sheriff and his deputy, jail is like an office and rooming house. Crawford talks Bond into giving him half ownership in his saloon. Bond was planning to offer Crawford the same proposition. Bond would be able to commit crimes while having the iron clad alibi of being locked in jail. Crawford falls in love with Gwynne, who is in love with wildcat oilman Patric Knowles. Crawford starts a protection agency for all the saloon owners, but Ralf Harolde refuses to join. Afterwards, his establishment is dynamited. Bond has options on all leases around Knowles' property. Having inside knowledge that Knowles will bring in a gusher, Bond wants drilling stopped on Knowles' well until Bond can pick up those options. Crawford sends for conman Andy Devine to get him to purchase a half interest in Gwynne's newspaper. This would allow him to put pressure on Gwynne to stop editorial attacks on the saloons and gambling houses. Knowing Knowles needs money to continue drilling, Bond sends for Carrillo to purchase an interest in Knowles' oil well. Knowles turns Carrillo down, as Bennett has provided monetary assistance. Bond sends men to stop Knowles from drilling, and they drop a shell into the well. The shell explodes, and water gushes to the surface. The townsmen turn angry and plan to lynch both Crawford and Bond. Devine knows it's time to leave, and Carrillo goes with him. Harolde hides in Crawford's office with plans to shoot him. Bond leaves jail and comes to the saloon to retrieve money and the oil leases. Harolde overhears how Crawford has been duped and that Bond is responsible for the lawlessness. Crawford engages Bond in a tough, brutal fight, which Bond wins. As Bond starts to leave, Harolde shoots him. The mob grabs Crawford, but Harolde intercedes. Crawford is told to leave town. On the train, he's joined by Bennett, who has seventeen thousand dollars—Devine persuaded Carrillo to return the money.

NOTES AND COMMENTARY: *Sin Town* was originally scheduled as a starring vehicle for Marlene Dietrich. Robert Stack was to have played the romantic lead opposite Anne Gwynne, but he turned the part down because his role was secondary to Constance Bennett and Broderick Crawford's. The script was rewritten, and Stack initially gave his approval but then changed his mind. The studio put Stack on suspension and assigned Patric Knowles to the part.

After *Sin Town*, Broderick Crawford would leave western features until resurfacing in *Bad Men of*

Tombstone (Allied Artists, 1949). 1949 was a good year for Crawford, who won a Best Actor Academy Award for his outstanding performance as Willie Stark in *All the King's Men* (Columbia, 1949). Crawford is perhaps best known as Lt. Dan Mathews in the syndicated TV series *Highway Patrol* (1955–59).

REVIEWS: "*Sin Town* proceeds to provide plenty of adventure entertainment." (*Variety*, 9/30/42); "*Sin Town* is directed with vigor, and the result is an entertaining little package." (*The Motion Picture Guide*, Nash and Ross)

SUMMATION: *Sin Town* is a slightly above average action melodrama. Broderick Crawford and Ward Bond make fine antagonists, who finally end up battling each other in an impressive knockdown, drag-out fistfight. Constance Bennett is okay, but the script fails to give her much screen time. The action is adequate, but the story suffers by making Crawford's character totally unlikable. There's the rub: what redeeming quality does Bennett see in Crawford? Ray Enright's direction keeps the story moving, so some holes in the screenplay are quickly passed over.

HE WROTE SIX-SHOOTER LAW AND SET IT TO MUSIC!

The Singing Outlaw

Universal (January 1938)

CAST: Scrap Gordon, **Bob Baker**; Joan McClain, **Joan Barclay**; Longhorn, **Fuzzy Knight**; Cueball Quayley, **Harry Woods**; Sheriff Haight, **Carl Stockdale**; Teton Joe, **LeRoy Mason**; Colonel, **Robert Card**; Sheriff, **Ed Piel**; Deputy Ed, **Glenn Strange**// Jim, **Budd Buster**; Groom, **Ralph Lewis**; Cowhand, **Art Mix**; Marshal Sam Fairfax, **Jack Montgomery**; Deputy Pete, **Jack Kirk**; Lucy Harris, **Georgia O'Dell**; Horseshoe Jim, **Robert McKenzie**; Deputy, **Jack Rockwell**; Wedding Guest, **Lafe McKee**

CREDITS: Director, **Joseph H. Lewis**; Assistant Director, **Glenn Cook**; Story/Screenwriter, **Harry O. Hoyt**; Editor, **Charles Craft**; Art Director, **Charles Clague**; Cinematographer, **Virgil Miller**; Sound, **Robert Pritchard** and **Jesse Bastian**; Musical Director and Arranger, **Frank Sanucci**

SONGS: "Branding Days"—sung by **Bob Baker**; "When the Roundup Days Are Over"—sung by **Bob Baker** and **male chorus**; "When the Roundup Days Are Over" (reprise)—sung by **Bob Baker**; "There's a Ring Around the Moon" (Allan)—sung by **Bob Baker and chorus**; and "I'm a Young Cowboy"—sung by **Bob Baker**

LOCATION FILMING: Kernville, California

RUNNING TIME: 57 min.

STORY: Bob Baker rides to Wyoming to buy a small ranch and marry Joan Barclay. Harry Woods, the Singing Bandit, has just held up a train and is being tracked by U.S. Marshal Jack Montgomery. After shooting Montgomery in the back, Woods spots Baker; and when he draws near, orders him to stop. Baker fires and jumps from his horse. Woods and Baker fight, first with guns and then with fists, with Woods the winner. Woods plans to impersonate the marshal and bring Baker in as the train robber. As Woods prepares to shoot Baker, Montgomery revives long enough to shoot Woods before he dies. Baker takes the marshal's identification and believes somehow he killed Woods. Arriving at his destination, Sheriff Carl Stockdale takes Baker for the marshal. Baker decides to impersonate the train robber and infiltrate the gang terrorizing the area. Stockdale is not certain of Baker and decides to trail him. One of the deputies finds a loose horse with Montgomery's papers and learns that Baker is not a marshal. Stockdale arrests Baker and places him in a jail cell next to bandit leader LeRoy Mason, who was arrested on a minor charge. Baker tells Mason he knows where they can get ten thousand dollars. This is the money Baker had saved to buy a ranch, and is hidden at Barclay's ranch. Mason's men break Mason and Baker out of jail. Baker rides to the Barclay ranch, followed by two deputies and Mason and his men. Mason lays siege to the ranch house, killing the two deputies. Baker then tricks Mason into bringing his men into the house, where he gets the drop on the gang. Stockdale arrives with a posse and takes the gang to jail. Baker's pal, Fuzzy Knight, brings proof that Woods and Montgomery shot each other. Baker and Barclay plan to buy a ranch and get married.

NOTES AND COMMENTARY: Fuzzy Knight plays a humorous scene at the end of the picture: seeing Bob Baker hesitate to kiss Joan Barclay, Knight says, "If you ain't going to kiss her, I will." And Knight does—twice.

The working title of *The Singing Outlaw* was *Renegade Wranglers*.

REVIEWS: "Vocal ability of Bob Baker is worked into the story, along with an atmosphere of action and unusual camera work." (*Variety*, 12/29/37); "A routine plot that is helped somewhat by good direction and exceptional photography." (*The Motion Picture Guide*, Nash and Ross)

SUMMATION: *The Singing Outlaw* is only an average western, with an overly complicated story and some plot discrepancies (e.g. why didn't Harry Woods just ambush Bob Baker when he'd just shot Jack Montgomery in the back?). Baker handles the role adequately, but it's a shame Baker had to lose his first screen fight. The villainy is minor; Woods is dispatched quickly and LeRoy Mason doesn't have enough screen time to make much of an impact. Fuzzy Knight, with basically a character part again, is the best actor in this one. Director Joseph H. Lewis directs competently and utilizes innovative camera angles, but the sub-par script does this feature in.

It Takes a CROSBY *to Tame the Old West... By Song*

The Singing Sheriff

Universal (October 1944)

CAST: Bob Richards, **Bob Crosby**; Caroline, **Fay McKenzie**; Fuzzy, **Fuzzy Knight**; Lefty, **Iris Adrian**; Seth, **Samuel S. Hinds**; Vance, **Edward Norris**; Jonas, **Andrew Tombes**; Squint, **Joe Sawyer**; Butch, **Walter Sande**; Ivory, **Doodles Weaver**; Dancers, **Pat Starling** and **Louis DaPron**; Spade Cooley and his Orchestra (includes **Deuce Spriggins, Tex Williams** and **Carolina Cotton**)// Outlaws, **Rex Lease, Ethan Laidlaw** and **Pierce Lyden**; Bus Station Manager, **Bob McKenzie**; Bailiff, **Syd Saylor**; Nurse, **Jean Trent**; Assistant Stage Manager, **Donald Kerr**

CREDITS: Director, **Leslie Goodwins**; Producer, **Bernard W. Burton**; Story, **John Grey**; Screenwriters, **Henry Blankfort** and **Eugene Conrad**; Editor, **Edward Curtiss**; Art Director, **John B. Goodman** and **Abraham Grossman**; Set Decorators, **Russell A. Gausman** and **Leigh Smith**; Cinematographer, **Charles Van Enger**; Gowns, **Vera West**; Sound, **Bernard B. Brown** and **Robert Pritchard**; Musical Director, **Sam Freed, Jr.**

SONGS: "Who's Next" (Wicks and Lava)—sung by **Iris Adrian**; "Reach for the Sky" (James and Miller)—sung by **Bob Crosby and Female Chorus**; "When a Cowboy Sings" (Franklin)—sung by **Bob Crosby**; "You Look Good to Me" (James and Miller)—sung by **Iris Adrian and Fuzzy Knight**; "Reach for the Sky" (reprise)—by **Bob Crosby**; "Ida Red" (traditional)—sung by **Deuce Spriggins, Tex Williams** and **Carolina Cotton** with **Space Cooley and His Orchestra**; "Whispering" (Coburn)—danced by **Pat Starling** and **Louis DaPron** with **Spade Cooley and His Orchestra**; "Who Broke the Lock" (traditional)—sung by **Deuce Spriggins** with **Spade Cooley and His Orchestra**; "Another Night" (George and Bibo)—sung by **Bob Crosby**; "Story of a Bad Man of the West"—sung by **Bob Crosby, Fuzzy Knight, Iris Adrian** and **chorus**.

LOCATION FILMING: Corriganville, California

RUNNING TIME: 60 min.

STORY: As sheriff Samuel S. Hinds is about to arrest Joe Sawyer for murder, he is wounded by one of Sawyer's underlings. Hinds asks Deputy Fuzzy Knight to send for his son, Walter Sande, who he has not seen since childhood. Sande had sent a picture of his pal, singing star Bob Crosby in a cowboy outfit, as himself. When Sande becomes ill, he asks Crosby to pose as Hinds' son. Hinds makes Crosby a Deputy Sheriff of Elbow Bend. Crosby agrees because he has fallen for Sande's sister, Fay McKenzie. Lawyer Edward Norris is courting McKenzie. An immediate jealousy arises between Crosby and Norris. Crosby gives Sawyer and his gang 24 hours to get out of town. Sawyer makes an attempt on Crosby's life, and Crosby decides to leave town before he gets killed. Sawyer's men are robbing the bus station when Crosby arrives. Crosby, accidentally, foils the robbery; and Knight and a posse round up the robbers. Upon leaving Hinds' ranch, Crosby left a note stating that he's not Hinds' son. McKenzie reads the note before Crosby can return and destroy it, having decided to stay and stop the lawlessness. Crosby discovers Norris is the real leader of the gang, and he can have Norris and his gang put away for murder if the body can be uncovered. Sawyer makes another attempt on Crosby's life but fails and is captured. Using a ruse, Knight finds the body. Sawyer implicates Norris, who tries to escape but runs into Sande and is captured. Sande, recovered from his illness, returned to Elbow Bend to reunite himself with Hinds. Crosby and McKenzie decide to get together.

NOTES AND COMMENTARY: When Edward Norris was making *The Singing Sheriff*, he was invited to a party. One of the guests, a former Russian nobleman, brought his '37 Jaguar, which was robins-egg blue with leather interior. Norris was impressed and stopped to look at the automobile. The nobleman wanted to sell the vehicle to Norris. The nobleman asked Norris if he was working. Norris replied he was working at Universal. The nobleman suggested Norris take the car to the studio to see how he liked it and gave him the keys. Norris recalled, "I was tempted and I took it to work. Right next to the sound stage I was on, was a western. All the cowboys saw this car. My leading lady (Fay McKenzie) and I were going to have lunch. I would take her in the car and we would go out. Filled right to the top of the doors was horse dung. I looked around and said, 'We can't take this.' So we had lunch and I came back in. I said, 'What in the world has happened here.' Everybody thought it was very funny, except me. I either had to buy this car or turn it back. So I had it cleaned. There were stains on that white leather. I had to redo that. That was five hundred bucks. In those days, that was a lot of money. That was a week's salary for me. I had to give it back."

Commenting on Bob Crosby, Edward Norris said, "Bing Crosby's brother, Bob, had a band. He was playing the lead. He was a bad actor, no good. He was always late. When you were looking for him, he was always on the phone talking to his bookie. He was making bets on the horses. One time I had an argument with him. I said, 'You'd better stay in the band because you're not going to make it in the picture business.' He said, 'Why not?' I said, 'We have to spend so much time looking for you. Every time you should be on the set, you're in the rest room or some place. You have to have a leash put on you.' Everybody thought that was funny."

Fay McKenzie didn't have many memories of *The Singing Sheriff*, but did recall one of the cast members: "There was a funny little character actress, Iris Adrian, in that. She became a really close friend of my older sister [Ida Mae McKenzie]. She was a riot. She was doing a lot of gangster movies in those days. I remember she did a number. The choreographer was Louis DaPron. In the early days, they were called 'dance directors.' Then the Director's Guild didn't want anybody else to be a director, so they had to be 'choreographers.'"

Carolina Cotton came to Hollywood to appear in the motion picture *Sing, Neighbor, Sing* (Republic, 1944). When she arrived, Cotton looked up entertainer and songwriter Johnny Marvin. Marvin was performing at the Hollywood Canteen, where he introduced her to bandleader Spade Cooley. Cooley needed a girl singer and hired Cotton. Cooley had been hired to appear with his orchestra in *Singing Sheriff*. Cotton has an eight-bar yodel solo in the song "Ida Red."

"Who Broke the Lock" was featured in the short film *Swingin' in the Barn* (Universal, 1940).

REVIEWS: "This is an unorthodox B western. Clearly intended as a satire on things western, it works best as a straight comedy." (*The Western*, Hardy); "A fair comedy for the duals." (*Variety*, 9/3/44)

SUMMATION: *The Singing Sheriff* is an amusing musical comedy western. Bob Crosby deftly handles the lead, both in song and dialogue delivery. Faye McKenzie makes an attractive heroine. Fuzzy Knight steals the show by taking care of the funny business in fine style. The songs are catchy and well performed by all concerned. Leslie Goodwins directs capably.

HE WAS BLAZING T.N.T. ON A DYNAMITE HORSE!
Rustlers fled the range when his whip-draw cracked down on them!

Smoke Tree Range

Universal (June 1937); A Buck Jones Production

CAST: Lee Cary, **Buck Jones**; Nan Page, **Muriel Evans**; Jim Cary, **John Elliott**; Teddy Page, **Dickie Jones**; Wirt Stoner, **Donald Kirke**; Gil Hawkins, **Ted Adams**; Pete, **Ben Hall**; Ma Kelly, **Mabel Colcord**; Sheriff Day, **Earle Hodgins**; Paso Wells, **Bob Kortman**; Sandy, **Edmund Cobb**; Sandy's Friend, **Eddie Phillips**; Dick, **Bob McKenzie**; Ferguson, **Slim Whitaker;** and "Silver Jr."// Pio, **Martin Garralaga**; Ranchers, **Charles King** and **Lee Phelps**; Outlaw, **Jim Corey**

CREDITS: Director, **Lesley Selander**; Story, **Arthur Henry Gooden**; Screenwriter, **Frances Guihan**; Editor, **Bernard Loftus**; Art Directors, **Ralph Berger** and **Frank Smith**; Cinematographers, **Allen Thompson** and **William Sickner**; Sound Supervisor, **L. John Myers**

LOCATION FILMING: Vasquez Rocks, Mojave Desert, California

RUNNING TIME: 59 min.

STORY: Muriel Evans and her brother, Dickie Jones, inherit land that the Smoke Tree Ranch has been using to graze their cattle. Evans and Buck Jones meet and begin to like each other until she sees Smoke Tree on his saddle, for she has received a note from Smoke Tree telling her to vacate her property. Smoke Tree foreman Ted Adams is working with saloon owner Donald Kirke to rustle cattle in the area. Smoke Tree owner John Elliott, thinking the occupants of Evans' ranch are squatters, sends Adams to evict Evans. B. Jones, Elliott's grandson, tries to tell Elliott that he can't control all the open range, and then stops Adams from evicting Evans. Kirke plans to gain possession of Evans' ranch and get rid of B. Jones and Elliott. Kirke has Evans and D. Jones kidnapped. B. Jones and Smoke Tree ranch hands begin to search for Evans and D. Jones. D. Jones frees Evans and himself from the isolated cabin that was their prison. Taking horses from their captors, Evans and D. Jones ride for safety but are spotted by hired gunman Robert Kortman and the rustlers. B. Jones spots the chase and joins Evans and D. Jones. B. Jones sends them to a hideout while he leads the outlaws away from them. When the outlaws pass, Evans and D. Jones ride for their ranch. B. Jones holes up in some rocks and starts a gunfight with the outlaws. At her ranch, Evans finds Elliott and tells Elliott his grandson is in trouble. Elliott and his men ride to the rescue and rout the rustlers. In the battle, Kortman is mortally wounded, but before he dies he identifies Kirke as the outlaw leader. B. Jones and Elliott ride to town and confront Kirke in his saloon. Unable to escape, Kirke fires at the two men and is cut down by bullets from B. Jones and Elliott. Elliott tells B. Jones that Evans begged him to come to his rescue. That's all Jones needs to send him to Evans' ranch.

NOTES AND COMMENTARY: Dickie Jones professes having no memories of working in the films he appeared as a child actor. He said he was too busy playing and having fun when not on camera. Jones just did his scenes and then went back to playing.

REVIEWS: "Better than usual Buck Jones western, filled with action." (*Variety*, 6/9/37); "Fine two-fisted action." (*The Motion Picture Guide*, Nash and Ross)

SUMMATION: *Smoke Tree Range* is a top flight "B" western, combining good characterization with some first rate action. Buck Jones is perfect as a cowhand who wants peace but is not afraid to take a stand. Muriel Evans handles the leading lady part well and shows the proper emotions. John Elliott plays the crusty ranch owner with a soft heart to a tee. Donald Kirke, Robert Kortman, Slim Whitaker and Ted Adams are capable villains. Adams impresses as a man who is tough but can be afraid of someone tougher. Lesley Selander directs firmly, utilizing the scenic backgrounds to great advantage while bringing a good story to the screen.

*A Smashing Western Crammed with Action, Drama and Mystery!
Fighting Ken Maynard in a Story Written by Himself*

Smoking Guns

Universal (June 1934); A Ken Maynard Production

CAST: Ken Masters, **Ken Maynard**; Alice Adams, **Gloria Shea**; Dick Evans, **Walter Miller**; Hank Stone, **Harold Goodwin**; Silas Stone, **William Gould**; Biff, **Bob Kortman**; Captain Adams, **Jack Rockwell**; Bob Masters, **Ed Coxen**; Slim, **"Slim" Whitaker**; Cinders, **Martin Turner**; Clementine, **Etta McDaniel;** and **"Tarzan, the Wonder Horse"**// Host at Dance, **Horace B. Carpenter**; Outlaws, **Hank Bell**, **Edmund Cobb**, **Jim Corey** and **Wally Wales**

CREDITS: Director, **Alan James**; Story, **Ken Maynard**; Screenwriter, **Nate Gatzert**; Editor, **Charles Harris**; Art Director, **Ralph Berger**; Cinematographer, **Ted McCord**; Sound Supervisor, **Earl Crain**

LOCATION FILMING: Bronson Canyon and Walker Ranch, California, and South America

RUNNING TIME: 62 min.

STORY: Ken Maynard accuses William Gould of framing his father, and Maynard declares he'll get the truth. Gould and Maynard fight; and in the struggle, Gould's son, Harold Goodwin, kills Gould and places the blame on Maynard. Maynard has been on the run and finally finds refuge in the swampland. Ranger Walter Miller tracks Maynard down and takes him prisoner. Maynard is happy to return and clear himself. Maynard could never find any trace of his father, or that he had ever served time in the penitentiary. As the two men return to civilization, Miller first succumbs to malaria and then is mauled by a crocodile. Gangrene sets in, and Maynard prepares to amputate Miller's leg. Miller writes a letter to his girl, Gloria Shea, and then commits suicide. Because of the striking resemblance between the two men, Maynard decides to impersonate Miller. Shea realizes that Maynard is not the man she loves, but after reading Miller's letter to her, begins to like Maynard and decides to help him. Goodwin is a rival for Shea's affections; and when he comes to escort her to a dance, he meets Maynard. Goodwin recognizes Maynard as the man he framed for his father's murder. Maynard gets word that his father, Ed Coxen, is alive in his old house. Coxen had found gold under the house and has been held prisoner by Goodwin and his partner, Slim Whitaker. Maynard goes to the house and rescues Coxen. Hearing that Maynard is in the house, Goodwin and his men ride there to take care of Maynard. Shea, knowing that Maynard is up against long odds, rides to the ranger station for help. Goodwin and his men corner Maynard. The rangers show up and take all the outlaws prisoner, except Goodwin. Shea has driven up to the house in a

Smoking Guns (1934) scene card: Walter Miller (*left*) and Ken Maynard in a jungle swampland. *Left border*, Ken Maynard.

wagon to make certain Maynard is unharmed. Goodwin takes control of the wagon as he tries to make his escape. Maynard pursues Goodwin, and, after rescuing Shea, jumps to the wagon and battles Goodwin. Maynard whips Goodwin in a brutal fistfight and brings him to justice. Maynard and Shea have fallen in love.

NOTES AND COMMENTARY: *Smoking Guns* was Ken Maynard's final film for Universal. Producer Sid Rogell wanted Maynard to reshoot several sequences in an attempt to make a better feature. Maynard refused. Universal president Carl Laemmle berated Maynard for making a bad picture and wanted Maynard to make changes. Maynard decided he'd quit first. Behind the scenes, Carl Laemmle, Jr. wanted Maynard out. The two men continually clashed over budgetary matters. Maynard's films consistently ran over ninety thousand dollars. In contrast, Buck Jones' films at Columbia were produced with budgets between twenty-five and thirty thousand. The bottom line was that Laemmle Sr. wanted Jones to star in westerns at Universal, and wanted to reduce the production costs. Maynard left Universal to make a feature, *In Old Santa Fe*, and a serial, *Mystery Mountain*, for Mascot for 1934 release. Jones became Universal's new cowboy star.

Between films, Ken Maynard flew to South America to hunt crocodiles. Maynard took home movies and wanted to use the footage in his next film. So the script was written to accommodate Maynard. Additionally, Maynard could now charge off the travel expense to the film's budget.

REVIEWS: "Actually rather fun if taken tongue-in-cheek." (*Western Movies*, Pitts); "An unusually bad western." (*Variety*, 8/14/34)

SUMMATION: *Smoking Guns* is only an average western, which is below par for Ken Maynard's second Universal series. The movie seems thrown together in the hopes that it would ultimately make sense. The script asks us to believe that Maynard could impersonate Walter Miller, with no one being the wiser. In fairness, Miller is only seen with a heavy beard. There are a lot of holes in the script during the South America sequence. For example, who took care of Tarzan while Miller was tracking down Maynard, and why did Miller abandon his canoe when he could have still used it? On Maynard's return to the town where he's wanted for murder, it's too easy for Maynard to clear things up. Maynard's screenplay doesn't have a definite flow, and that damages the storyline. Maynard and Miller's acting is not up to the demands of the script. Only Gloria Shea distinguishes herself. The film does have a certain "old dark house" atmosphere, however, and that makes it worth viewing.

SIX-GUNS BARK THEIR FURY!
...A blast of dynamite action ... as a dauntless daredevil rides the range for revenge!

Son of Roaring Dan

Universal (July 1940)

CAST: Jim Reardon, **Johnny Mack Brown**; Tick Belden, **Fuzzy Knight**; Jane Belden, **Nell O'Day**; Eris Brooke, **Jeanne Kelly**; Dan McPhail, **Robert Homans**; Stuart Manning, **Tom Chatterton**; Thorndyke, **John Eldredge**; Matt Gregg, **Ethan Laidlaw**; Brooks, **Lafe McKee**; Big Taylor, **Dick Alexander**; Charlie, **Eddie Polo**; Steve, **John Beach**; Tom, **Jack Shannon** and The Texas Rangers (**Robert "Captain Bob" Crawford, Edward "Tookie" Cronenbold, Francis "Irish" Mahaney** and **Roderic "Dave" May**)// Casey Waters, **Ralph Peters**; Judge, **Lloyd Ingraham**

CREDITS: Director, **Ford Beebe**; Associate Producer, **Joseph Sanford**; Screenwriter, **Clarence Upson Young**; Editor, **Paul Landres**; Cinematographer, **William Sickner**; Musical Director, **H.J. Salter**

SONGS: "Yippi-Ki-Yea"—sung by **the Texas Rangers**; "And Then I Got Married" (Carter and Rosen)—sung by **the Texas Rangers;** and "Let 'Er Buck, Powder River"—sung by **the Texas Rangers**

LOCATION FILMING: Morrison Ranch, California

RUNNING TIME: 63 min.

STORY: Johnny Mack Brown comes to town in the guise of Robert Homan's son to bring to justice John Eldredge, his father's murderer. Eldredge is behind the lawless activity in the area and an avowed enemy of Homans. Jeanne Kelly is an eyewitness to the murder of one of Homans' cowhands. Eldredge's second attempt to kidnap Kelly to prevent her testifying in court is successful. By a ruse, Brown rescues Kelly and gets her to court in time. Seeing that everything is lost, Eldredge empties his safe and attempts to make a getaway. Brown reaches Eldredge's office in time and bests him

Son of Roaring Dan (1940) scene card: As they prepare to make their getaway, Ethan Laidlaw (*left*) holds a gun on Johnny Mack Brown (*second left*) and Jeanne Kelly (*behind Brown*); John Eldredge (*third right*) holds a gun on the courtroom spectators; and an unidentified actor (*far right*) covers (*left to right*) unidentified actor, Fuzzy Knight, Tom Chatterton, Lloyd Ingraham and Chuck Morrison. Note: Chuck Morrison is not in the scene in the actual film.

in a rugged fistfight. Brown and Kelly plan to marry.

NOTES AND COMMENTARY: Joseph Sanford would gain greater fame as Joseph Gershenson, who would take charge of the Music Department at Universal.

Fred Graham doubled Johnny Mack Brown in the climactic fight with John Eldredge and Ethan Laidlaw.

"And Then I Got Married" would be sung by Fuzzy Knight in *Bad Men of the Border* (Universal, 1945).

Jeanne Kelly's character name in the credits is Brooke, but she's called Brooks in the film.

Jeanne Kelly would also be known as Jean Brooks in her screen career.

REVIEWS: "The story moves along very well to a stunning fist fight between Brown and crook Eldredge." (*The Motion Picture Guide*, Nash and Ross); "Well-tuned western, story moves at a good pace, is well plotted and considerable action is provided." (*Variety*, 8/14/40)

AUTHOR'S COMMENTS: *Son of Roaring Dan* is a top flight "B" western. Johnny Mack Brown is at his best, handling both action and dramatic scenes capably. Fuzzy Knight is a decided asset as Brown's sidekick. Knight's comedy in this film is funny without insulting the audience's intelligence. Nell O'Day, Jeanne Kelly, Robert Homans and John Eldredge head a first-rate supporting cast. Ford Beebe's direction is on the mark, as is the screenplay by Clarence Upson Young.

Flashing Sword Play and Dashing Action Interwoven with Charming Romance and THREE GREAT SONG HITS

Song of the Caballero

Universal (June 1930)

CAST: Juan, **Ken Maynard**; Anita, **Doris Hill**; Don Pedro, **Francis Ford**; Don Jose, **Gino Corrado**; Dona Louisa, **Evelyn Sherman**; Manuel, **Josef Swickard**; Andrea, Frank Rice; Bernardo, **William Irving**; Conchita, **Joyzelle**; and "Tarzan"

CREDITS: Director, **Harry J. Brown**; Assistant Director, **Mack V. Wright**; Story, **Kenneth C. Beaton** and **Norman Sper**; Screenwriters, **Bennett Cohen** and **Lesley Mason**; Editor, **Fred Allen**; Production Manager, **Sid Rogell**; Cinematography, **Ted McCord**; Recording Supervisor, **C. Roy Hunter**; Synchronization and Sound, **David Broekman**

SONGS: "Mi Caballero" (Seitman and Perry)

LOCATION FILMING: Walker and Monogram Ranches, California

RUNNING TIME: 72 min.

STORY: After receiving a delivery of gold, Gino Corrado is robbed by

Ken Maynard, a bandit who only steals from Corrado's family. Corrado and his men chase Maynard but the outlaw easily eludes the pursuers and returns to the cantina Corrado patronizes. Maynard strikes up an acquaintance with Joyzelle, Corrado's girlfriend. Joyzelle figures out that Maynard is the bandit who robbed Corrado. Doris Hill is traveling by stagecoach to marry Corrado. The coach stops at a vagabond camp, where Maynard is resting. Frank Rice, Maynard's sidekick, starts a run-a-way so he can kidnap Hill and bring her to Maynard. Maynard stops the coach and begins to get acquainted with Hill. As a reward, Francis Ford, Corrado's father, invites Maynard and Rice to the fiesta celebrating the betrothal of Corrado and Hill. Corrado intends to continue his romance with Joyzelle after his marriage to Hill. At the fiesta, Joyzelle tells Corrado that Maynard is the bandit. Corrado intends to capture Maynard immediately, but Ford interferes, telling Corrado that since Maynard is his guest, no harm can come to him until he leaves the rancho's gates. Hill sees Corrado kissing Joyzelle. Corrado begins to force himself on Hill but ceases at Maynard's interference. Hill, even though she has fallen in love with Maynard, intends to honor the marriage contract arranged by her father. Maynard victimizes Ford's household because Ford wronged his sister, Maynard's mother. Maynard leaves the hacienda but returns to rescue Hill from Corrado. Corrado learns of Maynard's return and, with his men, tries to capture him. Maynard's superior swordplay almost saves him, but Maynard is finally disarmed. Corrado is about to kill Maynard when Ford intervenes. Ford tells Maynard that he tried to find his mother; despite Maynard's bitterness, Ford lets him go free. As Maynard prepares to leave, he sees Ford's sincerity, and the men plan to work out their differences. Ford, knowing that Maynard and Hill are in love, gives them his blessing to marry.

NOTES AND COMMENTARY: The run-a-way coach scene would be used in Buck Jones' serial *The Red Rider* (Universal, 1934).

REVIEWS: "Okay Ken Maynard early talkie." (*Western Movies*, Pitts); "Fairly entertaining." (*Variety*, 7/9/30)

SUMMATION: *Song of the Caballero* is a poor Ken Maynard vehicle. Rousing swordplay at the finale can't compensate for the stilted dialogue and stilted acting. Even veteran Francis Ford cannot overcome the lines handed him, and Maynard looks very uncomfortable with his dialogue. Maynard is in fine form when in action, but, unfortunately, the action scenes are overshadowed by the dramatics. Maynard says it best when he states, "Have an end to words." Too bad that's said at the picture's end. The viewer gets the impression, during the dramatic scenes, that this is a filmed stageplay instead of a moving picture.

Hard Riding!
Fierce Fighting!
Roaring Romance!

Sons of the Saddle

Universal (August 1930)

CAST: Jim Brandon, **Ken Maynard**; Ronnie Stavnow, **Doris Hill**; Martin Stavnow, **Joseph Girard**; Harvey, **Carroll Nye**; "Red" Slade, **Francis Ford**; "Pop" Higgins, **Harry Todd**; and "**Tarzan**"

CREDITS: Director, **Harry J. Brown**, Story, **Bennett Cohen**; Screenwriters, **Bennett Cohen and Lesley Mason**; Editor, **Fred Allen**; Cinematographer, **Ted McCord**; Recording Engineer, **C. Roy Hunter**

SONGS: "Down the Home Trail With You" (Grossman and Handman)—sung by **Ken Maynard**; and "Trail Herd Song"—sung by **Ken Maynard**

RUNNING TIME: 76 min.

STORY: Ken Maynard, foreman of Joseph Girard's ranch, loves Doris Hill, Girard's daughter. Cowhand Carroll Nye also loves Hill, unknown to Maynard. Maynard is like an older brother to Nye, and he asks Nye to speak to Hill for him. Nye speaks for himself and is spurned by Hill. Upset, Nye decides to join Francis Ford's outlaw gang. Ford plans to raid Girard's ranch and rustle the herd. In the melee, Maynard tries, by force, to take Nye away from the gang. Maynard is unsuccessful; and in the raid, Nye is killed. With the aid of his horse Tarzan, Maynard checks the ensuing stampede. Ford tries to escape from Maynard in one of the ranch's wagons, unaware that Hill has been hiding there. In the chase, Ford loses control of the horses. Maynard rescues Hill just as the wagon plunges over a cliff, taking Ford to his death.

NOTES AND COMMENTARY: *Sons of the Saddle* was also released as a silent film.

"Down the Home Trail with You" was recorded by Maynard for Columbia Records.

REVIEWS: "Entertaining Ken Maynard vehicle." (*Western Movies*, Pitts); "Universal is demonstrating that good westerns can be made with application." (*Variety*, 8/30/30)

SUMMATION: The author was unable to view this western feature.

"Never a Law of Man or God North of 53!"
Roaring Adventure! Ruthless romance ... carved from the sin-splashed glory of the North's wildest, richest era!

The Spoilers

Universal (April 1942); Frank Lloyd Productions; A Charles K. Feldman Group Production

CAST: Cherry Malotte, **Marlene Dietrich**; McNamara, **Randolph Scott**; Glennister, **John Wayne**; Helen Chester, **Margaret Lindsay**; Dextry, **Harry Carey**; Bronco Kid, **Richard Barthelmess**; Banty, **George Cleveland**; Judge Stillman, **Samuel S. Hinds**; Flapjack, **Russell Simpson**; Wheaton, **William Farnum**; Idabelle, **Marietta Canty**; Mr. Skinner, **Jack Norton**; Clark, **Ray Bennett**; Bennett, **Forrest Taylor**; Deputy, **Art Miles**; Deputy, **Charles McMurphy**; Struve, **Charles Halton**; Marshal, **Bud Osborne**; Galloway, **Drew Demorest**// Restaurant Owner, **Robert McKenzie**; Prospector Looking for a Room, **Emmett Lynn**; Rooming House Owner, **Irving Bacon**; Mr. Montrose, **Chester Clute**; Robert W. Service (the Poet), **Robert W. Service**; Miner Standing at Poker Table, **Robert Barron**; Miner at Poker Table, **Harry Cording**; Disgruntled Miners, **Harry Woods** and **Mickey Simpson**; Captain, **Robert Homans**; Man in Jail, **Willie Fung**; Deputies, **William Haade** and **William Gould**; Kelly, **Lloyd Ingraham**; Mine Guard, **Tom Steele**

CREDITS: Director, **Ray Enright**; Assistant Director, **Vernon Keays**; Producer, **Frank Lloyd**; Associate Producer, **Lee Marcus**; Screenwriters, **Lawrence Hazard** and **Tom Reed**; Dialogue Director, **Gene Lewis**; Editor, **Clarence Kolster**; Art Directors, **Jack Otterson** and **John B. Goodman** and **Edward R. Robinson**; Set Decorator, **R.A. Gausman**; Cinematographer, **Milton Krasner**; Special Photographic Effects, **John P. Fulton**; Gowns, **Vera West**; Sound, **Bernard B. Brown** and **Robert Pritchard**; Musical Director, **Charles Previn**; Musical Score, **H.J. Salter**

SONG: "I'll Take You Home Again, Kathleen" (traditional) — sung by **barbershop quartet**

LOCATION FILMING: Topanga Canyon, California

RUNNING TIME: 87 min.

SOURCE: Novel "The Spoilers" by **Rex Beach**

STORY: John Wayne and Harry Carey return to Nome from Seattle to find that the small miners are being cheated out of their claims. Arriving with them are Judge Samuel S. Hinds and his niece, Margaret Lindsay. Wayne's arrival with Lindsay has caused Marlene Dietrich, owner of the Northern Saloon and Wayne's lover, to be consumed with jealousy. Hinds is supposed to bring law and justice to Nome but actually is in league with Gold Commissioner Randolph Scott to fleece the miners out of as much gold as possible.

Lindsay's role is to use her charms to persuade Wayne to let the courts settle the issue when there's a dispute over ownership. Carey wants to fight with guns but finally allows Wayne to have his way and let the courts make a decision. When Hinds rules in favor of a small miner, Wayne and Carey think justice will be served. There's a rude awakening when Hinds declares it will be ninety days before a decision can be made, which means a quarter million in gold can be mined before the claim reverts to Wayne and Carey. In going to Hind's room, Wayne finds Scott, Hinds and Linsay, and realizes he's up against a criminal combine. The safe from their mine was removed to the bank. Wayne, Carey and fellow miners break into the bank and retrieve the safe. When Marshal Bud Osborne investigates, Richard Barthlemess, who's deeply in love with Dietrich and hates Wayne, shoots Osborne in the back. Wayne is arrested for the murder and jailed. Scott plans a jailbreak in which Wayne will be killed as he walks out the back door. Dietrich learns of the plan and helps Wayne escape. Shots were fired, and Scott believes Wayne has been killed.

The Spoilers (1942) movie still: Marlene Dietrich feigns grief so Randolph Scott will not learn that the plot to kill John Wayne has failed. Marietta Canty looks on.

To give Wayne and Carey a chance to take back their mine by force, Dietrich feigns sorrow and has Scott take her to her room at the Northern Saloon. Wayne and Carey get their mine back and return to town to prevent Hinds from leaving on a boat to Seattle. Wayne learns that Scott is with Dietrich. As Wayne arrives, Scott is trying to force himself on her. A brutal fistfight follows, with the combatants fighting in Dietrich's room, across the balcony, down to the saloon floor, through the saloon out into the muddy streets before Wayne finally whips Scott. Dietrich tells Wayne he's won her.

NOTES AND COMMENTARY: John B. Goodman and Jack Otterson (art directors) and Russell A. Gausman and Edward R. Robinson (set decorators) received an Academy Award Nomination for Art-Set Decoration.

There were three previous screen entries of Rex Beach's *The Spoilers*. The first two were silent films, in 1914 with William Farnum and Tom Santschi in a Selig release, and a 1923 Goldwyn production with Milton Sills and Noah Beery (Sr.). The first sound entry came from Paramount in 1930 with Gary Cooper and William Boyd. This is not the Boyd of Hopalong Cassidy fame but an actor known as, but not billed as, William "Stage" Boyd. Universal-International remade the story in 1956 with Jeff Chandler and Rory Calhoun.

The film deviated from Beach's story in these aspects: Glennister is in love with Helen Chester, who is a dupe, not an ally of McNamara. The Bronco Kid, who is in love with Cherry Malotte, is Chester's long lost brother. Malotte was a former girlfriend of Glennister and does not own the Northern Saloon. The climactic fight occurs in a lawyer's office and not in the Northern.

At the beginning of the movie, prospector Emmett Lynn looks for a room. Rooming house owner Irving Bacon is turning Lynn away when a shot rings out and a body falls down the stairs. Bacon looks at the body and says, "That's Lee Marcus. You can have his room." This is an inside joke, as Lee Marcus was the associate producer for this film.

In the Northern Saloon, Marlene Dietrich encounters a poet at one of the balcony tables. The poet is Robert W. Service in a cameo bit. Service was famous for his Yukon poetry, with "The Shooting of Dan McGrew" and "Clancy of the Mounted" as two of his most memorable poems.

In the outstanding fistfight at the film's conclusion, Eddie Parker doubled John Wayne, and Allen Pomeroy doubled Randolph Scott.

There was ethnic humor in the film. When Marlene Dietrich learns that the boat from Seattle has arrived in Nome with John Wayne and Harry Carey as passengers, Dietrich's maid, played by Marietta Canty, remarks, "I sure hopes there's some colored folks on that boat. I'm getting mighty tired of pretending Eskimos are from Virginia."

Later in the film, after the bank robbery, Wayne comes to Dietrich's room with his face blackened with cork, and Canty thinks he an

African-American. Canty remarks, "You ain't no colored boy. You're washable." Wayne responds, "Let's get rid of some of the Alabama tan."

"I'll Take You Home Again, Kathleen" was previously used in *West Bound Limited* (Universal, 1937) and later in *The Daltons Ride Again* (Universal, 1945).

REVIEWS: "A first rate production, cast, direction and plenty of action." (*Variety*, 4/15/42); "Boasting three of Hollywood's biggest names and one of the most brutal fight scenes to hit the screen, *The Spoilers* manages to elevate itself above the B-western status it might otherwise have been relegated to." (*The Motion Picture Guide*, Nash and Ross)

SUMMATION: Okay, the fistfight at the picture's conclusion is a humdinger, but is the picture any good? Yes, *The Spoilers* is a good northern western, well-paced, well-directed and well-acted. While both Wayne and Scott give nice performances, it's Marlene Dietrich and Harry Carey who steal the acting honors. Dietrich conveys her wide range of emotions both with dialogue and her expressive face. Carey, as a no-nonsense old-timer, brings some welcome, unforced humor to the proceedings while taking care of the serious side in fine style. Director Ray Enright is a good action director, and his forthright style is perfect for this story. As the icing on the cake, a very well staged, though highly improbable, brawl brings the story to its happy conclusion. Action fans, don't miss this one!

---

*WHOOPEE-
The King of Cowboys is Here—
You'll ride with Hoot in a wild country, face to face with a
band of tough rustlers. SEE IT.*

Spurs

Universal (August 1930)

CAST: Bob Merril, **Hoot Gibson**; Peggy Bradley, **Helen Wright**; Pop Merril, **Bob Homans**; Tom Marsdan, **Philo McCullough**; Pecos, **Cap Anderson**; Buddy Hazlet, **Buddy Hunter**; Shorty, **PeeWee Holmes**; Indian Joe, **William Bertram**// Mr. Bradley, **Frank Clark**; Blackie, **Pete Morrison**; Eagle-Claw, **Artie Ortego**

CREDITS: Director/Screenwriter, Reeves Eason; Producer, **Hoot Gibson**; Editor, **Gilmore Walker**; Art Director, **David Garber**; Cinematographer, **Harry Neumann**; Recording Supervisor, **C. Roy Hunter**; Synchronization & Score, **David Broekman**

SONG: "Sleep, Baby, Sleep" (Rodgers)—sung by **PeeWee Holmes**

LOCATION FILMING: Lone Pine, California

RUNNING TIME: 60 min.

STORY: After Buddy Hunter's fa-

Spurs (1930) scene card: Hoot Gibson (***center***) and Philo McCullough (***left***) argue while Helen Wright and Frank Clark (***black hat***) watch attentively.

ther's murder, rancher Bob Homans gives Hunter a place to stay on his ranch. Hoot Gibson, Homans' son, with his sidekick PeeWee Holmes, invade a rustler stronghold to bring back William Bertram, who is accused of the crime. After rustler Cap Anderson and most of his men leave, Gibson and Holmes capture Bertram and two other members of the gang and take them to Holmes' shack for safekeeping. Gibson finds out that Bertram is not the man responsible for the murder. Homans' foreman, Philo McCullough, murdered Hunter's father because he found a secret entrance to the rustlers' stronghold. Gibson, lacking the necessary proof to have McCullough arrested, tells both McCullough and Homans that he also knows the secret entrance. That night, as Gibson and his sweetheart, Helen Wright, go to Holmes' shack, there is an unsuccessful attempt to shoot Gibson. The next day, the big rodeo is being held, with a pair of silver spurs and a thousand dollar prize going to the top cowboy. After the rodeo is over, the sheriff and his posse are planning to storm the outlaw stronghold, with Gibson taking care of the deadly machine gun trained on the entrance. Gibson rides the toughest horse in the rodeo contest. After the ride, Gibson and McCullough argue, and McCullough is taken into custody. Gibson sent Holmes and Hunter to Holmes' shack to bring in the outlaws. The outlaws have worked their way loose from their bonds and take Holmes and Hunter prisoner. Gibson finds that his friends have been captured and that Anderson and his men are aware the sheriff and his posse are going to raid the stronghold. Riding furiously, Gibson arrives at the stronghold before Anderson and his men. Gibson rescues Holmes and Hunter, and then, using the rustler's machine gun, shoots down Anderson and one of his men. Gibson, Holmes and Hunter split a five thousand dollar reward for breaking up the rustlers' gang. Wright tells Gibson he won the spurs and the prize money. Gibson now has the time to romance Wright.

NOTES AND COMMENTARY: *Spurs* was also released as a silent feature.

Buddy Hunter, who had appeared with Hoot Gibson in *Mounted Stranger* (Universal, 1930), had a short-lived career. After appearing in two Ken Maynard vehicles, *Sunset Trail* (Tiffany, 1932) and *King of the Arena* (Universal, 1933), his motion picture career was over.

Marsdan was spelled Mardsan in the film's credits.

REVIEWS: "Action western. Begins at a fast clip and keeps up the pace." (*Variety*, 9/3/30); "Exciting and well-done early Hoot Gibson sound film." (*Western Movies*, Pitts)

SUMMATION: *Spurs* is a good western, slightly marred by an ending that could have used more suspense. Hoot Gibson delivers a nice performance as the unconventional cowboy who somehow comes out on top. PeeWee Holmes chips in with a good performance as Gibson's sidekick, garnering laughs without portraying the dunce. The other actors do a capable job. Cinematographer Harry Neumann captures the beauty of Lone Pine, California, to the picture's benefit. Director Reeves Eason paces the film smartly but could have tightened up the climactic scenes at the outlaw hideout.

HIS SCORCHING GUNS BRING LAW TO THE ROADS!

Stagecoach Buckaroo

Universal (February 1942)

CAST: Steve, **Johnny Mack Brown**; Clem, **Fuzzy Knight**; Molly, **Nell O'Day**; Nina, **Anne Nagel**; Kincaid, **Herbert Rawlinson**; Braddock, **Glenn Strange**; Blinky, **Ernie Adams**; Denton, **Henry Hall**; Simpson, **Lloyd Ingraham**; Higgins, **Frank Brownlee**; Sheriff, **Jack C. Smith**; Blatz, **Harry Tenbrook**; Hogan, **"Blackie" Whiteford**; and the Guardsman// Poker Player,

Frank Ellis; Bartender, Hank Bell; Outlaw, **Kermit Maynard**

CREDITS: Director, **Ray Taylor**; Associate Producer, **Will Cowan**; Screenwriter, **Al Martin**; Editor, **Maurice Wright**, Art Directors, **Jack Otterson and Ralph M. DeLacey**; Set Decorators, **R.A. Gausman**; Cinematographer, **Jerome Ash**; Sound, **Bernard B. Brown and Hal Bumbaugh**; Musical Director, **H.J. Salter**

SONGS: "Don't You Ever Be a Cowboy" (Rosen and Carter)—sung by **Fuzzy Knight**; "Get Along Little Dogies"—sung by **the Guardsman**; "Just Too Gosh Darn Bashful" (Rosen and Carter)—sung by **Fuzzy Knight** and **Nell O'Day**; "Red River Valley" (traditional)—sung by **Fuzzy Knight** and **Nell O'Day;** and "Put It There" (Rosen and Carter)—sung by **the Guardsman**

LOCATION FILMING: Iverson, California

RUNNING TIME: 58 min.

SOURCE: Story "Shotgun Messenger" by **Arthur St. Clair**

STORY: When Anne Nagel mistakenly identifies Johnny Mack Brown as a stagecoach bandit, he and his sidekick, Fuzzy Knight, are arrested and jailed. The actual bandit, Glenn Strange, incites the townspeople into a lynch mob and takes Brown and

Stagecoach Buckaroo (1942) scene card: Nell O'Day tells Johnny Mack Brown (*center*) and Fuzzy Knight that Anne Nagel has been kidnapped.

Knight from the jail. Nell O'Day, daughter of stageline owner Henry Hall, discovers that Brown and Knight are innocent and stops the hanging just in time. When Hall is killed in a stagecoach holdup, Brown and Knight decide to help out O'Day. Nagel thinks saloon owner Herbert Rawlinson is her father and confides in him when gold is being shipped. Rawlinson, the actual leader of the bandits, passes this information to Strange and his gang. Brown decoys the outlaws by pretending to carry a gold shipment, while O'Day and Nagel transport the shipment instead. Nagel tells Rawlinson of the change in plans. Strange and his men kidnap O'Day and Nagel and take them and the money to Rawlinson's hideout. O'Day escapes and reaches Brown. Brown brings Rawlinson to justice.

NOTES AND COMMENTARY: With the completion of this film, Nell O'Day left the series. O'Day brought to the productions competent (and at times more so) acting, wonderful horsemanship, a fine singing voice and a touch of light comedy. O'Day began to freelance, appearing in the serial *Perils of the Royal Mounted* (Columbia, 1942), and then was featured with the Range Busters (Ray "Crash" Corrigan, John "Dusty" King and Max "Alibi" Terhune), Tim Holt, the Three Mesquiteers (Bob Steele, Tom Tyler and Jimmie Dodd) and finally the Texas Rangers (Dave "Tex" O'Brien, Jim Newill and Guy Wilkerson) before retiring from the screen. O'Day and Jimmie Dodd had been cast as sister and brother in Johnny Mack Brown's *Law and Order* (Universal, 1940).

"Don't You Ever Be a Cowboy" was sung by Jimmie Dodd in *Twilight on the Prairie* (Universal, 1944). "Get Along, Little Dogies" was featured in *Little Joe, the Wrangler* (Universal, 1942) and *Marshal of Gunsmoke* (Universal, 1944). "Red River Valley" was heard in *Sandflow* (Universal, 1937), *Law for Tombstone* (Universal, 1937) and *The Silver Bullet* (Universal, 1942).

REVIEWS: "A superior Brown series Western." (*The Western*, Hardy); "Western is far above the average, very good." (*Variety*, 7/15/42)

AUTHOR'S COMMENTS: A marvelous "B" western. Johnny Mack Brown's character acted more like a regular human being, from refusing to ride blindly out to discover the origin of some shots to declining a job as shotgun messenger when the stage line obviously needed his help. Brown finally takes the job when he realizes that had he taken the job earlier, it would have probably saved O'Day's father's life. Brown handles the acting and action requirements in capable fashion. Sidekick Fuzzy Knight is saddled with two "funny" bits, the hot frying pan and hornet's nest incidents, which could have been eliminated but probably drew laughs from the younger audiences. O'Day, the third member of Universal's unofficial trio, has her riding and singing talents shown to good advantage. In fact, the songs in this opus are very enjoyable and add to the picture's charm. Director Ray Taylor generates some suspense in the action sequences, to the picture's betterment. Don't miss this one.

*His Barking Guns Spoke the Law of the WEST!
...and his bullets wrote the periods!*

Stone of Silver Creek

Universal (April 1935); A Charles Buck Jones Production

CAST: T. William Stone, **Charles Buck Jones**; Lola, **Noel Francis**; Timothy Tucker, **Niles Welch**; Martha Mason, **Marion Shilling**; Nancy Raymond, **Peggy Campbell**; George J. Mason, **Murdock MacQuarrie**; Graves, **Rodney Hildebrand**; Simmons, **Harry Semels**; Jimmy, **Grady Sutton**; Ben, **Kerman Cripps**; Tom Lucas, **Frank Rice**// Station Agent, **Robert McKenzie**; Cowboy in Saloon; **Hank Bell**; Gambling Patron, **Lew Meehan;** and "Silver"

CREDITS: Director, **Nick Grinde**; Producer, **Irving Starr**; Story, **R.R. Harris**; Screenwriter, **Earl Snell**; Editor, **Bernard Loftus**; Art Director, **Ralph Berger**; Cinematographers, **Ted McCord** and **Joe Novak**; Sound Supervisor, **Buddy Myers**

SONGS: "Let's Put Two and Two Together"—sung by **Noel Francis**; "Nearer My God to Thee" (Adams and Mason)—sung by **Buck Jones** and chorus

LOCATION FILMING: Vasquez Rocks, California

RUNNING TIME: 62 min.

STORY: Rodney Hildebrand and Harry Semels get Murdock MacQuarrie drunk and cheat him out of his money and mining claim in a crooked card game. Saloon owner Buck Jones intervenes and wins the claim and money. Jones gives MacQuarrie his money back in exchange for half interest in the claim. Jones wants to finance modern mining equipment to make the claim pay off. Hildebrand and Semels make an unsuccessful attempt to take the money back from Jones. Marion Shilling, MacQuarrie's daughter, doesn't want Jones as a partner in her father's mine because she believes Jones is a sinner. MacQuarrie tells preacher Niles Welch how Jones saved his claim. Welch convinces Shilling that Jones is a worthy partner, and he also begins to see Jones in a new light. Welch has in the past refused Jones' monetary aid for his church. Jones needs a new entertainer for his saloon and writes east for a performer like Peggy Campbell, with whom he is still in love. Campbell, who is still in love with Jones and broke up with Jones because of malicious gossip, finds out about the job and decides to go to Silver Creek and see Jones. Out walking and thinking about Shilling, with whom he's fallen in love, Welch overhears Hildebrand and Semels planning to rob Jones' saloon. Welch tells Jones and decides to talk the men out of the robbery. Jones tells Welch he'd better talk to the men at the point of a gun. Welch then buys a gun. Noel Francis, who runs the saloon in Jones' absence, tells Hildebrand and Semels that

Jones is out of town. Francis alerts Jones, who has been hiding nearby. Welch tries to prevent the robbery but is shot in the arm. The holdup men race from the saloon, with Jones in pursuit. Welch follows with the sheriff and a posse. Jones catches up to the robbers and engages them in a gunfight. Welch wounds Hildebrand as he attempts to shoot Jones in the back. Jones then sneaks up on Semels and captures him. Playing cupid, Jones gets Welch and Shilling together. Returning to the saloon, he hears Campbell singing and tells her he should have never let her go.

NOTES AND COMMENTARY: Marion Shilling didn't particularly care for her role in *Stone of Silver Creek*. She thought the part was too goody-goody, not what she liked to play.

When Marion Shilling asked veteran actor Niles Welch's advice on furthering her career. Welch retorted, "Wear expansion pads in your bra."

Marion Shilling remembered Buck Jones was an excellent poker player, and $5000 could change hands in an afternoon. She liked Jones' sense of humor and related a joke he liked to tell: "A minister had a regular routine of Sunday afternoon visits to his parishioners. On a particular Sunday afternoon, he paid a visit

Stone of Silver Creek (1935) movie still: Buck Jones (*right*) battles Harry Semels.

to a farmhouse. The farmer's wife offered the minister a little sherry. The minister declared that he only consumed non-alcoholic drinks and asked for a glass of milk. The farmer's wife went to the kitchen to get the milk and because the minister looked a little tired decided to add a small amount of bourbon. Finally, she made the decision to add a good shot and took the milk to the minister. The minister took a big gulp and declared happily, 'God, what milk!'"

Peggy Campbell sings a song at the picture's finale. The title could be "Let Me Hold You Closely in My Arms for Tonight, Dear," or "For Tonight May Never Come Again," or even something else.

REVIEWS: "Cleverly written and quickly paced." (*The Motion Picture Guide*, Nash and Ross); "Rates a row of notches above the usual Buck Jones opus." (*Variety*, 4/10/35)

SUMMATION: *Stone of Silver Creek* is a superior "B" western. From an excellent story by R.R. Harris and screenplay by Earl Snell, this austere tale served up in the William S. Hart tradition serves the actors nicely. The script allows for good characterizations, and the principals respond accordingly. In particular, Buck Jones, Noel Francis and Niles Welch can be commended for their performances. Little action is shown, but is not needed until the action packed final reel. Director Nick Grinde proves he's up to the job of putting this fine story on the screen.

Around Her Swept a Storm of Hate and Passion!
Lovely Lupe! Fiery maiden of the frozen north! Luring! Tempting!
Toying with the surging passions of two strong, love-crazed men!

The Storm

Universal (August 1930)

CAST: Manette Fachard, **Lupe Velez**; Dave Stewart, **Paul Cavanagh**; Burr Winton, **William Boyd**; Jacques Fachard, **Alphonse Ethier**; Johnny, **Ernest Adams**

CREDITS: Director, **William Wyler**; Screenwriters, **Wells Root, Tom Reed and Charles A. Logue**; Cinematographer, **Alvin Wyckoff**; Recording Engineers, **Joseph P. Lapis and C. Roy Hunter**

SONG: "Chansonnette of Pierrot and Pierrette"—sung by **Lupe Velez**

LOCATION FILMING: Truckee (the High Sierras), California

RUNNING TIME: 80 min.

SOURCE: Play "Men Without Skirts" by **Langdon McCormick**

STORY: William Boyd and Paul Cavanagh travel to Boyd's cabin in the Canadian Northwest. During the winter, Alphonse Ethier and his daughter, Lupe Velez, take refuge in Boyd's cabin. Ethier has been mortally wounded by the Mounted Police. Before he dies, Ethier asks Boyd and Cavanaugh to take care of Velez. Both men fall in love with Velez, and their relationship becomes strained. Low on food, Boyd goes for help during a storm. In love with Boyd, Velez starts after him. Cavanaugh brings the lovers to safety.

NOTES AND COMMENTARY: *The Storm* was previously filmed by Universal in 1922 with House Peters, Virginia Valli and Matt Moore in the leads.

The William Boyd of *The Storm* is not the William Boyd of Hopalong Cassidy fame. Most historians refer to this film's star as William "Stage" Boyd.

The Storm was originally scheduled to shoot on location in Sonora, California. Due to the lack of snow, the site was changed to Truckee in the High Sierras.

REVIEWS: "Standard screen version of the Landgon McCormick novel with a well staged avalanche." (*Western Movies*, Pitts); "Rates as a fairly good programmer strictly on merit." (*Variety*, 8/27/30)

SUMMATION: This film was unavailable for viewing by the author.

MILES AND MILES OF DANGER, DRAMA, LOVE!
Wild horses and wilder men on the vast mesas of Arizona—in a drama of life against life!

Stormy

Universal (October 1935); A Henry MacRae Production

CAST: Stormy, **Noah Beery, Jr.**; Kerry, **Jean Rogers**; Trinidad, **J. Farrell MacDonald**; Stuffy, **Raymond Hatton**; Craig, **Walter Miller**; Deem, **Fred Kohler**; Greasy, **James Burtis**; the Arizona Wranglers (**L.F. Costello, Charles Hunter, John Jackson, John Luther, Curtis McPeters, Cal Shores** and **Glenn Strange**); "Rex, King of Wild Horses"; "Rex Junior"// Mr. Mack, **Harry Woods**; Monte, **Monte Montague**; Conductor, **Robert Homans**; Cowboy, **Bud Osborne**

CREDITS: Director, **Louis Friedlander**; Story, **Cherry Wilson**; Screenwriters, **Ben Grauman Kohn** and **George Plympton**; Editor, **Murray Seldeen**; Art Director, **Ralph Berger**; Cinematographer, **Richard Fryer**; Photographic Effects, **John P. Fulton**; Sound, **Gilbert Kurland**; Musical Director, **Heinz Roemheld**

SONGS: "Old Chisholm Trail" (traditional)–sung by **the Arizona Wranglers**; "A Cowboy's Dream" (O'Malley)—sung by **the Arizona Wranglers**

LOCATION FILMING: Oak Creek Canyon, California, and Sedona and the Painted Desert, Arizona

RUNNING TIME: 68 min.

STORY: Noah Beery, unable to stay with his beloved mare and her colt, Rex Jr., finds temporary refuge on a ranch owned by J. Farrell MacDonald and Fred Kohler. MacDonald owns a herd of wild horses and refuses to allow Kohler to destroy them to make room for additional cattle on the ranch. A train wreck throws the mare and Rex Jr. into the rangeland where the wild herd roams. Beery finds the mare dead but is able to capture Rex Jr. Beery builds a "hidden" corral away from the ranch and begins to train the horse, with the help of Kohler's daughter, Jean Rogers. Rogers and Beery begin to fall in love. Soon the colt grows into a handsome stallion, Rex. Rex begins running with the wild horses and is captured by Kohler's foreman, Walter Miller. Brought back to the ranch, Miller attempts to tame Rex by beating him. Beery stops Miller, but Rex is locked in the barn. Beery turns Rex loose. Kohler is furious and demands MacDonald kick Beery off the ranch. MacDonald refuses and tells Kohler that he will adopt Beery and leave the ranch to him. When MacDonald rides to start the adoption procedure, Kohler sends men to ambush him. A shot topples MacDonald from his horse and down a steep embankment. Rex finds the wounded man, and MacDonald sends Rex to find Beery. Beery and Rogers have been searching for Rex and find him at the "hidden" corral. MacDonald is brought to the "hidden" corral to convalesce. Kohler orders his cowboys to round up the wild horses so they can be slaughtered. Rex causes the wild herd to stampede back to the wild horse range. Kohler spots Beery, who has been trying to prevent the roundup. Beery sees that Kohler is in the path of the stampeding horses and tries to warn him. Kohler, intent only on shooting Beery, fires a shot, wounding him. Kohler then sees the horses bearing down on him and tries to ride out of danger. Kohler's horse stumbles, and Kohler is thrown to the ground to be trampled by the wild horses. Beery and Rogers decide to return Rex to the wild, but Rex comes back to the ranch.

NOTES AND COMMENTARY: Director Louis Friedlander was better known in his career as Lew Landers.

Rex was pictured as a lovable horse in his films. In reality, Rex was quite mean and vicious, a killer horse who was responsible for injuring many wranglers.

Footage from *Stormy* was utilized in *Scouts to the Rescue* (Universal, 1939) and *Wild Beauty* (Universal, 1946).

The song "A Cowboy's Dream" is sung to the tune of 'My Bonnie Lies Over the Ocean" and would later be sung by Tex Ritter, with Johnny Bond and His Red River Boys, in *Oklahoma Raiders* (Universal, 1944). "The Old Chisholm Trail" was featured in *Parade of the West* (Universal, 1930), *The Fiddlin' Buckaroo* (Universal, 1933) *The Phantom Rider* (Universal, 1936) and *The Old Chisholm Trail* (Universal, 1942).

REVIEWS: "Well made and entertaining melodrama." (*Western Movies*, Pitts); "Except for an effective stampede of horses in the final reel, *Stormy* has nothing to distinguish it from run-of-the-mill sagebrush sagas." (*Variety*, 12/11/35)

SUMMATION: *Stormy* is a heartwarming yet action filled horse story set in the West. Noah Beery, Jr. and Jean Rogers head an impressive cast. Beery is convincing as a young man who loves horses, especially Rex. Rogers gives a nice performance as a young woman who realizes she loves Beery more than she loves her father, Fred Kohler. In the supporting cast, J. Farrell MacDonald, as a horse-loving rancher, and Kohler, his partner who wants the horses removed from the range, are particular standouts. Cinematographer Richard Fryer captures the magnificent scenic backgrounds that enhance the story. Louis Friedlander directs with a steady and capable hand, and the result is a much better than average film.

BAD Men! WILD Horses!
— Both were alike to this man of steel!

Strawberry Roan

ALTERNATE TITLE: **Flying Fury**; Universal (October 1933); A Ken Maynard Production

CAST: Ken Masters, **Ken Maynard**; Alice Edwards, **Ruth Hall**; Bart Hawkins, **Harold Goodwin**; Shanty, **Frank Yaconelli**; Big Jim Edwards, **James Marcus**; Colonel Brownlee, **William Desmond**; Curley, **Charles King**; Beef, **Jack Rockwell**; Bat, **Bob Walker**; Slim, **Bill Patton**; and "Tarzan"// Ranch Hands, **Buck Bucko, Ben Corbett** and **Art Mix**

CREDITS: Director, **Alan James**; Story/Screenwriter, **Nate Gatzert**; Editor, **Chas. Harris**; Cinematographer, **Ted McCord**; Sound Supervisor, **Earl Crain**

SONGS: "Strawberry Roan" (Vincent & Howard)—sung by **Ken Maynard**

LOCATION FILMING: Kernville, Red Rock Canyon and Newhall, California

RUNNING TIME: 59 min.

SOURCE: Poem "Strawberry Roan" by **Curley Fletcher**

STORY: Cowhands Ken Maynard, Frank Yaconelli and Charles King find work when ranch owner James Marcus needs men to hunt down and break the Strawberry Roan. Marcus thinks the Roan has been driving off his best horses, but actually his foreman, Harold Goodwin, is behind the rustling. Maynard is happy to work on the ranch because he and Marcus' daughter, Ruth Hall, are in love. Ranch owner William Desmond offers the deed to his ranch as a prize to the man who can ride the Roan. Goodwin doesn't want the Roan captured because it will end his criminal activities. Maynard and

Hall capture the Strawberry Roan. No rider is able to stay on the horse the first day. Goodwin will be the first rider for the second day, so that night he takes the Roan out of the corral and has one of his men choke the animal so Goodwin will be able to ride him. While the Roan is being tortured, Goodwin plans to move all the stolen horses so they can be sold. Maynard and Hall take a moonlight ride, and Maynard sees the horses being moved and decides to investigate. Goodwin fires at Maynard, causing the horses to stampede through Marcus' ranch, wreaking havoc. Marcus, Desmond and the cowboys ride after the Roan and capture him. Desmond is about to shoot the Roan when Maynard interferes. Maynard tells Marcus that Goodwin is behind the rustling activities, and that his shot caused the stampede. Goodwin, who has rejoined the ranch hands, is captured. Maynard makes a case to allow him to ride the Roan and does so after a wild ride. Maynard wins the deed to Desmond's ranch and the ownership of the Strawberry Roan. Maynard and Hall give the Roan his freedom and the couple make plans to marry.

NOTES AND COMMENTARY: Fred Howard and Nat Vincent adapted

Strawbery Roan (1933) movie still: Frank Yaconelli (*left*), Ken Maynard and Charles King look for jobs.

Curley Fletcher's poem and added music to produce a classic western song. When the sheet music was released, Fletcher's name was listed as one of the songwriters.

Ken Maynard owned the rights to the song "The Strawberry Roan." Gene Autry wanted to use the song for his production of *The Strawberry Roan* (Columbia, 1948) and arranged for Columbia to purchase the screen rights. The plots of the Maynard and Autry films were different, however.

The Strawberry Roan was the title of a British National Films, Ltd. released in 1944. The film had a different story line than the two western films.

The Saalfield Publishing Company published a novelization of "The Strawberry Roan" as a children's book and a movie tie-in in 1934.

Footage from *The Devil Horse* (Pathe, 1926) was used in the wild horse sequences.

REVIEWS: "Full of action, music and good humor." (*Western Movies*, Pitts); "Plot thread too thin to gain great interest, but it abounds in physical action." (*Variety*, 12/12/33)

SUMMATION: *Strawberry Roan* is a winner. This is easily one of Ken Maynard's best westerns. Ted McCord's camerawork catches the action perfectly, especially in the fight scenes, whether it's man vs. man or horse vs. horse. Look at the scene where Tarzan protects Maynard and Ruth Hall from being trampled by stampeding horses. Alan James' screenplay is simple but straightforward, and is highly entertaining. James even depicts the crude ranch humor of the cowboys. Maynard's acting is satisfactory, but the film receives a big boost from the performances of Frank Yaconelli, Charles King and Hall.

IT'S THE ROOT-ZOOT WEST!
...with your favorite Stage, Screen and Radio merry-makers
...In a Jive-Jammed Round-Up of Joy!

Strictly in the Groove

Universal (January 1943)

CAST: Sally Monroe, **Mary Healy**; Bob Saunders, **Richard Davies**; Durham, **Leon Errol**; Pops, **Shemp Howard**; Dixie, **Grace McDonald**; Ozzie, **Ozzie Nelson**; Cathcart, **Franklin Pangborn**; R.C. Saunders, **Russell Hicks**; Martha, **Martha Tilton**; Skat, **Eddie Johnson**; Russ Monroe, **Charles Lang**; Jimmie, **Jimmie Davis**; **Jimmy Wakely and his Cowboy Band** (with **Johnny Bond**); the Dinning Sisters (**Ella Lucille, Eugenia Day** and **Virginia Moy Dinning**); Diamond Solid-Aires (Leo Diamond, Abe Diamond, Buddy

Raye, Maurice Pineman and Jerry Geller); Cowboy Singer, Kenny Stevens; and the Ozzie Nelson Orchestra// Professor Blake, Tim Ryan; Phone Girl, Frances Morris; Big Boy, Ralph Dunn; Pearl, Helen Deverell; McClelland, Lloyd Ingraham; Angry Man, Neely Edwards; Cactus, Charles R. Moore

CREDITS: Director, Vernon Keays; Associate Producer, Joseph Sanford; Screenwriters, Kenneth Higgins and Warren Wilson; Editor, Edward Curtiss; Art Directors, Jack Otterson and Ralph M. DeLacy; Set Decorator, R.A. Gausman; Gowns, Vera West; Cinematographer, John W. Boyle; Sound, Bernard B. Brown and Joe Lapis; Musical Director, Charles Previn; Dance Director, John Mattison

SONGS: "I Never Knew" (Pitts, Egan and Marsh)—sung by Martha Tilton and Ozzie Nelson; "Happy Rovin' Cowboy" (Nolan)—sung by Jimmy Wakely and His Cowboy Band; "Miss You" (Tobias and Tobias)—sung by Mary Healy and Richard Davies; "Central Avenue Shuffle" (Nelson)—played by the Ozzie Nelson Orchestra; "Ridin' On" (McHugh and Adamson)—sung by Kenny Stevens; "Buffalo Gals" (Traditional)—sung by Jimmy Wakely and His Cowboy Band; "The Pretty Girl Milking Her Cow" (Traditional)—sung by the Dinning Sisters; "Sweethearts or Strangers" (Davis and Wayne)—sung by Jimmie Davis; "Be Honest with Me" (Autry and Rose)—sung by the Dinning Sisters; "Dancing on Air" (Rosen and Carter)—sung by Martha Tilton and danced by Grace McDonald and Eddie Johnson; "Someone Else Is Taking My Place" (Howard, Ellsworth and Morgan)—sung by Ozzie Nelson and Martha Tilton; "Elmer's Tune" (Albrecht, Gallop and Jurgens)—sung by the Dinning Sisters; and "You Are My Sunshine" (Davis and Mitchell)—sung by Jimmie Davis, the Dinning Sisters and Mary Healy, performed by the Diamond Solid-Aires, and danced by Grace McDonald and Eddie Johnson

RUNNING TIME: 60 min.

STORY: Businessman Russell Hicks wants his son, Richard Davies, to help him run a chain of restaurants and lodges. Davies is more interested in playing piano with Ozzie Nelson's orchestra. Hicks orders Davies to work at Hicks' Circle S dude ranch in Arizona. Davies takes Nelson's band and candy store proprietor Shemp Howard to Arizona. Through trickery, he gets all the band members jobs at the dude ranch. Still trying to get a break in the music business, Davies has Howard work on rich cattleman Leon Errol to finance a radio show for the band. The plan fails when Hicks learns that Davies is still playing music and fires him. Davies talks rival dude ranch manager Mary Healy into opening a nightclub and featuring the band. Hicks has an option on Healy's place and grows incensed when he hears that music will be featured. Arriving in Arizona, Hicks calls on his old friend Errol, who persuades Hicks to attend the nightclub opening. Howard thinks he knows Hicks and Errol, and he finally remembers that the two men were once second-rate vaudevillians. The nightclub opening is a success. Howard talks Hicks into adding music to his restaurants, and Errol into sponsoring a radio program for the band. Davies and Healy have fallen in love and plan to marry.

NOTES AND COMMENTARY: *Strictly in the Groove* marked Jimmie Davis' first screen appearance. Davis was in California to record songs for Decca records when he was asked to appear in the movie. At the time, Davis had been elected Police Commissioner of Shreveport, Louisiana. Davis would appear in support of Charles Starrett at Columbia before becoming Governor of Louisiana. During his first term, on vacation, Davis starred in *Louisiana* (Monogram, 1947), his life story. Afterwards, Davis played the lead in a musical western, *Mississippi Rhythm* (Monogram, 1949). He will always be remembered for the song "You Are My Sunshine," which he wrote with Charles Mitchell and later recorded.

"Ridin' On" is a retitling of the song. "Ridin' Home," which was sung in *Desperate Trails* (Universal, 1939), *Road Agent* (Universal, 1941), and *Tenting Tonight on the Old Camp Ground* (Universal, 1943), and later was played in *Senorita from the West* (Universal, 1945).

Mary Healy married Peter Lind Hayes. The two starred on radio, television and in nightclubs for many years.

REVIEWS: "Minor filmusical for duals." (*Variety*, 11/11/42); "Fair Universal programmer musical western." (*Western Movies*, Pitts)

SUMMATION: *Strictly in the Groove* is strictly in the groove. Okay, the plot is bare-boned to the point of almost nonexistence but the music and comedy are so exuberant that who cares? It's unusual to find so many good songs in one picture, and the comedy provided by both Shemp Howard and Leon Errol is quite amusing. An enjoyable film.

A TWO-FISTED BLAST of FURY!

Sudden Bill Dorn

Universal (November 1937); A Buck Jones Production

CAST: Bill Dorn, **Buck Jones**; Lorna Kent, **Noel Francis**; Diana, **Evelyn Brent**; Cap Jenks, **Frank McGlynn, Sr.**; Ken Fairchild, **Lee Phelps**; Mike Bundy, **Harold Hodge**; Fontana, **Ted Adams**; Maggie, **Mabel Colcord**; Hank Smith, **Wm. Lawrence**; Stock Morgan, **Tom Chatterton**; Curly O'Connor, **Ezra Paulette**; Don Francisco, **Carlos J. de Valdez**; Joe Bishop; Sheriff, **Chas. Le Moyne**; and "Silver"// Bud Williams, Red Hightower; Tony, **Adolph Milar**

CREDITS: Director, **Ray Taylor**;

Story, **Jackson Gregory**; Screenwriter, **Frances Guihan**; Art Director, **Ralph Berger**; Editor, **Bernard Loftus**; Cinematographers, **Allen Thompson** and **John Hickson**; Sound Supervisor, **L. John Myers**

SONGS: "Everything is Swingin' (Way Up Thar)"—sung by **Red Hightower**; "Don't Jump the Gun"—sung by **Noel Francis;** and "Moonbeams"—sung by **Harold Hodge**

LOCATION FILMING: Kernville, California

RUNNING TIME: 60 min.

STORY: Rancher Buck Jones and his friends have been taken in by Harold Hodge's fraudulent oil scheme. Jones finds that Hodge has been seen in Bordertown, where he tells the townspeople he knows where gold can be found. Believing in Hodge and wanting to stake gold claims of their own, the townspeople, led by Lee Phelps, prevent Jones from exacting his revenge on Hodge. Hodge's partner is murdered, and singer Noel Francis is falsely accused of the crime. The crime is forgotten as Hodge tells the men that gold can be found on Ghost Mountain, and a mad rush to Ghost Town ensues. Jones takes Francis to her aunt's ranch and discovers that the aunt has died and Hodge is claiming ownership of the

Sudden Bill Dorn (1937) movie still: Noel Francis comforts a battered but victorious Buck Jones.

ranch. Francis refuses to leave the ranch, and Jones finds that Hodge cannot produce a deed. Hodge seems to have romantic designs on Francis, incurring the jealousy of Hodge's lover, Evelyn Brent. To drive Francis off her ranch, Brent has men dynamite and set fire to all the buildings except the ranch house. The townspeople realize the gold strike is a hoax. Jones finds evidence that Hodge murdered his partner. In the wreckage, Jones' pal, Frank McGlynn, Sr., discovers that the actual location of the gold strike is Francis' ranch. Hodge rides to the ranch, planning to take possession. Jones also arrives, and the two men wage a vicious fistfight, with Jones emerging victorious. Jones and Francis realize they're in love with each other.

NOTES AND COMMENTARY: *Sudden Bill Dorn* was the final Universal starring film for Jones. Jones had been negotiating a new three-year contract. The studio was not in good financial shape and could not agree to Jones' demands. Jones was irritated that he would not receive the same salary as his friend William Boyd in the Hopalong Cassidy series at Paramount, since in the exhibitor's polls he was the number one screen cowboy. Offered a better contract by Monroe Shaff to star in six films to be distributed by Columbia, Jones left Universal. In 1941 Jones would return to Universal to co-star with Dick Foran and Leo Carrillo in the serial *Riders of Death Valley*.

The song "Moonbeams" was sung by LeRoy Mason in Buck Jones' *When a Man Sees Red* (Universal, 1934). It seems that only the bad guy is allowed to sing this musical number.

Receiving thirteenth billing is actor Joe Bishop, who apparently only received screen credit for this film and for *Boss of Lonely Valley* (Universal, 1937). The author was unable to determine Bishop's character name for either film.

REVIEWS: "Plenty of action, but pacing off." (*The Motion Picture Guide*, Nash and Ross); "Fair actioner." (*Western Movies*, Pitts)

SUMMATION: *Sudden Bill Dorn* is a confused, disjointed film with few action sequences until the final fistic confrontation between Buck Jones and Harold Hodge at the story's climax. To further complicate matters, Jones' performance wavers from bold heroics to forgettable comedy sequences. Noel Francis, usually better served in Jones' vehicles, is adequate but unfortunately allows herself to be atrociously garbed. Overall, Hodge makes a weak villa, and therefore it's quite a surprise to find him a formidable foe in the rugged fight with Jones. Frances Guihan's screenplay ill serves the actors, with plot threads presented and abruptly dropped. This is a disappointing Jones entry.

He Said It with Bullets!
His Shootin' Irons, His Horse and His Fists Knew All the Answers!

Sunset of Power

Universal (January 1936); A Buck Jones Production

CAST: Cliff Lea, **Buck Jones**; Ruth Brannum, **Dorothy Dix**; Neil Brannum, **Charles Middleton**; Page Cothran, **Donald Kirke**; Red, **Ben Corbett**; Coley, **Charles King**; Bud Rolfe, **Wm. Lawrence**; Rosita, **Nina Compana**; Doctor, **Murdock MacQuarrie**; Mack, **Allan Sears**; Grocer, **Bob McKenzie**; Indian Joe, **Joe Delacruze**// Andreas, **Eumenio Blanco**; Cowhand, **Glenn Strange**

CREDITS: Director, **Ray Taylor**; Story, **J.E. Grinstead**; Screenwriter, **Earle Snell**; Editor, **Bernard Loftus**; Art Director, **Ralph Berger**; Cinematographers, **Allen Thompson** and **Herbert Kirkpatrick**; Sound, **Buddy Myers**

LOCATION FILMING: The French Ranch and the Walker Ranch, California

RUNNING TIME: 66 min.

STORY: Dorothy Dix, granddaughter of powerful ranch owner Charles Middleton, returns to the West after an eight year absence. Middleton treats Dix harshly and will not allow the servants to coddle her. Middleton is disappointed that the last of his family is a girl and thinks leading a Spartan life will toughen her up sufficiently so she can run his ranch. Dix finds that none of the servants will speak to her since Middleton has threatened death to any one who does. Middleton decides the ranch needs a foreman and asks Donald Kirke to take the job. A thousand cattle are missing, and Middleton expects Kirke to get to the bottom of the problem. Dix meets ranch hand Buck Jones when she has a riding accident, and immediately likes him. Middleton expects Dix and Kirke to marry. Marriage to Kirke is unacceptable to Dix, and she begins riding with Jones and telling him her troubles. Jones thinks Middleton will change his mind before the wedding. Jones believes Kirke is behind the rustling scheme. Kirke senses that Jones is onto him and arranges to have Jones ambushed. Kirke's henchman, Allan Sears, shoots the wrong man and, in turn, is shot by the murdered man's partner. Jones decides to leave the ranch, accompanied by his two pals, Ben Corbett and Charles King. They take refuge in a deserted cabin that Jones has stocked with provisions. Before Dix can marry Kirke, Jones, in disguise, leads Middleton and Kirk on a wild chase while Corbett and King take Dix to the cabin. At the cabin, Dix finds proof that Jones was the mystery man responsible for breaking up the wedding, and the two fall in love. Jones goes to town, arranges to meet Middleton, and forces him to listen to his accusation that Kirke is the leader of the rustlers. Jones forces rustler Joe de la Cruz to admit Kirke's part in the scheme. Jones and Middleton go to the saloon to confront Kirke. A gunfight ensues, in which Middleton is wounded and Kirke killed. Middleton names Jones his new foreman and apologizes to Dix for making her unhappy, now realizing that Dix will marry Jones, who will run the ranch.

NOTES AND COMMENTARY: Appearing as a masked avenger in *Sunset of Power* was the inspiration for Buck Jones' character in his serial *The Phantom Rider* (Universal, 1936). The difference: in the serial Jones dresses in white, while his character in the feature film is garbed in black.

REVIEWS: "Interesting and well made Buck Jones vehicle." (*Western Movies*, Pitts); "A better-than-average series entry for Jones." (*The Motion Picture Guide*, Nash and Ross)

SUMMATION: This is a very good "B" western. Good acting highlights *Sunset of Power*, which came from a fine story by J.E. Grinstead and top-notch screenplay by Earle Snell. Charles Middleton excels as a "ruthless" ranch owner, and his performance dominates the picture. Dorothy Dix, the recipient of a well-written role, easily meets the demands of the script. Buck Jones, cast as a hero who has doubts about how matters will be resolved, handles the part quite well. Jones' pals, Ben Corbett and Charles King, deliver some effective light humor, more appreciated by the adult audience. Director Ray Taylor paces the film nicely, stressing story over action without loss of interest by the audience, young or old.

THESE ARE THE GIANTS!
…who built America, who changed the course of the world and gave humanity a new foothold on romance, a new inspiration to love!… Whose mighty story is told in …
SUTTER'S GOLD
THE PICTURE THAT CAN NEVER DIE!

Sutter's Gold

Universal (April 1936); An Edmund Grainger Production

CAST: Johan Sutter, **Edward Arnold**; Pete Perkin, **Lee Tracy**; Countess Elizabeth Bartoffski, **Binnie Barnes**; Anna Sutter, **Katharine Alexander**; Captain Kettleson, **Montague Love**; Marshall, **Addison Richards**; Captain Alvarado, **John Miljan**; Kit Carson, **Harry Carey**; Sutter's son, **William Janney**; Sutter's daughter, **Nan Grey**; General Rotscheff, **Robert Warwick**; General Fremont, **Morgan Wallace**; Alverado's son, **Allen Vincent**// John Sutter, Age 8, **Ronnie Crosby**; King Kamehamehe, **Mitchell Lewis**; Lars, **Harry Cording**; Lt. Bacalenakoff, **Gastin Glass**; General Ramos, **Billy Gilbert**; Smythe, **Sidney Bracey**; Attorney for the State of California, **Jonathan Hale**; 1st Newsboy, **Tommy Bupp**; 2nd Newsboy, **Dickie Jones**

CREDITS: Director, **James Cruze**; Screenwriters, **Jack Kirkland**, **Walter Woods** and **George O'Neill**; Editor, **Philip Cahn**; Art Director, **Albert S. D'Agostino**; Technical Director, **Tito Davison**; Cinematographer, **George Robinson**; Special Cinematography, **John P. Fulton**; Gowns, **Brymer**; Sound, **Gilbert Kurland**; Orchestrator, **Clifford Vaughan**; Musical Score, **Franz Waxman**

RUNNING TIME: 94 min.

SOURCE: Novel by **Blaise Cendras**, by arrangement with Bruno Frank

STORY: Falsely accused of murder, Edward Arnold leaves his wife, Katherine Alexander, and their children in Switzerland to settle in New York City. In New York, Arnold and Lee Tracy become fast friends. Arnold's desire is now to go to California. Because of the winter weather, Arnold and Tracy have to catch a boat to the Sandwich Islands, and from there take a boat to California. He gets Captain Montague Love to allow him to book passage. Once on board, Arnold discovers that Love's vessel is a slave ship headed for South America. Tracy, who had thought about staying behind, finally comes aboard. When rations get low, Love and mate Harry Cording decide to throw the islanders overboard. Arnold incites a mutiny and takes control of the ship. When the ship nears the California coast, Arnold, Tracy and the Islanders go ashore. Arnold makes an agreement with Mexican general John Miljan to settle land in California. After three years, when all is bleak, Russian General Robert Warwick sells Arnold all the resources of their colony as the Russians leave California. As the resources are being transferred, Arnold meets and falls in love with Countess Binnie Barnes. Arnold's colony is doing well until one of Arnold's workers, Addison Richards, discovers gold and mistakenly tells Tracy. Tracy tells too many people, and the workers take over in their craze for gold. With Arnold's fortunes on the decline, Barnes decides to leave Arnold's compound for San Francisco. Tracy sends for Alexander and Arnold's son, William Janney, and Arnold's daughter, Nan Grey. Alexander has contracted tropical fever. Before Alexander dies, she makes Arnold pledge to have the courts return his lands. Janney is a lawyer and works through the court system, which finally decides in favor of Arnold. The people now living on those lands riot and the decision is reversed, but not before Janney is killed in a riot. Arnold and Tracy spend sixteen years in Washington, D.C. being shuffled from one bureaucrat to another. The newspaper boys play a cruel joke and shout that Arnold has regained his property. When Arnold buys a paper and learns it was a joke, it's too much for his system. Arnold collapses and dies.

NOTES AND COMMENTARY: *Sutter's Gold* would prove to be the beginning of the end for the Laemmle regime at Universal. This was an expensive picture that proved a box office disaster. When *Show Boat* (1936)

ran into financial difficulties while in production, the studio was forced to reorganize. Standard Capital purchased Universal, and the company became known as the New Universal.

Both the shipboard and western segments of *Mutiny on the Blackhawk* utilized some of the story line and footage from *Sutter's Gold*.

Edward Arnold appeared in this film by arrangement with B.P. Schulberg.

REVIEWS: "Lavish production and cast still leave something to be desired." (*Variety*, 4/1/36); "Lavish but dull story." (*The Motion Picture Guide*, Nash and Ross)

SUMMATION: *Sutter's Gold* is overblown, episodic and generally uninteresting. Edward Arnold, for the most part, plays the role either too cute or too dumb, and it's hard to believe Sutter could be a success at anything. Lee Tracy, a competent actor when he assays a character with a quick quip, plays this role like he had been drinking, whether the scene called for this effect or not. Binnie Barnes' acting is entirely superficial. Nowhere does anyone convince the audience to feel any emotion they're enduring. The episodic nature of the story line works against the film; at no time do you really get a sense of reality. Director James Cruze is unable to make Jack Kirkland, Walter Woods and George O'Neill's sorry screenplay work. In the end, when the newspaper boys play a cruel joke on Arnold, it's like the same thing was played on the audience.

They Rode to Live ... Shot to Kill!
On the thunderous trail of the overland mail!

Tenting Tonight on the Old Camp Ground

ALTERNATE TITLE: *Tenting Tonight;* Universal (February 1943)

CAST: Wade Benson, **Johnny Mack Brown**; Bob Courtney, **Tex Ritter**; Si Dugan, **Fuzzy Knight**; Kay Randolph, **Jennifer Holt**; Talbot, **John Elliott**; Judge Higgins, **Earle Hodgins**; Zeke Larkin, **Rex Lease**; Duke Merrick, **Lane Chandler**; Matt Warner, **Alan Bridge**; Ed Randolph, **Dennis Moore**; Pete, **Tom London**; Deputy Snell, **Bud Osborne**; Sheriff, Lyton Brent; Smokey, **Reed Howes**; Stage Driver, **George Plues**; Sleepy Martin, **Hank Worden**; and **the Jimmy Wakely Trio (Jimmy Wakely, Johnny Bond** and **Scotty Harrel)**

CREDITS: Director, **Lewis D. Collins**; Associate Producer, **Oliver Drake**; Story, **Harry Fraser**; Screenwriter, **Elizabeth Beecher**; Editor, **Charles Maynard**; Art Directors,

Jack Otterson and **Ralph M. DeLacy**; Set Decorators, **R.A. Gausman** and **A.J. Gilmore**; Cinematographer, **William Sickner**; Gowns, **Vera West**; Sound, **Bernard B. Brown** and **Jess Moulin**; Musical Director, **H. J. Salter**

SONGS: "Tenting Tonight on the Old Camp Ground" (Kittredge)—sung by **the Jimmy Wakely Trio**; "Drinks Are on the House" (Rosen and Carter)—sung by **the Jimmy Wakely Trio**; "Cielito Lindo" (traditional)—sung by **Jennifer Holt and the Jimmy Wakely Trio**; and "Ridin' Home" (McHugh and Adamson)—sung by **Tex Ritter and the Jimmy Wakely Trio**

LOCATION FILMING: Agoura, Iverson Ranch and Corriganville, California

RUNNING TIME: 62min.

STORY: Alan Bridge, attempting to build a road for the stage line to travel to Silver Bow, is beset by accidents and outlaw raids. Tex Ritter is sent west to investigate. Bridge tells Ritter that the road can't be completed unless a short cut to Silver Bow is found. Former mail service employees Johnny Mack Brown and Dennis Moore are looking for jobs. Bridge hires Brown to find a short cut and get the road completed in time for a test run. Brown has thirty days to succeed. Brown hires Moore to set up the final relay station. Outlaws led by Reed Howes, under orders from Rex Lease, raid the station, steal the horses and shoot Moore. Moore lives long enough to tell Brown who shot him. Brown and Ritter go to town. Howes and Brown meet, and, in a gun duel, Brown shoots Howes just as the stage coach pulls into town with Moore's sister, Jennifer Holt. In a callous manner, from one of Lease's henchmen, Holt learns that Moore has been killed. Ritter puts the blame on Brown for having Moore working by himself. Holt refuses to listen to Brown's explanations and turns to Ritter for comfort. To further damage the stage line's chances of success, Lease has Lane Chandler erect a tent saloon on public property adjacent to the construction camp. Drinks on credit entice the stage line workers, and Holt is hired as an entertainer. Lawyer Fuzzy Knight, a friend of Brown, gets the idea of assigning the prisoners in the local jail to work on the road. The road is nearly completed when a stage rolls into camp with inspector John Elliott to see if Bridge has met the deadline. Chandler realizes the stage might make it through and decides to lead an attack on the stage to prevent it from reaching Silver Bow. Learning that the final leg of the route will be over a dry wash, the driver, George Plues, backs out; and Elliott thinks it's too risky to attempt. Holt, who has learned the truth about her brother's murder and has warned Brown that the stage will be attacked, volunteers to ride as a passenger. Brown decides to drive the stage. Intimidated by Holt's action, Elliott climbs aboard. With Ritter and Knight and some of the men as outriders, the journey begins. Chandler and his men attack. Ritter, Knight and the men retaliate. Ritter captures Chandler, who confesses that Lease is behind the scheme, while Knight and the boys round up the gang members. The stage reaches Silver Bow safely, and Bridge is awarded the mail contract. Brown stays on with the stage line, and romance begins to blossom between Brown and Holt.

NOTES AND COMMENTARY: A *Daily Variety* headline in July 1943 stated that Jimmy Wakely had been hurt in an accident on the film set. Wakely and Bond were to be extras in a scene and were to walk across a street as Johnny Mack Brown and Tex Ritter raced into town. The two started across the street when Brown came racing by, hell-bent-for-leather. Wakely froze because he had no idea where Ritter and his horse, White Flash, were. As fate would have it, Wakely was directly in Ritter's path. Ritter tried to bring White Flash to a halt but not before there was a collision. Wakely, fortunately, was knocked into some soft dirt a few feet away. Ritter was genuinely apologetic and happy to see Wakely wasn't really hurt.

Tenting Tonight on the Old Camp Ground was remade as *The Old Texas Trail* (Universal, 1945) with Rod Cameron.

"Ridin' Home" had been heard in many Universal westerns such as *Desperate Trails* (Universal, 1939) with Johnny Mack Brown and Bob Baker, and *Road Agent* (Universal, 1941) with Dick Foran. "The Drinks Are on the House" was sung by Vyola Vonn in the serial *Winners of the West* (Universal, 1940). "Cielito Lindo" had been presented in *The Masked Rider* (Universal, 1941) and *Road Agent* (Universal, 1941).

Lane Chandler was a western star in the early thirties, toplining feature films for Big 4, Syndicate, Kent and Empire.

Fuzzy Knight's funny business is inspired by his mail order book "How to Be a Lawyer in Six Easy Lessons." Those viewers down on lawyers will eat this up, and lawyers themselves might register a chuckle or two.

REVIEWS: "One of the best of the Brown-Ritter series Westerns." (*The Western*, Hardy); "One of the better Brown and Ritter westerns." (*The Motion Picture Guide*, Nash and Ross)

SUMMATION: *Tenting Tonight on the Old Camp Ground* is a good, well-paced "B" western. Johnny Mack Brown and Tex Ritter make good antagonists who finally stand shoulder-to-shoulder to get the stage line through. Jennifer Holt does her usual fine job, singing a number and reacting naturally to the circumstances that befall her. Fuzzy Knight has some inspired comedy scenes as a not-so-brilliant lawyer. Lewis D. Collins directs briskly, keeping the action and story lines moving nicely.

Tom and his new pony, TONY, JR., in the best talking picture Tom's ever made...
Fast and furious action from start to finish...
a plot that will keep you on edge all the way through...
A WESTERN WITH A WALLOP!

Terror Trail

Universal (February 1933)

CAST: Tom Munroe, **Tom Mix**; Norma Laird, **Naomi Judge**; Bernie Laird, **Arthur Rankin**; Colonel Ormsby, **John St. Polis**; Sheriff Judell, **Frank Brownlee**; "Lucky" Dawson, **Raymond Hatton**; Tad McPherson, **Francis McDonald**; Tim McPherson, **Robert Kortman**; Shay, **Lafe McKee**// Prisoner, **Jay Wilsey**; Outlaw at Hideout, **Bud Osborne**; Posse Member, **Hank Bell**

CREDITS: Director, **Armand Schaefer**; Screenwriter, **Jack Cunningham**; Editor, **Russell Schoengarth**; Cinematographer, **Daniel B. Clark**

LOCATION FILMING: Lone Pine, Bronson Canyon and French Ranch, California

RUNNING TIME: 57 min.

SOURCE: Story "Riders of Terror Trail" by **Grant Taylor**

STORY: Tom Mix is asked by the Governor of Arizona to break up an outlaw gang, the Paint Horse Riders, who have been terrorizing the Silver County area. John St. Polis, head of the vigilante committee, and Sheriff Frank Brownlee are the gang's leaders. Mix brings in four members of the gang, but the outlaws are released from jail during the night. In addition, all the horses, including Tony, are stolen from the livery stable, except the horse owned by St. Polis. Gambler Raymond Hatton has a hunch the horses will show up at Naomi Judge's ranch. Judge's brother, Arthur Rankin, wrangles horses for the Paint Horse Riders. Rankin wants to quit, but St. Polis won't let him. The horses show up at the ranch. Rankin tells Mix that he found the horses wandering on the range. Mix, who has begun to fall in love with Judge, tells her to believe her brother. The outlaws strike again, holding up a stagecoach. Working alone, Mix finds a clue at the robbery scene, and tracks down and captures Rankin and three other gang members. The outlaws break jail, but Rankin rides to Judge's ranch instead of joining the gang. The outlaws ride to the ranch to prevent Rankin from talking. St. Polis has led a posse to the ranch and has captured Rankin with the intent to lynch him. Mix arrives at the ranch and makes Rankin his prisoner. The gang comes to the ranch, and a pitched battle begins between the inhabitants in the ranch house and the outlaws. St. Polis, under a flag of truce, goes to speak to the outlaws, and it looks like he's taken captive. Rankin admits to Mix and the posse members that St. Polis is the secret leader of the gang. With Tony's help, Mix rides clear of the ranch. Locating the outlaws' horses, he exchanges them with unbroken mustangs. Hatton brings a large posse to Judge's ranch. Outnumbered, the gang members try to escape but are no match for the wild horses, and are easily captured. Mix places handcuffs on St. Polis' wrists, and the outlaw gang's reign of terror is broken. Using his influence with the Governor, Mix plans to have Rankin paroled and released to Judge's custody. Mix and Judge now have time to spend time together, with Hatton betting they'll be married shortly.

NOTES AND COMMENTARY: *Terror Trail* was the title of an 18-chapter serial released by Universal in 1921, and would be used by Columbia for a Charles Starrett Durango Kid entry in 1946.

A novelization of *Terror Trail* was published as a Big Little Book by the Whitman Publishing Company as a children's book and movie tie-in.

REVIEWS: "Well produced western and it has that action." (*Variety*, 2/14/33); "Entertaining Tom Mix vehicle, although not up to par with some of his other Universal works." (*Western Movies*, Pitts)

SUMMATION: *Terror Trail* is another entertaining entry in the Tom Mix Universal series. Mix is fun to watch as he brings a star presence to this otherwise above average film. Raymond Hatton stands out in the capable supporting cast. The film moves nicely and is greatly enhanced by the magnificent location scenery.

See Tom and "Tony" Outwit the Smartest Band of Outlaws the West Had Ever Known.

The Texas Bad Man

Universal (June 1932)

CAST: Tom Logan, **Tom Mix**; Nancy Keefe, **Lucille Powers**; Milton Keefe, **Willard Robertson**; Gore Hampton, **Fred Kohler**; Captain Carter, **Joe Girard**; Yat Gow, **Tetsu Komai**; Chester Bigelow, **Edward Le Saint**; and "Tony"// Gang Member, **Bud Osborne**; Ranger, **Richard Alexander**; John Andrews, **Francis Sayles**; Bank Patron, **Edmund Cobb**

CREDITS: Director, **Edward Laemmle**; Producer, **Carl Laemmle, Jr.**; Associate Producer, **Stanley Bergerman**; Story/Screenplay, **Jack Cunningham**; Scenario Editor, **Richard Schayer**; Film Editor, **Philip Cahn**; Supervising Film Editor, **Maurice Pivar**; Art Director, **Thomas F. O'Neill**; Cinematographer, **Daniel B. Clark**; Recording Supervisor, **C. Roy Hunter**; Special Effects, **John P. Fulton**

LOCATION FILMING: Joshua Tree National Monument, California

RUNNING TIME: 63 min.

STORY: Tom Mix, undercover lawman, has the job of breaking up a well-organized bandit gang. Mix holds up a stagecoach and takes the payroll. Bandit henchman Fred Kohler, intending to rob the stage with his gang, pursues Mix. After hiding the money, Mix surrenders to Kohler. Kohler decides to take him to his boss, Willard Robertson. Robertson will allow Mix to stay under his protection for one-half of the payroll money. Mix agrees and brings the money to Robertson. Mix disguises himself as a Mexican caballero so he can go into the town of San Luis. On his way to town, Mix meets Lucille Powers. Powers sees a wanted poster with Mix's picture, but, immediately liking the cowboy, tries to persuade Mix to change his ways. In town, Mix finds that Robertson, in his guise of a respected businessman, is Powers' brother. Robertson later warns Mix to stay away from his sister. Because the stage lines are afraid to transport large sums of money, the San Luis bank has $250,000 in its vault. Robertson plans to rob the bank and, in the process, have one of his men kill Mix. Robertson's gang holds up the bank, but Mix foils the plot to kill him. As the bank robbers leave the bank, rangers are in place to

Texas Bad Man (1931) scene card: Tom Mix (*left*) battles Fred Kohler. *Left border*, Tom Mix; *right border*, Tom Mix on Tony.

bring them to justice. Kohler had already escaped by the back door and exchanges the money sack with a dummy sack at Robertson's store. The rangers see Kohler ride out of town, and pursue and shoot him out of the saddle. Mix goes to Robertson's house to arrest him. Powers pleads with Mix to let her brother escape. Robertson, seeing Powers has distracted Mix, pulls a gun and fires at Mix. Robertson's shot misses Mix, but Mix's shot hits Robertson. As Robertson tries to shoot again, rangers' shots mortally wounds the outlaw leader. With his dying breath, Robertson asks Mix to take care of Powers. Mix asks Powers to live at his sister's ranch, reminding her that he will be there frequently. Powers thinks this is a wonderful idea.

NOTES AND COMMENTARY: A novelization of *The Texas Bad Man* was published in 1934 as a Five Star Library Book by Engle-Van-Wiseman as a children's book and a movie tie-in.

REVIEWS: "Tom Mix gets the breaks on this one and scores strongly. Too good to be wasted on a double bill." (*Variety*, 9/27/32); "Very good Tom Mix vehicle." (*Western Movies*, Pitts)

SUMMATION: *The Texas Bad Man* is a superior "B" western for Tom Mix. Aided by Jack Cunningham's fine screenplay, all the actors perform admirably, headed by Willard Robertson's outstanding performance as an intelligent bandit leader with a Napoleonic complex. Robertson brings a subtlety and complex shading to the role that allows the audience to feel a certain sympathy for Robertson in his demise. Daniel B. Clark's cinematography enhances the action sequences, especially the brilliantly staged bank holdup. Edward Laemmle's direction is first rate.

BRANDED! Like One of His Own Steers,
He Bore the Stigma of His Father's Guilt!
RUSTLERS! HORSES! GUNS! POSSES! FIGHTS! RACES!

The Throwback

Universal (September 1935); A Buck Jones Production

CAST: Buck Saunders, **Buck Jones**; Muriel Fergus, **Muriel Evans**; Ford Cruze, **George Hayes**; Jack Thorne, **Bryant Washburn**; Milt Fergus, **Eddie Phillips**; Spike Travis, **Paul Fix**; Saunders' Foster Father, **Charles K. French**; Tom Fergus, **Frank LaRue**; Sheriff, **Bob Walker**; Jim Saunders, **Earl Pingree**; Buck as a boy, **Allan Ramsay**; Muriel as a girl, **Margaret Davis**; Milt as a boy, **Bobbie Nelson**; Spike as a boy, **Mickey Martin**; and "**Silver**"// Stockdale, **Carl Stockdale**; Race Patron, **Lafe McKee**; Messenger, **Jim Corey**

CREDITS: Director, **Ray Taylor**;

Story, **Cherry Wilson**; Screenwriter, **Frances Guihan**; Art Director, **Ralph Berger**; Editor, **Bernard Loftus**; Cinematographers, **Allen Thompson** and **Herbert Kirkpatrick**; Sound Supervisor, **Buddy Meyers**

LOCATION FILMING: Agoura, Vasquez Rocks, California

RUNNING TIME: 60 min.

STORY: After a long absence, Buck Jones returns to King City, primarily to see his childhood sweetheart, Muriel Evans. Jones' father had been killed as a rustler and most of the townspeople think Jones will follow in his father's footsteps. Only a friend of Jones' father, George Hayes, and Evans are happy to see him. Evans' father, Frank LaRue tries, unsuccessfully to run Jones out of town. Jones takes up residence on his father's ranch. Evans' brother, Eddie Phillips, and his friend, Paul Fix, have been rustling cattle in the King City area and plan to frame Jones for their crimes by planting stolen cattle in Jones' corral. Jones is arrested for rustling, but he has found a matchbox in the corral. In jail, Jones shows the matchbox to Evans, who tells Jones the box belongs to Phillips. Bailed out of jail, Jones begins to amass evidence against the real culprits. Working with Jones, Hayes en-

The Throwback (1935) movie still: Muriel Evans (*right*) visits Buck Jones in jail as Sheriff Bob Walker watches.

tices Phillips into a card game in which Phillips runs up a huge gambling debt. Hayes tells Phillips he wants his money immediately. Phillips rifles his father's safe, but finds no money. Evans witnesses this act and follows Phillips as he leaves the ranch. Going to Fix, Phillips tells them they have to rustle and sell cattle that night. Jones alerts LaRue, Sheriff Bob Walker and Cattleman's Detective Bryant Washburn, who meet him at the scene of the rustling activity. The men close in. Fix is shot but Phillips escapes. As he dies, Fix admits he was behind the rustling activity but refuses to name his partner. Jones rides after Phillips and catches him. As Jones starts to take Phillips to jail, Evans shows up and threatens to shoot Jones unless he allows Phillips to escape. He refuses; and Evans shoots Jones, wounding him. Phillips rides away, and Evans rushes to Jones' side. Only Jones, Evans and Hayes know the truth about Phillips, and they decide not to tell Larue. Jones and Evans plan to wed.

NOTES AND COMMENTARY: With this film, Buck Jones began his second season with Universal. The series created a new opening, with Jones riding to the camera and rearing up on Silver as Jones' name flashes across the screen. Also, Jones used a new theme song, "Hoofbeats," over the opening credits. Jones also utilized this music for his radio show.

George Hayes appeared in *The Throwback* and *SilverSpurs* (Universal, 1936) before settling into his role of Windy Halliday in the Hopalong Cassidy series. Hayes finally left the Cassidy series after the 1938–39 season and signed a contract with Republic Pictures, where as "Gabby" he became Roy Rogers' best-known sidekick. Most film historians rate Hayes as the best of the comic sidekicks. Although Smiley Burnette was the first sidekick to show up in the *Motion Picture Herald's* Top Ten Money-Making Stars poll, Hayes consistently made the list from 1943 through 1952, and again in 1954, with a second place finish in 1945.

REVIEWS: "Story avoids the usual cliché of westerns, and all concerned turn in a fine job." (*The Motion Picture Guide*, Nash and Ross); "Plenty of production, good support and nice acting job by Buck Jones gives this one virtual deluxe rating." (*Variety*, 11/6/35)

SUMMATION: Again producer Buck Jones comes up with a strong "B" western, with a storyline that avoids the usual clichés. The acting is above the usual caliber seen in series westerns, led by a fine performance by Jones. Jones flawlessly conveys his emotions in well-written scenes with Muriel Evans and George Hayes. Evans also shines as she handles difficult scenes usually not asked of the leading ladies. Hayes, who would become one of the premier movie sidekicks, perhaps the best of that breed, registers strongly as a basically decent man who works with the lawless element. Cherry Wilson's story and Frances Guihan's resulting screenplay are excellent. Director Ray Taylor knows he has a good story and doesn't disappoint.

Tree-Topping Thrills! Axe Slashing Action!

Timber

Universal (August 1942)

CAST: Quebec, **Leo Carrillo**, Arizona, **Andy Devine**; Kansas, **Dan Dailey, Jr.**; Yvette Lacour, **Marjorie Lord**; Pierre Lacour, **Edmund MacDonald**; Dan Crowley, **Wade Boteler**; Jules Fabian, **Nestor Paiva**; Pop Turner, **Paul Burns**; Joe Radway, **James Seay**; Ann Burrows, **Jean Phillips**; Bill Cormack, **William Hall**; Sandy, **Walter Sande**// Mill Worker, **Murdock MacQuarrie**; Jerome K. Osborne, **Guy Usher**; Disgruntled Logger, **Ethan Laidlaw**; Henchman, **Anthony Warde**; Loggers, **Frank Hagney**, **Eddie Dew**, **James Westerfield** and **Ernie Adams**; Doctor, **Lloyd Ingraham**; Police Officer, **Stanley Blystone**

CREDITS: Director, **Christy Cabanne**; Associate Director, **Ben Pivar**; Story, **Larry Rhine** and **Ben Chapman**; Screenwriter, **Griffin Jay**; Editor, **Otto Ludwig**; Art Director, **Jack Otterson** and **Ralph M. DeLacy**; Set Decorators, **R.A. Gausman** and **J. Andrew Gilmore**; Cinematographer, **Jack McKenzie**; Sound, **Bernard B. Brown** and **Glenn Anderson**; Music Director, **H.J. Salter**

RUNNING TIME: 58 min.

STORY: Logging operations are being sabotaged by foreign agents to prevent needed lumber from reaching shipyards. The lumberyard owner tells mill boss Leo Carrillo and yard boss Andy Devine the lumber has to get through. Devine proposes firing all workers who won't produce. New workers are hired, and Carrillo and Devine's old friend, Dan Dailey, Jr., signs on. Dailey is given the job of driving the lumber trucks down a narrow steep road to the mill. At the logging camp, Edmund MacDonald, his sister Marjorie Lord, and best friend William Hall, receive jobs. Dailey and Lord are instantly attracted to each other. Dailey and MacDonald are government operatives assigned to stop the sabotage. Shopkeeper Paul Burns, leader of the sabotage operations, learns who Dailey really is and plans to have him killed on his next night trip. Dailey gets MacDonald to take his trip so he can date Lord. MacDonald sees headlights coming toward him as he heads downhill and swerves off the road to avoid a head-on collision. MacDonald is killed. MacDonald's friend, Hall, blames Dailey. Hall is found murdered, and office manager James Seay, in the employ of the saboteurs, unsuccessfully tries to place the blame on Dailey. After another truck crashes, the other drivers are afraid to take the run. Carrillo, Devine and Dailey decide to drive with Carrillo on the next trip. From a sound-activated toy in Devine's office, Dailey surmises how the accidents happen. With Devine driving a station wagon, Dailey catches up and transfers to Carrillo's truck. As Dailey climbs into the cab with Carrillo, headlights are seen. The truck crashes through a large mirror. When activated, the truck's air horn caused the mirror to swing across the road. Dailey, Carrillo and Devine go to Burns' store. Burns and his men put up a fight but are no match for the trio. Dailey is put in charge of the lumberyard, with Lord as his secretary.

NOTES AND COMMENTARY: At one lower end New York movie house, *Timber* was booked with a western feature and a chapter of the serial *The Great Alaskan Mystery* (Universal, 1944). That particular episode was made up almost entirely of footage from *Timber*. The audience was stunned, and the management changed the bill the next day.

Dan Dailey was a contract player on loan from Metro-Goldwyn-Mayer. This would be Dailey's first starring role. Later in 1942, Dailey entered the service. On his return to Hollywood, Dailey was signed by 20th Century Fox, became a star and received an Academy Award nomination for his performance in *When My Baby Smiles at Me* (20th Century Fox, 1948). Other notable Dailey performances can be seen in *Meet Me at the Fair* (Universal-International, 1953) and *It's Always Fair Weather* (Metro-Goldwyn-Mayer, 1955).

REVIEWS: "A compact package of outdoor melodramatics that will provide fast and logical action entertainment." (*Variety*, 8/12/42); "Much better than average release." (*Hollywood Reporter*, 8/10/42)

SUMMATION: *Timber* is an exciting logging saga that generates moments of genuine suspense. Dan Dailey, Jr. joins Leo Carrillo and Andy Devine in this outing, adding a welcome light touch to the proceedings. Carrillo and Devine give their usual fine performances, with a particular nod to Devine for the delicate shadings he adds to his acting scenes. Christy Cabanne directs hell bent for leather and delivers a very entertaining story.

---

*First Western Epic Since the Days of the Silent Screen!
The King of the Saddle in a blazing Western drama in which he outwits
a gigantic cattle-stealing scheme!*

Trail Drive

Universal (September 1933); A Ken Maynard Production

CAST: Ken, **Ken Maynard**; Virginia, **Cecilia Parker**; Honest John, **William Gould**; Thirsty, **Frank Rice**; Blake, **Bob Kortman**; Aunt Martha, Fern Emmett; Marshall, **Jack Rockwell**; Jamison, **Lafe McKee**; and "Tarzan"// Dad, **Horace B. Carpenter**; Bucko, **Al Bridge**; Banker, Wallis Clark; Frank, **Frank Ellis**; Ben, **Ben Corbett**; Chick, **Slim Whitaker**; Cowboy, **Art Mix**; Musician at Camp Fire, **Jack Kirk**; Hank, **Hank Bell**; Steve, **Wally Wales**

CREDITS: Director/ Story/ Screenwriter, **Alan James**; Editor, **Charles Harris**; Cinematographer, **Ted McCord**; Sound, **Earl Crain**

SONGS: "Trail Herd" (Maynard) — sung by **Ken Maynard**

LOCATION FILMING: Kernville, and the Miller and Lux Ranch, California

RUNNING TIME: 60 min.

STORY: Ken Maynard arrives in Sweetwater to find the cattlemen unable to sell their cattle. No buyer will make any type of bid. Maynard tells the cattlemen that he'll talk to his boss, William Gould, and find the answer to the problem. Unknown to Maynard, Gould has men intimidating the cattle buyers so he will be able to buy the cattle with script instead of money. Gould plans to sell the cattle and not redeem the script. Maynard, believing in Gould, takes the responsibility for driving the cattle to New Mexico and seeing the cattlemen will be paid in full before the steers leave Texas. Sheriff Jack Rockwell discovers Gould's plan and rides with a posse to prevent the cattle from leaving Texas soil. Gould's henchman tries to get Maynard to

The Trail Drive (1933) movie still: Ken Maynard (*right*) catches up with swindler William Gould.

move the cattle at a faster pace. Maynard refuses, and Kortman makes an unsuccessful attempt to take over as trail boss. Maynard decides to hold the herd and ride into town to talk to Gould. Cattle owner Cecilia Parker, who is in love with Maynard, decides to follow him. Maynard discovers that Gould is trying to cheat the cattlemen, and is captured after a furious struggle. Parker is also detained. With Herculean effort, Maynard gets free and rescues Parker. Maynard gets back to the herd, but before they can be turned back to Sweetwater, Kortman and his men stampede the herd across the river into New Mexico. Gould has sold the cattle, and the buyers are waiting for the herd. Maynard rounds up Gould and forces him to face the cattlemen. Fearing the cattlemen will lynch him, Gould surrenders the money to redeem the script. Maynard lets Gould ride back to Texas, where Kortman shoots Gould for the money he's carrying. Maynard and Parker now have time to renew their romance.

NOTES AND COMMENTARY: To obtain permission to use cattle from the famous Miller and Lux ranch for the trail drive sequences, Ken Maynard's unit filmed a two-reel short about life on the ranch.

Cecilia Parker is best known for her role as Mickey Rooney's older sister, Marian, in the Andy Hardy series from 1937 to 1942, and in the final entry, *Andy Hardy Comes Home* (Metro-Goldwyn-Mayer, 1958).

REVIEWS: "A good story and typical Ken Maynard standards of action make this top notch feature a must for the star's fans." (*Western Movies*, Pitts); "One of the best looking of Maynard's series Westerns thanks to cinematographer McCord who responds to the simplicity of director James' story with a set of epic images that give the film the feel of a silent western." (*The Western*, Hardy)

SUMMATION: *Trail Drive* is a very good Ken Maynard vehicle. Though merely adequate in the acting department, Maynard certainly knows how to deliver the action goods. The film highlights Maynard at his riding, fighting and shooting best. Cecilia Parker makes a comely heroine, and William Gould scores a bullseye as Maynard's adversary, Honest John. In addition, some neat plot elements help to elevate director Alan James' fine screenplay.

"The Vigilantes Are Coming!"
... The most terrifying words of a lawless era ... as the reddest pages of the West leap to thrilling life!

Trail of the Vigilantes

Universal (December 1940)

CAST: Kansas (Tim Mason), **Franchot Tone**; Dawson, **Warren William**; Swanee, **Broderick Crawford**; Meadows, **Andy Devine**; Bolo, **Mischa Auer**; Sheriff Korley, **Porter Hall**; Barbara Thornton, **Peggy Moran**; George Preston, **Samuel S. Hinds**; Thornton, **Charles Trowbridge**; Lefty, **Paul Fix**; Phil, **Harry Cording**; Joe, **Max Wagner**// Conductor, **Victor Potel**; Medicine Show Owner, **Earle Hodgins**; Store Owner, **Robert McKenzie**; Bartender, **Lew Kelly**; Deputy Sheriff, **Ralph Dunn**; Telegrapher, **George Chandler**; Wagon Driver, **Hank Bell**

CREDITS: Director, **Allan Dwan**; Assistant Director, **Vernon Keays**; Screenwriter, **Harold Shumate**; Editor, **Edward Curtiss**; Art Directors, **Jack Otterson** and **Harold MacArthur**; Set Decorator, **R.A. Gausman**; Cinematographers, **Joseph Valentine** and **Milton Krasner**; Gowns, **Vera West**; Sound, **Bernard B. Brown** and **Robert Pritchard**; Music Director, **H.J. Salter**

LOCATION FILMING: Lake Sherwood, Walker Ranch, Lone Pine, Kernville, Iverson, Corriganville and Tuolumme County, California

RUNNING TIME: 75 min.

STORY: Special investigator Franchot Tone journeys to Peaceful Valley to investigate the lawlessness of the vigilantes. Tone makes friends with Charles Trowbridge's ranch hands, Broderick Crawford and Andy Devine. Crawford gets jobs on the ranch for Tone and medicine show entertainer Mischa Auer. Tone meets Warren William and immediately suspects him of orchestrating the lawless activity. At Trowbridge's ranch, his daughter, Peggy Moran, immediately falls in love with Tone. Tone searches William's office and finds a crucial ledger. William is unsuccessful in preventing Tone from taking the ledger. William has Tone arrested; but his pals, Crawford, Devine and Auer, break Tone out of jail. Learning that the outgoing stage carries all the ranchers' savings to purchase grazing lands, Tone thinks William's men will hold up the stage. Approaching the stagecoach, the men see the coach being robbed. Giving chase, Tone and his pals are unable to catch the bandits but recover the money. Tone brings the money to the ranchers, not knowing Auer has taken the ledger Tone has concealed in his saddle. The ranchers think Tone held up the stagecoach until Crawford shows up with the ledger and puts things straight. William had been with the ranchers until he received word the stage coach robbery went sour and started back to town. With him is Peggy Moran, unhappy because she thinks she's in love with an outlaw. The ranchers race to town to bring William and his gang to justice. William and his men hole up in the saloon. Tone and his pals investigate while the ranchers wait at the edge of town. Tone's horse acts up and plunges into the saloon, wreaking havoc. With this diversion, Crawford, Devine and Auer gain entrance and begin taking care of the gang with their fists. Tone gets the drop on William, but Crawford smashes down an office door into Tone, which allows William to make a break across the rooftops. Crawford gives chase while Tone searches for Moran. William falls to his death trying to get away from Crawford. Tone finds Moran trussed up in a closet and realizes he loves her. With the reward money, Tone buys a ranch, marries Moran and hires Auer as his foreman. Crawford and Devine dress in eastern clothes and travel to Kansas City to see what fortune holds for them.

NOTES AND COMMENTARY: Peggy Moran recalled that Franchot Tone had previously been cast in sophisticated roles, and now he was asked to portray a cowboy in *Trail of the Vigilantes*. Initially, Universal wanted Tone to play opposite Nancy Kelly, fresh from a Broadway triumph. Tone wasn't familiar with Kelly, so scenes from *One Night in the Tropics* (Universal, 1940) were shown to him. Moran was also in the scene. Afterwards, Tone said she was great; but he was talking about Moran, not Kelly. So Moran won the part in the film.

Peggy Moran remembers she was cast as a man-crazy girl, always running after men. Moran commented, "I never had to run after men, but in these pictures I always did."

Peggy Moran had looked up to Franchot Tone as a romantic man. When Moran made this picture, she and Tone started dating. Moran recalled that Tone was smitten with her. Tone told her he hadn't felt that way since his marriage to Joan Crawford. Even at that time, Moran felt she had made a romantic commitment to Henry Koster, who had directed her in *First Love* (Universal, 1939) and *Spring Parade* (Universal, 1940). Moran eventually married Koster and retired from the motion picture business, appearing only in cameo roles in her husband's films.

Peggy Moran commented, "It was really a spoof on westerns. When I'm stolen by the heavy, Warren William, Franchot Tone has a line, 'Don't tell me they've stole the girl.' I think the picture was a big hit in the modern cities, like New York or Chicago. Small towns didn't quite get it. They were used to their straight westerns."

Director Allan Dwan struck Peggy Moran as a nice man. Moran said, "In many of the pictures that I made, I might have been able to become a star. When I played in all those pictures, if I remembered the lines they said, 'Print it.' That's about the help I got."

In talking about the scene in which all the principals became stuck in mud trying to rescue a calf, Moran recalled, "I remember being stuck in the mud. For purely female reasons it was tough on me. I can't explain exactly why. You can use your imagination, being stuck in the mud up to your waistline. Unpleasant."

Footage from *Trail of the Vigilantes* was later used in the Kirby Grant western *Rustler's Roundup* (Universal, 1946), the serial *The Scarlet Horseman* (Universal, 1946) and the Tex Williams featurette *Western Courage* (Universal-International, 1950).

The Broderick Crawford chase sequence was later recycled for *Road Agent* (Universal, 1941) and *Gunman's Code* (Universal, 1946).

REVIEWS: "Fast action western drama with overtones of comedy and undertone of satire." (*Variety*, 12/11/40); "Pleasant blend of humor and action." (*Western Movies*, Pitts)

SUMMATION: *Trail of the Vigilantes* is a delightful comedy western that doesn't forget to deliver the action goods. Franchot Tone, Broderick Crawford, Andy Devine and Mischa Auer give engaging performances and make a fine quartet of outlaw-busters. Peggy Moran does a nice job as the spunky rancher's daughter who sets her cap for Tone. Warren William makes a properly nasty villain. Allan Dwan brings in a most enjoyable feature.

A TWO-GUN TROUBLE SHOOTER RIDDING the RANGE of RUSTLERS!

Trail to Gunsight

Universal (August 1944)

CAST: Dan Creede, **Eddie Dew**; Bill Hollister, **Lyle Talbot**; Horatius, **Fuzzy Knight**; Barton, **Ray Whitley**; Mary Wagner, **Maris Wrixon**; Tim Wagner, **Buzz Henry**; Clementine, **Marie Austin**; Ma Wagner, **Sarah Padden**; Duke Ellis, **Glenn Strange**; Bert Nelson, **Ray Bennett**; Reb Tanner, **Charles Morton**; Sheriff Morgan, **Forrest Taylor**; Ray Whitley's Bar-6 Cowboys// Wagner, **Terry Frost**; Gunsight Sheriff, **Jack Clifford**

CREDITS: Director, **Vernon Keays**; Associate Producer, **Oliver Drake**; Story, **Jay Karth**; Screenwriter, **Bennett Cohen**; Additional Dialogue, **Patricia Harper**; Editor, **Russell Schoengarth**; Art Directors, **John B. Goodman** and **Abraham Grossman**; Set Decorators, **Russell A. Gausman** and **Leigh Smith**; Cinematographer, **Maury Gertsman**; Gowns, **Vera West**; Sound, **Bernard B. Brown** and **Joe Lapis**; Musical Director, **Paul Sawtell**

SONGS: "Slumbertime Out on the Prairie" (O. Drake) — sung by Eddie Dew; "Chuck Wagon Blues" (Jackson, Walters and Lillie) — sung by Ray Whitley and his Bar-6 Cowboys; "Old Nevada Trail" (Carol) — sung by **Ray Whitley**; and "I Ain't Got a Gal to Come Home To" (O.

Drake)—sung by **Eddie Dew** and **Ray Whitley**

LOCATION FILMING: Agoura, California

RUNNING TIME: 58 min.

STORY: Three of Glenn Strange's men, led by Ray Bennett, rob the bank. The outlaws are chased by a posse led by Deputy Sheriff Eddie Dew. When the bandits split up, Dew and a newcomer to town, Fuzzy Knight, trail Bennett. Strange is waiting for his gang at Terry Frost's ranch. Frost wants nothing to do with Strange. Bennett arrives at the ranch just ahead of Dew and Knight. A gunfight ensues, and Frost attempts to capture Strange; but Strange gains the upper hand and shoots Frost. Strange and Bennett are able to slip away. Dew enters the cabin and finds Frost's dead body. Dew believes he killed Frost. Frost's son, Buzz Henry, rides up. Dew tells him Frost was killed while battling the bank robbers. Dew resigns to take Henry to his mother, Maris Wrixon, and grandmother, Sarah Padden, in Gunsight. Deputy Marshal Lyle Talbot suspects Dew might have taken the bank money since it was not recovered. Strange and Bennett go to Gunsight, planning to steal Padden's cattle. Dew tells Wrixon and Padden that Frost died a hero. Knight and Dew sign on to help Padden. Strange, Bennett and Talbot also sign on as cowhands. Strange finds out Talbot is a lawman. Strange wants Dew to help with the rustling scheme and threatens to tell Wrixon and Padden he killed Frost if he refuses. Dew pretends to go along but plans to stop Strange. Dew thinks Strange and Bennett might have been in the cabin when Frost was killed. Some of the stolen money has shown up in Gunsight. Strange plants some of the stolen money in Dew's bunk. Dew finds the money and plans to take it to the sheriff. Strange tells everyone that Dew killed Frost, and Talbot arrests Dew. Henry comes to the jail to shoot Dew and Knight, but Dew convinces Henry to release them so the can thwart Strange's plan to rustle Padden's cattle. Dew and Knight ride to stop Strange, and Henry rides for Talbot and a posse. Together, Dew, Knight and Talbot bring Strange and his gang to justice. Strange admits he shot Frost.

NOTES AND COMMENTARY: Eddie Dew here receives his first starring role since his short-lived series at Republic in 1943. Dew inherited the Rod Cameron role, with Lyle Talbot in support. Dew signed on as second lead, with Cameron as top cowboy, in *Trigger Trail* (Universal, 1944), and would revert to co-star status for four more entries, beginning with *Riders of the Santa Fe* (Universal, 1944).

REVIEWS: "Passable Eddie Dew western with the slick Universal look." (*Western Movies*, Pitts); "Nothing unusual to be found here." (*Motion Picture Guide*, Nash and Ross)

AUTHOR'S COMMENTS: *Trail to Gunsight* is a nicely paced western feature. With better fighting technique, Eddie Dew might have made a first rate western star. Too bad someone didn't show Dew how to throw effective and realistic punches.

Fuzzy Knight does well as a sidekick, except in the scenes where he has to go through some "funny" business with a hypnotic eye. Thank goodness these are mercifully brief. Lyle Talbot's talents are wasted as the secondary hero. The rest of the cast acquit themselves nicely. Director Vernon Keays does well with a somewhat familiar story.

REVENGE ON THE RANGE!
...blasting the brawling badlands!

Trail to Vengeance

ALTERNATIVE TITLE: *Vengeance;* Universal (November, 1945)

CAST: Jeff Gordon, **Kirby Grant**; Hungry Huggins, **Fuzzy Knight**; Dorothy Jackson, **Poni Adams**; Horace Glumm, **Tom Fadden**; Bully, **John Kelly**; Foster Felton, **Frank Jaquet**; Sheriff Morgan, **Stanley Andrews**; Bart Jackson, **Walter Baldwin**; Alice Gordon, **Beatrice Gray**// Cattle Herder, **Roy Brent**; Outlaws, **Pierce Lyden** and **Dan White**

CREDITS: Director / Producer, **Wallace W. Fox**; Screenwriter, **Bob Williams**; Editor, **Russell Schoengarth**; Art Directors, **John B. Goodman** and **Abraham Grossman**; Set Decorators, **Russell A. Gausman** and **Ralph Warrington**; Cinematographer, **Maury Gertsman**; Sound, **Bernard B. Brown** and **William Hedgcock**; Musical Director, **Mark Levant**

SONGS: "On the Trail of Tomorrow" (Carter and Rosen)—sung by **a male chorus;** and "Huckleberry Pie" (Carter and Rosen)—sung by **Fuzzy Knight**

LOCATION FILMING: Corriganville and Agoura, California

RUNNING TIME: 58 min.

STORY: Kirby Grant rides, with his sidekick Fuzzy Knight, to visit his brother, who is engaged in a power struggle with rancher Walter Baldwin. Grant's brother has been murdered, and Baldwin has been arrested. Banker Frank Jaquet begins foreclosure on Grant's brother's ranch because he holds an overdue note on the property. Widow Beatrice Gray can't comprehend this situation, since there is sufficient money in a bank in Colorado. Grant wants an extension, but Jaquet initially refuses. Undertaker Tom Fadden intercedes and persuades Jaquet to comply. Fadden is behind a scheme to gain control of Gray's and Baldwin's ranches. Because of Jaquet's criminal past, Fadden makes use of his talents as a forger. Fadden has his henchman, John Kelly, hold up the stage and take the money which would pay off the mortgage. This act leads Grant to believe that Baldwin is innocent. Grant begins to work with Baldwin's daughter, Poni Adams, to prove Baldwin's innocence and bring

Trail to Vengence (1945) title card: *Left*, Fuzzy Knight, Poni Adams; *right*, Kirby Grant; *lower right*, Kirby Grant delivers a strong right to the jaw of John Kelly.

to justice his brother's murderer. Fadden has Kelly break Baldwin out of jail, leave a forged confession stating Baldwin murdered Grant's brother, and bring him to Fadden's undertaker parlor. Finding Baldwin gone, Grant, Knight and Adams go to see Jacquet. Grant and Adams demand to know if there is a mortgage on Baldwin's ranch. Jaquet acknowledges there is a mortgage, but Grant finds evidence that Jacquet is a forger. Jacquet breaks down and names Fadden as the man behind the scheme. Grant arrives at the undertaker parlor just in time to prevent Fadden from embalming Baldwin. Fadden makes an escape in his buggy. Grant gives chase, and Fadden's buggy disengages from the horse and plunges over a steep embankment, carrying Fadden to his death. Grant and Adams plan to marry.

NOTES AND COMMENTARY: Jane Adams recalled an amusing incident that occurred when she first viewed the finished film. "I had met my love, [he would be] my husband for over fifty years, and we went to Grauman's Chinese Theater. It was a 'B' picture. I was the 'B'. I'm sort of a loving person. I don't like any violence or anything in my life. I had to use this gun. I had to practice and practice to twirl that gun. When I picked that gun up to use it in the movie, my [future] husband—it was a serious scene—just roared. You could hear him all over the theater. It was so unlike me."

Fuzzy Knight sang "Huckleberry Pie" in *Rawhide Rangers* (Universal, 1941) which starred Johnny Mack Brown. "On the Trail of Tomorrow" was previously heard in *West of Carson City* (Universal, 1940) and *Arizona Cyclone* (Universal, 1941).

This film's trail drive footage would later be utilized in the Tex Williams featurette *Cheyenne Cowboy* (Universal-International, 1949).

REVIEWS: "Standard Kirby Grant vehicle for Universal." (*Western Movies*, Pitts)

SUMMATION: *Trail to Vengeance*'s well-written screenplay offers ample opportunity to allow Kirby Grant to shine as a western star. Screenwriter Bob Williams, who penned many of the fine stories for the Allan "Rocky" Lane series at Republic, is in good form here. What a hoot to have a minion (John Kelly) who likes to sleep in a coffin! Sidekick Fuzzy Knight does well, and deftly keeps the comedy routines from overshadowing the story. Leading lady Poni Adams gets a chance to do a little acting as well as being decorative, and does fine on both counts. This is a good western.

The King of the Saddle!
See ridin' roarin' fightin' Hoot speed over the plains.
See him battle big-city thugs, outwit his treacherous rival,
rescue the beautiful girl, thrill you in a hundred ways.

Trailing Trouble

Universal-Jewel (March 1930)

CAST: Ed King, **Hoot Gibson**; Molly Blake, **Margaret Quimby**; "Pop" Blake, **William McCall**; Buck Saunders, **Pete Morrison**; Red Gillis, **Bob Perry**; Ming Toy, **Olive Young**// Bill Dobson, **William Dyer**

CREDITS: Director, **Arthur Rosson**; Producer, **Hoot Gibson**; Screenwriter, **Harold Tarshis**; Editor, **Gilmore Walker**; Art Director, **David Garber**; Cinematographer, **Harry Neumann**; Recording Engineer, **C. Roy Hunter**; Synchronization & Score, **David Broekman**

LOCATION FILMING: Alabama Hills, Lone Pine and the Iverson Ranch, California

RUNNING TIME: 57 min.

SOURCE: Story "Hand 'Em Over" by **Arthur Rosson**

STORY: Ranch owner William McCall puts cowhand Hoot Gibson in charge of delivering horses to William Dyer in Kansas City and collecting $5000 in return. Gibson likes

McCall's daughter, Margaret Quimby, but is known to have a roving eye. Quimby warns Gibson that if he gets into any trouble on the trip, she might marry Gibson's rival for her affections, Pete Morrison. After Dyer pays off Gibson, Morrison conspires with Dyer to take the money away from Gibson. On his way to the public library, Gibson sees a gang attempting to abduct Olive Young. The gang, led by Bob Perry, and Young are working with Dyer and Morrison. Through all obstacles, Gibson rescues Young, but Gibson thinks that in doing so he's killed Perry and the police are now after him. Gibson and Young elude the police, and, as they part, Young steals the money from Gibson. Immediately, Young has a change of heart and goes to the train to return the money to Gibson. Morrison gets Young to board the train. The train pulls out as Gibson reaches the train yards. Gibson hides in a plane that will fly over McCall's ranch, and he parachutes to earth. Gibson is at the ranch when Young shows up to return the money. Young identifies Morrison as the man who made the arrangements to have Gibson robbed. Morrison is arrested, and Quimby and Gibson finally get together.

NOTES AND COMMENTARY: Interestingly enough, the book Hoot Gibson tells Margaret Quimby he read at the library was "All Quiet on the Western Front." This was an obvious plug for the Universal's big film at that time. *All Quiet on the Western Front* (Universal, 1930) received four Academy Awards (best picture, director, screenwriting and cinematography).

REVIEWS: "Pleasant Hoot Gibson vehicle, not too complicated but plenty of fun for his fans." (*Western Movies*, Pitts); "A delightful picture." (*The Western*, Hardy)

SUMMATION: *Trailing Trouble* is a top notch Hoot Gibson western. Gibson is in good form delivering action and comedy, with director Arthur Rosson mixing in some solid suspense. The rest of the cast performs adequately, with the exception of Pete Morrison, who has trouble delivering some of his lines. Screenwriter Harold Tarshis plays fast and loose with the probability of Gibson finding a plane to take him back to the ranch. Otherwise, Tarshis' screenplay is on target.

Dynamite in the Saddle!

Trigger Trail

Universal (July 1944)

CAST: Clint Farrell, **Rod Cameron**; Echo, **Fuzzy Knight**; Sheriff Bob Reynolds, **Eddie Dew**; Ann Catlett, **Vivian Austin**; Slade, **Lane Chandler**; Rance Hudson, **George Eldredge**; Chip, **Buzz Henry**; Silas Farrell, **Davidson Clark**; Bender, **Michael Vallon**; Waco, **Dick Alexander**; Joe Kincaid, **Jack Rockwell**; Tug Catlett, **Budd Buster;** and Ray Whitley's Bar-6 Cowboys// Gilroy, **Ray Whitley**; Stage Driver, **Bud Osborne**; Hogan, **Jack Ingram**; Townsman, **Ray Jones**; Outlaw, **Artie Ortego**

CREDITS: Director, **Lewis D. Collins**; Associate Producer, **Oliver Drake**; Screenwriter, **Ed Earl Repp**; Additional Dialogue, **Patricia Harper**; Editor, **Milton Carruth**; Art Directors, **John B. Goodman** and **Abraham Grossman**; Set Decorators, **Russell A. Gausman** and **Leigh Smith**; Cinematographer, **William Sickner**; Gowns, **Vera West**; Sound, **Bernard B. Brown** and **Jess Moulin**; Musical Director, **Paul Sawtell**

SONGS: "Trail Dreamin'" (O. Drake, Wakely and Rosen)—sung by **Ray Whitley and His Bar-6 Cowboys**; "I'm Headin' for My Oklahoma Home" (Hamilton and Mays)—sung by **Eddie Dew and Ray Whitley's Bar-6 Cowboys**; "Twilight on the Prairie" (Whitley)—sung by **Fuzzy Knight;** and "Long About Sundown" (Marvin)—sung by **Ray Whitley and His Bar-6 Cowboys**

LOCATION FILMING: Corriganville and Iverson, California

RUNNING TIME: 59 min.

STORY: Ranchers are being run off their spreads on the Comanche Strip. The land is needed for a railroad right-of-way. Davidson Clark sends for his son, lawyer Rod Cameron, to help the ranchers in their trouble. Clark has been given thirty days to vacate his ranch by George Eldredge. Cameron drafts a petition to allow the ranchers to keep their lands. Eldredge begins a reign of terror to prevent the homesteaders from living up to the law. The government sends an agent to stop all land transfers, pending an investigation. Eldredge has his henchman, Richard Alexander, kill the agent. Cameron decides to investigate the scene of the crime and catches another henchman, Lane Chandler, retrieving the spent cartridge. Cameron takes Chandler to jail and finally breaks him down. When Cameron goes to bring Sheriff Eddie Dew to listen to the confession, Alexander kills Chandler. Cameron is blamed for the crime and sentenced to work on the road gang. Telegrapher Vivian Austin receives a telegram stating all evictions are illegal. Fuzzy Knight notices that Eldredge has been informed of the telegram's content.

Trigger Trail (1944) scene card: Eddie Dew (*left center*) holds a gun on Rod Cameron as Lane Chandler ministers to Budd Buster.

When Eldredge leaves town, Knight follows and is captured. Knight hears Eldredge tell his men that they are going to raid the Clark ranch and burn it to the ground. Knight escapes and rides to the road camp. Dew deputizes Cameron and other ranchers, and they ride to Clark's ranch, which is under siege. Cameron, Dew and the posse arrive just in time. Cameron and Dew defeat Eldredge and Alexander in fistfights. The posse rounds up the other gang members. The settlers are allowed to keep their lands, and Cameron and Austin have time for romance.

NOTES AND COMMENTARY: Vivian Austin commented on Rod Cameron: "He was a nice fellow, everybody liked him. He was polite. I was his girl. In those days, women did not have a helluva lot to do in westerns. Even though you have the lead, you haven't got a helluva lot to do."

Asked about her riding ability, Vivian Austin replied, "I was a very good rider. My husband was Glenn Austin, who was a polo player and he carried nine goals. He and I used to ride in the Hollywood hills a lot. I used to ride his horses and help him exercise them."

Universal had previously used this title for a 1921 Jack Perrin entry.

"Trail Dreamin'" was also sung in *Boss of Hangtown Mesa* (Universal, 1942) and *The Lone Star Trail* (Universal, 1943).

REVIEWS: "Well produced and entertaining Rod Cameron series vehicle." (*Western Movies*, Pitts); "Routine oater action and fine for fans of the genre." (*Motion Picture Guide*, Nash and Ross)

SUMMATION: *Trigger Trail* is a solid Rod Cameron western. Cameron and Eddie Dew make an engaging heroic duo, and Fuzzy Knight brings a nice comedic touch to the proceedings. George Eldredge, Lane Chandler and Richard Alexander effectively handle the villainy. Chandler, in particular, registers strongly in the scene that suggests that he will hang for murder. Lewis D. Collins directs smoothly and keeps the story on track. William Sickner's camerawork showing a horse and rider galloping across the plains is breathtaking.

Hoot knows his trigger tricks—and lots of others. You'll know when he outsmarts the wildest, toughest bunch of bad men that ever raised ruckus. Surprise twists that will leave you gasping—and laughing at the discomfited henchmen. Lots of riding, too—as only Hoot knows how!

Trigger Tricks

Universal-Jewel (June 1930)

CAST: Tim Brennan, **Hoot Gibson**; Betty Dawley, **Sally Eilers**; Thomas Kingston, **Bob Homans**; Joe Dixon, **Jack Richardson**; Nick Dalgus, **Monte Montague**; Jack Thompson, **Neal Hart**; Ike, **Max Asher**; Mike, **Walter Perry**// Outlaw, **Ben Corbett**

CREDITS: Director/Story, **Reeves Eason**; Producer, **Hoot Gibson**; Editor, **Gilmore Walker**; Art Director, **David Garber**; Cinematographer, **Harry Neumann**; Recording Engineer, **C. Roy Hunter**; Synchronization & Sound, **David Broekman**

Location FILMING: Agoura Ranch, California

RUNNING TIME: 60 min.

STORY: Texas Ranger Hoot Gibson takes over the job of foreman of Sally Eilers's sheep ranch to avenge his brother's death. Gibson immediately suspects cattleman Bob Homans of being behind the trouble between the cattleman and the sheepmen, and the death of his brother. Working undercover, Gibson also gets hired by Homans to work on Eilers ranch in order to spy on her. Sheepherder Monte Montague is in league with Homans and has been stealing Eilers' sleep. Gibson discovers Montague's treachery and plans to bring Homans and his men to justice. Through trickery, Gibson captures Homans. Gibson convinces Homans to confess and then has time to show his affection for Eilers.

NOTES AND COMMENTARY: At

Trigger Tricks (1930) scene card: Hoot Gibson tries to discover who's behind the trouble between the cattlemen and the sheepmen; *left border*, Hoot Gibson; *right* (*circle*), Sally Eilers, Hoot Gibson.

one point Gibson refers to secondary character "Nick Dalgas," played by Monte Montague, as a "wop sheepherder." This is not something that would be tolerated by a hero in later years.

REVIEWS: "The western has suspense. Gunplay and fist fights are lacking. However, it should not prove a disappointment to the western fan" (*Variety*, 6/25/30); "Lighthearted Hoot Gibson film." (*Western Movies*, Pitts)

SUMMATION: Director Reeves Eason paces this average western nicely, but the story would have had more impact if more action had been forthcoming. Gibson fires one shot, throws no punches and engages in little hard riding. The actors' performances are generally okay, but Gibson and leading lady Sally Eilers at times have trouble delivering long passages of dialog.

*HE'D RATHER FIGHT A MAN TO DEATH—
THAN SQUEAL ON HIM!*

Trouble at Midnight

Universal (January 1938)

CAST: Kirk, **Noah Beery, Jr.**; Tony, **Larry Blake**; Catherine, **Catherine Hughes**; Marion, **Bernadene Hayes**; Elmer, **Louis Mason**; Goff, **Earl Dwire**; Benson, **Charles Halton**; Cordeen, **Frank Melton**; Dick, **Henry Hunter**; Dick, **George Humbert**; Sheriff, **Harlan Briggs**; DeHoff, **Edward Hearn**; Doctor, **Harry C. Bradley**// Ranch Hand, **Tom Steele**; Bradley, **Ernie Adams**

CREDITS: Director, **Ford Beebe**; Associate Producer, **Barney A. Sarecky**; Screenwriters, **Ford Beebe** and **Maurice Geraghty**; Editor, **John Rawlins**; Art Director, **Ralph DeLacy**; Cinematographer, **Jerome Ash**; Sound, **Jesse T. Bastian** and **Lawrence Aicholtz**; Musical Director, **Charles Previn**

RUNNING TIME: 68 min.

SOURCE: Story "Night Patrol" by **Kimball Herrick**

STORY: Dairyman Noah Beery, Jr. believes that organized gangsters are rustling valuable dairy cows. He believes that it's only a matter of time before their area is targeted and wants to organize a night patrol. Only newspaperman Earl Dwire backs Beery, and the City Council votes against the idea. A wounded gangster, Larry Blake, arrives at the ranch and is about to be arrested, but Beery covers for him. Blake had saved Beery's brother's life in World War I. Under Beery's influence, Blake starts to enjoy ranch life but refuses to squeal on his former comrades. The gangsters finally raid the area and frame Blake as a participant. Blake is arrested, but Beery persuades Sheriff Harlan Briggs to let him escape to help round up the rustlers. The gangsters raid Beery's ranch. Beery and Blake engage the gangsters in a gun battle and try to hold them until Briggs can arrive with a posse. Even though wounded, Blake shoots the leader. The posse arrives and the rest of the gangsters are rounded up. Both Beery and Blake have love interests whom they plan to marry.

NOTES AND COMMENTARY: World War I footage from *All Quiet on the Western Front* (Universal, 1930) and *The Road Back* (Universal, 1937) was used in *Trouble at Midnight*. Interestingly, both Noah Beery, Jr. and Larry Blake had roles in *The Road Back*.

Catherine Hughes sometimes received on-screen billing as Kay Hughes.

REVIEWS: "Highly efficient and entertaining 'B' melodrama." (*Western Movies*, Pitts); "Largely thrown together, it will snake its way into the lower action brackets and find its forte in the duals where another film carries the bulk of the matinee load." (*Variety*, 11/10/37)

SUMMATION: *Trouble at Midnight* is a neat gangster melodrama with a western setting. Director Ford Beebe takes a familiar plot line and, with a talented cast, makes this film pleasant entertainment. Noah Beery, Jr. comes across well as the straightforward hero. Larry Blake has a tendency to overact slightly as the bad guy who reforms under Beery's influence, but the reformation is convincing. Catherine Hughes and Bernadene Hayes are attractive heroines; but Hayes has the better part and she handles it quite well. Earl Dwire, as the newspaper editor, and Harlan Briggs, as the sheriff, play believable characters while adding some necessary humor to the story.

---

*She's a'swingin' in the Saddle
He's a Cow-Cow Boogie Boy!
Rhythm rides the range with herds of laughs ... and sizzlin' songs!*

Twilight on the Prairie

Universal (July 1944)

CAST: Bucky, **Johnny Downs**; Sally, **Vivian Austin**; Cactus, **Leon Errol**; Ginger, **Connie Haines**; Phil, **Eddie Quillan**; Jackson, **Jack Teagarden**; Chuck, **Jimmie Dodd**; Gainsworth, **Milburn Stone**; Jed, **Olin Howland**; Hank, **Perc Launders**; Jason, **Dennis Moore**; Texas Bill, **Ralph Peters**; Jack Teagarden's Orchestra; Eight Buckaroos; Foy Willing & the Riders of the Purple Sage

CREDITS: Director, **Jean Yarbrough**; Producer, **Warren Wilson**; Story, **Warren Wilson**; Screenwriter, **Clyde Bruckman**; Editor, **Fred R. Feitshans, Jr.**; Art Directors, **John B. Goodman** and **Abraham Grossman**; Set Decorators, **Russell A. Gausman** and **E.R. Robinson**; Cinematographer, **Jerome Ash**; Gowns, **Vera West**; Sound, **Bernard B. Brown** and **Charles Corrall**; Music, **Hans Salter**

SONGS: "Where the Prairie Meets the Sky" (Carter and Rosen)—sung by **Johnny Downs**; "Little Brown Jug" (Winner)—sung by **Connie Haines**; "Sip Nip Song" (George and Weisberg)—sung by **Jack Teagarden, Johnny Downs, Jimmie Dodd** and **Eddie Quillan**; "I Get Mellow in the Yellow of the Moon" (Dodd)—sung by **Jimmie Dodd**; "The Blues" (Teagarden)—sung by **Jack Teagarden**; "Let's Love Again" (Carter and Rosen) —sung by **Connie Haines**; "Salt Water Cowboy" (Evans)—sung by **Connie Haines**; "And Then" (Mitchell and Stept)—sung by **Connie Haines** and **Johnny Downs**; "Don't You Ever Be a Cowboy" (Carter and Rosen)— sung by **Jimmie Dodd**; "No Letter Today" (Brown)—sung by **Foy Willing and the Riders of the Purple Sage**; "Texas Polka" (Halderman, Knight and Porter)—sung by **Connie Haines** and **Jimmie Dodd**

RUNNING TIME: 62 min.

STORY: Johnny Downs and his musical group have become a radio sensation with their western songs. Signed to make a picture in Hollywood, the group takes a flight west. The government commandeers the plane and forces it to land in the small Texas town of Little Lip. Downs and his musicians are stranded. There are no rooms and only enough food for residents. Foreman Leon Errol is looking for cowhands to work on Vivian Austin's ranch to brand and round up the cattle. Needing food and lodging, Downs and his group sign on. Some of the townspeople recognize the troupe as a famous Western group. Austin thinks this is a publicity stunt, but Downs assures her otherwise. Milburn Stone, the movie studio head, thinks that this is a great publicity stunt and orders Downs to stay on the ranch until they're needed in Hollywood. Before all the work is completed, Downs is called back to Hollywood. In Hollywood, Downs insists the film should be shot on location at Austin's ranch in Texas, and Stone reluctantly agrees. Downs has scenes inserted into the film depicting branding and a cattle roundup, which takes care of the work Austin needed to have done. Austin realizes Downs did this because he's in love with her. Seeing that Downs is a little shy, Errol tells Downs to kiss Austin, which he does. Austin and Downs realize they love each other.

NOTES AND COMMENTARY: Jazz great Jack Teagarden, needing work, was signed by Universal to make sound effects for two cartoons, *The Pied Piper of Basin Street* (Universal, 1944) and *The Sliphorn King of Polaroo* (Universal, 1945). While at the studio, Teagarden and his band made their appearance in *Twilight on the Prairie*.

The song "Don't You Ever Be a Cowboy," was sung by Fuzzy Knight in *Stagecoach Buckaroo* (Universal, 1942). "Where the Prairie Meets the Sky" had been featured in *Bad Man from Red Butte* (Universal, 1940) and *Frontier Law* (Universal, 1943). "Little Brown Jug" can be heard in *Law for Tombstone* (Universal, 1937).

Look closely at the montage scene of cowboys rounding up cattle, and you can see western great Buck Jones.

REVIEWS: "Plenty of songs fill this typically glossy Universal programmer." (*Western Movies*, Pitts); "Perfunctory cowboy musical that manages to pack 12 typical cowpoke songs into just over an hour." (*The Motion Picture Guide*, Nash and Ross)

SUMMATION: *Twilight on the Prairie* misses the mark with a weak story burdened by an uneven quality of songs. Jazz great Jack Teagarden is an unexpected delight, providing an ingratiating performance and wonderful singing and playing of his trombone. Foy Willing and the Riders of the Purple Sage chip in with a smooth rendition of "No Letter Today." Leon Errol does the best he can with the tired material he's handed. Vivian Austin makes a beautiful heroine. Overall, the film is best forgotten, except by fans of the various stars.

*The West Goes Ga-Ga with a Six-Gun Saga
...of Bullets and Ballads and Beauties!*

Under Western Skies

Universal (January 1945)

CAST: Katie, **Martha O'Driscoll**; Tod, **Noah Beery, Jr.**; King Randall, **Leo Carrillo**; Willie Wells, **Leon Errol**; Sheriff Wyatt, **Irving Bacon**; Professor Moffat, **Ian Keith**; Charity, **Jennifer Holt**; Faith, **Edna Mae Wonacott**; Mayfield, **Earle Hodgins**; Barton Brothers, **Shaw and Lee**; Maybelle, **Dorothy Granger**; Neil Matthews, **Jack Rice**// Lulu, **Gladys Blake**; Outlaws, **Frank Lackteen, Jack Ingram** and **Jack Casey**; Hank, **Perc Launders**; Mrs. Simms, **Claire Whitney**; Prudence, **Nan Leslie**; Mr. Jonathan, **George Lloyd**; Stable Owner, **Donald Kerr**; Preacher, **Eddy Waller**; Bartender, **Guy Wilkerson**

CREDITS: Director, **Jean Yarbrough**; Producer, **Warren Wilson**; Story, **Stanley Roberts**; Screenwriters, **Stanley Roberts and Clyde Bruckman**; Editor, **Arthur Hilton**; Art Director, **John B. Goodman**; Set Decorations, **Russell A. Gausman** and **Victor A. Gangelin**; Cinematographer, **Charles Van Enger**; Gowns, **Vera West**; Sound Director, **Bernard B. Brown**; Sound Technician, **William Fox**; Music Director, **H.J. Salter**

SONGS: "Under Western Skies" (Rosen and Carter)—sung by **Martha O'Driscoll, Ian Keith, Leon Errol, Jack Rice and Gladys Blake**; "Don't Go Making Speeches" (Rosen and Carter)—sung by **Martha O'Driscoll**; "Swanee" (Foster)—danced by **Al Shaw** and **Sam Lee**; "Oh, You Kid" (Rosen and Carter)—sung by **Dorothy Granger and chorus**; "An Old Fashioned Girl" (Rosen and Carter)—sung by **Martha O'Driscoll**; "Cowboy's Prayer" (Rosen and Carter)—sung by **Martha O'Driscoll** and **chorus**; "Don't Go Making Speeches" (reprise)—sung by **Martha O'Driscoll and chorus**; and "Under Western Skies" (reprise)—sung by **Martha O'Driscoll and chorus**

LOCATION FILMING: Burro Flats and Iverson, California

RUNNING TIME: 57 Min.

STORY: Leon Errol's traveling troupe arrives in the town of Rimrock. Fearless sheriff Irving Bacon tells Errol they can't use the Opera House for their show. The ladies of Rimrock dislike show people. Errol's daughter, Martha O'Driscoll, arranges to have the show play at the saloon. O'Driscoll takes a buckboard to deliver handbills through the community, and a wheel comes off. Schoolteacher Noah Beery, Jr. repairs the buckboard and the two feel an immediate attraction. That night, as the show is playing, bandit king Leo Carrillo and his men show up. Bacon tells Carrillo to leave, even though Bacon's eyesight is poor and he can hardly see the outlaw gang. A brawl erupts between the townspeople and Carrillo's men. Beery, who was in the audience, carries O'Driscoll out of the melee. At the Sunday church service, Carillo's henchmen, Jack Ingram and Frank Lackteen, kidnap O'Driscoll and take her to the outlaw camp. Because Bacon didn't shoot at the fleeing outlaws, his badge is taken away. Beery straps on his six guns and rides to O'Driscoll's rescue. Carrillo tells O'Driscoll he plans to reform and turn away from a life of crime. O'Driscoll is given a horse and sent back to town. Ingram, Lacteen and the other henchmen rebel and begin a gunfight with Carrillo. Beery arrives and helps Carrillo. Sharp shooting from Beery and Carrillo ends the lives of the henchmen. Carrillo rides away, and Beery is stuck with the dead bodies. Beery doesn't want his prowess with a six-shooter known to the townspeople. The bodies are brought to town, and Beery and Bacon place them in the saloon. Bacon begins firing his guns. The townspeople, seeing the dead men, think Bacon is a hero. The sheriff's badge is returned to Bacon. Bacon tells the people that O'Driscoll lured the men into Rimrock so he could deal with them. O'Driscoll and Beery get married.

NOTES AND COMMENTARY: Leo Carrillo's character is listed as King Randall in the credits but is called King Carlos throughout the film.

The veteran vaudeville team of Al Shaw and Sam Lee plays the Barton Brothers.

REVIEWS: "Cut and dried story, dialogue, acting and direction add up to a rather unentertaining film." (*Variety*, 1/3/45); "Universal tunefilm below par." (*Hollywood Reporter*, 12/29/44)

SUMMATION: *Under Western Skies* comes in as a below average musical western. Not even the talented Martha O'Driscoll and Noah Beery, Jr. can save this one. O'Driscoll looks fine and sings some forgettable songs well. Beery is okay as a mild-mannered schoolteacher who really is a crack shot. Leo Carrillo's talents are wasted as a bandit king who suddenly decides to leave his life of crime. The screenplay by Stanley Roberts and Clyde Bruckman doesn't make much sense, and the songs and comedy are not good enough to make up for it. Ashes and switches to whoever made the decision to cast the beautiful Jennifer Holt as a "plain Jane." Jean Yarbrough, usually adept in comedy situations, can't do much with this one.

A Great Western Picture
The Star Who's As Big As All Outdoors!
First Talking and Singing Picture
The voice of the WEST with its galloping hoofs, its roar of prairie wagons, the crack of whips, the red-blooded dialogue of the ropin', ridin' daredevils
and Best of All, the Songs of the Cowboys!

The Wagon Master

Universal-Jewel (September 1929); A Ken Maynard Production

CAST: The Rambler, **Ken Maynard**; Sue Smith, **Edith Roberts**; Bill Hollister, **Frederick Dana**; Jake Lynch, **Tom Santschi**; Jacques Frazelle, **Al Ferguson**; Billie Hollister, **Jack Hanlon**; Buckeye Pete, **Bobby Dunn**; Grasshopper Jim, **Frank Rice**; Stuttering Sam, **Whitehorse**//"**Tarzan**"

CREDITS: Director, **Harry Joe Brown**; Story, **Marion Jackson**; Screenwriters, **Marion Jackson and Leslie Mason**; Editor, **Fred Allen**; Cinematographer, **Ted D. McCord**; Sound, **C. Roy Hunter**

RUNNING TIME: 70 min.

LOCATION FILMING: Lone Pine, California

STORY: Tom Santschi controls food prices in various mining com-

The Wagon Master (1929) herald: *Left*, Ken Maynard; *center*, Ken Maynard, Al Ferguson, Edith Roberts; *right* (*top*), Edith Roberts, Ken Maynard; *right* (*bottom*), Edith Roberts and Ken Maynard on Tarzan.

munities. Frederick Dana decides to bring food to Gold Hill and break Santschi's monopoly. Ken Maynard joins the wagon train. On the trek, Edith Roberts' horse runs away and Maynard rescues her. Dana's second-in-command, Al Ferguson, is actually working for Santschi. Ferguson murders Dana and expects to take command of the wagon train. Maynard takes over and thwarts Santchi's attempts to stop the train. In addition, both Maynard and Ferguson vie for Roberts' attentions. A showdown results between Maynard and Ferguson, with Maynard besting Ferguson in a whip fight. Maynard races to Gold Hill in time to prevent the miners from signing an exorbitant contract with Santschi.

NOTES AND COMMENTARY: Through *The Wagon Master* has talking sequences and a musical score, it was also released as a silent picture. Maynard refused to add sound to his films until Carl Laemmle agreed that Universal would cover the added expense.

Stock footage from *The Wagon Master* was used in the serials *Mystery Mountain* (Mascot, 1934) and *The Roaring West* (Universal, 1935). In *The Roaring West*, Ken Maynard and his horse Tarzan can easily be seen in place of star Buck Jones and Silver.

REVIEWS: "Ken Maynard part-talkie is a pleasant affair." (*Western Movies*, Pitts); "High above the usual cow land picture." (*Variety*, 10/2/29)

SUMMATION: This is one of eight Universal feature films that the author was unable to view.

A RAILROADIN' FOOL!
He ran a runaway mountain train out of breath, switched himself into romance and a happy siding for life!

West Bound Limited

Universal (July 1937)

CAST: Dave, **Lyle Talbot**; Janet, **Polly Rowles**; Pop, **Frank Reicher**; Joe, **Henry Brandon**; Howard, **Henry Hunter**; Dispatcher, **William Lundigan**// District Superintendent, **George Cleveland**; Tommy, **Tom Steele**; Engineer, **J.P. McGowan**; Baker, **William Royle**; Chuck, **Charles Murphy**; Carter, **Monte Vandergrift**; Head Dispatcher, **Lew Kelly**

CREDITS: Directory/Story, **Ford Beebe**; Associate Producer, **Henry MacRae**; Screenwriter, **Maurice Geraghty**; Editor, **Phil Cahn**; Art Director, **Ralph DeLacey**; Cinematographer, **Elwood Bredell**; Sound, **Robert Pritchard** and **Jesse T. Bastian**; Musical Director, **Charles Previn**; Sound Effects, **John P. Fulton**

SONG: "I'll Take You Home Again, Kathleen" (traditional)—sung by **Polly Rowles**

LOCATION FILMING: Santa Cruz

County (Felton Depot and Zayante), California

RUNNING TIME: 66 min.

STORY: The night train brings both a payroll and a coffin to station operator Lyle Talbot. A man, hiding in the coffin, attempts to steal the payroll. A fight ensues, the thief's shirt is torn, and Talbot sees an unusual tattoo on the man's forearm. In a short chase, Talbot shoots the man in the shoulder. During the fight, a setting to hold a train was removed, and the train crashes head on into another train. Talbot is arrested for manslaughter, and the jury refuses to believe his story of the fight with a robber. En route to prison, Talbot leaps from the train and escapes. On the run, Talbot interrupts a tense confrontation between Polly Rowles, daughter of Frank Reicher, the local day station manager, and Henry Brandon, the night station manager. Reicher has a heart attack, and Talbot takes over to save Reicher's railroad pension. Talbot is given lodging at Reicher's home. Talbot and Rowles begin to fall in love. Brandon's jealousy is so intense that when he learns that Talbot is accused of being responsible for a train wreck, Brandon informs railroad authorities. In a confrontation with Brandon, Talbot learns the sheriff is coming to arrest him. Talbot starts to leave, but Brandon pulls a pistol and forces Talbot to stay. Talbot starts a terrific fight with Brandon. Meanwhile, a runaway freight train is headed for a head-on collision with a passenger train. Talbot wins the fight with Brandon and wants Brandon to derail the runaway train while he makes his escape. Brandon's arm was broken in the fight, and he passes out. Talbot realizes he can't leave, and is able to derail the runaway and prevent the disaster. When Brandon's arm is tended to, Talbot sees the unusual tattoo and realizes Brandon was the mysterious robber. Talbot tells the sheriff that Brandon has a bullet scar in his right shoulder. Brandon is arrested, and Talbot will be cleared of any wrongdoing. Talbot and Rowles plan to marry.

NOTES AND COMMENTARY: Henry Brandon endeared himself to serial buffs with his villainous performances. Brandon portrayed "the Cobra" in *Jungle Jim* (Universal, 1937), "Blackstone" in *Secret Agent X-9* (Universal, 1937), "Captain Lasca" in *Buck Rogers* (Universal, 1939) and his coup-de-grace, the sinister "Fu Manchu" in *Drums of Fu Manchu* (Republic, 1940).

"I'll Take You Home Again, Kathleen" would later be used in *The Spoilers* (Universal, 1942) and *The Daltons Ride Again* (Universal, 1945).

REVIEWS: "Nice little programmer; lightweight railroad saga but not without thrills and suspense." (*Variety*, 11/17/37); "An exciting, but minor, railway tale." (*The Motion Picture Guide*, Nash and Ross)

SUMMATION: *Westbound Limited* is a good little action drama with a first-rate performance by Lyle Talbot. Polly Rowles holds her own as Talbot's love interest. The chemistry is right between the two stars, and their romance develops naturally. Frank Reicher adds humor in a well-acted role as Rowles' father. Through Ford Beebe's fine direction, plenty of suspense is built up in the climactic sequence in which two trains are headed straight toward each other. This is a good story (despite a too pat ending) that stresses Talbot's characterization over action.

BLAZING ON TO THE GOLD RUSH!
...With guns smoking and fists flying they fought their way to the pay dirt!

West of Carson City

Universal (May 1940)

CAST: Jim Bannister, **Johnny Mack Brown**; Nevada, **Bob Baker**; Banjo, **Fuzzy Knight**; Millie Harkins, **Peggy Moran**; Mack Gorman, **Harry Woods**; Judge Harkins, **Robert Homans**; Lem Howard, **Al K. Hall**; Bill Tompkins, **Roy Barcroft**; Drag, **Charles King**; Breed, **Frank Mitchell**; Sleepy, **Eddie Cobb**; Larkin, **Jack Roper**; Slim, **Ted Wells**; Pete, **Jack Shannon**; Singing Cowhands, **the Four Singing Notables** // Snicker Joe, **Ernie Adams**; Heavy, **Victor Potel**; Stagecoach Robber, **Kermit Maynard**; Land Salesman, **Donald Kerr**; Man on Horseback with Note, **Richard Cramer**; Witness, **Al Bridge**

CREDITS: Director, **Ray Taylor**; Story, **Milton Raison**; Screenwriters, **Milton Raison, Sherman Lowe** and **Jack Bernhard**; Editor, **Louis Sackin**; Art Directors, **Jack Otterson** and **Harold MacArthur**; Set Decorator, **R.A. Gausman**; Sound, **Bernard B. Brown** and **Robert Pritchard**; Musical Director, **Hans J. Salter**

SONGS: "Let's Go" (Carter and Rosen)—sung by **the Four Singing Notables** and **Bob Baker**; "On the Trail of Tomorrow" (Carter and Rosen)—sung by **Bob Baker** and **the Four Singing Notables;** and "On the Trail of Tomorrow" (reprise)—sung by **Bob Baker** and **the Four Singing Notables**

LOCATION FILMING: Agoura and Iverson, California

RUNNING TIME: 56 min.

STORY: Gold is found in the ghost town of Ridgeville. As the town rebuilds, a lawless element, led by Harry Woods, takes control. Rancher Johnny Mack Brown breaks up a stagecoach robbery and meets passengers Judge Robert Homans and his attractive daughter, Peggy Moran. Woods arranges perjured testimony to free the bandits. undaunted by this setback, Homans and Brown begin to bring law and order to the community. After thwarting an ambush by Woods' henchman, Brown gives Woods and his men 24 hours to leave town. Woods retaliates by having Homans and Moran kidnapped in order to draw Brown into a trap. Brown affects a rescue and then leads his men into town. In a furious free-for-all, Brown and his men overpower Woods and his gang, and now Brown can spend time with Moran.

NOTES AND COMMENTARY: Continuity was not this production's strong suit: After giving his pistol to Peggy Moran, Johnny Mack Brown chases badman Charles King. Brown's only weapon is a rifle. Initially in the chase, Brown is shown without the rifle, but the pistol is back in his holster. Then things are righted, and the rifle is back in Brown's hand, with his holster empty.

Peggy Moran learned to ride for her role in Gene Autry's *Rhythm of the Saddle* (Republic, 1938). Her agent told her to say she knew how to ride, then go out and learn. Moran said, "I went to some riding academy for a few days. My fanny got so sore, I couldn't sit down. I had to eat from the mantle." In her first riding scene, Moran couldn't stop her horse and ended up in the next set. To film the scene, riders had to hold her horse on both sides in a way that wouldn't be caught by the camera in order to stop her. Moran stated, "That's the way I learned to ride."

Recalling her gunplay scenes in *West of Carson City*, Peggy Moran said, "I remembered, also, things like shooting a gun. I remember that I had to try to hide the fact that everytime the gun went off, I would blink. That was hard for me to do." I guess they had to take the shot when I didn't blink."

"Let's Go" would be heard in *Arizona Cyclone* (Universal, 1941) and *Arizona Trail* (Universal, 1943). "On the Trail of Tomorrow" would be sung in *Arizona Cyclone* and *Trail to Vengeance* (Universal, 1945).

REVIEWS: "Entertaining and well made Johnny Mack Brown vehicle" (*Western Movies*, Pitts); "Trimly contrived western of gold rush days, stacking up with the strongest outdoor epics turned out by the studio" (*Variety*, 5/8/40)

SUMMATION: *West of Carson City* is a slightly above average "B" western. The film moves briskly but is marred by some continuity lapses, as noted above, and the script plays fast and loose with time elements (e.g. Johnny Mack Brown has just returned to his ranch but states that he's been back a few days). The acting is standard for a western programmer. The fistfights are merely adequate, with the exception of an above average donnybrook between Brown and Harry Woods. Peggy Moran makes an attractive heroine.

A Battling Fool Drilling Killers with Death-Tipped Slugs!

Western Trails

Universal (June 1938)

CAST: Bob, **Bob Baker**; Alice, **Marjorie Reynolds**; Ben, **John Ridgely**; Rudd, **Carlyle Moore, Jr.**; Williams, **Forrest Taylor**; Indian Joe, **Franco Corsarro**; Dad Mason, **Bob Burns**; Bartender, **Jack Rockwell**; "Smokey"; "Wimpy"; "Apache"// Outlaw, **Jack Kirk**; Station Master Williams, **Murdock MacQuarrie**; Stage Guard, **Jack Ingram**; Bud (Harmonica Player), **Oscar Gahan**

CREDITS: Director, **George Waggner**; Assistant Director, **Glenn Cook**; Story/Screenplay, **Norton S. Parker**; Editor, **Charles Craft**; Art Director, **Charles Clague**; Set Decorator, **Albert Greenwood**; Cinematographer, **Harry Neumann**; Sound, **Charles Carroll** and **Edwin Wetzel**; Musical Director/ Arranger, **Frank Sanucci**

SONGS: "I Long for the Hills of Wyoming" (Allan)—sung by **Bob Baker**; "Ridin' Down That Utah Trail" (Allan)—sung by **Bob Baker, Marjorie Reynolds, Forrest Taylor** and **John Ridgely**; "When a Cowboy's Day Is Done" (Allan)—sung by **Bob Baker**; "A Cowboy's Life Is a Life of Ease" (Allan)—sung by **Bob Baker**; and "Riding the Trail Again" (Allan)—sung by **Bob Baker**, accompanied by **Oscar Gahan**

LOCATION FILMING: Iverson's Ranch, California

RUNNING TIME: 58 min.

STORY: Bob Baker returns home to find that his father, Bob Burns, has been murdered by Carlyle Moore, Jr., the leader of a vicious outlaw gang terrorizing the area. Chasing after the bandits, Baker is ambushed by Moore. Baker is taken to the cabin of John Ridgely, a stagecoach driver, to recuperate. Marjorie Reynolds, whom Ridgely loves, nurses Baker back to heath. Baker and Reynolds begin to fall in love. Baker has reservations because of his friendship with Ridgely. Moore and Reynolds are brother and sister. To give Ridgely a chance to propose to Reynolds, Baker takes Ridgely's stage run, which is carrying a large gold shipment. Moore and his gang attack the stage, but Baker's quick thinking prevents the robbery. Baker knows Moore is behind the robberies and murder of his father, but has no proof. Realizing Baker is getting close, Moore poisons Ridgely's mind against Baker, telling Ridgely that Baker is trying to steal Reynolds' affections. Baker obtains proof that Moore killed his father and leaves a note telling Ridgely he's leaving the area after he settles with Moore. Ridgely meets Baker at his cabin, and Baker tells him he's going to town to meet Moore. When Baker saddles his horse, Ridgely unloads Baker's six-shooter. After Baker leaves, Ridgely sees the note and realizes the mistake he's made. Moore and a confederate,

Jack Rockwell, are waiting in town for Baker. Rockwell hides in a hayloft, waiting for the chance to shoot Baker in the back. Baker and Moore meet in the dusty street. Before the two men can draw, Ridgely arrives and shoots Moore. Rockwell then shoots Ridgely in the back. Finding his gun empty, Baker grabs Ridgely's pistol and puts an end to Rockwell's murderous intentions. Baker decides to ride out; but Reynolds catches up to him, and both know they'll ride side by side forever.

NOTES AND COMMENTARY: *Western Trails* is a remake of the John Wayne vehicle *The Dawn Rider* (Lone Star/Monogram, 1935).

In the closing credits, Jack Rockwell's character designation is "Bartender." In the film, Rockwell is never seen in a saloon.

Bob Baker would sing "Ridin' Down the Utah Trail" in his final solo starring film, *The Phantom Stage* (Universal, 1939). The song title would be reworked to become "Ridin' Down That Old Texas Trail" for *The Old Texas Trail* (Universal, 1944).

Some of this film's background music was lifted from Universal's horror and serial productions.

REVIEWS: "Formula makes it a standard gunplay affair. With a little more skillful handling of detail, this film could have been an A western." (*Variety*, 6/29/38); "Okay singing oater in the Bob Baker series." (*Western Movies*, Pitts)

SUMMATION: *Western Trails* is a good Bob Baker vehicle. Baker has a little more to do that usual in the acting department, and he handles it well. John Ridgely and Marjorie Reynolds add nice support. Ridgely plays Baker's best friend and rival for Reynolds' affection, and his wavering between friendship to jealousy is convincing. Reynolds effectively balances her affections between Baker and Ridgely, and shows her torment in her decision making. This is one of George Waggner's better directorial efforts.

The Indians are coming! ... The prairie's afire!
White men worse than Indians are in ambush! ... Ride 'im, cowboy—in
this most exciting movie that's hit the screen in a dog's age!

The Wheels of Destiny

Universal (February 1934); A Ken Maynard Production

CAST: Ken Manning, **Ken Maynard**; Mary, **Dorothy Dix**; Rocky, **Philo McCullough**; Pinwheel, **Frank Rice**; Bill, **Jay Wilsey**; Dad, **Ed Coxen**; Scalp-Em-Alive, **Fred Sale, Jr.**; Red, **Fred MacKaye**; Ed, **Jack Rockwell**; Deacon, **William Gould**; Trapper, **Nelson McDowell**; Chief War Eagle, **Big Tree**; and "**Tarzan**"// Joe, **Horace B. Carpenter**; Pioneer

Woman, **Helen Gibson**; Outlaw, **Slim Whitaker**

CREDITS: Directed: **Alan James**; Story/Screenwriter, **Nate Gatzert**; Editor, **Charles Harris**; Cinematography, **Ted McCord**; Sound Supervisor, **Earl Crain**

SONG: "Wheels of Destiny" (Maynard)—sung by chorus; and "Wheels of Destiny" (Maynard)—hummed by **Dorothy Dix** and played by **Ken Maynard**.

LOCATION FILMING: Lone Pine, and Miller & Lux Ranch, California

RUNNING TIME: 64 min.

STORY: Jay Wilsey has a map to a gold claim in California and returns home to bring settlers to the new land. Wilsey gives the map to Ed Coxen for safekeeping. Fred MacKaye, spying on Wilsey, sees the map placed in a strong box. MacKaye reports to the outlaw leader, Philo McCullough, who decides to steal the map. After Wilsey leaves for the settler's camp, McCullough lays siege to Coxen's hotel. Ken Maynard and his pal, Frank Rice, are traveling to the town so Maynard can meet Wilsey's sister, Dorothy Dix. Settler Jack Rockwell makes a break from the hotel to get help from Wilsey and the settlers, but stops to tell Maynard about Coxen's predicament. Maynard and Rice ride to the hotel and keep the outlaws at bay until help arrives. After the fight, Maynard meets Dix and it's love at first sight. Maynard and Rice decide to travel back to California. McCullough and his men are allowed to join the group, even though Maynard thinks they were the men who tried to steal Wilsey's map. On the journey, Maynard finally finds proof that McCullough was behind Wilsey's trouble. The outlaws are set loose on the trail, with the admonition not to come near the wagon train. McCullough stirs up the Indian tribe by stampeding the buffalo herd. The Indians think members of the wagon train are the guilty ones, so they ride to wipe out the settlers. The Indians attack the train, but with Maynard's guidance the Indians are driven off. A band of Indians find the outlaws who started the buffalo stampede and wipe them out. Only Philo McCullough, who was watching the train, escapes. Maynard gets the wagon train across the river and out of Indian territory to safety. McCullough makes one last attempt to steal the map from Coxen's wagon, but the wagon breaks loose from the team of horses and carries him to his death. Maynard and Dix plan to make their life together.

NOTES AND COMMENTARY: A novelization of *Wheels of Destiny* was published as a Five Star Library Book by Engle-Van-Wiseman Book Corporation as a children's book and a movie tie-in. Ken Maynard wrote a brief afterward for the book.

Fred Sale, Jr.'s character name in the opening and closing credits was listed as "Scalp-Em-Alive." "Freddie" would have been more appropriate, as this is what he's called throughout the film.

Footage from *The Flaming Frontier* (Universal, Universal, 1926), *The Indians Are Coming* (Universal, 1930) and other Universal films was recycled for this feature.

Jay Wilsey, using the name Buffalo Bill, Jr., starred in western films for various independent producers from the silents to the early sound era.

Tex Harding was seen as the second lead in eight Durango Kid features for Columbia in the 1945–46 season. Harding was the brother of leading lady Dorothy Dix.

REVIEWS: "Top notch Ken Maynard film." (*Western Movies*, Pitts); "Little variation from the accepted formula of oater material." (*The Motion Picture Guide*, Nash and Ross)

SUMMATION: *Wheels of Destiny* is a stirring "mini-epic" of a wagon train trek to California. Ken Maynard is perfect as the "wagon boss," and Dorothy Dix does a neat job as the heroine. The rest of the cast handles their parts admirably. Stock footage is used to good advantage to enhance the action sequences. Alan James directs capably, and the result is a highly enjoyable movie.

He's a Man's Man
Buck JONES in His Greatest Picture

When a Man Sees Red

Universal (November 1934); A Charles Buck Jones Production

CAST: Buck Benson, **Charles Buck Jones**; Mary Lawrence, **Peggy Campbell**; Barbara, **Dorothy Revier**; Dick, **Le Roy Mason**; Ben, **Syd Saylor**; Mandy, **Libby Taylor**// Jim, the Station Agent, **Horace B. Carpenter**; Sheriff, **Jack Rockwell**; Mr. Radcliff, **Frank LaRue**; Deputy, **Frank Ellis**; Outlaw, **Bob Kortman**; Preacher, **Charles K. French**

CREDITS: Director/ Screenwriter, **Alan James**; Producer, **Irving Starr**; Story, **Basil Dickey**; Editor, **Bernard Loftus**; Art Director, **Ralph Berger**; Cinematographer, **Ted McCord**; Sound, **Buddy Meyers**

SONGS: "La Cucurachia" (traditional)—played by a **Mexican quartet**

LOCATION FILMING: Kernville and Red Rock Canyon, California

RUNNING TIME: 60 min.

STORY: Buck Jones goes east to persuade Peggy Campbell to come west to visit her uncle. In Jones' presence, Campbell receives a telegram notifying her that her uncle has died. Campbell comes west for the reading of the will and finds that Jones is now her guardian. Jones chases a rustler, LeRoy Mason, who eludes Jones by diving into a river. Campbell pulls Mason out of the river. Mason tells Campbell he's an officer of the law, and Jones is a rustler. When Jones arrives on the scene, Campbell tells Jones that Mason works for her at the ranch. When Campbell refuses to discharge Mason, Jones throws him off the ranch. Jones receives a note from Campbell telling him that she is going to see Mason. Jones follows. Realizing there will be a fight, Jones' pal, Sid Saylor, and a sheriff's posse follow Jones. From a distance, Jones sees Campbell meet Mason. Mason tries to force Campbell to marry him. Campbell tries to escape, calling for Jones. Meanwhile, Mason's gang is rustling Campbell's cattle. The posse arrives and takes Mason's men into custody. As Jones goes to Campbell's aid, Mason shoots him in the shoulder. Jones perseveres and faces Mason, knocking him down before collapsing to the ground. As Mason takes aim to shoot Jones, Saylor shoots Mason. Jones and Campbell realize they are made for each other.

NOTES AND COMMENTARY: Dorothy Revier and Buck Jones were close friends. In addition to appearing in *When a Man Sees Red*, Revier starred with Jones in *Thrill Hunter* (Columbia, 1933), *The Fighting Ranger* (Columbia, 1934) and *The Cowboy and the Kid* (Universal, 1936).

Le Roy Mason sings a love song to Peggy Campbell. Possible titles could be "Sad Dreams," "Glad Dreams" or "Moonbeams."

Syd Saylor was billed as Sid.

REVIEWS: "Over laden with class and skimpy in excitement." (*Variety*, 1/22/35)

SUMMATION: Buck Jones' second Universal western is only average fare. The story is top heavy with the taming of the beautiful heir, to the detriment of the western action. Jones again proves he can act as well as handle the action chores. Peggy Campbell is effective as the sophisticated young woman who learns the ways of the west. Syd Saylor adds some good light comedy, and Le Roy Mason makes a handsome villain. Although the story is slight, Jones' presence and the effective cinematography of Ted McCord brings the film up to par, but no further.

BANDITS WHO HELD A NATION AT BAY!
A country-side up in arms ... whole towns terror-stricken ... as the most daring desperadoes in history strike again!

When the Daltons Rode

Universal (July 1940)

CAST: Tod Jackson, **Randolph Scott**; Julie King, **Kay Francis**; Grat Dalton, **Brian Donlevy**; Caleb Winters, **George Bancroft**; Bob Dalton, **Broderick Crawford**; Ben Dalton, **Stuart Erwin**; Ozark Jones, **Andy Devine**; Emmett Dalton, **Frank Albertson**; Ma Dalton, **Mary Gordon**; Rigby, **Harvey Stephens**; Sheriff, **Edgar Dearing**; Wilson, **Quen Ramsey**; Nancy, **Dorothy Granger**; Photographer, **Bob McKenzie**; Hannah, **Fay McKenzie**; Judge Swain, **Walter Soderling**; Minnie, **Mary Ainslee**; District Attorney, **Erville Alderson**; Annabella, **Sally Payne**; Suzy, **June Wilkins**// Man at Livery Stable, **Edgar Buchanan**; Surveyors, **Harry Cording, Bob Kortman** and **Ethan Laidlaw**; Pete Norris, **Robert Dudley**; Annabella's Brother, **James Flavin**; Deputies on Train, **William Gould** and **Walter Long**; Ed Pickett, **James C. Morton**; Pete, **Pat West**; Clerk of the Court, **Forrest Taylor**; Deputy, **Jack Clifford**; Lyncher, **Tom London**; Doctor, **Lafe McKee**

CREDITS: Director, **George Marshall**; Assistant Director, **Vernon Keays**; Screenwriter, **Harold Shumate**; Editor, **Ed Curtiss**; Art Directors, **Jack Otterson** and **Martin Obzina**; Set Decorator, **R.A. Gausman**; Cinematography, **Hal Mohr**; Gowns, **Vera West**; Sound, **Bernard B. Brown** and **Robert Pritchard**; Musical Director, **Charles Previn**; Musical Score, **Frank Skinner**

LOCATION FILMING: Tuolumme County and Iverson, California

RUNNING TIME: 80 min.

SOURCE: Story "When the Daltons Rode" by **Emmett Dalton and Jack Jungmeyer, Sr.**

STORY: On his way to Oklahoma, lawyer Randolph Scott stops in a small Kansas town to see Mary Gordon and her sons, Brian Donlevy, Broderick Crawford, Stuart Erwin and Frank Albertson. Scott is talked into setting up practice in Kansas and quickly falls in love with Kay Francis. Francis, although engaged to Crawford, begins to fall in love with Scott. Harvey Stevens, with the Kansas Land and Development Company, is re-surveying land as part of a land grab scheme to take over the farmers' ranches. When an attempt is made to survey Gordon's farm, an altercation develops, leaving one surveyor dead. Erwin is arrested for murder. Scott defends Erwin, but circumstances are stacked against him, and Crawford helps Erwin escape. While Crawford and his brothers are hideout, all the major crimes in the area are blamed on them. To obtain money to fight their case in court, Crawford and his brothers rob a stagecoach carrying the Land and Development Company's payroll. Gordon's ranch is burned to the ground, and Albertson goes into town to check on Gordon and is captured. Stevens stirs up a lynch mob, but Scott manages take Albertson to the jail, where Crawford and his brothers are waiting. In the brothers' flight from town, Erwin is captured and gunned down by Stevens. Donlevy returns to town and shoots Stevens. The brothers become outlaws, robbing both stagecoaches and trains. Crawford wants Francis to go with him to South America, but Francis refuses and tells him she loves Scott. Scott discovers that honest citizen George Bancroft is behind the land grab scheme. Bancroft plans to sell the land to the railroad. Crawford wants no more robberies, but Donlevy plans to hold up the town bank before leaving the area. From his office window, Bancroft sees Donlevy, Albertson and their men enter the bank and notifies Sheriff Edgar Dearing. In the meantime, Crawford encounters Scott, planning to kill him. Francis and Gordon intervene. Gordon's tears bring Crawford to his senses and he realizes Scott is the man for Francis. Crawford sees his brothers and their gang trapped by Dearing and the townspeople and quickly joins them. In the gang's attempt to escape, Bancroft begins shooting the men down. All the gang members are killed or mortally wounded. Scott comes out into the street and Bancroft aims his rifle at him. In his dying moments, Crawford shoots Bancroft. Scott and Francis now are able to marry.

NOTES AND COMMENTARY: Commenting on *When the Dalton's Rode* and the fact she was one of Andy Devine's many girlfriends, Fay McKenzie said, "I remember that I had a fight with another girl over him. It was a catfight, but I won. He was a cute guy, a darling guy, funny and dear."

Fay McKenzie remarked about her role, "I loved it. The idea to work opposite Andy Devine was very exciting to me."

When the Daltons Rode was Edgar Buchanan's first appearance in a western film. In his long and distinguished career, he would appear in over fifty outdoor sagas, as well as portraying "Red Conners" in the Hopalong Cassidy television series from 1949 to 1951.

REVIEWS: "Slick Universal feature that has more action than plot." (*Western Movies*, Pitts); "Speedy and actionful melodrama of western outlawry, Solid adventure entertainment." (*Variety*, 7/31/40)

SUMMATION: Though a whitewashed account of the Dalton gang's activities, *When the Daltons Rode* is nevertheless an exciting, well made western. Nominal leads Randolph Scott and Kay Francis are quite adequate in their roles, but Broderick Crawford steals the show, with Andy Devine's performance coming in a close second. The film impresses with two memorable sequences the first shows the Daltons hopping on a train with a posse in full pursuit, and the second: showcases the outstanding stunt of the Daltons riding horses off a moving train. (The only sour note from that scene was Crawford's jump, which was lifted from a John Wayne Lone Star/Monogram "B" western.)

The Stampede KIiller!
outcast boy...
outlaw horse...

Wild Beauty

Universal (August 1946)

CAST: Dave Morrow, **Don Porter**; Linda Gibson, **Lois Collier**; Sissy, **Jacqueline deWit**; Gordon Madison, **Robert Wilcox**; Barney, **George Cleveland**; John Andrews, **Dick Curtis**; Johnny, **Robert "Buzzy" Henry**; and "Wild Beauty"// Ed, **Hank Patterson**; Winnie, **Eva Puig**; Mrs. Anderson, **Isabel Winters**; Roy, **Pierce Lyden**; Gus, **Roy Brent**

CREDITS: Director and Producer, **Wallace W. Fox**; Screenwriter, **Adele Buffington**; Editor, **D. Patrick Kelly**; Art Directors, **Jack Otterson** and **Abraham Grossman**; Set Decorators, **Russell A. Gausman** and **Leigh Smith**; Cinematographer, **Maury Gertsman**; Gowns, **Rosemary Odell**; Hair Stylist, **Carmen Dirigo**; Makeup, **Jack P. Pierce**; Sound, **Bernard B. Brown** and **Jess Moulin**; Music, **Frank Skinner**; Musical Director, **Paul Sawtell**

SONG: "My Country 'Tis of Thee" (traditional)—sung by **children's chorus**

LOCATION FILMING: Red Rock Canyon, California

RUNNING TIME: 59 min.

STORY: Schoolteacher Lois Collier, with her companion Jacqueline deWit, comes west by stagecoach to teach at an Arizona Indian reservation. The coach almost collides with an Indian boy, Robert "Buzzy" Henry, who's racing to the reservation to find Dr. Don Porter. Henry has found an injured colt, Wild Beauty, on the range. Between the efforts of Porter and Henry, Wild Beauty makes a full recovery. Henry returns the colt to the wild horse herd that roams the reservation. Through a misunderstanding, Porter asks Collier to resign, but with Henry's intervention, Porter relents. Porter and Collier begin to fall in love. As Porter is getting up the nerve to propose, Collier's old boyfriend, Robert Wilcox, arrives to try to persuade Collier to return east. Rancher Dick Curtis gives Wilcox a place to stay. The two men discuss the wild horse herd. Wilcox tells Curtis there's a market for horse hides. Curtis decides to stampede the horses into a box canyon he owns. Once the horses are off the reservation, they're no longer under the protection of the government. Curtis' cowhands stampede the horses into the canyon. While in school, Henry has a premonition that Wild Beauty and the herd are in trouble and rides to help. A Curtis henchman, Pierce Lydon, shoots the boy, wounding him. Collier tells Porter, and Porter finds the wounded Henry. When told Henry may still be alive, Curtis goes to finish him off. Wild Beauty is able to open the gate of the corral holding

380 WILD BEAUTY

Wild Beauty (1946) half sheet. Center, "Wild Beauty," right (top to bottom), Robert "Buzzy" Henry, Lois Collier, Don Porter.

the horses and stampedes the herd toward the reservation. Curtis is caught in the path of the stampede. Curtis' horse panics and throws Curtis. The horses trample Curtis. Porter returns to the reservation and confronts Wilcox. The men fight, with Porter emerging triumphant. Porter puts Wilcox on a stagecoach heading east. Henry recovers from his wound and resumes his friendship with Wild Beauty. Porter and Collier marry.

NOTES AND COMMENTARY: Footage from *Stormy* (Universal, 1935) was used in the wild horse herd sequences. The famous horses Rex and Rex Jr. can easily be seen.

In the fight scene between Don Porter and Robert Wilcox, Dale Van Sickel doubles Porter.

"My Country 'Tis of Thee" can be heard in *Mountain Justice* (Universal, 1930) and *Lady from Cheyenne* (Universal, 1941).

REVIEWS: "Pretty fair family-oriented programmer." (*Western Movies*, Pitts)

AUTHOR'S COMMENTS: *Wild Beauty* is an above average horse picture set in the west. The acting by Don Porter, Lois Collier, Robert "Buzzy" Henry and the rest of the cast is up to par. Wallace W. Fox directs with an eye toward solid family entertainment.

Guns and Spurs!
He "fanned" his gun to shoot faster and cooler!

Wild West Days

Universal (June 1937)

CAST: Kentucky, **John Mack Brown**; the Dude, **George Shelly**; Lucy Munro, **Lynn Gilbert**; Mike, **Frank Yaconelli**; Trigger, **Bob Kortman**; Keeler, **Russell Simpson**; Doc Hardy, **Walter Miller**; Buckskin, **Charles Stevens**; Larry Munro, **Frank McGlynn**; Purvis, **Francis McDonald**; Steve, **Al Bridge**; Red Hatchet, **Chief Thunderbird**; Mouth Organ Kid, **Robert McClung**; Sheriff, **Ed LeSaint**; Judge Lawrence, **Joseph W. Girard**; Dorry, **Jack Clifford**; Brady, **William Royle**; Tobe Driscoll, **Bruce Mitchell**; Chan, **Miki Morita** // First Wagon Train Boss, **Lafe McKee**; Dawson, **Ralph Lewis**; Bauldeen, **Bud Osborne**; Johnny, **Sidney Bracey**; Blacksmith, **Frank Ellis**; Outlaw, **Ben Corbett**; Indian, **Iron Eyes Cody**; Bartender, **Monte Montague**; Prospector, **Pat O'Malley**; Settlers, **Horace B. Carpenter** and **Bud Osborne**; Townsmen, **Hank Bell** and **Tex Cooper;** and "Starlight"

CREDITS: Directors, **Ford Beebe** and **Cliff Smith**; Associate Producers, **Henry MacRae** and **Ben Koenig**; Screenwriters, **Wyndham Gittens**, **Norman S. Hall** and **Ray Trampe**; Supervising Editor, **Saul A. Goodkind**; Editors, **Alvin Todd** and **Louis Sackin**; Art Director, **Ralph DeLacy**; Cinematography, **Richard Fryer**

SONGS: "Get Along Little Pony" (Kellogg)—sung by **George Shelly**; "Song of the Sage" (Kellogg)—sung by **George Shelley** and "Turkey in the Straw" (traditional)—played by **Bob McClung**

LOCATION FILMING: Kernville and Vasquez Rocks, California

RUNNING TIME: 265 min.

CHAPTER TITLES: 1. Death Rides the Range, 2. The Redskins' Revenge, 3. The Brink of Doom, 4. The Indians Are Coming, 5. The Leap for Life, 6. Death Stalks the Plains, 7. Six-Gun Law, 8. The Gold Stampede, 9. Walls of Fire, 10. Circle of Doom, 11. The Thundering Herd, 12. Rustlers and Redskins, 13. Rustlers' Roundup

SOURCE: Novel "Saint Johnson" by **W.R. Burnett**

STORY: John Mack Brown and his three friends, George Shelly, Frank Yaconelli and Bob Kortman, arrive at the Circle D ranch to help Frank McGlynn stand against a wave of lawlessness. Newspaper editor Russell Simpson is the leader of the Secret Seven and the brains behind the lawless activity. McGlynn has found platinum on his ranch, which Simpson wants for himself. Through accomplice Charles Stevens, Simpson uses the Indians in his quest. Brown, McGlynn and McGlynn's sister, Lynn Gilbert are captured by the Indians. The Indians trade McGlynn to Stevens for rifles but plan to burn Brown and Gilbert at the stake. Kortman and Yaconelli effect a rescue. Surviving many harrowing adventures, Brown finally rescues McGlynn. To make McGlynn record his mining claim, Simpson starts a gold rush. Brown, knowing the gold rush is a fake, convinces the men that it's all a hoax before McGlynn's platinum claim is discovered. Simpson plans to bankrupt McGlynn by running off his herd of horses, which would force McGlynn to record his claim. Shelly, Yaconelli and Kortman stop the rustlers. Yaconelli turns the herd before it reaches the badlands. Outlaw leader Al Bridge and a member of the Secret Seven, Bruce Mitchell, discover the platinum vein but decide not to tell Simpson. Mitchell shoots Bridge and offers to buy McGlynn's ranch. McGlynn accepts. Bridge is only wounded and reports to Simpson, who orders Stevens to kill Mitchell. During the murder attempt, Brown captures Stevens and Mitchell, and takes possession of the deed to the Circle D. Mitchell returns the ranch to McGlynn. Brown finally figures out Simpson is behind the villainy and captures him. Brown, Yaconelli and Kortman ride on to new adventures, but Shelly stays behind to marry Gilbert.

NOTES AND COMMENTARY: W.R. Burnett's novel had been filmed previously as *Law and Order* (Universal, 1932) with Walter Huston, and would be remade as *Law and Order* (Universal, 1940) with Johnny Mack Brown, and again as *Law and Order* (Universal-International, 1953) with Ronald Reagan.

Kay Kellogg's song "Get Along Little Pony" would find service in *Forbidden Valley* (Universal, 1938) and *Oklahoma Frontier* (Universal, 1939). The Jimmy Wakely Trio sang "Song of the Sage" in *Deep in the Heart of Texas*. "Turkey in the Straw" was played by Ken Maynard on his fiddle in *The Fiddlin' Buckaroo* (Universal, 1933).

Bud Osborne plays two roles in this serial, a meaty role as an outlaw and a non-speaking part as a settler traveling with the wagon train in Chapter One.

Sidney Bracey plays Russell Simpson's mute typesetter, Johnny. In Chapter Eight, Walter Miller calls him Charlie.

Footage from Hoot Gibson's *The Flaming Frontier* (Universal, 1926) is used liberally for the Indian attack scenes.

REVIEWS: "Plenty of action, noise and kid appeal." (*Variety*, 8/4/37); "Fast moving cliffhanger." (*Western Movies*, Pitts)

SUMMATION: *Wild West Days* is a top-flight western serial containing plenty of good action sequences, and decent cliffhanger chapter endings and resolutions. John Mack Brown makes a formidable western hero and receives excellent support from sidekicks Bob Kortman, on the right side of the law this time, and Frank Yaconelli. The villainy rests in the capable hands of Russell Simpson, Charles Stevens and Al Bridge. Screenwriters Wyndham Giddens, Norman S. Hall and Ray Trampe have fashioned a good script, and directors Ford Beebe and Cliff Smith bring it to the screen in fine fashion.

Blasting for Black Gold!
They Gambled Everything for Sudden Riches!
That Was the Chance They Took, Recklessly Gambling with Death!

The Wildcatter

Universal (June 1937)

CAST: "Lucky" Conlon, **Scott Colton**; Helen Conlon, **Jean Rogers**; "Smiley," **Jack Smart**; Julia Frayne, **Suzanne Kaaren**; Tom Frayne, **Russell Hicks**; Johnson, **Ward Bond**; Torrance, **Wallis Clark**; Joe Tinker, **Jack Powell**// Ed, **Milburn Stone**; Real Estate Agent, **William Gould**; Bill Webster, **Bob McKenzie**; Pearl, **Louise Beavers**

CREDIT: Director, **Lewis D. Collins**; Associate Producer, **George Owen**; Story, **Tom Van Dycke**; Screenwriter, **Charles A. Logue**; Editor, **Frank Gross**; Art Directors, **Jack Otterson** and **Loren Patrick**; Cinematographer, **Stanley Cortez**; Sound, **Jess A. Moulin** and **Jesse T. Bastian**; Musical Director, **Charles Previn**; Special Effects, **John P. Fulton**

RUNNING TIME: 58 min.

STORY: An oil strike brings Scott Colton and his pal Jack Smart to Texas. Colton and Smart take a 24-hour option on a property. While gambling, Colton turns a hundred dollars into a substantial amount. Colton also meets oilman Russell Hicks' daughter, Suzanne Kaaren. Colton neglects to mention that he's married to Jean Rogers. With time running short, Colton makes the decision to "shoot" the well. The effort proves fruitless, as the well is dry. Hicks offers Colton the chance to drill his well. Hicks is setting up an oil well scam by making the oil field seem worthless so the wildcatters will sell their leases at a nominal price. Not realizing his agreement with Hicks is not on the up-and-up, Colton drills in earnest and brings in a gusher. Now Hicks wants multiple rigs set up to bring in as much oil as possible. Smart worries that an underground lake of water may ruin the oil field if not handled properly. Colton becomes ruthless in his desire to put as many rigs as possible to work. Hicks tells Kaaren to keep Colton away from the field so "accidents" can happen to the leases he doesn't control. If those leases are not worked for a twenty-four hour period, Hicks can take control. Wildcatter Ward Bond believes Colton is responsible for the accidents and goes after him with a gun. Every wildcatter is ruined. Bond catches up with Colton, but Colton persuades Bond to allow him to see Hicks. Hicks boasts that he's responsible for the "accidents." Colton passes the information to Bond and then returns to the oil field. The irate wildcatters are about to kill Colton when Bond shows up and tells the crowd Hicks is responsible. Hicks comes to the field; and Colton tells him the wildcatters will "shoot" their wells, disturbing the underground lake and thereby ruining the field. Realizing the wildcatters are serious, Hicks concedes and promises to put the wildcatters' leases back in working condition. Hicks wants to hire Colton on a permanent basis, but Bond wants Colton as a partner. Colton accepts Bond's offer.

NOTES AND COMMENTARY: Scott Colton also received billing as Scott Kolk. Kolk had the leading role in the serial *Secret Agent X-9* (Universal, 1937).

Jack Smart, under the name J. Scott Smart, won fame as Dashiell Hammett's famous sleuth Brad Runyon in the radio series *The Fat Man*. Smart also brought Runyon to the big screen in *The Fat Man* (Universal-International, 1951).

REVIEW: "Light stuff, stiffly acted." (*Variety*, 6/16/37); "Okay Universal dual bill item." (*Western Movies*, Pitts)

SUMMATION: *The Wildcatter* is an interesting oil melodrama about ruthless activities on a Texas oil field. Scott Colton, unfortunately, does not make a dynamic hero, to the film's detriment. Jean Rogers is only adequate as Colton's suffering wife. Jack Smart steals the show as Colton's portly sidekick. Director Lewis Collins keeps the slight story moving to its satisfactory conclusion.

HEROES OF THE IRON HORSE!
Daring redskins and renegades to blaze the rail trail to the West!

Winners of the West

Universal (July 1940)

CAST: Jeff Ramsey, **Dick Foran**; Claire Hartford, **Anne Nagel**; Tex Houston, **Tom Fadden**; Jim Jackson, **James Craig**; King Carter, **Harry Woods**; Snakeye, **Charles Stevens**; John Hartford, **Edward Keane**; Raven, **Trevor Bardette**; Tim, **Edgar Edwards**; Bill, **William Desmond**; Logan, **Roy Barcroft**; Lacey, **Charles Whitaker**; Rita, **Vyola Vonn**; Jenny, **Evelyn Selby**; Chief War Eagle, **Chief Yowlatchie**// "Smoky"; Blade, **Chuck Morrison**; Hacienda Sentry, **Bud Osborne**; Maddox, **Edmund Cobb**; Indian, **Iron Eyes Cody**; Marshal Bowers, **Ed Cassidy**; Joe, **Frank Ellis**; Webb, **Tom London**; Craig, **Earle Douglas**; Rooney, **Harry Tenbrook**; Workman with Liquor, **Bob Kortman**; Greeley, **James Farley**; Wagon Driver, **Ken Terrell**; Army Captain, **Al Bridge**; Senator Dodson, **James Blaine**; Townsmen, **Jim Corey**, **Horace B. Carpenter** and **Hank Worden**

CREDITS: Directors, **Ford Beebe** and **Ray Taylor**; Associate Producer, **Henry MacRae**; Screenwriters, **Geo. H. Plympton**, **Basil Dickey** and **Charles R. Condon**; Dialogue Director, **Jacques Jaccard**; Supervising Editor, **Saul A. Goodkind**; Editors, **Alvin Todd**, **Louis Sackin** and **Joseph Glick**; Art Director, **Harold H. MacArthur**; Cinematographers, **Jerome Ash**, **William Sickner** and **John Hickson**

SONG: "The Drinks Are On the House" (Rosen and Carter)—sung by **Vyola Vonn**

LOCATION FILMING: Tuolumme County and Agoura, California

RUNNING TIME: 247 min.

CHAPTER TITLES: 1. Redskins Ride Again, 2. The Wreck at Red River Gorge, 3. The Bridge of Disaster, 4. Trapped by Redskins, 5. Death Strikes the Trail, 6. A Leap for Life. 7. Thundering Terror, 8. The Flaming Arsenal, 9. Sacrificed by Savages, 10. Under Crashing Timbers, 11. Bullets in the Dark, 12. The Battle of Blackhawk, 13. Barricades Blasted

STORY: Harry Woods is the self-appointed ruler of the territory from Hell Gate Pass through Sunset Mesa, and plans to stop any effort to build a railroad through this area. Chief engineer Dick Foran, with his pals Tom Fadden and James Craig, is determined to see that the railroad goes through. Woods, using the half-breed Charles Stevens, enlists the Indians' help in sabotaging the railroad. Woods has his chief henchmen, Charles Stevens, Edmund Cobb and Chuck Morrison, dress as Indians and lead the Indians' attacks on railroad properties, destroying work trains, bridges and other supplies. Foran blunts the renegades' success at every turn. Woods twice kidnaps railroad president Edward Keane's daughter, Anne Nag, in attempts to force Keane to build his railroad around Woods' territory. Each time, Foran rescues Nagel before Keane can sign such an agreement. Luring Keane to Black Hawk, Woods holds Keane prisoner to draw Foran into his clutches. Foran brings all the railroaders into Black Hawk, and they begin a pitched battle with Woods' henchmen. The railroaders gain the upper hand, and Woods decides to retreat to his hacienda, taking Keane with him. Foran rescues Keane and then pursues Woods and his men. Woods sets up an ambush while he rides to the hacienda to bring back ammunition. Foran gets to the hacienda and faces Woods. Both men draw, and Foran shoots the gun from Woods' hand. Foran puts down his gun, and the two men fight, with Foran winning a lengthy and rugged battle. Meanwhile, Charles Stevens tries to incite the Indians against all whites, but Chief Yowlatchie realizes he's been duped and inflicts a fatal punishment on Stevens. Yowlatchie now wants peace and is willing to testify against Woods. The railroaders wipe out Woods' men, defeating the lawless element. Under Foran's leadership, the railroad is completed. Foran and Nagel marry.

NOTES AND COMMENTARY: With Johnny Mack Brown now Universal's top cowboy star, Dick Foran replaced Brown as the western lead in the studio's annual Western serial. Ironically, in 1942 Foran and Brown both appeared in Abbott and Costello's *Ride 'Em Cowboy* (Universal, 1942), with Foran as the top cowboy hero in this one.

In the climactic fistfight between Dick Foran and Harry Woods, Eddie Parker doubles Foran (though Cliff Lyons was Foran's riding double), and Fred Graham doubles Woods.

The cliffhanger ending of Chapter Nine, as Foran's horse stumbles, was used earlier in Chapter Four. I would imagine someone at Universal didn't think the kids in the audience would have good memories.

From *Destry Rides Again* (Universal, 1939), the song "Little Joe" can be heard in some of the serials saloon sequences. "The Drinks Are on the House" would later be used in *Tenting Tonight on the Old Camp Ground* (Universal, 1943).

REVIEWS: "Lightning fast Universal cliffhanger marred by excessive stock footage." (*Western Movies*, Pitts)

SUMMATION: *Winners of the West* is a good, fast-paced western serial. The acting is okay in general, with Harry Woods' performance deserving of special mention. Woods is properly authoritative and proves why he's regarded as one of the top western badmen of all time. Dick Foran makes for a good western hero, handling the action requirements in fine style. Directors Ford Beebe and Ray Taylor keep the proceedings moving, with hardly any breaks in the action. Two minor blemishes (both in the final chapter) mar the production. First, the climactic battle between the railroaders and badmen takes place entirely off-camera; and, second, the two-plus minutes of footage showing the completion of the railroad is just unnecessary filler.

MURDER and MYSTERY! RISKS and ROMANCE! TORRENTS and THRILLS in the GREAT GEYSER MURDER MYSTERY!

Yellowstone

(September 1936)

CAST: Dick Sherwood, **Henry Hunter**; Ruth Foster, **Judith Barrett**; "Pay-Day," **Andy Devine**; Hardigan, **Alan Hale**; James Foster, **Ralph Morgan**; Marty Ryan, **Monroe Owsley**; Franklin Ross, **Rollo Lloyd**; Old Pete, **Raymond Hatton**; Radell, **Paul Harvey**; "Dynamite," **Paul Fix**; Singing Cowboy, **Michael Loring**// George, **Jim Thorpe**; Desk Clerk, **Eddie Acuff**; Ranger, **House Peters, Jr.**, Fong, **Willie Fung**

CREDITS: Director, **Arthur Lubin**; Producer, **Val Paul**; Story, **Arthur Phillips**; Screenwriters, **Jefferson Parker, Stuart Palmer** and **Houston Branch**; Editor, **Maurice E. Wright**; Art Directors, **Jack Otterson** and **John F. Ewing**; Cinematographer, **Milton Krasner**; Special Effects, **John P. Fulton**; Gowns, **Vera West**;

Sound, **Homer Tasker**; Musical Director, **Herman Heller**

SONGS: "From the Land of Sky Blue Waters" (Cadman); "Is It True What They Say About Dixie" (Caesar)—sung by male quartet; and "Joggin' Along" (Actman and Loesser) —sung by **Michael Loring**

LOCATION FILMING: Yellowstone National Park, and Jenny Lake at the Grand Teton National Park, Wyoming

RUNNING TIME: 63 min.

STORY: After eighteen years in prison, Ralph Morgan returns to Yellowstone National Park to retrieve stolen payroll money. Judith Barrett, Morgan's daughter, arrives to be with her father. Also showing up are gangsters Monroe Owsley and Paul Fix, detective Alan Hale and botanist Rollo Lloyd. Morgan is murdered, and the blame falls on park ranger Henry Hunter, who is in love with Barrett. Hunter, with Barrett's help, finds the loot and discovers that Hale is the murderer. Hale is killed as he tries to murder Hunter and Barrett. Hunter and Barrett resume their romance.

NOTES AND COMMENTARY: *Yellowstone* was the third picture in House Peters, Jr. long career. Peters made 88 feature films, as well as appearing in over 50 television series. In 1958, Peters was television's original Mr. Clean. Peters remembered he had the part of a forest ranger in *Yellowstone,* and that most of his good scenes were cut from the final release print. He thought the studio did a fine job in constructing a replica of Old Faithful on the lot.

Determining where *Yellowstone* was filmed proved to be more difficult than it sounds. Correspondence with Lee Whittlesey, archivist for Yellowstone National Park, garnered these remarks: "I cannot confirm that any of the film was shot here in Yellowstone. Everything that I can remember of it appears to have been shot on a cheap Hollywood set. The shots of 'Old Faithful Inn' were not done at OFI (Old Faithful Inn) at all, but rather in a wooden building somewhere else. Old Faithful geyser was ridiculously referred to as "Old Bess," and none of the shots of it were taken in the park. Instead, all appear to have been taken on a paper mache set. The geyser appears to be paper mache."

On the film itself, Whittlesey commented, "In my opinion it was poorly written, poorly acted and poorly produced."

Actually, *Yellowstone* was filmed at the park. Additionally, a movie still purchased from Universal notes that scenes were filmed at Jenny Lake in the Grand Teton National Park.

REVIEWS: "A routine mystery melodrama whose chief claim to distinction is that it uses the geysers of Yellowstone Park in its murder plot and the scenery of the park for background." (*Hollywood Reporter*, 9/3/36); "Fairly good actioner with some nice mystery elements." (*Western Movies*, Pitts)

SUMMATION: *Yellowstone* is an average murder mystery with a Western setting. The story holds the interest, but the denoument is too hurried the screenwriters refuse to play fair by withholding clues that would give the viewer a fighting chance to guess the killer's identity. Judith Barrett and Raymond Hatton are standouts among the cast members, while Andy Devine's talent is wasted in a supposedly comedic role. Of special note is cinematographer Herman Heller's outstanding photography, which captures the beauty of Yellowstone.

The Western Short Films of Universal

Universal was most prolific in its release of short films in the 1929-30 season, with 26 new releases (13 episodes of the Northwest Mounted Police series with Ted Carson, and 13 episodes of the Pioneer Kid series with Bobby Nelson) and 26 re-releases (from the 1924-25 season). Though these are all silent films, they're included here in order to generate a complete filmography of the Universal films of the sound era.

In researching the short films, the author encountered three titles that *seemed* to be westerns, *Rock-a-Bye Cowboy* (1933), *Western Cowgirl* (1943) and *Melody Stampede* (1945). These titles, however, do not appear in *Shoot-Em-Ups* (Arlington House, 1978)—nor are they designated as westerns in *Universal Pictures* (Arlington House, 1977)—so they are not included here.

Only two short films, *Swingin' in the Barn* and *Frontier Frolic*, were available for viewing.

1. The Boy and the Bad Man
(September 1929)
CAST: **Bobby Nelson; Edmund Cobb**
CREDITS: Director, **Jack Nelson**
RUNNING TIME: 20 min.
NOTES AND COMMENTARY: Bobby Nelson was a child actor in films, primarily western, from 1926 until 1937. Over the course of his career, Nelson appeared with western greats Hoot Gibson, Ken Maynard, Buck Jones, Johnny Mack Brown and Bob Steele. Nelson left motion pictures to become a public accountant.

Bobby Nelson received billing as both Bobbie Nelson and "Little Bobbie" Nelson

The Boy and the Bad Man was the first of 13 entries in the Pioneer Kid Series.

2. The Red Rider (September 1929)
CAST: **Ted Carson**
CREDITS: Director, **Josef Levigard**
RUNNING TIME: 20 min.
NOTES AND COMMENTARY: It is

rumored that Ted Carson was German and lacked a command of the English language. With the advent of sound, Carson's career ended.

The Red Rider was the first of 13 entries in the Northwest Mounted Police series. Universal liked the title and had used it for a Jack Hoxie film in 1925 and a Buck Jones serial in 1934. None of the stories were related.

Josef Levigard was also billed as Joseph Levigard.

3. ***Waif of the Wilderness*** (October 1929)
   CAST: **Bobby Nelson**
   CREDITS: Director, **Jack Nelson**
   RUNNING TIME: 20 min.

4. ***Man of Daring*** (October 1929)
   CAST: **Ted Carson**
   CREDITS: Director, **Josef Levigard**
   RUNNING TIME: 20 min.

5. ***The Kid Comes Thru*** (November 1929)
   CAST: **Bobby Nelson**
   CREDITS: Director, **Jack Nelson**
   RUNNING TIME: 20 min.

6. ***The Border Wolf*** (November 1929)
   CAST: **Ted Carson**
   CREDITS: Director, **Josef Levigard**
   RUNNING TIME: 20 min.

7. ***Orphan of the Wagon Trails*** (November 1929)
   CAST: **Bobby Nelson; Edmund Cobb**

Ted Carson (photograph courtesy of Bill McDowell).

   CREDITS: Director, **Jack Nelson**
   RUNNING TIME: 20 min.

8. ***The Red Coat's Code*** (December 1929)
   CAST: **Ted Carson**
   CREDITS: Director, **Josef Levigard**
   RUNNING TIME: 20 min.

9. ***Dangerous Days*** (December 1929)
   CAST: **Bobby Nelson; Edmund Cobb; Marjorie Bonner; Walter Shumway**
   CREDITS: Director, **Jack Nelson**
   RUNNING TIME: 20 min.

10. ***Trail of the Pack*** (January 1930)

CAST: Ted Carson
CREDITS: Director, Josef Levigard
RUNNING TIME: 20 min.

11. *The Last Stand* (January, 1930)
CAST: Bobby Nelson
CREDITS: Director, Jack Nelson
RUNNING TIME: 20 min.

12. *The Badge of Bravery* (February 1930)
CAST: Ted Carson
CREDITS: Director, Josef Levigard
RUNNING TIME: 20 min.

13. *The Post of Honor* (February 1930)
CAST: Bobby Nelson
CREDITS: Director, Jack Nelson; Screenwriter, William Lester
RUNNING TIME: 20 min.

14. *Crimson Courage* (March 1930)
CAST: Ted Carson
CREDITS: Director, Josef Levigard
RUNNING TIME: 20 min.

15. *The Danger Claim* (March 1930)
CAST: Bobby Nelson
CREDITS: Director, Jack Nelson; Screenwriter, Basil Dickey
RUNNING TIME: 20 min.

16. *Law in the Saddle* (April 1930)
CAST: Ted Carson
CREDITS: Director, Josef Levigard
RUNNING TIME: 20 min.

17. *Six Gun Justice* (April 1930)
CAST: Bobby Nelson; Ted Wells
CREDITS: Director, Jack Nelson; Screenwriter, George Morgan
RUNNING TIME: 20 min.

18. *Crooked Trails* (May 1930)
CAST: Ted Carson
CREDITS: Director, Josef Levigard; Screenwriter, Basil Dickey
RUNNING TIME: 20 min.

19. *Alias the Bandit* (May 1930)
CAST: Bobby Nelson
CREDITS: Director, Jack Nelson; Screenwriter, Harry Crist
RUNNING TIME: 20 min.
NOTES AND COMMENTARY: Harry Crist would become better known to western fans as Harry Fraser.

20. *Wolf's Fangs* (May 1930)
CAST: Ted Carson
CREDITS: Director: Josef Levigard; Screenwriter, George Morgan
RUNNING TIME: 20 min.

21. *The Battling Kid* (June 1930)
CAST: Bobby Nelson
CREDITS: Director, Jack Nelson
RUNNING TIME: 20 min.

22. *The Redcoat's Romance* (June 1930)
CAST: Ted Carson
CREDITS: Director, Josef Levigard; Screenwriter, Basil Dickey
RUNNING TIME: 20 min.

23. *Son of Courage* (July 1930)
CAST: Bobby Nelson
CREDITS: Director, Jack Nelson; Screenwriter, Carl Krusada
RUNNING TIME: 20 min.

24. *The Man Hunter* (July 1930)
CAST: **Ted Carson**
CREDITS: Director, **Josef Levigard**
RUNNING TIME: 20 min.

25. *The Pony Express Kid* (August 1930)
CAST: **Bobby Nelson**
CREDITS: Director, **Jack Nelson**
RUNNING TIME: 20 min.

26. *The Lightning Rider*
CAST: **Ted Carson**
CREDITS: Director, **Josef Levigard**
RUNNING TIME: 20 min.

27. *Discontented Cowboys* (October 1930)
CAST: **George Sidney; Charles Murray; Monte Collins; Roger Gray**
CREDITS: Director, **Albert Ray**; Screenwriters, **Ralph Ceder** and **James Mulhauser**
RUNNING TIME: 18 min.
NOTES AND COMMENTARY: The working title for this short was *Dude Ranch*.

28. *Swingin' in the Barn* (May 1940)
CAST: **Texas Jim Lewis and His Band; King Sisters; Maidie and Ray; Fred Scott; Vernon and Draper; Lucille Walker; Forrest and Towne; Chester Gunnels; Hill-Billyettes**
CREDITS: Director, **Larry Ceballos**: Cinematographer, **William Sickner**; Editor, **Milton Carruth**; Sound Supervisor, **Bernard Brown**; Musical Director, **Charles Previn**
SONGS: "My Big Mountain Hill Billy Bill"—sung by **Lucille Walker**; "Who Broke the Lock" (traditional)—sung by **Tex Jim Lewis and His Band**; "I Like Mountain Music" (Cavanaugh and Weldon)—sung by the **King Sisters**; "I've Sold My Saddle for an Old Guitar" (Allen and Rogers)—sung by **Fred Scott**; and "Good Old Mountain Music"—sung by the **King Sisters**
RUNNING TIME: 19 min.
STORY: Fred Scott is rehearsing some musicians for the dance at Chester Gunnels' barn. Tex Jim Lewis wants to join the group but Scott won't let him. Lewis falls asleep and dreams he's the star of the show.
NOTES AND COMMENTARY: Fred Scott had his own western series for Spectrum from 1936 to 1939, with twelve entries. Scott was billed as "the Silvery Voiced Buckaroo."
"Who Broke the Lock" would be heard in *The Singing Sheriff*, with Deuce Spriggins singing in front of Spade Cooley's Orchestra. The song, "I've Sold My Saddle for an Old Guitar" was composed by Flemming Allen, who wrote most of the songs for Bob Baker's Universal westerns. The King of the Cowboys, Roy Rogers, later also received credit for writing the song. Rogers recorded the song for Decca in 1941, and it is considered one of his best early recordings.
SUMMATION: *Swingin' in the Barn* is fast entertainment. The highlight is Fred Scott's rendition of "I've Sold My Saddle for an Old Guitar."

29. *Frontier Frolic* (October 1946)
CAST: **Bob Wills and His Band**;

Paula Kelly and the Modernaires; Tommy Duncan, the McKinney Sisters; Pat Starling

CREDITS: Director, **Lewis D. Collins**; Producer, **Will Cowan**; Editor, **D. Patrick Kelly**; Cinematographer, **Ernest Miller**; Sound Director, **Bernard B. Brown**; Musical Director, **Milton Rosen**

SONGS: "Texas Playboy Rag" (Wills)—played by **Bob Wills and the Texas Playboys**; "La Cucaracha" (traditional)—sung by **Paula Kelly and the Modernaires**; "I Betcha My Heart I Love You" (Miller and Van Sciver)—sung by **the McKinney Sisters, with Bob Wills and the Texas Playboys**; "Western Medley"— danced by **Pat Starling** and played by **Bob Wills and His Texas Playboys**; "San Antonio Rose" (Wills)— sung by **Tommy Duncan with Bob Wills and His Texas Playboys**; "Coffee Five, Doughnuts Five (Coffee and Doughnuts Ten)" (Dickinson and Giberling)—sung by **Paula Kelly and the Modernaires** and "Good Bye Liza Jane" (Duncan)—sung by **Tommy Duncan, Bob Wills, and the McKinney Sisters, with the Texas Playboys**

RUNNING TIME: 15 min.

STORY: This is a musical short featuring the talents of Bob Wills and the Texas Playboys, Paula Kelly and the Modernaires, the McKinney Sisters, Pat Starling and Tommy Duncan in seven musical numbers.

NOTES AND COMMENTARY: This was the last big screen appearance for Bob Wills. Wills had been featured in western films since his appearance in *Take Me Back to Oklahoma* (Monogram, 1940) with Tex Ritter. His most memorable roles came in his eight entries in Russell Hayden's Columbia series in which Wills was Hayden's co-star.

Universal called Bob Wills' musical aggregation simply "His Band" instead of the Texas Playboys, as was the custom. Some of the musicians who appeared on-screen were Lester Barnard, Jr., Noel Boggs, Millard Kelso, Louis Tierney and Luke Wills.

"La Cucaracha" was heard earlier in *When a Man Sees Red* (Universal, 1934), *Law for Tombstone* (Universal, 1937), *Outlaw Express* (Universal, 1938) and *Boss of Bullion City* (Universal, 1941).

SUMMATION: *Frontier Frolic* is an entertaining short. It's always a pleasure to see the King of Western Swing, Bob Wills, on the screen. Even though Paula Kelly and the Modernaires deliver their musical numbers in entertaining and professional fashion, it would have been nicer to have seen just the unbridled Wills and his group. Wills is not allowed to deliver his "Ah-hahs" and call out his musicians' names. Too bad, for it prevented this short from becoming a classic.

30. *Tumbleweed Tempos* (December 1946)

CAST: **Spade Cooley and His Orchestra**

CREDITS: Director/Producer, **Will Cowan**; Musical Director, **Milton Rosen**

RUNNING TIME: 15 min.

In the 1929-30 season, Universal re-released 26 western short films:

1. **The Lone Round-Up** with Jack Daugherty (September 1929). Original release date: May 1924
2. **The Boss of Bar 20** with William E. Lawrence (September 1929). Original release date: May 1924
3. **Blue Wing's Revenge** with William E. Lawrence (October 1929). Original release date: June 1924
4. **A Sagebrush Vagabond** with William E. Lawrence (October 1929). Original release date: August 1924
5. **Flying Eagle** with William E. Lawrence (November 1929). Original release date: July 1924
6. **Red Raymond's Girl** with Pete Morrison (November 1929). Original release date: July 1924
7. **Between Fires** with Edmund Cobb (December 1929). Original release date: September 1924
8. **A Race for a Ranch** with Billy Sullivan (December 1929). Original release date: November 1924
9. **The College Cowboy** with Joe Bonomo (January 1930). Original release date: September 1924
10. **The Ropin' Venus** with Josie Sedgwick (January 1930). Original release date: July 1925
11. **The Way of the West** with Billy Sullivan (February 1930). Original release date: January 1925
12. **The Storm King** with Edmund Cobb (February 1930). Original release date: March 1925
13. **Queen of the Roundup** with Josie Sedgwick (March 1930). Original release date: June 1925
14. **The Whip Hand** with Billy Sullivan (March 1930). Original release date: January 1925
15. **Dynamite's Daughter** with Josie Sedgwick (March 1930). Original release date: August 1925
16. **The Pronto Kid** with Edmund Cobb (April 1930). Original release date: June 1925
17. **The Fighting Schoolmarm** with Josie Sedgwick (April 1930). Original release date: August 1925
18. **The Loser Wins** with Billy Sullivan (May 1930). Original release date: February 1925
19. **The Wild West Wallop** with Edmund Cobb (May 1930). Original release date: April 1925
20. **The Best Man** with Josie Sedgwick (June 1930). Original release date: August 1925
21. **Loaded Dice** with Edmund Cobb (June 1930). Original release date: March 1925
22. **The Boundary Line** with Fred Humes (July 1930). Original release date: October 1925
23. **The Fighting Terror** with Billy Sullivan (July 1930). Original release date: February 1925
24. **A Close Call** with Edmund Cobb (August 1930). Original release date: May 1925
25. **Seeing Red** with Billy Sullivan (August 1930). Original release date: January 1925
26. **The Bashful Whirlwind** with Edmund Cobb (August 1930). Original release date: April 1925

Alphabetical Listing of Universal Sound Westerns

1. *Arizona Cyclone* with Johnny Mack Brown, **November 1941**
2. *Arizona Trail* with Tex Ritter, **September 1943**
3. *Bad Man from Red Butte* with Johnny Mack Brown, **May 1940**
4. *Bad Men of the Border* with Kirby Grant, **September 1945**
5. *Badlands of Dakota* with Robert Stack, **September 1941**
6. *Battling with Buffalo Bill* with Tom Tyler, **November 1931**
7. *Beyond the Pecos* with Rod Cameron, **April 1945**
8. *Black Aces* with Buck Jones, **September 1937**
9. *Black Bandit* with Bob Baker, **September 1938**
10. *Border Brigands* with Buck Jones, **June 1935**
11. *Border Wolves* with Bob Baker, **February 1938**
12. *Boss of Boomtown* with Rod Cameron, **May 1944**
13. *Boss of Bullion City* with Johnny Mack Brown, **January 1941**
14. *Boss of Hangtown Mesa* with Johnny Mack Brown, **August 1942**
15. *Boss of Lonely Valley* with Buck Jones, **November 1937**
16. *Boss Rider of Gun Creek* with Buck Jones, **November 1936**
17. *Bury Me Not on the Lone Prairie* with Johnny Mack Brown, **March 1941**
18. *Can't Help Singing* with Deanna Durbin, **December 1944**
19. *Canyon Passage* with Dana Andrews, **July 1946**
20. *Cheyenne Roundup* with Johnny Mack Brown and Tex Ritter, **April 1943**
21. *Chip of the Flying U* with Johnny Mack Brown, **November 1939**
22. *Clancy of the Mounted* with Tom Tyler, **January 1933**
23. *Code of the Lawless* with Kirby Grant, **October 1945**
24. *The Concentratin' Kid* with Hoot Gibson, **October 1930**
25. *Courage of the West* with Bob Baker, **December 1937**
26. *Courtin' Wildcats* with Hoot Gibson, **December 1929**
27. *The Cowboy and the Kid* with Buck Jones, **May 1936**

28. *Cowboy in Manhattan* with Frances Langford, **April 1943**
29. *The Crimson Trail* with Buck Jones, **March 1935**
30. *The Daltons Ride Again* with Alan Curtis, **November 1945**
31. *Deep in the Heart of Texas* with Johnny Mack Brown and Tex Ritter, **September 1942**
32. *Desperate Trails* with Johnny Mack Brown, **September 1939**
33. *Destry Rides Again* with Tom Mix, **April 1932**
34. *Destry Rides Again* with Marlene Dietrich and James Stewart, **Dec. 1939**
35. *Diamond Frontier* with Victor McLaglen, **October 1940**
36. *Empty Saddles* with Buck Jones, **December 1936**
37. *The Fiddlin' Buckaroo* with Ken Maynard, **July 1933**
38. *Fighting Bill Fargo* with Johnny Mack Brown, **December 1941**
39. *The Fighting Legion* with Ken Maynard, **April 1930**
40. *Flaming Frontiers* with John Mack Brown, **May 1938**
41. *Flaming Guns* with Tom Mix, **December 1932**
42. *For the Service* with B. Jones, **May 1936**.
43. *Forbidden Valley* with Noah Beery, Jr., **February 1938**
44. *The Fourth Horseman* with Tom Mix, **September 1932**
45. *Frisco Sal* with Susanna Foster, **February 1945**
46. *Frontier Badman* with Robert Paige, **August 1943**
47. *Frontier Gal* with Yvonne De Carlo, **December 1945**
48. *Frontier Law* with Russell Hayden, **November 1943**
49. *Ghost Town Riders* with Bob Baker, **December 1938**
50. *Gordon of Ghost City* with Buck Jones, **August 1933**
51. *The Great Alaskan Mystery* with Milburn Stone, **1944**
52. *Guilty Trail* with Bob Baker, **October 1938**
53. *Gun Justice* with Ken Maynard, **December 1933**
54. *Gun Town* with Kirby Grant, **January 1946**
55. *Gunman's Code* with Kirby Grant, **August 1946**
56. *Hell's Heroes* with Charles Bickford, **January 1930**
57. *Heroes of the West* with Noah Beery, Jr., **June 1932**
58. *Hidden Gold* with Tom Mix, **November 1932**
59. *Honor of the Range* with Ken Maynard, **April 1934**
60. *Honor of the West* with Bob Baker, **January 1939**
61. *The Indians Are Coming* with Tim McCoy, **October 1930**
62. *The Ivory-Handled Gun* with Buck Jones, **November 1935**
63. *King of the Arena* with Ken Maynard, **June 1933**
64. *The Lady from Cheyenne* with Loretta Young, **April 1941**
65. *Lasca of the Rio Grande* with Leo Carrillo, **November 1931**
66. *The Last Stand* with Bob Baker, **April 1938**
67. *Law and Order* with Walter Huston, **March 1932**
68. *Law and Order* with Johnny Mack Brown, **November 1940**
69. *Law for Tombstone* with Buck Jones, **October 1937**
70. *Law of the Range* with Johnny Mack Brown, **June 1941**
71. *Lawless Breed* with Kirby Grant, **August 1946**
72. *Left Handed Law* with Buck Jones, **April 1937**
73. *The Lightning Express* with Lane Chandler, **June 1930**

74. *Little Joe, the Wrangler* with Johnny Mack Brown and Tex Ritter, **November 1942**
75. *The Lone Star Trail* with Johnny Mack Brown and Tex Ritter, **August 1943**
76. *The Long Long Trail* with Hoot Gibson, **October 1929**
77. *Lucky Larkin* with Ken Maynard, **March 1930**
78. *Man from Montana* with Johnny Mack Brown, **September 1941**
79. *Man from Montreal* with Richard Arlen, **March 1940**
80. *Marshal of Gunsmoke* with Tex Ritter and Russell Hayden, **January 1944**
81. *The Masked Rider* with Johnny Mack Brown, **October 1941**
82. *Men of Texas* with Robert Stack, **July 1942**
83. *Men of the Timberland* with Richard Arlen, **June 1941**
84. *The Mighty Treve* with Noah Beery, Jr., **April 1937**
85. *Moonlight and Cactus* with the Andrew Sisters, **September 1944**
86. *Mountain Justice* with Ken Maynard, **May 1930**
87. *The Mounted Stranger* with Hoot Gibson, **February 1930**
88. *Mutiny on the Blackhawk* with Richard Arlen, **August 1939**
89. *My Little Chickadee* with Mae West and W.C. Fields, **February 1940**
90. *My Pal, the King* with Tom Mix, **August 1932**
91. *North to the Klondike* with Broderick Crawford, **January 1942**
92. *Oklahoma Frontier* with Johnny Mack Brown, **October 1939**
93. *Oklahoma Raiders* with Tex Ritter, **March 1944**
94. *The Old Chisholm Trail* with Johnny Mack Brown and Tex Ritter, **December 1942**
95. *The Old Texas Trail* with Rod Cameron, **December 1944**
96. *The Oregon Trail* with Johnny Mack Brown, **May 1939**
97. *Outlaw Express* with Bob Baker, **June 1938**
98. *Outlawed Guns* with Buck Jones, **July 1935**
99. *Overland Mail* with Lon Chaney, Jr., **September 1942**
100. *The Overlanders* with Chips Rafferty, **December 1946**
101. *Parade of the West* with Ken Maynard, **January 1930**
102. *The Phantom Rider* with Buck Jones, **July 1936**
103. *The Phantom Stage* with Bob Baker, **February 1939**
104. *Pony Post* with Johnny Mack Brown, **December 1940**
105. *Prairie Justice* with Bob Baker, **November 1938**
106. *Ragtime Cowboy Joe* with Johnny Mack Brown, **September 1940**
107. *Raiders of Ghost City* with Dennis Moore, **July 1944**
108. *Raiders of San Joaquin* with Johnny Mack Brown and Tex Ritter, **June 1943**
109. *Ramrod* with Joel McCrea, **May 1947**
110. *Rawhide Rangers* with Johnny Mack Brown, **July 1941**
111. *The Red Rider* with Buck Jones, **July 1934**
112. *Renegades of the Rio Grande* with Rod Cameron, **June 1945**
113. *Ride 'Em Cowboy* with Buck Jones, **September 1936**
114. *Ride 'Em Cowboy* with Abbott and Costello, **February 1942**
115. *The Rider of Death Valley* with Tom Mix, **May 1932**
116. *Riders of Death Valley* with Dick Foran, **July 1941**
117. *Riders of Pasco Basin* with Johnny Mack Brown, **April 1940**

118. *Riders of the Santa Fe* with Rod Cameron, **November 1944**
119. *Road Agent* with Dick Foran, **December 1941**
120. *Roaring Ranch* with Hoot Gibson, **April 1930**
121. *The Roaring West* with Buck Jones, **July 1935**
122. *Rocky Rhodes* with Buck Jones, **September 1934**
123. *The Royal Mounted Rides Again* with Bill Kennedy, **October 1945**
124. *Rustlers of Red Dog* with Johnny Mack Brown, **January 1935**
125. *The Rustlers' Roundup* with Tom Mix, **March 1933**
126. *Rustler's Roundup* with Kirby Grant, **August 1946**
127. *Salome, Where She Danced* with Yvonne De Carlo, **April 1945**
128. *Sandflow* with Buck Jones, **February 1937**
129. *The Scarlet Horseman* with Peter Cookson, **January 1946**
130. *Scouts to the Rescue* with Jackie Cooper, **1938**
131. *Senor Americano* with Ken Maynard, **November 1929**
132. *Senorita from the West* with Allan Jones, **October 1945**
133. *The Silver Bullet* with Johnny Mack Brown, **August 1942**
134. *Silver Spurs* with Buck Jones, **January 1936**
135. *Sin Town* with Constance Bennett, **September 1942**
136. *The Singing Outlaw* with Bob Baker, **January 1938**
137. *The Singing Sheriff* with Bob Crosby, **October 1944**
138. *Smoke Tree Range* with Buck Jones, **June 1937**
139. *Smoking Guns* with Ken Maynard, **June 1934**
140. *Son of Roaring Dan* with Johnny Mack Brown, **July 1940**
141. *Song of the Caballero* with Ken Maynard, **August 1930**
142. *Sons of the Saddle* with Ken Maynard, **August 1930**
143. *The Spoilers* with Marlene Dietrich, **April 1942**
144. *Spurs* with Hoot Gibson, **August 1930**
145. *Stagecoach Buckaroo* with Johnny Mack Brown, **February 1942**
146. *Stone of Silver Creek* with Buck Jones, **April 1935**
147. *The Storm* with Lupe Velez, **August 1930**
148. *Stormy* with Noah Beery, Jr., **October 1935**
149. *Strawberry Roan* with Ken Maynard, **October 1933**
150. *Strictly in the Groove* with Richard Davies, **January 1943**
151. *Sudden Bill Dorn* with Buck Jones, **November 1937**
152. *Sunset of Power* with Buck Jones, **January 1936**
153. *Sutter's Gold* with Edward Arnold, **April 1936**
154. *Tenting Tonight on the Old Camp Ground* with Johnny Mack Brown and Tex Ritter, **February 1943**
155. *Terror Trail* with Tom Mix, **February 1933**
156. *Texas Bad Man* with Tom Mix, **June 1932**
157. *The Throwback* with Buck Jones, **September 1935**
158. *Timber* with Leo Carrillo, **August 1942**
159. *The Trail Drive* with Ken Maynard, **September 1933**
160. *Trail of the Vigilantes* with Franchot Tone, **December 1940**
161. *Trail to Gunsight* with Eddie Dew, **August 1944**
162. *Trail to Vengeance* with Kirby Grant, **November 1945**
163. *Trailing Trouble* with Hoot Gibson, **March 1930**

164. *Trigger Trail* with Rod Cameron, **July 1944**
165. *Trigger Tricks* with Hoot Gibson, **June 1930**
166. *Trouble at Midnight* with Noah Beery, Jr., **January 1938**
167. *Twilight on the Prairie* with Johnny Downs, **July 1944**
168. *Under Western Skies* with Martha O'Driscoll, **January 1945**
169. *The Wagon Master* with Ken Maynard, **September 1929**
170. *West Bound Limited* with Lyle Talbot, **July 1937**
171. *West of Carson City* with Johnny Mack Brown, **May 1940**
172. *Western Trails* with Bob Baker, **June 1938**
173. *The Wheels of Destiny* with Ken Maynard, **February 1934**
174. *When a Man Sees Red* with Buck Jones, **November 1934**
175. *When the Daltons Rode* with Randolph Scott, **July 1940**
176. *Wild Beauty* with Don Porter, **August 1946**
177. *Wild West Days* with Johnny Mack Brown, **June 1937**
178. *The Wildcatter* with Scott Colton, **June 1937**
179. *Winners of the West* with Dick Foran, **July 1940**
180. *Yellowstone* with Henry Hunter, **September 1936**

Chronological Listing of Universal Sound Westerns

1. *The Wagon Master* with Ken Maynard, **September 1929**
2. *The Long Long Trail* with Hoot Gibson, **October 1929**
3. *Senor Americano* with Ken Maynard, **November 1929**
4. *Courtin' Wildcats* with Hoot Gibson, **December 1929**
5. *Hell's Heroes* with Charles Bickford, **January 1930**
6. *Parade of the West* with Ken Maynard, **January 1930**
7. *The Mounted Stranger* with Hoot Gibson, **February 1930**
8. *Lucky Larkin* with Ken Maynard, **March 1930**
9. *Trailing Trouble* with Hoot Gibson, **March 1930**
10. *The Fighting Legion* with Ken Maynard, **April 1930**
11. *Roaring Ranch* with Hoot Gibson, **April 1930**
12. *The Lightning Express* with Lane Chandler, **June 1930**
13. *Mountain Justice* with Ken Maynard, **May 1930**
14. *Trigger Tricks* with Hoot Gibson, **June 1930**
15. *Song of the Caballero* with Ken Maynard, **August 1930**
16. *Sons of the Saddle* with Ken Maynard, **August 1930**
17. *The Storm* with Lupe Velez, **August 1930**
18. *Spurs* with Hoot Gibson, **August 1930**
19. *The Indians Are Coming* with Tim McCoy, **October 1930**
20. *The Concentratin' Kid* with Hoot Gibson, **October 1930**
21. *Lasca of the Rio Grande* with Leo Carrillo, **November 1931**
22. *Battling with Buffalo Bill* with Tom Tyler, **November 1931**
23. *Law and Order* with Walter Huston, **March 1932**
24. *Destry Rides Again* with Tom Mix, **April 1932**
25. *The Rider of Death Valley* with Tom Mix, **May 1932**
26. *Heroes of the West* with Noah Beery, Jr., **June 1932**
27. *Texas Bad Man* with Tom Mix, **June 1932**
28. *My Pal, the King* with Tom Mix, **August 1932**

29. *The Fourth Horseman* with Tom Mix, **September 1932**
30. *Hidden Gold* with Tom Mix, **November 1932**
31. *Flaming Guns* with Tom Mix, **December 1932**
32. *Clancy of the Mounted* with Tom Tyler, **January 1933**
33. *Terror Trail* with Tom Mix, **February 1933**
34. *Rustlers' Roundup* with Tom Mix, **March 1933**
35. *King of the Arena* with Ken Maynard, **June 1933**
36. *The Fiddlin' Buckaroo* with Ken Maynard, **July 1933**
37. *Gordon of Ghost City* with Buck Jones, **August 1933**
38. *The Trail Drive* with Ken Maynard, **September 1933**
39. *Strawberry Roan* with Ken Maynard, **October 1933**
40. *Gun Justice* with Ken Maynard, **December 1933**
41. *The Wheels of Destiny* with Ken Maynard, **February 1934**
42. *Honor of the Range* with Ken Maynard, **April 1934**
43. *Smoking Guns* with Ken Maynard, **June 1934**
44. *The Red Rider* with Buck Jones, **July 1934**
45. *Rocky Rhodes* with Buck Jones, **September 1934**
46. *When a Man Sees Red* with Buck Jones, **November 1934**
47. *Rustlers of Red Dog* with Johnny Mack Brown, **January 1935**
48. *The Crimson Trail* with Buck Jones, **March 1935**
49. *Stone of Silver Creek* with Buck Jones, **April 1935**
50. *Border Brigands* with Buck Jones, **June 1935**
51. *Outlawed Guns* with Buck Jones, **July 1935**
52. *The Roaring West* with Buck Jones, **July 1935**
53. *The Throwback* with Buck Jones, **September 1935**
54. *Stormy* with Noah Beery, Jr., **October 1935**
55. *The Ivory-Handled Gun* with Buck Jones, **November 1935**
56. *Sunset of Power* with Buck Jones, **January 1936**
57. *Silver Spurs* with Buck Jones, **January 1936**
58. *Sutter's Gold* with Edward Arnold, **April 1936**
59. *For the Service* with Buck Jones, **May 1936**
60. *The Cowboy and the Kid* with Buck Jones, **May 1936**
61. *The Phantom Rider* with Buck Jones, **July 1936**
62. *Ride 'Em Cowboy* with Buck Jones, **September 1936**
63. *Yellowstone* with Henry Hunter, **September 1936**
64. *Boss Rider of Gun Creek* with Buck Jones, **November 1936**
65. *Empty Saddles* with Buck Jones, **December 1936**
66. *Sandflow* with Buck Jones, **February 1937**
67. *Left Handed Law* with Buck Jones, **April 1937**
68. *The Mighty Treve* with Noah Beery, Jr., **April 1937**
69. *Smoke Tree Range* with Buck Jones, **June 1937**
70. *Wild West Days* with Johnny Mack Brown, **June 1937**
71. *The Wildcatter* with Scott Colton, **June 1937**
72. *West Bound Limited* with Lyle Talbot, **July 1937**
73. *Black Aces* with Buck Jones, **September 1937**
74. *Law for Tombstone* with Buck Jones, **October 1937**

CHRONOLOGICAL LISTING   403

75. *Sudden Bill Dorn* with Buck Jones, **November 1937**
76. *Boss of Lonely Valley* with Buck Jones, **November 1937**
77. *Courage of the West* with Bob Baker, **December 1937**
78. *The Singing Outlaw* with Bob Baker, **January 1938**
79. *Trouble at Midnight* with Noah Beery, Jr., **January 1938**
80. *Forbidden Valley* with Noah Beery, Jr., **February 1938**
81. *Border Wolves* with Bob Baker, **February 1938**
82. *The Last Stand* with Bob Baker, **April 1938**
83. *Flaming Frontiers* with John Mack Brown, **May 1938**
84. *Western Trails* with Bob Baker, **June 1938**
85. *Outlaw Express* with Bob Baker, **June 1938**
86. *Black Bandit* with Bob Baker, **September 1938**
87. *Guilty Trail* with Bob Baker, **October 1938**
88. *Prairie Justice* with Bob Baker, **November 1938**
89. *Ghost Town Riders* with Bob Baker, **December 1938**
90. *Honor of the West* with Bob Baker, **January 1939**
91. *The Phantom Stage* with Bob Baker, **February 1939**
92. *Scouts to the Rescue* with Jackie Cooper, **1938**
93. *The Oregon Trail* with Johnny Mack Brown, **May 1939**
94. *Mutiny on the Blackhawk* with Richard Arlen, **August 1939**
95. *Desperate Trails* with Johnny Mack Brown, **September 1939**
96. *Oklahoma Frontier* with Johnny Mack Brown, **October 1939**
97. *Chip of the Flying U* with Johnny Mack Brown, **November 1939**
98. *Destry Rides Again* with Marlene Dietrich and James Stewart, **Dec. 1939**
99. *My Little Chickadee* with Mae West and W.C. Fields, **February 1940**
100. *Man from Montreal* with Richard Arlen, **March 1940**
101. *Riders of Pasco Basin* with Johnny Mack Brown, **April 1940**
102. *West of Carson City* with Johnny Mack Brown, **May 1940**
103. *Bad Man from Red Butte* with Johnny Mack Brown, **May 1940**
104. *Winners of the West* with Dick Foran, **July 1940**
105. *Son of Roaring Dan* with Johnny Mack Brown, **July 1940**
106. *When the Daltons Rode* with Randolph Scott, **July 1940**
107. *Ragtime Cowboy Joe* with Johnny Mack Brown, **September 1940**
108. *Diamond Frontier* with Victor McLaglen, **October 1940**
109. *Law and Order* with Johnny Mack Brown, **November 1940**
110. *Pony Post* with Johnny Mack Brown, **December 1940**
111. *Trail of the Vigilantes* with Franchot Tone, **December 1940**
112. *Boss of Bullion City* with Johnny Mack Brown, **January 1941**
113. *Bury Me Not on the Lone Prairie* with Johnny Mack Brown, **March 1941**
114. *The Lady from Cheyenne* with Loretta Young, **April 1941**
115. *Men of the Timberland* with Richard Arlen, **June 1941**
116. *Law of the Range* with Johnny Mack Brown, **June 1941**
117. *Riders of Death Valley* with Dick Foran, **July 1941**
118. *Rawhide Rangers* with Johnny Mack Brown, **July 1941**
119. *Badlands of Dakota* with Robert Stack, **September 1941**
120. *Man from Montana* with Johnny Mack Brown, **September 1941**

121. *The Masked Rider* with Johnny Mack Brown, **October 1941**
122. *Arizona Cyclone* with Johnny Mack Brown, **November 1941**
123. *Fighting Bill Fargo* with Johnny Mack Brown, **December 1941**
124. *Road Agent* with Dick Foran, **December 1941**
125. *North to the Klondike* with Broderick Crawford, **January 1942**
126. *Ride 'Em Cowboy* with Abbott and Costello, **February 1942**
127. *Stagecoach Buckaroo* with Johnny Mack Brown, **February 1942**
128. *The Spoilers* with Marlene Dietrich, **April 1942**
129. *Men of Texas* with Robert Stack, **July 1942**
130. *The Silver Bullet* with Johnny Mack Brown, **August 1942**
131. *Boss of Hangtown Mesa* with Johnny Mack Brown, **August 1942**
132. *Timber* with Leo Carrillo, **August 1942**
133. *Deep in the Heart of Texas* with Johnny Mack Brown and Tex Ritter, **September 1942**
134. *Sin Town* with Constance Bennett, **September 1942**
135. *Overland Mail* with Lon Chaney, Jr., **September 1942**
136. *Little Joe, the Wrangler* with Johnny Mack Brown and Tex Ritter, **November 1942**
137. *The Old Chisholm Trail* with Johnny Mack Brown and Tex Ritter, **December 1942**
138. *Strictly in the Groove* with Richard Davies, **January 1943**
139. *Tenting Tonight on the Old Camp Ground* with Johnny Mack Brown and Tex Ritter, **February 1943**
140. *Cheyenne Roundup* with Johnny Mack Brown and Tex Ritter, **April 1943**
141. *Cowboy in Manhattan* with Frances Langford, **April 1943**
142. *Raiders of San Joaquin* with Johnny Mack Brown and Tex Ritter, **June 1943**
143. *Frontier Badman* with Robert Paige, **August 1943**
144. *The Lone Star Trail* with Johnny Mack Brown and Tex Ritter, **August 1943**
145. *Arizona Trail* with Tex Ritter, **September 1943**
146. *Frontier Law* with Russell Hayden, **November 1943**
147. *Marshal of Gunsmoke* with Tex Ritter and Russell Hayden, **January 1944**
148. *The Great Alaskan Mystery* with Milburn Stone, **1944**
149. *Oklahoma Raiders* with Tex Ritter, **March 1944**
150. *Boss of Boomtown* with Rod Cameron, **May 1944**
151. *Trigger Trail* with Rod Cameron, **July 1944**
152. *Twilight on the Prairie* with Johnny Downs, **July 1944**
153. *Raiders of Ghost City* with Dennis Moore, **July 1944**
154. *Trail to Gunsight* with Eddie Dew, **August 1944**
155. *Moonlight and Cactus* with the Andrew Sisters, **September 1944**
156. *The Singing Sheriff* with Bob Crosby, **October 1944**
157. *Riders of the Santa Fe* with Rod Cameron, **November 1944**
158. *Can't Help Singing* with Deanna Durbin, **December 1944**
159. *The Old Texas Trail* with Rod Cameron, **December 1944**
160. *Under Western Skies* with Martha O'Driscoll, **January 1945**
161. *Frisco Sal* with Susanna Foster, **February 1945**
162. *Beyond the Pecos* with Rod Cameron, **April 1945**

163. *Salome, Where She Danced* with Yvonne De Carlo, **April 1945**
164. *Renegades of the Rio Grande* with Rod Cameron, **June 1945**
165. *Bad Men of the Border* with Kirby Grant, **September 1945**
166. *Senorita from the West* with Allan Jones, **October 1945**
167. *Code of the Lawless* with Kirby Grant, **October 1945**
168. *The Royal Mounted Rides Again* with Bill Kennedy, **October 1945**
169. *The Daltons Ride Again* with Alan Curtis, **November 1945**
170. *Trail to Vengeance* with Kirby Grant, **November 1945**
171. *Frontier Gal* with Yvonne De Carlo, **December 1945**
172. *Gun Town* with Kirby Grant, **January 1946**
173. *The Scarlet Horseman* with Peter Cookson, **January 1946**
174. *Canyon Passage* with Dana Andrews, **July 1946**
175. *Rustler's Roundup* with Kirby Grant, **August 1946**
176. *Wild Beauty* with Don Porter, **August 1946**
177. *Lawless Breed* with Kirby Grant, **August 1946**
178. *Gunman's Code* with Kirby Grant, **August 1946**
179. *The Overlanders* with Chips Rafferty, **December 1946**
180. *Ramrod* with Joel McCrea, **May 1947**

Selected Bibliography

Books

Aaronson, Charles S. *The International Motion Picture Almanac*. New York: Quigley Publications, 1965.

Adams, Les, and Buck Rainey. *The Shoot-Em-Ups*. New Rochelle, N.Y.: Arlington House, 1978.

Alicoate, Jack. *Film Daily Yearbook of Motion Pictures 1930–1947*. New York: Ayer Company Publishers.

Barbour, Alan G. *Cliffhanger*. Secaucas, N.J.: Citadel Press, 1977.

———. *The Serial, Vol. 3 & 4*. Kew Gardens, N.Y.: Alan G. Barbour.

Beach, Rex E. *The Spoilers*. New York: A.L. Burt Company, Publishers, 1906.

Bickford, Charles. *Bulls, Balls, Bicycles & Actors*. New York: Paul S. Eriksson, Inc., 1965.

Bloom, Ken. *Hollywood Song: The Complete Film and Musical Companion*. New York: Facts on File, Inc., 1995.

Blottner, Gene. *Universal-International Westerns, 1947–1963*. Jefferson, N.C., and London: McFarland & Company, Inc., 2000.

Bond, Johnny. *The Tex Ritter Story*. New York: Chappell & Co., Inc., 1976.

Coglan, Frank, Jr. *They Still Call Me Junior*. Jefferson, N.C., and London: McFarland & Company, Inc., 1993.

Copeland, Bobby J. *Bill Elliott: "The Peaceable Man."* Madison, N.C.: Empire Publishing, Inc., 2000.

———. *The Bob Baker Story*. Oak Ridge, Tenn.: BoJo Enterprises.

De Carlo, Yvonne, with Doug Warren. *Yvonne: An Autobiography*. New York: St. Martin's Press, 1987.

Drake, Oliver. *Written Produced and Directed*. Baldwyn, Miss.: Outlaw Press, Inc., 1990.

Fitzgerald, Michael G. *Universal Pictures*. New Rochelle, N.Y.: Arlington House, 1977.

Fleming Allan's Folio of Bob Baker Western Songs. Portland, OR: American Music, Inc., 1939.

Hardy, Phil. *The Western*. New York: William Morrow and Company, Inc., 1983.

Higham, Charles, and Joel Greenberg. *The Celluloid Muse: Hollywood Directors Speak*. New York: Signet, 1969.

Hirschhorn, Clive. *The Universal Story*. New York: Crown Publishers, 1983.

Jacobs, Larry. *Big Little Books, a Collector's Reference and Guide*. Paducah, Ky.: Collectors Books, division of Schroeder Publishing Co., Inc., 1996.

Luke Short's Best of the West. New York: Zebra Books/Kensington Publishing Corp., 1983.

Maltin, Leonard. *Movie and Video Guide*. New York: Signet, 1995.

_____. *Movie Comedy Teams*. New York: Signet, 1970.

Miller, Don. *Hollywood Corral*. New York: Popular Library, 1976.

Mulholland, Jim. *The Abbott and Costello Book*. New York: Popular Library, 1975.

Nash, Jay Robert, and Stanley Ralph Ross. *The Motion Picture Guide*. Chicago: Cinebooks, Inc., 1985.

The New York Times Film Reviews, 1913–1968. New York: New York Times and Arno Press, 1970.

Nivens, Francis M. *The Films of Hopalong Cassidy*. Waynesville, N.C.: World of Yesterday, 1988.

Parris, Barry. *Louise Brooks*. New York: Alfred A. Knopf, 1989.

Peters, House, Jr. *Another Side of Hollywood*. Madison, N.C.: Empire Publishing, Inc., 2000.

Pitts, Michael R. *Western Movies*. Jefferson, N.C., and London: McFarland & Company, Inc., 1986.

Rainey, Buck. *The Life and Films of Buck Jones: The Sound Era*. Waynesville, N.C.: World of Yesterday, 1992.

Rooney, Mickey. *Life Is Too Short*. New York: Villard Books, 1991.

Rothel, David. *Those Great Cowboy Sidekicks*. Waynesville, NC: World of Yesterday, 1984.

Rutherford, John A., and Richard B. Smith III. *More Cowboy Shooting Stars*. Madison, N.C.: Empire Publishing, Inc., 1992.

Serra, C.G. *Lasca del Rio Grande*. Barcelona, Spain: Biblioteca Films.

Service, Robert W. *The Best of Robert Service*. New York: Dodd, Mead & Company.

Smith, Jay D., and Leonard Guttridge. *Jack Teagarden: The Story of a Jazz Maverick*. DaCapo Press, 1988.

Terhune, Albert Payson. *Treve*. New York: Grosset and Dunlap Publishers, 1924.

Townsend, Charles R. *San Antonio Rose: The Life and Music of Bob Wills*. Urbana and Chicago: University of Illinois Press, 1976.

Wakely, Linda Lee. *See Ya' Up There, Baby: The Jimmy Wakely Story*. Canoga Park, Calif.: Shasta Records, 1992.

Webster's New World Dictionary. Cleveland and New York: World Publishing Company, 1966.

Weill, Gus. *You Are My Sunshine: The Jimmie Davis Story*. Gretna, La.: Pelican Publishing Company, 1991.

Weiss, Ken. *To Be Continued*. New Rochelle, N.Y.: Love's Labor Press, 2000.

_____, and Ed Goldberg. *To Be Continued—*. New York: Crown Publishers, 1972.

Zinman, David. *Saturday Afternoon at the Bijou*. New Rochelle, N.Y.: Arlington House, 1973.

Periodicals

Boyd Magers' Serial Report (Albuquerque, New Mexico)
Boyd Magers' Western Clippings (Albuquerque, New Mexico)
Classic Images (Muscatine, Iowa)
Hollywood Reporter (Hollywood, California)
Screen Facts (Kew Gardens, New York)
Western Review (Alamonte Springs, Florida)
Yesterday's Saturdays (Lubbock, Texas)

Newspapers

Allentown Morning Call (Allentown, Pennsylvania)
Bethlehem Globe-Times (Bethlehem, Pennsylvania)
Daily Progress (Charlottesville, Virginia)
The New York Times (New York, New York)

Richmond Times Dispatch (Richmond, Virginia)
The Virginian-Pilot (Norfolk, Virginia)

Miscellaneous

Don't Fence Me In: Western Music's Early Golden Era (album liner notes—Rounder Records CD-1102)
Song of the Civil War (album liner notes—CMH Records CD-8028)
Tumbleweed: Bob Baker, Universal Singing Cowboy (album liner notes—compiled and recorded by Bill Russell)

Index

Abbott, Bud 254–256, 385
Abbott and Costello 253, 254–256, 385
"Abide with Me" 42
Abrahams, Maurice 235
"Ace in the Hole" 108
"Aches and Pains" 57
Acuff, Eddie 386
Adams, Ernie 45, 96, 97, 107, 164, 180, 227, 229, 230, 236, 260, 265, 286, 319, 324, 346, 362, 370
Adams, Jane 4, 61–68, 133, 134, 164, 165, 185, 235, 279, 280, 281, 283, 354–356
Adams, Kathryn 9–11, 45, 47, 244, 245
Adams, Les 1, 3
Adams, Poni *see* Adams, Jane
Adams, Ted 41, 94, 159, 260, 262, 303, 305, 306, 331
Adams, Victor 288
"Adios Vaqueros" 171
Adler, Fay 198
Adrian, Iris 150, 303, 305
Adventures of Captain Marvel 37, 60
Adventures of Ozzie and Harriett 243
Aicholtz, Lawrence 362
Ainslee, Mary 377
Ainsworth, Virginia 276
"Ain't Got Nothin' and Nothin' Worries Me" 40, 54
Akst, Albert 101, 278

Alba, Maria 134, 136
Albertson, Frank 376
Albright, Hardie 189
Alden, Eric 13
Alderson, Erville 11, 51, 150, 190, 377
Aldrich, Charles T. 150
Alexander, Dick *see* Alexander, Richard
Alexander, Katherine 335
Alexander, Richard 17, 35, 38, 39, 48, 51, 52, 75, 84, 98, 150, 156, 157, 176, 207, 250, 260, 264, 265, 273, 281, 293, 309, 341, 358, 360
Alias Billy the Kid 208
Alias the Bandit 391
All Quiet on the Western Front 5, 357, 362
All the King's Men 301
"All the Things I Wanna Say" 293
Allen, Fleming 66, 67, 392
Allen, Fred 96, 175, 193, 224, 292, 311, 313, 367
Allen, Harry 106
"Along the Rio Grande" 250
Alper, Murray 191
"Am I in Love" 293
"Amigo Mio" 216
Anchors Aweigh 50
"And Then" 363
"And Then I Got Married" 15, 310
Anderson, Captain 106, 317

Anderson, Glenn 38, 108, 230, 234, 250, 346
Anderson, Mable 196
Andre, Lona 31, 33
Andrews, Dana 51, 52, 54
Andrews, Del 134
Andrews, Laverne 191
Andrews, Maxene 191
Andrews, Patty 191, 192
Andrews, Stanley 61, 63, 74, 104, 203, 204, 354
Andrews Sisters 191–193
Andy Hardy 18, 349
Andy Hardy Comes Home 349
Ankers, Evelyn 203, 204
Ankrum, Morris 254, 265
Anna Christie 135
"Another Night" 303
Anthony, Stuart 31
"Any Moment Now" 48
Apache (horse) 216, 232, 372
Appel, Sam 15
Applebaum, Irving 269, 276
Arabian Nights 39
Archer, John *see* Bowman, Ralph
Ardigan, Art 246
Arizona 221, 288
Arizona Bushwackers 27
Arizona Cyclone (1934) 11
Arizona Cyclone (1941) 9–11, 13, 95, 356, 371
Arizona Trail 11–13, 112, 182, 371
Arizona Wranglers 325

411

Arlen, Richard 2, 178–180, 189–190, 196–198
Armand, Eddie 241
Armendariz, Pedro 136
Armida 15, 17
Armstrong, Robert 272, 275
Arno, Sigfried 88
Arnold, Edward 6, 150, 197, 335, 337
"As the Old Chuck-wagon Rolls Along" 143
As the World Turns (TV series) 42
Ascher, Max 257
Ash, Jerome 46, 79, 98, 101, 159, 191, 205, 213, 230, 234, 260, 266, 273, 286, 320, 362, 363, 385
Asher, Max 360
Askam, Earl 89, 297, 298
Astor, Gertrude 31, 89
Atchley, Hooper 128
Ates, Roscoe 48, 231
"A-Tisket, A-Tasket" 254
Atwill, Lionel 236, 237, 239
Auer, Mischa 84, 86, 87, 350, 352
Auster, Islin 85
Austin, Frank 260
Austin, Gene 198, 199
Austin, Glenn 359
Austin, Marie 35, 352
Austin, Vivian 35, 37, 38, 358, 359, 363, 364
Austin, William 191
Autry, Gene 6, 7, 78, 91, 329, 371
Ayers, Mitch 191
Aylesworth, Arthur 284, 299

Bacon, Irving 48, 314, 316, 365
Bad Man from Red Butte 13–15, 55, 86, 118, 235, 364
Bad Men of the Border 15–17, 311
Bad Men of Tombstone 301
Badge of Bravery 391
Badlands of Dakota 7, 17–19, 132, 182, 188, 239

Baker, Bob 7, 13–15, 30, 31, 34, 35, 56, 57, 58, 64–67, 72, 79–81, 107, 119–121, 126, 127, 142–144, 154–156, 205, 207, 212, 216, 217, 219, 227–230, 232, 233, 235, 254, 262, 263, 301, 302, 339, 370, 372, 392
Baker, Graham 241, 243
Baker, Lorin 71
Baker, Tex *see* Baker, Bob
Balcon, Michael 222, 223
Baldra, Chuck 119, 232
Baldwin, Walter 354
"Bananas Make Me Tough" 164, 176
Bancroft, George 376
Banderas, Antonio 221
Bane, Holly 241, 243
Bank Robbery 250
Banks, Lionel 241
Banton, Travis 51, 113
Barclay, Don 17, 216, 217
Barclay, Joan 301, 302
Barcroft, Roy 13, 54, 56, 98, 183, 184, 209, 213, 234, 260, 370, 384
Bardette, Trevor 241, 384
Barker, Jess 74, 293
Barnard, Lester, Jr. 393
Barnes, Binnie 335, 337
Barnes, Charles E. 146, 147, 162
Barnes, Eddie 140, 142
Barrat, Robert 104, 105
Barrett, Judith 386, 388
Barrie, Judith 139
Barron, Robert 17, 35, 38, 39, 54, 55, 219, 236, 314, Barrymore, Diana 111, 112
Barrymore, John 38
Barthelmess, Richard 314
Barton, Finis 201
The Bashful Whirlwind 394
Bastian, Jesse 34, 64, 262, 301, 362, 368, 383
Bates, Barbara 281
Bates, Les 96, 97, 193, 194
The Battling Kid 391
Battling with Buffalo Bill 20, 21
Baxter, Warner 5

"Be Honest with Me" 330
Beach, Guy 273
Beach, John 309
Beach, Rex 314, 316
Beale, Frank 291
"The Bears Give Me the Bird" 46, 116
Beaton, Kenneth C. 311
"Beautiful Dreamer" 111, 209
Beavers, Louise 383
"Bed Down, Bed Down, Little Dogies" 262
Beebe, Ford 111–113, 144, 167, 183, 185, 205, 207, 213, 219, 222, 260, 262, 263, 309, 311, 362, 368, 369, 381, 382, 384, 385
Beecher, Elizabeth 169, 295, 337
Beecher, Janet 186
Beery, Noah 196, 198, 219, 221, 222, 316
Beery, Noah, Jr. 74, 76, 104, 105, 111, 112, 137, 138, 190, 219, 221, 222, 260, 278, 279, 325, 327, 362, 363, 365, 366
Beery, Noah, Sr. *see* Beery, Noah
Beggs, Lee 246
Bell, Hank 17, 31, 32, 35, 57, 91, 98, 128, 140, 156, 205, 225, 246, 254, 262, 269, 279, 281, 307, 320, 322, 340, 348, 350, 381
Bell, Marjorie 12, 142–144
Bell, Rex 20, 21
Bellamy, Madge 122–124
Bellamy, Ralph 186
Belmore, Lionel 88
"Beloved" 108
Benedict, Billy 198, 200
Benedict, Howard 113
Bennett, Charles M. 286
Bennett, Constance 299–301
Bennett, Helen 272, 285
Bennett, Ray 124, 129, 180, 314, 352
Bennison, Andrew 57, 79
Berger, Hal 148, 150
Berger, Ralph 25, 31, 42, 44, 70, 73, 90, 91, 140,

146, 148, 161, 165, 218, 226, 252, 269, 271, 276, 284, 297, 305, 307, 322, 325, 332, 334, 344, 375
Bergerman, Stanley 83, 101, 106, 257, 341
Bergman, Helmer 291
Beringer, Carl 286
Bernard, Joseph 239
Bernard, Sam 288
Bernhard, Jack 370
Bernoudy, Jane 153
Bernstein, Isadore 83, 84, 102
Berrell, George 136
Bertram, William 317
"Beside the Rio Tonto Shore" 254
Best, Willie 150, 152
The Best Man 394
Between Fires 394
Bevins, Clem 225
Bey, Turhan 107, 109, 110
Beyond the Last Frontier 172
Beyond the Pecos 22–24, 118, 134, 177
Beyond the Seven Seas 22
Biberman, Abner 281, 283
Bickford, Charles 134–137, 260, 261
"Big Corral" 205
Big Tree 373
Billington, Francelia 195
Birch, Paul 273, 286
Birnbaum, Irving 124, 236, 273, 286
Birtles, Dora 223
Bischoff, Samuel 152
Bishop, Joe 41–43, 331, 333
Bishop, Julie 59, 138
Black Aces 25–29
Black Bandit 30, 31, 208, 233
Blackwell, Carlyle 107
Blaine, James 94, 96, 97, 100, 176, 177, 205, 207, 213, 215, 260, 384
Blake, Gladys 365
Blake, Larry 362, 363
Blanco, Eumenio 334
Blandick, Clara 48, 113
Blankfort, Henry 75, 303

"Blaze Away, Cowboy" 34
Blazing the Overland Trail 238
Bleifer, John 73, 74
Bletcher, Billy 84
Blomberg, J. Edward 281
Blottner, Charles 4
"Blow the Man Down" 22
Blue, Jean 222
Blue, Monte 203, 204, 260
The Blue Dalhia 242
"Blue Danube" 281, 293
Blue Wing's Revenge 394
"The Blues" 363
Blystone, Stanley 96, 146, 224, 230, 269, 285, 346
Boardman, True 254
The Bobby Darin Story 240
Bogart, Humphrey 206
Boggs, Noel 393
The Bold Caballero 221
Bolger, Jack A., Jr. 15, 181
Bond, Johnny 7, 11–13, 31, 37, 45, 54, 56, 76, 95, 116, 117, 169, 171, 180–183, 185, 207, 208, 209, 230, 239, 329, 326, 337, 339
Bond, Ward 51, 52, 54, 73, 74, 299, 301, 383
Bonham, Guy 17
Bonner, Marjorie 390
Bonomo, Joe 20, 67, 394
Border Brigands 31–33, 93
Border Buckaroos 36
The Border Wolf 390
Border Wolves 34, 35
Borradaile, Osmond 222, 224
The Boss of Bar 20 394
Boss of Boomtown 35–38
Boss of Bullion City 38, 39, 162, 217, 393
Boss of Hangtown Mesa 39–41, 56, 172, 212, 263, 360
Boss of Lonely Valley 41–43, 333
Boss Rider of Gun Creek 44, 45
Boteler, Wade 150, 254, 346

Botiller, Dick 183, 213, 250, 288
Bouk, Ray 148, 150
The Boundary Line 394
The Bounty Hunter 243
Bower, B.M. 57, 58
"Bowlegged Bill" 34
Bowles, Phil 286
Bowman, Earl W. 173
Bowman, Ralph 97, 100
The Boy and the Bad Man 389
Boyd, William 6, 139, 140, 243, 333
Boyd, William (stage) 316, 324, 325
Boyle, Charles P. 113, 116
Boyle, John W. 19, 254, 330
"The Boys in the Back Room" 85
Boy's Life 289
Bracey, Sidney 335, 381, 382
Bradley, Harry C. 362
Brady, Edward 97, 128
Branch, Houston 386
Brand, Max 83, 84, 85, 86
"Branding Days" 301
Brandon, Henry 368, 369
Bredell, Elwood *see* Bredell, Woody
Bredell, Woody 48, 50, 104, 105, 368
Brennan, Walter 106, 136, 156, 158, 173, 174, 278
Brent, Evelyn 331
Brent, Linda 254
Brent, Lyton 337
Brent, Roy 15, 61, 76, 239, 354, 379
Bretherton, Howard 250, 252
Bricker, George 203
The Bride Wasn't Willing 113
Bridge, Al 17, 88, 94, 98, 140, 150, 162, 186, 198, 205, 206, 244, 265, 337, 347, 370, 381, 382, 384
Bridge, Alan *see* Bridge, Al
Bridges, Lloyd 51, 52, 54, 241

Briggs, Harlan 198, 362, 363
Brinley, Charles 73
Briskin, Irving 249
Brissac, Virginia 74, 84
Broadbent, Aida 71
Brodie, Don 178
Broekman, David 63, 67, 135, 144, 193, 195, 268, 311, 317, 356, 360
Brooks, Jean *see* Kelly, Jeanne
Brooks, Louise 89–91
Brooks, Richard 186, 299
Brooks, Ted 136
Brown, Bernard B. 9, 12, 13, 15, 17, 22, 30, 35, 38, 40, 46, 48, 51, 54, 57, 61, 71, 75, 76, 79, 85, 88, 94, 108, 111, 113, 116, 119, 126, 129, 133, 143, 159, 162, 164, 169, 171, 176, 178, 181, 183, 186, 189, 191, 196, 199, 203, 205, 207, 209, 211, 213, 228, 230, 232, 234, 239, 244, 250, 254, 262, 264, 266, 279, 281, 293, 295, 299, 303, 314, 320, 330, 338, 346, 350, 352, 354, 358, 363, 365, 370, 377, 379, 392, 393
Brown, Edward B. 151
Brown, Forrest 41
Brown, Harry J. 96, 97, 164, 175, 193, 194, 224, 291, 292, 311, 31, 367
Brown, John Mack *see* Brown, Johnny Mack
Brown, Johnnie Mack *see* Brown, Johnny Mack
Brown, Johnny Mack 7, 8, 9–11, 12, 13–15, 24, 38, 39, 41, 45, 47, 48, 54–56, 57, 58, 62, 76, 77, 79–81, 94–96, 97, 99, 100, 138, 147, 152, 158, 159, 160, 162, 163, 165, 169, 170, 171, 172, 176–178, 182, 183–185, 188, 205–207, 209, 210, 213–215, 229, 230, 231, 234–236, 238, 239–241, 244–246, 254, 256, 262, 263, 276, 277, 280, 288, 295–297, 309–311, 319–321, 337, 339, 370, 371, 381, 382, 385
Brown, Kenneth 176, 177
Brown, Loren 84
Brown, Milton 195
Brown, Raymond 25
Browne, Lucille 20, 21, 148
Brownie (horse) 9, 94, 95, 230
Brownlee, Frank 260, 319, 340
Bruce, David 48, 281, 283
Bruckman, Clyde 363, 365, 366
Bruggerman, George 107
Brunette, Fritzi 276
The Brute Man 273
Bryant, Nana 48
Brymer 336
Buchanan, Edgar 377, 378
Buck Privates 256
Buck Rogers 368
The Buckaroo Kid 101
Bucko, Buck 91, 327
Bucko, Roy 91
Bud 'n Ben 233
Buffalo Bill 243
Buffalo Bill, Jr. *see* Wilsey, Jay
"Buffalo Gal" 140, 193, 205, 330
Buffington, Adele 15, 16, 379
Bumbaugh, Hal 94, 254, 320
Bupp, Tommy 336
Burbridge, Betty 207–209
Burgess, Dorothy 152
Burke, Orrin 225
Burnett, W.R. 156, 159, 381, 382
Burnette, Smiley 265, 345
Burns, Bob 119, 268, 372
Burns, Fred 96, 100, 106, 195, 224, 244
Burns, Paul E. 189, 190, 272, 275, 346
Burrud, Billy 70, 71
Burson, Polly 115
Burtis, James 325
Burton, Bernard W. 303

"Bury Me Not on the Lone Prairie" 46
Bury Me Not on the Lone Prairie 45–48, 118
Busch, Mae 257
Bush Christmas 223
Buster, Budd 54, 55, 61, 76, 165, 180, 209, 236, 239, 250, 264, 279, 281, 286, 301, 358, 359
Butch 'n Buddy 169, 176, 177
Butler, Roy 116, 250

Cabanne, Christy 178, 180, 196, 198, 346, 347
Cactus Mack and His Saddle Tramps 226
Cagney, James 206
Cahn, Edward L. 156, 158
Cahn, Philip 15, 106, 156, 191, 254, 293, 336, 341, 368
Cain, Ted 254
Calhoun, Rory 238, 316
"Californ-I-ay" 49
"Call of the Range" 22, 116, 133, 176
Calleia, Joseph 198, 201
Callejo, Cecilia 216, 217, 281
The Calloping Dude 58
Camargo, Anita 79
Cameron, Rod 8, 16, 22–24, 35–38, 39, 80, 112, 113–116, 211, 213, 242, 250, 251, 264, 265, 281, 283, 296, 339, 353, 358–360
Campana, Nina 216
Campbell, Daphne 222
Campbell, Peggy 322, 324, 375
Campeau, Frank 25, 34, 89, 152
Candy and Coco 198, 199
Cansino, Carmella 183, 254
"Cansinoble, Cansinita and Chiapanacas" 183
"Can't Help Singing" 48, 49
Can't Help Singing 1, 8, 48–50

Canty, Marietta 314–317
Canutt, Yakima 20
Canyon Passage 8, 51–54
Canyon Passage (novel) 51
Captain America 212
"Captain Jinks of the Horse Marines" 140
Card, Robert 154, 301
Cardwell, James 51
"A Carefree Cowboy" 239
Carey, Harry 5, 81, 93, 136, 156–158, 314, 316, 317, 335
Carey, Harry, Jr. 136
Carleton, Claire 72, 113, 129
Carlisle, Robert 257
Carlson, Richard 168
Carlson, Walter 17
Carlyle, Richard 193
"Carmencita" 183
Carmichael, Hoagy 51, 54
Carny, Mary 160
Carolina 49
Carpenter, Horace B. 9, 98, 119, 128, 148, 216, 218, 269, 284, 307, 346, 373, 375, 381, 385
Carr, Trem 66
Carradine, Keith 136
Carrillo, Leo 111, 113, 134, 152, 186, 187, 191–193, 197, 260, 261, 265–267, 299, 333, 346, 347, 365, 366
Carroll, Charles 111, 154, 191, 216, 372
Carroll, Virginia 183
Carruth, Milton 51, 85, 189, 358, 392
Carson, Jack 84
Carson, Sunset 208
Carson, Ted 389, 390, 391, 392
Carson City 243
Carter, Everett 47
Caruth, Burr 70
Casey, Jack 250, 365
Cason, John 236
Cassell, Wally 241
Cassidy, Ed 34, 45, 75, 79, 97, 216, 234, 244, 260, 262, 273, 285, 384
Castle, Nick 254

Castle, William 203
Catlett, Walter 71
Cavan, Danny 44
Cavanaugh, Hobart 190
Cavanaugh, Paul 324
Cebalos, Larry 392
Ceder, Ralph 392
Cendras, Blaise 336
"Central Avenue Shuffle" 330
Cerf, Norman A. 124, 207, 236, 273, 286
The Chadwick Family 107
Champion, Gower 143
Champion, Marge 120, 143
Chandler, George 350
Chandler, Jeff 316
Chandler, Lane 5, 167, 178, 186, 205, 213, 230, 264, 265, 273, 293, 337, 339, 358–360
Chaney, Lon 7, 17, 74, 76, 111, 113, 203–205, 219, 221, 222, 260, 261, 288
Chaney, Lon, Jr. *see* Chaney, Lon
Channing, Ruth 218
Chanslor, Roy 75
"Chansonnette of Pierrot and Pierrette" 324
Chapman, Ben 346
Charters, Spencer 104, 150
Chatterton, Tom 44, 219, 221, 222, 230, 284, 309, 310, 331
Chesebro, George 75, 85, 180, 203, 205, 262, 281
Chevret, Lita 284, 285
Cheyenne Cowboy 356
Cheyenne Roundup 14–15, 41, 54–56
"Chiapanecas" 192
Chief Many Treaties *see* Hazlett, Bill
Chief Thunderbird 20, 102, 137, 144, 381
Chief Thundercloud 98, 100, 102, 219, 236, 276
Chief Yowlatchie 51, 384
Chinook (dog) 16
Chip of the Flying U (1914) 58

Chip of the Flying U (1926) 58
Chip of the Flying U (1939) 57, 58, 67, 72, 81, 93, 161, 245, 263
Chip of the Flying U (novel) 57
Christine, Virginia 170, 211, 236–239, 285, 288
"Christmas Eve at Pilot Butte" (story) 80
"Chuck Wagon Blues" 352
Chung, Wong 159
Churchill, Edward 271
"Cielito Lindo" 183, 195, 266, 338
Circus Boy 294
The Cisco Kid 5, 24, 192
Citizen Kane 132
Clague, Charles 34, 64, 154, 216, 289, 301, 372
Clancy of the Mounted 3, 4, 59, 60
Clancy of the Mounted (poem) 59, 316
Clark, Charles H. 104
Clark, Daniel B. 83, 84, 106, 107, 139, 257, 259, 278, 340, 341, 343
Clark, Davidson 358
Clark, Frank 268, 317, 318
Clark, Frank Howard 278
Clark, Harvey 41, 43, 44, 45, 89, 160
Clark, Mamo 196
Clark, Steve 279
Clark, Wallis 139, 201, 202, 348, 383
Clarke, Grant 235
Clary, Charles 175
Clatworthy, Robert 48, 108
Clemente, Steve 59, 148
"Clementine" 239
Clements, Marjorie 211
Cleveland, George 48, 71, 73, 119, 121, 227–230, 293, 294, 314, 368, 379
Clichy, Martin 167
Clifford, Jack 9, 124, 168, 211, 219, 234, 260, 293, 352, 377, 381
Clifton, Elmer 54, 76, 79, 116, 118, 209, 210, 239

416 INDEX

The Climax 109
Cline, Edward F. 191, 193, 199, 201
Cline, Wilfred 144
Clive, Iris 250
A Close Call 394
Clute, Chester 51, 314
"C'Mere Baby" 192
Cobb, Edmund 15, 20, 59, 61, 76, 122, 124, 137, 138, 144, 146, 176, 190, 209, 211, 230, 236, 237, 246, 249, 250, 252, 260, 276, 278, 279, 281, 285, 288, 305, 307, 341, 370, 384, 389, 390, 394
Coby, Fred 285
Cochran, Dorcas 94
Code of the Lawless 16, 61–63
Cody, Bill, Jr. 13, 79, 85, 213, 215, 288, 291
Cody, Iron Eyes 44, 148, 213, 219, 230, 254, 257, 288, 381, 384
Cody, William F. 20, 144
"Coffee Five, Doughnuts Five" 393
Coglan, Frank, Jr. 288, 290, 291
Cohen, Bennett 22, 96, 176, 177, 193, 224, 291, 311, 313, 352
Colcord, Mabel 305, 331
The College Cowboy 394
Collier, Lois 379, 380
Collins, Lewis D. 124, 169, 170, 191, 207, 209, 211, 213, 236, 239, 241, 273, 275, 286, 288, 337, 339, 358, 360, 383, 384, 393
Collins, Monte 108, 392
Collins, Monty *see* Collins, Monte
Collins, Ray 48
Colton, Scott 383, 384
Combo, Clyde 222
"Come All Ye Faithful" 108
Come On Danger (1932) 208
Come On Danger!(1942) 208
Come to the Stable 151

"Comin' Round the Mountain" 161
Compana, Nina 334
Compton, Joyce 276, 277
The Concentratin' Kid 63, 64
Condon, Charles R. 384
Conflict 2
Conlin, Jimmy 198
Connell, Jack 260, 262
Connors, Buck 122, 134
Conover, Harry 283
Conrad, Eddy 178
Conrad, Eugene 191, 303
Cook, Evelyn 169
Cook, Glenn 30, 34, 64, 119, 126, 143, 154, 216, 228, 232, 301, 372
Cook, Mary Lou 254
Cookson, Peter 7, 285, 287, 288
Cooley, Spade 283, 293, 294, 303, 305, 392, 393
Cooper, Courtney Riley 80
Cooper, Gary 223, 316
Cooper, George 225, 227, 252, 253
Cooper, Jackie 186, 188, 288, 290, 291
Cooper, Tex 35, 51, 111, 129, 137, 150, 186, 236, 381
Corbett, Ben 25, 67, 89, 91, 96, 102, 128, 137, 140, 146, 160, 327, 334, 335, 348, 360, 381
Corby, Ellen 285
Cord, Robert 262
Cording, Harry 17, 45, 84, 111, 124, 150, 159, 160, 196, 213, 219, 221, 222, 244, 245, 254, 314, 335, 350, 377
Cordova, Fred 183
Corey, Jeff 150, 203, 241
Corey, Jim 45, 67, 68, 96, 122, 124, 137, 144, 152, 162, 165, 195, 219, 225, 246, 268, 276, 305, 307, 343, 384
Cormack, Dorothy 213
Corrado, Gino 291, 292, 311

Corrall, Charles 363
Correll, Mady 209, 210
Corrigan, D'Arcy 156
Corrigan, Lloyd 203
Corrigan, Ray "Crash" 321
Corsarro, Franco 372
Cortez, Stanley 17, 383
Costello, L.F. 325
Costello, Lou 254–256, 385
Cotton, Carolina 303, 305
The Count of Monte Cristo 89
The Countess of Monte Cristo 110
Courage of the West 58, 64–67, 81, 93, 127, 161, 245
Courtin' Calamity 69
Courtin' Wildcats 67–69
Cowan, Lester 198
Cowan, Will 9, 94, 162, 176, 183, 244, 320, 393
The Cowboy and the Kid 70, 71, 376
Cowboy Holiday 252, 253, 256
Cowboy in Manhattan 1, 58, 71–73, 132, 245
"A Cowboy Is Happy" 72, 129, 244
"A Cowboy's Dream" 207, 325
"Cowboy's Lament" 77
"A Cowboy's Life Is a Life of Ease" 372
"A Cowboy's Prayer" 365
"Cowboy's Song for Sale" 30
Cowles, Jules 137
Cox, Buddy 64
Cox, Morgan B. 111, 236, 239, 266, 273, 286
Coxen, Ed 128, 148, 307, 373
Coyote Canyon 35
Craft, Charles 34, 64, 154, 216, 301, 372
Craig, James 159, 160, 288, 384
Crain, Earl 91, 128, 140, 307, 327, 348, 374
Cramer, Richard 64, 102,

156, 205, 246, 249, 257, 370
Crane, Earl *see* Crain, Earl
Craven, Frank 150, 152
Craven, James 169
Crawford, Broderick 17, 19, 186, 188, 203–205, 299–301, 350, 352, 376, 378
Crawford, Joan 351
Crawford, Kathryn 63, 64, 193, 194, 291, 292
Crawford, Robert "Captain Bob" 57, 162, 205, 234, 244, 309
Crehan, Joseph 124, 126, 186, 273
Crimson Courage 391
The Crimson Trail 73, 74
Cripps, Kernan 70, 71, 297, 322
Crisp, Donald 241
Crist, Harry 391
Crizer, Tom J. 201
Crockett Family 276
Cronenbold, Edward "Tookie" 57, 162, 205, 234, 244, 309
Cronjager, Edward 51, 54
Crooked Trails 391
Crosby, Bob 143, 303–305
Crosby, Marshall 222
Crosby, Ronnie 335
Cross, Alexander 160, 162
"Cross-Eyed Kate" 234
Crump, Irving 289
Cruze, James 336, 337
"La Cucaracha" 38, 161, 216, 375, 393
Cummings, Robert, Sr. 205
Cunard, Grace 106, 137, 276
Cunningham, Jack 101, 106, 257, 259, 340, 341, 343
Curran, Charles 191
Currie, Louise 129–132
The Curse of Capistrano 221
Curtis, Alan 74, 76, 107, 108, 110
Curtis, Dick 9–11, 164, 165, 234, 236, 285, 379
Curtiss, Edward 107, 151, 159, 162, 199, 250, 299, 303, 330, 350, 377
Cutler, Victor 51

Dabney, Virginia 41, 42
D'Agostino, Albert S. 336
Dailey, Dan *see* Dailey, Dan, Jr.
Dailey, Dan, Jr. 197, 346, 347
Daily, Dean 148
The Daltons Ride Again 7, 74–76, 112, 317, 368
Dana, Frederick 367
"Dancing on Air" 330
The Danger Claim 391
Dangerous Days 390
A Dangerous Game 197
D'Antonio, Carmen 84
DaPron, Louis 303, 305
Darcy, Ann 276
D'Arcy, Roy 218
Darin, Bobby 240
The Darkening Trail 45
Darling, W. Scott 299
Darr, Vondell 288, 290, 291
Darwell, Jane 186
Daugherty, Jack 394
Davidson, Tito 336
Davidson, William B. 150, 198
Davies, Richard 265, 329, 330
Davis, Boyd 254
Davis, George Gibson 292
Davis, Jimmie 329–331
Davis, Margaret 343
The Dawn Rider 373
Dean, Eddie 13, 94, 95, 118, 200, 231
Dean, Jimmie 11, 13, 116, 118, 180, 207
Dearing, Edgar 376
De Carlo, Yvonne 39, 113–116, 281–283, 294
"Deep in the Heart of Texas" 77
Deep in the Heart of Texas 41, 76–79, 188, 382
Deep in the Heart of Texas (working title) 188
"Defective Detective from Deadwood" 264
DeFore, Don 241, 243
DeGarro, Harold 84
Dekker, Albert 281, 283
DeLacey, Ralph *see* DeLacy, Ralph M.
Delacruz, Joe *see* de la Cruz, Jose
de la Cruz, Jo *see* de la Cruz, Jose
de la Cruz, Jose 134, 136, 205, 334
DeLacy, Ralph M. 9, 11, 40, 54, 71, 79, 94, 98, 111, 124, 169, 171, 176, 183, 189, 196, 203, 205, 209, 213, 254, 260, 266, 295, 320, 330, 338, 346, 362, 368, 381
De La Motte, Marguerite 219
Dell, Claudia 81, 82, 84
de Montez, Rico 183
Demorest, Drew 314
D'Ennery, Guy 183
DeRosas, Enrique 284
de Segurola, Andre 48
Desmond, William 20, 21, 22, 45, 48, 54, 59, 111, 122, 124, 137, 171, 219, 246, 269–271, 276, 278, 279, 295, 327, 384
Desperate Trails (1921) 81
Desperate Trails (1939) 58, 67, 79–81, 93, 161, 245, 267, 294, 331, 339
Destry 86
Destry of Death Valley 259
Destry Rides Again (1932) 6, 81–84, 86, 172, 259
Destry Rides Again (1939) 7, 84, 84–87, 170, 176, 212, 231, 265, 386
Destry Rides Again (novel) 83, 85
De Toth, André 241–243
Deutsch, Adolph 241
de Valdez, Carlos J. 331
Deverell, Helen 39, 330
The Devil Horse 279, 329
The Devil Is Driving 18

"The Devil's Gonna Laugh" 12
Devine, Andy 2, 17, 51, 54, 76, 83, 84, 107, 109, 110, 111, 113, 113, 116, 134, 156, 158, 178–180, 189, 190, 196–198, 203, 204, 265–267, 299, 346, 347, 350, 352, 378, 386, 388
Devine, Denny 51
Devine, Tad 51
Dew, Eddie 17, 22, 23, 80, 172, 211, 213, 250–252, 264, 265, 346, 352, 353, 358–360
de Wit, Jacqueline 191, 379
Diamond, Abe 329
Diamond, Leo 329
Diamond Frontier 88, 89, 158
Diamond Solid-Aires 329, 330
Diary of a Lost Girl 90
Dickey, Basil 59, 98, 122, 137, 213, 215, 226, 246, 260, 262, 269, 276, 375, 289, 384, 391
Dickinson, Dick 30, 119, 143
Dietrich, Marlene 2, 7, 84–87, 170, 178, 212, 300, 314–317
Dimsdale, Howard 293
Dinning, Ella Lucille 329
Dinning, Eugenia Day 329
Dinning, Virginia Moy 329
Dinning Sisters 329, 330
Dirigo, Carmen 51, 113, 133, 164, 279, 379
Discontented Cowboys 392
Dix, Dorothy 334, 335, 373–375
Dix, Richard 17–19, 132
"Dixie" 193
"Do the Oo La La" 164, 234
Dodd, James *see* Dodd, Jimmie
Dodd, Jimmie 159, 160, 321, 363

Dodge, Mary 93
Dolan, Jack 124, 236, 273, 286
Dolenz, George 272, 274
Dominguis, Joe 216
The Domino Kid 238
Donaldson, Don 241
Donlevy, Brian 51, 52, 54, 84, 376
Donnelly, Ruth 198
"Don't Go Making Speeches" 365
"Don't Jump the Gun" 332
"Don't You Ever Be a Cowboy" 320, 363
"The Door of Your Heart" 133
Dorn, Philip 88, 89
Dorrell, Dick 34, 35
Douglas, Earle 384
Douglas, George 264, 265
"Down an Old Spanish Trail" 250
"Down by the Silvery Rio Gande" 153
"Down in the Valley" 192
"Down in Union County" 224
"Down That Old Home Trail" 119
"Down the Home Trail with You" 313
"Down the Road to Santa Fe" 228
Downing, Rex 30
Downs, Johnny 363
Drake, Claudia 164, 165, 235
Drake, Oliver 11, 22, 35, 36, 40, 54, 76, 116, 118, 169, 171, 180, 207, 209, 211, 239, 250, 251, 264, 295, 296, 337, 352, 358
Driftin' River 231
"Drinks Are on the House" 338, 385
Drums of Fu Manchu 368
Dude Ranch 392
Dudley, Robert 377
Duff, Warren 150
Duggin, Jan 198
Dumbrille, Douglas 74, 254, 278, 279

Duncan, Kenne 54
Duncan, Tommy 393
Dunn, Bobbie 224, 367
Dunn, Bobby *see* Dunn, Bobbie
Dunn, Eddie 113, 254, 281
Dunn, Ralph 79, 81, 150, 288, 293, 330, 350
Duprez, Frank 153
Durand, David 288, 291
Durbin, Deanna 8, 48–50, 109
"Dusty an' Dry" 30, 232
"Dusty Trails" 22
Duval, Diane 59, 137, 138
Duval, Leon 59
Dwan, Allan 350–352
Dwan, Dorothy 96
Dwire, Earl 362, 363
Dyer, Bill *see* Dyer, William
Dyer, William 128, 356
Dynamite (dog) 144
Dynamite's Daughter 394

Eason, B. Reeves 161, 268, 269, 281, 317, 319, 360, 361
Eason, Breezy *see* Eason, B. Reeves
Eason, W.B. *see* Eason, B. Reeves
Eckhardt, Oliver 70
Eddie Dean Trio 94, 118
Eddy, Nathaniel 276
Edwards, Edgar 384
Edwards, Neely 330
Eggerton, Joseph 94, 150
Eight Buckaroos 363
Eilers, Sally 173, 268, 269, 360, 361
"Elbow Room" 48
Eldredge, George 48, 111, 113, 116, 171, 207, 209, 211, 236, 239, 273, 275, 358, 360
Eldredge, John 15, 309–311
Ellery Queen 107
Elliott, Bill (Wild Bill) 24, 78, 182, 231
Elliott, John 207, 239, 305, 306, 337
Ellis, Frank 9, 34, 38, 67,

79, 91, 96, 98, 119, 122, 142, 143, 144, 154, 159, 169, 176, 180, 186, 193, 198, 205, 213, 244, 262, 299, 320, 348, 375, 381, 384
Ellis, John 88, 189
"Elmer's Tune" 330
Emert, Oliver 113
Emmett, Daniel Decatur 194
Emmett, Fern 79, 347
Empty Saddles 89–91
Enfield, Hugh 122, 124
Engle, Billy 171
Enright, Ray 186, 188, 299, 301, 314, 317
Ernest, George 81
Errol, Leon 71, 329, 331, 363, 364, 365
Erwin, Stuart 376
Escape from Hong Kong 15, 118
Esquire Magazine 283
"Estrellita" 292
Ethier, Alphonse 44, 156, 324
Eureka Stockade 223
Evans, Muriel 41, 43, 44, 45, 160, 269–271, 297, 299, 305, 306, 343, 345
Everly Brothers 210
"Everything Is Swingin'" 332
Ewing, John F. 386

Fadden, Tom 84, 111, 272, 354, 384
Fain, Matty 41, 165, 167
Fairbanks, Douglas 221, 292
Fairchild, Edgar 48, 293
Fargo Phantom 230
Farley, James 67, 98, 116, 175, 244, 260, 295, 384
Farley, Jim *see* Farley, James
Farmer, Frances 17–19, 132
The Farmer's Daughter 151
Farnum, Franklyn 140
Farnum, William 39, 76, 79, 100, 102, 111, 186, 188, 295, 314, 316

Farrell, Cliff 218
The Fat Man 384
The Fat Man (radio series) 384
Fay, Dorothy 232, 233
Faye, Alice 72, 235
Faye, Randall 152
Fegan, John 222
Feitshans, Fred, Jr. 71, 111, 363
Feldman, Charles K. 314
Fellows, Edith 257, 259
Ferguson, Al 5, 22, 167, 168, 246, 264, 271, 276, 281, 293, 367
Ferguson, Frank 51
Fernside, John 222
Fessier, Michael 113
The Fiddlin' Buckaroo 33, 58, 67, 81, 91–93, 158, 161, 210, 225, 227, 245, 326, 382
Field, Sylvia 281
Fields, Stanley 81, 84, 150, 271, 272
Fields, W.C. 198–201
Fighting Bill Fargo 94–96, 118, 172
Fighting Legion 96, 97
The Fighting Ranger 376
The Fighting Schoolmarm 394
The Fighting Terror 394
Fighting with Kit Carson 277
Finn, Jonathan 150
The Firefly 294
First Love 351
Fiske, Bert 107, 173
Fiske, Robert 159
Fitzgerald, Ella 14, 254, 256
Fitzgerald, Michael 2
Fitzpatrick, Herbert 70
Fix, Paul 73, 196, 271, 343, 350, 386
Flaherty, Pat 178, 180
Flame of New Orleans 2
The Flaming Frontier 21, 100, 102, 145, 215, 288, 374, 382
Flaming Frontiers 97–100, 138, 145, 277
Flaming Guns 100–102

Flaming Guns (novel) 101
Flash Gordon's Trip to Mars 261
Flavin, James 254, 377
Fleischer, Stanley 153
Fletcher, Curley 327, 329
Flint, Sam 35, 154
Floyd, Larry 4
Flying Eagle 394
Flying Fury 327
Foley, Jack 20, 124, 137
For the Service 3, 102, 103, 145
Foran, Dick 7, 134, 197, 198, 201, 221, 254, 256, 260, 261, 265–267, 288, 333, 339, 384–386
Foran, John 104
Forbidden Valley 104, 105, 206, 382
Ford, Francis 20, 21, 59, 81, 88, 122, 137, 144, 146, 195, 196, 257, 311, 312, 313
Ford, John 81, 136
Ford, Tennessee Ernie 210, 212
Forest, William 236
"Forget Your Boots and Saddles" 162
Forman, Tom 98
Forrest and Towne 392
Foster, Lewis 48
Foster, Preston 241, 243
Foster, Susanna 107–110
Foulger, Byron 196
Four Faces West 243
Four Singing Notables 370
The Fourth Horseman 106, 107, 121
Fowler, Art 11, 116
Fowler, Jack 96
Fox, Wallace W. 15, 16, 61, 129, 132, 133, 134, 164, 165, 264, 265, 279, 280, 354, 379, 380
Fox, William 186, 196, 365
Foxe, Earle 81
Francis, Kay 376, 378
Francis, Noel 165–167, 201, 322, 324, 331–333
Francis, Owen 178
Franey, Billy 91, 96

Franey, Wm. *see* Franey, Billy
Frank, Bruno 336
Frank, Christian 201
Frank, Fred 51, 150, 186, 281
Frank, Jerry 276
Frankenstein 202
Franklin, Paul 94
Fraser, Harry 209, 337, 391
Frazer, Robert 25, 165, 166, 297
Free Rangers 66, 67
Freed, Sam, Jr. 303
French, Charles K. 64, 73, 83, 225, 246, 276, 343, 375
Friedkin, Joel 236
Friedlander, Louis 246, 249, 276, 277, 325–327
Friend, Cliff 192
Frisco Kate 109
Frisco Sal 107–110, 132
Fritzsche, William 48, 51, 113, 281
From Here to Eternity 212
"From the Land of Sky Blue Waters" 387
Frontier 186
Frontier Badmen 7, 76, 111–113, 210, 265
Frontier Frolic 39, 162, 217, 389, 392, 393
Frontier Gal 7, 8, 39, 113–116
Frontier Law 7, 15, 24, 95, 116–118, 134, 177, 181, 364
Frost, Martin 196
Frost, Terry 162, 211, 352
Fryer, Richard 246, 269, 276, 325, 327, 381
Fulton, Joan 113
Fulton, John P. 12, 113, 314, 325, 336, 341, 368, 383, 386
Fung, Willie 17, 34, 35, 203, 205, 314, 386

"Gabby, the Lawyer" 13
Gahan, Oscar 64, 372
Gale, Joan 218
Gallaudet, John 265
Galli, Eole 269
Gan, Chester 198, 244, 246
Gangelin, Paul 75
Gangelin, Victor A. 281, 365
Garber, David 63, 67, 173, 195, 268, 317, 356, 360
Garbo, Greta 135
Gardner, Ava 110
Gargan, Edward 124
Garralaga, Martin 216, 217, 305
Garrick, Gene 129, 130, 236
Gatzert, Milton 246, 276
Gatzert, Nate 91, 128, 140, 269, 276, 307, 327, 374
Gausman, R.A. 9, 11, 13, 15, 17, 22, 35, 38, 40, 46, 48, 51, 54, 57, 61, 71, 75, 76, 79, 85, 88, 94, 108, 111, 113, 116, 129, 133, 151, 159, 164, 169, 171, 176, 178, 180, 183, 186, 189, 191, 196, 199, 203, 205, 207, 209, 211, 230, 234, 239, 250, 254, 262, 264, 266, 279, 281, 293, 295, 299, 303, 314, 316, 320, 330, 338, 346, 350, 352, 354, 358, 363, 365, 370, 377, 379
Gausman, Russell A. *see* Gausman, R.A.
Geldart, Clarence 271
Geller, Jerry 330
George, Gladys 150, 152
Geraghty, Gerald 17, 107, 111, 299
Geraghty, Maurice 362, 368
"Geraldine" 94, 116
Gerard, Jos. *see* Girard, Joseph W.
Gershenson, Joseph *see* Sanford, Joseph
Gertsman, Maury 15, 22, 61, 129, 133, 164, 250, 264, 279, 352, 354, 379
"Get Along, Little Dogies" 169, 181, 205, 320
"Get Along, Little Pony" 104, 205, 381
The Ghost Rider 277

Ghost Town Riders 107, 119–121
Gibson, Diana 225
Gibson, Helen 374
Gibson, Hoot 5, 6, 8, 14, 21, 58, 63, 64, 67–69, 100, 101, 102, 145, 149, 173–175, 195, 196, 215, 268, 269, 278, 279, 317–319, 356, 357, 360, 361, 382, 389
Gibson, Tom 273, 286
Gilbert, Billy 84, 121, 335
Gilbert, Eugenia 67–69
Gilbert, Jody 48, 254
Gilbert, Lynn 381
Giles, Lem 35
Gilman, Fred 63, 129
Gilmore, A.J. 169, 171, 209, 239, 299, 338, 346
Gilmore, J. Andrew *see* Gilmore, A.J.
Girard, Joe *see* Girard, Joseph W.
Girard, Joseph W. 67, 91, 93, 146, 218, 252, 313, 341, 381
Girl of the Oregon Trail 49
"Git Along" 57
Gittens, Wyndham 98, 104, 105, 289, 381, 382
"Give Me My Saddle" 254
"Give Me the Life of a Cow-boy" 228
Glass, Gastin 335
The Glass Key 242
Glendon, Frank 246
Glidden, Frederick Dilley *see* Short, Luke
Glosup, Jimmie Dean *see* Dean, Jimmie
Gluck, Joseph 98, 213, 219, 260, 384
G-Men Vs. the Black Dragon 36
Gober, Mildred 70
The Godchild 136
Godsoe, Harold 241
"Going Home" 226
"Going to Have a Big Time Tonight" 17
Gold Hunters of the North 203, 205

INDEX   421

Gold Strike 107, 121
Golitzen, Alexander 51, 281
"La Golondrina" 181, 183
Gomez, Thomas 48, 74, 107, 108, 110, 111, 113
Gone with the Wind 26
"Good Bye Liza Jane" 393
"Good Little Bad Little Lady" 108
"Good Old Mountain Music" 392
Goodall, Grace 41
Gooden, Arthur Henry 305
Goodkind, Saul A. 6, 98, 211, 213, 219, 226, 246, 260, 269, 276, 279, 289, 381, 385
Goodman, John B. 11, 15, 22, 35, 48, 51, 61, 71, 75, 107, 111, 113, 116, 129, 151, 171, 180, 191, 207, 211, 250, 264, 281, 293, 303, 314, 316, 352, 354, 358, 363, 365
Goodrich, Marcus 191
Goodwin, Aileen 26, 27
Goodwin, Harold 113, 234, 285, 287, 307, 327
Goodwins, Leslie 303, 305
Gordon, Mary 134, 376
Gordon of Ghost City 122–124, 272
Gottlieb, Alex 254
Gould, Charles S. 17, 107
Gould, William 128, 176, 219, 234, 262, 263, 307, 314, 347–349, 373, 377, 383
Graham, Fred 61, 311, 386
Graham, Malcolm 284
Grainger, Edmund 335
Granger, Dorothy 71, 150, 203, 365, 376
Granstedt, Greta 167
Grant, John 254
Grant, Kirby 8, 15, 16, 19, 61–63, 80, 129–132, 133, 134, 164, 165, 185, 235, 245, 267, 279, 280, 352, 354–356
Grant, Marshall 88

Granville, Bonita 293, 294
Gray, Beatrice 354
Gray, Franklin 151
Gray, Roger 392
Grayson, Charles 191
The Great Alaskan Mystery 2, 124–126, 190, 347
The Great Northern Mystery 124
The Great West That Was (book) 20, 144
Green, Alfred E. 17, 19
Green, Billy 107, 108, 110
Green, Howard 173
Greene, Joseph J. 11, 211
Greene, W. Howard 48, 50, 281
Greenwood, Albert 30, 119, 126, 143, 216, 228, 232, 372
Gregory, Jackson 332
Grey, John 303
Grey, Nan 261, 335
Gribbon, Eddie 139, 225
Grieve, Helen 222
Grinde, Nick 31, 322, 324
Grinstead, J.E. 334, 335
Gross, Frank 17, 104, 122, 191, 266, 383
Grossman, Abraham 11, 15, 22, 35, 61, 116, 129, 180, 207, 264, 293, 303, 352, 354, 358, 363, 379
The Guadalajara Trio 38, 182, 183
Guard, Kit 107
The Guardsman 319, 320
The Guiding Light 42
Guihan, Frances 25, 42, 44, 45, 70, 90, 161, 165, 167, 252, 284, 305, 332, 333, 344, 345
Guilfoyle, James 260, 262
Guilfoyle, Paul 285, 287, 288
Guilty Trail 127
Guilty Trails 67, 126, 127
Gun Justice (1927) 129
Gun Justice (1933) 128, 129
Gun Town 19, 72, 110, 129–132, 245
Gunfighters 118

Gunman's Code 24, 118, 133, 134, 160, 165, 177, 267, 352
Gunnels, Chester 392
Guns A-Blazin' 156, 158
The Guns of Will Sonnet 174
Gunsmoke 126
Guys and Dolls 86
Gwynne, Anne 13, 111, 113, 178, 179, 186, 188, 205, 207, 254, 256, 265, 267, 299, 300

Haade, William 273, 275, 314
Hackathorne, George 100
Hackett, Carl *see* Hackett, Karl
Hackett, Karl 38, 51, 57, 58, 98, 100, 133, 164, 176, 177, 178, 213
Hadley, Reed 178, 180, 265
Hagney, Frank 39, 140, 186, 293, 346
Haines, Connie 363
Hale, Alan 386
Hale, Jonathan 336
Hale, Monte 164
Hall, Al K. 370
Hall, Ben 305
Hall, Charlie 156
Hall, Henry 39, 57, 75, 219, 239, 319
Hall, Jon 39, 115
Hall, Norman S. 381, 382
Hall, Porter 350
Hall, Russell 198
Hall, Ruth 100, 102, 327, 329
Hall, Thurston 196
Hall, William 260, 346
Hallett, Beresford 222
Halperin, Victor 171
Halton, Charles 150, 314, 362
Hamblin, Stuart 65
Hamilton George, IV 210
Hamilton, J. Frank 186
Hamilton, Mahlon 44
Hamilton, Margaret 198, 201
Hammett, Dashiell 384

Hand 'Em Over 356
Hanlon, Jackie 149, 224, 225, 367
Hansen, Eleanor 97, 100
"Happiness Corral" 94
"Happy Rovin' Cowboy" 330
Harburg, E.Y. 50
Harding, Tex 375
Hardy, Phil 1
Hardy, Stuart 104
"Hark the Herald Angels Sing" 108
Harlan, Kenneth 76, 94, 213
Harlan, Otis 193, 224, 257
Harlan, Russell 241, 243
Harmon, John 88
Harmony Trail 95
Harolde, Ralf 299
Harper, Patricia 61, 239, 286, 352, 358
Harrel, Scotty 54, 76, 169, 171, 209, 239, 337
Harris, Charles 91, 128, 140, 148, 307, 327, 348, 374
Harris, Joe 136
Harris, R.R. 322, 324
Harris, Roy 162, 163, 189, 190, 203, 205, 219, 244, 246
Harrison, Carey 61
Hart, Hal 250
Hart, Jerome 162
Hart, Neal 360
Hart, William S. 24, 45, 324
Harte, Jerome 260
Hartman, Edmund 88, 89
Hartmann, Edmund L. 254
Harvey, Paul 386
The Harvey Girls 53
Haskell, Al 183
"Hatches and the Morgans" 239
Hathaway, Joan 254
Hatton, Raymond 93, 106, 134, 137, 139, 156–158, 276, 277, 325, 340, 341, 386, 388
Hatton, Rondo 273, 275
Have a Heart 294

Haworth, Joseph 113, 272, 275, 281
Haycox, Ernest 51
Hayden, Harry 107
Hayden, Russell 7, 80, 95, 116–118, 172, 180–183, 393
Haydon, Julie 208
Hayes, Bernadene 362, 363
Hayes, George 45, 297, 343, 345
Hayes, Linda 189
Hayes, Peter Lind 331
Hayes, W. Donn 88
Hayward, John Nugent 222
Hayward, Susan 51–54
Hayworth, Rita 208
Hazard, Lawrence 314
Hazel 243
Hazlett, Bill 98, 126, 127, 216, 219, 221, 276
Hazlett, William *see* Hazlett, Bill
Head, Edith 241
"Headin' for the Ole Corral" 143
"Headin' Home" 119
Healy, Mary 329–331
Hearn, Edward 44, 134, 198, 362
Heart of the Rio Grande 78
"Heave Ho My Lads, Heave Ho" 191
Hedgcock, William 12, 51, 76, 79, 88, 113, 151, 264, 281, 354
Heimel, Otto 198
Heller, Herman 387, 388
Hello, Frisco, Hello 235
Hell's Heroes 134–137
Henderson, Ray 22
Henie, Sonja 109, 110
Henry, Buzz *see* Henry, Robert "Buzzy"
Henry, Robert "Buzzy" 352, 358, 379, 380
Herbert, Hugh 17
Herman, Ace 124, 236
Heroes of the West 100, 137, 138
Herrick, Kimball 362

Hervey, Irene 84, 294
"Hi' Falutin' Cowboy" 232
Hicks, Russell 254, 329, 383
Hickson, John 20, 42, 73, 122, 137, 161, 162, 226, 332, 385
Hidden Gold (1932) 139, 140
Hidden Gold (1940) 139
"Hidden Valley" 226
Higgins, Kenneth 330
Higgins, Rose 241
"High, Wide and Handsome" 22
Hightower, Red 41, 42, 331, 332
Highway Patrol 301
Hildebrand, Rodney 20, 322
Hill, Doris 311, 313
Hill, Riley 163, 190, 246
Hill, Robert F. 169
Hill-Billyettes 392
Hilliard, Ernest 44
Hillyer, Lambert 22, 24
Hilton, Arthur 83, 365
Hinds, Samuel S. 17, 84, 104, 107, 108, 110, 124, 150, 190, 254, 265, 303, 314, 350
Hobart, Rose 51
Hobbes, Halliwell 51
Hodge, Harold 160, 165, 284, 331–333
Hodgins, Earl *see* Hodgins, Earle
Hodgins, Earle 13, 38, 76, 94, 96, 98, 107, 116, 129, 154–156, 159, 160, 171, 172, 209, 264, 265, 279, 305, 337, 350, 365
Hoffman, Otto 198
Hohl, Arthur 281
Holden, Fay 51
Holland, Dick 41–43
Holland, Willard 75, 236, 273, 286
Holland, William 48
The Hollywood Reporter 4
Holman, Harry 295
Holmes, PeeWee 100, 193, 278, 317, 319

Holmes, Stuart 201
Holt, Jennifer 22, 23, 54–56, 71, 76, 77, 116, 169, 171, 180–183, 185, 207, 209, 210, 239, 241, 250–252, 264, 265, 295, 337–339, 365, 366
Holt, Tim 208, 321
Homans, Bob *see* Homans, Robert E.
Homans, Robert E. 22, 63, 111, 309, 311, 314, 317, 325, 360, 370
"Home" 192
"Home on the Plains" 126
"Home on the Range" 284
"Honky-Tonk" 49
Honor of the Range 140–142, 194
Honor of the West 142–144
Hoosier Hot Shots 192
Hopalong Cassidy 6, 27, 80, 118, 139, 217, 243, 333, 345, 377
Hopkins, Anthony 221
Hopton, Russell 93, 156, 158
Horne, Victoria 285, 288
Horsley, D.S. 51, 54
Horton, Lester 108, 281
House, Don 45
Houston, George 238
Houston, Paul 219
How to Succeed in Business Without Really Trying 86
Howard, Edward M. 15, 61, 62, 113, 285
Howard, Fred 328, 329
Howard, Frederic 81, 82, 106
Howard, Shemp 191, 329, 331
Howdy Cowboy 268
Howes, Reed 107, 119, 142, 227, 337
Howland, Olin *see* Howlin, Olin
Howlin, Olin 48, 293, 294, 363
Hoxie, Jack 390

Hoyt, Harry O. 59, 122, 154, 301
"Huckleberry Pie" 244, 354
Hudson, Daral 273
Hughes, Catherine 362, 363
Hughes, J. Anthony 88
Hughes, John J. 156
Hughes, Kay *see* Hughes, Catherine
Hugo, Mauritz 279, 285
Hulten, George P. 292
Hultman, Rune H. 61
Humbert, George 38, 362
Humes, Fred 269, 394
Humphrey, Harry 159
Hunter, Buddy 195, 317, 319
Hunter, C. Roy 20, 63, 67, 83, 96, 135, 137, 144, 153, 156, 173, 193, 195, 224, 257, 268, 311, 313, 317, 324, 341, 356, 360, 367
Hunter, Charles 325
Hunter, E.M. Inman 222
Hunter, Henry 104, 362, 368, 386
Hurst, Paul 175, 193, 194, 201, 202
Hussy, Jim 288
Huston, John 156, 158
Huston, Walter 93, 156–158, 382
Hutton, Betty 235
Hutton, Beulah 20
Hymer, Warren 84

"I Ain't Got a Gal to Come Home To" 352
"I Betcha My Heart I Love You" 393
"I Don't Like No Cows" 230
"I Get Mellow in the Yellow of the Moon" 363
"I Had a Gal and Her Name Was Sue" 57
"I Just Got In" 108, 129
"I Like Mountain Music" 392
"I Long for the Hills of Wyoming" 372

"I Love Someone on the Texas Prairie" 90
"I Never Knew" 330
"I Plumb Forget" 162
"I Want My Man of the Golden West" 63
I Want to Live 53
"I Would Love You" 15
"I'd Rather Be Footloose and Free" 239
"I'd Saddle My Pony" 169
"Ida Red" 303
"I'll Build a Ranch House on the Range" 64
I'll Cry Tomorrow 53
"I'll Remember April" 254
"I'll Take You Home Again, Kathleen" 75, 314, 368
I'll Tell the World 15, 118
"I'm a Happy Cowboy" 46
"I'm a Texas Cowboy" 57
"I'm a Young Cowboy" 301
I'm from Arkansas 13
"I'm Getting Married in the Morning" 51
"I'm Headin' for My Oklahoma Home" 358
"I'm the Son of a Son of a Son of a Gunman" 250
"I'm Tying Up My Bridle to the Door of Your Heart" 262
"I'm Weeping Alone" 17
Imhof, Roger 150
In Old Arizona 5
In Old California 196
"In Old Oklahoma" 205
In Old Oklahoma 206
In Old Santa Fe 308
In the Navy 256
Ince, John 83, 152
Ince, Ralph 156
Incendiary Blonde 235
The Indians Are Coming 6, 21, 100, 144–146, 158, 374
Ingraham, Lloyd 13, 85, 89, 150, 198, 205, 230, 295, 309, 310, 314, 319, 330, 346

Ingram, Jack 11, 22, 23, 30, 35, 38, 113, 116, 171, 172, 207, 209, 236, 239, 260, 285, 358, 365, 372
The Invisible Woman 38
Ireland, John (actor) 223
Ireland, John (composer) 223, 224
Irving, Ernest 223
Irving, William 311
"Is It True What They Say About Dixie" 387
"It Ain't So Rosy on the Range" 119
"It's a Ranger's Life" 244
It's Always Fair Weather 347
Ivano, Paul 293
"I've Got to See Texas Just Once More" 171
"I've Sold My Saddle for an Old Guitar" 392
The Ivory Handled Gun 146, 147, 163

Jaccard, Jacques 124, 219, 260, 384
"Jack and Jill" 61
Jack Teagarden's Orchestra 363
Jackson, Felix 48, 85, 86
Jackson, John 325
Jackson, Marion 175, 367
Jackson, Selmer 273
Jacquet, Frank 22, 354
James, Alan 98, 100, 128, 129, 140, 142, 148, 150, 289, 291, 307, 327, 329, 348, 349, 374, 375
James, Alfred P. 102, 271
James, John 238, 250, 251
James, Walter 134
Janney, William 335
January, Lois 64–66
Jarrico, Paul 189
Jay, Griffin 189, 346
Jean, Gloria 109
Jeffers, Ray L. 22, 250
Jenkins, Allen 84
Jenks, Si 198
The Jesters 17
Jewell, Isabell 150
Jimenez, Soledad 15, 104

Jimmy Wakely and His Cowboy Band 329, 330
Jimmy Wakely and His Rough Riders 45, 46, 182, 230, 231
Jimmy Wakely Trio 54, 55, 76, 77, 95, 169, 171, 209, 239, 337, 338, 382
Joe Palooka 192
"Joggin' Along" 387
"Johnny's Coming Home Today" 113
Johnson, Eddie 329, 330
Jolley, I. Stanford 116, 118, 207
Jones, Allan 293, 294
Jones, Arthur V. 94
Jones, Buck 6, 7, 8, 24, 25–29, 31–33, 41, 43, 44, 45, 70, 71, 73, 89–91, 102, 103, 122–124, 146, 147, 160–162, 163, 165–167, 218, 219, 225, 227, 246–249, 252, 253, 260, 261, 269–271, 272, 284, 285, 297–299, 305, 306, 308, 309, 312, 322–324, 331–333, 334, 335, 343–345, 364, 368, 375, 376, 389, 390
Jones, Charles *see* Jones, Buck
Jones, Charles Buck *see* Jones, Buck
Jones, Clifford 102, 103
Jones, Dickie 34, 84, 305, 306, 336
Jones, Jack 294
Jones, Ray 264, 358
Jose Cansino Dancers 183
Jowett, Anthony 51
Joyzelle 311
Judge, Naomi 340
Jungle Jim 368
Just Pals 70
"Just Too Gosh Darn Bashful" 320
Justice Rides Again 81

Kaaren, Suzanne 383
Kalmus, Natalie 48, 51, 113, 281
Kane, Sandra 196
Karth, Jay 22, 352

Katch, Kurt 281
Kayser, Carl 222
Keach, Stacy 108, 293
Keane, Edward 31, 44, 102, 384
Keays, Vernon 11, 13, 17, 85, 180, 314, 330, 350, 352, 354, 377
Keene, Edw. *see* Keane, Edward
Keene, Tom 208
Keep 'Em Flying 256
Keith, Brian 227
Keith, Ian 365
Keith, Robert 83, 84
Kellaway, Cecil 88, 89
Kellogg, Cecil 57, 122
Kellogg, Kay 105, 206, 382
Kelly, D. Patrick 133, 286, 379, 393
Kelly, Jeanne 17, 94, 95, 176, 177, 260, 261, 309–311
Kelly, John 198, 354–356
Kelly, Lew 140, 265, 350, 368
Kelly, Nancy 351
Kelly, Patrick 219
Kelly, Paula 393
Kelly, Robert 167
Kelso, Edmund 213, 215
Kelso, Millard 393
Kendall, Cy 285, 287
Kennedy, Bill 7, 272, 274, 275
Kennedy, Daun 272, 281
Kennedy, Edgar 124–126, 152
Kennedy, Tom 191
Kenny, Colin 213
Kent, Ted 35, 48, 153, 203
Kenton, Erle C. 203, 205
Kern, Jerome 50
Kerr, Donald 303, 365, 370
Kettle Creek 193
Keyes, Stephen 207
The Kid Comes Thru 390
"Kid from Laredo" 154
King, Charles 17, 25, 46, 70, 97, 98, 146, 162, 164, 165, 205, 213, 218, 225, 230, 269, 305, 327, 329, 334, 335, 370, 371
King, Joe 84

King, John "Dusty" 321
King of the Arena 148–150, 225, 319
King of the Range 149
King of the Rodeo 58
King Sisters 392
Kings Men 176
Kinskey, Leonid 48, 50
Kirk, Jack 34, 64, 91, 92, 126, 127, 140, 142, 144, 154, 216, 227, 232, 285, 301, 348, 372
Kirke, Donald 106, 139, 252, 305, 306, 334
Kirkland, Jack 336, 337
Kirkpatrick, Herbert 44, 90, 91, 146, 147, 252, 284, 285, 297, 334, 344
Kirkwood, James 150, 201
Kit Carson 36
Knags, Skelton 88
Knibbs, Henry H. 195
Knight, Fuzzy 7, 9–13, 15, 17, 22–24, 34, 35, 37, 38, 39–41, 45–48, 54, 56, 57, 58, 61–63, 64, 66, 67, 72, 76, 77, 79–81, 94, 95, 107, 110, 113, 114, 116, 118, 124, 126, 129, 131, 132, 133, 134, 154, 156, 159, 160, 162, 163, 164, 165, 169, 170, 171, 172, 176, 178, 180–183, 185, 198, 205–207, 209, 210, 211–213, 215, 229, 230, 231, 234, 235, 239, 244–246, 250–252, 262, 264, 265, 279, 280, 293, 294, 295–297, 301, 302, 303, 305, 309–311, 319–321, 337, 339, 352, 354–356, 358, 360, 364, 370
Knight, Harlan 269, 270
Knott, Lydia 271
Knowles, Patric 299, 300
Knox, Elyse 191, 193
Koenig, Ben 381
Kohler, Fred 31–33, 91, 93, 102, 104, 105, 106, 107, 134, 136, 137, 140–142, 257, 259, 325, 327, 341, 342
Kohler, Fred, Jr. 39

Kohler, Fred, Sr. *see* Kohler, Fred
Kohn, Ben Grauman 325
Kolk, Scott *see* Colton, Scott
Kolster, Clarence 186, 314
Komai, Tetsu 341
Kortman, Bob 25, 46, 73, 94, 146, 148, 149, 159, 162, 205, 207, 244, 284, 285, 305, 306, 307, 340, 347, 375, 381, 382, 384
Kortman, Robert *see* Kortman, Bob
Kosleck, Martin 124
Koster, Henry 351
Kramer, Cecile 241, 243
Kramer, Vernon W. 129
Krasner, Milton 88, 151, 178, 186, 314, 350, 386
Kruger, Alma 190
Krusada, Carl 391
Kurland, Gilbert 325, 336
Kyne, Peter B. 98, 100, 101, 122, 135, 137, 137, 138

Lackteen, Frank 48, 59, 111, 113, 137, 138, 165, 191, 192, 278, 285, 365
Ladd, Alan 6, 132, 168, 242
Laddie (dog) 88
"Ladies from Paree" 151
The Lady from Cheyenne 7, 150–152, 194, 380
Laemmle, Carl 5, 6, 134, 173, 249, 308, 336, 368
Laemmle, Carl, Jr. 5, 83, 135, 249, 308, 341
Laemmle, Edward 152, 341, 343
Laidlaw, Ethan 15, 46, 75, 107, 122, 150, 159, 162, 169, 171, 180, 186, 189, 207, 219, 260, 279, 303, 309–311, 346, 377
Laine, Frankie 210
Lake, Veronica 241–243
La Marr, Margaret 246
Lamb, Ande 250, 264, 265
Lamont, Charles 113, 116, 266, 267, 281, 283
Lancaster, Burt 242

Landers, Lew *see* Friedlander, Louis
Landres, Paul 9, 13, 38, 75, 94, 176, 230, 234, 244, 293, 309
Lane, Allan "Rocky" 356
Lane, Bruce 297
Lane, Charles 254
Lane, Nora 175
Lane, Richard 196, 254
Lang, Charles 329
Lang, Melvin 38
Langford, Frances 58, 71–73
Lanning, Frank 136
Lapis, Joe 48, 71, 119, 143, 199, 207, 228, 324, 330, 352
Lapis, Joseph *see* Lapis, Joe
LaRue, Frank 116, 165, 225, 262, 343, 375
La Rue, Lash 200
Lasca (1913) 153
Lasca (1919) 153
Lasca (poem) 153
Lasca del Rio Grande 4
Lasca of the Rio Grande 3, 152, 153
Lassie 294
The Last Frontier 221
The Last Stand 154–156, 391
Latham, Dwight 17
Launders, Perc 124, 363, 365
La Verre, Mert *see* Merton, John
Law and Order (1932) 83, 93, 145, 156–158, 382
Law and Order (1940) 134, 158, 159, 160, 280, 321, 382
Law and Order (1953) 158, 160, 382
Law for Tombstone 39, 58, 67, 81, 93, 160–162, 166, 217, 245, 285, 296, 321, 364, 393
Law in the Saddle 391
Law of the Range 14, 162, 163, 170, 245, 296
Lawless Breed 164, 165, 178, 185

Lawless Clan 164
Lawrence, W.E. *see* Lawrence, William E.
Lawrence, William E. 25, 44, 89, 165, 252, 297, 331, 334, 394
Lawson, Priscilla 225
Lease, Rex 39, 61, 113, 186, 236, 279, 285, 295, 303, 337
Leddy, Arthur D. 75, 129
Lee, Duke 63, 100, 106
Lee, Eddie 113
Lee, Ruth 75
Lee, Sam 365, 366
Left Handed Law 161, 165–167
LeMoyne, Chas. (Charles) 25, 89, 144, 160, 165, 225, 252, 331
Len Nash and His Country Boys 193
Lenard, Grace 295
Lenhart, Bill "Bull Fiddle" *see* Lenhart, Billy
Lenhart, Billy 176, 177
Leonard, Sheldon 113, 116
LeSaint, Edward 83, 139, 196, 213, 341, 381
Leslie, Nan 365
Lester, William 391
"Let 'Er Buck, Powder River" 310
"Let's Go" 9, 12, 370
"Let's Love Again" 363
"Let's Put Two and Two Together" 322
Letters to Loretta 151
Levant, Mark 15, 129, 354
Levigard, Josef 389, 390, 391, 392
Levigard, Joseph *see* Levigard, Josef
Lewis, Forrest 285
Lewis, Gene 186, 257, 299, 314
Lewis, George J. 48, 236, 265, 299
Lewis, Joseph H. 9, 11, 34, 35, 40, 41, 64, 67, 154, 156, 295, 296, 301, 302
Lewis, Mitchell 335
Lewis, Ralph 285, 301, 381
Lewis, Sheldon 128

Lewis, Tex Jim *see* Lewis, Texas Jim
Lewis, Texas Jim 13, 15, 392
Life and Times of Judge Roy Bean 158
The Lightning Express 2, 3, 4, 5, 167, 168
The Lightning Rider 392
Linaker, Kay 4, 25–29, 186–188
Lindsay, Margaret 106, 107, 314
Litel, John 74, 186, 188, 281
"Little Brown Jug" 161, 363
"Little Joe " 85, 169
"Little Joe, the Wrangler" 13, 169, 176, 211
Little Joe, the Wrangler 86, 169, 170, 178, 182, 321
"Little Sweetheart of the Rio Grande" 209, 262, 295
Lively, William 11, 35, 38, 129, 132, 133, 180, 211, 212
Livingston, Bob 221, 238
Lloyd, Frank 150, 152, 314
Lloyd, George 48, 107, 196, 273, 275, 365
Lloyd, Rollo 386
Loaded Dice 394
Loder, John 88, 89
Loesser, Frank 86
Loft, Arthur 111, 262, 263
Loftus, Bernard 25, 31, 42, 44, 70, 73, 90, 161, 146, 165, 218, 252, 284, 297, 305, 322, 332, 334, 344, 375
Logue, Charles A. 324, 383
London, Jack 203, 205
London, Tom 30, 57, 64, 122, 126, 134, 152, 189, 213, 225, 269, 337, 377, 384
The Lone Avenger 97
The Lone Ranger (TV series) 294
The Lone Ranger 294

The Lone Rider 238
Lone Round-Up 394
The Lone Star Trail 41, 9, 171, 172, 360
"Lonely Love" 293
Long, Walter 377
"Long About Sundown" 358
The Long Long Trail 5, 173–175
"Looney Cowboy Band" 262
Lord, Marjorie 346
"Lorena" 113
The Loretta Young Show 151
Loring, Michael 386, 387
"Lorita" 216
Lorraine, Louise 167, 195, 196
Lorraine, Robert Locke 107
The Loser Wins 394
Lost City of the Jungle 118, 287
"Lost Doggies" 154
"Lou Lou Louisana" 293
Louisana 331
Love, Montague 335
Lowe, Sherman 9, 46, 133, 159, 160, 162, 169, 183, 185, 230, 231, 234, 260, 262, 266, 279, 370
Lubin, Arthur 254, 256, 386
Lucas, Jimmie 260
Lucas, Wilfred 234
Lucky Larkin 3, 5, 175
Lucky Ralston 159
Ludwig, Otto 54, 164, 346
Luke, Keye 203, 204
Lundigan, William 368
Luther, John 325
Lux Radio Theatre (radio series) 283
Lydecker, Howard and Theodore 288
Lyden, Pierce 15, 61, 236, 286, 303, 354, 379
Lynn, Emmett 265, 314, 316
Lyons, Cliff 113, 269, 386
Lyons, Colette 107, 108, 110

INDEX 427

MacArthur, Harold 17, 38, 46, 57, 75, 76, 88, 159, 162, 178, 211, 219, 230, 234, 236, 239, 244, 250, 262, 273, 286, 299, 350, 370, 385
MacDonald, Edmund 84, 346
MacDonald, Ian 241
MacDonald, J. Farrell 64, 67, 325, 327
MacDonald, Jeanette 109, 294
Mack, Cactus 102, 225, 226, 325
Mack, Tommy 71
MacKaye, Fred 25, 128, 276, 373
MacQuarrie, Murdock 119, 126, 142, 150, 176, 196, 227, 230, 232, 322, 334, 346, 372
MacRae, Henry 20, 59, 98, 104, 122, 124, 137, 144, 146, 167, 213, 219, 225, 246, 260, 269, 272, 276, 278, 279, 289, 325, 368, 381, 384
The Mad Stampede 153
Mahaney, Francis "Irish" 57, 162, 205, 234, 244, 309
Maidie and Ray 392
Mailes, Charles Hill 168
Mala 196
The Maltese Falcon 158
Malvern, Paul 71, 203
Man from Montana 24, 81, 86, 118, 134, 165, 170, 176–178, 280
Man from Montreal 178–180, 197
The Man Hunter 392
Man in the Saddle 243
Man in the Wilderness 158
Man of Daring 390
Manheim, Het 122
Mann, E.B. 44
Maran, Francisco 196
"March" 49
Marcus, James 140, 148, 327
Marcus, Lee 314, 316
Mario, Frank 279

Marion, Beth 102, 103, 297
The Mark of Zorro (1920) 221
The Mark of Zorro (1940) 221
Marked Men 136
Marker, Harry 134
Marlowe, Jerry 178
Marshal of Gunsmoke 7, 19, 112, 118, 170, 180–183, 185, 231, 321
Marshall, George 85–87, 377
Martin, Al 320
Martin, Charles M. 161, 165
Martin, Chris-Pin 152
Martin, Marian 150
Martin, Mickey 343
Martin, Nora Lou 39, 40, 295
Martin, Scoop 239
Marvin, Johnny 305
The Mask of Zorro 221
The Masked Rider 165, 182, 183–185, 251, 267, 339
Mason, James 173, 174, 225, 227
Mason, James (British actor) 227
Mason, Jim 63
Mason, LeRoy 216, 217, 295, 296, 301, 302, 333, 375, 376
Mason, Lesley 96, 175, 193, 224, 291, 292, 311, 313, 367
Mason, Leslie *see* Mason, Lesley
Mason, Louis 362
The Master Key 238
Mattison, John 330
Mattox, Martha 106, 137
May, Roderic "Dave" 57, 162, 205, 234, 244, 309
Maynard, Charles 46, 337
Maynard, Ken 5, 6, 8, 14, 33, 74, 91–93, 95, 96, 97, 128, 129, 140–142, 145, 147, 148–150, 158, 175, 193, 194, 224, 225, 245, 249, 270, 291, 292,

307–309, 311, 312, 313, 319, 327–329, 347–349, 367, 368, 373–375, 382, 389
Maynard, Kermit 9, 17, 38, 46, 54, 57, 85, 94, 111, 159, 176, 230, 234, 262, 279, 320, 370
McCall, William 356
McCarroll, Frank 133, 159, 234, 286
McCarthy, Earl 59
McCarty, Henry 291
McCauley, W.H. 79
McClung, Robert 381
McClure, Bud 91
McConnell, Gladys 224
McConville, Bernard 54
McCord, Ted 91, 93, 96, 128, 129, 140, 148, 150, 175, 193, 194, 224, 271, 292, 307, 311, 313, 322, 327, 329, 348, 367, 374, 375, 376
McCormick, Langdon 324
McCormick, Merrill 20, 94, 119, 122, 295
McCoy, Tim 6, 8, 21, 144, 146
McCrea, Joel 24, 243
McCulley, Johnston 219, 221
McCullough, Philo 85, 137, 138, 317, 318, 373
McDaniel, Etta 307
McDonald, Francis 15, 51, 189, 340, 381
McDonald, Grace 329, 330
McDonough, Joseph A. 198
McDowell, Bill 4
McDowell, Nelson 156, 278, 373
McEvoy, Renny 293
McGaugh, Wilbur 144, 146
McGlynn, Frank 381
McGlynn, Frank, Sr. 102, 218, 219, 269–271, 331
McGowan, J.P. 31, 168, 246, 249, 252, 276, 291, 292, 297, 368

McGowan, Robert *see* McGowan, J.P.
McGuire, Kathryn 173
McHugh, Matt 71, 225, 281
McKay, Wanda 236
McKee, Lafe 13, 70, 96, 102, 122, 128, 144, 146, 148, 225, 257, 262, 269, 276, 301, 309, 340, 343, 347, 377, 381
McKenna, Dudley 67
McKenzie, Bob 25, 61, 84, 91, 102, 128, 252, 257, 297, 301, 303, 305, 314, 322, 334, 350, 377, 383
McKenzie, Eva 119
McKenzie, Fay 119–121, 303–305, 377, 378
McKenzie, Ida Mae 305
McKenzie, Jack 346
McKenzie, Robert *see* McKenzie, Bob
McKinney, Florine 169
McKinney, Myra 13, 15
McKinney Sisters, the 393
McLaglen, Victor 88, 89
McLeod, Victor 17, 38, 39, 46, 159, 160, 183, 185, 279
McMichael, Joe 254
McMichael, Judd 254
McMichael, Ted 254
McMurphy, Charles 176, 314
"McNamarra's Band" 17
McPeters, Curtis *see* Mack, Cactus
McWade, Margaret 104
Meadows, Denny *see* Moore, Dennis
Medicine Bend 168
Meehan, Lew 31, 70, 146, 159, 322
Meek, Donald 198, 201
Meet Me at the Fair 347
Melford, George 198
Melody Stampede 389
Melton, Frank 362
Men of Destiny 186
Men of Texas 78, 186–188
Men of the Timberland 189, 190, 197
Men Without Skirts 324

Merch, Mary 70
Merkel, Una 84, 86
Merrick, Lynn *see* Merrick, Marilyn
Merrick, Marilyn 234, 235
Merrill, Bob 293
The Merry Macs 254, 256
Merton, John 246, 249
"Mexican Hat Dance" 183, 250
Meyer, Buddy *see* Myers, Buddy
Meyers, Buddy *see* Myers, Buddy
"Mi Caballero" 311
"Mi Morina" 38
Michigan Kid 115
Middleton, Charles 89, 97, 100, 334, 335
Midnight Raiders 207
The Mighty Treve 1, 2, 3, 190, 191
Milar, Adolph 331
Mile-a-Minute 264
Miles, Art 314
Miljan, John 335
Millard, Helen 106
Miller, Charles 75, 133, 279, 280
Miller, Ernest 393
Miller, Ivan 288
Miller, Sidney 288, 290
Miller, Virgil 301
Miller, Walter 41, 122, 124, 128, 146, 147, 246, 247, 249, 269, 270, 271, 276, 277, 307–309, 325, 381, 382
Mills, Felix 90
The Misfits 158
"Miss You" 330
Mississippi Rhythm 331
"Mr. Moon" 57, 72
Mitch Ayers and His Orchestra 191, 192
Mitchell, Beverlee 35
Mitchell, Bruce 381
Mitchell, Charles 331
Mitchell, Frank 13, 370
Mitchell, Guy 168
Mitchum, Bob 171, 172, 242
Mix, Art 13, 20, 137, 140,

156, 246, 276, 301, 327, 348
Mix, Tom 6, 8, 58, 71, 81–84, 86, 100, 102, 106, 107, 121, 139, 140, 149, 172, 201–203, 257–259, 278, 279, 340, 341–343
"A Modern Monte Cristo" (story) 88
Modernaires 393
Moehring, Kansas 111
Moffitt, Jack 241, 243
Mohr, Hal 85, 110, 281, 377
Money Madness 168
Monk, Thomas 64
Montague, Monte 6, 75, 137, 144, 218, 246, 249, 271, 276, 325, 360, 361, 381
Montague, Monty *see* Montague, Monte
Montana Justice 176
Montez, Maria 38, 39, 115
Montgomery, Jack 34, 64, 154, 301, 302
Monty, Harry 254
"Moonbeams" 332, 376
Moonlight and Cactus 191–193
"Moonlight Sonata" 22
Moore, Bill 196
Moore, Carlyle 216
Moore, Carlyle, Jr. 330, 372
Moore, Charles R. *see* Moore, Carlyle, Jr.
Moore, Constance 34, 154, 196
Moore, Dennis 7, 11–13, 48, 116, 118, 172, 182, 207, 209, 236–239, 246, 249, 251, 297, 299, 337, 363
Moore, Ida 264
Moore, Matt 325
Moore, Roy 139
Moore, Vin 246, 276
Moran, George 198
Moran, Peggy 350–352, 370, 371
"More and More" 49
More Cowboy Shooting Stars 3

INDEX   429

Morey, Elaine 162
Morgan, George 391
Morgan, Ralph 124, 188, 386
Morita, Miki 381
Morrell, George 119, 279
Morris, Chester 136
Morris, Frances 330
Morrison, Charles *see* Morrison, Chuck
Morrison, Chuck 9, 11, 17, 57, 58, 160, 262, 310, 384
Morrison, Pete 67, 317, 356, 357, 394
Morton, Charles 352
Morton, Danny 133, 134, 272, 285, 287
Morton, James C. 377
Moss, Bill 219
The Motion Picture Guide (book) 3
Moulin, Jess 9, 13, 22, 35, 46, 54, 57, 61, 75, 104, 116, 133, 159, 162, 169, 171, 176, 183, 189, 205, 209, 211, 213, 239, 244, 295, 338, 358, 379, 383
Moulin, Jesse *see* Moulin, Jess
Moulton, Buck 9, 11, 94, 234
Mountain Justice 5, 142, 152, 193, 194, 245, 380
Mountains Are My Kingdom 104
The Mounted Stranger 195, 196
Mower, Jack 91, 148
Muir, Gavin 281
Muir, Lewis 235
Mulhall, Jack 71, 288, 299
Mulhauser, James 139, 392
Mummert, Danny 293
Murdoch, Henry 222
Murphy, Audie 86, 105, 168
Murphy, Charles 213, 368
Murphy, George 72
Murphy, Horace 79, 98, 205, 213
Murray, Charles 392
Murray, Jack 183

Muse, Clarence 299
The Music Man 152
The Music Man (play) 152
Mutiny in the Arctic 2
Mutiny on the Blackhawk 1, 196–198, 337
My Baby Smiles at Me 347
"My Big Mountain Hill Billy Bill" 392
"My Cincinnati (Ohio)" 206
"My Country 'Tis of Thee" 151, 193, 379
My Foolish Heart 53
"My Gal She Works in a Laundry" 151, 295
My Little Chickadee 198–201, 285
"My Old Paint Pony an' Me" 30
My Pal the King 201–203
"My Pretty Quadroon" 91, 156
"My Proud Beauty" 35
"My Saddle Serenade" 181, 230
Myers, Buddy 25, 31, 42, 44, 70, 90, 146, 161, 165, 218, 252, 271, 284, 297, 305, 322, 332, 334, 344, 375
Myers, Henry 85
Myers, L. John *see* Myers, Buddy
The Mysterious Mr. M 238, 287
The Mysterious Stranger 61
Mystery Mountain 147, 309, 368

Nagel, Anne 88, 89, 198, 265, 266, 319, 384
Nancy Drew 294
Nancy Drew, Reporter 294
Nash, Len 193
National Barn Dance 19
Natteford, Jack 73, 139, 201, 279
Neal, Frances 208
Neal, Paul 299
"Nearer My God to Thee" 322

Neitz, Alan J. *see* James, Alan
"Nelly Bly" 207
Nelson, Billy 71, 293
Nelson, Bobbie *see* Nelson, Bobby
Nelson, Bobby 20, 148, 268, 343, 389, 390, 391, 392
Nelson, Jack 389, 390, 391, 392
Nelson, "Little Bobbie" *see* Nelson, Bobby
Nelson, Ozzie 329, 330
Neptune's Daughter 86
Nestell, Bill 96, 97
Neumann, Harry 34, 63, 79, 119, 124, 142, 153, 154, 156, 173, 181, 195, 216, 227, 236, 268, 317, 319, 356, 360, 372
Neumann, Kurt 201
Nevada Trail 76, 86, 112, 265
Neville, Jack 146, 147, 218
Neville, John T. *see* Neville, Jack
New Christy Minstrels 210
Newill, Jim 321
Newman, Harry 76, 79
Night Patrol 362
Nincent, Nat 93
"Ninety-Nine Days" 36
"No Letter Today" 363
Nolan, Herman 106
Norman, Leslie A. 222
Norris, Edward 303, 304
North, Jay Robert 3
North to the Klondike 203–205
Norton, Grace 76
Norton, Jack 314
Norvello, Jay 48, 124
The Notables 9, 159
Novak, Joe 322
Nye, Carroll 313

"O Tannebaum" 281
Oakman, Wheeler 268
The Oaksresa 150
Oberon, Merle 109
O'Brien, Dave "Tex" 172, 182, 321

430 INDEX

O'Brien, George 6, 168, 208
O'Brien, Mary 191
O'Brien, Pat (Warners star) 218
O'Brien, Pat J. 45, 47, 98, 218, 219, 269
Obzina, Martin 85, 191, 199, 377
O'Conner, Frank 143
O'Connor, Bob 183, 234
O'Connor, Frank 45
O'Day, Nell 9–11, 38, 39, 45, 47, 48, 72, 94, 159, 160, 162, 165, 176, 183, 185, 230, 231, 234, 235, 244, 246, 280, 309, 311, 319–321
O'Dea, Allan 241
O'Dell, Georgia 34, 126, 301
Odell, Rosemary 133, 164, 293, 379
O'Donnell, Joseph 273, 286
O'Driscoll, Martha 74, 365, 366
"Oh, Promise Me" (story) 122
Oh Promise Me (working title) 139
"Oh, Susanna" 57, 64, 79, 91, 161, 244
"Oh, You Kid" 365
Oklahoma Frontier 81, 104, 205–207, 382
Oklahoma Kid 206
Oklahoma Raiders 207–209, 233, 326
"Oklahoma's Oke with Me" 159
"Old Chisholm Trail" 91, 92, 209, 224, 226, 325
The Old Chisholm Trail 93, 112, 209, 210, 225, 227, 265, 296, 326
"An Old Fashioned Girl" 365
"Old Nevada Trail" 352
"The Old Oaken Bucket" 269
The Old Texas Trail 41, 86, 170, 178, 211–213, 339, 373

"Ole Buttermilk Sky" 51
O'Malley, Kathleen 281
O'Malley, Pat 76, 77, 162, 381
"On the Trail of Tomorrow" 9, 354, 370
One Night in the Tropics 351
One Touch of Venus 110
O'Neil, Ella see O'Neill, Ella
O'Neill, Ella 20, 59, 98, 122, 137, 138, 226, 246, 269, 276, 278, 289
O'Neill, George 336, 337
O'Neill, Thomas F. 83, 122, 246, 257, 341
Operation Neptune (TV series) 42
The Oregon Trail 213–215, 221, 276, 287
Orphan of the Wagon Trails 390
Ortego, Artie 22, 269, 276, 317, 358
Osborne, Bud 20, 45, 58, 73, 94, 100, 106, 122, 139, 144, 146, 162, 180, 234, 246, 249, 260, 271, 276, 278, 279, 314, 325, 337, 340, 341, 358, 381, 382, 384
Oscar, John 67, 167
O'Shea, Jack 107, 113, 239
O'Shea, Oscar 34, 293, 294, 299
Otterson, Jack 9, 13, 17, 38, 40, 46, 54, 57, 76, 79, 85, 88, 94, 104, 133, 151, 159, 162, 164, 169, 176, 178, 183, 186, 189, 196, 199, 203, 205, 209, 230, 234, 239, 244, 254, 262, 266, 279, 295, 299, 314, 316, 320, 330, 338, 346, 350, 370, 377, 379, 383, 386
"Out in Califor-ni-a" 216
"Out on the Lone Star Trail" 209
"Out on the Open Range" 207
"Out on the Santa Fe" 262

"Out on the Texas Plains" 165
Outlaw Express 39, 162, 216, 393
Outlawed Guns 218, 219
Outlawed Marshal 206
Overland Mail 7, 14, 219–222
Overland Stage Robbery 90
The Overlanders 1, 8, 222–224
Overman, Jack 113
Ovey, George 269
Owen, George 383
Owsley, Monroe 386
Ozzie Nelson Orchestra 330

Pabst, G.W. 90
Padden, Sarah 104, 241, 352
Pagan, Peter 222
Pagano, Ernest 113
Page, Bradley 17
Paige, Robert 48–50, 71–73, 109, 111, 112
Paiva, Nestor 241, 281, 346
Pal (horse) 144
Palance, Jack 136
Palmer, Stuart 386
Palmer, Tex 142, 143, 227, 230
Pals of the Golden West 39, 40, 295
"Pals of the Prairie" 162
Pandora's Box 90
Pangborn, Franklin 329
"Pappy Was a Gunman" 40
Parade of the West 3, 93, 149, 150, 224, 225, 227, 326
Pardner (horse) 20
Parker, Cecilia 128, 129, 140–142, 347, 349
Parker, Eddie 81, 160, 171, 172, 234, 288, 316, 386
Parker, Jefferson 386
Parker, Murray 299
Parker, Norton S. 34, 64, 154, 216, 217, 372
Parkinson, Cliff 241

INDEX   431

Parnell, Emory 150
Parrish, Helen 219, 221, 222
Pascal, Ernest 51
Pasternak, Joe 84
Patric, Gil 54
Patrick, Loren 383
Patterson, Hank 285, 379
Patterson, Walter 195
Patton, Bill 327
Patton, Virginia 51
Paul, Val 191, 386
Paulette, Ezra 35, 41, 160, 161, 331
Payne, Sally 150–152, 377
Payne, Stephen 25
Payson, Ed 260
The Pearl of Death 273
"Pedro, the Gay Vaquero" 250
Pelly, William Dudley 69
Pendleton, Gaylord 189, 190
Pendleton, Steve *see* Pendleton, Gaylord
"Percy" 108
Perez, Paul 98
Perils of the Royal Mounted 321
Perils of the Wilderness 238
Perkins, Albert R. 191
Perrin, Jack 359
Perry, Bob 356
Perry, Pascale 128
Perry, Walter 360
Pershing, Frank 219
Peters, House 325
Peters, House, Jr. 386, 387
Peters, Ralph 51, 254, 309, 363
Peterson, Dorothy 51
Peterson, Gus 126, 232
The Phantom 37, 60
The Phantom of the West 21
The Phantom Rider 93, 210, 225–227, 326, 335
The Phantom Stage 212, 227–230, 373
Phelps, Jimmy 126, 232
Phelps, Lee 41, 44, 165, 236, 284, 288, 305, 331

Phelps, Willie 65
Philharmonic Orchestra 223, 224
Phillips, Arthur 386
Phillips, Bernard 25
Phillips, Eddie 146, 305, 343
Phillips, Jean 346
Phillips, Jimmy 154
Phillips, Joe 76
Phillips, Michael J. 281
Phipps, Charles Z. 219
The Pied Piper of Basin Street 364
Piel, Ed *see* Piel, Edward, Sr.
Piel, Edward, Sr. 81, 148, 262, 301
Pierce, Jack P. 48, 51, 75, 109, 113, 133, 164, 279, 281, 379
Pierce, James 167
Pierson, Carl 30, 119, 126, 143, 228, 232
Pineman, Maurice 330
Pingree, Earl 343
Pirates of Monterey 39, 115
Pitts, Michael 1
Pitts, ZaSu 81
Pivar, Ben 178, 18, 196, 266, 346
Pivar, Maurice 83, 153, 156, 257, 341
Plues, George 9, 35, 76, 77, 159, 234, 295, 337
Plunkett, Walter 48
Plympton, George H. 20, 98, 122, 124, 137, 144, 213, 215, 226, 246, 260, 262, 269, 276, 289, 325, 384
Poff, Lon 67
Poland, Joseph Francis *see* Poland, Joseph
Poland, Joseph 289, 297
Polk, Rudolph 241
"Polly Wolly Doodle" 211
Polo, Eddie 309
Pomeroy, Allen 316
"Pony Express" 216
Pony Express Days 217
The Pony Express Kid 392
Pony Post 182, 230, 231

Porter, Don 379, 380
The Post of Honor 391
Potel, Victor 57, 241, 350, 370
Powell, Jack 383
Powers, John 241
Powers, Lucille 341
Powers, Richard 124
Prairie Justice 31, 143, 208, 232, 233
Prairie Outlaws 95
Prairie Pirates 11
Preston, Robert 150, 152
"Pretty Girl Milking Her Cow" 330
Previn, Charles 57, 71, 79, 85, 104, 151, 196, 199, 213, 254, 289, 314, 330, 362, 368, 377, 383, 392
Price, Alonzo 104, 260
Price, Hal 252
Price, Stanley 71, 111
"Pride of the Prairie" 143
Pritchard, Robert 17, 30, 34, 67, 85, 126, 154, 178, 203, 232, 266, 293, 301, 303, 314, 350, 368, 370, 377
"Private Cowboy Jones" 72
The Pronto Kid 394
Prosser, Hugh 39, 41, 61, 62
Public Cowboy No.1 265
Puig, Eva 379
Purcell, Dick 211, 212
Purcell, Gertrude 85
The Purple Monster Strikes 238
"Put It There" 320
Putnam, Nina Wilcox 106

Quartero, Nena 165
Queen of the Roundup 394
Quigley, Robert 128
Quillan, Eddie 191, 363
Quimby, Margaret 356, 357
Quirt, Charley 35

Raboch, Al 73, 271, 272
A Race for a Ranch 394
Rafferty, Chips 222, 223

Ragan, Michael *see* Bane, Holly
"Ragtime Cowboy Joe" 234
Ragtime Cowboy Joe 80, 165, 234–236, 280
The Raiders 27
Raiders of Ghost City 19, 236–239, 287
Raiders of San Joaquin 239–241
Raines, Ella 109
Rainey, Buck 1, 3
Raison, Milton 370
Ralph, Jessie 150
Rambeau, Marjorie 281
The Ramblin' Kid 173
The Ramblin' Kid (novel) 173
Ramrod 2, 241–243
Ramrod (novel) 241, 242
Ramsay, Allan 343
Ramsey, Quen 376
Randall, Jack 273
Randall, Rebel 299
Randle, Karen 113, 281
Randolph, Isabelle 254
The Range Busters 238, 321
Ranger (horse) 234, 235
"Rangers' Song" 64
Rankin, Arthur 340
Ransome, Frank 222
Rawhide Rangers 58, 67, 72, 81, 93, 132, 161, 194, 244–246, 356
Rawlins, John 189, 190, 219, 222, 362
Rawlinson, Herbert 9, 180, 207, 319
Ray, Albert 79, 80, 81, 205, 392
Ray, Allene 144, 146
Ray, Joey 225
Ray Whitley's Bar-6 Cowboys 22, 35, 36, 37, 210, 211, 250, 264, 352, 358
Raye, Buddy 330
"Reach for the Sky" 303
Read, Barbara 190
Ready to Ride 217
Reagan, Ronald 158, 160, 382
Rebel (horse) 58

The Red Badge of Courage 158
The Red Coat's Code 390
The Red Head from Sun Dog 247, 249
The Red Raiders 145
Red Raymond's Girl 394
The Red Rider (1925) 390
The Red Rider (1929) 389
The Red Rider (1934) 6, 246–249, 272, 312, 390
Red River Boys 7, 11–13, 31, 37, 116, 117, 180, 181, 185, 207, 208, 326
"Red River Valley" 161, 284, 295, 320
The Redcoat's Romance 391
Redman, Frank 167
Redmond, Harry, Jr. 241, 243
Reed, Marshall 285
Reed, Tom 134, 153, 156, 158, 314, 324
Reeves, Bob 167
Reeves, Jim 210
Regas, George 20, 21, 165, 288
Reicher, Frank 368, 369
Reinhart, Dick 45, 230
Renaldo, Duncan 61, 192
Renegade Ranger 208
Renegade Wranglers 302
Renegades of the Rio Grande 185, 250–252, 296
Renfrew of the Mounted 168
Repp, Ed Earl 244, 269, 358
Repp, Edward Earl *see* Repp, Ed Earl
"Restin' Beside the Trail" 64
Revier, Dorothy 70, 71, 375, 376
Rex (horse) 224, 325–327, 380
Rex Jr. (horse) 325, 380
Reynolds, Craig *see* Enfield, Hugh
Reynolds, Marjorie 30, 31, 120, 126, 127, 227, 372, 373

Rhine, Larry 57, 346
Rhythm of the Saddle 371
Riano, Rennie 48
Rice, Florence 152
Rice, Frank 31, 33, 91, 93, 96, 146, 147, 148, 193, 224, 246, 311, 322, 347, 367, 373
Rice, Jack 189, 365
Richards, Addison 17, 178, 186, 198, 236, 272, 275, 335
Richards, Frank A. 133, 164, 279
Richardson, Jack 128, 360
Richmond, Warner 213
Rickaby, Ruth 260
Ricketts, Tom 122, 124
Ricks, Archie 173
"Ride Along" 260
Ride 'Em Cowboy (1936) 252, 253, 256
Ride 'Em Cowboy (1942) 14, 253, 254–256, 385
"Ride 'Em Cowboy" 254
"Ride 'Im Cowboy" 159
"Ride On" 57
Ride to Hangman's Tree 110
"Ride, Ride, Ride" 231
The Rider of Death Valley 257–259
The Riders of Death Valley (1932) 257, 259
Riders of Death Valley (1941) 259, 260–262, 333
Riders of Oklahoma 207
Riders of Pasco Basin 41, 58, 262, 263
Riders of San Joaquin 239
Riders of Terror Trail 340
Riders of the Desert 257, 259
Riders of the Purple Sage 363, 364
Riders of the Santa Fe 4, 76, 112, 210, 264, 265, 296, 353
Ridgely, John 104, 105, 372, 373
Ridges, Stanley 51
Ridgeway, Fritzi 134
"Ridin' Down That Utah Trail" 228, 372

INDEX 433

"Ridin' Down to Santa Fe" 12
"Ridin' Home" 79, 266, 293, 338
Ridin' Kid from Powder Ridge 196
"Ridin' Kid from Powder Ridge" (story) 195
"Ridin' On" 330
"Ridin' the Owl Hoot Trail" 34
"Ridin' the Range Again" 154
"Ridin' the Trail Again" 34, 372
"Riding Down That Old Texas Trail" 211
Riding Shotgun 243
Riedel, Richard H. 51, 113, 186
"Ring Around the Moon" 126
Ritter, Tex 7, 8, 11–13, 15, 19, 24, 36, 41, 54–56, 76–79, 80, 111, 112, 118, 169, 170, 171, 172, 180–183, 188, 207, 209, 210, 212, 233, 238, 239, 240, 283, 326, 337–339, 393
Rivero, Julian 190, 216
Rix, Jack 222
Rixey, John W. 164, 279
Roach, Joe 137
Road Agent (1941) 81, 134, 185, 238, 265–267, 294, 331, 339, 352
Road Agent (1952) 267
The Road Back 362
Road to Reno 4
Roaring Ranch 268, 269
The Roaring West 269–271, 368
Roberts, Beatrice 285
Roberts, Edith 367
Roberts, Jason 288
Roberts, Lee 285
Roberts, Stanley 365, 366
Robertson, Willard 189, 198, 257, 341, 343
Robins, Sam 13, 183, 185
Robinson, Dewey 88, 156
Robinson, E.R. *see* Robinson, Edward R.

Robinson, Edward R. 48, 54, 76, 314, 316, 363
Robinson, Frances 79, 81, 104, 105, 262, 263
Robinson, George 113, 116, 134, 137, 219, 286, 299, 336
Roc, Patricia 51, 52
Roche, Betty 198
Rochelle, Claire 89
Rock-a-Bye Cowboy 389
Rockefeller, "Bobo" *see* Sears, Barbara
"Rockin' and Reelin'" 254
Rockwell, Jack 22, 30, 45, 75, 91, 111, 124, 126, 127, 128, 140, 148, 162, 218, 219, 230, 232, 236, 237, 260, 265, 271, 284, 285, 301, 305, 327, 347, 358, 372, 373, 375
Rocky Rhodes 271, 272
Roemheld, Heinz 325
Rogell, Albert 257, 259
Rogell, Sid 193, 308, 311
Rogers, Jean 325, 327, 383, 384
Rogers, Roy 7, 65, 152, 345, 392
"Rogue River Valley" 51
Rooney, Mickey 201–203, 349
Roosevelt, Buddy 106, 269
Roosevelt, Franklin D. 290
Root, Wells 324
"Rootin' Tootin' Cowboy" 54
Roper, Jack 98, 100, 198, 370
Roper, John *see* Roper, Jack
The Ropin' Venus 394
Roquemore, Henry 70, 171, 239
Rose, Jackson 156
Rose, Sherman A. 241
"Rose of the Hills" 55
"Rose of the Prairie" 232
Rosemond, Clinton 17
Rosen, Milton 47, 61, 133, 164, 279, 393
Ross, Stanley Ralph 3
Rosson, Arthur 63, 100,

139, 140, 173, 195, 196, 356, 357
Roth, Gene 16, 24, 236
Rothafel, Robert C. 269
"Rovin' Gambler" 209, 281
Rowan, Dan 260
Rowles, Polly 368, 369
Roy, Rosalie 59
Royal, Charles 122, 144
The Royal Mounted Rides Again 272–275
Royle, William 97, 178, 179, 368, 381
Rubin, Stanley 88, 89
Rudy Sooter and the Californians 262
Ruggles, Charlie 241
Ruhl, Bill *see* Ruhl, William
Ruhl, William 88, 124, 288, 291
Rush, Dick 70, 122, 227, 269
Russell, Albert 64
Russell, J. Gordon 167
Rustler's Hideout 279
Rustlers of Red Dog 276, 277
Rustler's Roundup 177, 235, 279, 280, 296, 352
The Rustlers' Roundup 278, 279
Rutherford, Ann 17–19
Rutherford, Jack 97, 265
Ryan, Frank 48, 50
Ryan, Pat 110
Ryan, Tim 330

Sackin, Louis 57, 79, 98, 205, 213, 219, 226, 260, 262, 289, 370, 381, 385
Sacks, Howard and Judith 194
A Sagebrush Vagabond 394
Saigon 242
St. Claire, Arthur 38, 39, 133, 266, 320
Saint Johnson 158
Saint Johnson (novel) 156, 159, 381
St. Polis, John 148, 340
Sale, Fred, Jr. 373, 374

Salome, Where She Danced 8, 210, 281–283, 294
"Sal's Got a Wooden Leg" 224
"Salt Water Cowboy" 363
Salter, H.J. 9, 13, 17, 38, 40, 46, 48, 54, 76, 88, 94, 111, 113, 159, 162, 169, 171, 176, 178, 181, 183, 189, 203, 205, 209, 230, 239, 244, 262, 266, 295, 299, 309, 314, 320, 338, 346, 350, 363, 365, 370
Salter, Hans J. *see* Salter, H.J.
"San Antonio Rose" 393
Sande, Walter 74, 303, 346
Sandflow 161, 284, 285, 296, 321
Sanford, Joseph 13, 309, 311, 330
Sanford, Ralph 189
Santley, Frank 269
Santschi, Tom 316, 367
Sanucci, Frank 30, 34, 64, 119, 126, 143, 154, 216, 228, 232, 301, 372
Sarecky, Barney A. 362
Sareky, Lou 203
Saturday Evening Post 51
Sawtell, Paul 12, 22, 116, 207, 211, 250, 264, 352, 358, 379
Sawyer, Joe 71, 150, 178, 180, 236, 237, 239, 287, 303
Sawyer, Joseph *see* Sawyer, Joe
Saxton, Charles 63
Sayles, Francis 341
Saylor, Syd 107, 303, 375
The Scarlet Horseman 285–288, 352
Schaefer, Armand 340
Schayer, Richard 83, 84, 152, 156, 201, 341
Schoen, Vic 191
Schoengarth, Russell 169, 239, 278, 281, 340, 352, 354
"Schubert's Serenade" 22
Schulberg, B.P. 337
Schumann-Heink, F. 201

Schuster, Harold 88, 89
Scola, Kathryn 150
Scott, Fred 177, 392
Scott, Randolph 8, 242, 243, 314–317, 376, 378
Scott, Wallace 51, 54
Scout (horse) 98, 288
Scouts to the Rescue 2, 288–291, 326
Searl, Jack 198
Sears, Allan 44, 89, 102, 334
Sears, Barbara 15, 16, 61
Seay, James 254, 346
Secret Agent X-9 (1937) 368, 384
Secret Service in Darkest Africa 36
Sedgwick, Josie 394
"Seeing Nellie Home" 193
Seeing Red 394
Seidel, Tom 191
Selander, Lesley 26, 27, 29, 44, 45, 89, 91, 165, 167, 252, 253, 284, 285, 305, 306
Selander, Leslie *see* Selander, Lesley
Selbie, Evelyn 88, 126, 384
Selby, Evelyn *see* Selbie, Evelyn
Seldeen, Murray 325
Sells, Paul 11, 116, 180, 207
Seltzer, Charles Alden 297
Selwynne, Clarissa 201
Semels, Harry 271, 322, 323
"Send Me a Man, Amen" 191
Senor Americano 291, 292
Senorita from the West 8, 267, 283, 293, 294, 331
Sepulvada, Carl 9, 169, 239
Service, Robert W. 59, 314, 316
Sessons, Almira 48
"Set 'Em Up Joe" 113
Shady Lady 24, 110
Shaff, Monroe 333
Shane, Maxwell 71
Shannon, Fay 119, 121
Shannon, Frank 244, 245

Shannon, Harry 51
Shannon, Jack 176, 309, 370
Sharpe, Davy 262
Shaw, Al 365, 366
Shaw, Frank 48
Shaw, Janet 11, 285
Shaw and Lee 365
Shayer, Richard 257
She Done Him Wrong 142
Shea, Gloria 91–93, 158, 307, 309
Shelly, George 381
Shelton, Marla 225, 227
Sheriff of Gunsmoke 180
Sherman, Evelyn 311
Sherman, Harry 27, 45, 241–243
Sherwood, George 209, 219, 281
"She's Only a Bird in a Gilded Cage" 140
Shilling, Marion 246–249, 322, 323
Shipman, Helen 225, 227
The Shoot-Em-Ups 1, 3, 389
The Shoot-Em-Ups Ride Again 1
The Shooting of Dan McGrew 316
Shores, Cal 325
Short, Dorothy 230
Short, Luke 241, 242
Short, Robin 236
Shotgun Messenger 320
Show Boat (1936) 6, 336
Shumate, Harold 17, 186, 254, 350, 377
Shumway, Lee 25, 45, 146, 165, 218, 225, 271
Shumway, Walter 390
Sickel, Dale Van 380
Sickner, William 11, 13, 17, 25, 29, 31, 35, 38, 54, 57, 73, 111, 116, 124, 165, 169, 171, 207, 209, 211, 213, 218, 219, 220, 236, 239, 260, 262, 269, 276, 289, 291, 305, 309, 338, 358, 360, 385, 392
Sidney, George 392
Sierra 105
"Silent Night" 108, 135

Sills, Milton 316
Silver (horse) 25, 31, 41, 44, 70, 73, 74, 89, 102, 122–124, 161, 218, 225, 246, 252, 260, 269, 271, 284, 297, 322, 331, 345, 368
Silver Bullet (1934) 296
Silver Bullet (1942) 161, 210, 265, 280, 285, 295–297, 321
Silver Butte 185
Silver Jr. (horse) 165, 246, 249, 305
"Silver Saddle" 51
Silver Spurs 297–299, 345
Silverspurs 297
Simmons, Beverly 113, 116
Simmons, Michael L. 196
Simpson, Mickey 39, 314
Simpson, Russell 79, 81, 156, 314, 381, 382
Sin Town 299–301
Sinclair, Bertha "Muzzy" see Bower, B.M.
Sinclair, Diane 278, 279
"Sing" 192
Sing Me a Song of Texas 37
Sing, Neighbor, Sing 305
The Singing Outlaw 301, 302
Singing Sheriff (1939) 143
The Singing Sheriff (1944) 143, 303–305, 392
"Singing Swinging Cowboy" 42
Siodmak, Curt 107
"Sip Nip Song" 363
6-Bar Cowboys 7, 37, 208
"Six Gun Dan" 162
Six Gun Justice 391
Skelton, Tiny 269, 270
Skinner, Frank 48, 51, 75, 85, 113, 151, 199, 254, 377, 379
Skirball, Jack H. 150
Sky Bandits 168
Sky King 16
Sky Raiders 125
Slade, Michael 98
Slattery's Hurricane 242
Slavan, Brad see Slavan, Buster

Slavan, Buster 198, 200
"Sleep, Baby, Sleep" 317
Slezak, Walter 281, 283
The Sliphorn King of Polaroo 364
Slosser, Ralph 273
"Slumbertime Out on the Prairie" 352
Slye, Leonard 65; see also Rogers, Roy
Smart, J. Scott see Smart, Jack
Smart, Jack 383, 384
Smart, Ralph 222
Smash-Up: The Story of a Woman 53
Smith, Al 140
Smith, Cliff 381, 382
Smith, Frank 25, 44, 305
Smith, Jack C. 39, 213–215, 319
Smith, L.R. see Smith, Leigh
Smith, Lee R. see Smith, Leigh
Smith, Lee see Smith, Leigh
Smith, Leigh 11, 35, 51, 111, 116, 164, 180, 191, 207, 264, 279, 293, 303, 352, 358, 379
Smith, Paul Gerard 191
Smith, V.O. 273
Smoke Tree Range 305, 306
Smokey (horse) 260, 372, 384
Smoking Guns 6, 307–309
Snell, Earle 322, 324, 334, 335
Snowdens, the 194
Snyder, Ray 22, 113, 129, 171, 209, 264, 271
Soderling, Walter 234, 236, 377
"Someone Else Is Taking My Place" 330
Son of Courage 391
Son of Roaring Dan 16, 62, 309–311
Song of the Caballero 249, 311, 312
"Song of the Prairie" 40, 262

"Song of the Sage" 77, 381
"Song of the Trail" 64, 126
"Song of the Trail Drive" 234
Sons of the Saddle 3, 313
Sooter, Rudy 89, 90, 262
Sosso, Pietro 61
Sothern, Hugh 88
"Sourwood Mountain" 193, 244
Spade Cooley's Orchestra 283, 293, 294, 303, 392, 393
Spearman, Frank H. 167, 168
Sper, Norman 311
Spiers, Arch 222
The Spoilers (1914) 316
The Spoilers (1923) 316
The Spoilers (1930) 316
The Spoilers (1942) 7, 76, 287, 314–317, 368
The Spoilers (1956) 316
The Spoilers (novel) 314, 316
Spriggins, Deuce 303, 392
Spring Parade 351
Spurs 317–319
Stack, Robert 17–19, 132, 186–188, 300
Stagecoach Buckaroo 161, 170, 182, 285, 296, 319–321, 364
Stagecoach Line 211
Stallings, Lawrence 281
Standish, Schuyler 30
Stanley, Ed see Stanley, Edwin
Stanley, Edwin 88, 196, 288, 291
Stanley, Forrest 257, 259
Stanley, Louise 213–215
Stark, Irving 271
Starlight (horse) 381
"Starlight on the Prairie" 30, 207, 232
Starling, Pat 303, 393
Starr, Irving 31, 73, 322, 375
Starrett, Charles 24, 177, 331, 341
"Stars of the Midnight Range" 12

State Fair (1945) 50
Staub, Ralph 57, 58
"Stay Away from My Heart" 12
Steele, Bob 95, 259, 321, 389
Steele, Mrs. 268
Steele, Tom 98, 172, 219, 314, 362, 368
Steele, William 84, 122
Steir, Kenneth 3
Stephens, Harvey 376
Stevens, Charles 15, 79, 97, 98, 104, 213, 214, 219, 221, 288, 381, 382, 384
Stevens, Kenny 330
Stevens, Onslow 51, 137, 138
Stevenson, Houseley 241
Stewart, James 7, 84, 86, 87
Stewart, Peggy 208
Stewart, Roy 278
Stockdale, Carl 64, 73, 218, 146, 160, 271, 301, 343
Stoloff, Ben 83
Stone of Silver Creek 322–324
Stone, Lewis 136
Stone, Milburn 7, 74, 124–126, 272, 274, 275, 363, 383
The Storm (1922) 325
The Storm (1930) 3, 324, 325
Storm, Jerome 67
The Storm King 394
Stormy 93, 208, 210, 225, 227, 261, 291, 325–327, 380
"Story of a Bad Man of the West" 303
Strang, Harry 171, 211
Strange, Glenn 9, 11, 15, 17, 30, 34, 64, 104, 119, 120, 126, 142, 144, 154–156, 161, 169, 227, 250, 252, 260, 301, 319, 325, 334, 352
Strange, Robert 9
Stranger Wore a Gun 243
Strawberry Roan (1933) 327–329

The Strawberry Roan (1944) 329
The Strawberry Roan (1948) 329
Strawberry Roan (poem) 327
"Strawberry Roan" 327
Strawn, Arthur 266
Strayer, Frank 293
"Streets of Laredo" 35
Strictly in the Groove 1, 81, 142, 194, 267, 294, 329–331
Strong, Gene 241
Stutenroth, Gene 15, 16, 22, 24, 51
Sudden Bill Dorn 43, 331–333
Sullivan, Billy 394
Sullivan, C. Gardner 134
Summerville, Slim 152
"Sundown Trail" 181
Sundown Trail 11
Sunrise, Lee 254
Sunset of Power 334, 335
Sunset Trail 319
Sutter's Gold 1, 6, 197, 198, 291, 335–337
Sutton, Grady 322
Sutton, Kay 178, 180
"Swanee" 365
Swartz, Kenneth 133
"Sweet Genevieve" 77
"Sweethearts or Strangers" 330
Swickard, Josef 44, 284, 311
"Swing Your Sweetheart" 49
Swingin' in the Barn 305, 389, 392
Sylos, Ralph 15

Taggart, Ben 12, 219
Take Me Back to Oklahoma 393
Talbot, Lyle 129, 131, 132, 352–354, 368–370
Taliaferro, Hal 30, 31, 116, 126, 127, 162, 169, 225, 232, 233, 241, 286
Tambert, Elmer 104
Tamiroff, Akim 48, 50
Tannen, William 189

Tarshis, Harold 61, 356, 357
Tarzan (horse) 9, 93, 96, 128, 140, 148, 175, 194, 224, 270, 291, 307, 309, 311, 313, 327, 329, 347, 367, 368, 373
Tasker, Homer 387
Taylor, Ferris 57, 88, 104
Taylor, Forrest 22, 30, 35, 57, 64, 119–121, 126, 142, 154, 213, 216, 219, 227, 232, 314, 352, 372, 377
Taylor, Grant 340
Taylor, Kent 74, 76
Taylor, Libby 375
Taylor, Ray 13, 15, 17, 20, 21, 35, 38, 39, 41, 43, 46, 54, 56, 59, 70, 71, 75, 76, 94, 96, 98, 100, 122, 124, 137, 138, 146, 147, 159, 160, 162, 163, 171, 172, 176, 178, 218, 219, 226, 227, 230, 231, 234, 236, 244, 245, 260, 262, 269, 270, 273, 275, 286, 288, 289, 291, 297, 299, 320, 321, 331, 334, 335, 343, 344, 370, 384, 385
Taylor, Robert 242
Teagarden, Jack 363, 364
Teal, Ray 51, 219, 230, 236, 241
Tenbrook, Harry 137, 138, 205, 219, 234, 276, 319, 384
Tenting Tonight 337
"Tenting Tonight on the Old Camp Ground" 338
Tenting Tonight on the Old Camp Ground 41, 81, 185, 212, 267, 294, 331, 337–339, 386
Terhune, Albert Payson 191
Terhune, Max "Alibi" 321
Terrell, Ken 384
Terror Trail (1921) 341
Terror Trail (1933) 340, 341
Terror Trail (1946) 341
Terry, Don 197, 219, 222
Terry, Robert 284

Terry, Sheila 271, 272
The Tex Ritter Story
    (book) 182
"Texas" 35
The Texas Bad Man
    341–343
"Texas Playboy Rag" 393
Texas Playboys 393
"Texas Polka" 363
"Texas Prairie" 161
The Texas Rangers 57,
    104, 119, 162, 205, 206,
    234, 244, 309, 310
The Texas Rangers (series)
    7, 36, 172, 182, 287, 321
Texas Road Agent 265
Texas Terror 127
Thalasso, Arthur 142
"That's the Way I Am"
    279
"Then We Go Ridin'" 244
"There's a Ring Around
    the Moon" 301
"These Hazy, Lazy Old
    Hills" 293
This Gun for Hire 242
This Is Darin 240
Thomas, Bernard 133
Thomas, Charles 260
Thomas, William L. 59,
    71
Thompson, Allen 25, 29,
    31, 42, 44, 70, 90, 91,
    102, 146, 147, 161, 162,
    165, 218, 219, 226, 252,
    284, 285, 297, 305, 332,
    334, 344
Thompson, Allen Q. *see*
    Thompson, Allen
Thompson, Hank 210
Thompson, Robert 239
Thorne, William L. 269
Thorpe, James *see*
    Thorpe, Jim
Thorpe, Jim 20, 22, 122,
    146, 201, 225, 246, 247,
    249, 276, 386
"Those Happy Old Days"
    133, 159
3 Godfathers 136
Three Godfathers (1916)
    136
Three Godfathers (1936)
    136

"Three Godfathers"
    (story) 135
Three Men from Texas 217
The Three Mesquiteers (series) 90, 321
Thrill Hunter 376
Thrilling Ranch Stories
    (magazine) 73, 218
The Throwback 343–345
Thunder Cloud *see* Chief
    Thundercloud
Thunder Over the Plains
    243
The Tie That Binds 98,
    100, 137, 138
Tierney, Louis 393
Tilton, Martha 329, 330
Timber 1, 125, 190, 197,
    212, 346, 347
To Be Continued 4
Todd, Alvin 11, 20, 98,
    122, 124, 137, 144, 180,
    213, 219, 226, 236, 260,
    269, 273, 276, 286, 289,
    381, 385
Todd, Ann 84
Todd, Edward 137, 144,
    226, 246, 269, 276
Todd, Harry 67, 96, 122,
    175, 313
Tolhurst, Stan 222
Tombes, Andrew 48, 113,
    116, 303
Tombragel, Maurice 124,
    189, 266
Tone, Franchot 350–352
Toney, Jim 213
Tony (horse) 82, 83, 106,
    201, 202, 257, 259, 278,
    341, 342
Tony, Jr. (horse) 100, 139
Toomey, Regis 236
Tourneur, Jacques 51, 53,
    54
Tracy, Lee 197, 335, 337
The Trail Blazers 14
"Trail Dreamin'" 40, 171,
    358
Trail Drive 347–349
"Trail Dust" 211
"Trail Herd" 348
"Trail Herd Song" 313
Trail of Terror 36
Trail of the Pack 390

Trail of the Vigilantes 7,
    238, 280, 350–352
Trail to Gunsight 352–354
"Trail to Mexico" 207
Trail to Vengeance 11, 165,
    245, 354–356, 371
Trailing Trouble 356, 357
Trampe, Ray 381, 382
Travis, Merle 211, 212
*The Treasure of the Sierra
    Madre* 158
Trent, Jean 113, 281, 299,
    303
Trent, Philip *see* Jones,
    Clifford
Treve (novel) 191
Trigger Trail (1921) 359
Trigger Trail (1944) 41,
    172, 353, 358–360
Trigger Tricks 360, 361
Trouble at Midnight 362,
    363
Trowbridge, Charles 196,
    350
Truesdale, Howard 173
Truex, Ernest 281
Tuffy (dog) 190
Tumbleweed Tempos 393
Tummel, William 75, 113
"Turkey in the Straw" 91,
    381
Turner, George 211
Turner, Lana 109
Turner, Martin 119, 120,
    307
Tuttle, W.C. 247, 249, 271
Tuttle, Wesley 11–13,
    116–118, 180, 207
"Twilight on the Prairie"
    358
Twilight on the Prairie 15,
    118, 161, 321, 363, 364
Twins of the West 31
Two-Gun Troubadour 177
Tyler, Dick 73
Tyler, Tom 8, 20, 21, 35,
    37, 38, 59, 60, 296, 321

"Under Western Skies"
    365
Under Western Skies 365,
    366
The Unforgiven 158
Universal Pictures 1, 3, 389

The Universal Story 3
Urecal, Minerva 84, 191
Usher, Guy 190, 299, 346

Valentine, Joseph 199, 350
Valle, Gil 254, 299
Valli, Virginia 325
Vallon, Michael 39, 116, 171, 172, 180, 209, 239, 295, 358
Vandergrift, Monty 368
Van Dycke, Tom 383
Van Enger, Charles 9, 40, 75, 94, 107, 109, 162, 176, 183, 203, 244, 273, 295, 303, 365
The Vanishing Westerner 164
Van Slyke, Arthur 25, 30, 34, 160, 216, 284
Vaughan, Clifford 336
Vaughan, Dorothy 88
Vaughn, Kerry 113, 281
Velasco, Dr. Mavel 4
Velez, Lupe 324
Vengeance 354
Verdera, Clare 150
Vernon and Draper 392
Victor/Victoria 152
Vigilante War 263
The Vigilantes Return 115
Vincent, Allen 335
Vincent, June 48
Vincent, Nat 328, 329
The Virginian (1929) 97
Visoroff, Michael 148
Vogan, Emmett 17, 150, 236, 288, 293
Von Hemert, Ted 108, 211
Vonn, Viola 165, 234, 339, 384, 385
"Vote for Cal Dixon" 279
"Vote for Emily Morgan" 295

Waggenheim, Charles 111, 236, 281, 299
Waggner, George 17, 30, 31, 107, 110, 119–121, 126, 127, 143, 144, 186, 216, 227, 230, 232, 233, 299, 372, 373
Wagner, Max 35, 350

Wagner, William 278
The Wagon Master 3, 270, 367, 368
"Wah-Hoo!" 191
Waif of the Wilderness 390
"Wake Up Jacob" 254
Wakely, Jimmy 24, 45, 46, 54, 55, 76, 95, 112, 142, 169, 171, 182, 200, 209, 230, 238, 239, 251, 329, 330, 337–339, 382
Wales, Wally 11, 14, 31, 148, 225, 227, 233, 276, 307, 348
Walker, Baby 268, 269
Walker, Bob *see* Walker, Robert
Walker, Francis 160
Walker, Gilmore 63, 67, 173, 195, 268, 317, 356, 360
Walker, Lucille 162, 392
Walker, Robert 91, 96, 165, 271, 327, 343
Wallace, Morgan 198, 335
Waller, Eddy 97, 111, 178, 196, 236, 239, 265, 279, 299, 365
Walters, Luana 252, 253, 265
Wanger, Walter 51, 281, 282
Wanzer, Arthur 156
Ward, Edward 108, 281
Ward, Luci 236
Warde, Anthony 57, 58, 124, 125, 205, 346
Warden, Jack 136
Ware, Edward 186
Warrington, Ralph 61, 354
Warwick, Robert 335
Washburn, Bryant 299, 343
Washington, Blue 148, 175, 193, 224
Watson, W.W. 213, 215
Watt, Harry 222, 224
Waxman, Franz 336
"Way Back in Oklahoma" 230
The Way of the West 394
Wayne, Billy 299
Wayne, John 2, 8, 66, 71,

73, 127, 136, 215, 287, 314, 316, 317, 378
"We Are the Rangers" 161
"We Want Hornsby" 13
"We Want Rawlins" 55
"Wearing of the Green" 91
Weaver, Doodles 303
Weaver, Marjorie 124–126
Webb, Ira S. 40, 71, 273, 295
Webb, R.S. 186
Weed, Leland "Tumble" *see* Baker, Bob
Weiss, Fred 168
Welch, Niles 89, 102, 146, 322–324
"Welcome Home" 94, 171
"Welcome to the Empty Saddle Ranch" 90
"Well, Need I Say More" 72
Wells, Jacqueline 59, 60, 138
Wells, Ted 370, 391
Welsch, Howard 75
"We're Brandin' Today" 228
"We're Rollin' Today" 228
West, Dr. James P. 290
West, Joseph 30, 31, 119, 121, 126, 127, 143, 228, 230, 232, 233
West, Mae 142, 198–201
West, Pat 377
West, Vera 9, 17, 71, 75, 85, 88, 94, 108, 111, 151, 176, 178, 183, 186, 196, 199, 203, 239, 254, 266, 279, 281, 299, 303, 314, 330, 337, 350, 352, 358, 363, 365, 377, 386
West, Wilton 73
West Bound Limited 2, 76, 317, 368–370
West of Carson City 11, 13, 55, 356, 370, 371
West of Laramie 177
Westerfield, James 346
The Western 1, 3
Western Caravans 177
Western Courage 160, 352
Western Cowgirl 389
Western Film Annual 231

INDEX   439

"Western Medley" 393
Western Movies 1, 3
"The Western Trail" 176, 279
Western Trails 212, 372, 373
The Westerner 174
Weston, Doris 57, 58
Wetzel, Edwin 104, 154, 216, 372
"What a Change in the Weather" 293
"What Is Love" 113
"Wheels of Destiny" 374
The Wheels of Destiny 145, 373–375
Whelan, Arleen 241
"When a Cowboy Sings" 303
"When a Cowboy's Day Is Done" 372
When a Man Sees Red 39, 162, 217, 333, 375, 376, 393
When the Daltons Rode 7, 376–378
"When the Roundup Days Are Over" 301
"Where the Prairie Meets the Sky" 13, 117, 363
Where's Charley (play) 86
The Whip Hand 394
"Whispering" 303
Whispering Smith (1916) 168
Whispering Smith (1948) 168
Whispering Smith (novel) 168
Whispering Smith (TV series) 168
Whispering Smith Speaks 168
"Whispering Smith Speaks" (story) 167
Whispering Smith vs. Scotland Yard 168
"Whistle Your Blues to a Bluebird" 71
The Whistler 283
Whitaker, Charles *see* Whitaker, Slim
Whitaker, Slim 30, 31, 46, 91, 96, 97, 98, 100, 137, 140, 148, 161, 162, 169, 180, 207, 225, 232, 234, 260, 262, 269, 276, 295, 305, 306, 307, 348, 374, 384
White, Dan 11, 22, 129, 180, 236, 354
White, Leo 268
White Flash (horse) 339
White Hell of Pitz Palu 125
Whiteford, Blackie 94, 102, 319
Whitehorse 367
Whitley, Ray 7, 22, 35, 36, 192, 208, 210, 211, 250, 264, 352, 353, 358
Whitney, Claire 57, 295, 365
Whitney, Peter 51
Whitten, Tom 178, 180
Whittlesey, Lee 387
"Who Broke the Lock" 303, 392
"Who's Next" 303
Wilcox, Robert (actor) 379, 380
Wilcox, Robert (editor) 144
Wild Beauty 152, 194, 326, 379, 380
Wild Beauty (horse) 379, 380
Wild Horse Roundup 208
Wild Horse Stampede 14
Wild West 95
Wild West Days 79, 93, 105, 158, 160, 206, 277, 381, 382
The Wild West Wallop 394
The Wildcatter 2, 383, 384
Wildfire 95
Wiley, Jan 113
Wilke, Robert 75
Wilkerson, Billy 107
Wilkerson, Guy 273, 285, 287, 321, 365
Wilkins, June 377
William, Warren 350, 352
Williams, Bill 36
Williams, Bob 164, 165, 354, 356
Williams, Charles 150
Williams, Eric 222
Williams, Guinn "Big Boy" 196, 198, 260, 261
Williams, Tex 11, 35, 86, 107, 112, 121, 160, 177, 185, 212, 217, 230, 265, 293, 303, 352, 356
Williams, Walt 233
"Willie of the Valley" 199
Willing, Foy 363, 364
Willis, Matt 273
Willis, Norman 13, 15, 17, 111
Wills, Bob 392, 393
Wills, Henry 22, 264
Wills, Luke 393
Wills, Walter 142
Wilsey, Jay 269, 270, 340, 373, 375
Wilson, Cherry 89, 284, 325, 344, 345
Wilson, Clarence H. 79, 81, 100
Wilson, Lois 156, 257–259
Wilson, Warren 71, 330, 363, 365
Wimpy (dog) 232, 372
Windheim, Marek 71
Winkler, Ben 241
Winkler, Robert 262, 263
Winners of the West 221, 288, 339, 384–386
Winniger, Charles 84–87
Winters, Isabel 379
Wire, Harold C. 273
With a Song in My Heart 53
Withers, Grant 183, 246, 249
Wolfe, Bill 11, 198, 265
Wolf's Fangs 391
Wonacott, Edna Mae 365
Wood, Robert 241
"Wooden Leg Pete" 9
Woodruff, Frank 71, 73
Woods, Al 285
Woods, H.L. *see* Woods, Harry
Woods, Harry 38, 39, 48, 54, 56, 64, 66, 67, 76, 79, 150, 156, 180, 183, 225, 227, 276, 277, 301, 302, 314, 325, 370, 371, 384, 386

Woods, Walter 336, 337
Worden, Hank 41, 57, 119, 121, 164, 337, 384
A World Apart (TV series) 42
Worth, Harry 70, 71
Worthington, William 159
Wrather, Jack 294
Wright, Helen 317, 318
Wright, Mack V. 193, 311
Wright, Maurice 39, 76, 178, 189, 196, 295, 320, 386
Wright, Will 71, 281
Wright, William Lord 144
Wrixon, Maris 352
Wyckoff, Alvin 324
Wyler, William 129, 134–137, 324

Wynters, Charlotte 146, 147
Wyoming (1941) 18
"Wyoming Moon" 34

Yaconelli, Frank 89, 90, 165, 206, 224, 291, 292, 327, 329, 381, 382
Yarbo, Lillian 84
Yarbrough, Jean 363, 365, 366
Yellowstone 2, 386–388
Yesterday's Saturday 3
"Yippi-Ki-Yea" 310
York, Chick 241
"You Are My Sunshine" 330
"You Look Good to Me" 303

Young, Carleton 17, 30, 126, 142, 144, 216, 219, 232
Young, Clarence Upson 203, 309, 311
Young, Loretta 74, 150–152
Young, Olive 356
Young, Polly Ann 73, 74
You're a Sweetheart 72
"You've Got That Look" 85
Yukon Flight 168

Zane, Edgar 116, 124, 236, 273, 286
Zorro's Fighting Legion 221

www.ingramcontent.com/pod-product-compliance
Lightning Source LLC
Chambersburg PA
CBHW051202300426
44116CB00006B/415